THE TRACKS WE LEAVE

Ethics *and* Management Dilemmas *in* Healthcare

Ethics *and* Management Dilemmas *in* Healthcare

Frankie Perry

ACHE Management Series

Library of Congress Cataloging-in-Publication Data is on file at the Library of Congress, Washington, DC.

ISBN: 978-1-64055-451-1

The paper used in this publication meets the minimum requirements of American National Standard for Information Sciences—Permanence of Paper for Printed Library Materials, ANSI Z39.48-1984. ♾™

Manuscript editor: Lori Meek Schuldt; Cover designer: Carla Nessa; Layout: Integra

Found an error or a typo? We want to know! Please e-mail it to hapbooks@ache.org, mentioning the book's title and putting "Book Error" in the subject line.

For photocopying and copyright information, please contact Copyright Clearance Center at www.copyright.com or at (978) 750-8400.

Health Administration Press
A division of the Foundation of the American
    College of Healthcare Executives
300 S. Riverside Plaza, Suite 1900
Chicago, IL 60606-6698
(312) 424-2800

We will be known forever by the tracks we leave.

—*Native American proverb*

Contents

Epilogue: Follow-up on the Cases

Foreword

FRANKIE PERRY HAS succeeded in creating an ethics book that is practical, pragmatic, and thought-provoking. The judicious use of actual cases, issue discussions, and thoughtful essays on related topics makes for interesting and meaningful reading. This book not only serves the individual reader but also provides the basis for roundtable and classroom discussions. An epilogue, rare in books of this type, provides some closure on each of the cases. This is real life tied together with solid contributions to our literature to help all of us improve our perspective on ethical situations.

This book is quite timely. Complications in healthcare delivery, complex business transactions, conflicts of interest, and the vastly expanding list of issues relating to bias confound our daily life as healthcare executives. Every organization faces these and other ethical problems constantly. Understanding these problems and acting proactively to prevent them are critical skills for any executive. The breadth of this book goes far beyond the cases and provides a foundation for enhancing existing ethics education programs or creating new ones. Once read, this book will be a very useful reference tool for any institution's effort to deal with and prevent ethical dilemmas. Furthermore, this book should find a home in many graduate and undergraduate classes as both a text and a foundation for case discussions.

Creating a book of this type requires a special person. Frankie Perry approached this effort with outstanding preparation. Ms. Perry has held hospital positions from staff nurse through nursing supervision to top hospital management. From her hospital executive role, she joined the staff of the American College of Healthcare Executives (ACHE). Once again, she rose through the ranks to serve the professional society as executive vice president and as staff representative to the ACHE ethics committee. Implementing and preserving the ACHE *Code of Ethics* is the focus of the work of the ethics committee, which in turn becomes a major part of the role of the staff representative. This includes extensive analysis and action over violations of the *Code*. This is the exceptional perspective of Frankie Perry, which serves as a key to the value of this excellent book.

I have high hopes for this book and its effect on our profession, in both the practice and the academic communities. I know it will assist all readers to more effectively fulfill their responsibilities as healthcare executives, as professionals in other healthcare roles, or as students aspiring to leadership and service roles in healthcare.

—Stuart A. Wesbury Jr., PhD, LFACHE

Preface

EVOLUTION IS A progression of interrelated phenomena. Society is continuously evolving, and as an institution of society, healthcare is evolving as well. Thoughtful people have studied this evolution and helped develop rules of conduct for each new paradigm. Our sense of morality also changes, and the old rules of moral behavior do not always apply. On a fundamental level, people need and want guidance and standards to help them "do the right thing."

Nowhere is this evolution more evident than in the complex field of healthcare management. Healthcare as a microcosm of society reacts and responds to societal events. Continual advances in technology, changes in healthcare financing, increasing consumer needs and expectations, the proliferation of socioeconomically induced health problems, ever-expanding public scrutiny and litigation, and the debate over healthcare reform all contribute to the significant complexity of healthcare. The decision-making process in healthcare management has become more complicated, and healthcare executives may sometimes waver in their confidence that they are making ethically responsible decisions.

Amid this turmoil of constant change, healthcare executives frequently find themselves in uncharted waters where the ethical "rules" may be unclear. Real-life ethical dilemmas are complex. Rarely do such dilemmas involve a single ethical issue. More often, numerous intertwined issues—involving many stakeholders with diverse values—clamor for attention. Ambiguities abound; resolutions to ethical dilemmas do not come easily.

More than a decade ago, Friedman (2012) suggested that future ethics issues would surround access to care, informed consent for participation in accountable care organizations, insurance discrimination, power shifts, scope-of-practice issues, the drive to maximize profits, end-of-life issues, privacy and security of health information, and a focus on thinking communally. Friedman said then that healthcare leadership would need to be "able to justify one's decisions on ethical grounds as well as fiscal ones to be successful."

It would appear that recent history has proven Friedman right. Today health-care management struggles with ethical decisions in the wake of power shifts within the healthcare system whereby more and more healthcare decisions appear to be driven by healthcare insurers and more and more healthcare costs are attributed to escalating usage and prices of pharmaceuticals.

PART I

Part I of this book deals with ethics as a leadership imperative. It has been said that "character is at the core of leadership." Indeed, when we hear of the leadership failures of industry titans, corporate executives, politicians, religious leaders, and others, we find that these failures are often ones of character and the lack of a personal moral compass. Healthcare executives are not exempt from such failures. Part I discusses the ethical responsibilities of healthcare executives and makes the case for committing resources to establish an ethical culture and infrastructure in one's organization wherein ethical decision making becomes standard practice.

PART II

Part II presents cases that reflect the realities of healthcare management, the diversity of special interests, and the competing values and moral conflicts that challenge the healthcare executive. Many of the cases examine the ethical responsibilities of managers as stewards of valuable organizational and community resources. Each case is followed by a description of the ethics issues inherent in the situation presented and a discussion of these interrelated issues. These cases and discussions are intended to stimulate thoughtful analysis and reflection that will help readers successfully navigate the quagmire of ambiguity that ethical dilemmas can present.

The names of the people, places, and institutions in the case studies and examples used in this book are fictional. Any real people, places, or institutions referenced in this book are ones that have been publicly identified in the news or media, and appropriate attributions have been made here.

PART III

Part III stresses the importance of establishing policies and infrastructure components that support an ethical culture and integrating ethical decision making into the way of doing business. For most of the cases in part II, a relevant chapter can be found in part III that expands on the issues in the case and enriches the discussion.

EPILOGUE

For those who wish to know if and how the ethical issues in the case studies were resolved and what happened subsequently, the epilogue provides follow-up on cases presented in part II.

I have drawn all the cases from real-life experiences. They represent the kinds of management dilemmas and moral challenges that confront healthcare managers on a day-to-day basis. Thoughtful analysis of these cases, and exploration of strategies that deal effectively with the issues they present, will better prepare healthcare managers to successfully address similar issues in the future. If such thoughtful reflection helps you anticipate and forestall situations comparable to the ones presented here, then this book will have served its purpose. If, having read this book, you are more apt to add a discussion of ethical implications to your decision-making process, then even better.

And finally, I hope that you will become ever more aware that good management requires morally sound management decisions. Ignoring the ethical implications of management decisions can be disastrous—to the organization, to the community, to patients and clients, and to the careers of healthcare managers.

INSTRUCTOR RESOURCES

This book's instructor resources include PowerPoint presentations, a quiz, additional cases, case analysis instructions, and websites of interest.

For the most up-to-date information about this book and its instructor resources, go to ache.org/HAP and search for the book's order code (2505I).

This book's instructor resources are available to instructors who adopt this book for use in their course. For access information, please e-mail hapbooks@ache.org.

REFERENCE

Friedman, E. 2012. "The Ethics of Change: Making the Right Decisions in a Shifting System." *Hospitals & Health Networks Daily*. Published October 2. www.hhnmag.com/hhnmag/HHNDaily/HHNDailyDisplay.dhtml?id=8200007092.

Acknowledgments

MUCH HAS BEEN written about ethics and how it applies to healthcare management and delivery. Significant contributions to the literature have been made by John Griffith, Austin Ross, John Worthley, Laura Nash, Paul B. Hofmann, William A. Nelson, Emily Friedman, and others whose valuable work has found its way into this book. To them I owe a debt of gratitude.

My 28 years of hospital experience, first as a nurse and then as an administrator, and several years as executive vice president and staff representative to the ethics committee of the American College of Healthcare Executives, made it clear to me that much still needs to be written to help healthcare managers successfully navigate the sometimes murky paths to ethical decisions.

I humbly submit this work to the collection of ethics literature for healthcare managers, knowing that much has been written but also that there can never be too much written on this important subject.

PART I

The Leadership Imperative

CHAPTER 1

Understanding Your Ethical Responsibilities

HEALTHCARE LEADERS AND those aspiring to be leaders must recognize first and foremost that character and integrity constitute the very cornerstone of leadership. Organizations have failed and promising careers have been derailed when ethics have been relegated to secondary importance or, worse yet, ignored in the pursuit of more bottom-line considerations. Healthcare managers must understand their role and responsibility in creating an ethical healthcare environment that is honest, just, and always in the best interests of those being served. Whether you are the CEO, an assistant administrator, a department head, a program manager, or a clinician, if you are "in charge," you have the ultimate responsibility for establishing the culture and setting the standards of conduct in your sphere of influence.

This task is not always an easy one. Nor is it easy for well-intentioned managers to always make ethical decisions themselves. For this reason, healthcare managers must recognize the importance of ensuring that organizational resources are available to assist them and their staff in making ethical decisions.

Now and then, managers may question the difference between morals and ethics. People generally agree that the terms *ethics* and *morals* are interchangeable. Even professional ethicist Bruce Weinstein (2018), CEO of the Institute for High Character Leadership, says that business leaders can use the terms interchangeably, with the caveat that they must be clear about what they want to accomplish; instead of talking about "ethics" or "morals," they should refer to what the terms are broadly about: "doing the right thing, leading an honorable life, and acting with high character."

Those who do see a difference between ethics and morals often define *ethics* as an external set of standards for conduct, usually established by an institution (e.g., an organization, business, or religion). Codes of ethics provide professional or legal guidelines for physicians, nurses, lawyers, healthcare managers, and the like. Conduct that violates these codes typically incurs punishment of some sort by the profession or licensing agency. *Morals*, on the other hand, are often defined as the internal compass of right and wrong that guides an individual's beliefs and behaviors (Diffen 2023).

Recognizing the cultural, racial, religious, and professional diversity in a healthcare organization, management must clearly establish the values espoused by the organization and the norms of ethical conduct required of all.

BARRIERS TO ETHICAL DECISION MAKING

In our book *Healthcare Leadership Excellence: Creating a Career of Impact*, James A. Rice and I identify some of the common barriers to ethical decision making and seven pitfalls for managers to avoid (Rice and Perry 2013, 29–37). We then make recommendations for building a solid culture and infrastructure to support ethical decision making throughout the organization. The following summarizes those pitfalls and our recommendations for overcoming them:

1. *Failing to recognize that ethics and management decisions are interrelated.* Management decisions are too often based solely on financial data, market share, and other bottom-line considerations without regard to ethical implications. Ethics and management are, in fact, not only closely related but also inseparable (exhibit 1.1).
2. *Failing to recognize that management decisions directly affect clinical care.* Operational decisions must take into account how actions affect patient safety and healthcare needs.
3. *Failing to integrate ethics into the way you conduct business.* Ethical standards must be more than a well-crafted values statement published in the annual report. They must be incorporated into the work life of every staff member throughout the organization, from the boardroom to housekeeping.
4. *Failing to understand that just because something is legal does not mean it is ethical.* Pushing legal boundaries does not build leadership character. Wise leaders recognize that the role of the attorney is to advise regarding the law; the healthcare leader must decide what is morally right.

Exhibit 1.1: Relationship Between Ethics and Management

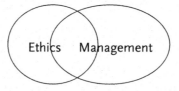

Ethics   Management

---

5. *Believing you are above the rules and laws of others.* Hubris is often at the root of unethical behavior. Leaders cannot operate by one set of standards and expect their employees to function under different, higher ones.

6. *Rushing to judgment.* Ethical mistakes are often the result of hasty decisions made without reflection and consultation with others. Aspiring leaders may mistakenly believe that rapid, independent decisions are expected of them and are the mark of a leader. Technology has further compounded our time crunch. Healthcare managers who are hard pressed for time suffer from information overload. Always-on, multitasking work environments leave little time for thoughtful analysis of ethical dilemmas and the implications of decisions.

7. *Believing that when everyone else does it, you can do it, too.* The creep of moral relativism, in which the standards of right and wrong are mere products of time and culture, may become more pronounced during economic downturns and as healthcare is confronted with new challenges. If everyone else is bending the rules, don't we need to do the same to remain competitive? Experienced healthcare leaders know that bending the rules for short-term gains may have long-term negative consequences. Inevitably, questionable legal or ethical behavior has a price. Actions will come to light and competitive gains will be lost.

So, how do you avoid these pitfalls and build an ethical infrastructure and an organizational culture that make ethics the only acceptable way of doing business?

OVERCOMING BARRIERS TO ETHICAL DECISION MAKING

Ethics leader Paul Hofmann says (quoted in Rice and Perry 2013, 26), "Organizational culture always has been and always will be largely determined for better or worse by the CEO." While this is certainly true, middle managers, supervisors, and other staff have a responsibility to promote and model ethical decisions in their sphere of influence and to advocate for an infrastructure that supports ethics in their corporate organization. Management at all levels of the organization will be looked to for what is acceptable behavior within the organizational workplace. The corporate culture of an organization is defined by its policies, its practices, and the allocation of its resources, but perhaps most visibly by its leadership and their actions. This is definitely a case where the age-old adage holds true—"actions speak louder than words." What the leadership and the management of the organization encourage, reward, punish, overlook, and tolerate speaks volumes about the corporate culture of the organization and what is expected of its employees.

Managers can promote ethical conduct in their organization by taking the following steps:

1. Establish ethical standards, expectations, and a written code of conduct. Rethink the code of conduct regularly to ensure that it is *current* with ethical demands. Think about the importance of this in terms of pandemics and climate change and how unprepared many organizations were for the ethical challenges that these presented—or artificial intelligence, quantum computing, and other technologies looming in the future and the ethical dilemmas they may present.
2. Hire ethical people. Consider presenting ethical dilemmas as part of your organization's interview process. Include an ethics dimension in performance appraisals.
3. Cultivate a relationship with a trusted colleague within or outside your organization who can provide candid, honest feedback regarding the appearance of your personal and professional conduct. Invite colleagues to continually review and enhance your organization's ethical culture.
4. Serve as a role model of ethical standards.
5. Complete an ethics self-assessment from time to time and address areas that need improvement (see appendix A for the Ethics Self-Assessment of the American College of Healthcare Executives).
6. Establish an ethics committee to address both clinical and business ethics issues. Consider expanding the role of the traditional ethics committee in scope and function and in membership to ensure that it can comprehensively and capably serve as a needed resource for both management and clinicians. Expanding the role of ethics committees acknowledges the impact that management decisions have on patient care.
7. Require ethics training and education of all employees and staff. Ensure that training and education are up-to-date and widely disseminated. Use of real-life cases has proven to be an especially effective teaching methodology.
8. Ensure compliance with ethical standards that includes enforcement, reprimands for improper actions, and rewards for ethical conduct.
9. Create an ethical environment with fair and equitable personnel practices and workforce reduction policies—one that is free from harassment, discrimination, and pressure to perform or ignore illegal or unethical actions.
10. Address impairment in the workplace with education, reporting mechanisms, counseling, and treatment options.
11. Integrate patients' rights into operations. Implement patient advocacy and customer service programs.
12. Adopt a framework for ethical decision making consistent with the mission, vision, and values of the organization.

THE IMPORTANCE OF CULTIVATING A "LEARNING ORGANIZATION"

As the case studies in part II of this book demonstrate, many moral dilemmas are the result of management mistakes and the reluctance of executives, managers, or employees to own up to these mistakes and be accountable for their actions. Many organizations have a "blame and shame" culture, wherein the punishment may far outweigh the mistake and where organizations fail to learn from their missteps. In such a culture, employees learn very quickly to hide their mistakes and thus compound potential ethical dilemmas.

In contrast, a "learning organization" takes a systems approach rather than a personal one and, through such mechanisms as root cause analysis, attempts to locate the cause of errors and make changes in the system to prevent errors from occurring again. A learning organization provides venues for employees to candidly explore ethical concerns and conflicts and ask questions without fear of retribution or scorn. In such an organization, underrecognized ethical issues may come to light. Hofmann identifies three such issues that warrant attention and discussion (summarized in Buell 2009, 56):

1. *Promoting unrealistic expectations on the part of the public that an organization can do more than it can deliver.* Promoting unrealistic expectations is an issue that calls for organizations to closely examine their marketing and advertising claims to make certain they are valid. Written ethical guidelines for advertising and marketing must be developed and enforced. These guidelines must avoid any and all dishonest or unrealistic claims for healthcare treatments or outcomes. This is especially important when contracting with public relations and marketing agencies for this work.
2. *Rationalizing inappropriate or incompetent behavior.* Rationalizing inappropriate or incompetent behavior can have a negative effect on patient safety and quality of care. It certainly has a dispiriting effect on staff morale and productivity.
3. *Failing to acknowledge mistakes.* Failing to acknowledge mistakes is not only unethical in and of itself; it also means that the mistake may not be avoided in the future or, in the case of medical errors, that the patients affected may suffer further harm because important information was withheld from them.

ADOPTING AN ETHICAL DECISION-MAKING FRAMEWORK

Those who study decision making consider the ability to make decisions with farsighted consequences a "strangely underappreciated skill" (Johnson 2018, 13).

History offers many examples of decision-making strategies. Charles Darwin, for example, used two columns to organize the pros and cons of his actions, while Benjamin Franklin used what he called "prudential algebra" to assign a numerical value to each item on his list of pros and cons (Johnson 2018). The ancient Persians made important decisions by deliberating them "once while drunk and once while sober" (Rothman 2019).

Today's decision makers draw on more sophisticated methods. Decision Sciences Institute (DSI) is an association of interdisciplinary researchers whose members "aim to understand and improve the judgment and decision-making capabilities of individuals, groups, and organizations across all areas of human enterprise" (DSI 2023). Through conferences, publications, and job placements, DSI shares the latest research and opportunities in decision science.

No one denies that decision making is fraught with problems and uncertainties. Nowhere is this more evident than in today's dynamic healthcare environment. However, one thing that philosophers and researchers tend to agree on is that "sound decisions flow from values" (Rothman 2019). Experienced healthcare executives know this to be unequivocally true. Successful healthcare organizations have adopted and follow an ethical decision-making framework. A decision-making framework can help employees recognize an ethical problem and encourage them to question the ethics of actions and decisions—both their own and those of others. If an ethical issue is not recognized, it cannot be addressed.

Healthcare managers are confronted with ethical dilemmas on a daily basis. Most of the time, they make the right decisions unconsciously and do the right thing. For the most part, those who work in healthcare are decent, moral individuals who are attracted to the healthcare field because they wish to contribute something of value to society. Nevertheless, they occasionally make errors in judgment, detrimental decisions, and unintentional mistakes. More often than not, mistakes are the result of the barrage of decisions that must be made by managers who are pressed for time and strained by the demands of the job. Decisions are made without any opportunity for the sort of thoughtful reflection or consultation with others that might permit managers to consider the implications of their proposed actions, including unintended consequences—a law of nature long observed by social scientists. Taking the time to fully explore the unintended consequences of medical, scientific, and technological breakthroughs before putting them into practice is critically important today. Healthcare organizations that rush to employ practices involving artificial intelligence, quantum computing, and the like must fully understand and be prepared to deal with the ethical issues that may directly arise and those that may arise from the unintended consequences of the decision making surrounding these new advances.

Theoretical constructs and ethical decision-making frameworks abound, but as the busy practitioner knows only too well, the exigencies of time and place often preclude their proper usage. Competing priorities prohibit "seeking out diverse perspectives, challenging . . . assumptions, [and] making an explicit effort to map the variables" (Johnson 2018, 186). Healthcare managers are simply expected to know all the answers, to make decisions quickly and authoritatively, and to lead their staff down a path of moral integrity.

This book is intended to provide some practical guidance to healthcare managers who are confronted with these challenges. What useful thought process can healthcare managers employ to make this task easier? What steps can they take to move staff in the direction of ethically sound decisions?

The process suggested here for arriving at such decisions is a relatively simple one—a series of questions that healthcare managers can ask to determine whether additional time or resources need to be brought to bear on the decision-making process and the situation at hand. These questions focus on identifying the issues in any particular situation, as well as the stakeholders, colleagues, resources, and organizational impact surrounding those issues (exhibit 1.2):

- *Issues.* What are the ethical issues in this situation? Relatively few situations involve a single issue. More often, the ethical dilemma comprises several interrelated issues. Each issue must be isolated and thoughtfully explored.
- *Stakeholders.* Which persons or groups will be affected by this situation and the actions taken? What will each feel is in their best interest?
- *Colleagues.* Which trusted colleagues may have insights, experiences, and knowledge to share relating to this matter? Can they be consulted in confidence?
- *Resources.* What resources are available? Does the organization have a mission statement? Values statement? Ethics committee? Ethics officer? Code of conduct? Compliance officer? Guiding principles? Policies? Laws? Regulations? Decision-making models? Legal counsel?
- *Organizational impact.* What will be the effect on the organization that pays the executive's salary and has expectations that the executive will act in its best interests?

Leaders must exercise caution to avoid assuming that if no law, rule, regulation, or policy addresses an action, then the action must be ethical. This is simply not true. Moral individuals do not need situations to come with written instructions to do the responsible thing.

Exhibit 1.2: Issues Wheel

Nash (2009) offers the following 12 questions for examining the ethics of a business decision:

1. Have you defined the problem accurately?
2. How would you define the problem if you stood on the other side of the fence?
3. How did this situation occur in the first place?
4. To whom and to what do you give your loyalty as a person and as a member of the corporation?
5. What is your intention in making this decision?
6. How does this intention compare with the probable results?
7. Whom could your decision or action injure?
8. Can you discuss the problem with the affected parties before you make your decision?
9. Are you confident that your position will be as valid over a long period of time as it seems now?
10. Could you disclose without qualm your decision or action to your boss, your CEO, the board of directors, your family, or society as a whole?
11. What is the symbolic potential of your action if understood? If misunderstood?
12. Under what conditions would you allow exceptions to your stand?

Hosmer (1995) discusses ten ethical principles that can help healthcare executives determine an ethical course of action:

1. *Self-interests.* Never take any action that is not in the long-term self-interests of yourself or the healthcare organization to which you belong.

2. *Personal virtues.* Never take any action that is not honest, open, and truthful and that you would not be proud to see reported widely in national newspapers and on television.
3. *Religious injunctions.* Never take any action that is not kind and that does not build a sense of community, a sense of all of us working together for a commonly accepted goal.
4. *Government requirements.* Never take any action that violates the law, for the law represents the minimal moral standards of our society.
5. *Utilitarian benefits.* Never take any action that does not result in greater good than harm for the society of which you are a part.
6. *Universal rules.* Never take any action that you would not be willing to see others, faced with the same or a closely similar situation, also be free to take.
7. *Individual rights.* Never take any action that abridges the agreed-upon and accepted rights of others.
8. *Economic efficiency.* Always act to maximize profits subject to legal and market constraints, for maximum profits are the sign of the most efficient production.
9. *Distributive justice.* Never take any action in which the least among us are harmed in some way.
10. *Contributive liberty.* Never take any action that will interfere with the right of all of us to self-development and self-fulfillment.

Nelson (2005, 10–13) provides an eight-step process reflecting procedural justice:

1. *Clarify the ethical conflict.* What is the specific ethical question or conflict? If the question or conflict is not an ethical one, it should be referred to another person or process.
2. *Identify all the affected stakeholders and their values.* Who are the individuals or programs affected by the ethical question?
3. *Understand the circumstances surrounding the ethical conflict.* Identify the economic, patient care, legal, and community concerns.
4. *Identify the ethical perspectives relevant to the conflict.* Explore the relationship of the ethical question to professional codes, ethics literature, and the organization's policies and procedures.
5. *Identify options for action.* What is the ethical reasoning for each?
6. *Select among the options.* Is the selected option practical? Does it have a clear ethical foundation? Does one ethical concept or stakeholder value appear to be stronger than the others?

7. *Share and implement the decision.* Organizational decisions should be publicly disclosed along with the ethical reasons behind them.

8. *Review the decision to ensure that it achieved the desired goal.* If it becomes clear that the course of action did not achieve the anticipated outcome, then the organization should reconsider the decision and explore other options based on the current information.

In chapter 17, Joan McIver Gibson provides detailed guidance and a helpful elliptical diagram for identifying values and applying values-based decision making to the analysis of ethics situations (see exhibit 17.4 in that chapter). She also provides a tool for a "values analysis on the fly" when time is short but values still must be considered (see exhibit 17.5 in chapter 17).

Before codes of conduct and ethical frameworks for decision making were available, the young hospital administrators who reported to me looked to me for sage advice on how to do the right thing when they were on call. They knew that they could call me if they really got into trouble, but they also knew I expected them to have a plan of action when they did call. To help them formulate this plan of action, I gave them four simple questions to apply to any situation:

1. What action is in the best interests of the patient(s) involved?
2. What action is in the best interests of the organization?
3. If this action is taken, what is the worst possible thing that can happen?
4. What is my contingency plan to deal with all possible ramifications of the action?

Although this thought process did not easily solve every problem, my objective was to focus the administrator's thinking on what was best for the patient and the organization (instead of on subjective concerns, such as personal power, authority, or control) in solving the problem at hand. For the most part, it worked—the process did lend itself to the quick resolution of the kinds of problems an administrator tends to see at three o'clock in the morning.

Whichever strategy healthcare managers use to arrive at a sound ethical decision, they must examine all the consequences of each action considered. The key to ethical decisions is an awareness of the need to ask thoughtful questions and to take the time to formulate ethically sound answers. Doing so will help healthcare managers avoid hasty decisions that are not always attentive to the ethical implications of actions taken. Aristotle considered contemplation the best activity, remarking that "it is the most continuous, since we can contemplate truth more continuously than we can do anything" (Ross 2023).

Hofmann reminds us that managers of character and integrity demonstrate certain behavioral traits (Buell 2009, 54). They are ethically conscious of ethical dimensions and implications. They are ethically committed to doing the right thing. They are ethically competent, possessing the knowledge and understanding required to make ethically sound decisions. They are ethically courageous even when actions may not be accepted with enthusiasm or endorsement. They are ethically consistent and do not make inconvenient exceptions. They are ethically candid, open, and forthright and are active advocates for ethical analysis and conduct.

A wise and experienced healthcare executive whom I know once observed that "working in healthcare gives you the opportunity to do something ethical every day."

TOOLS

To further assist healthcare managers in future decision making, the appendixes at the end of the book include the following:

- American College of Healthcare Executives Ethics Self-Assessment (appendix A)
- American College of Healthcare Executives *Code of Ethics* (appendix B)

REFERENCES

Buell, J. M. 2009. "Ethics and Leadership." *Healthcare Executive* 24 (3): 54–56.

Decision Sciences Institute (DSI). 2023. "About DSI: Mission Statement." Accessed September 3. https://decisionsciences.org//about/.

Diffen. 2023. "Ethics vs. Morals." Diffen.com. Accessed September 3. www.diffen.com/difference/Ethics_vs_Morals.

Hosmer, L. T. 1995. "Brief Summaries of Ten Ethical Principles." *Academy of Management Review* 20 (2): 396–97.

Johnson, S. 2018. *Farsighted: How We Make the Decisions That Matter the Most.* New York: Riverhead Books.

Nash, L. L. 2009. *Ethics Without the Sermon.* Boston: Harvard Business School Publishing.

Nelson, W. A. 2005. "An Organizational Ethics Decision-Making Process." *Healthcare Executive* 20 (4): 9–14.

Rice, J. A., and F. Perry. 2013. *Healthcare Leadership Excellence: Creating a Career of Impact*. Chicago: Health Administration Press.

Ross, W. D. (trans.). 2023. "Nicomachean Ethics by Aristotle: Book X." MIT Internet Classics Archive. Accessed September 3. http://classics.mit.edu/Aristotle/nicomachaen.10.x.html.

Rothman, J. 2019. "The Art of Decision Making." *New Yorker*, January 21, 27–28.

Weinstein, B. 2018. "Is There a Difference Between Ethics and Morality in Business?" *Forbes*. Published February 27. www.forbes.com/sites/bruceweinstein/2018/02/27/is-there-a-difference-between-ethics-and-morality-in-business/.

CHAPTER 2

The Business Case for Ethics Management

HEALTHCARE LEADERS KNOW that ethics management is not merely a nice thing to do. Ethics management has a business case. McNamara (2023) says that managing ethics in the workplace

- improves society;
- helps maintain a moral course in turbulent times;
- cultivates strong teamwork and productivity;
- supports employee growth and meaning;
- helps ensure that policies are legal;
- helps prevent criminal acts "of omission" and lowers fines if such acts occur;
- helps with quality management, strategic planning, and diversity management;
- promotes a strong public image;
- provides overall benefits in legitimizing managerial actions, strengthening organizational culture, improving trust, supporting consistency in quality of service, and cultivating greater sensitivity to values; and, most important,
- is the right thing to do.

McNamara does not mention in this list that morally sound management decisions are also financially prudent. Doing the right thing to begin with is much less costly than cleaning up the mess—and sometimes the litigation—that unethical behavior leaves in its wake. Morally sound management decisions save time, effort, and resources in the long run.

In 1991, the US Congress passed the Federal Sentencing Guidelines for Organizations, which apply to all for-profit and not-for-profit organizations with ten or more employees, including healthcare organizations. With a few revisions, the guidelines have essentially remained the same. The guidelines hold an organization responsible for the wrongful acts of its employees if they are acting in their official capacities, whether the organization or its managers knew about the illegal actions or not. An organization can be held liable for the acts of its employees even when an employee acts in ways that defy organizational policy or employee training. Fines and jail sentences can be handed down to the organization, the employees involved, and the managers and executives as well.

If the organization has an effective ethics and compliance program, fines and penalties may be significantly reduced. An additional and sometimes overlooked benefit of ethics management is that it saves the organization time, effort, and resources in the recruitment and retention of talent. Competent physicians and employees want to work with ethical managers who inspire them and challenge them to achieve high levels of ethical performance. They do not want to work with unethical leaders and suffer "guilt by association" or have to compromise their own moral principles. The ability to attract and retain a high-quality workforce has become increasingly important as healthcare organizations face critical labor shortages. These labor shortages are especially dire among clinical staff—physicians and nurses who have their own professional codes of conduct that make them less tolerant of working with unethical management.

Patients, too, value honest and trustworthy care and will seek organizations and clinicians they feel they can trust. Likewise, vendors and insurers want to do business with reputable organizations and credible administrators they can trust. Wise healthcare executives know that they must be personally and professionally ethical to enjoy and prosper in their many business and professional relationships (Perry 2012, 16).

A common theme often mentioned in the management literature is the significance of "trustworthiness" as an attribute of successful leadership. Organizations and their leaders who can be trusted thrive in the business sense. Ethical conduct builds trust within the organization and within the community served.

Experience tells us that successful relationships in which all parties benefit are built on trust. Effective managers are honest and trustworthy, and they model these attributes consistently over time. Management guru Warren Bennis advises, "Trust is the emotional glue that binds followers and leaders together" (AZ Quotes 2023a). He also notes, "Trust is the lubrication that makes it possible for organizations to work" (AZ Quotes 2023b).

Trust must be earned. Successful managers are consciously aware of this and intentionally examine their everyday actions to make certain they are ones that generate and sustain trust.

So how does a manager build trust and become "trustworthy"?

My experience has led me to the following conclusions. My advice is simple:

- Say what you will do—and do what you say!! *Over time!!* It takes a long time to build trust but unfortunately very little time to lose it.
- Your staff, your partners, and your community will learn by your actions over time that you can be trusted to do what you said you were going to do.
- Be willing to admit when you make a mistake.
- Be a skilled listener.

Most important, always make decisions that are in the best interests of patients, clients, and the organization and in keeping with its mission and ethical values. Never allow your personal interests to outweigh those of the organization. Focus on the work! Your colleagues and those you manage will learn to trust your decisions and follow your lead.

Simply put, managing ethics in the workplace is good management, and there is a strong business case for an ethical corporate culture. It saves time, effort, and resources in the long run. The wise stewardship of resources is a paramount responsibility of leadership in any organization, but especially in a healthcare organization whose mission is to serve humanity.

In an address to an assembly of healthcare executives, noted journalist and political analyst Juan Williams (2010) challenged healthcare leaders to extend their leadership role, to work at changing society to make it a more ethical and more civil environment in which people are more concerned for one another. Such an effort will advance productivity and the responsible stewardship of valuable resources throughout organizations, making society a better place for all.

REFERENCES

AZ Quotes. 2023a. "Warren G. Bennis: Trust Is the Emotional Glue That Binds Followers and Leaders Together." Accessed September 13. www.azquotes.com/quote/1345207.

———. 2023b. "Warren G. Bennis: Trust Is the Lubrication That Makes It Possible for Organizations to Work." Accessed September 13. www.azquotes.com/quote/23987.

McNamara, C. 2023. "Ethics Management Guide: Toolkit for Ethical Managers." Free Management Library. Updated June 19. http://managementhelp.org/businessethics/ethics-guide.htm.

Perry, F. 2012. *Healthcare Leadership That Makes a Difference: Creating Your Legacy.* Self-study course. Chicago: Health Administration Press.

Williams, J. 2010. "American Leadership: The Inspiration and Power Behind Proven Leaders." Malcolm T. MacEachern Memorial Lecture presented at the American College of Healthcare Executives Congress on Healthcare Leadership, Chicago, March 23.

PART II

Case Studies and Moral Challenges

CHAPTER 3

Medical Errors: Paradise Hills Medical Center

CASE STUDY

Paradise Hills Medical Center was a 500-bed teaching hospital in a major metropolitan area of the South. It was known throughout a tristate area for its comprehensive oncology program and served as a regional referral center for thousands of patients suffering from various forms of malignant disease.

Paradise Hills was affiliated with a major university and had residency programs in internal medicine, surgery, pediatrics, obstetrics and gynecology, psychiatry, radiology, and pathology—all fully accredited by the Accreditation Council for Graduate Medical Education. In addition, Paradise Hills had an oncology fellowship program, a university-affiliated nursing program, and training programs for radiology technicians and medical technologists. All these teaching programs were highly regarded and attracted students from across the nation.

Paradise Hills enjoyed an enviable reputation. It was respected for its high-quality care; its state-of-the-art technology; and its competent, caring staff. Although Paradise Hills was located in a highly competitive healthcare community, it boasted a strong market share for its service area. Its patients also provided significant referrals to the surgery, pediatrics, and radiology programs.

Paradise Hills was a financially sound institution with equally strong leadership. Its past successes could be attributed in large part to its aggressive, visionary CEO and his exceptionally competent management staff.

But all was not as well as it seemed at Paradise Hills. Although the oncology program still enjoyed a healthy market share of 75 percent, it had been slowly and steadily declining from a peak of 82 percent two years earlier. In addition, the program's medical staff was aging, and some of its highest-admitting physicians were contemplating retirement. The oncology fellowship program had been established a few years previously to address this situation, but unfortunately the graduates of this program had so far elected not to stay in the community. Of most concern to the CEO and his staff was the fact that the hospital's primary competitor had recently recruited a highly credentialed oncology medical group practice from the Northeast and had committed enormous resources to strengthening its own struggling cancer care program.

The previous week, Paradise Hills's board of trustees had held its monthly meeting, with a fairly routine agenda. However, during review of a standard quality assurance report, one of the trustees inquired about a section of the report indicating that 22 oncology patients had received radiation therapy dosages in excess of what had been prescribed for them. It was explained that the errors had occurred because of a flaw in the calibration of the linear accelerator and that the medical physicist responsible for the errors had been asked to resign his position. Another trustee then asked if the patients who had received the excessive radiation had been told about the errors. The CEO responded that it was the responsibility of the medical staff to address this issue, and they had decided not to inform the patients about the errors. The board did not agree that the medical staff were solely responsible for informing the patients about the errors and requested that the administrative staff review both the hospital's ethical responsibility to these patients and its liability related to the incident, and report back to the board within two weeks.

The CEO and his management staff responsible for the radiology department and the oncology program met with the medical staff department chairs for internal medicine and radiology, the program medical directors for oncology and radiation therapy, and the attending oncologists. The CEO related the board's discussion about the errors and the board's request that the actions taken be reviewed, specifically the decision not to inform the affected patients.

All the physicians agreed that the adverse effects of the accidental radiation overdose on the patients were unknown. The oncologists argued that the patients should not be told of the incident, asserting that cancer patients did not want or need any more bad news. "Let's face it—these patients are terminal," they said. "Informing them about this error will only confuse them and destroy their faith and trust in their physicians and in the hospital." Furthermore, they claimed, informing the patients of the errors could unnecessarily frighten them to the extent that they might refuse further treatment, which would be even more detrimental to them. Besides, the physicians argued, advising the patients of potential ill effects just might induce those symptoms through suggestion or excessive worry. Every procedure has its risks, the radiology department chair insisted, and these patients signed an informed consent.

Physicians know what is best for their patients, the attending oncologists maintained, and they would monitor the patients in question for any ill effects. The department chair for internal medicine was of the opinion that the incident was clearly a patient–physician relationship responsibility and not the business of the hospital. Besides, the radiology chair added, informing the patients would "just be asking for malpractice litigation."

The medical director for the oncology program then suggested that the board of trustees and the management staff "think long and hard" about the public relations effect that disclosing the incident would have on the oncology program. "Do you really think patients will want to come to Paradise Hills if they think we're incompetent?" he asked.

The CEO conceded that he supported the position of the medical staff in this matter and that he, too, was concerned about preserving the image of the oncology program. But, he said, his hands were tied because the board clearly considered this an ethical issue that would have to be referred to the hospital's ethics committee for its opinion.

The physicians noted that if indeed the ethics committee subsequently recommended that the patients be informed, then realistically that responsibility would rest with the patients' primary care physicians and not with any of them.

ETHICS ISSUES

Truth telling: Is there a difference between lying to a patient and withholding the truth? Does it matter to the patient whether the act is one of omission or commission?

Justice and fairness: Is it fair to these patients to withhold information about their clinical treatment and any potential risks inherent in the accidental overdose?

A patient's right to know: Do these patients have a right to know about this incident? Do these patients have a right to know so that they may make informed therapeutic choices? Can not informing the patients affected by this radiation overdose be reconciled with the patients' bill of rights?

Adherence to the organization's mission statement, ethical standards, and values statement: Are the actions being considered in this case consistent with the hospital's mission statement, ethical standards, and values statement?

Adherence to professional codes of ethical conduct: Are the actions being considered in this case consistent with the codes of ethical conduct promulgated by the professional organizations and associations representing physicians, healthcare executives, and hospitals?

Discrimination against a class of patients: Does labeling these patients as "terminal" invalidate their self-determination? Does it limit their ability to participate in their choice of treatment options? Does discrimination against terminal patients give tacit permission to discriminate against other diverse groups, such as the aged, immigrants, or LGBTQ+ people?

Management's role and responsibility: What are the role and responsibility of hospital management in this matter? What are the role and responsibility of the hospital CEO specifically?

Legal implications: What are the legal implications of the actions being considered for the hospital? For the physicians involved? Does withholding information about this medical treatment and its potential risks from the patients involved constitute medical malpractice? In the view of the legal system, is this action indeed fraud? Has the hospital's management considered the liability exposure for fraud that is not covered under medical malpractice insurance?

Other legal aspects to be considered relate to specific liability and employment issues. Who employs and supervises the medical physicist? Who pays the medical physicist, and who asked him to resign? Is the medical director for radiation oncology, who typically prescribes radiation therapy dosages, an employee of the hospital or an independent contractor? If the medical director is a contract physician, does the contract stipulate that he hires and pays the medical physicist? Should it? Is the medical director responsible for the actions of the medical physicist whether the medical physicist is employed by the medical director or not? Finally, who owns the linear accelerator used in this case?

Organizational implications: How will the actions being considered in this case affect the oncology program? The hospital as a whole? The hospital staff?

Ethical decision-making framework: Can the actions being considered in this case be justified within an acceptable ethical decision-making framework?

DISCUSSION

Truth Telling, and Justice and Fairness

The fundamental issue in this case seems to be one of truth telling. Is it not a basic tenet of all ethical relationships that individuals and organizations tell the truth? Is it not the "right" thing to do?

The physicians in this case have argued that telling the truth would cause more harm than good—that not sharing this incident with their patients is, in fact, in their patients' best interest. This position assumes that the patients will never find out about the incident or that they will die without the incident ever coming to light. From a practical standpoint, this eventuality may indeed be the case. But on closer examination, is this scenario likely? Consider the number of healthcare workers who interact with a patient on any given day and have access to the patient's medical record. In a teaching hospital, that number is likely to be higher. The prescribed radiation therapy and the received radiation therapy are a matter of medical record. Incident reports and quality assurance reports are also a matter of record. Is it realistic to believe that staff will not have questions about the incident and, worst-case scenario, inadvertently discuss it with the affected patient? Given the great number of staff, physicians, and trustees who are privy to this information, is maintaining a "conspiracy of silence" even possible? Is it right for the hospital to attempt to cover up the error?

In the event that the patients or their families find out about the incident after the fact, what then? What effect will this knowledge have on their opinions of the physicians and the hospital?

Clearly, human relationships are built on the communication of information. If the information shared is not truthful, there can be no trust. Unfortunately, not telling the entire truth in a situation usually means additional shading of the truth or outright lying when questions arise. An individual or institution that betrays the trust on which relationships are built is no longer credible. This betrayal of trust can be especially problematic in healthcare, where patient compliance and positive health outcomes depend on patients' trust in their healthcare providers.

In the Paradise Hills case, lying or withholding the truth carries enormous risk for undermining the image of the physicians and the hospital. If the incident is discovered by the patients or their families, the physicians and the hospital could be accused of attempting to cover up the incident, which could prove disastrous both in the judgment of the community and in a court of law. Recent political scandals are a tragic reminder that the public will not quietly stand for deceitfulness.

However, the intent in withholding information could arguably be to protect the patients from unnecessary stress and anxiety, not unlike the "white lies" used to spare someone's feelings in everyday life. Is this a fair comparison? Using the Golden Rule as a guide, if you or a loved one were the patient, would you want to know the truth about the incident? Or would you wish to be spared the anxiety?

In the assessment of Elisabeth Kübler-Ross (1969, 32), the psychiatrist renowned for her theory of the five stages of grief, "the question should not be stated, 'Do I tell my patient?' but should be rephrased as, 'How do I share this knowledge with my patient?'" Kübler-Ross believed that "the way in which the bad news is communicated is . . . an important factor which is often underestimated and which should be given more emphasis in the teaching of medical students and supervision of young physicians." Does her assessment apply in this case?

Much in the literature supports the notion that what matters is not so much what is said as how it is said and in what context. Medical information should be presented by a physician with whom the patient has a trust relationship, and nursing staff should be in attendance so that they can prompt the patient to ask questions of the doctor before the doctor leaves or answer such questions after the doctor has gone. While this solicitude may seem like a small thing to do, in today's rushed environment nurses may not be expected or have time to make rounds with physicians. To further compound the situation, in teaching hospitals the patient may feel overwhelmed by a large entourage of house staff, and in nonteaching hospitals a hospitalist whom the patient does not know well may be designated to inform the patient about the medical error. Some might suggest that the risk manager or hospital attorney should be in attendance when a patient is informed about an error. This consideration must be weighed against any alarm or apprehension their presence may generate. When multiple patients need to be informed individually about an error, using scripted information—or at least talking points—may be wise to ensure that all patients receive the same information.

A relevant study by Iezzoni and colleagues (2012) presented some startling revelations about physician attitudes:

> Approximately one-third of physicians did not completely agree with the need to disclose serious medical errors to patients, almost one-fifth did not completely agree that physicians should never tell a patient something untrue, and nearly two-fifths of physicians did not completely agree that they should disclose their financial relationships with drug and device companies to patients. Just over one-tenth said they had told patients something untrue in the previous year.

The researchers concluded:

> Our findings raise concerns that some patients might not receive complete and accurate information from their physicians, and doubts about whether patient-centered care is broadly possible without more widespread physician endorsement of the core communication principles of openness and honesty with patients.

The study suggests that healthcare professionals could use more education and training about truth telling in patient-centered care. Patients need information and to have all their questions answered in a straightforward, concerned manner to be able to participate appropriately in their treatment options and to comply with medical instructions. The increasing diversity of both patient populations and healthcare professionals further complicates communications. For more on managing diversity and the ethical implications it presents, see chapter 19.

A Patient's Right to Know

Do the patients in the Paradise Hills case have a right to know about the error and how it may potentially affect them? In an effort to encourage patients to become active participants in their care, the American Hospital Association (AHA 2003) created *The Patient Care Partnership* brochure and made it available to healthcare organizations to provide to their patients. The brochure states:

> Our hospital works hard to keep you safe. We use special policies and procedures to avoid mistakes in your care and keep you free from abuse or neglect. If anything unexpected and significant happens during your hospital stay, you will be told what happened, and any resulting changes in your care will be discussed with you.

How does this standard of conduct apply to the radiation therapy incident at Paradise Hills? The management team and the physicians involved should review its applicability. Their review should consider the patients' and their family members' interpretation of the standard as well.

As healthcare becomes more outcomes driven, "transparency is not only the right thing to do, but also the pragmatic thing to do," according to Toby Cosgrove (2013), past president and CEO of Cleveland Clinic. Cleveland Clinic was a pioneer in transparency. Its patients have "a clear window into their medical information" through universal access to medical records during their entire care process. After they go home, patients can go online and sign in to MyChart to review all their care, renew prescriptions, make appointments, and consult with their doctor's office. When patients have such immediate and ongoing access to their medical records, physicians and other clinicians have no choice but to keep patients informed of all aspects of their care, including medical errors. This access makes patients active partners in the care process and provides them with the information they need to make informed decisions about their care and treatment, including what actions to take when medical errors occur. The staff at Cleveland Clinic believed in the early 2010s that patients have a right to know and that this kind of transparency holds the staff accountable and makes them better (Cosgrove 2013). Cleveland Clinic became a model for transparency, with similar patient programs being adopted throughout the country. Today it is common practice for patients to have universal access to their medical records, often through what is identified as the "patient portal" on the hospital's website.

Do patients and their families have a right to know when a medical error has occurred during the course of their treatment? A look at the history of medical errors—the acknowledgment that they occur, the number of lives they claim, and national efforts to decrease their incidence—is instructive, as the following section discusses.

Adherence to the Organization's Mission Statement, Ethical Standards, and Values Statement

The Institute of Medicine report *To Err Is Human: Building a Safer Health System* (Kohn, Corrigan, and Donaldson 1999) claimed that medical errors in the nation's hospitals, clinics, and physician offices account for the deaths of nearly 100,000 Americans each year. Not surprisingly, this landmark report was covered extensively by the media, which in turn prompted a rapid political response. Congressional hearings, a report from the Quality Interagency Coordination Task Force (2000) titled *Doing What Counts for Patient Safety: Federal Actions to Reduce Medical Errors and Their Impact*, and a major policy speech by President Bill Clinton on reducing medical errors soon followed.

In his speech, President Clinton introduced a national action plan to reduce preventable medical errors by 50 percent within five years (Pilla 2000). This action plan called for

- $20 million for the creation of a Center for Quality Improvement and Patient Safety to sponsor research and education in reducing errors;
- new regulations requiring all 6,000 hospital participants in the Medicare program to implement patient safety programs to reduce medical errors;
- development of a national, state-based system for reporting medical errors, including mandatory reporting of preventable errors causing death or serious injury and voluntary reporting of other medical errors, such as "near misses";
- support of legislation that protects provider and patient confidentiality without undermining existing tort remedies; and
- new steps to specifically reduce medication errors.

This national action plan signaled government intervention in a domain that previously had been notorious for "policing its own," where medical errors had been kept secret for fear of malpractice litigation, where those committing medical errors were blamed and punished, and where the prevailing standard for prevention of medical errors was to educate those involved in the hope that such errors would not happen again.

To change what some observers called a "conspiracy of silence," the Institute of Medicine and the Quality Interagency Coordination Task Force recommended further actions, as presented by the Quality Interagency Coordination Task Force (2000):

- Health plans involved in the Federal Employees Health Benefits Program were required to implement patient safety programs.
- Employers were to incorporate patient safety performance into their healthcare purchasing decisions.
- Periodic relicensing and reexamination of physicians and nurses by state boards would include knowledge of and competence in patient safety practices.
- Healthcare organizations would establish a goal of continually improved patient safety.
- Healthcare organizations would implement proven medication safety practices.
- Accrediting bodies such as The Joint Commission would review organizational efforts to minimize errors and promote patient safety.
- Computerized medical records would be implemented and integrated with drug ordering and administrative systems.

For healthcare providers, perhaps the most disconcerting of these recommendations was the mandatory reporting of medical errors to patients and their families. No responsible healthcare professional will argue about the need for strategies to reduce medical errors and ensure patient safety, but the notion of placing the organization and its staff at risk for malpractice litigation was worrisome.

Yet, in his policy address, President Clinton stated, "People should have access to information about a preventable medical error that causes serious injury or death of a family member, and providers should have protections to encourage reporting and prevent mistakes from happening again" (Pilla 2000). Is the expectation that healthcare institutions and medical professionals will report their errors unreasonable? More to the point, is the fear of litigation sufficient justification for withholding the truth from those affected by medical errors? Any reasonable healthcare manager will respond, "Of course not." The patient must always be the first priority. And yet, knowing the right thing to do may be easier than actually doing the right thing.

The Institute of Medicine report *To Err Is Human* had recommended that Congress create a Center for Patient Safety within the Agency for Healthcare Research and Quality (AHRQ 2003) to

- set national goals for patient safety, track progress in meeting those goals, and issue an annual report to the president and Congress on patient safety; and
- develop knowledge and understanding of errors in healthcare by developing a research agenda, funding centers of excellence, evaluating methods for identifying and preventing errors, and funding dissemination and communication activities to improve patient safety.

In addition, AHRQ (2003) was authorized to establish a comprehensive patient safety initiative to

- identify the causes of preventable healthcare errors and patient injury in healthcare delivery;
- develop, demonstrate, and evaluate strategies for reducing errors and improving patient safety; and
- disseminate such effective strategies throughout the healthcare industry.

AHRQ's Center for Quality Measurement and Improvement was renamed in 2001 as the Center for Quality Improvement and Patient Safety (AHRQ 2023), which now

- conducts and supports user-driven research on patient safety and healthcare quality measurement, reporting, and improvement;
- develops and disseminates reports and information on patient safety and healthcare quality measurement, reporting, and improvement;
- collaborates with stakeholders across the healthcare system to implement evidence-based practices, accelerating and amplifying improvements in quality and safety for patients; and
- assesses patient safety and healthcare quality to ensure continuous learning and improvement.

Despite these agencies' best efforts, little seemed to have changed to stem the tide of medical errors. In fact, many studies suggest the problem is only getting worse. A 2012 US Department of Health and Human Services (HHS) report found that one in seven Medicare patients died or was harmed by hospital care (Greider 2012). A 2018 Johns Hopkins study found that deaths from medical errors exceed 250,000 per year and remain the third-leading cause of death in the United States (Sipherd 2018). And the Leapfrog Group (2023) indicates that "upwards of 200,000 people die every year from hospital errors, injuries, accidents, and infections. . . . Today alone, more than 500 people will die because of a preventable hospital error." A recent Yale School of Medicine study suggests that the previously reported numbers of patient deaths from medical errors have been too high, and it puts the number at closer to 22,000 per year (Hathaway 2020) Yet in 2023, the *New England Journal of Medicine* published a study finding that nearly one in four patients who are admitted to hospitals in the United States will experience harm (Bates et al. 2023).

Even more disconcerting, as much as 86 percent of harm to Medicare patients from errors goes unreported, according to the US Department of Health and Human Services (HHS 2012). This failure to report errors is not surprising, given that many hospitals have been unwilling or unable to transform their facilities into learning organizations rather than punitive ones. No wonder *American Medical News* has claimed that a "fear of punitive response to hospital errors lingers" (O'Reilly 2012a), citing an AHRQ survey that found 67 percent of healthcare professionals said they are concerned that mistakes are held in their personnel files, and fewer than 50 percent feel free to question decisions or actions of superiors.

The cost of medical errors has received an increasing amount of media attention in recent years, and the numbers are staggering. One study put the annual cost of medical errors in the United States near $1 trillion (Goedert 2012). In 2008, in an effort to reduce the cost of medical errors to the government, Medicare adopted a policy of "no pay for never events" (medical errors that should never happen). This "ethical and patient safety imperative" seems to have induced hospital leaders to focus more on patient safety and fostered more collaboration among healthcare professionals (O'Reilly 2008, 2012b).

Despite all the pressures to disclose medical errors so that they can be analyzed and prevented in the future, an overriding fear of litigation still exists. Citing a study that found that 43 percent of 127 families who sued their healthcare providers after perinatal injuries were motivated by revenge or suspicion of a cover-up, Kraman and Hamm (1999) argued in an oft-cited scholarly article that honesty is the best policy in risk management. The authors reported on the experiences of one Department of Veterans Affairs medical center that implemented a policy of full disclosure of medical errors to patients and families (in the presence of a family attorney, if the family so desired). The medical center initiated this practice because staff believed it was "the right thing to do." They also found that this honest approach resulted in unanticipated financial benefits to the medical center when lower-cost settlements began replacing higher-cost litigation. This study remains the definitive scholarly work that provides evidence supporting full disclosure of medical errors.

Surgeon and health policy expert Marty Makary, MD, determined that most medical errors are caused by "inadequately skilled staff, errors in judgement or care, a system defect, or a preventable adverse effect" (Sipherd 2018). The compendium of causes includes "computer breakdowns, mix-ups with the doses or types of medications administered to patients, and surgical complications that go undiagnosed" (Sipherd 2018). Makary admonishes healthcare managers to blame the system rather than individuals (Sipherd 2018).

A number of strategies have aimed to help healthcare managers reduce medical errors. Technology, such as computerized physician order entry and electronic medical records, has certainly proven useful. Incentive awards encourage employees to be alert to errors and report them; Mount Sinai Hospital in New York, for example, gives a "Good Catch Award" to employees who detect potential and existing errors. Encouraging patients to take charge of their healthcare by downloading a healthcare app to access their medical information, asking questions, seeking second opinions, and bringing a friend or relative along to doctor visits so that they can ask questions, too—all have merit in helping to reduce medical errors (Sipherd 2018).

A word about transparency may be in order here. *Transparency* has become the buzzword for all that is right. Transparency is advocated in business, government, and healthcare (especially recently). It has been argued that a lack of transparency leaves flaws unchecked and systems uncorrected.

What kind of information, and how much, is appropriate to disclose? And to whom should it be disclosed? A political commentator recently questioned the wisdom of too much transparency, arguing that the public is getting bogged down in the minutiae and that backdoor bickering and grandstanding are obscuring the real issues the public needs to grapple with. Transparency needs to be tempered with judgment. The CEO of one not-for-profit organization proudly spoke of his philosophy that "dirty laundry needs to be aired," but some influential members resigned from the organization because they believed he was publicly sharing too much detail about internal staff conflicts that leadership should have handled quietly.

A case can be made that the greatest positive effect of transparency is that the mere idea of it directs an organization's culture and activities in ways that can withstand public scrutiny whether the public needs to know about them or not. Transparency should lead to resources being committed to activities that are in the best interests of patients and the community being served. As a physician once put it during a discussion about transparency, "If you're going to be naked, you'd better be buff." Although the language may be brash, the advice is good.

Today's managers must consider more than just how their actions would play on CNN. Thanks to social media, an organization's actions may quickly become the latest viral internet sensation, with a series of unintended consequences.

Adherence to Professional Codes of Ethical Conduct

Do the existing codes of ethical conduct promulgated by the professional organizations and associations representing physicians, healthcare executives, and hospitals require that the incident at Paradise Hills be fully disclosed to the patients involved? The *Code of Medical Ethics* of the American Medical Association (AMA 2023) states:

> In the context of health care, an error is an unintended act or omission or a flawed system or plan that harms or has the potential to harm a patient. Patients have a right to know their past and present medical status, including conditions that may have resulted from medical error. Open communication is fundamental to the trust that underlies the patient-physician relationship, and physicians have an obligation to promote patient welfare and safety. Concern regarding legal liability should not affect the physician's honesty with the patient.

Even when new information regarding the medical error will not alter the patient's medical treatment or therapeutic options, individual physicians who have been involved in a (possible) medical error should:

(a) Disclose the occurrence of the error, explain the nature of the (potential) harm and provide the information needed to enable the patient to make informed decisions about future medical care.

(b) Acknowledge the error and express professional and compassionate concern towards patients who have been harmed in the context of health care.

(c) Explain the efforts that are being taken to prevent similar occurrences in the future.

(d) Provide for continuity of care to patients who have been harmed during the course of care, including facilitating transfer of care when a patient has lost trust in the physician.

Physicians who have discerned that another health care professional (may have) erred in caring for a patient should:

(e) Encourage the individual to disclose.

(f) Report impaired or incompetent colleagues in keeping with ethics guidance.

As professionals uniquely positioned to have a comprehensive view of the care patients receive, physicians must strive to ensure patient safety and should play a central role in identifying, reducing and preventing medical errors. Both as individuals and collectively as a profession, physicians should:

(g) Support a positive culture of patient safety, including compassion for peers who have been involved in a medical error.

(h) Enhance patient safety by studying the circumstances surrounding medical error. A legally protected review process is essential for reducing health care errors and preventing harm.

(i) Establish and participate fully in effective, confidential, protected mechanisms for reporting medical errors.

(j) Participate in developing means for objective review and analysis of medical errors.

(k) Ensure that all investigation of root causes and analysis of error leads to measures to prevent future occurrences and that these measures are conveyed to relevant stakeholders.

The *Code of Ethics* of the American College of Healthcare Executives (ACHE 2022) states:

> The healthcare executive shall conduct professional activities with honesty, integrity, respect, fairness and good faith in a manner that will reflect well upon the profession. . . . The healthcare executive shall, within the scope of his or her authority, work to ensure the existence of a process that will advise patients or others served of the rights, opportunities, responsibilities and risks regarding available healthcare services.

These ethical standards provide clear guidance to those wrestling with the ethical dilemma at Paradise Hills. As professionals, the physicians must disclose and discuss medical errors with their patients. The executives at Paradise Hills must determine whether their actions are consistent with the ethical standards that apply to them.

In 2017, ACHE joined forces with the Lucian Leape Institute of the Institute for Healthcare Improvement and National Patient Safety Foundation to create *Leading a Culture of Safety: A Blueprint for Success*—an evidence-based, practical resource that provides tools and proven strategies for healthcare leaders seeking to develop a safe environment for patients at every level of their organization (exhibit 3.1). The document's goals and strategies, both foundational and sustaining, are organized around six leadership domains, each of which requires the focus and commitment of the CEO:

1. Establish a compelling vision for safety.
2. Build trust, respect, and inclusion.
3. Select, develop, and engage your board.
4. Prioritize safety in the selection and development of leaders.
5. Lead and reward a just culture.
6. Establish organizational behavior expectations.

Exhibit 3.1: Six Domains for Developing a Culture of Safety

Source: ACHE (2023).

The safety *Blueprint* also includes a self-assessment tool that organizations can use to evaluate their strengths and weaknesses in this arena and to better plan where resources should be deployed (Wagner 2019). Several prominent healthcare leaders have testified to the *Blueprint*'s merit and usefulness in their organizations (Wagner 2019). The complete document can be downloaded from the ACHE website (see ACHE 2023) along with other valuable resources, tools, and best practices for building a culture of safety.

The guidance offered here supports the argument that ethical matters involving patient–physician relationships are, in fact, the business of hospital management and cannot be relegated to the medical staff alone. Senior-level healthcare managers must work in direct partnership with the medical staff to provide the safest possible care environment for patients.

Understanding the Medical Staff Perspective

That the physicians at Paradise Hills take a different view is not surprising. A basic understanding of the medical staff orientation helps explain why physicians adamantly protect what they consider to be their professional province.

Physicians typically enjoy a supreme position in the hospital's organizational hierarchy. They generally establish and maintain the rules that regulate most patient care in the hospital, and they serve as gatekeepers in admitting patients to the healthcare system. Once patients are admitted for care, they and their caregivers are required to follow "doctor's orders." Physicians thus set the standards for patient care. According to this classic view, physicians are granted the authority to define illness because they possess "a body of knowledge that defines and constructs the roles to be played in the context of the institution" (Berger and Luckmann 1967, 67). Roles make it possible for institutions to exist. The role physicians play inducts them into specific areas of knowledge, not only in the narrower cognitive sense but also in the sense of norms, values, and even emotions. This knowledge may become so internalized that physicians consider the role "an inevitable fate for which [they] may disclaim responsibility." Thus, they might say, "I have no choice in the matter, I have to act this way because of my position" (Berger and Luckmann 1967, 76).

Physicians learn their role through a complex socialization process that begins when they enter medical school. The rigors and expense of medical school, the admission requirements, the protégé system, and the collegial bonds of the medical profession all reflect occupational socialization. On completion of medical school, the symbolic universe of physicians includes elaborate rights, obligations, standard practices, and a role-specific vocabulary. Physicians are now socialized to play the role as definers of reality for patients (Berger and Luckmann 1967, 91).

The effects of this socialization on the moral reasoning of medical students was the subject of an important study conducted by Hébert, Meslin, and Dunn (1992) at the University of Toronto. Students in all four years of medical school participated in the study; the first-year students completed the survey during their medical school orientation. The research instrument presented four clinical scenarios, and the respondents were asked to list the ethical issues in each. Significantly, the fourth-year students identified far fewer ethical issues than the first-year students did. The researchers concluded that "these studies show a disturbing pattern; the ethical sensitivity of medical students seems to decrease with more time in medical school. Is this the consequences of medical socialization and is it harmful?"

Thus, physicians approach the world very differently than hospital administrators do. "Physicians tend to be doers, reactive, independent, solo decisionmakers, business owners," whereas hospital administrators "tend to be planners, proactive, participative, collaborative problem solvers, business stewards" (Peck 2012). Physicians tend to focus on individual patients, whereas administrators focus on the overall organization. To work together successfully, they must reach agreement that what is good for individual patients and what is good for the organization are one and the same.

In any discussion about the role of physicians, some attention must be given to professionalism. Professionals, such as physicians, lawyers, accountants, and healthcare executives, have a number of characteristics in common. They typically form associations, establish licensing or certifications, require specialized education, codify standards of conduct, have their own language, and promote professional autonomy and self-regulation. These characteristics tend to foster exclusivity and place professionals in a position of dominance in society. Some observers will argue that physicians' position of dominance is justified because they must make life-and-death decisions. Advocates of patient self-determination, however, claim that physician dominance is detrimental—that the health status of individuals or populations can improve only when they have a better understanding of health promotion, disease prevention, and disease management.

At Paradise Hills, the physicians believe that matters of patient care fall strictly in their domain because of occupational socialization and the professional dominance they enjoy.

Discrimination Against a Class of Patients

Labeling the patients in the Paradise Hills case as "terminal" and treating them differently from the way other groups in similar situations are treated is arguably a form of discrimination. Situations where withholding information because of class distinctions appears to be the norm can place decision makers on a slippery slope because allowing this action with one group may be taken as permission to replicate it among other groups. Treating certain patients differently can be especially dangerous in healthcare organizations, whose patient, employee, and professional populations are increasingly diverse.

Who decides if withholding information from a particular patient or group is appropriate? As the population ages and resources become increasingly scarce, the debate about limiting treatment options for older people will rage on. This issue is not new; when dialysis and kidney and heart transplants were introduced in the 1960s, the same discussions took place. Around the same time, ethics committees were finding their way into the hospital setting. However, costs are now central to the discussions, so more conflicts are likely to occur. When the issues at stake involve "priceless" lives and the cost–benefit analysis of treatments, the following questions are likely to come into consideration:

- Does extended quality of life for the individual matter?
- Does the individual's contribution or future contribution to society matter? For example, is treating a rocket scientist different from treating a homeless person?
- Where does self-determination fit into the equation?
- Do "believers" of a certain religion or sect get priority over "nonbelievers"?
- Do patients born in the United States get priority over immigrants?
- What about those who have increased health risks because of what they do to their bodies—substance abusers, alcoholics, smokers, or the obese?
- Does it matter who is paying the bill—government, insurance, or private pay?
- When dealing with older adults, are all 75-year-olds equal physically, mentally, emotionally, and intellectually?
- Who should participate in these decisions?

These same questions may be asked in the future to determine whether costly medications or procedures should be part of the treatment plan for any patient, not just those of a particular group. Clearly, the ethical implications of these decisions will weigh heavily on the minds of healthcare managers faced with the responsibility of developing organizational structures to deal with such issues. A national conversation about this topic is necessary, one that does not allow political interests and hysteria to influence the discussion. Healthcare executives must take the lead in framing the discussion and in developing language and terminology that allow the discussion to take place without talk of "death panels."

Management's Role and Responsibility

What are the role and responsibility of hospital management in the Paradise Hills case? What are the role and responsibility of the hospital CEO specifically? A literal interpretation of the standards of ethical conduct promulgated by ACHE and the AHA (as presented earlier in this chapter) would indicate that the role of the CEO in this case is burdensome because the CEO must balance complex needs and conflicting interests. In fulfilling all his duties, the CEO has responsibilities to the governing board, the institution, the medical staff, the employees, the community, the patients, the profession, and himself.

The CEO's mandate is to carry out the policies of the governing board, which include ensuring compliance with the board-approved ethical standards for the practices of the institution. The CEO is likewise charged with the responsibility of ensuring that the institution operates in ways that are consistent with its mission and values statements.

Partnering with the Medical Staff

The management staff at Paradise Hills have a strong working relationship with the medical staff. The oncology physicians have been especially loyal and committed to Paradise Hills, and in return hospital management has provided them with the resources and technology they need to practice state-of-the-art medicine. It has been a win–win situation for Paradise Hills. The CEO is determined to arrive at a solution to this problem that will preserve the existing medical staff–management relationship. Not incidentally, he knows he must avoid alienating these community-based physicians, whose patients are vital to the financial viability of the hospital.

Leadership hospitals generally embrace the core belief that medical staff participation is essential to the successful operations and strategic planning of the institution. Management in such an institution enthusiastically integrates medical staff participation into its way of doing business, fosters ongoing dialogue with physicians, and recognizes the medical staff as a needed resource. The CEO at Paradise Hills has worked to develop such an environment and is staunch in his resolve that the medical staff must be full and active participants in this ethical decision making. The CEO believes that a satisfactory solution to this incident must not violate confidentiality of patient information, must not infringe on or threaten patient–physician relationships, and must not precipitate a lawsuit. He knows that to secure these objectives, he must work closely with the medical staff and avoid an adversarial confrontation. The physicians must be full partners in the analysis and resolution of the problem. Their voice in the proceedings must be heard and attended to. The outcome must be one in which they have been allowed to exercise some element of control.

Fortunately, the CEO at Paradise Hills is armed with the primary prerequisite to successful partnering with the medical staff: They trust him. To solve this ethical problem successfully, he must be well prepared with solid facts, a well-thought-out rationale for action, and a commitment and plan to deal with all consequences of the actions taken.

The CEO and management staff must also recognize that medical errors take their toll on the physicians and other staff who are involved in an incident. Management must therefore take measures to assist staff in appropriately coping with medical errors.

Leadership

In this case, as in all ethical matters, the CEO has enormous leadership responsibility. The CEO is responsible for the ethical culture in the organization, implementing the standards of ethical conduct, and serving as an ethical role model for staff. While clinical professionals may bring their own codes of conduct to the workplace, management must set the tone for how business is conducted, how professionals interact, and how patients are served.

In their classic text *Leaders*, Bennis and Namus (1985, 186) are clear on this point: "The leader is responsible for the set of ethics or norms that govern the behavior of people in the organization. Leaders set the moral tone." Nancy Schlichting, former CEO of Henry Ford Health System, says (quoted in Rice and Perry 2013, 33), "The greatest deterrent to unethical behavior is values-driven leadership. When people stand for something and there are visible symbols of those values for all to see, they hold it up and measure against it. Employees look at what the leaders are doing and they feel free to come forward and challenge behaviors that do not meet that standard."

According to renowned ethicist Paul B. Hofmann (quoted in Rice and Perry 2013, 38), "the consistent and absolute intolerance of unethical behavior" is a leadership responsibility. "A policy of zero tolerance means swift action is taken when it occurs, regardless of organizational status. Prerequisites include a comprehensive and unambiguous code of conduct that is well disseminated and understood; no disconnect between the rhetoric and reality of organizational values; [and] behavior of all organizational leaders and staff members that is always above reproach." The significance of the leader as a role model should not be underestimated. Through their behavior, leaders define what is acceptable and what is not. Others in the organization will seek to emulate those behaviors to gain favor or status.

Ethical problems are a true managerial dilemma because they often represent conflict between an organization's financial performance and its responsibilities to the community and the patients it serves. In the Paradise Hills case, will telling the patients about the errors reduce the public's trust in the organization and dissuade patients from being treated there? Will telling the patients about the errors alienate the physicians and induce them to admit their patients to other facilities? This case, like all ethical problems, requires that the CEO, his management team, and the medical staff think through the consequences of their actions on multiple dimensions using ethical analysis as well as bottom-line considerations. While the task is complex and the conflicts may appear insurmountable, Bennis and Namus (1985, 186) remind us that "leaders are persons who are able to influence others; this influence helps to establish the organizational climate for ethical conduct; ethical conduct generates trust; and trust contributes substantially to the long-term success of the organization."

The Betsy Lehman Case

A real-life case that is strikingly similar to the Paradise Hills incident involved Betsy Lehman and the Dana-Farber Cancer Institute.

Betsy Lehman was a health news reporter for the *Boston Globe*, and her husband was a scientist at the Dana-Farber Cancer Institute. She died in December 1994 while undergoing chemotherapy at Dana-Farber. Her overdose error was discovered in February 1995 during a medical records review. This tragic case underscores the interrelatedness of management, clinical care, and ethics and drives home the point that leadership cannot delegate risk management but must make risk management its own responsibility.

The Betsy Lehman case has been considered a landmark event in the evolution of national attention given to medical errors. It was certainly well publicized. The *Boston Globe* broke the story in March 1995 with the headline "Doctor's Orders Kill Cancer Patient." An ABC News special with Barbara Walters and Dr. Timothy Johnson, "Betsy Lehman and Medical Errors in U.S. Hospitals," aired in July 1995. Even Lucian Leape, long considered a pioneer advocate for patient safety, appeared on national television as an authority on the prevalence and causes of medical errors. Notably, the Institute of Medicine report *To Err Is Human* was published a few years later, in November 1999, and patient safety initiatives—including federal legislation intended to reduce medical errors—soon followed.

A root cause analysis of the Betsy Lehman case revealed the breakdown of a complex medication process compounded by a lack of communication, illegible physician handwriting, and professional arrogance. Although the human loss in this case was immeasurable, the organization also suffered a public relations crisis that had an extensive negative impact on merger negotiations; staff morale; clinical trials; donations; and the recruitment of physicians, nurses, and researchers. Both The Joint Commission and the state of Massachusetts placed Dana-Farber on probation, affecting both its Medicare reimbursement and its ability to treat patients. This case was published by Harvard Business School and is used as a teaching tool in university programs throughout the United States (Bohmer and Winslow 1999).

REFERENCES

Agency for Healthcare Research and Quality (AHRQ). 2023. "Center for Quality Improvement and Patient Safety." Reviewed June. www.ahrq.gov/cpi/centers/cquips/index.html.

———. 2003. "AHRQ's Patient Safety Initiative: Breadth and Depth for Sustainable Improvements." Chapter 3 in *AHRQ's Patient Safety Initiative: Building Foundations, Reducing Risk.* Updated December. www.ahrq.gov/research/findings/final-reports/pscongrpt/index.html (content no longer available).

American College of Healthcare Executives (ACHE). 2023. *Leading a Culture of Safety: A Blueprint for Success.* Accessed August 24. www.ache.org/about-ache/our-story/our-commitments/leading-for-safety/blueprint.

———. 2022. *Code of Ethics.* As amended December 5. www.ache.org/about-ache/our-story/our-commitments/ethics/ache-code-of-ethics.

American Hospital Association (AHA). 2003. *The Patient Care Partnership: Understanding Expectations, Rights and Responsibilities.* Accessed September 3, 2023. www.aha.org/system/files/2018-01/aha-patient-care-partnership.pdf.

American Medical Association (AMA). 2023. "Promoting Patient Safety." *Code of Medical Ethics* Opinion 8.6. Accessed September 3. www.ama-assn.org/delivering-care/ethics/promoting-patient-safety.

Bates, D. W., D. M. Levine, H. Salmasian, A. Syrowatka, D. M. Shahian, S. Lipsitz, J. P. Zebrowski, L. C. Myers, M. S. Logan, C. G. Roy, C. Iannaccone, and M. L. Frits. 2023. "The Safety of Inpatient Healthcare." *New England Journal of Medicine* 388: 142–53.

Bennis, W., and B. Namus. 1985. *Leaders: The Strategies for Taking Charge.* New York: Harper and Row.

Berger, P. L., and T. Luckmann. 1967. *The Social Construction of Reality.* Garden City, NY: Anchor Books.

Bohmer, R. M. J., and A. Winslow. 1999. "The Dana-Farber Cancer Institute." Harvard Business School Case 699-025. Revised July. www.hbs.edu/faculty/Pages/item.aspx?num=304.

Cosgrove, T. 2013. *Transparency: A Patient's Right to Know.* Commentary, Institute of Medicine. Published May 17. https://nam.edu/wp-content/uploads/2015/06/RighttoKnow.pdf.

Goedert, J. 2012. "Study Pegs Cost of Medical Errors Near $1 Trillion Annually." HealthData Management. Published October 19. www.healthdatamanagement.com/news/medical-errors-economic-cost-study-hospitals-45134-1.html (content no longer available).

Greider, K. 2012. "The Worst Place to Be If You're Sick." *AARP Bulletin.* Published March. http://pubs.aarp.org/aarpbulletin/201203_DC?pg=10 (content no longer available).

Hathaway, B. 2020. "Estimates of Preventable Hospital Deaths Too High, New Study Shows." Yale News. Published January 25. https://news.yale.edu/2020/01/28/estimates-preventable-hospital-deaths-are-too-high-new-study-shows.

Hébert, P. C., E. M. Meslin, and E. V. Dunn. 1992. "Measuring the Ethical Sensitivity of Medical Students: A Study at the University of Toronto." *Journal of Medical Ethics* 18 (3): 142–47.

Iezzoni, L. I., S. R. Rao, C. M. DesRoches, C. Vogeli, and E. G. Campbell. 2012. "Survey Shows That at Least Some Physicians Are Not Always Open or Honest with Patients." *Health Affairs* 31 (2): 383–91.

Kohn, L. T., J. M. Corrigan, and M. S. Donaldson (eds.). 1999. *To Err Is Human: Building a Safer Health System.* Washington, DC: National Academies Press.

Kraman, S. S., and G. Hamm. 1999. "Risk Management: Extreme Honesty May Be the Best Policy." *Annals of Internal Medicine* 131 (12): 913–67.

Kübler-Ross, E. 1969. *On Death and Dying.* New York: Macmillan.

Leapfrog Group. 2023. "Errors, Injuries, Accidents, Infections." Leapfrog Hospital Safety Grade. Updated May 3. www.hospitalsafetygrade.org/what-is-patient-safety/errors-injuries-accidents-infections.

O'Reilly, K. B. 2012a. "Fear of Punitive Response to Hospital Errors Lingers." *American Medical News.* Published February 20. www.amednews.com/article/20120220/profession/302209938/2/.

———. 2012b. "Medicare's No-Pay Rule Sharpens Infection-Control Efforts." *American Medical News.* Published May 14. www.amednews.com/article/20120514/profession/305149943/6/.

———. 2008. "No Pay for 'Never Events' Becoming Standard." *American Medical News.* Published January 7. www.amednews.com/article/20080107/profession/301079966/7/.

Peck, C. 2012. "Better Hospital–Physician Partnerships." *Hospitals & Health Networks Daily.* Published April 5. www.hhnmag.com/hhnmag/HHNDaily/HHNDailyDisplay.dhtml?id=9270008713 (content no longer available).

Pilla, L. 2000. "Clinton Introduces Plan to Reduce Medical Errors." Nurses.com. Published February 22. www.nurses.com/doc/Clinton-Introduces-Plan-to-Reduce-Medical-Err-0001 (content no longer available).

Quality Interagency Coordination Task Force. 2000. *Doing What Counts for Patient Safety: Federal Actions to Reduce Medical Errors and Their Impact.* Accessed September 4, 2023. http://archive.ahrq.gov/quic/report/mederr2.htm.

Rice, J., and F. Perry. 2013. *Healthcare Leadership Excellence: Creating a Career of Impact.* Chicago: Health Administration Press.

Sipherd, R. 2018. "The Third Leading Cause of Death in US Most Doctors Don't Want You to Know About." CNBC. Updated February 28. www.cnbc.com/2018/02/22/medical-errors-third-leading-cause-of-death-in-america.html.

US Department of Health and Human Services (HHS). 2012. *Hospital Incident Reporting Systems Do Not Capture Most Patient Harm.* Report no. OEI-06-09-00091. Published January. https://oig.hhs.gov/oei/reports/oei-06-09-00091.pdf.

Wagner, K. 2019. "Executing on Your Safety Priorities." *Healthcare Executive* 34 (2): 17–23.

CHAPTER 4

Conflicting Moral Demands:
Qual Plus HMO

CASE STUDY

For ten years, Jim Goodrich had been the chief operating officer (COO) of Qual Plus, a successful not-for-profit, staff-model managed care organization (MCO) with 275,000 members in a major metropolitan area on the West Coast. The organization was so financially successful, in some measure thanks to Jim's efforts, that it was about to embark on the construction of a $12 million corporate office complex to house its business activities. As COO, Jim was responsible for the planning and development of the project, the purchase of the land, and the presentation of the construction proposal to the 12-member board of directors.

Now that the board had given the project a green light, the board's building and grounds committee needed to select a general contractor and submit the construction contract to the board for its approval. The committee-established selection criteria for the general contractor included demonstrated quality of work, ability to meet construction deadlines and work within budget, financial solvency, and competitive costs. Only local firms known to adhere to ethical business practices were asked to bid on the project.

The request for bids indicated that all bids had to be sealed and delivered by noon on December 9 to the COO's office. Bids received after this designated time or not in this designated manner would not be considered. The committee was scheduled to meet at 1:00 p.m. that day to open the bids, review them, and select a general contractor to submit for board approval.

Dan Smith had served on the building and grounds committee for a number of years. Well liked by the other members of the board, he had been appointed to this committee because, as the owner of Smith Masonry, he had expert knowledge of construction and related fields.

At the appointed time, the committee met, opened the bids, and began its review. Of the bids received, three met all criteria. The costs associated with two of the bids were close. The cost of the third bid, offered by Acme Construction, was considerably higher. Dan was visibly shaken. Knowing that Acme subcontracted with Dan's firm for masonry work, Jim assumed Dan would declare a conflict of interest and abstain when it came time for a vote. Jim did not anticipate what happened next.

As the discussion was about to begin, Dan moved that the committee take a ten-minute recess before continuing its deliberations. When the committee reconvened, Dan made a motion that the three contractors who had made the final cut be offered the opportunity to submit a "final" bid within 24 hours. The committee would then reconvene the next day to review these final bids. Jim was astonished at the motion and at its immediate support from the rest of the committee and questioned the rationale, legality, and ethical implications of the proposed action. He was told quite simply that because all three finalists were being given the same opportunity, it should not be considered illegal or improper. As for rationale, the committee believed that Acme Construction, which met all of the other criteria, may have inadvertently made a calculation error that placed its bid so much higher than the other two finalists. Dan indicated that it would, in fact, be unfair and unethical not to allow a final bid from a contractor known to be competitive in pricing and highly regarded in the building community when the difference in bid was obviously great enough to be a miscalculation. The motion was quickly called, and the vote was unanimous that "final" bids would be sought from the three contractors.

Jim was shocked and angry that the board committee would take action that he believed to be blatantly unethical, if not illegal. Furthermore, as the executive responsible for this project, he was expected to concur with their decision, an expectation that he was uncomfortable with and believed to be in conflict with his responsibility as an administrator. As soon as he was in his office, Jim called the organization's attorney and reviewed the committee action with him. When asked about the legality of this action, the attorney said he believed it to be a bit unusual but not illegal. Jim suspected that the attorney was reluctant to explore the matter more fully because it was individual board members' actions that were being questioned, rather than the action of the board as a whole.

At this point, Jim knew he had to report the events of the afternoon to Brent Williams, his boss. Brent had been CEO of Qual Plus since its inception 15 years ago and had the unfailing support of the board of directors. Jim liked Brent, and his reporting relationship with him had been mutually satisfying. Brent trusted Jim and gave him latitude to run the operations of the organization. At times Jim felt that Brent might play a little fast and loose with propriety, but the issues were always personal ones that did not really affect Jim or the operations of the organization. Rumors had circulated that Brent's home had been remodeled at no cost to him through Dan's largesse and that his automobiles were provided at no cost to him by another board member. He was also known to vacation often in a luxury condo in the Caribbean owned by yet another board member. More disturbing to Jim, however, was the fact that Brent's administrative assistant took care of all his personal errands and was often gone from the office for extended periods.

When Jim told Brent about the committee action, Brent dismissed it with a shrug. "It's a board committee—it's their call," he said. Jim persisted and told Brent that he was not comfortable with the committee's actions, especially because he was the one expected to execute their decision. He said he intended to request an opinion from the Qual Plus ethics committee. Brent appeared agitated at this suggestion and said abruptly, "I would not recommend that, but if you feel you must, go ahead. Just remember, it's your job that's on the line here." He then stood up, indicating that the discussion was over.

Jim was disappointed with Brent's reaction. With a mortgage, twin daughters in college, a son in high school, and a wife with professional ties to the community, Jim was not prepared to relocate. He doubted he could match his current salary in another position. Brent and the board had been extremely generous with his compensation package. Jim did not want to jeopardize his position at Qual Plus. On the other hand, he was seriously troubled by his dilemma.

He called the chair of the organization's ethics committee, who said she did not believe this situation fell within the purview of her committee because it was a board action. However, she agreed to poll her committee and get back to Jim with a response by late afternoon. Jim was not surprised when she called back to say that her committee agreed with her earlier assessment. Jim had come to the conclusion that no one at Qual Plus was ready to take on the board members over this issue. Frustrated, Jim knew that he was expected to keep his mouth shut and carry out the board committee's wishes. He also knew that if he did this, he would be violating his personal principles and would make himself vulnerable to future expectations of unethical behavior.

ETHICS ISSUES

Conflict of interest: Do Dan's actions constitute a flagrant conflict of interest? Does Qual Plus have an organizational policy on conflicts of interest that specifically provides guidance and direction for governing board members?

Management's role and responsibility: What are management's role and responsibility in this matter? Specifically, what is the role of the CEO related to actions of governing board members? Have Brent's special relationships with board members compromised his position and authority as CEO? Is management's primary responsibility to the governing board or to the organization?

Use of organizational resources: Is having the administrative assistant perform personal business for the CEO an appropriate use of organizational resources? Is it appropriate for the CEO to accept personal favors of such value as home remodeling, luxury cars, and vacations from board members?

Adherence to the organization's mission statement, ethical standards, and values statement: Are the actions of the Qual Plus board committee consistent with the organization's mission statement, ethical standards, and values statement? What about Jim's reaction and Dan's reaction?

Adherence to professional codes of ethical conduct: Are the actions here consistent with the codes of conduct promulgated by the professional organizations and associations representing healthcare executives, governing board members, and MCOs?

Organizational implications and evaluating the effectiveness of ethics committees: What is the role of the Qual Plus ethics committee in this situation? What does it say about the organizational culture if so many staff and governing board members appear to find the board committee's action to be acceptable? What effects do the actions of the leadership at Qual Plus have on the organizational culture?

Conflicting moral demands: What is the responsibility of a healthcare executive when they are asked to do something that they feel is unethical? What is the responsibility of a healthcare executive when they observes their boss or others acting unethically? How does the healthcare executive reconcile professional and personal ethical demands when they are in conflict with one another?

Legal implications: Does the action of the board committee in this case constitute a violation of the organization's bid process? Is any aspect of the action illegal? What is the responsibility of the organization's attorney in this case? Is the misuse or waste of charitable or community resources a legal concern, as well as unethical?

Justice and fairness: Even if it is not illegal, is the board committee's action fair to the other contractors who participated in good faith in the bid process as stated in the written request for bids?

DISCUSSION

Conflict of Interest

What is a conflict of interest? According to the *Encyclopedia of American Law*, the term *conflict of interest* is "used to describe the situation in which a public official or fiduciary who, contrary to the obligation and absolute duty to act for the benefit of the public or a designated individual, exploits the relationship for personal benefit, typically pecuniary" (Gale Cengage Learning 2010). In healthcare, a conflict of interest typically arises when an individual or group, such as a board of trustees, has been entrusted with the assets of an organization but acts for personal gain rather than in the organization's best interests. A conflict of interest may be present if even the potential for personal gain exists. Conflicts of interest are very real dangers, both to organizations and to careers. Healthcare managers must always be mindful of potential clashes between their professional obligations and personal interests because even the appearance of a conflict of interest can be damaging.

The American College of Healthcare Executives (ACHE) believes that conflicts of interest are significant enough to warrant reference in two of its policy statements. In its "Considerations for Healthcare Executive–Supplier Interactions," ACHE (2016) states:

> In interacting with current and potential suppliers, healthcare executives must act in ways that merit trust, confidence and respect, while fulfilling their duties to the public, their organizations and the profession. Further, it is important to avoid even the appearance of conflicts of interest that may seem to unduly advantage the healthcare executive, the organization or the supplier. Thus, healthcare executives must demonstrate the utmost integrity and embrace the need for transparency in interactions with suppliers.

In its policy statement "Ethical Decision Making for Healthcare Executives," ACHE (2021) states:

> Ethical decision making is required when the healthcare executive must address a conflict or uncertainty regarding competing values, such as personal, organizational, professional and societal values. . . . Healthcare organizations should have resources that may include ethics committees, ethics consultation services, and written policies, procedures, frameworks and guidelines to assist them with the ethics decision-making process. With these organizational resources and guidelines in place, the best interests of patients, families, caregivers, the organization, payers and the community can be thoughtfully and appropriately evaluated in a timely manner.

State licensures for professionals also may include standards of conduct that address conflicts of interest.

Conflicts of interest most often involve money. A conflict of interest becomes an issue when an individual's personal ties could influence their professional judgment or when an individual is in a position to influence the business of the organization in ways that could lead to personal gain or that of close family or friends. In some cases, individuals may be quick to exercise caution when their own personal gain is at issue but lax toward the gain of others in their realm of family, friends, or, more significantly, those in authority. However, the same principle applies.

Healthcare executives who know they are not doing anything wrong may not consider the appearance of impropriety as seriously as they should. Sometimes, the healthcare executive may be so close to the issue that they cannot see how their actions appear to others and may not realize that their actions are unfair to legitimate stakeholders because their conflict of interest favors other parties. Of particular relevance in the Qual Plus case is this value of fairness and how it relates to the other general contractors who have fulfilled the criteria required by the organization's formal bid process. Corporate policies and procedures should, above all, be fair to all parties concerned.

Conflicts of interest seem to feature in newspaper headlines with increasing regularity amid the ever-changing complexities of the US healthcare system and in American society where some people find it acceptable to stretch the limits of the law and propriety for economic or personal advantage. Legal and ethical implications will continue to multiply as more and more hospitals and physicians contract for services, as employers and insurers contract with hospitals and physician groups, and as issues of third-party payers, corporation-sponsored research, physician investments, mergers, and the like complicate the relationships involved.

Avoiding Conflicts of Interest

Conflicts of interest and the appearance of impropriety are easier to avoid than to explain. Academic health centers and universities, in particular, are aware of conflicts of interest associated with physicians' entrepreneurial activities and academic research, especially when funded by corporations. Many universities require that individuals, upon hire and periodically thereafter, disclose significant financial, personal, and professional relationships that may represent potential conflicts between their academic role and outside interests. Teaching organizations routinely require that faculty refrain from promoting services or products that bring them personal gain, financial or otherwise.

Governing board members of healthcare organizations are typically required to complete and sign an annual conflict-of-interest disclosure form, noting any financial interests or governing responsibilities they may have in businesses or entities that transact with the healthcare organization. Some organizations include conflict-of-interest clauses in senior-level executive contracts. Healthcare executives have a responsibility to abide by these standards even if they are not required to sign any conflict-of-interest agreement, however. They also must remember that the standards apply when close family or friends have a substantial interest in businesses that interact with the healthcare organization. When conflicts of interest are present, those with the conflicts should always recuse themselves from any decision making related to the entity.

While formal agreements are effective in preventing conflicts of interest from becoming major problems, informal realities in each organization also have a considerable impact on how business is conducted and what behavior is considered appropriate. Corporate norms, social groups, role modeling, and interpersonal relationships all play a role in determining behaviors. The burden of responsibility for ethical conduct in the organization is placed on the leaders of the organization, who ultimately are accountable for the corporate culture.

Professional codes of conduct usually address conflicts of interest. The ACHE policy statements cited earlier address the professional responsibilities of healthcare executives. The American Medical Association (AMA) also takes seriously its role in mitigating conflicts of interest among physicians. It publishes guidelines on conflicts of interest, conflicts of interest in biomedical research, managing conflicts of interest in the conduct of clinical trials, and financial relationships with industry in continuing medical education. Among the top ten ethical issues that the AMA urges educators to teach medical students are how to manage conflicts of interest versus obligations in education, clinical practice, and research and the reporting of incompetent or unethical behaviors by colleagues. (AMA 2020).

In defining the responsibility of governing boards related to conflicts of interest, the Association of Governing Boards (AGB) is clear. In the preface to its *Statement on Conflict of Interest*, it says that "in light of a number of high profile conflict of interest violations across the not-for-profit sector, there is a pressing need for boards to conduct thorough and periodic reviews of their conflict of interest policies and to ensure adherence" (AGB 2013, 2). One of the AGB's conflict-of-interest principles states (AGB 2013, 4):

> If reasonable observers, having knowledge of all of the relevant circumstances, would conclude that the board member has an actual or apparent conflict of interest in a matter related to the institution, the board member should have no role for the institution in the matter.

The principles go on to say (AGB 2013, 4):

> When a board member is barred by actual or apparent conflict of interest from voting on a matter, ordinarily the board member should not participate in or attend board discussion of the matter, even if to do so would be legally permissible. If, however, the board determines that it would significantly serve the interests of the board to have the conflicted board member explain the issue or answer questions, the board, if legally free to do so, may consider whether to invite the board member for that limited purpose. Any resulting invitation should be recorded in the minutes of the meeting.

The AGB principles also require that board members promptly disclose any real or apparent conflicts of interest and recommend that an organization's management annually inform its board of "major institutional relationships and transactions" to facilitate disclosure of conflicts of interest that may be present (AGB 2013, 5).

Although these principles are directed at governing board members, they are also instructive for healthcare managers because they address the organization's responsibility to educate board members on these standards of responsibility and to ensure that board policies address conflicts of interest. Managers who fail to ensure ethical standards of board conduct put the organization in danger of harm to its reputation and to the people who are part of it, whether they are personally guilty of unethical conduct or not.

Because it generally falls to senior management to plan and coordinate board orientation and continuing education, ensuring that the board's conflict-of-interest policy is current, well understood, and appropriately implemented is an essential part of that responsibility. It is also the law: "Having a conflict of interest policy [for governing boards] is also a legal requirement under federal law and some state laws. . . . Nonprofits that allow conflicts of interest to continue may be subject to penalties toward the affected board director, the organization or both" (Price 2018).

The *New York Times* published an article about a report that leaders at Memorial Sloan Kettering Cancer Center had violated conflict-of-interest policies. The report revealed that Sloan Kettering had "inadequate oversight and a lack of established protocols for examining whether employees' and executives' affiliations with corporations could result in biased results that favored a company's products" (Ornstein and Thomas 2019). The law firm conducting the review of Sloan Kettering said that although they found no "conscious decision to engage in misconduct by the hospital's executives or board members," they did find that "processes and controls for the review and management of senior executive and board-level conflicts were deficient and resulted in instances of noncompliance"

(Ornstein and Thomas 2019). Sloan Kettering was quick to respond with comprehensive policy changes and a commitment to transparency, including disclosure of financial interests on the organization's website. This incident serves as a reminder to all healthcare executives that conflicts of interest can be damaging to an organization—whether they are perceived or real, and whether intentional misconduct is involved or not.

A Formal and Fair Bid Process

Organizational conflict-of-interest policies and procedures should be written to provide guidance for employees and staff and help them define and avoid difficult situations. A formal bid process typically embodies this kind of protection for staff and ensures fair and equal treatment of vendors. The process and the selection criteria should be well publicized, and bids should be solicited from the broadest range of potential providers. The bids should be sealed and kept confidential, and they should be opened and reviewed simultaneously. Under no circumstances should one vendor know another's bid. The perception of wrongdoing must be avoided. Rumors of unethical business practices, even if untrue, can damage the reputation of the organization and cause it to lose future business. Improperly disclosing confidential information of one vendor to another could even be cause for litigation.

To ensure the integrity of the bid process, a blind consideration of all bids on merit, without identifying names, could be undertaken. If any question of conflict of interest remains, the individual involved should recuse themself from any decision making or discussion that may influence others' votes, to avoid the appearance of preferential treatment or bid rigging.

Clearly, policies, procedures, codes of conduct, and the like will help healthcare managers avoid problems associated with conflicts of interest. Equally important is candid, open discussion among coworkers and professional colleagues when questions of conflict of interest arise. This kind of honest dialogue can help substantially to eradicate any perceptions of wrongdoing before they develop.

Healthcare organizations should be judicious in selecting whom they partner with in their business transactions. It is not just a matter of money; the mission and values of the business partner also must be considered. Healthcare organizations must take care to align themselves only with ethical organizations.

Management's Role and Responsibility

Generally, executive leaders in healthcare organizations are expected to be "servant leaders"—that is, to serve the needs of their organization and its stakeholders. However, this leadership style may become problematic if the demands of patients, clients, governing board members, or others in the organization conflict with one's personal values. When a board member uses their board appointment to acquire personal financial gain, to obtain confidential information, or to secure favorable treatment for family or friends, it presents an ethical dilemma for the healthcare executive. Strong, capable leadership can handle this situation without compromising personal integrity. Occasions may arise when a healthcare executive must compromise personal preferences or close relationships for the good of the organization, but such compromise is different from sacrificing personal values or standards of ethical conduct. A CEO's responsibility to the organization also outweighs their responsibility to any individual board member. Having clearly written and well-understood policies for the conduct of the governing board is one way to preempt unreasonable and sometimes unethical requests from individual board members.

So, what should Brent have done in the case of Qual Plus? An appropriate and ethical approach in this situation may have been for the CEO and the board chair to discuss the situation and then meet privately with the board member in question to review the inappropriateness of his actions related to the bid process. Of course, this approach assumes that the CEO has previously implemented guidelines and codes of conduct for the organization and the board, including signed documents of conflict-of-interest disclosures. This approach also assumes that the CEO has been a visible role model for ethical conduct throughout the organization and the community and has included ethics education as part of the board's orientation and continuing education. Certainly, if these structural mechanisms were in place, questionable ethical practices like the one surrounding the Qual Plus bid process would not have occurred.

Further complicating the situation at Qual Plus and Brent's leadership abilities has been Brent's poor behavior as an effective role model. He dismisses Jim's concerns with little thought. He does not take the situation or Jim's discomfort with it seriously and shows no support or willingness to pursue an analysis of the ethical implications of the board committee's actions.

Use of Organizational Resources

In the Qual Plus case, the CEO's cavalier personal use of organizational resources sends a signal to employees and staff that such misuse is acceptable. He uses his administrative assistant as his personal valet, while the organization pays her salary and reaps small benefit from her time "at work." He drives luxury cars and takes frequent Caribbean vacations. He has created the impression of a lavish lifestyle garnered from being an executive of an HMO—and this at a time when the rising costs of healthcare and efforts to reduce those costs loom high on the national agenda. The CEO has provided fertile ground for the appearance of impropriety and suspicions that other questionable business practices may just not be visible. MCOs, like other healthcare institutions, are vulnerable to public scrutiny and accountability because they receive public benefits in the form of tax exemptions. Any suggestion that the organization's operations and business practices involve conflicts of interest, unethical practices, or profit making at whatever cost may threaten its tax status.

Executives with reputations for excess have been in trouble with the law, the government, and the public. The political and corporate worlds provide us with too many examples to list here. Healthcare executives are not exempt from temptation. Prominent, successful leaders can be found in the headlines and across the internet captured in humiliating, unethical, and sometimes illegal acts. More often than not, their misdeeds involve financial or sexual transgressions that can be traced to hubris—the arrogant belief that they deserve special treatment and perks and that they are above the rules of ordinary people. Unfortunately, great leaders sometimes possess major character flaws.

At Qual Plus, the propriety of the gifts and favors Brent receives from board members is also questionable. Gift giving is a reciprocal act, in which the recipient is expected to express gratitude in some way—by a subsequent gift, favor, or special consideration. In this case, what could the board members who had been presenting the gifts to Brent reasonably expect in return? The answer, as any experienced senior-level manager knows, is political considerations and personal favors. Brent is on dangerous ground because he may develop a sense that he is beholden to the gift givers and expected to provide favors that compromise his obligations to the organization and to the other board members. Such a feeling may, in some part, account for Brent's reluctance to challenge the board committee's actions at Qual Plus—a reluctance that is mirrored by that of the ethics committee and the attorney representing Qual Plus. The staff and employees in an organization take their cues from the CEO and the role modeling that the CEO demonstrates on a day-to-day basis. Such is the power of example. The CEO has the responsibility for establishing an ethical culture in the organization, implementing standards of ethical conduct, educating trustees and staff on these standards, and fulfilling the organization's ethical responsibilities to its community. The CEO must conduct their personal and professional life in an ethical manner worthy of emulation. Healthcare leaders must set high standards and then lead by example. Leaders must practice the standards that they expect of their employees and staff, who will follow what is lived rather than what is written. This is true regardless of the scope of a manager's sphere of influence. We have all known pillars of excellence within organizations. Chances are these departments have managers who set and live high ethical standards. While clinicians may bring their own codes of conduct to the workplace, management must set the tone for how business is conducted, how professionals interact, and how patients and clients are served. The culture of the organization quickly teaches newcomers what is acceptable, what is rewarded, and what is frowned upon.

Leadership creates the organizational culture, and the culture at Qual Plus appears to be toxic. Why do those in leadership positions sometimes behave in such obviously wrong ways? What impact does leadership behavior have on the organization? Savvy executives never underestimate the far-reaching influence of leadership throughout the organization. Leaders at the top are role models, and those under them will seek to emulate them in an effort to gain favor in the management hierarchy. Wise leaders will consider how to influence managers and informal leaders throughout the organization in positive ways.

Adherence to the Organization's Mission Statement, Ethical Standards, and Values Statement

While an organization must have a code of conduct, clear ethical standards must also be articulated and well understood by all members of the organization. Formal education of staff, trustees, physicians, vendors, and suppliers must ensure that everyone knows the ethical rules governing the organization and that everyone plays by them. Each program decision, resource allocation, personnel practice, corporate policy, and so forth, whether at the board level or below, must be undertaken only after the ethical implications have been examined and found to meet the organization's standards. In an ethical culture, staff are encouraged to question decisions and probe for the ethics issues that may be present. Forums for discussion and mechanisms for consultation contribute to sound ethical decisions.

A major responsibility of the CEO in the development of an ethical culture is educating trustees. Because trustees are typically community members, often in business, the board must have a clear conflict-of-interest policy. The governing board must mandate that all trustees declare any conflicts of interest and abstain from voting whenever decisions of the board would bring business advantages to them, either directly or indirectly. Policies related to competitive bidding procedures must be clear and information kept confidential.

Most trustees are aware of their fiduciary responsibilities to the organization. Too often, however, financial decisions may be reached without a full understanding of their ramifications. Trustees have an ethical responsibility to make informed financial decisions and to spend the organization's resources wisely. The healthcare executive must assist trustees in fulfilling this obligation by providing complete information and recommending continuing education when needed.

Information regarding patients, clients, physicians, staff, suppliers, and the organization must be treated as confidential by trustees unless otherwise specified. Frequently, trustees may be asked by friends or family to provide information that must be kept in confidence. A clear confidentiality policy must be in place and well understood. All board members must be educated regarding the Health Insurance Portability and Accountability Act and its requirements.

Only a few of the areas requiring trustee education are mentioned here. These areas were chosen because of their relevance to the case in point. However, some CEOs fail to make board education the priority that they should. Some fear that a strong, effective board may challenge their authority. Experienced executives know that a well-educated board is needed to move an organization forward. As governing boards become increasingly accountable for quality of care, financial oversight, and other important challenges, healthcare executives must take very seriously their responsibility to ensure their organization has an effective board in place.

Adherence to Professional Codes of Ethical Conduct

ACHE (2023) offers an Ethics Self-Assessment tool to help healthcare executives evaluate their areas of ethical strength and opportunities for improvement (see appendix A). Among the assessment's many statements for personal reflection are three that are relevant to the Qual Plus case:

1. I have a routine system in place for board members to make full disclosure and reveal potential conflicts of interest.
2. I personally disclose and expect board members, staff members, and clinicians to disclose any possible conflicts of interest before pursuing or entering into relationships with potential business partners.
3. I advocate ethical decision making by the board, management team, and medical staff.

The Ethics Self-Assessment is one of several tools available to help healthcare executives develop an ethical corporate culture and create management strategies and programs that support ethical decision making.

The best practices of other healthcare organizations can provide valuable guidance, too. In particular, healthcare organizations that focus on performance excellence will not fail to have an ethical culture. Malcolm Baldrige National Quality Award winners share their best practices willingly through both personal contacts and webinars that cover such topics as leadership, quality, and innovation. Henry Ford Allegiance Health (HFAH) has a strong and comprehensive code of conduct that leaves no doubt about the values its staff should practice and the importance of complying with its principles. Titled "Living Our Values: A Guide to Doing the Right Thing for the Right Reason," the HFAH code makes the organization's standards of conduct clear to all staff, who are required to formally attest to their understanding of, and duty to uphold, the code (Henry Ford Health System 2023). The code includes a brief test that employees can take to assess their knowledge of the standards; common healthcare scenarios are presented, questions are asked, and answers follow with rationale. Significantly, leadership at HFAH does not abdicate its personal or professional responsibility to abide by its code of conduct; a letter from CEO Georgia Fojtasek that accompanies the code of conduct states that "our values are timeless and should be embraced by all members of the HFAH team, including our Board, executives, staff, physicians, volunteers, partners and suppliers" (Henry Ford Health System 2023).

Compliance programs provide an opportunity to combine the responsibilities of compliance and ethics management in an organization. While a compliance program may address some ethical issues, separate compliance and ethics programs should be established that complement one another. Conduct that is legal may not be ethical, even though to be ethical an organization must comply with legal mandates.

A paramount responsibility of leadership in an organization, especially in a healthcare organization whose mission is to serve humanity, is to create a corporate culture where sound ethical decisions are a way of life. As professionals, healthcare executives must commit themselves to a set of standards higher than the morals of the marketplace.

Organizational Implications and Evaluating the Effectiveness of Ethics Committees

Historically, ethics committees and ethics consultants in healthcare organizations were called on to assist in resolving ethical issues related to end of life, access to treatment, and the like. Typically, the majority of committee members were clinicians, and the knotty issues brought to these committees were clinical in nature.

As the "business" of healthcare delivery has become more complicated, the lines between clinical and business ethical issues frequently blur. Healthcare executives are confronted with more ambiguities, potential for ethical dilemmas, and uncharted waters than ever before. Ethics committees can serve as a valuable sounding board to test ideas and explore potential solutions to ethical dilemmas, and they can be especially helpful to CEOs who may be removed from day-to-day operations.

However, to be prepared to deal with such multifaceted issues as managed care contracting, mergers and acquisitions, compliance, physician investment, and the like, ethics committees must regularly review their scope and function, as well as their member composition. Expanding the responsibilities of the ethics committee to include addressing organizational issues and providing advice and counsel to healthcare managers is imperative. Healthcare managers familiar with the clinical issues may be inexperienced with the business issues they now encounter. If ethics committees have not expanded their purposes, they may not be used where the greatest need exists.

For a number of reasons, an ethics committee may not be used as effectively as it should be. Staff and employees may not understand what the committee's role and functions are, what issues it deals with, or how to refer questions or concerns to it. They may be uncomfortable suggesting that the organization's actions, contemplated or otherwise, may not be ethical. They may not know that the committee's deliberations are confidential. They may believe the committee deals only with clinical issues because membership typically includes physicians and nurses. Management needs to address these issues through staff education and increased visibility of the committee's work.

Ethics committees play an important role in ensuring that an organization is meeting its obligations to patients, clients, and the community. If a healthcare organization is to make sound ethical decisions on a daily basis, its ethics committee must be readily accessible to staff and its effectiveness must be regularly evaluated. Chapter 25 offers practical strategies for evaluating the effectiveness of ethics committees and useful insights on committee self-assessment.

Conflicting Moral Demands

Ethical dilemmas in healthcare are seldom one-dimensional and are rarely, if ever, under the control of a single well-meaning manager. By definition, a dilemma implies conflicting choices with different consequences, usually undesirable. The conflicting moral demands of one's boss and one's conscience are a major challenge for the most ethical of healthcare managers. This dilemma lies at the heart of the matter in the Qual Plus case.

In December 2018, the Ethics and Compliance Initiative (ECI) released a report titled "A Global View at How Stronger Ethics Cultures Have a Favorable Impact on Ethics Outcomes." The report's encouraging findings showed that the actions and behaviors of employees are significantly influenced by a strong ethical culture, and that employees are more likely to report wrongdoing in an organization when a strong ethical culture is in place.

In the United States, 95 percent of employees in a strong ethical culture seek guidance when unsure of what ethical action to take, whereas only 49 percent of employees in a weak ethical culture do so (ECI 2023). In a strong ethical culture,

99 percent of employees feel prepared to handle situations that could lead to ethical violations, compared to only 24 percent in a weak ethical culture (ECI 2023).

More discouraging were data that 22 percent of US employees felt pressure to compromise their personal standards during the previous 12 months, and that 30 percent personally observed misconduct in the workplace. Not surprisingly, as pressure to compromise standards increased, misconduct also increased. Perhaps the most alarming finding was that 76 percent of US employees personally reported ethical misconduct during the previous 12 months (ECI 2023).

Those who did not report ethical violations cited the following reasons: 74 percent feared that reporting would not be confidential; 69 percent did not believe corrective action would be taken; 64 percent could not report anonymously; and 63 percent feared being labeled a "snitch." The study indicated that 53 percent of those who reported ethical violations did, in fact, experience retaliation. The retaliation most often affected those in top management positions (ECI 2023).

As expected, strong management commitment and vocal support for ethics were positive indicators for overall workplace integrity. The ECI (2023) study identified six critical elements for an effective ethics and compliance program:

1. Written standards of workplace integrity
2. Training on the standards of workplace integrity
3. Ability to seek feedback and advice related to workplace integrity
4. Confidential or anonymous reporting mechanism
5. Workplace integrity as part of the performance appraisal process
6. Formal process to discipline violations of the code of conduct

Of the US employees responding to the 2018 survey, 41 percent said all six of these elements were in place at their organization; 47 percent said some of these elements were present; and 12 percent said none of them were present or they didn't know (ECI 2023).

As mentioned, misconduct is more prevalent in organizations with weak ethical cultures. An organization's culture may condone unethical conduct simply by overlooking it. Sometimes overlooking seemingly small examples of unethical behavior gives a colleague the green light to misbehave in bigger ways. In contrast, questioning the colleague and challenging their actions can alert them to an opportunity for behavior modification.

So what do you do when someone in authority asks you to act unethically? Standing up for what is right is always commendable, but before you do so, you must calculate the costs and the unintended consequences of your actions. Most people cannot afford to stand up for their principles lest they lose their job, especially during an economic recession. Of those who are reluctant to report wrongdoing, many fear retaliation of some kind.

Indeed, an employee facing this dilemma is at great personal risk if they refuse to perform unethical acts and if, as in the Qual Plus case, those in authority are the CEO and board members who control the employee's job and, to some extent, future career. Aside from potentially losing his job, what other considerations must weigh heavily on Jim's decision? What about his family obligations, his children's education, and his wife's ties to the community? Jim believes he would have difficulty matching his current compensation package if he were fired. Is this a valid consideration in his decision making? Are his personal well-being and the well-being of his family separate from morality? How would he explain his termination, if that should occur? What about his references for new employment? Would he be labeled as "not a team player"? Is he the only one who sees anything wrong? Would all the parties involved deny any wrongdoing if the situation were made public? Does Jim have any personal liability if he acts unethically?

On the other hand, if Jim acquiesces to the board committee's requests and takes action that he deems unethical, what consequences can he expect? Jim knows that he will have difficulty living with himself if he makes that decision. It will be a terrible blow to his self-esteem. He worries that if he complies with the committee's wishes, he will be expected to abandon his principles in future decisions—in essence, be "held hostage" by this action in whatever unethical murky situations lie ahead. Most employees simply give in under this kind of pressure and become "organization people."

A physician who was asked about a similar dilemma responded, "I'm not so narcissistic that I would stand firm in my righteousness while my family starved." Perhaps he was exaggerating, but his comment makes an interesting point: One's moral obligations are complex. There are no simple answers. An experienced senior-level executive in a multinational corporation, when told of the physician's remark, immediately replied, "He's using his family as a rationalization for not doing the difficult thing." He went on to explain that he had been with a company that gave very large bonuses to its top senior executives (himself included) but at the same time told the executives to cut the salaries of all their direct reports. When he complained that this was unfair, he was told the decision had been made. He decided he couldn't live with that and resigned. It took him three months to find another position, but he said he never regretted his decision and his family supported him in it. Although we do not know all of the circumstances in either the physician's or the executive's case, we can appreciate that they both faced challenging dilemmas and that a number of considerations entered into their decisions.

Given all the risks involved, can a senior-level manager defy authority more easily than an administrative assistant can? Who has more to lose? Being asked to ignore or participate in ethical misconduct presents challenges at all levels of the organization. Resolution is difficult for any employee, and the difficulty is only intensified by personal circumstances.

The federal government recognizes the difficulty that employees face when they are asked to do something unethical or when they observe unethical conduct on the part of their coworkers. In 1991, Congress passed the Federal Sentencing Guidelines for Organizations (USSC 2023). The guidelines apply to all for-profit and not-for-profit organizations, associations, corporations, and the like; mandate strict punishment for those convicted of federal crimes; and hold an organization responsible for the wrongful acts of its employees if the employees are acting in their official capacities. The guidelines include fines for the organizations and jail sentences and/or fines both for those involved and for managers and executives, whether they knew about the illegal actions or not. If the company has an effective ethics and compliance program, penalties may be significantly reduced. Complementing the ECI criteria discussed earlier, the Federal Sentencing Guidelines indicate that criteria for an effective program include

- compliance standards and procedures,
- oversight by high-level personnel,
- due care in delegating authority,
- training programs that communicate ethical standards and ensure compliance,
- internal auditing and reporting systems,
- consistent enforcement of standards through disciplinary measures, and
- measures to prevent recurrence of offenses.

The Federal Sentencing Guidelines expect organizations to train and counsel employees to act lawfully and ethically. The guidelines also require that employees be able to report suspected violations without fear of reprisal. Employees of most organizations are guaranteed further protection against reprisal when they disclose actions that violate federal statutes; Title VII of the Civil Rights Act, the Age Discrimination in Employment Act, and the Occupational Safety and Health Act all contain antiretaliation protection. Government agencies such as the Environmental Protection Agency, the Department of Health and Human Services, and the Antitrust Division of the Department of Justice have developed model compliance programs, programs for self-reporting, and programs for amnesty.

The act of whistle-blowing has become even more complicated with the passage of two federal laws. The False Claims Act of 1986 and the Sarbanes-Oxley

Act of 2002 seek to recover government funds from organizations found guilty of misdeeds and to provide financial rewards for whistle-blowers in amounts that can be substantial. The potential rewards have caused some employees to make premature or false claims and have caused others to question the motivation of some whistle-blowers interested more in money than in "doing the right thing."

Friedman (2007) provides some solid advice for those who may consider whistle-blowing:

- Have some basis in fact.
- Don't wait until the evidence is overwhelming.
- Listen to the concerns of people closest to the situation.
- Don't try to cover the situation up; someone will find out.
- Support your colleagues who blow the whistle.
- Make your report to the appropriate individual or entity, starting internally.
- Respect that confidential sources must remain confidential.
- Consider whether the organization's culture provides protection for whistle-blowers.
- Understand the consequences of your decision.
- Decide if whistle-blowing is worth it.

While some protection exists for those who do not wish to participate in unethical or illegal acts or stand by while they observe others participate, risks remain. Healthcare managers who find themselves in a dilemma must carefully weigh both current and future consequences of their actions on themselves personally as well as on family, colleagues, and those for whom they are a role model. We all make choices that we believe we can live with, but rarely does compromising our principles come to a good end.

Knowing the right thing to do is easier than doing the right thing. Some managers may choose simply to remove themselves from a situation that requires them to compromise their principles and their personal value system. Others may decide to "ride it out" and allow freedom and flexibility to work out problems. Sometimes this course of action is an acceptable one. But healthcare managers ought to think carefully through the difficult choices before them and consider both the short- and long-term consequences of their decisions for their organizations, their families, and their careers.

Kolhatkar (2019) chronicles the personal and professional toll that whistle-blowing has taken on some who have suffered through it. The experience can involve financial strain, emotional stress, marital tension and divorce, and stress-related illnesses such as shingles, autoimmune disorders, depression, migraines, and insomnia. Many whistle-blowers have lost their jobs and have been unable to get another. One individual said he would not advise others to become whistle-blowers. Many people believe whistle-blowers do it for the money, but in fact they are most often motivated by a sense of frustration and moral outrage (Kolhatkar 2019).

Healthcare policy experts have noted that "fraud left unchecked is the greatest threat to government funded health care programs" (Kolhatkar 2019). Those with the courage to endure the personal toll of whistle-blowing can feel pride in knowing that "the government recovered nearly $2.6 billion from the health care industry in 2017, much of it thanks to whistle-blowers" (Kolhatkar 2019). This should be a call to action for all healthcare managers to eliminate any hint of fraud within their organizations.

REFERENCES

American College of Healthcare Executives (ACHE). 2023. "Ethics Self-Assessment." Accessed September 7. www.ache.org/about-ache/our-story/our-commitments/ethics/ethics-self-assessment.

———. 2021. "Ethical Decision Making for Healthcare Executives." Ethical policy statement. Approved by Board of Governors December 6. www.ache.org/about-ache/our-story/our-commitments/ethics/ache-code-of-ethics/ethical-decision-making-for-healthcare-executives.

———. 2016. "Considerations for Healthcare Executive–Supplier Interactions." Ethical policy statement. Approved by Board of Governors November 14. www.ache.org/about-ache/our-story/our-commitments/policy-statements/considerations-for-supplier-interactions.

American Medical Association (AMA). 2020. "The Top 10 Ethical Issues Students Should Be Taught." Published February 14. www.ama-assn.org/education/accelerating-change-medical-education/top-10-ethical-issues-students-should-be-taught.

Association of Governing Boards (AGB). 2013. *AGB Board of Directors' Statement on Conflict of Interest with Guidelines on Compelling Benefit*. Published April. http://agb.org/sites/default/files/agb-statements/statement_2013_conflict_of_interest.pdf (content no longer available).

Ethics and Compliance Initiative (ECI). 2023. "Global Business Ethics Survey: Interactive Maps; 2018 Benchmark on Workplace Ethics; Global View Ethics Outcomes." Accessed September 7. www.ethics.org/knowledge-center/interactive-maps.

Friedman, E. 2007. "Hear That Long, Lonesome Whistle Blow." *Hospitals & Health Networks Daily*, October 2.

Gale Cengage Learning. 2010. *Encyclopedia of American Law,* 3rd ed. Vol. 14, *Dictionary of Legal Terms.* Farmington Hills, MI: Gale Cengage Learning.

Henry Ford Health System. 2023. "Living Our Values: A Guide to Doing the Right Thing for the Right Person." Henry Ford Allegiance Health. Accessed September 7. www.henryford.com/-/media/files/henry-ford/locations/allegiance/hfah-code-of-conduct.pdf.

Kolhatkar, S. 2019. "The Personal Toll of Whistle-Blowing: Why One Physician Took the Risk of Becoming an FBI Informant to Expose Alleged Medicare Fraud." *New Yorker.* Published February 4. www.newyorker.com/magazine/2019/02/04/the-personal-toll-of-whistle-blowing.

Ornstein, C., and K. Thomas. 2019. "Memorial Sloan Kettering Violated Conflict-of-Interest Rules, Report Finds." *New York Times.* Published April 4. www.nytimes.com/2019/04/04/health/memorial-sloan-kettering-conflicts-.html.

Price, N. 2018. "Conflict of Interest Policy for Nonprofit Boards." *Board Effect* (blog). Published April 18. www.boardeffect.com/blog/conflict-of-interest-policy-for-nonprofit-boards/.

US Sentencing Commission (USSC). 2023. "Sentencing of Organizations." Chapter 8 of the USSC *Guidelines Manual.* Accessed September 7. www.ussc.gov/Guidelines.

CHAPTER 5

Gender Discrimination: Community Medical Center

CASE STUDY

Community Medical Center was a 200-bed acute care facility located in an afflu-ent suburb of a major metropolitan area in the Midwest. The hospital was highly regarded in the community, especially for its obstetrics program and innovative birthing center, its ambulatory care program, and its geriatrics center. The hospital was supported by a large group practice of young, well-trained primary care phy-sicians who occupied an adjacent medical office building owned by the hospital. Despite turmoil in healthcare delivery during the past ten years, Community Medi-cal Center had remained financially strong. Indeed, it had prospered in an environ-ment that had recently become dominated by managed care.

Community Medical Center was well positioned for such changes. Its financial stability, its strong primary care base, and its modern facilities predicted success. In addition, its location among rolling meadows and its proximity to an exclusive golf course made the hospital a desirable place of employment for professional and nonprofessional staff alike.

John Waverly had been the CEO of Community Medical Center for five years. After conducting a national search, the hospital's governing board had aggressively recruited John, who at 42 years old had been an up-and-coming healthcare manage-ment organization executive on the West Coast. The board still congratulated itself on its foresight and wisdom. John was just what Community needed to make the hospital a major player in the then emerging managed care market. The hospital thrived under John's leadership and compensated him well for his efforts. In addi-tion, John continued to enjoy the favor of a governing board that, although conser-vative, remained supportive of his innovative management style. John was the envy of his peers in other, more beleaguered healthcare institutions and, at age 47, he felt good about his professional achievements and status.

In retrospect, his decision to take the CEO position at Community Medical Center had been a good one. At the time of his recruitment, John had had major reservations about relocating to the Midwest, especially to the conservative community surrounding Community Medical Center. He hadn't been sure his wife and children would easily adjust. Indeed, they had never fully embraced this community, a fact that continued to be a source of tension in John's life.

In the beginning, John had also been uneasy about his credentials and unsure about how well his educational background would translate to the delivery side of healthcare. John knew he would have to work especially hard to compensate for his lack of hospital experience.

Six months ago, John hired a bright, ambitious postgraduate fellow from a prestigious university program in hospital administration. At the time, John was about to enter into discussions with two powerful healthcare financing and delivery systems nearby, both of which wanted Community Medical Center to become a part of their multihospital structure. John knew that these discussions and evaluations of any proposals they submitted would be time-consuming and would require a great deal of research and preparation. Having a capable postgraduate fellow on board to perform staff work appeared to be a win–win situation. The arrangement would provide both valuable experience for the fellow and a welcome resource for the organization. John especially liked the idea of working with someone who was well schooled in the latest academic trends in healthcare administration.

Over the past six months, the partnership proved to be as fruitful as expected. The CEO and his young protégée worked closely together for long hours and weekends, and Community Medical Center benefited greatly from their hard work. John and his protégée found themselves celebrating success after success. It was a most enjoyable partnership. She admired and respected John; he was flattered by her admiration. He found himself seeking out opportunities to spend more and more time with her. She began to accompany him to all his meetings, even those unrelated to her assigned projects. He looked for educational conferences in attractive locations, where the two of them enjoyed fine dining and upscale accommodations.

Now her fellowship was nearing its close, and she approached John about her future career plans. Her performance evaluations had been outstanding, as indeed had been her accomplishments. Community Medical Center had profited greatly from her efforts, and she fully expected to be awarded a permanent position. After all, many of her peers had already received job offers from their fellowship organizations even though they had no significant accomplishments to report from their fellowship experiences. John had been an outstanding mentor, and her admiration and respect for him bordered on hero worship.

John was not unprepared for this discussion. After much thought, he had decided it would not be prudent for him to offer her a position at Community Medical Center. He candidly explained the situation to her. Her performance had been outstanding, many had noted her professionalism, and she was a brilliant strategist. But, he said, he was personally attracted to her and he felt this attraction was reciprocated. He believed that if they continued to spend time together, this attraction would escalate to a physical relationship. He offered to help her in her job search by providing impeccable references and contacting his colleagues in progressive, innovative organizations where her talents would be showcased.

She was astonished and humiliated. In view of her accomplishments and her close working relationship with John, she assumed a position was a given. She felt used and betrayed. Angry, she said this treatment constituted nothing other than sexual harassment. John believed this remark was an idle threat and that reason would overcome her emotional outburst.

The following day, John received a phone call from a member of the governing board informing him that an executive session of the board had been scheduled to discuss "this appalling situation" and the action that should be taken to avert a lawsuit. He told John to be prepared to respond to the allegations at this meeting, and if they were accurate, he should consider resigning to spare the hospital any adverse publicity.

John was surprised by the call and by the tone of the conversation, but he felt confident that he had done nothing wrong. In fact, he believed he had honestly appraised the potential dangers of his relationship with the fellow and had avoided any misconduct. He believed his actions had been in the best interests of the organization and that the governing board would agree.

ETHICS ISSUES

Legal implications: Do John's actions in this situation constitute sexual harassment? If so, are John and the hospital both liable for his actions? Could this situation be viewed as a case of gender discrimination? Does it matter?

Adherence to the organization's mission statement, ethical standards, and values statement: Are John's actions in this situation consistent with the hospital's ethical standards and values?

Adherence to professional codes of ethical conduct: Is John's conduct in this situation consistent with the professional codes of ethics as promulgated by the professional organizations representing healthcare executives and hospitals?

Organizational implications: Have organizational resources been used prudently? Has this situation, including John's actions specifically, had any effect on other employees in the organization? Have the image and reputation of the organization been affected by this situation? How significant an impact might this situation have on the operations and success of the organization? Are there financial implications to John's actions?

Leadership responsibilities: Was John's conduct in this situation consistent with the role and responsibility inherent in the position of CEO of a healthcare organization?

Expectations of a mentorship program: What are the role and responsibilities of a mentor? Of a protégé? On completion of a postgraduate fellowship, what can each of the participants expect to have achieved? In this case, has the postgraduate fellowship met or failed its expectations?

Justice and fairness: Has the postgraduate fellow in this case been treated fairly? Is John being treated fairly by the governing board, considering his candor and honesty regarding the situation?

Community values: Has John taken sufficient consideration of community standards and values into account? What about the board, when identifying their expectations of the CEO and the needs of his family? When new staff members are recruited to a community, how important are the standards and expectations that the community may have for its professionals?

DISCUSSION

Legal Implications

The fundamental question in this case may well be: Did John, in fact, do anything wrong? Formal allegations of sexual harassment may be forthcoming. Do John's actions here constitute sexual harassment? John would vehemently deny any explicit or implicit actions or expressions that would suggest sexual harassment. He admits to his attraction to the fellow but insists that the long hours worked together, the meetings, and the out-of-town conferences were work related and that she was never coerced to spend this time with him. Indeed, he would argue that she seemed to be attracted to him and, in fact, to have encouraged his attentions with frequent flattery and expressions of gratitude for the time and effort he was putting into her fellowship experience.

Some might argue that John's superior position as CEO gives him a power advantage that "implies" coercion, overt or not. But if John and his protégée both willingly and actively participated in this relationship, does that not imply acceptable activity between two consenting adults? And as such, would this relationship not be consistent with prevailing societal norms and therefore lack coercion?

If John is not guilty of sexual harassment, then perhaps he is guilty of sexual misconduct. However, John and the fellow did not engage in any sexual or physical activity. In fact, no expression of desire or intimacy was involved. To himself, John would admit flirtation, but nothing more. Is attraction not acted on a form of sexual misconduct—adultery of the heart, so to speak, as admitted publicly by former president Jimmy Carter? Some religious beliefs delineate clearly between desire or intention and action. These beliefs suggest that the action is what is "sinful," and if the "evil" desires are overcome by will and hence not acted on, such behavior may be considered virtuous. In this case, John chose not to take the relationship to the next level—assuming that the choice was his alone to make, that is.

Or is this gender discrimination? Would this postgraduate fellow have been offered a position with the organization if she had been a man? High-performing postgraduate fellows are not guaranteed a position on completion of the fellowship, but offering a position is a common practice among healthcare organizations. An American College of Healthcare Executives (ACHE) study found that 63 percent of postgraduate fellows surveyed were offered a position following their fellowship (ACHE 2010). However, 90 percent of the postgraduate fellowship group surveyed expected to be offered a position. While healthcare executives will admit that postgraduate fellowships are a great source of new talent for an organization, mentors are wise to clearly state at the outset that there is no guarantee a position with the organization will be offered at the end of the fellowship.

Were there financial improprieties in this situation? Were the out-of-state conferences necessary, or were they merely boondoggles? Is it wrong to consider these conferences in upscale locations as a well-deserved and appropriate reward for high-performing staff who may be putting in long hours in uncompensated or lowly compensated positions, especially when conferences are infrequent and have educational merit?

Is John's conduct in this case simply an example of bad judgment? Were his actions motivated by a sense of power and a belief that his status and accomplishments placed him above the need to avoid any appearance of impropriety? John would argue that his actions were always in the best interests of the organization. He can cite significant accomplishments as a result of this mentor–protégé relationship. According to John, his intentions were always to serve as a diligent preceptor, and he believes the fellowship has been an educationally rewarding experience for the fellow. He is stunned that anyone on the governing board would consider his actions to be anything other than in the best interests of the organization. After all, for the good of the organization he denied a position to this fellow. John believes the only thing he may be guilty of is misplaced honesty, and he greatly regrets admitting his attraction to the postgraduate fellow.

In their upcoming review of this case, the governing board members must, to the extent possible, set aside personal standards of conduct and rely on the hospital's standards and policies and on professional codes of ethics if they are to make a fair and just assessment of the situation. Is it likely they will be able to do so?

Movie mogul Harvey Weinstein made the cover of the October 23, 2017, issue of *Time* magazine amid multiple accusations of sexual harassment of well-known and not-so-well-known women. The Me Too movement, which aimed to raise awareness of the pervasiveness of sexual abuse, began to spread virally through the hashtag #MeToo in the fall of 2017 as literally thousands of women—including many celebrities and public figures—went public with allegations of sexual harassment against men in the corporate and business world. Actor-comedian Bill Cosby was found guilty on April 26, 2018, of three counts of sexual assault. A vast number of Americans viewed the televised congressional hearings of Supreme Court nominee Brett Kavanaugh on September 27, 2018, as Christine Blasey Ford testified under oath that Kavanaugh had sexually assaulted her when they were teenagers. Yet some of the most shocking and outrageous examples of sexual misconduct surround former US presidents Bill Clinton and Donald Trump. Clinton was publicly accused of sexual assault and misconduct and settled a sexual harassment suit with one of his accusers in 1998. But Trump became the first US president to be indicted. In 2023, a jury found Trump guilty of sexual abuse and defamation and ordered him to pay $5 million in damages in a civil case in which a writer claimed in her 2019 book that he had raped her in an incident during the 1990s and Trump subsequently called her account a "hoax," prompting her to sue for defamation; the jury's verdict "marked the first time a former president has been found civilly liable for sexual misconduct" (Reiss and Gregorian 2023). In another case involving sexual misconduct, Trump in April 2023 pleaded not guilty to a 34-count criminal indictment charging him with falsifying business records in connection with a hush money payment made to adult film actress Stormy Daniels days before the 2016 presidential election; his trial was set to begin on March 4, 2024 (El-Bawab and Katersky 2023).

These events, along with many others like them, have signaled what some observers have called a "cultural shift" in the way sexual misconduct is viewed by the public (Kusisto 2020).

Adherence to the Organization's Mission Statement, Ethical Standards, and Values Statement

To resolve the issues of this case, access to the hospital's ethical standards and values would be advantageous. Indeed, assistance in the resolution of ethical questions is ample justification for written standards of ethical practice in an organization.

Such written standards also provide valuable guidelines for an organization's day-to-day professional and business operations.

The governing board and senior management of Community Medical Center have a moral responsibility to establish the ethical standards that guide the organization's operations. Legal and accreditation requirements address this obligation as well.

Emanating from the hospital's mission statement, these ethical standards frequently reflect the mission of the organization in responding to the needs of its community and the prevailing standards of behavior in its community. In this particular case, no such written standards of ethical conduct or values statement are in place, but Community Medical Center's mission statement does reference "family values" in its stated commitment to serve its community through state-of-the-art programs in family practice, obstetrics and gynecology, and geriatrics. The service area for Community is family oriented, religious, and conservative, and the board members representing this community reflect these same values. Under these circumstances, is it safe to assume that John's behavior will be judged in the same framework as that of his colleagues in other healthcare organizations? If not, is this disparate treatment fair?

When recruiting John to be the CEO of Community Medical Center, did the board make clear the community's standards and expectations for its professionals? Did the board take into account how significantly the job performance of the hospital's CEO would depend on the satisfactory adjustment of his family, given that the CEO would be spending considerable time away from home on work-related activities? If not, is the board acting fairly now?

Typically, healthcare organizations are a vital and visible part of any community. They serve the community's healthcare needs, but they are also a source of employment and an economic force in the community. Accordingly, leaders of healthcare organizations are expected to be pillars of the community. Disregarding community values can be career limiting, or at least embarrassing, for the CEO and other senior-level staff. For example, in one Michigan hospital with a board chair who was a retired plant manager for Chevrolet, a vice president made the mistake of parking his foreign-made automobile in the hospital parking lot and was publicly chastised at the board meeting for disloyalty to the community.

Adherence to Professional Codes of Ethical Conduct

ACHE's *Code of Ethics* provides guidelines for the ethical conduct of healthcare executives (see appendix B). It identifies standards of ethical behavior for healthcare executives in their professional and personal relationships, especially when their "conduct directly relates to the role and identity of the healthcare executive." The *Code* advises that healthcare executives should serve as "moral advocates and models" and should "act in ways that will merit the trust, confidence and respect" of all. In doing so, "healthcare executives should lead lives that embody an exemplary system of values and ethics" (ACHE 2022, preamble). If these standards are to be applied to the Community Medical Center case, the key word here may be "exemplary."

In the section on the healthcare executive's responsibilities to employees, the *Code* obligates healthcare executives to promote "a healthy work environment which includes freedom from harassment, sexual and other, and coercion of any kind" and "a culture of inclusivity that seeks to prevent discrimination on the basis of race, ethnicity, religion, gender, sexual orientation, age or disability" (ACHE 2022, section IV, C, D).

Organizational Implications

Are financial improprieties evident in John's actions? The answer to this question must follow a careful review of the hospital's policies related to educational conferences and business travel. Adherence to these policies must be uniform among the staff, including the CEO.

Has this situation, and John's behavior specifically, had any effect on other employees in the organization? Regardless of how discreet the individuals in any "special" relationship may be, the relationship is usually quickly perceived by most of the staff who have contact with the participants—particularly when the CEO is involved, because of his high visibility. Such special relationships are often a frequent topic of office gossip and speculation. They are bound to be an unneeded distraction at best and a threat to the credibility of management at worst. Regardless of what the participants may believe, favoritism, physical attractions, and flirtations are always obvious to outside observers and do affect the functioning of the organization, however negligible in some cases.

If office rumors filter outside the organization into other, more public domains, as they often do, the image of the organization and the effectiveness of the CEO may suffer. These considerations have prompted many organizations to establish policies limiting or prohibiting workplace liaisons. Gloria Allred, the highly sought-after lawyer for sexual harassment and discrimination cases, was once quoted as saying, "There is an epidemic of sexual harassment and discrimination against women in companies all across America" (Kolhatkar 2012). Indeed, according to the US Equal Employment Opportunity Commission (EEOC 2018), 25,605 sex discrimination charges and 6,696 sexual harassment charges were filed in 2017. Allred has been highly successful in prosecuting such cases. She says, "Some very intelligent men can be so successful in business and so stupid in the workplace" (Kolhatkar 2012).

In 2018, the EEOC received 7,609 sexual harassment charges—a 13.6 percent increase over 2017 (EEOC 2019). There may be a correlation between the Me Too movement, which gained momentum in fall 2017, and this rise in data. Certainly, less stigma is now attached to reporting such incidents, and those who believe themselves to be victims may be less reluctant to do so. Healthcare managers need to ensure that proper education and training regarding sex discrimination and sexual harassment are mandatory for all staff.

Leadership Responsibilities

Effective leaders have certain characteristics in common: vision, integrity, intelligence, initiative, interpersonal skills, ethics, and flexibility, to name a few. Leaders are expected to serve as positive role models, to motivate staff and employees, to be committed to the organization's mission and goals, to be responsive to the community's needs, to establish ethical standards, and to be of strong moral character.

The higher the leader is in the organization, the more important and visible her moral character becomes. The moral character of the leader can serve as the standard for acceptable behavior, or it can destroy the organization's reputation and effectiveness. At Community Medical Center, John's preferential treatment of the postgraduate fellow has eroded staff morale, and rumors about the relationship are fraying his credibility. Healthcare executives, especially CEOs, may liberally reward their immediate subordinates for jobs well done, while others in the organization may perform equally well yet go unrewarded. Executives may be oblivious to the effect that this behavior has on the remainder of the staff.

It's lonely at the top. Unfortunately, to be effective, a leader must willingly take on this hardship. Too often, the job is just not that much fun. The leader may enjoy friendship and confidences among professional colleagues in other organizations (noncompetitors, of course), but not in their own organization without the risk of compromising their position.

Further complicating the role and responsibilities of leaders is the issue of professional power. When you are the boss and have the power to reward others (or not), do your subordinates always tell you the truth, or do they tell you what they think you want to hear? Some subordinates may want nothing other than to please you (the superior) and be liked by you. Taken to extremes, the subordinate may begin to adopt your manner of dress, appearance, and work habits. If the behavior borders on the obsequious, the subordinate may be ridiculed by other employees and called a "yes man" or even worse. Some subordinates who exhibit this behavior seek career advancement; others simply want to be closer to those in authority.

The behavior of the superior in this dynamic can be interesting as well. Whereas some bosses may feel flattered and enjoy such behavior, others may dismiss it and seek more original thinking and intellectual challenge from their subordinates. As in all circumstances, the boss takes the lead in defining the patterns of behavior that will prevail in an organization.

An additional source of power for executives, whether in healthcare or the corporate world, comes from the rituals and symbols that define the "executive office" and impart power to those who inhabit it. Berger and Luckmann (1967, 91), pioneers in the sociological theory of symbolic interactionism, posit that all reality is socially constructed by the interactions of the participants. They believe that symbols and rituals structure and influence these interactions and distribute power accordingly. The corner office, the executive furniture, the Mont Blanc pens, the executive attire, and the framed diploma all signify authority and set the executives apart from the less powerful employees. No wonder many executives seek to keep these tokens of power in place.

Executives often underestimate the level of power that they exercise. In fact, it can be dangerous when the powerful are unaware of the power they wield. Equally dangerous, however, is when the powerful become so aware and so seduced by power that they act in arrogant disregard of the norms, laws, and standards intended for everyone in a profession, an organization, or a society. Hubris—excessive pride or self-inflation—and the downfalls that result from it are often noted in mythology and history. In Greek mythology, the hero aspiring to be like the gods was usually punished by death. In modern times, examples abound of political figures who believed they were above the law and suffered a demolished career and reputation as a result. Less conspicuous but more common in healthcare management are the highly regarded and committed leaders who develop a sense of entitlement regarding the "perks" of their position as a result of the long hours and personal sacrifices that they have endured.

Finally, some healthcare leaders struggle with a desire to do the right thing in the face of ethical dilemmas and ambiguities. The close scrutiny of their actions in their organization, in the healthcare field, and in the media and the community at large makes them especially vulnerable to questions.

Effective leaders are self-aware. They reflect on their words and actions, and on the effect they have on others and their organizations. Chinese philosopher Lao Tzu said, "Knowing others is wisdom; knowing yourself is enlightenment." Leaders are not always perfect, but they must be open to learning new communication styles and leadership strategies. Successful leaders seek to understand their strengths and weaknesses and work toward improving those areas that need it. They know that if they want high-performing teams, they must model the behaviors they wish their staff to emulate. Effective leaders are moral leaders who promote morality among their subordinates.

A multitude of resources provide ethical guidance, including professional organizations, university programs, publications, educational programs, ethics consultants, networking, and the internet. However, the best source of guidance remains the organization's mission statement, which should help define the ethical standards of the organization and provide a sense of purpose and direction to staff.

Stanford professor of organizational behavior Roderick Kramer (2003) suggests that leaders ask themselves the following questions from time to time to determine if they are in danger of reckless behavior:

1. Are you spending most of your time plugging holes and papering over cracks?
2. How do you respond to those annoying dissenting voices in your organization?
3. Whom can you really trust to tell you "the emperor has no clothes"?
4. Do you have delusions of grandeur?
5. Are you too greedy for your own good?
6. Is this a good time to pause and consider doing something different (or even nothing at all)?

The situation at Community Medical Center points out the very real need for healthcare leaders at all levels to have a trustworthy confidant who can advise and alert them when their actions are questionable and may have untoward consequences. Some managers fail to seek such advice because their insecurity or naivete does not invite criticism. But effective leaders must be able to anticipate the consequences of personal and professional actions both on their careers and on their organizations. Wise managers will seek out a respected and trustworthy staff member, colleague, or friend who can offer candid criticism in confidence.

In the Community Medical Center case, should the fellow be considered blameless in what appears to be an escalating personal relationship? Perhaps not. One would think that having completed a graduate program, the fellow would be mature enough to recognize inappropriate behavior, whether her own or that of others. Nevertheless, university programs should include professionalism and ethical conduct as important components of coursework. Regardless of the fellow's responsibility, however, the power equation of superior–subordinate tips the balance of blame toward the CEO mentor.

Sex Discrimination and Sexual Harassment

Sex discrimination is against the law and has been since Congress passed the Civil Rights Act of 1964. This law, along with various state and local statutes, prohibits discrimination based on race, sex, religion, age, and national origin. Title VII of the Civil Rights Act of 1964 prohibits discrimination in private employment with respect to compensation and the terms, conditions, and privileges of employment. These include hiring, firing, promotion, transfer, job training, and apprenticeship decisions. The Civil Rights Act of 1991 awarded to victims of such discrimination the right to jury trials and compensatory and punitive damages (EEOC 2023a). The EEOC is the federal agency established to administer the law.

In 2009, President Barack Obama signed the Lilly Ledbetter Fair Pay Act, a law named for an Alabama woman who, at the end of her 19-year career as a supervisor at Goodyear Tire and Rubber, discovered that she had been paid less than men in the same position. Her claim was originally denied by the US Supreme Court, which said she should have filed her suit within 180 days (six months) of the date that Goodyear first paid her less. This law resets the six-month statute of limitations every time the worker receives a paycheck (EEOC 2023b).

Sex discrimination was not part of the Civil Rights Act of 1964 as it was originally written. Gender was added at the last minute by conservative southern opponents of the bill who thought that something as "ludicrous" as equality of the sexes would surely cause the bill to founder. The bill passed and became law, but the EEOC took no action against sex discrimination in employment for several years until pressure from the women's movement made it an issue. A case was subsequently made that sexual harassment is, in fact, a form of sex discrimination. In 1980, the EEOC defined sexual harassment as a form of sex discrimination prohibited by the Civil Rights Act, and in 1986, the Supreme Court held that sexual harassment on the job was a form of sex discrimination (Lazar and Volberg 2019).

Although the Community Medical Center case involved a male CEO and a female postgraduate fellow, it could have occurred in reverse, with a female CEO and a male postgraduate fellow, or with two individuals of the same sex. The significant issue here is one of "power of authority."

In the case of Community Medical Center, an examination of the possibility of disparate treatment because of gender may be in order. If an employee is treated less favorably because of gender, or if they are treated both differently and less favorably, disparate treatment and discrimination may be involved. The complainant must show that the employer intended to discriminate because of gender. That is, the employee must show that they were qualified and applied for a job or promotion that the employer was seeking to fill, that they were denied, and that the employer continued to seek applications. The employer does not need to prove a lack of discrimination. Employers are given a great deal of latitude in this area and can disguise questionable employment practices as business decisions. The complainant, on the other hand, must show direct evidence, such as derogatory statements by the employer; comparative evidence, such as similar situations where others were treated more favorably; or evidence that the employer acted contrary to its own policies (Lazar and Volberg 2019; Outten, Rabin, and Lipman 1994).

While sexual harassment is a form of sex discrimination, it is not always as easy to define. Typically, the legal issues focus on whether the conduct in question is sexual in nature, unreasonable, severe, and unwelcome. Title VII of the Civil Rights Act considers sexual harassment as unwelcome sexual conduct of two types: (1) quid pro quo, or sexual favors for job benefits, and (2) hostile work environment, wherein the employee is forced to endure unpleasant conduct because of gender. In quid pro quo situations, the harasser must be one who has authority over the victim's job and benefits. In hostile work environments, any conduct of a sexual nature that interferes with an employee's work is considered hostile (Lazar and Volberg 2019; Outten, Rabin, and Lipman 1994).

Most experts agree that a key determinant of sexual harassment is whether the conduct is unwelcome, but this perception is not always readily apparent. The EEOC (2010) has stated that "because sexual attraction may often play a role in the day-to-day social exchange between employees, the distinction between invited, uninvited but welcome, offensive but tolerated, and flatly rejected advances may well be difficult to discern." Italie (2013) asks, "Are workplace compliments focused on looks or other personal details like dress ever OK? When do such remarks rise to actionable harassment or become worthy of a friendly rebuff or a trip to HR?" In the opinion of compliance experts, human resources managers, and labor lawyers, "tone, context, and a pattern of behavior are everything when it comes to unwanted remarks" (Italie 2013). Some compliments mean nothing; others aim to change the power dynamic between two individuals.

Office romances are an inevitable fact of life. Some people attribute them to the greater number of women now in the workforce; others point to the fact that many workers are putting in longer hours. According to a CareerBuilder survey, almost 39 percent of workers have dated a coworker, and of those, nearly 17 percent have dated a coworker at least twice (Singh 2013). Despite the prevalence of office affairs, a Society for Human Resource Management survey found that only 13 percent of companies have a policy on workplace romance, perhaps because many human resources managers believe a formal policy would intrude too much on employees' personal lives (Singh 2013).

When my millennial graduate students were given the assignment to write their organization's policy on coworker dating, the results were surprisingly across-the-board, ranging from no policy at all to a strict prohibition. Those advocating for no policy were adamant that it is inappropriate for an organization to legislate the personal behavior of adult employees. Those advocating for strict prohibition expressed concern about the negative impact that dating a coworker could have on the organization in the event of breakups, rejections, or relationships that turn hostile. Other student policies struck a middle ground, with most allowing coworker dating but not between superiors and subordinates and not within the same department.

Workplace romances, real or imagined, have an impact on the work environment. They change the dynamics and chemistry between workers. The perception of favoritism can erode productivity and morale. When a breakup occurs, negative fallout brings unwanted tension.

Affairs between managers and subordinates are the most dangerous liaisons. The manager undermines their authority, jeopardizes working relationships with other reports, and is often seen as having a conflict of interest. Despite a perception of favoritism, the subordinate may, in fact, be treated less favorably in an attempt to cover up the relationship. Coworkers may view that subordinate as an informant and avoid them. The subordinate may not have access to the information or teamwork they need to do their job effectively. Charges of sexual harassment against someone in authority are often scrutinized more closely than others because of the possible abuse of power.

Although other managers may not be so fortunate, many CEOs have survived office affairs and not been fired for sexual misconduct. Governing boards sometimes appear to be more interested in financial performance than in their CEO's sexual escapades. Still, in a widely publicized scandal, the CEO of Beth Israel Deaconess Medical Center in Boston was fined $50,000 by the hospital's board for his "lapses in judgment" in a personal relationship with a female employee (Kowalczyk 2010b, 2010c). This action followed an investigation of an anonymous complaint letter to the board alleging inappropriate hiring practices and sexual relationships involving the CEO and hospital employees. In spite of this "punitive" fine and the board's public "expression of their disappointment" in its CEO, the board declared "unanimous continued confidence" in his leadership of the medical center. The board cited his "exemplary record . . . , the current performance of the hospital, [and] his role as the chief architect of the hospital's leading position in quality and safety" in a public statement concerning its actions (Kowalczyk 2010c).

These public statements notwithstanding, some dissension among board members regarding its decision was reported, and the board subsequently asked the Massachusetts attorney general's office to review its decision and determine whether it had appropriately fulfilled its responsibility in its handling of the matter. In September 2010, the attorney general found "no evidence of misuse or abuse of charitable funds" in the hiring or compensation of the employee with whom the CEO admitted to having a personal relationship (Massachusetts Office of the Attorney General 2010).

However, the report of the attorney general continued:

> The predictable and unfortunate result of combining personal and professional relationships within a workplace environment means decisions made regarding the employee's hiring, transfer, pay, bonuses, and performance reviews will always be subject to the perception they may have been influenced as much by the personal relationship . . . as by her own professional performance. The outstanding reputation of an organization and its CEO are valuable assets of any charitable organization. The personal relationship between the CEO and the employee, which continued throughout her tenure despite repeated expressions of concern by senior staff and certain board members, clearly damaged his reputation, and of greater concern, endangered the reputation of the institution and its management.

The attorney general's review further concluded that the hospital board had acted appropriately in its investigation and deliberations but indicated that the board should have taken earlier disciplinary action given the CEO's continued personal relationship after repeated expressions of concern by senior staff and some board members. The attorney general subsequently urged the board of Beth Israel Deaconess Medical Center to do "some soul searching" about the CEO's ability to continue leading the hospital (Kowalczyk 2010a). The CEO stayed on for a few months and then announced his retirement in January 2011, claiming his resignation was unrelated to the controversy of the previous year.

Much can be learned from this unfortunate incident. Personal relationships, especially those of a sexual nature, will not go unnoticed by hospital staff and employees, and the perception of favoritism and unlimited access to the boss will have negative consequences. In this incident, the anonymous complaint letter was signed "concerned employees of BIDMC." The fallout from a tarnished institutional image, although not immediately apparent, may negatively affect future donor support or recruitment of professional and clinical talent. The energy and resources committed to investigation of the allegations and management of the public relations related to this incident may have been diverted from more pressing, patient-centered activities.

Like John at Community Medical Center, the CEO of Beth Israel Deaconess Medical Center had served as a mentor to the employee in question, who, like the fellow at Community, was by all accounts a competent healthcare manager with positive performance reviews. A close mentoring relationship requires that the mentor wisely establish boundaries that keep the relationship at a professional level; neither CEO in these scenarios was attentive to boundaries. Finally, wise healthcare executives pay attention when colleagues tell them their behaviors are being perceived as inappropriate and potentially harmful to the organization.

Sexual misconduct, and especially charges of sexual harassment, can be costly to an organization. Employers are almost always responsible for the actions of a superior when a subordinate files such charges. The average cost of defense against a sexual harassment claim can range from $75,000 to $150,000 if the organization wins the case. If it loses, the typical cost is $175,000–$250,000 but can surpass $150,000,000 (Sims 2018). And these are just the direct costs; indirect costs include diminished work performance, lower productivity, and poorer employee health, as well as staff turnover and harm to the organization's image. Fox News paid $45 million over the course of just one year to address the fallout of former anchor Bill O'Reilly's history of sexual harassment (Sims 2018). The total cost of settlements and awards to US organizations in 2012 exceeded $356,000,000 (EEOC 2016). There can be no doubt that sexual harassment is "unethical . . . illegal . . . and really, really expensive" (Sims 2018).

In addition to the direct and indirect costs of sexual harassment to an organization, the less tangible (but perhaps even more detrimental) effects of sexual harassment claims are distrust of management in general and an erosion of faith in society's institutions. Questions, such as the following, remain as to how far the costs of sexual harassment claims extend beyond the individual companies directly involved:

- Does the publicity surrounding settlements foster complaints in other organizations?
- Are more false claims filed because the complainant despises the boss, was rejected by a superior, was humiliated or made to feel inferior, hates the company, or is just seeking financial gain?
- Is the government overregulating the workplace?
- Are sexual harassment claims making our society more litigious—and driving up healthcare costs?

All these questions should be part of the discussion. But regardless, sexual harassment is against the law, and the employer is responsible for establishing strong policies that prohibit it in the workplace; effective investigative procedures; and comprehensive training programs for all employees, managers, and governing board members.

Sexual harassment is not a simple issue, and its complexities make it a major ethical challenge for organizations. Smart organizations will meet this challenge and commit the necessary resources to create a working environment free from harassment because they know that, in many ways, it is costly not to do so.

Expectations of a Mentorship Program

Corporate leaders often rank mentoring second only to education as a significant factor in their success. In interviews with 21 nationally prominent healthcare executives, a respected mentor was often credited with early guidance and instilling a sense of purpose in them (Rice and Perry 2013, 57). The executives interviewed indicated that they, in turn, have cultivated their effectiveness as mentors by intentionally developing leadership teams and by sharing relevant career experiences with their direct reports. They believe in the power of mentoring and expect that those whom they mentor will mentor others in turn.

The mentor's protégé is often a postgraduate fellow. A postgraduate fellowship is "a preceptor-directed program designed to nurture independence and experiential learning by an individual who has recently obtained a master's degree" (ACHE 2023a). A fellowship provides an opportunity for the protégé or fellow to gain real-world experience in their professional field, to refine skills, to test academic concepts, and to learn about the dynamics and politics of organizations. ACHE encourages healthcare organizations to offer postgraduate fellowships as a way for healthcare executives to give back to their field. To spur interest and promote access to postgraduate fellowships, ACHE provides detailed resources on logistics, compensation and benefits, recruiting, onboarding, and assessment of fellowship candidates (ACHE 2023b).

The preceptor or mentor is typically a senior-level executive who is interested in teaching and sharing experiences, insights, and knowledge with young professionals embarking on their careers. Some view mentoring as a mechanism whereby executives can contribute to their field and assist in the professional development of future colleagues.

To be effective, the mentor must be an emotionally secure individual who possesses high ethical standards and values and behaves in a rational, consistent manner. These traits are important because the mentor serves as a role model and teaches by example. Protégés often adopt the behaviors and value systems of their mentors and retain this learned work philosophy throughout their careers. Early careerists may pattern their professional lives after that of their mentors. Seen in this light, mentoring provides the executive with considerable responsibility, as well as an opportunity to prepare healthcare leaders of the future.

Because of position and experience, the mentor can provide the direction and guidance that the protégé needs to achieve career goals. The mentor serves as a teacher and protector and provides learning opportunities. The mentor makes it safe for the protégé to make mistakes but intervenes when circumstances become difficult or complex. Effective mentors are good teachers, enjoy a favorable professional reputation and network of colleagues, and commit the necessary time to the relationship. Time is a precious commodity in the life of an executive, and mentoring takes time. Minimally, the mentor must plan the fellowship experience, assign meaningful projects, confer with the protégé at least weekly to assess progress, and provide honest evaluation. Most important, the protégé must have access to the mentor.

Having access to the boss sometimes creates problems among other employees, who may feel that the protégé enjoys special privileges. The perception of favoritism is just one of the pitfalls of mentoring. Mentors must also avoid teaching only what they believe to be true. They must encourage their protégés to be critical thinkers and to challenge their ideas and methods. Mentors who teach thoughtful questioning and tactful disagreement will provide their protégé with valuable interpersonal skills. Collaborating closely, sharing thoughts, and spending a lot of time together can predispose the principal participants in a fellowship to a romantic attraction. This possibility could be one reason some male executives may be reluctant to mentor women.

Given that currently most CEOs are men, gender could be a potential barrier to desirable mentorship situations for women. Further limiting mentorship opportunities for women is the unfortunate reality that women executives who rise to the top are often reluctant to mentor other women (Tahmincioglu 2010). Women face other barriers as well: Male managers may have more access than female managers to informal executive networks, which tend to be the dominant organizational coalitions that provide access to mentors. It is no myth that a great deal of business is conducted on the golf course and other predominantly male social venues. The prevalence of this dynamic makes it especially important for women to interact with senior-level executives through fellowships, membership in professional societies such as ACHE, service on local or state healthcare committees, and the like. The absence of such executive interaction diminishes a woman's ability to develop the network needed for career advancement.

A series of interviews with more than 30 senior executives in the financial world found that "many are spooked by #MeToo and struggling to cope" (Tan and Porzecanski 2018). These executives are avoiding working with women—and in some cases even hiring them—which may be contributing to "gender segregation" in corporate finance. Male executives in other industries are "walking on eggshells," too, as they check their behavior around women to protect themselves from what they consider to be "unreasonable political correctness" (Tan and Porzecanski 2018). This phenomenon has been called "the Pence Effect," after former US Vice President Mike Pence, who has said that he avoids dining alone with any woman other than his wife. This series of interviews indicates that the Me Too movement is creating hurdles for working women, whose career advancement would benefit from mentoring—and as long as most CEO positions are held by men, women will continue to be at a disadvantage, and organizations may lose valuable talent (Tan and Porzecanski 2018).

The medical profession is sounding the alarm about this backlash as well. In a *New England Journal of Medicine* article, "Men's Fear of Mentoring in the #MeToo Era—What's at Stake for Academic Medicine?" researcher Sophie Soklaridis and colleagues cite a Lean In sexual harassment backlash survey of 3,000 US adults that found that "some men have stopped meeting alone with women, and others will not meet with women they do not know well or who are considered to be their subordinates." Soklaridis and her colleagues tell us this attitude has created a fear of mentoring in medicine, which has serious consequences because women represent nearly one-half of medical school graduates but only 16 percent of medical school deans (Soklaridis et al. 2018).

The sports industry, too, is not immune to the impact of the Me Too movement. Dallas Mavericks owner Mark Cuban commissioned an investigation of the Mavericks front office that revealed a toxic workplace culture, prompting Cuban to donate $10 million to groups dedicated to stopping domestic violence and developing women leaders in the sports industry. He hired a new CEO—a woman—to clean up the mess created by years of incompetent leadership and hostile working conditions for women on the organization's staff (Pilon 2018).

Even in publishing, more and more prominent men have been the subject of allegations of sexual misconduct. An increasing number of publishers are now including a "morality" clause in their contracts that permits them to terminate a book contract with authors accused of "widespread public condemnation . . . that materially diminishes the sales potential of the work" (Shulevitz 2019).

Executive-level interaction and mentorship that crosses gender lines does carry risk for inappropriate sexual behavior on the part of one or both of the participants. Recognizing this risk, the American Medical Association (AMA 2023b) has published guidelines for preventing sexual harassment that include a code of behavior for teacher–learner relationships in medical education. This code of behavior notes that "the teacher–learner relationship should be based on mutual trust, respect and responsibility. This relationship should be carried out in a professional manner, in a learning environment that places strong focus on education, high quality patient care and ethical conduct." The teacher is expected to provide "instruction, guidance, inspiration, and leadership in learning" (AMA 2023b). The learner is expected to make the effort to acquire the necessary knowledge and skill to become an effective professional. In addition to defining and prohibiting sexual harassment, the AMA (2023a) specifically addresses consensual amorous relationships between medical supervisors and trainees, noting that the fundamental imbalance of power between the two partners and the possibility of biased evaluations, either positively or negatively, make these relationships unethical. "Sexual relationships between medical supervisors and trainees are not acceptable, even if consensual," the code states. "The supervisory role should be eliminated if the parties wish to pursue their relationship" (AMA 2023a).

Despite the time, energy, and resources needed to establish and participate in mentoring younger, less experienced healthcare managers, valuable benefits accrue to the mentor and to the organization from mentoring. Mentoring requires mentors to objectively analyze their way of addressing an issue, examine their choice of actions more closely, and stay current with best practices in the field (Perry 2012).

Clayton M. Christensen, an influential management expert, asked the Harvard Business School class of 2010, "How will you measure your life?" His own answer to this question was the following (Christensen 2010):

> Management is the most noble of professions if it's practiced well. No other occupation offers as many ways to help others learn and grow, take responsibility and be recognized for achievement, and contribute to the success of a team. More and more MBA students come to school thinking that a career in business means buying, selling, and investing in companies. That's unfortunate. Doing deals doesn't yield the deep rewards that come from building up people. I've concluded that the metric by which God will assess my life isn't dollars but the individual lives I've touched. . . . Don't worry about the level of individual prominence you have achieved; worry about the individuals you have helped become better people.

REFERENCES

American College of Healthcare Executives (ACHE). 2023a. "The Basics: Q&A." Accessed September 21. www.ache.org/career-resource-center/seek-new-opportunities/postgraduate-fellowships/fellowship-resources/the-basics-q-and-a.

———. 2023b. "Postgraduate Fellowships." Accessed September 21. www.ache.org/career-resource-center/seek-new-opportunities/postgraduate-fellowships.

———. 2022. *Code of Ethics*. As amended December 5. www.ache.org/about-ache/our-story/our-commitments/ethics/ache-code-of-ethics.

———. 2010. "Administrative Residencies and Postgraduate Fellowships in Healthcare Administration." Published May 12. www.ache.org/-/media/ache/career-resource-center/administrative-residencies-and-postgraduate-fellowships.pdf.

American Medical Association (AMA). 2023a. "Sexual Harassment in the Practice of Medicine." Opinion 9.1.3 of the AMA *Code of Medical Ethics*. Accessed September 21. www.ama-assn.org/delivering-care/ethics/sexual-harassment-practice-medicine.

———. 2023b. "Teacher–Learner Relationship in Medical Education." AMA Policy H-295.955. Accessed September 21. https://policysearch.ama-assn.org/policyfinder/detail/H-295.955?uri=%2FAMADoc%2FHOD.xml-0-2254.xml.

Berger, P. L., and T. Luckmann. 1967. *The Social Construction of Reality*. Garden City, NY: Anchor Books.

Christensen, C. M. 2010. "How Will You Measure Your Life?" *Harvard Business Review*. Published July. http://hbr.org/2010/07/how-will-you-measure-your-life/ar/pr.

El-Bawab, N., and A. Katersky. 2023. "Timeline: Manhattan DA's Stormy Daniels Hush Money Case Against Donald Trump." ABC News. Published August 28. https://abcnews.go.com/Politics/timeline-manhattan-district-attorney-case-donald-trump/story?id=98389444.

Italie, L. 2013. "Sexism Walks a Fine Line." *Albuquerque Journal*, May 12, H2.

Kolhatkar, S. 2012. "Why They All Want Gloria Allred." *Bloomberg Businessweek*, July 19.

Kowalczyk, L. 2010a. "AG Urges Beth Israel to Rethink CEO's Fitness." *Boston Globe*, September 2.

———. 2010b. "Hospital Chief Sorry for 'Poor Judgment.'" *Boston Globe*, April 27.

———. 2010c. "Levy Is Fined $50,000 for Lapses in Judgment." *Boston Globe*, May 4.

Kramer, R. M. 2003. "The Harder They Fall." *Harvard Business Review* 81 (10): 58–66.

Kusisto, L. 2020. "Weinstein Verdict Signals Cultural Shift on Sexual Assault." *Wall Street Journal*, February 20.

Lazar, W. S., and D. I. Volberg. 2019. "Sexual Harassment in the Workplace." Outten & Golden. Accessed August 26. www.outtengolden.com/sites/default/files/sexual_harassment_in_the_workplace.pdf (content no longer available).

Massachusetts Office of the Attorney General. 2010. "Letter from Assistant Attorney General Jed M. Nosal to Chairman Stephen Kai, Beth Israel Deaconess Medical Center." Published September 1. www.mass.gov/ago/docs/nonprofit/findings-and-recommendations/beth-israel-hosptial-review-090110.pdf (content no longer available).

Outten, W. N., R. J. Rabin, and L. R. Lipman. 1994. *The Basic ACLU Guide to the Rights of Employees and Union Members*, 2nd ed. Carbondale: Southern Illinois University Press.

Perry, F. 2012. *Healthcare Leadership That Makes a Difference: Creating Your Legacy*. Self-study course. Chicago: Health Administration Press.

Pilon, M. 2018. "How to Clean Up a #MeToo Mess." *Bloomberg Businessweek*, December 24.

Reiss, A., and D. Gregorian. 2023. "Trump Found Liable for Sexually Abusing and Defaming E. Jean Carroll in Civil Trial and Is Ordered to Pay $5 Million." NBC News. Published May 9. www.nbcnews.com/politics/donald-trump/jury-reaches-verdict-e-jean-carroll-rape-defamation-case-trump-rcna82778.

Rice, J., and F. Perry. 2013. *Healthcare Leadership Excellence: Creating a Career of Impact.* Chicago: Health Administration Press.

Shulevitz, J. 2019. "Must Writers Be Moral? Their Contracts May Require It." *New York Times.* Published January 4. www.nytimes.com/2019/01/04/opinion/sunday/metoo-new-yorker-conde-nast.html.

Sims, K. 2018. "Harassment: The Costs to Your Business Can Be Dizzying." *Compli* (blog), KPA. Published January 24. www.compli.com/blog/harassment-the-dizzying-costs-for-your-business/.

Singh, R. 2013. "HR—the Third Umpire in Office Romance." People Matters. Published April 22. www.peoplematters.in/articles/learning-curve/hr-the-third-umpire-in-office-romance.

Soklaridis, S., C. Zahn, A. Kuper, D. Gillis, V. H. Taylor, and C. Whitehead. 2018. "Men's Fear of Mentoring in the #MeToo Era." *New England Journal of Medicine* 379 (23): 2270–74.

Tahmincioglu, E. 2010. "Women Still Reluctant to Help Each Other." NBC News. Updated July 6. www.nbcnews.com/id/wbna38060072.

Tan, G., and K. Porzecanski. 2018. "For Women, Working Life Gets Tougher." *Albuquerque Journal,* December 9.

US Equal Employment Opportunity Commission (EEOC). 2023a. "The Civil Rights Act of 1991." Accessed September 21. www.eeoc.gov/eeoc/history/civil-rights-act-1991.

———. 2023b. "Lilly Ledbetter Fair Pay Act of 2009 (Original Text)." Accessed September 21. www.eeoc.gov/lilly-ledbetter-fair-pay-act-2009-original-text.

———. 2019. "EEOC Releases Fiscal Year 2018 Enforcement and Litigation Data." Press release, April 10. www.eeoc.gov/eeoc/newsroom/release/4-10-19.cfm.

———. 2018. "EEOC Releases Fiscal Year 2017 Enforcement and Litigation Data." Press release, January 25. www.eeoc.gov/eeoc/newsroom/release/1-25-18.cfm.

———. 2016. "Select Task Force on the Study of Harassment in the Workplace." Published June. www.eeoc.gov/eeoc/task_force/harassment/report.cfm.

———. 2010. "Enforcement Guidance: Policy Guidance on Current Issues of Sexual Harassment." Revised June 28. www.eeoc.gov/eeoc/publications/upload/currentissues.pdf (content no longer available).

CHAPTER 6

Physician Impairment: University Hospital

CASE STUDY

University Hospital had long been designated as the Level I trauma center serving a tricounty area of a northwestern state. It enjoyed a favorable reputation among healthcare professionals and the public it served. Its teaching, research, and patient care programs were of the highest caliber. Its trauma center was nationally known for its excellent medical staff, and the resident physicians who trained there were in demand across the country when they graduated from the program.

Jan Adams had been the second-shift operating room (OR) supervisor for ten years. She knew her job and was well liked and highly respected by staff and physicians alike. She made certain that the surgeons followed protocol and never got out of hand. She probably knew more about the skill levels of the surgical staff than most of the surgeons themselves.

Jan liked working second shift and liked working with trauma patients. She received a great deal of satisfaction from the lifesaving immediacy so visible with trauma patients.

Friday nights had always been the busiest of the week for trauma, and this Friday was no exception. The helicopter was on its way in with a 42-year-old man who had been in an automobile accident, struck head-on by a drunk driver going the wrong way on the interstate.

The resident physician, Dr. Truman, was already scrubbing, as were the two other house staff who would be assisting. The scrub nurse and circulating nurse had the room set up and were waiting. Dr. Spalding, the trauma surgeon on call, was on his way to the hospital, and the anesthesiologist was setting up when the patient arrived. Things looked grim—lots of bleeding, vitals fading. Dr. Truman quickly prepped and draped the unconscious patient and readied to make his incision. Although Dr. Spalding had not yet arrived, Dr. Truman knew he had to proceed if the patient was going to make it.

Jan was concerned that Dr. Spalding had not yet arrived. As the trauma surgeon on call, he was responsible for being in attendance when a resident performed surgery. Jan tried calling him several more times but received no response. She considered calling the surgeon on second call but was reluctant to cause any problems for Dr. Spalding. She checked to see how the surgery was going and waited. The patient's ruptured spleen had been removed, and his lacerated liver was being repaired. He was still losing blood, and the residents were looking for additional sources of the bleeding.

Almost three hours had elapsed when Dr. Spalding finally arrived. As Jan began to brief him on the patient's status, she noticed the unmistakable odor of alcohol. This was not the first time Dr. Spalding had arrived in the OR smelling of alcohol while on call. He was known to have a drink or two, but no one had ever questioned his operating skill. In fact, Jan had said that if it were her or one of her family members on that operating table, there was no surgeon she'd rather have operating than Dr. Spalding. He was a superb teacher as well; the residents consistently voted him "Faculty of the Year." He was well liked, confident but never arrogant, and always considerate of the staff. The scrub nurses would volunteer to work overtime if it meant the opportunity to scrub for him.

This Friday night was different. His speech was slurred, and Jan knew he was drunk. She suggested they talk in the doctors' lounge, and once there, she gave him coffee and told him she thought it best if he stayed in the lounge instead of scrubbing in. When she went back into the OR, they were closing and the patient was stable. Jan breathed a sigh of relief, believing a crisis had been averted.

On Saturday morning, she received a call at home from the vice president of nursing, who had been contacted by a reporter from the local newspaper. He said the reporter had information that emergency surgery had been performed the night before on a critical patient by a physician-in-training because the surgeon showed up drunk. He was giving University Hospital an opportunity to comment before he contacted the patient's family. The story would appear in that afternoon's newspaper.

ETHICS ISSUES

Patient safety: What is the hospital's responsibility for the safety of the patients entrusted to its care? Of the licensed professionals administering that care?

Impaired healthcare professionals: When caring for patients, what is the responsibility of healthcare professionals related to impairment—their own and that of others?

Adherence to professional codes of ethical conduct: Were the actions in this case consistent with the professional codes of conduct for physicians? For nurses? For resident physicians?

Adherence to the organization's mission statement, ethical standards, and values statement: Were Jan's actions consistent with the organization's mission statement, ethical standards, and values statement? Were Dr. Spalding's?

Management's role and responsibility: What are Jan's role and responsibility as the OR supervisor in this situation? What is senior management's responsibility following this incident?

Failure to apply hospital policies in a fair and equitable manner: Could the way Jan treated Dr. Spalding in this case be perceived as favoritism? What are the repercussions of favoritism on staff morale? On staff performance? On management credibility? On the culture of the OR?

Legal implications: What is the hospital's liability for allowing a resident to perform surgery without the supervision of an attending physician? What is Jan's liability? What are the legal implications of failing to follow hospital policies and protocols consistently? How will this surgery be billed?

Implications for graduate medical education: What are the implications of this incident for the surgical residency program? Should the program director for surgery education have been notified?

Organizational implications: How will this incident be perceived by the public? What will its effect on the organization be? What effect will Jan's actions have on the staff and culture of the OR? Does this incident involve issues related to compliance with regulatory or accrediting agencies? What will the patient or his family be told about his surgery?

DISCUSSION

Patient Safety

Patient safety must be the primary concern and focus in this case. It can never be trumped by personal or organizational loyalties. The mission, values, and code of ethical conduct of this and all healthcare organizations must clearly identify patient safety as the institution's primary goal, ahead of all other goals and activities. "Do no harm" is clear in both the Hippocratic oath and the codes of conduct of professional healthcare disciplines. Hospital policies need to be clear and specific about this point and absolutely must focus on patient care and safety to merit the public's trust.

Impaired Healthcare Professionals

In addition to drugs and alcohol, causes of impairment among healthcare professionals may include mental or emotional instability, cognitive dysfunction, physical limitations, and the mental or physical effects of aging. Aging may become more of an issue as an increasing proportion of the population, which includes many brilliant and capable physicians, grows older. Although the University Hospital case deals with an impaired physician, impairment can occur at all levels of the clinical staff and throughout the organization.

Abuse of alcohol and drugs is a national issue that has significant social, financial, and ethical implications. Substance abuse crosses all socioeconomic lines, but the problem is particularly serious in healthcare because healthcare professionals are responsible for the health, well-being, and safety of patients and can ill afford to have their competence and judgment compromised by addiction. Healthcare professionals are also looked up to as role models of healthy lifestyles and behaviors, and they must take this role seriously. Professional impairment has both direct consequences (harm to patients) and indirect ones (erosion of public trust and confidence in the profession). Therefore, the ethical obligations of organizations—and everyone who works in them—in matters of substance abuse and those affected by it are considerable. Research suggests that at some point during their careers, one in ten physicians will abuse drugs or alcohol, and about 20 percent of nurses have been found to struggle with an addiction to alcohol or drugs (Addiction Center 2023). For healthcare professionals, narcotics such as oxycodone and fentanyl also are among the drugs most frequently abused (Addiction Center 2023).

The opportunity and availability of substances and knowledge about drugs and their effects may be a contributing factor. According to the Addiction Center (2023), "what sets doctors and nurses apart from other professionals is their accessibility to highly sought-after drugs—because it's easier for them to get the drugs, it's easier to create or feed an addiction." Although some observers may dispute this prevalence of substance abuse, no one can deny the dangers of substance abuse among healthcare professionals who have been entrusted with the lives of patients in their care. Admitting to substance abuse and seeking treatment may be problematic for healthcare professionals, whose livelihood, like that of airline pilots, depends on the trust of the public. Healthcare professionals who abuse substances often suffer in isolation that is enabled by the silence of coworkers, who fear that reporting a colleague may cause that colleague to lose professional credibility or license to practice.

Having organizational policies and programs in place that provide help and access to treatment for impaired individuals is therefore all the more important.

Early detection, reporting, and treatment will not only protect the impaired individual from embarrassment but will also safeguard patients from undue harm. A solid, trusting relationship with a surgery department chair, residency program director, or chief of staff can be valuable to an administrator who, confidentially and for the good of the individual physician as well as the hospital, could ask that an investigation be undertaken to determine if a problem exists and if early intervention is needed. The Addiction Center (2023) encouragingly reports that "the rate at which doctors and nurses suffer from addiction may be high, but this subgroup of people also has a high rate of recovery when they get treatment."

Although healthcare is an extremely rewarding occupation, it is also a very stressful one, especially for those on the front lines of patient care who often must work long hours and cope with the sadness associated with death and dying patients. A VITAL WorkLife and Cejka Search survey (2019b) of US physicians presented the following statistics:

- Almost 87 percent of physicians report feeling moderately to severely stressed and burned out on an average day.
- Nearly two-thirds of the survey's respondents said that their stress levels had increased moderately to dramatically over the past three years.
- Fourteen percent said that they left their practice because of stress.
- The top four causes of work-related stress were administrative demands of the job, long hours, on-call requirements, and worry about malpractice lawsuits.
- Only 15 percent of those surveyed said their organization helps them cope with stress or burnout.

Further complicating matters, physicians may view alcohol or drugs as a way to reduce stress and fatigue.

Physician stress has implications for the entire organization and the patients treated there. It can result in disruptive physician behaviors, which have an impact on staff morale and productivity, staff turnover, and—most alarming—patient safety. A follow-up VITAL WorkLife and Cejka Search (2019a) study of physicians found substantive ways healthcare organizations can increase physician engagement and satisfaction, reduce physician stress, and subsequently help reduce addiction. When physician respondents in this survey were asked what was most important to them that healthcare organizations could help control, they indicated the following:

- Respect for their competency and skills
- Feeling that their opinions and ideas are valued

- Good relationships with their physician colleagues
- Good work–life balance
- A voice in how their time is structured and used

A companion study of healthcare administrators showed that although respondents understood the importance of these components, they overstated how effectively their organizations were addressing them (VITAL WorkLife and Cejka Search 2019a).

For good reason, healthcare leaders need to pay attention to physician stress and provide programs that address this growing problem. Wise healthcare managers recognize that healthy clinicians must care for patients and will seek solutions that are compatible with physicians' schedules and that have the support and sanction of the medical staff. Dealing with physician stress is much easier than dealing with alcohol and substance abuse. Time and money are better spent addressing the causes of physician stress and impairment than managing the consequences.

In a landmark report titled *A Crisis in Health Care: A Call to Action on Physician Burnout*, the Massachusetts Medical Society, the Massachusetts Health and Hospital Association, the Harvard T. H. Chan School of Public Health, and the Harvard Global Health Institute declared a call to action for healthcare institutions to address the physician burnout crisis at the systemic and institutional levels. The report identified three major recommendations for healthcare organizations (Jha et al. 2019):

> Institutions should immediately improve access to and expand health services for physicians, including mental health services. Physicians should be encouraged to take advantage of such services in order to prevent and, as needed, manage the symptoms of burnout.

> In the medium term, addressing the burnout crisis will require significant changes to the usability of electronic health records (EHRs), including reform of certification standards by the federal government; improved interoperability; the use of application programming interfaces (APIs) by vendors; dramatically increased physician engagement in the design, implementation, and customization of EHRs; and an ongoing commitment to reducing the burden of documentation and measurement placed on physicians by payers and health care organizations.

> Finally, to successfully address the crisis in the long term, the appointment of executive-level chief wellness officers (CWOs) is essential. CWOs must be tasked with studying and assessing physician burnout at their institutions, and with consulting physicians to design, implement, and continually improve interventions to reduce burnout.

The report concluded that "physician burnout is a public health crisis that urgently demands action by health care institutions, governing bodies, and regulatory authorities. If left unaddressed, the worsening crisis threatens to undermine the very provision of care, as well as eroding the mental health of physicians across the country."

A 2018 perspective in the *New England Journal of Medicine* had another recommendation. Author Leo Eisenstein said, "To fight burnout, organize," and recommended that physicians look to collective bargaining for the prevention programs they need.

The frustration that physicians voice related to the medical practice changes that they believe have been thrust upon them must be addressed by healthcare organizations if they are to continue to fulfill their mission and obligations to the community. "EHR adoption, decreased time with patients, excessive documentation, increased regulations that create administrative burden, the proliferation of imperfect performance measures and increased patient volumes" have significantly contributed to physician burnout (Van Dyke 2019, 11). Physicians most often see newly required administrative tasks as interfering with their time with patients. Many complain that this is not the medical practice they trained for, and some even opt for early retirement. Van Dyke (2019, 12) tells us that "the rationale for addressing burnout is now clear" and cites research that links physician burnout to "lower quality, increased costs, turnover and alarming rates of clinician suicide and depression." She advocates for creating an organizational culture that supports physicians and relieves them of administrative burdens as much as possible.

As a first step in creating such a culture, management must recognize the critical nature of the issue and work with medical staff leaders to develop specific initiatives that address various facets of the problem. Such initiatives may be as fundamental as assigning certain documentation responsibilities to medical assistants; triaging e-mail messages before physicians read them; and implementing more user-friendly and less time-consuming technologies for physician tasks that cannot be delegated. Addressing work–life balance and implementing wellness programs may be more complicated, but they are necessary and pay great dividends in patient care.

"Promoting an ethical practice environment" is an essential component of reducing clinician stress (Van Dyke 2019, 18). Having policies in place that identify ethical standards of conduct and providing counsel on ethical questions will reduce uncertainty and conflicts that may arise in the delivery of healthcare.

The COVID-19 pandemic certainly exacerbated clinician burnout, and staff wellness programs have become a high administrative priority, not "just a nice thing to do."

Adherence to Professional Codes of Ethical Conduct

Most healthcare organizations, professional societies, and associations have addressed the issue of drug and alcohol abuse and impaired healthcare professionals in ethical policy statements, codes of conduct, human resources policies, and the like. The "Impaired Healthcare Executives" ethical policy statement of the American College of Healthcare Executives (ACHE 2022) reminds us that impairment results in more than just personal damage to the abuser and their family. Impairment affects an organization, colleagues, patients, and clients, as well as the profession, community, and society as a whole. Impairment typically leads to misconduct, incompetence, unsafe or unprofessional behavior, and errors in judgment. The organization may suffer from a loss of public confidence and support. The ACHE policy statement defines the ethical obligations of the healthcare executive, which include the following mandates (ACHE 2022):

- Maintain a personal health that is free from impairment.
- Refrain from all professional activities if impaired.
- Seek assistance, whenever there is uncertainty, in understanding whether impairment exists.
- Expeditiously seek treatment if impairment occurs.
- Follow organizational procedures for reporting and addressing impairment in clinicians and other staff.

In addition, "healthcare executives should have an organization-wide mechanism that prevents, reviews, addresses and supports impaired executives" (ACHE 2022).

The current opinion of the American Medical Association (AMA 2011) on the reporting of impaired colleagues says that "physicians have an ethical obligation to report impaired . . . colleagues in accordance with the legal requirements in each state." The opinion states that "physicians' responsibilities . . . include timely intervention to ensure that these colleagues cease practicing and receive appropriate assistance from a physician health program. Ethically and legally, it may be necessary to report an impaired physician who continues to practice despite reasonable offers of assistance and referral to a hospital or state physician health program." An impaired physician who does not enter a treatment program should be reported directly to the state licensing authority.

Both the ACHE and the AMA policies emphasize treatment as the first solution, and the AMA policy clearly says that impaired physicians must be reported to the appropriate authorities if they do not enter treatment programs or if they continue to demonstrate impairment in professional activities. Given the medical staff "chain of command" in the hospital setting, in the case of University

Hospital, Jan could have appropriately reported Dr. Spalding to the chief of the department of surgery, and Dr. Truman should have reported him to the program director for the surgery residency.

The *Code of Ethics for Nurses* of the American Nurses Association (ANA 2015) is clear on nurses' responsibility to "promote, advocate for, and protect the rights, health, and safety of the patient." The nurse's highest duty is always to the patient. The ANA position on reporting impairment is based on this provision of its code of ethics: "When . . . impaired practice is not corrected and continues to jeopardize patient well-being and safety, nurses must report the problem to the appropriate external authorities such as practice committees of professional organizations, licensing boards, and regulatory or quality assurance agencies. Some situations are sufficiently egregious as to warrant the notification and involvement of all such groups and/or law enforcement." When a nurse suspects a colleague is impaired, the nurse's duty is to take action to protect patients and to help the impaired individual receive treatment (ANA 2015).

Management's Role and Responsibility

The healthcare organization's mission statement and ethical standards almost certainly address the hospital's responsibility for the safety of patients and the delivery of high-quality healthcare. The mission statement and standards mandate that management address the issue of impairment in the workplace with programs that protect the patient and ensure a work environment that is conducive to effective patient care.

Progressive discipline for substance abuse is the norm in most healthcare organizations today, and many organizations have employee assistance programs (EAPs). But EAPs are not always the answer. They still carry some stigma, and some employees fear that entering such a program will damage their career. Even though EAPs ensure confidentiality, many employees avoid them for fear that their problem will become public. In addition, insurance does not always cover the costs of an EAP, so employees may have to pay out of pocket.

For impaired professionals who want more anonymity than their hospital's treatment program provides, some states have recovery programs that promise confidentiality. For example, the Michigan legislature has established the Health Professional Recovery Program (HRRP 2023) to offer healthcare professionals a confidential, nondisciplinary approach to support recovery from substance abuse, chemical addiction, and mental illness.

An effective substance abuse program must have clear policies, developed through a collaborative process, that clearly identify why drug and alcohol abuse is unacceptable in the organization and what actions need to be taken when it occurs. The collaboration should include representatives of human resources, legal counsel, safety departments, medical staff, and employees. If the organization is unionized, a union representative should be included as well. The program that is implemented must fit the organization, its culture and philosophy, and its business activities.

The program should include easy access to a reporting system, which may function more effectively if it is anonymous. As in the case at University Hospital, coworkers may be reluctant to report an impaired colleague, especially one whom they like and respect. They may not want to get him into trouble or hamper his career. They may be reluctant to report him for fear he may have his privileges suspended, lose his licensure, or be reported to the National Practitioner Data Bank.

Concerned coworkers may think they do not have many options when dealing with an impaired colleague. They may urge the individual to seek treatment or ask someone close to that person to intervene. But if the impaired healthcare professional does not refrain from professional activity, they must be reported to protect the patients receiving care from the organization. Colleagues and coworkers must recognize that although reporting an impaired professional is difficult, early intervention will protect the individual from doing harm to themself and others.

Having effective programs and policies in place is never enough. Management must make certain that those policies and procedures are well known and followed by staff. The most commonly abused workplace substance—alcohol—is especially dangerous because it is not illegal, it is socially accepted, and supervisors and coworkers tend to overlook its abuse. Coworkers may even rationalize a colleague's misconduct by telling themselves, "He was drunk at the time." But being drunk never justifies unethical, incompetent, or erratic behavior. Employees must be made well aware of the dangers that being under the influence of alcohol poses for patients. Similarly, although marijuana, or cannabis, has been legalized for recreational use in nearly half the states in the United States (ProCon 2023), working while impaired by it is unacceptable for the same reasons.

As the second-shift OR supervisor, Jan is the manager in this case and has responsibility for reporting incidents beyond her remedy or control to the next in command—administratively, medically, or both. Nurses are expected to be reliable in assuming this responsibility. Some time ago, a surgeon was overheard saying that physicians rely on nurses to report unethical conduct because "nurses have a more highly developed conscience than physicians." Whether or not this statement is true, physicians are not relieved of their burden of responsibility for the safety of patients or their compassion for colleagues in need. Some physicians may believe that their scope of responsibility is limited to their own patients; others may simply wish to avoid conflict. This attitude is not surprising—most physicians, even those who are employed by a hospital, view themselves as independent practitioners and strongly believe in personal accountability. Bujak (2008, 75) tells us, "Physicians define quality as 'the way I take care of [my] patients.'" In a sense, this implies that others in the organization can take care of other matters. However, the AMA (2011) makes it clear that physicians have an ethical obligation to report impaired colleagues to the appropriate bodies.

Physicians apparently are not the only ones who rank nurses high on the ethical scale. A Gallup poll found that nurses were the professionals whom Americans consider most honest and ethical. They were ranked ahead of pharmacists, doctors, engineers, and all others (Brenan 2018). Licensed nurses have sworn to uphold a code of ethics that, for most, means "they have a nonnegotiable set of moral standards that govern the way they interact with patients, patients' families and other medical professionals" (Lyder 2011). Healthcare executives should take advantage of this perception of ethical superiority and consider nurses among their most valuable advocates when developing an ethical organizational culture.

Failure to Apply Hospital Policies in a Fair and Equitable Manner

Applying the same standards of behavior and discipline to high-performing staff as to moderate-performing staff may be difficult, especially in the case of a staff member who is well liked. However, the consequences of inconsistency can be far-reaching. The OR staff who witnessed Jan's accommodating treatment of Dr. Spalding may perceive her actions as favoritism because she likes Dr. Spalding so much. What effect may Jan's actions have on the morale and culture of the OR and on the behavior and performance of other physicians and OR staff? Could their performance suffer, taking a back seat to efforts at making sure that Jan likes them? What kind of role modeling does this case involve? The adverse effects of favoritism on staff morale, productivity, and teamwork are predictable, and favoritism lowers the bar for everyone as far as standards of conduct are concerned.

Legal Implications

As the legal analysis of this case in chapter 15 observes, failure to follow existing hospital policies or to apply hospital policies consistently can be difficult to defend in a court of law. In this case, two policies were ignored: the policy regarding on-call surgeons and the one related to impaired professionals. Jan may also have exposed the organization to future litigation, if different standards and disciplinary actions are applied in future incidents involving other staff members or physicians. Leadership actions always have broader implications than may at first appear to be the case.

Implications for Graduate Medical Education

The high quality of patient care for which teaching hospitals are known can erode if those hospitals do not conform to the highest ethical standards. Public trust in teaching hospitals can give way to fear and uncertainty if healthcare professionals are unknown to the patient. The public has been educated to believe that (1) physicians-in-training are closely supervised by practicing physician specialists and subspecialists who are board certified in their particular fields and (2) patient care is delivered in an environment of intellectual inquiry that fosters the state-of-the-art practice of medicine.

If a physician-in-training performs unsupervised surgery, the action invites mistrust of the institution and its healthcare professionals. It also threatens the certification of the residency program by the Accreditation Council for Graduate Medical Education (ACGME), which can have financial implications for the teaching hospital. An ACGME ruling requires that residents and faculty in training programs inform patients about a resident's role in the patient's surgery (ACGME 2017). A faculty physician who arrives in surgery intoxicated only compounds this mistrust, further erodes the integrity of the program, and compromises the credibility of the institution that would allow such misconduct. Because teaching hospitals receive public benefits such as tax exemptions, training support, and research grants, they must do their utmost to preserve the public's trust and confidence. More information on ethics issues in graduate medical education can be found in chapter 27.

Organizational Implications

Reisor (1994, 28) suggests that "institutions have ethical lives and characters just as their individual members do." He cautions that the day-to-day interactions in a healthcare organization must reflect the values that it professes. To illustrate his point, he examines some of the contradictions often seen in academic health centers. For example, faculty may lecture medical students on the need to treat indigent patients the same as the insured but then turn the care of indigents over to residents; hospitals may build special facilities for the wealthy and ignore the poor in the neighborhood; faculty may instruct medical students to treat people with dignity but then treat those medical students as nonpersons; and administrators may call for cooperation while undermining competitors. Contradictions between what institutions say and what they do breed cynicism among employees and staff as well as public mistrust of the institution (Reisor 1994).

In the case of University Hospital, Jan's tolerance of Dr. Spalding's intoxication while on call has not gone unnoticed by the OR staff. Her failure to report him or to call the surgeon on second call has surely cost her the respect of her staff.

What about Dr. Truman and his responsibility as the resident in this case? Dr. Truman may be in a more precarious situation because resident physicians rely on teaching physicians for their evaluations. Many residents also stay where they train and rely on faculty physicians there for references and referrals.

The accreditation bodies that review residency programs are interested in the policies and procedures that ensure sound educational practices, and accreditation decisions affect the funding of residency programs. Dr. Spalding's behavior is not just a personal matter; it is also a program matter. As a teacher, Dr. Spalding has a responsibility to serve as an ethical role model. In this case, he is teaching that unsafe patient care is acceptable.

Dr. Truman and Jan demonstrate misplaced loyalty in this case. As healthcare professionals, they should have their primary loyalty be to the patient. The codes of conduct for the professions of both medicine and nursing are clear on this point. But both Jan and Dr. Truman like and respect Dr. Spalding's skill as a surgeon. Their respect for him has muddied their decision and also raises the question of fairness. Would Jan and Dr. Truman be as reluctant to report a surgeon whom they did not like or respect? Probably not. Is this fair? When we like someone, we tend to favor that person, sometimes overlooking weaknesses that we would not overlook in others or allowing outstanding attributes to eclipse flaws. Dr. Spalding may have a drinking problem, but his contributions to the hospital and the teaching program are significant. This kind of rationalization can be dangerous; it is reminiscent of the declaration in George Orwell's cautionary novel *Animal Farm* that "all . . . are equal, but some . . . are more equal than others."

The elitist culture of the OR is a contributing factor in this case. The OR is a restricted area where professionals, especially surgeons and nurses, work closely together, bond with one another, and depend on one another. They are isolated from the rest of the hospital, its rules, and its bureaucracy, and they enjoy a less formal atmosphere. (As someone once remarked, "What do you expect? They work in pajamas.") This isolation and elitist attitude can pose a challenge for administrators, who need to be visible and also ensure that OR staff are made to feel a part of the larger organization and accountable to the same policies and standards of behavior.

Much can be learned from identifying and investigating near-miss situations like the one at University Hospital—incidents that caused no harm, but could have.

REFERENCES

Accreditation Council for Graduate Medical Education (ACGME). 2017. "ACGME Common Program Requirements." Accessed September 16. www.acgme.org/Portals/0/PFAssets/ProgramRequirements/CPRs_2017-07-01.pdf (content no longer available).

Addiction Center. 2023. "Addiction in Medical Professionals." Updated April 13. www.addictioncenter.com/addiction/medical-professionals/.

American College of Healthcare Executives (ACHE). 2022. "Impaired Healthcare Executives." Ethical policy statement. Revised December. www.ache.org/about-ache/our-story/our-commitments/ethics/ache-code-of-ethics/impaired-healthcare-executives.

American Medical Association (AMA). 2011. "AMA Code of Medical Ethics' Opinions on Physicians' Health and Conduct: Reporting Impaired, Incompetent, or Unethical Colleagues." Opinion 9.031 of the AMA *Code of Medical Ethics.* Published October. https://journalofethics.ama-assn.org/article/ama-code-medical-ethics-opinions-physicians-health-and-conduct/2011-10.

American Nurses Association (ANA). 2015. *Code of Ethics for Nurses with Interpretive Statements.* Published January. www.nursingworld.org/coe-view-only.

Brenan, M. 2018. "Nurses Again Outpace Other Professions for Honesty, Ethics." Gallup. Published December 20. https://news.gallup.com/poll/245597/nurses-again-outpace-professions-honesty-ethics.aspx.

Bujak, J. S. 2008. *Inside the Physician Mind: Finding Common Ground with Doctors.* Chicago: Health Administration Press.

Health Professional Recovery Program (HRRP). 2023. "About Us." Accessed September 22. https://hprp.org/.

Eisenstein, L. 2018. "To Fight Burnout, Organize." *New England Journal of Medicine* 379(6): 509–11.

Jha, A. K., A. R. Illif, A. A. Chaoui, S. Defossez, M. C. Bombaugh, and Y. R. Miller. 2019. *A Crisis in Health Care: A Call to Action on Physician Burnout.* Massachusetts Medical Society, Massachusetts Health and Hospital Association, Harvard T. H. Chan School of Public Health, and Harvard Global Health Institute. Accessed September 16. www.massmed.org/News-and-Publications/MMS-News-Releases/Physician-Burnout-Report-2018/ (content no longer available).

Lyder, C. H. 2011. "Nurses at the Forefront of Change." *Hospitals & Health Networks Daily.* Published November 7. www.hhnmag.com/hhnmag/HHNDaily/HHNDailyDisplay.dhtml?id=3820003826 (content no longer available).

ProCon. 2023. "State by State Recreational Marijuana Laws." Encyclopedia Britannica. Updated June 5. https://marijuana.procon.org/legal-recreational-marijuana-states-and-dc/.

Reisor, S. J. 1994. "The Ethical Life of Healthcare Organizations." *Hastings Center Report* 24 (6): 28–35.

Van Dyke, M. 2019. "Battling Clinician Burnout: Fighting the Epidemic from Within." *Healthcare Executive* 34 (1): 10–19.

VITAL WorkLife and Cejka Search. 2019a. "Vital WorkLife and Cejka Search Physician Engagement Survey." Accessed March 24. www.physicianwellnessservices.com/news/engagementsurvey.php (content no longer available).

———. 2019b. "VITAL WorkLife and Cejka Search Physician Stress and Burnout Survey." Accessed March 24. www.physicianwellnessservices.com/news/stresssurvey.php (content no longer available).

CHAPTER 7

Workforce Reduction:
Hillside County Medical Center

Glenn A. Fosdick

CASE STUDY

Hillside County Medical Center was a 475-bed public teaching hospital located in an urban setting in the Midwest. It served a city of approximately 250,000 people in a county whose total population was 500,000. Its primary local competition consisted of two regional hospital systems, both not-for-profit. Because of its urban location and its historical status as the county hospital, Hillside provided a significant portion (approximately 70 percent) of the uncompensated care for the community. Nevertheless, it received no financial subsidies from the city or the county.

For many years, Hillside had been the main tertiary center providing specialized care in high-risk obstetrics, Level III neonatal intensive care, and pediatric intensive and specialized care including pediatric oncology. In addition, Hillside was the regional provider for kidney transplants, burn services, and emergency medicine, experiencing close to 80,000 emergency department (ED) visits per year. Hillside's services had been augmented over the previous four years by the development of the region's first American College of Surgeons–verified trauma program. Hillside was affiliated with a major university medical school, with residencies in internal medicine, pediatrics, med/peds, and obstetrics, and had a shared program with other hospitals in radiology and orthopedics. Furthermore, it had recently added an emergency medicine residency program.

Because Hillside was a public hospital, its board was strongly committed to the community and the hospital's mission. A number of programs had been developed that increased patient access and the hospital's ability to meet its community health needs, including a large clinic providing primary and urgent care services in the community's most underserved area. Unfortunately, because of the low reimbursement from outpatient Medicaid and the high percentage of uninsured who were served, the clinic experienced significant financial losses.

Like most hospitals, Hillside had prospered until about 2010, when changes in reimbursement and increasing competition began to affect it. Hillside was also heavily unionized; nine unions represented 86 percent of its employees, resulting in higher-than-average benefit and pension costs. After multiple strikes and work actions, Hillside had lost market share to its competitors. As its competitors grew stronger, Hillside started to face significant financial challenges, which culminated in 2015 in a financial loss of close to $7 million. Through the recruitment of new leadership, enhanced strategic planning, and marketing, the organization had been able to correct itself and make significant progress. However, over the past several years, it had again faced increasing financial concerns. The dilemma Hillside now faced reflected the variety of problems that were common to most hospitals. These problems resulted from a number of specific issues, including decreasing reimbursement, uncompensated care, increasing competition, rising personnel costs, and a depressed economy.

The largest unknown facing Hillside was the exact impact that ongoing healthcare reform would have on the hospital. Like other healthcare providers, Hillside was experiencing decreased reimbursement and increased vulnerability to financial penalties for quality, satisfaction, and performance issues. In addition, the replacement of inpatient care with ambulatory services seemed to be escalating.

Reform was also affecting Hillside's reimbursement from Medicaid, which represented approximately 25 percent of the hospital's business. Because Hillside served a high percentage of uninsured and Medicaid patients, it was eligible for Disproportionate Share Hospital (DSH) payments. The Affordable Care Act (ACA) had placed an increasingly high percentage of Medicaid care into competitive regional and statewide Medicaid contracts because the state had decided to expand Medicaid eligibility. DSH payments to Hillside were decreasing accordingly.

All healthcare providers faced unique challenges, unknown in other industries, that were further complicated by insurance exchanges and other adaptations associated with healthcare reform. Although the ACA decreased the number of uninsured, the amount of uncompensated care that Hillside provided had increased over the previous three years. Strategic analysis by the hospital suggested that, at least locally, this was partly the result of the US economy: The instability of the job market had resulted in a higher percentage of jobs that did not provide health insurance benefits.

Hillside also faced the difficulty, common to all healthcare providers, of actually collecting the payment due for services provided. The financial pressures that insurers faced appeared to encourage them to find ways to make billing more difficult, to find justification for denying claims, and in many circumstances to engineer significant delays in providing reimbursement for services that were properly billed.

Furthermore, Hillside faced increasing challenges from nonhospital competitors in diagnostic and treatment areas that historically had been financially advantageous to the hospital. These areas included ambulatory, surgical, and diagnostic centers, such as magnetic resonance imaging (MRI) facilities and dialysis centers owned and operated on a proprietary basis.

Like most hospitals, Hillside faced the challenge of keeping its patient census as high as it had been in the past. Reductions in reimbursement for patients who stayed longer than the appropriate time, expanded competition both regionally and nationally, and increasing use of ambulatory services to treat patients in such areas as chemotherapy, surgery, and diagnostic scenarios all complicated Hillside's ability to maintain its average daily census.

At the same time, hospitals and other healthcare providers were experiencing dramatic increases in the costs associated with providing care. Drug expenditures continued to rise, and the prices of medical, surgical, and other supplies continued to experience inflationary increases that exceeded annual reimbursement adjustments.

Further concerns were government mandates and accreditation standards that required additional staff for non–patient care activities. For example, the implementation of the federal APC (ambulatory patient classification) outpatient billing system had necessitated the hiring of additional coders to comply with increased mandates for medical record requirements.

Hospitals also faced an intensely competitive environment for the recruitment and retention of healthcare personnel. Perhaps the most significant concern was the future availability of registered professional nurses. The average age of nurses nationally was 50 years. Although the American Association of Colleges of Nursing had reported an increase in enrollment in baccalaureate programs in recent years, this increase might not be sufficient to meet the projected demand for nursing services.

This nursing crisis had been neutralized somewhat by the lethargic economy, which had temporarily discouraged employees from retiring. However, when the economy improved, the turnover rate would surely be higher than average and nursing resources would be depleted. As pressure for financial control and clinical improvement mounted, fewer qualified personnel would be interested in taking on these issues. Other shortages could occur among ultrasound technicians, pharmacists, and radiation therapy personnel. These shortages required Hillside to regularly reexamine its pay and benefits package to ensure that it was competitive and capable of attracting the right kind of personnel.

Another concern was the increasing number of professional nursing staff who worked for nurse staffing agencies. These agencies allowed nurses more independence and control over when and how many hours they worked, including on weekends and holidays, usually at the expense of benefits and pension plans. This situation contributed to a shortage of staff available to work unattractive hours, and the agency nurses' higher hourly rates resulted in additional costs to the hospital.

These difficulties in recruiting nurses and the financial requirements of tight staffing had increased the need for overtime and mandatory overtime. Not only did overtime mean higher costs, but concerns about the strain on staff and the effect of excessive overtime on the quality of clinical care had also prompted the state legislature to develop controls regarding the use of overtime. Increased overtime also stimulated reaction from unions, resulting in strikes and other work actions.

All these pressures combined to create the difficulties that Hillside now faced. The CEO and management staff had examined their situation and realized that unless significant changes were made quickly, Hillside would cease to be financially viable. The CEO also recognized that these issues were more important now than in the past. His board, like many, had increasingly identified the hospital's operating margin and financial performance as the primary indicators of the management team's effectiveness.

Recognizing the critical importance of swiftly and properly addressing these financial concerns, the CEO called his senior management team together. He had decided that, to ensure the best results, the issue needed to be addressed from a corporatewide standpoint and all senior management personnel had to be involved.

Because of the matter's financial significance, the chief financial officer (CFO) took the initiative. She noted that, as in most healthcare organizations, the highest portion of expense was associated with staff. For example, under the current salary and benefits package, the average employee cost Hillside approximately $75,000 per year. Even with the costs of unemployment liabilities and potential severance programs, she argued, reductions in the workforce were the safest and best-known method of reducing financial deficiencies.

The vice president for human resources reminded the group that in most union contracts and many state labor codes, seniority was a key determinant in workforce reductions. At Hillside, for example, the contracts with key unions, such as nursing, stipulated that seniority be determined on a hospitalwide basis. She noted that some of the least senior nursing staff were located in critical areas, such as the ED and operating rooms, where their services were essential for continuing financial productivity. She also pointed out that many unions closely monitored the comparative numbers affected from each union and the ratios of reduction to management personnel, which could have implications for labor stability.

The vice president for nursing and the vice president for medical affairs collectively announced that patient care could not be compromised and that inappropriate reductions in these areas would have a critical effect on the organization's clinical capability and reputation. The vice president for operations questioned the effect on community projects, such as the clinic, and asked whether other approaches could be taken. The CEO pondered these questions as he contemplated the right approach to address Hillside's situation successfully.

The CEO tried to identify the dynamics of healthcare that distinguished it from other industries. Although other industries also faced the need for employee reductions, those environments did not incorporate the multifaceted responsibilities of the healthcare institution. Certainly financial performance, while important, was not the only criterion that must be measured. The CEO knew that Hillside needed to ensure that proper care was provided and available to those who sought it. In no other business did a person receive a service before identifying how payment for that service would be provided. In fact, mandates from the federal government prohibited assessment of financial status prior to providing emergency medical care.

Hillside's mission statement clearly defined its responsibilities to improve the health of the community. Because the vast majority of hospitals in the United States, like Hillside, had either not-for-profit or public tax status, they were required to provide services in some cases that did not conform to the usual business standards. Unfortunately, all too often the public perception was that this requirement was not being met.

The CEO reminded himself that most people did not believe that the quality of care had improved. In fact, one recent study had found that 40 percent of Americans thought the quality of care had declined over the past five years. The CEO felt strongly that Hillside needed to live up to its mission, and he knew that as a public hospital Hillside would be under close scrutiny to see that it did.

ETHICS ISSUES

Organizational implications: What is the most appropriate and ethical method of addressing the organization's potential financial shortcomings? To whom should the CEO listen as he determines the appropriate course of action? Should he include others beyond senior management? If so, whom?

Adherence to the organization's mission statement, ethical standards, and values statement: Does the best approach reflect and adhere to the responsibilities of the organization's mission? How does the CEO prioritize financial viability as compared with clinical quality, organizational mission, and community responsibilities?

Management's role and responsibility: Is workforce reduction the only answer or even the best answer to addressing financial difficulties? Does workforce reduction ensure that all levels and groups in the organization share the effect of and exposure to these difficulties? Can workforce reduction successfully address financial deficiencies without compromising clinical needs? Should the CEO examine other options to address the organization's financial concerns? Does the approach ensure that the effect of the decision does not create even bigger difficulties in the long run?

Clinical quality: Should the decision to cut back be determined from a clinical viewpoint or a business viewpoint?

DISCUSSION

Participation in Problem Resolution

A fundamental question is: Who should participate in the resolution of this problem? Is it enough that the CEO has sought input from the key members of his senior management staff?

A hospital is unique in that the stakeholders involved in and influenced by its actions are very important. With a problem of this magnitude, should the stakeholders be involved and, just as important, can they help? To determine the answer to this question, one must first identify who the stakeholders are, how they may be affected, and what the potential positive and negative ramifications of their involvement may be.

Medical Staff

Because the medical staff have a dominant role in the hospital as a customer, provider of care, leader, and political force, the discussion should begin with them. Any change in clinical staffing or services will directly influence the care provided to their patients, so concerns regarding these issues are to be expected and understood. In addition, the medical staff have evolved as an informal (and sometimes formal) representative for hospital staff; they will likely hear all the rumors (accurate or not), know the staff's fears, and, in many cases, attempt to defend and protect the staff. Such attempts may include discussion with board members or use of the formal medical staff structure to react to any considered changes or reductions. Because workforce reduction is difficult to do without affecting services, in some circumstances their concerns may be legitimate. More important, the medical staff can be valuable when determining how to address this problem.

The CEO must understand that the medical staff will be affected and should be a part of the process in some way. The medical staff can be defensive and disruptive, or they can be collaborative. Because financial problems are unfortunately common in healthcare, members of the medical staff no longer think of staff reductions as inconceivable. Accordingly, the CEO may identify this challenge as one that requires the combined efforts of both the medical staff and management. The CEO should start by educating and sharing his concerns with the medical staff in a variety of settings. Using the formal structure, beginning with the medical executive committee, is beneficial. However, informal discussions at departmental meetings or with key individual physicians are essential.

The medical staff can contribute greatly to the resolution of the problem. Reductions in length of stay, selection and use of medical and surgical supplies, and increases in admissions are possible and may be preferable alternatives to losing popular staff or important services. Finally, involvement in these tough decisions may enhance the medical staff's appreciation that, after thorough analysis, the chosen approach is the most feasible one.

Governing Board Members

The board will be involved in the formal approval stages of the process, but they may provide value in the decision phase as well. Because workforce reduction is increasingly common in other industries, some board members may have experience in this area. The CEO must be willing to use all available expertise to accomplish staff reductions with the least negative effect. The more involved the board is, the more support this matter will receive and the better prepared board members will be when responding to any personal inquiries they may receive regarding actions taken.

Unions

Although unions have historically been more common in public hospitals, they are active throughout healthcare. The overall number of unionized workers increased from 2016 to 2017 (Chen 2018), and it is predicted that union membership will continue to grow because of uncertainties in the job market. The increasing involvement of unions has required senior managers to develop new skills to work successfully in a union environment.

Although the most common approach taken by US managers when planning workforce reduction is to notify unions of the plan for reductions, the CEO should strongly consider involving union leadership at an earlier stage of the process. Sharing the problem and identifying it as an issue common to all parties may direct negative feelings away from the hospital and management and focus attention on the external forces that are causing the financial problems. In addition, union leadership may have valuable input.

The CEO of Hillside recalled hearing about one organization in similar circumstances that spent more than 30 hours in one week with key union leaders examining the entire operating budget and seeking feedback on each line item. From this process, the organization was able to implement a number of sound ideas for reducing costs that it might not have conceived on its own. Just as important, involving union leadership in solving the problem demonstrated the difficulty that management was facing and its desire to reduce costs in the best and fairest manner possible.

Essential to the success of this approach with union leadership and employees are the following actions:

- The first cuts must be made at the level of vice president, associate administrator, or senior departmental director.
- No particular department or segment of the organization should be exempt from workforce reduction, unless this exemption is completely justifiable.
- If possible, the same percentage of managers and employees should be dismissed.
- Managers should exhibit and communicate to their employees the sacrifices that they, too, are making as a result of the workforce reduction.

These actions will allow union leaders to return to their respective constituents with a strong appreciation of the challenge involved and the intent of management to address it fairly. This appreciation could also be important considering how union leadership may respond to the media. In many cases, a hospital's ability to provide adequate and safe care may be criticized after a reduction in workforce. Such criticism may cause a further reduction in volume and the need for additional cost and staff reductions. However, if union leadership has participated in the process and is comfortable that the actions taken were required, that the actions were fair and consistently executed, and that the focus of the institution remains on the patient, a supportive response from union leadership is possible.

Employees
Progressive and beneficial feedback from employees is also desirable. Giving employees the opportunity to identify cost-saving opportunities, educating them about what will happen if costs cannot be reduced, and incorporating them in the process where possible all have the potential to identify new approaches and to avoid mistrust of management. Communication with employees is critical as the issue develops. Rumors, misinformation, and anger toward management are not beneficial and are typically disruptive and counterproductive.

The CEO is responsible for defining guidelines that ensure all staff resources are incorporated in the process, even over the recommendations of members of management who prefer to make these decisions the "easy way." Fear of politically affecting the process and delaying needed reductions is common, and while such caution has merit, this is not the time for management to be autocratic. If the rationale for workforce reduction is not communicated well and honestly, the negative impact on employee morale and productivity can be devastating.

Exploring Other Options

A critical aspect of workforce reduction is determining that it is the right or only approach to address the organization's financial difficulties. A common premise is that the desired goal is reducing costs. That premise is not accurate. The primary goal is to improve overall financial viability. The organization is measured on its financial viability, which is essential to its long-term success. The CEO should remember that if cutting costs were the only goal, then closing all the nursing units would do the trick—a large percentage of costs would be eliminated. However, the corresponding loss of revenue obviously precludes that approach. Financial viability can be improved via two avenues: reducing costs and increasing revenues. All too frequently, the focus in healthcare has been on cost reduction.

Although the overall high costs of healthcare certainly support cost reduction, it is not always the best direction for the organization and the community it serves. The CFO often makes cost reduction a primary strategy for several good reasons:

- It is clearly the fastest method of addressing financial concerns.
- It is the most reliable and measurable method in the short run. As the CFO at Hillside pointed out, even when the unemployment insurance and severance costs are incorporated, the savings from workforce reduction are well defined and expedient.
- In healthcare today, the costs of care often exceed reimbursement.

However, the CEO's duty is to consider cost reduction as only one option and ensure that all possibilities are explored for the long-term success of the organization.

In the case of Hillside, one such possibility may be a review of its public status. Although transforming a public hospital to a not-for-profit one may be difficult and expensive, the option is not uncommon. A move of this type has some distinct financial advantages and some potential disadvantages. For example, public hospitals in many states are constrained in their ability to invest cash reserves, which during a highly productive financial market can result in significant limitations on potential returns from investments. In addition, eliminating the public hospital status may increase the hospital's ability to refine its benefit or pension status to a more competitive one that is parallel to those of not-for-profit hospitals. On the negative side, losing its public status could reduce Hillside's access to certain DSH payments and other benefits that have been identified for public hospitals. In sum, Hillside should examine all aspects to determine the value and potential impact of this transformation.

The organization should also examine the potential for reducing or eliminating clinical programs in the hospital itself. Although historically the strategic approach has been to provide as many types of services as possible, maintaining programs with decreasing volume and expensive qualifications and support needs may not be beneficial. However, services can remain open, with no clinical loss to the community, through collaboration with other providers.

For example, a collaborative effort between two organizations may allow one service to be reduced at one facility in return for another service being dropped at the other. Both facilities may thereby expand their volume and potentially increase their profit margin. The CEO and senior management must not be limited by historical protocol. The fact that other hospitals have "always provided" certain services does not mean they cannot change. A progressive and well-planned effort to reduce duplication of services and commit to their delivery by one provider may be well received by insurers, local industry leaders, and the community. While the physicians and staff currently providing these services may voice some concerns, their concerns may be minimal compared with those caused by the continued reduction of an organization's overall capability.

Revenue Enhancement

In today's competitive healthcare environment, identifying opportunities to expand revenue has become increasingly challenging. Efforts should revolve around several key areas:

1. Ensure that payment is received on a timely basis and at the highest amount for services rendered. Opportunities in this area include reviewing the present billing system to identify departmental performance. This assessment includes the following at minimum:
   a. *Days in receivables (compared with state and national averages).* Changes in performance over the past 24 months may reflect problems that have grown or emerged in the recent past.

b. *Charge rates.* An external review of charge rates may identify possible areas of improvement, particularly in areas such as operating rooms and ambulatory facilities.

c. *Analysis of individual insurance agreements.* Analysis of insurance agreements may result in renegotiation of certain contracts or separation from others.

d. *Internal analysis of charging programs.* Analysis of charging programs will ensure that charges are developed on a timely basis for all services rendered.

2. Review patient volume to ensure that the highest volume of patients is obtained for each service rendered.

a. An in-depth inspection of admission rates by physician and service, combined with a yearly analysis of market share data, will identify changes or opportunities in volume. It will also give the CEO information to discuss with the medical staff when identifying strategic priorities for the recruitment or placement of new physicians. The CEO should also examine the ages of the medical staff to identify needs for future recruitment.

b. An analysis of patient satisfaction scores is important because it may reveal factors affecting patient volume. Recognizing the competitive environment requires a clear assessment of the present facilities and a commitment on the part of staff to enhance customer service.

c. New or additional service opportunities should be explored in depth to identify all available revenue sources. The CEO should examine each of these areas in detail with the appropriate staff. Because of the competitive nature of healthcare, finding new revenue-producing programs is not easy. The proverbial "low-hanging fruit" has probably been picked, and new programs may require significant investment or a time delay before profits are realized. However, revenue generation is a key responsibility of the CEO to move the organization forward.

To make investments of this type at this time requires the confidence of the board and medical staff and may be criticized by union leaders or other employees. The CEO is responsible for keeping these important stakeholders focused on the vision of the organization's long-term success and for ensuring that other stakeholders appreciate that the actions being taken do not reflect a short-range crisis but rather an industry direction.

Clinical Quality

One challenge facing Hillside's CEO is determining if any contemplated workforce reduction will affect the quality of the organization's clinical care. The board, CEO, and senior management must appreciate the need for high quality and understand that quality issues do not allow much room for flexibility.

The 1999 Institute of Medicine report *To Err Is Human* noted that "at least 44,000 people, and perhaps as many as 98,000 people, die in hospitals each year as a result of medical errors" and that medication errors are costly: "2 of every 100 admissions experienced a preventable, adverse drug event resulting in increased hospital costs of $4,700 per admission" (Kohn, Corrigan, and Donaldson 1999). More recent studies have suggested that errors remain high and that many issues around substandard care persist (Leapfrog Group 2023; Sipherd 2018).

These efforts require the CEO to analyze every move in a workforce reduction effort to ensure that the organization's clinical quality is not compromised. The challenges associated with the expanding demands of clinical capability and decreasing reimbursement do not excuse the organization from performing at a consistent and standard level of quality. A new level of understanding and use of information is required, along with a collaborative working relationship with the medical staff, nursing leadership, and senior management. A series of reactive decisions may compromise the organization's ability to maintain an acceptable level of care.

Community Health

The organization's commitment to community health programs must be given priority. Assessments should take into account the potential for improved health and efficiencies, as well as the possibility of a reduction in programs. The CEO at Hillside must, for example, carefully examine the clinic providing care to the underserved population. At a time when the organization's overall future viability is at stake, programs of this type may be deemed unaffordable. On the other hand, such programs may incur front-end financial losses but also entail significant admissions and laboratory and diagnostic tests that add financial value to the organization. The entire financial contribution of this type of program must be examined to determine its true bottom-line impact on the organization. Identifying what will happen if this program is not in operation is also valuable. Eliminating the program may have a real potential cost if, for example, patients use the ED instead, which would result in overcrowding and delays in admissions and care for more emergent patients.

Finally, other options for retaining a valuable program should be examined. Is it possible, for example, to share the costs of the program with other healthcare providers? Are grants or governmental funds available that may provide support for a program that contributes to the overall health of the community? Could an existing, federally funded health clinic in the community take over the operation of the Hillside clinic and make it eligible for financial support?

Closing a program of this type may also have a political cost. Underserved communities have become extremely sensitized through ongoing experiences of having services reduced or eliminated, and they may criticize the closure in the media, to community leaders, or in other ways, such as picketing. These concerns must be considered when measuring the true cost of reducing such services.

Collaboration

Financial challenges provide an opportunity for organizations like Hillside to examine the possibility of increased collaboration with competitors. Because the financial difficulties experienced by healthcare organizations are almost universal, competing hospitals are likely facing these challenges as well. In these circumstances, opportunities may exist for the organizations to work collectively and merge certain services to avoid duplication, reduce costs, and enhance the overall quality of programs provided. Opportunities may include programs such as jointly run MRI or other radiological test centers, centralized laboratory systems, and support services such as laundry, freestanding security, and ambulance services. In addition, a strategic assessment may be made of programs that are offered at multiple hospitals and possible collaborations explored.

A joint operating agreement, which allows both institutions to work together and share the savings achieved by avoiding duplication, could formalize this collaboration. For example, an agreement between Hillside and Behavioral Medicine Services resulted in the closure of a freestanding outpatient behavioral center at one facility and the closure of the inpatient pediatric adolescent unit at the other. The end result was significant savings and improved utilization by both parties.

Leadership

The financial problems experienced by Hillside are common in healthcare. Decreases in revenue, increases in costs, and reductions in inpatient volume have required institutions such as Hillside to deal with significant threats to their financial viability, in many cases necessitating immediate action and tough decisions. To some degree, the climate has moved the healthcare industry closer in parallel to other industries in the United States. No longer is the healthcare system a stable industry that does not experience layoffs and workforce reductions. Rather, the dramatic pressures coming from the government, insurance companies, and industry have made it one of the most complicated and uncertain industries in our society.

These challenges require healthcare executives to become better leaders and more sophisticated managers capable of making tough decisions. Financial challenges combined with the expansion of healthcare unions, managed care, and increasing pressure on and from physicians now demand that healthcare executives develop the skills necessary to work collaboratively with medical staff, union leaders, and employees. Healthcare managers must enhance their ability to lead the institution in the strategic planning process, take the strategic vision that evolves, sell it to the primary stakeholders, and make it work. Once key services are defined, executives must be able to monitor and measure these programs to determine if and when they need enhancements or reductions. Recognizing their obligation to community service, leaders must ensure that financially successful programs can pay for those that are not self-sustaining.

As changes take place and outside influences affect the industry, healthcare executives must lead their institutions in the right direction. Too often, actions of external decision makers have had an unforeseen effect on organizations. For example, as the government has encouraged the closure of hospital beds and services, it has ignored the impact on the hospital's ED services. Because of the reduction of reimbursement for home and long-term healthcare, many of the home health agencies in the United States have closed, and many long-term care providers are facing significant financial problems. These fiscal challenges are magnified as states prolong the approval process for qualifying Medicaid applicants for nursing home services, delaying the discharge process and lengthening hospital lengths of stay. The CEO is responsible for addressing these challenges successfully and ethically without compromising the clinical care the institution provides.

Although many parallels to other industries can be made, the expectations for providers of healthcare are significantly different. Moving a hospital to another community to reduce costs is not an option. Turning away patients who require emergency care because of their financial status is unethical, ill advised, and illegal. Healthcare executives must deal with these challenges in a more compassionate way than leaders in other industries would. The willingness of large corporations to cut tens of thousands of jobs to enhance the profit margins of their stockholders is only too well known. To deal with financial concerns, healthcare executives must start by asking themselves whether they have done everything possible to effectively reduce costs, improve financial performance, and enhance their services to make them more attractive to consumers. If they cannot convince themselves of this, they must not take the easy way out and cut staff. The ability to deal with these issues well will separate the successful and ethical executive from the rest of the pack.

REFERENCES

Chen, M. 2018. "Millennials Are Keeping Unions Alive." *The Nation*. Published February 5. www.thenation.com/article/archive/millennials-are-keeping-unions-alive/.

Kohn, L. T., J. M. Corrigan, and M. S. Donaldson (eds.). 1999. *To Err Is Human: Building a Safer Health System*. Washington, DC: National Academies Press.

Leapfrog Group. 2023. "Errors, Injuries, Accidents, Infections." Leapfrog Hospital Safety Grade. Updated May 3. www.hospitalsafetygrade.org/what-is-patient-safety/errors-injuries-accidents-infections.

Sipherd, R. 2018. "The Third Leading Cause of Death in US Most Doctors Don't Want You to Know About." CNBC. Updated February 28. www.cnbc.com/2018/02/22/medical-errors-third-leading-cause-of-death-in-america.html.

CHAPTER 8

Nurse Shortage:
Metropolitan Community Hospital

CASE STUDY

Metropolitan Community Hospital (MCH) was in trouble. The nurse shortage, a problem throughout the country, had reached epidemic proportions at MCH. While all four of the other hospitals in town were experiencing nurse shortages as well, none of the competing hospitals was facing the crisis that confronted MCH. For the first time in her 12-year tenure at MCH, Jane MacArthur, MCH's chief nursing officer (CNO), was beginning to feel a little insecure about her position. In fact, she was updating her resume and had begun to consider new opportunities.

MCH was a 250-bed, privately owned, not-for-profit hospital located in the heart of a midsize city on the East Coast. The four other hospitals in town ranged from 200 to 400 beds and included an investor-owned hospital (part of a national chain), a county hospital, a Catholic hospital (part of a regional network), and another privately owned community hospital. All these facilities had been aggressively competing for the limited number of nurses in the geographic area, and no matter what strategies it employed or how many resources it committed to the task, MCH was clearly losing to the competition. In the past two years, the five area hospitals had engaged in a bidding war in terms of salaries, sign-on bonuses, and benefits such as relocation expenses, tuition reimbursement, and healthcare coverage for domestic partners. MCH simply could not match the deep pockets of some of its competitors. The nurse turnover rate at MCH had reached 25 percent as nurses left MCH to take more lucrative positions at competing hospitals.

Case originally published in a slightly different format in Mistakes in Healthcare Management: Identification, Correction and Prevention, *edited by Paul B. Hofmann and Frankie Perry. Copyright ©* *2005 Cambridge University Press. Reprinted with permission.*

MCH's geographic location was an additional recruiting obstacle. Its urban neighborhood was perceived to be a high-crime area, and although statistics disproved this notion, the idea persisted among the predominantly young female nurse population. Jane was aware of this perception, but because it was not supported in fact, she dismissed it as not needing her attention.

As more and more foreign-born nurses were recruited to MCH and as an increasingly higher percentage of agency staff were used, the budget overrun for nurse staffing had reached record proportions. The board had become impatient with Jane's attempts at justifying this cost overrun. The board chair declared, "We can no longer tolerate explanations for the problem. We need solutions."

The problem had become more significant than just cost overruns. The nurse-to-patient ratio on the medical/surgical units at MCH was 1 to 12, an unacceptable level by any standard for both patient safety and quality of care. Patient and family complaints had increased dramatically over the past year. Adverse events had also increased, and John Fairfield, the hospital's legal counsel, who had never been one of Jane's supporters, was quick to remind the CEO and the MCH board that the source of these potential litigations was failure to remedy the nurse shortage.

Two years earlier, when Eugene Wellborn was hired as CEO at MCH, the nurse shortage was identified as a problem but did not rank high on the board's list of priorities for Eugene to tackle. In fact, the board chair had assured Eugene that Jane was unquestionably competent and could be relied on to resolve the issue satisfactorily. The message was clear that nursing took care of itself and that Jane had the board's full confidence. In retrospect, Eugene wished he had not hesitated in dealing with the issue. The nurse shortage now occupied a huge proportion of his daily schedule and usurped time and energy he could be spending on the hospital's other pressing agenda items. Hardly a day passed that Eugene did not have to deal with an irate patient, family member, or physician.

The nurse shortage at MCH had been the primary topic of discussion at last month's general medical staff meeting and had been accompanied by threats of diverting patient admissions to competing hospitals if the situation did not improve immediately. Jane was quick to point out that physicians were a major part of the problem and one of the reasons she was having difficulty recruiting and retaining nurses.

The medical staff enjoyed strong political clout and expected others to defer to them on questions of authority, facility planning, and patient care. Past administrations had abdicated many of their responsibilities related to patient care and seemed indifferent to issues other than the financial viability of the institution and its public image in the community. Attracting physicians had been a priority in the recent past, and Eugene's predecessor had spent every Wednesday afternoon on the golf course with prominent members of the executive medical staff committee.

Eugene left this kind of relationship building to Carter Sims, MCH's young, ambitious chief operating officer (COO). For his part, Eugene believed his role and responsibility as CEO was to focus on the external environment. He needed to develop collaborative relationships and coalitions throughout the community if MCH was to survive into the future. This was his strong belief and the mandate he had received from the board.

Nevertheless, Eugene was troubled by the powerful position of the medical staff and agreed with Jane that the behavior of some of the physicians contributed to the exodus of nurses. He had been reluctant to confront the medical staff leadership on this issue, believing that he needed to develop a stronger relationship with the physicians before taking on such an adversarial role.

To the nursing staff at MCH, this administrative posture suggested that nurses were not valued and were only supposed to follow the physicians' orders. In this environment, the physicians had become accustomed to behaving in an autocratic and sometimes disrespectful manner toward the nurses. John Fairfield had on more than one occasion cautioned Eugene about the legal implications of actions that he believed bordered on harassment. These incidents had fueled hostile outbursts between Jane and the chief of the medical staff, who she believed turned a blind eye to the physicians' inappropriate behavior.

In some ways, Jane's management style mirrored the autocratic, disrespectful approach toward the nursing staff favored by some physicians. Jane, on the other hand, saw herself as a "benevolent dictator," always ready to do battle in defense of her team. The nursing staff resented both of these higher authorities. Behind Jane's back, they referred to her as "the General," and they had even more derogatory nicknames for some of the physicians. The nurses believed that they did all the work and reaped none of the rewards. They had no authority or control over their work and no participation in the decision making about patient care. They received no recognition or respect for the physically and emotionally stressful work they were expected to perform without regard to personal or professional preferences. Their work schedules were frequently modified, overtime was often required, and they were arbitrarily pulled from their work units to float in unfamiliar, understaffed areas of the hospital.

The informal leaders among the nursing staff had begun to talk about organizing. Some of them had complained to Carter Sims, the COO, but it seemed that the administration's answer to the nurses' complaints was to throw money at the problem. Carter was overheard to say, "If we pay them enough, they'll be happy." That did seem to be the case with the foreign-born nurses that MCH recruited. They seemed willing to tolerate the unpleasant working conditions if the pay was good. This difference of opinion created resentment among the US-born nurses, who believed the foreign-born nurses were encouraging unfair treatment by allowing themselves to be exploited. This resentment spawned a lack of cooperation and tension among the nurses that patients observed. Eugene knew it was just a matter of time before news of the disruptive environment at MCH reached the community and he heard about it at the Rotary Club.

The only patient care units in MCH that operated peacefully and efficiently were the emergency room, the operating room, and the intensive care unit. The physician–nursing coalitions in those patient care units made them untouchable. Both Jane and the attending physicians knew better than to antagonize the skilled, experienced, and confident nurses whom the medical directors of those units considered irreplaceable. Indeed, those nurses were considered more competent and more valuable than some of the attending physicians whose patients were treated there.

As Eugene pondered the situation at MCH, he knew he must take action, and he knew it was not going to be pleasant.

ETHICS ISSUES

Patient safety: Has the shortage of nurses responsible for direct patient care threatened patient safety at MCH? If the nurse shortage continues to go unaddressed, will patient safety be further compromised? What effect does the nurse shortage have on the public image of the institution and the willingness of patients to seek care there? What effect does the nurse shortage have on future recruitment and retention of nurses? Do nurse-to-patient staffing ratios have implications for hospital licensure or accreditation?

Adherence to the organization's mission statement, ethical standards, and values statement: Are the actions of the senior executive team at MCH consistent with the organization's mission, code of ethics, and values?

Management's role and responsibility: What ethical responsibility does the management of a healthcare organization have to focus on mission, model ethical conduct, and support patient-centered care?

Ethical responsibilities to employees: What is the ethical responsibility of healthcare executives in the provision of a safe working environment that is free from harassment and discrimination?

Disruptive physician behaviors: What effect has the disruptive behavior of physicians had on recruitment and retention of nurses? On patient care? On the culture of the organization?

Legal implications: What is the hospital's liability for failing to address safe patient care? For failing to address a hostile work environment?

DISCUSSION

Patient Safety

Patient safety must always be the primary focus and concern of any healthcare organization. The presence of an adequate number of direct caregivers with appropriate skills is critical to the safety of patients. Nurses are often the sole professional staff attending to patients 24 hours a day, 7 days a week in the hospital setting. As such, nurses serve as clinical coordinators of patient care, addressing vital patient needs and ensuring that other healthcare professionals, including physicians, are contacted and informed of patient requirements and medical status in a timely manner. Nurses also monitor the safety and well-being of their assigned patients and serve as a conduit for communication and interactions with patients and family members. A shortage of these key caregivers requires serious attention.

Because nurses play highly visible roles, a shortage of nurses can be alarming to the public and contribute to negative perceptions of an organization. Such perceptions may impede the recruitment and retention of nurses and deter patients from seeking care at that institution.

In addition, depending on the state in which the institution is located, nurse-to-patient staffing ratios may have a significant effect on licensure. In 2004, California became the first state to implement minimum nurse-to-patient ratios in acute care hospitals. A report released by the Agency for Healthcare Research and Quality (AHRQ) of the US Department of Health and Human Services documenting the California experience found that "state-mandated nurse staffing levels alleviate workloads leading to lower patient mortality and higher nurse satisfaction" (AHRQ 2012). The American Nurses Association (ANA 2023) reports that as of March 2022, 16 states addressed nurse staffing in hospitals through either laws or regulations. Staffing effectiveness is on the radar at the national level as more and more stories about patient safety and the costs associated with medical errors and hospital accidents flood the media and as nurse advocacy groups continue their fight to encourage states to pass legislation that mandates safe nurse staffing levels.

Adherence to the Organization's Mission Statement, Ethical Standards, and Values Statement

In this case, the senior managers at MCH seem to have completely lost sight of the organization's mission and its responsibility to the community it serves. Focus on the mission of the hospital, which should be paramount, has been replaced by focus on self-interests. Eugene, the CEO, has blindly taken his marching orders from the governing board and concentrated all his energies on the external environment, leaving the internal operations of the organization to flounder. Is he more concerned about pleasing the board than fulfilling his obligation to the organization? Although the CEO may serve at the pleasure of the board, both the CEO and the governing board must be committed to the best interests of the organization they serve. Eugene's failure to conduct a thorough assessment of the organization's operations and senior staff, identify areas in need of attention, and set priorities is a failure of leadership. When leaders focus on mission, they must also pay attention to the people they need to carry out that mission, and Eugene has failed to do both.

Management's Role and Responsibility

The most pressing issue at MCH is the nurse shortage, and yet the organization's failure to conduct an in-depth analysis of the crisis is evident. A thorough analysis would have revealed the need to address the factors underlying the problem, such as disruptive behaviors among physicians, autocratic nursing leadership, lack of inclusiveness and respect, a negative work environment, cultural differences among nurses, and the perception that MCH is located in a high-crime area.

Equally pressing is the need for a careful evaluation of senior management to determine whether they are capable of functioning as a team to tackle the organization's problems and carry out its mission of patient care. The senior staff have established beneficial relationships with people who would champion them and their positions—the COO with the medical staff, the CNO with influential board members, and the CEO with the board and community leaders. Those alliances promote individual interests at the expense of the organization's mission. Leadership must create a culture that encourages teamwork and integrates the efforts of all staff to achieve organizational goals.

People drive an organization and contribute to its success or failure. According to Russell and Greenspan (2005, 86), "The biggest mistake managers consistently make is to recognize that they have the wrong person in a key position and fail to do something about it." Replacing a staff person who is unable to do the job is difficult, especially if the person has been in the position for a long time or has friends on the board or the medical staff.

The situation can also be problematic if you have personally hired the person, particularly if you provided a premium hiring package because you were impressed with the person's credentials, experience, or potential. You must admit that you made a mistake. That situation is examined in the Heartland Healthcare System case in chapter 9.

Decisions about people always seem to be the most difficult but are especially crucial to the success of the organization. In his national bestseller *Good to Great*, consider Jim Collins's observation: "The executives who ignited the transformations from good to great [companies] did not first figure out where to drive the bus and then get people to take it there. No, they first got the right people on the bus (and the wrong people off the bus) and then figured out where to drive it" (Collins 2001, 41).

Ethical Responsibilities to Employees

Healthcare managers, regardless of their areas of responsibility, often find the management of people to be the most challenging part of their jobs. Mastering skills in finance, planning, marketing, information technology, and the like is less difficult for most managers than dealing with the people-related problems and conflicts that arise in the work environment. Adding to the complexity is the diversity of today's workforce and the various values, ethics, and cultural perspectives that influence how each employee sees the world. The healthcare manager must be sensitive to those differences and clearly establish the ethical principles and behaviors that are acceptable when dealing with patients, clients, and coworkers. Perhaps even more important, the healthcare manager must actually practice those principles and behaviors when dealing with employees. Healthcare managers are usually acutely aware of their ethical responsibilities to patients, clients, the organization, and the community, but all too often they overlook their ethical responsibilities to the people they manage.

The leadership of an organization establishes the ethical culture in which work is performed and patient care is provided. In healthcare, the clinical staff administer patient care, but management is responsible for creating an environment in which top-quality, effective patient care is delivered. At MCH, Eugene has failed miserably in fulfilling this responsibility. He has focused on the external environment and allowed the internal culture to lapse into a muddle of adversarial relationships, negativity, and distrust. Such a culture will produce patient complaints and staff shortages. Working in such an environment holds little reward. The *Code of Ethics* of the American College of Healthcare Executives (ACHE 2022) is clear about the ethical responsibilities of healthcare executives in this regard:

Healthcare executives have ethical and professional obligations to the employees they manage that encompass but are not limited to:
A. Creating a work environment that promotes ethical conduct
B. Providing a work environment that encourages a free expression of ethical concerns and provides mechanisms for discussing and addressing such concerns

C. Promoting a healthy work environment which includes freedom from harassment, sexual and other, and coercion of any kind, especially to perform illegal or unethical acts

D. Promoting a culture of inclusivity that seeks to prevent discrimination on the basis of race, ethnicity, religion, gender, sexual orientation, age or disability

E. Promoting a clinical environment that intends to avoid discriminating behavior toward healthcare professionals and trainees from patients and families

F. Working to ensure there is a process in place to facilitate the resolution of conflicts that may arise between workforce members or the individual and the organization

G. Providing a work environment that promotes the proper use of employees' knowledge and skills

H. Providing a safe, healthy and equitable work environment

I. Ensuring clinicians and other staff are not subject to violence or any form of preventable harm by patients, family members or visitors

J. Promoting a culture in which employees are provided fair compensation and benefits based upon the work they perform

The management at MCH has also failed to address the perception that the hospital is located in a high-crime neighborhood. Although this perception is not based in fact, "reality is what it is perceived to be" (Berger and Luckmann 1967), and if left unchallenged, perceptions can become accepted as truth. Management has a responsibility to address this issue with facts and to make high-profile changes to ensure that patients, visitors, and staff feel safe and secure in the hospital and its surrounding area.

As mentioned, MCH's management has neglected to complete a comprehensive analysis of the factors leading to its nurses' dissatisfaction and resignations. Valuable information could have been gained from exit interviews. A competitive market analysis of salaries and benefits would have been helpful. Focus groups and similar efforts might have shed light on the problem and potential solutions.

If MCH wishes to ensure its viability as a healthcare provider, it should model its approach to nursing on the Magnet Recognition Program, which was developed by the ANA in response to the nurse shortage of the 1980s. The American Nurses Credentialing Center (ANCC 2023) believes that Magnet organizations "will lead the reformation of health care; the discipline of nursing; and care of the patient, family and community." The program incentivizes healthcare organizations to improve nurse recruitment and retention by means of the 14 Forces of Magnetism, organized under five Magnet Model Components, that differentiate Magnet-recognized hospitals from other hospitals:

1. Transformational leadership
   - *Quality of nursing leadership (Force 1).* Are they strong, knowledgeable advocates for the staff?
   - *Management style (Force 3).* Do the leaders invite participation and feedback?
2. Structural empowerment
   - *Organizational structure (Force 2).* Is it decentralized with strong representation for nurses?
   - *Personnel policies and programs (Force 4).* Are salaries competitive? Are flexible schedules offered?
   - *Community and the healthcare organization (Force 10).* Does the hospital have a strong presence in the community?
   - *Image of nursing (Force 12).* Do other members of the healthcare team view the work of nursing as essential?
   - *Professional development (Force 14).* Is significant emphasis placed on in-service education, continuing education, and career development?
3. Exemplary professional practice
   - *Professional models of care (Force 5).* Are nurses given responsibility and authority?
   - *Consultation and resources (Force 8).* Are there adequate human resources?
   - *Autonomy (Force 9).* Are nurses allowed independent judgment?
   - *Nurses as teachers (Force 11).* Are nurses permitted and expected to incorporate teaching in all aspects of practice?
   - *Interdisciplinary relationships (Force 13).* Is a sense of mutual respect exhibited among all disciplines?
4. New knowledge, innovation, and improvements
   - *Quality improvement (Force 7).* Are nurses involved?
5. Empirical quality results
   - *Quality of care (Force 6).* Is it an organizational priority?

Pursuing Magnet recognition has merit. Premier hospitals throughout the nation seek to meet the requirements and earn this designation, which is an important element in *U.S. News & World Report* magazine's annual Best Hospitals list.

Nurses are the largest, most visible segment of a hospital's workforce and are widely recognized as the most crucial. A strong nursing staff leads to better outcomes for patients and less nurse attrition and turnover.

Disruptive Physician Behaviors

Disruptive and unprofessional physician behavior is more common than one might think. A national survey by the American Association for Physician Leadership

(AAPL; previously the American College of Physician Executives) reported that "more than 2 in 3 US doctors witness other physicians disrupting patient care or collegial relationships at least once a month; more than 1 in 10 say they see it every day" (Knox 2011). An organization representative said, "Our profession is still plagued by doctors acting in a way that is disrespectful, unprofessional and toxic to the workplace" (Knox 2011). The AAPL continues to address the problem of disruptive physician behaviors through its publications and educational programming. Another study of disruptive physician behaviors found that 80 percent of hospital workers, including doctors and nurses, said they had seen "yelling," "abusive language," "condescension," and "berating of colleagues"—and 25 percent of those surveyed said they saw such behavior weekly (Scheinbaum 2012).

The consequences of inappropriate behaviors are many and severe. They result in dysfunctional teams, reduced quality of patient care and medical outcomes, medical errors, poor nurse retention, and increased risk of litigation (Swiggart et al. 2009).

Contributing causes of inappropriate and damaging behavior are thought to be stress, long hours, red tape, and shrinking physician compensation. As a result of their socialization in medical school, physicians expect to be in control of situations, always be right, and never have their orders questioned. In the twenty-first century, however, they have lost more and more control over their practices, compensation, and way of life. In addition, stress is intrinsic to their profession, which requires them to deal with life-and-death situations and the ever-present threat of malpractice. But many physicians fail to develop the social relationships and good physical habits that might serve as stress relievers (Scheinbaum 2012).

Swiggart and colleagues (2009) found that failure to address physicians' disruptive behavior and a lack of consequences reinforce inappropriate conduct. Management may choose to ignore such behavior for many reasons. Perhaps the offender is a high admitter or the only practitioner of a desirable subspecialty. Perhaps administrators fear antagonizing the offender's colleagues or simply wish to avoid conflict. Under such circumstances, the disruptive behaviors are likely to continue and may even escalate. Finally, a physician's inappropriate behavior may be a symptom of a deeper underlying problem, such as addiction or physical or mental illness. Every instance of troublesome conduct requires early intervention to determine its causes.

The American Medical Association (AMA 2001) places responsibility on physicians to "report physicians deficient in character or competence." Physicians, however, may expect management to handle sensitive situations, especially if the offending physician is well connected politically and professionally. The Joint Commission (2021) is clear on this issue, as stated in a *Sentinel Event Alert*: "To assure quality and promote a culture of safety, health care organizations must address the problem of behaviors that threaten the performance of the health care team." The Joint Commission has required hospitals to incorporate codes of conduct into medical staff bylaws and medical agreements that declare zero tolerance for disruptive behavior and provide protections for those who report it (DerGurahian 2008). In its current standards, The Joint Commission (2023) requires hospital leaders to "develop a code of conduct that defines acceptable behavior and behaviors that undermine a culture of safety" and to "create and implement a process for managing behaviors that undermine a culture of safety."

When dealing with medical staff issues that require behavioral correction, disciplinary action, or cooperation, organizational leaders should collaborate closely with medical leaders and seek their help in pursuing change. Healthcare executives must clearly communicate the effects of disruptive physician behaviors, especially on patient care and staff retention, so that physicians understand how their patients will benefit from explicit methods of dealing with unprofessional conduct. All members of the medical staff must be familiar with policies and procedures pertaining to disruptive behaviors, reporting guidelines, and responsibilities of medical staff officers. Clear definitions of terms such as *discrimination,* *harassment,* and *disruptive behaviors* are especially important to ensure that staff recognize inappropriate conduct and know that it must be dealt with. Investigations of alleged inappropriate behaviors must be confidential and documented and must allow the physician in question to respond (Hofmann 2010). Interventions and corrective actions must follow allegations proven to be true.

To create a more productive, professional environment, some healthcare organizations have found it helpful to engage the services of an anger management consultant to help physicians learn to control their anger and modify their behavior. One such consultant has created a workbook, *The Practice of Control,* especially for physicians. It teaches that anger, which is often a precursor of disruptive behavior, is as personally harmful as smoking a pack of cigarettes a day (Scheinbaum 2012).

Hofmann (2010) found that the following management actions promote and support a productive, professional work environment:

1. Provide education and training about inappropriate conduct.
2. Survey staff about the work environment.
3. Enforce compliance with codes of conduct and policies regarding disruptive behavior.
4. Ensure a means for reporting concerns.
5. Promptly investigate allegations.
6. Give timely feedback about complaints.
7. Offer support services for physicians who behave improperly.

All such actions require a commitment from management to provide the necessary time and staff, but healthcare managers with foresight will recognize that the return on investment will be invaluable.

Legal Implications

At MCH, staff shortages, disruptive physician behaviors, conflicts, and poor communication among nurses of disparate cultures have created a negative work environment and an adversarial climate. Such conditions often lead to medical errors, patient dissatisfaction, and adverse patient events such as falls, surgical complications, hospital-acquired infections, and medication overdoses. Staff shortages and poor communication among caregivers threaten patient safety and set the stage for malpractice litigation. And nurses hesitate to question a volatile physician's order, even when doing so might prevent an adverse patient event.

The toxic work environment at MCH invites claims of discrimination and hostile working conditions. Sooner or later, disgruntled employees, patients, or families will decide that management is ignoring their complaints and will seek recourse. The resulting legal, political, and public relations damage will threaten MCH's very existence.

REFERENCES

Agency for Healthcare Research and Quality (AHRQ). 2012. "State-Mandated Nurse Staffing Levels Alleviate Workloads, Leading to Lower Patient Mortality and Higher Nurse Satisfaction." AHRQ Innovations Exchange. Updated October 10. http://innovations.ahrq.gov/content.aspx?id=3708 (content no longer available).

American College of Healthcare Executives (ACHE). 2022. *Code of Ethics*. As amended December 5. www.ache.org/about-ache/our-story/our-commitments/ethics/ache-code-of-ethics.

American Medical Association (AMA). 2001. "AMA Principles of Medical Ethics." Revised June. https://code-medical-ethics.ama-assn.org/principles.

American Nurses Association (ANA). 2023. "Advocating for Safe Staffing." Accessed October 30. www.nursingworld.org/practice-policy/nurse-staffing/nurse-staffing-advocacy/.

American Nurses Credentialing Center (ANCC). 2023. "Magnet Model—Creating a Magnet Culture." Accessed October 30. www.nursingworld.org/organizational-programs/magnet/magnet-model/.

Berger, P. L., and T. Luckmann. 1967. *The Social Construction of Reality*. Garden City, NY: Anchor Books.

Collins, J. 2001. *Good to Great: Why Some Companies Make the Leap . . . and Others Don't*. New York: HarperCollins.

DerGurahian, J. 2008. "Behavioral Watchdogs: Joint Commission Standard Targets Unruly Staff." *Modern Healthcare* 38 (28): 8–9.

Hofmann, P. B. 2010. "Fulfilling Disruptive-Behavior Policy Objectives: Leaders Must Promptly Address Improper Clinician Behavior." *Healthcare Executive* 25 (3): 62–63.

Joint Commission. 2023. *Comprehensive Accreditation Manual for Hospitals*. Oakbrook Terrace, IL: Joint Commission Resources.

———. 2021. "Behaviors That Undermine a Culture of Safety." *Sentinel Event Alert*. No. 40. Updated June 18. www.jointcommission.org/-/media/tjc/documents/resources/patient-safety-topics/sentinel-event/sea-40-intimidating-disruptive-behaviors-final2.pdf.

Knox, R. 2011. "Doctors Behaving Badly? They Say It Happens All the Time." *Shots* (blog), NPR. Published May 25. www.npr.org/blogs/health/2011/05/28/136648516/doctorsbehaving-badly-they-say-it-happens-all-the-time.

Russell, J. A., and B. Greenspan. 2005. "Correcting and Preventing Management Mistakes." In *Management Mistakes in Healthcare: Identification, Correction and Prevention*, edited by P. B. Hofmann and F. Perry, 84–102. New York: Cambridge University Press.

Scheinbaum, C. 2012. "Doctors Without Boundaries: An Anger Management Pioneer Tries to Defuse Rageaholic Physicians." *Bloomberg Businessweek*, August 6.

Swiggart, W. H., C. M. Dewey, G. B. Hickson, A. J. R. Finlayson, and W. A. Spickard Jr. 2009. "A Plan for Identification, Treatment, and Remediation of Disruptive Behaviors in Physicians." *Frontiers of Health Services Management* 25 (4): 3–11.

CHAPTER 9

Information Technology Setback: Heartland Healthcare System

CASE STUDY

Jack Moore had been frustrated throughout most of his career. Information Technology (IT) had been breaking new ground in the medical and corporate worlds for more than 20 years, yet Jack found himself continually compromised by unimaginative bosses and organizations crippled by a lack of resources. But it looked as though things were about to change. Jack had recently been hired as the chief information officer (CIO) of Heartland Healthcare System, a successful multihospital system. It was his dream position.

The flagship 500-bed hospital was located in the major metropolitan area of a predominantly rural state in the Great Plains region. Heartland's five smaller hospitals of 50 or fewer beds were scattered throughout the rural regions of the state within a 100-mile radius of the flagship hospital. In addition, three specialty hospitals (heart, pediatrics, and orthopedics) thrived in the metropolitan area along with a very busy outpatient surgical center. The hospitals that made up the Heartland system were connected by a sophisticated helicopter transport service that quickly transported patients in need to the flagship hospital. The hospital system employed more than 5,000 staff members and 300 physicians, mostly subspecialists. An additional 900 private-practice physicians had privileges at Heartland. Heartland's staff included a sizeable number of nurse practitioners, who played a significant role in caring for the state's rural population and who also staffed a number of the primary healthcare clinics located in the metropolitan area.

When Jack was hired as CIO at Heartland, he was charged with two major responsibilities: (1) ensure access and interconnectivity of medical information among all of the system's hospitals, urgent care centers, primary care clinics, and private physician offices; and (2) determine whether to upgrade the existing patient financial system (PFS), which was slated to be discontinued by the current vendor, or move to a new vendor and completely replace the existing PFS with a new product. To make his job easier, he would report directly to the CEO.

Richard Smith had been the CEO of Heartland for more than 15 years and was largely responsible for the success of the health system. His one disappointment had been his inability to enhance the IT services available at Heartland. His failure to do so was in some measure attributable to John Forbes, the previous CIO, who was retiring after more than 20 years at Heartland and who was thought to be out of touch with the currently available technology. Richard had often berated himself for not investing more in IT and for not forcing early retirement on John to better achieve this goal.

Richard was pleased with his recruitment of Jack, who had very impressive IT credentials, although not in healthcare, and who seemed competent and eager to move Heartland into the next generation of IT. Richard assured Jack that the needed resources had been budgeted and approved to achieve rapid progress, based on an earlier feasibility study by a reputable IT consulting firm. Heartland had engaged the firm to conduct the study, and both Richard and the Heartland board had been pleased with the firm's work. The IT consultants had indicated in their study that the existing PFS system at Heartland could be upgraded to the new version for a cost of $8 million. An upgrade seemed like a reasonable solution to the immediate problem, but Jack believed it was a myopic strategy if Heartland were to move into future cutting-edge technologies necessary to maintain its command of the market. The plan certainly did not mesh with his personal ambition to build an IT system at Heartland that would be the envy of healthcare organizations across the Midwest. Eager to bring Heartland's system up-to-date as quickly as possible, Richard did not need much convincing of the wisdom inherent in Jack's strategy. Subsequently, a three-vendor search and formal bid process yielded a $40 million contract with MedCore to implement a completely new IT system that fully integrated all clinical and financial functions into a single platform, providing the desired interconnectivity throughout Heartland, its electronic medical records, and its PFS—in short, a comprehensive, state-of-the-art healthcare delivery platform.

As the project progressed, Jack hired Alan Atkins, a local independent contractor, to manage the implementation and conversion project. The project was a much more complex undertaking than Jack's previous experience had prepared him for, but he felt that with Alan's help, the project would move forward. As work progressed, Jack found himself relying more and more on Alan and his advice on managing the project. Alan began contracting for more and more staff time from his firm to work on the implementation, even though using Heartland IT staff would have been less expensive and certainly better for Heartland staff morale. The staff were beginning to grumble that they were being left out of the loop and did not know what was going on. The sense of being left out of the decision making on the implementation began to escalate as the accounting staff responsible for patient billing and the nursing staff responsible for patient care were ignored. The nursing staff became especially vocal in their chagrin at not being consulted as decisions were made that affected their patient care activities. The vice president (VP) for nursing wasted no time in making her concerns known to the CEO, but they were largely unheeded. Richard thought this was yet another example of the VP's marginal cooperation with other departments in the organization, a problem he had raised during her last annual performance review.

To the hospital staff, Jack and Alan seemed to be making decisions in isolation with the unflinching support of the CEO. To Richard, the hospital staff—especially nursing—were being resistant to change as usual and were attempting to thwart the progress necessary to bring Heartland's IT into the twenty-first century. As morale plummeted, speculation among the staff began to focus on the appropriateness of Alan's firm's business transactions with Heartland. The purchasing staff let it be known that Heartland had purchased 40 laptops from Alan's firm without a formal bid process. The information security officer complained that Alan's firm had not handed those laptops over to be encrypted per Heartland's information security policy. Making matters worse, Alan's staff were purportedly using real patient records to run test scenarios on their unencrypted laptops—a rumor that was confirmed when a contractor reported that his laptop had been stolen from his hotel room and Heartland was required to file a data breach notification.

Then the unthinkable happened. Two years into the contract and $35 million into the $40 million project, MedCore was sold to another company, which dropped the patient billing system product that was an integral part of the project. Nothing in the contract protected Heartland from this scenario. In an effort to minimize the financial loss, Jack went back to the original PFS vendor, who after much negotiation agreed that with the remaining budget of $5 million Heartland could pursue the original option of upgrading the existing system.

Richard was dumbfounded. Jack had recommended MedCore so strongly and was so confident that it was the perfect fit for Heartland. Following the initial shock of the disclosure, however, Jack was able to convince Richard that this unfortunate turn of events could not have been foreseen. As Jack put it, it was a minor setback that would not prevent Heartland from moving into the technology future they both desired.

In the aftermath of the MedCore debacle, Heartland hired Alan as its full-time manager of hardware support. Jack was shaken by the MedCore departure and believed that he needed Alan even more. It was common knowledge among the Heartland IT staff that Alan had no formal degree. Not only had Heartland waived the position's requirements for Alan, but it had also not posted the position.

Today, Richard still has high hopes that Heartland can acquire state-of-the-art technology like that of hardware system giants in the corporate world. Although he has less confidence in Jack and suspects that Jack is more interested in building his own personal technology empire, he does not necessarily see their goals as being mutually exclusive.

Heartland's IT staff clearly lack confidence in Jack's leadership ability. They see a firewall between IT management and the employees doing application support. The nursing staff believe that Jack has no concept of the health system's mission of patient care and no interest in involving patient care staff in technology planning and implementation. The accounting staff are convinced that Jack has no business savvy and does not adequately focus on business applications. In fact, one employee was recently overheard to say, "Jack is more intent on being a cutting-edge IT think tank than being an integral part of a hospital system whose job is to serve patients."

ETHICS ISSUES

Management's role and responsibility: What are Richard's role and responsibility in this case? What are Jack's? How does Richard's and Jack's treatment of the other senior staff inform the situation? Were project goals established with metrics to measure progress? Was appropriate accountability and oversight established for a project of this magnitude? Were contracting, purchasing, and human resources practices judicious and ethical? Who is accountable for the security breach that could easily have been avoided if established policy had been followed?

Organizational implications: Given the fiduciary obligation of administrators to their organization, how could Richard and Jack have avoided, or at least minimized, the damage caused by their IT plan running into difficulty? Who is more accountable—Jack, the CIO, for convincing Richard to change plans, or Richard, the CEO, for allowing himself to be swayed without conducting more due diligence? What is the board's role? What are the implications of this situation for quality improvement at Heartland? How will reimbursements be affected? Staff satisfaction? Patient satisfaction? What effect will this failed project have on future staff collaboration and productivity? On staff's trust of management?

Adherence to the organization's mission statement, ethical standards, and values statement: Are the actions in this case consistent with the organization's mission statement, ethical standards, and values statement? Was Jack unethical in his management of the IT project? Did Richard behave ethically in his obligations as CEO? Have personal goals and ambitions trumped the organization's mission and responsibility to the community?

Conflict of interest: What are the conflicts of interest in this case? Did Jack truly believe that the solution he proposed would provide greater benefit to Heartland and its patients? How might the situation have been different if Richard had examined the interests of all parties (including his own) in an objective way?

Use of consultants: What factors should be considered when hiring a consultant? What steps should be taken during the hiring process? Did Jack use his consultant effectively and appropriately? What could Jack have done to improve the situation?

Justice and fairness: How do issues of justice and fairness enter into this case? Did Jack manage personnel and other resources fairly? What role did bias play in the situation and its outcome? Did the relationship between Richard and Jack support or inhibit fair and just relationships with others? How did Jack's relationship with Alan affect members of the IT staff? How might the situation at Heartland have been different if Jack and Alan had listened to and engaged other leaders and staff?

DISCUSSION

by Pete Shelkin and Melissa Cole

This case tells the story of a CIO who lands his dream job and is looking forward to making his mark by raising his employer's IT infrastructure to a level that will be the envy of other health systems. Such opportunities can be great motivators because they challenge people to prove their abilities. However, this case also demonstrates that it takes more than desire and motivation to ensure success and that straying from the path to success can be easy once the first missteps are taken. Along the way, ethical challenges arise to which people can increasingly succumb as pressures mount.

The following discussion addresses the pitfalls of confusing one's own goals with those of an organization and the consequences of not knowing when to ask for or properly use help.

Management's Role and Responsibility

Before dealing with ethics, we need to discuss roles and responsibilities. In Richard's case, the board would consider his CEO responsibilities to include setting clear organizational direction, creating the management organization chart, staffing the executive team, ensuring that budgets are set and met, and making sure that decisions are well made and executed (White and Griffith 2019). Richard has further responsibilities to his management team, which include giving each executive clear direction in their specific area of responsibility, assessing performance, and providing coaching and guidance when necessary. Finally, as CEO, Richard is also responsible for ensuring that Heartland staff are empowered to do their jobs well and that all of Heartland's patients are treated justly. These actions will ensure that the community's trust is not violated and that patients are satisfied with the services they receive (Morrison 2016).

As a member of the senior executive team, Jack is responsible for achieving the goals that the CEO sets for him in ways that will ensure the best results. Those results are typically measured in terms of quality, costs, and benefits. As the CIO, Jack is also responsible for working closely with clinical leaders to ensure that he understands their needs and to prepare strategic and operational plans that take those needs into account. More important, in executing his plans he is expected to meet the clinicians' needs as closely as possible. Given unlimited wants and limited budgets, meeting their needs can be a difficult task, but the expectation is legitimate. Established models and practices show that this responsibility can be successfully fulfilled (White and Griffith 2019). Jack is also responsible for setting clear direction in the IT department and ensuring the just treatment of his staff (Petersen et al. 2018). Finally, as the most senior IT manager at Heartland, Jack has significant responsibility for ensuring that electronically stored protected health information is not accidently disclosed (Shay 2017; US Department of Health and Human Services [HHS] 2023).

The financial management function projects future needs, arranges to meet them, and manages the organization's assets and liabilities in ways that increase its profitability (White and Griffith 2019). Executives have a fiduciary responsibility to protect the resources of their institution. The loss of $35 million and two years of effort opens the door to charges that Heartland's administrators, particularly the CEO and CIO, have failed to uphold their fiduciary responsibility. The board may even ask questions about managerial malpractice and negligence when they learn that the contract with MedCore had no provisions protecting Heartland in the event that MedCore was sold. Although the CEO and Heartland's legal counsel may share in the blame, the CIO has primary responsibility to ensure that relatively common issues with IT vendors are identified and addressed in such an important IT contract.

Even if we lay the blame for the troubled IT project at the feet of the CIO, we must still ask what the CEO could have (or should have) done to minimize or even avoid the damage. Healthcare administrators are ethically bound to ensure that staff who work at their institutions are competent (Morrison 2016). This obligation is most clear in the areas of direct care delivery, where many staff are required to be licensed or certified and to stay up-to-date through continuing education. Although healthcare executives are not required to be licensed or certified, they are expected to be highly competent in their respective fields, and their managers are expected to validate that competency on a regular basis. A Joint Commission (2023) standard requiring that competency be assessed during orientation helps ensure that every staff member is able to perform and that larger challenges or problems will not develop.

In this context, we must ask why the CIO is able to persuade the CEO to ignore the $8 million budget that the board previously approved and to pursue a much more expensive strategy. And then, after the sale of MedCore, why is the CEO willing to believe that the debacle is only a minor setback? Finally, after the VP for nursing voices concerns about not being included in the process, how can the CEO continue to avoid questioning the CIO's ability to do his job?

While we may forgive Richard for seeing Jack in only his best light during the hiring process, ethical questions begin to arise in regard to Richard's response—or rather his lack of response—to warning signs about Jack's ability to take direction and his competency in general. At what point between the initial honeymoon period granted to a new hire and the catastrophic failure of the IT project did the CEO fail in his duty to ensure that Heartland had a competent CIO? Could following a schedule of required formal performance assessments that included gathering feedback from others at key intervals have helped the CEO keep the CIO on a course to success?

Organizational Implications

Clearly, the loss of $35 million and two years of effort will have a significant impact on Heartland. Not only have the goals of installing a new PFS and ensuring interconnectivity been delayed, but the benefits that could have been gained by spending that $35 million on other capital projects have also been forfeited. Even without further details about Heartland's financials, we have enough information about the size of the system and its operations to make some reasonable assumptions. For example, healthcare organizations with 5,000 employees have about $567.6 million in annual revenue (Computer Economics 2017). We can also assume that Heartland will want to maintain a 2 percent operating margin to achieve an A credit rating (Standard & Poor's Financial Services 2017).

Assuming that Heartland is like other midwestern hospital systems of its size, its $35 million loss would have amounted to writing off nearly all of its annual capital budget for the past two years. The lack of corresponding assets on the balance sheet will significantly drive down Heartland's margin and have an adverse effect on its financial and operating ratios. As substantial as the damage appears to be, the picture would be even worse if Heartland's financial performance were below average to begin with. The damage is sufficiently great that the CFO and the board's finance committee will have to make some tough decisions as they watch Heartland's ratios decline and its credit rating get downgraded.

The effect on Heartland will likely go beyond the damage to its financial statements and operating ratios and may extend to staff and patients alike. Questions that the CEO should anticipate hearing from the board include the following: What quality improvement initiatives were initially postponed to fund the IT projects, and will they now be postponed even further? Are quality metrics stagnating, or worse yet, declining, while improvement efforts await funding? If so, how will reimbursements be affected now that they are being tied to outcomes? The board may also want to know whether staff satisfaction is being affected by delays in improvements and whether patient satisfaction is being affected by quality issues, deterioration of the physical plant, or perceptions of outdated equipment. The losses resulting from Jack's actions have implications that reach far beyond the IT department.

Given the ethical obligation of administrators to serve in a fiduciary role, how might the CEO and CIO have avoided, or at least minimized, any negative consequences? Why has the original consulting report been discounted? The report was provided by a reputable firm, and the board is pleased with it. Heartland is planning to act on the report's recommendations until Jack arrives and convinces Richard to think bigger. In his enthusiasm to move Heartland into a cutting-edge IT future, Richard fails to exercise due diligence, such as having the consulting firm review Jack's new proposal and compare it with its earlier recommendation. If the consulting firm is truly reputable, and if Jack's plan has merit and is backed by facts, the firm could easily modify its recommendation in light of the new information and Jack's leadership. Given the effect of the change in plans, who is more accountable? What is the board's role? Have they approved the change in plans without asking questions of their own? As tends to be the case when leaders look back at massive failures, they may see many missed opportunities that might have ensured accountability and prudent corrections.

Questions also remain about how MedCore has been selected and how the project is managed within the organization. Whether the selection committee includes representatives of all stakeholders is unknown; however, Jack's exclusion of key stakeholders from decision making during the new system's implementation suggests that he also does not consider stakeholder input during the selection process. Ignoring stakeholder input is a primary cause of failure for IT projects (Acharya and Werts 2019). Given that Jack failed to use stakeholder input as the basis of his planning and decision processes, the project likely would have run into serious trouble even if MedCore had not been sold.

Finally, there will be tough questions to answer, as well as tough penalties to pay, for the Health Insurance Portability and Accountability Act (HIPAA) violation that resulted from the loss of an unencrypted laptop containing patient data. Because the organization knew about the noncompliance (as evidenced by the complaint of the information security officer) but took no action to correct it, the Office of Civil Rights of the US Department of Health and Human Services will consider this a Tier 4 violation—the most serious type of HIPAA violation, which carries the stiffest penalties (*HIPAA Journal* 2023). Financial penalties could easily run into the millions of dollars, and Heartland's reputation will also certainly be tarnished by the negative publicity that comes with public disclosure and notification (HHS 2023; Shay 2017).

Adherence to the Organization's Mission Statement, Ethical Standards, and Values Statement

Although we do not have access to Heartland's mission statement and strategic goals, we do know that Jack has two major responsibilities: achieving interconnectivity and upgrading or replacing the PFS. Jack's primary goals are probably tied directly to Heartland's strategic plan, which is—by definition and necessity—intended to support Heartland's mission and vision.

Jack clearly has not met the goals for which he was responsible. However, is failure unethical? One could easily argue that failing to meet a business goal is not in and of itself an ethical failure. To determine the existence of an ethical breach, we need to understand why a failure occurred. For instance, a failure might occur because an unethical person misrepresented their skills or experience to get a job. An obvious example of this in healthcare is someone who impersonates a physician and harms patients by giving bad advice and bungling procedures (Ellison 2018; Martyr 2018). However, Jack appeared to have impressive IT credentials when Heartland hired him and so does not seem guilty of outright fraud. Later we learn that Heartland's project was "a much more complex undertaking than Jack's previous experience had prepared him for." Nonetheless, Jack's willingness to take on such a difficult project would not necessarily be an ethical breach because eagerness to tackle ever greater challenges is often encouraged and admired in successful leaders.

What distinguishes an ethical failure from an unethical one is the motive involved (Collins 2018). Jack certainly wanted to make Heartland a successful showcase of technology, but he may have been motivated more by his ambitions than by a desire to support Heartland's mission. According to the opening paragraph, Jack "had been frustrated throughout most of his career" and felt that he had been "continually compromised by unimaginative bosses." Jack's personal ambition was "to build an IT system at Heartland that would be the envy of healthcare organizations across the Midwest." Jack's ambition raises questions about his adherence to Heartland's mission, which focuses on serving patients and, we can assume, makes no mention of causing competitors to be envious. In light of such information, Jack's motives may be questioned, along with the ethics of his priorities and actions.

Conflict of Interest

Conflict is not necessarily bad or unethical. In fact, many innovations have come about because people's perspectives conflicted with the status quo, and their interest in providing a more valuable product or service drove them to challenge accepted assumptions or previous decisions. Some people also discover that they are working for an unethical organization and seek to expose the unprincipled activities. Although such whistle-blowers are motivated by the conflict between their personal interests and their responsibilities to their employers, they are usually regarded as acting ethically. In the end, the determining factor is the whistle-blower's motivation: Is the individual focused primarily on personal gain or on the benefit to the organization?

In the case under consideration, the goals of the CIO, the CEO, and Heartland initially appear to be aligned: They all share the goal of using technology to move the health system into a productive and efficient future where quality rises and cost per unit of service declines. Conflict comes into play almost immediately, however, when the CIO decides that the board-approved solution is myopic and lobbies successfully to pursue an alternative strategy at a much higher cost. Where do the CIO's interests lie when he persuades the CEO, and presumably the board, to change direction? Does he believe that his solution will result in greater benefit to Heartland and its patients? Perhaps he does; however, we are told that a primary reason the CIO believes that the approved solution is shortsighted is that it does not mesh with his personal ambitions. When that is considered along with the statement in the opening paragraph that the CIO had felt "continually compromised by unimaginative bosses" throughout his career, we get a sense that while the parties' goals may be aligned, their motives may not be. The term *conflict of interest* is commonly used to describe such situations; perhaps the term *conflict of motive* can be thought of as the key to identifying a conflict of interest that is unethical.

In the Heartland case, other interests besides those of the CEO and CIO are at play as well. For example, the CIO's interests seem to conflict with those of the VP for nursing and her nursing staff, the accounting staff, and the IT staff. While mounting evidence suggests that the CIO's selfish motives are at the root of those conflicts, each interest should be examined on its own merits. All too often, a mob mentality can take over when a crisis reaches critical mass and people rally to find a scapegoat. To guard against a situation such as that at Heartland, people must avoid accepting the easy conclusion and falling into an ethical trap. The CEO's actions are evidence of this tendency: Instead of fully investigating the situation, Richard quickly dismisses the nursing VP's objections because he sees them as proof of her marginal cooperation. In fact, as the project gets deeper and deeper into trouble, the more others complain and the more they are ignored. How might the situation have been different had the CEO examined all parties' interests and assessed the validity of each perspective?

Use of Consultants

Healthcare leaders must frequently decide whether to use internal talent or outside expertise. Large IT projects are especially likely to call for such decisions because the needed skills and the duration of those needs usually differ greatly from the needs of day-to-day operations.

Ideally, when organizations hire consultants for temporary support and enhancement of their own staff, the staff gain valuable new knowledge and abilities. Laying the foundation for a successful collaboration requires input from the project's stakeholders to clearly define the scope of work to be accomplished, as well as thorough research by the in-house project manager to locate a consultant with the right skills, experience, and credentials. A contract is then negotiated that documents the scope, the deliverables (which should include knowledge transfer), and a clear timeline that includes project benchmarks. (Of course, use of consultants for open-ended operational activities would not require such a strict plan.)

At Heartland, the CIO seems not to have taken any of those steps when hiring his consultant. He instead hires a consultant who can make up for his own lack of experience: "This project was a much more complex undertaking than Jack's previous experience had prepared him for, but he felt that with Alan's help, the project would move forward." In short, Jack creates a situation that discourages the consultant from transferring the knowledge needed to sustain the new system because, from the consultant's perspective, doing so would bring an end to what has turned out to be an open-ended, lucrative project. In addition, the consultant's lack of credentials, compounded by his inability to connect with the VP for nursing and other leadership, leaves him open to criticism and takes a toll on staff morale. Clinical, accounting, and IT staff all feel left out of the decision making and therefore have no buy-in to the project or its success.

The Code of Professional and Ethical Conduct of the American Medical Informatics Association (AMIA) states (Petersen 2018):

> *Recognize technical and ethical limitations and seek consultation when needed, particularly in ethically conflicting situations.*

Has Jack followed the AMIA's code and admitted his technical shortcomings? On the surface, his choice to use a consultant implies that he recognizes the gap in his abilities. However, instead of expanding his own abilities or those of his staff, he appears to use company resources to keep his shortcomings covered up.

By failing to define the roles of his consultant and his IT staff, the CIO also opens the door to dissension and frustration: He does not engage his staff in the knowledge-building process, and his actions create a wedge as opposed to a bridge. Although he is ethically bound to ensure that the goals and activities of his department are aligned with Heartland's mission and vision, Jack's pursuit of his personal goals creates an environment that is counterproductive and distracting for his team. The CIO has painted himself into a corner and feels forced to convert what should have been a defined consulting project for Alan into a permanent job. By ensuring that Alan reports directly to him, Jack ultimately removes the need to improve on his own skills.

Justice and Fairness

Richard and Jack certainly have focused goals: move forward with replacing the PFS; create a legacy of supporting patient safety; and provide a fully integrated, state-of-the-art IT system for use by staff across the enterprise. Their vision is clear, and the resources they need seem readily available; yet when they begin working toward achieving those goals, they are unwilling to listen to stakeholders, especially those with differing views, and thus fail to find common ground.

All people have biases, and if pressed, most will admit to them. Fair and just leaders know how to identify potentially damaging biases and keep them in check. They also know that openly disclosing affiliations and financial ties helps clear blind spots, reduces liability, and increases the trust of staff and colleagues.

Consider why people develop a bias toward a favorite source of input. Is it because that person helps them come to the best conclusion and grow in the process? Or because that person fills a gap that they have and helps them avoid detection? Which reason better explains the relationship that Heartland's CIO has with the IT consultant? How may the CIO's waiving of Heartland's hiring criteria for the hardware support manager position be viewed by the IT staff, particularly those who may actually have qualifications for the position that the consultant lacks?

Managers may naturally gravitate toward one or two staff members when they seek advice. We all seek advice from people who have the skills and experience to help us. The way a manager responds to input from people other than trusted advisers can raise ethical questions, however, especially when that input conflicts with the manager's point of view. To be fair, the manager should listen to all opinions with an open mind. Clearly, Heartland's CIO has not done so. By failing to listen to those he viewed as critics and adversaries, he has failed to include information that may have helped him create the most serviceable IT system for all users (Acharya and Werts 2019).

Heartland's CIO and CEO have allowed their biases to influence whom they listened to. Would a strong focus on fair and equitable treatment have helped them avoid the compromising situation that they now find themselves in? Imagine if the CEO had listened without bias to nursing and accounting staff and put them in leadership roles on the project. Consider how working conditions might have changed in the IT department if the CIO had listened to his team as much as he listened to his consultant. In a fair and just organizational culture, an IT project would turn out quite differently than did the project at Heartland, where the CIO and CEO gave in to their biases.

Fairness does not imply consensus seeking or weakness, nor does it mean compromising on goals or outcomes. Ethical and just leaders do not choose sides—they maintain their vision of success for all. They bring dissenting voices together via shared goals. People often have differing opinions about "how." The true, ethical leader reminds them of "why."

Lessons Learned

The *Code of Ethics* of the American College of Healthcare Executives (2022) states:

> The fundamental objectives of the healthcare management profession are to maintain or enhance the overall quality of life, dignity and well-being of every individual needing healthcare service and to create a more equitable, accessible, effective and efficient healthcare system. Healthcare executives have an obligation to act in ways that will merit the trust, confidence, and respect of healthcare professionals and the general public.

It also enjoins us to "use this *Code* to further the interests of the profession and not for selfish reasons." These passages provide a good ethical framework for examining the case of Heartland Healthcare System.

In the Heartland case, the CEO and CIO are quite shortsighted as they move forward with system integration and modernizing the PFS. Despite many setbacks, the CEO remains satisfied with the CIO's performance and seems unable to respond to feedback from others to the contrary. While he has "an obligation to act in ways that will merit the trust, confidence, and respect" of his executive team, he does not listen to his VP for nursing and thus erodes her trust. He also minimizes the complaints of Heartland's information security officer, which may result in financial penalties and damage to the organization's reputation. Healthcare leaders must give everyone a chance to be heard, even when the motivation behind dissenting voices might be in question. In a highly engaged team, all ideas are not necessarily supported, but all voices are heard. Ensuring that level of engagement is the responsibility of every leader, especially the CEO.

At Heartland, the CIO becomes increasingly dependent on the consultant, and in doing so he allows the balance of power to shift away from his team and to an outsider. This dependence causes growing concern among others in the organization—concern that is compounded by the CIO's failure to consider their input. Leaders must communicate when their abilities are stretched. Asking for help is indeed a challenge. All people strive to appear competent, and many worry that by asking for assistance or admitting they do not have all the answers, they risk exposure—or worse, repercussions. Successful leaders understand their shortcomings and use help in targeted ways for specific results. Less successful leaders sometimes use help as a cover, hoping that the helper will solve all the problems before they fully manifest themselves and derail a project.

Following are steps to take when help is needed:

1. **Learn to recognize an error.** First, assess whether an error has been made. If so, immediately confer with an executive stakeholder who can assist with any course corrections. Ethical leaders monitor themselves, recognize errors, and model to staff how best to respond to mistakes.
2. **Be willing to seek specific help.** Identify personal strengths and weaknesses, and recognize when help is needed. Be specific about the help needed by clearly defining the tasks, roles, and outcomes sought. Be clear about what you know, what you need from others, and what you expect moving forward. By defining the need and the expectations, you make the distinction between using help and being helpless.
3. **Engage others.** Connect with others early and often to gather relevant information and develop strong employee involvement. This can be the

most valuable time you invest in a project because collaboration improves outcomes. By engaging others from the beginning, you may be able to prevent an error or avoid the need to ask for help later. If you recognize the need for a course correction, promptly acknowledge any error and then ask for help. Demonstrating humility and acknowledging what others can contribute will earn the trust needed to move forward.

4. **Request feedback.** Seek counsel from peers, stakeholders, and supervisors. Reach out to a mentor, ideally someone outside the organization, who has succeeded with similar projects. After making (and admitting to) an error, engage people of influence to ensure a turnaround and success.

5. **Remain open.** Keep firmly in mind that the concerns voiced by people you may perceive as resistant could have some validity. Get past your preconceptions and hear the true message. Do not alienate people whose support and guidance you may need in the future.

6. **Focus on the solution.** Once an error or misstep has been acknowledged, gather your team and begin working to correct it. Recognize that even individuals who have resisted your plans likely share your goal: to make the organization more successful. Focusing on the solution overcomes any unpleasantness caused by disagreement. Also, giving detractors a role in planning the solution ensures their buy-in, which will be critical not only for the success of the project but also for sustained operational success.

Healthcare IT is evolving at a rapid rate, and no one person can have expertise in every area. Acknowledge when additional expertise is needed and engage stakeholders to ensure adoption of proposals and their cost-effective implementation.

Perhaps the most significant ethical lapse by Heartland's CIO is to disregard his responsibility to identify when the project's demands have exceeded his technical ability or to draw on appropriate resources and stakeholders to ensure the project's success. By not engaging key stakeholders or asking for feedback and by attempting to do everything on his own (helped only by Alan), Jack has alienated all of the team members he needs to successfully define and implement his project. Ultimately, the ACHE *Code of Ethics* identifies healthcare leaders' responsibilities in six key areas (ACHE 2022):

1. The profession of healthcare management
2. Patients or others served
3. The organization
4. Employees
5. Community and society
6. Reporting of violations

When healthcare executives lose sight of their mission or lose their ethical grounding, they tend to make poor decisions. Poor decisions result in criticism, and if they fail to respond properly to justifiable criticism, they lose the trust of those they lead or serve. As Greer (2012) observed, "in the absence of trust, we try for control," and the Heartland case illustrates that trust cannot be won back simply through the exercise of control.

Ideally, we all have an ingrained set of ethics—an internal compass that helps us differentiate between right and wrong. When we find ourselves confronted by an ethical dilemma at work, we can reach into our professional toolbox, which includes our mentors, our colleagues, and our professional code of ethics. Our code of ethics is the foundation of all our activities, decisions, and behaviors; by broadening our perspective, it enables us to see beyond our personal interests and pursue higher goals.

The leaders in this case had wonderful intentions. When their project became too difficult for them, however, they reacted by trying to hold onto control instead of admitting that they needed help. Had they behaved ethically when problems arose instead of becoming entrenched in a battle for control, the outcome probably would have been much different.

Additional Thoughts and Reflections: Impact of 2020 Crisis Response

Editor's note: This final section is dedicated to the memory of coauthor Melissa Cole, a good friend and colleague, who passed away before we completed this update to the chapter.

We have reviewed the Heartland case where hospital leaders have failed in their roles, examined lessons learned from that failure, and discussed some suggestions for how those same mistakes could be avoided by others. Given our recent experiences with managing a significantly disruptive long-term event—the COVID-19 pandemic—as well as how that event has promoted modern workforces to establish remote and hybrid work models, let us now bring some additional topics into the discussion.

Strategy and Flexibility

As we learned in 2020, unexpected events can cause priorities, budgets, and resource availability to change dramatically in a very short time frame. What is management's responsibility in regard to balancing flexibility needed to manage a crisis with assuring that the long-term strategy remains a priority?

In addition to the management roles and responsibilities already addressed in the foregoing discussion, we must note that managers are also responsible for responding to unexpected challenges, including changing course when threats appear imminent. Health system managers are also responsible for having business continuity and disaster recovery plans so that the organization can remain functional in the event of a disaster (Joint Commission 2023; National Archives 2023).

Traditionally, when we think of the need for a flexible strategy, we think of changing demographics, emerging technology, or competitive forces in the local or regional market. When we think of disaster recovery, we tend to think of events that, while unlikely, can be defined and planned for such as a fire, earthquake, or even malicious destruction of resources such as cyberattacks made via malware or ransomware. However, self-inflicted issues such as making a poor business decision, or sudden overwhelming factors such as a deadly pandemic, are not what we typically think of when considering how to prepare and respond to the sudden, unexpected disappearance of budget funds or revenue sources.

Whereas the need to prepare for an unexpected, overwhelming, and disruptive event such as a pandemic is necessary, it is beyond the scope of the Heartland discussion. What is relevant, however, is the question of how to manage the risk that funds that were initially expected and budgeted for will suddenly no longer be available, as noted in the discussion topic "Organizational Implications," where we discuss the far-reaching implications of a $35 million loss. In light of the questions already posed, and imagining that the Heartland case were to take place in our postpandemic world, how might Richard apply more recent lessons to this case? In particular, what have recent experiences with adjusting strategy in response to crisis taught us about avoiding a crisis in the first place? The painful lessons of the past tend to motivate us to try harder to avoid repeating them in the future. Although we can't necessarily avoid something like a pandemic, what might Richard do to avoid a repeat of Jack's MedCore fiasco?

Communication

Even with all staff working on-site, issues such as staff feeling left out of the process and deteriorating relationships were factors in this case. With modern workforces trending toward remote and hybrid models, might these issues have become even more of a factor? Would leadership have even been aware of them? Leaders need to consider what they can do to promote communication and inclusion when facing contentious issues that involve teams working primarily from home offices.

It is well accepted that good communication skills are an essential part of a successful manager's tool kit. It is also well understood that nonverbal communication is often more important than the spoken word. Given that Jack's failures included failing to communicate and engage with his management peers or with his own departmental staff, it is easy to see how things might have been made even worse if Heartland's administrative leaders and staff were working remotely.

Prior to the postpandemic boom in remote workplace practices, people and teams would generally meet face-to-face in offices or conference rooms. Body language and facial expression were well-used communication devices, even if typically used subconsciously. With people working in close physical proximity, it was also quite easy to hold impromptu premeeting huddles while walking to a conference room with a colleague, and to hold quick one-on-one or small group follow-up conversations after a meeting to smooth bruised egos or dig deeper into why issues may be encountering resistance.

Although remote teleconferencing technology all but eliminates those benefits of in-person meetings, it also adds some benefits, such as making it easy to quickly reference publications, share documents, and collaborate on creating work products. Such technology also makes it not only possible, but quite simple, to have previously inaccessible outside experts join a meeting from anywhere in the world.

The Heartland case takes place before the major workplace changes that the recent pandemic response brought about, but it is not difficult to imagine that Jack's poor communication and collaboration efforts could have caused his peers and his staff to become even more frustrated and dissatisfied. Managers must make an extra effort to reach out and engage with others when managing a remote workforce. Revisiting the discussion sections on "Justice and Fairness" and "Lessons Learned" (especially point 3, "Engage others"), consider how the circumstances might have been different had the case taken place with Heartland's administrative leaders and IT department working primarily from home offices.

REFERENCES

Acharya, S., and N. Werts. 2019. "Toward the Design of an Engagement Tool for Effective Electronic Health Record Adoption." *Perspectives in Health Information Management* 16 (Winter): PMC6341416.

American College of Healthcare Executives (ACHE). 2022. *Code of Ethics*. Updated December 5. www.ache.org/about-ache/our-story/our-commitments/ethics/ache-code-of-ethics.

Collins, D. 2018. *Business Ethics: Best Practices for Designing and Managing Ethical Organizations*, 2nd ed. Los Angeles, CA: Sage.

Computer Economics. 2017. "Healthcare Services Sector Benchmarks." Chapter 11 in *IT Spending and Staffing Benchmarks 2017–2018*. Irvine, CA: Computer Economics.

Ellison, A. 2018. "Physician Imposter Allegedly Diagnosed Patient at California Hospital." *Becker's Hospital Review*. Published September 4. www.beckershospitalreview.com/legal-regulatory-issues/physician-imposter-allegedly-diagnosed-patient-at-california-hospital.html (content no longer available).

Greer, T. 2012. "Physician Hospital Integration in the 21st Century." Panel discussion held at the 5th Annual New Mexico Healthcare Managers Forum, Albuquerque, October 19.

HIPAA Journal. 2023. "What Are the Penalties for HIPAA Violations?" Accessed September 24. www.hipaajournal.com/what-are-the-penalties-for-hipaa-violations-7096/.

Joint Commission. 2023. *Comprehensive Accreditation Manual for Hospitals*. Oakbrook Terrace, IL: Joint Commission Resources.

Martyr, P. 2018. "A Brief History of Fake Doctors, and How They Get Away with It." *The Conversation*. Published April 9. https://theconversation.com/a-brief-history-of-fake-doctors-and-how-they-get-away-with-it-94572.

Morrison, E. E. 2016. *Ethics in Health Administration: A Practical Approach for Decision Makers*, 3rd ed. Burlington, MA: Jones & Bartlett Learning.

National Archives. 2023. "Code of Federal Regulations: Title 45, Subtitle A, Subchapter C, Part 164, Subpart C." Amended August 31. www.ecfr.gov/current/title-45/subtitle-A/subchapter-C/part-164/subpart-C.

Petersen, C., E. S. Berner, P. J. Embi, K. Fultz Hollis, K. W. Goodman, R. Koppel, C. U. Lehmann, H. Lehmann, S. A. Maulden, K. A. McGregor, A. Solomonides, V. Subbian, E. Terrazas, and P. Winkelstein. 2018. "AMIA's Code of Professional and Ethical Conduct 2018." *Journal of the American Medical Informatics Association* 25 (11): 1579–82.

Shay, D. F. 2017. "The HIPAA Security Rule: Are You in Compliance?" *Family Practice Management* 24 (2): 5–9.

Standard & Poor's Financial Services. 2017. *U.S. Not-for-Profit Health Care System Median Financial Ratios—2016 vs. 2015*. Published August 24. www.spratings.com/documents/20184/908554/US_PF_Event_Webcast_hc91417_art7.pdf (content no longer available).

US Department of Health and Human Services (HHS). 2023. "Cyber Security Guidance Material." Updated July 31. www.hhs.gov/hipaa/for-professionals/security/guidance/cybersecurity/index.html.

White, K. R., and J. R. Griffith. 2019. *The Well-Managed Healthcare Organization*, 9th ed. Chicago: Health Administration Press.

CHAPTER 10

Failed Hospital Merger:
Richland River Valley Healthcare System

CASE STUDY

The scenic Richland River meandered through historically prosperous Clay County. In the heart of this fertile valley lay the charming and picturesque city of Richland. The suburban area surrounding Richland, with its rolling hills and abundance of natural beauty, had attracted developers and now boasted elite resorts and retirement communities for the wealthy. The population of Clay County, including the city of Richland, was just under 500,000.

Clay County was proud of its healthcare services and touted them in its promotions to attract new industry to the area. The county had six hospitals—four in the city of Richland and two in the outlying suburban areas. Suburban Medical Center was a 150-bed general acute care hospital, and Community Behavioral Health Center was a 50-bed residential center with an innovative and highly regarded outpatient treatment center. In the city of Richland, the healthcare providers of choice for the vast majority of the population were Trinity Medical Center and Sutton Memorial Hospital. The other two general acute care hospitals in the city, both with fewer than 200 beds, were not considered major players in the healthcare arena of Clay County.

While both Trinity and Sutton Memorial were well-respected providers of high-quality healthcare, they were very different in mission and structure. Trinity Medical Center was a faith-based organization that was part of a larger, regional religious system. Its mission was to care for those in need regardless of their ability to pay,

---

and as a result, Trinity provided the vast majority of indigent care in Clay County. Its programs had been developed in response to the needs of the younger population it tended to serve. Enormous resources had been committed to its high-risk obstetrics program, neonatal intensive care unit, and pediatrics program with its attendant pediatrics intensive care unit. Trinity was also the designated Level I trauma center for the county and had committed considerable resources to its critical care programs, which included surgical and medical intensive care units and renal dialysis and burn units. In addition to its general medical and surgical units, it operated oncology, cardiology, and orthopedics programs, all supported by active outpatient clinics and rehabilitation programs. The professional personnel at Trinity, especially the nurses, were exceptionally loyal to the hospital and were highly skilled, competent, and compassionate. Although they were unionized, Trinity had implemented strong, effective management–employee programs, and the unions were committed to the continued success of the Trinity organization.

The J. Blair Sutton Memorial Hospital was a privately owned, richly endowed healthcare organization whose namesake had been the founder of Sutton Manufacturing and Construction Inc., a company that had brought great wealth to its founder and employment to many of the residents of Richland. The Sutton family was "old money" and had originally acquired its wealth from sawmills along the Richland River. J. Blair Sutton had been quick to respond to modern technologies, and when the time was right, he had diversified his holdings and entered commercial construction and the manufacturing of doors, windows, and lumber products. That was in the 1940s, and now the Sutton name and its products were known nationwide. To manage the family money, the Sutton progeny had moved from Richland to New York City, but the Sutton name still graced the streets of Richland on schools, avenues, plazas, and prominent buildings throughout the community.

J. Blair Sutton Memorial Hospital was one such legacy. The 275-bed acute care hospital was renowned throughout the state for its cardiology services, including a respected and successful open heart surgery program, an orthopedic surgery program specializing in hip replacements, and a cancer care program that had attracted nationally recognized oncologists and cancer surgeons. In addition to these "pillars of excellence," Sutton Memorial offered general medical/surgical, obstetrics, and pediatrics services, but these programs commanded fewer resources because the hospital's mission was to serve the healthcare needs of the "older" families of Clay County. The governing board of Sutton Memorial had no problem supporting this mission. After all, Trinity very capably and compassionately cared for the indigent in Clay County. Sutton Memorial's mission was to provide healthcare to those who continued to commit their personal wealth to enrich the Richland community. This mission was in keeping with J. Blair Sutton's personal philosophy, deeply rooted in American capitalism and the right of individuals to reap the rewards and privileges of their hard work. His philosophy did not abide government intervention of any kind, and accordingly, the Sutton Memorial board had done all that it could for as long as it could to legally avoid caring for Medicare and Medicaid patients. The hospital had operated on a cash basis until the recent past. This system was very appealing to the members of the Sutton Memorial board, the majority of whom were corporate executives with companies of international stature who had been recruited to the board by the influential Sutton family.

In contrast, the Trinity governing board comprised representatives of the community, the religious order, and local bank and corporate executives. These two governing boards, very different in philosophy, had little reason to interact. They did not travel in the same social circles, and the Sutton Memorial board members were most often out of town running their corporations in other states. The Sutton Memorial board met quarterly, while the Trinity board, with its local members, met monthly. The administrations of the two organizations seemed content with maintaining the status quo. After all, both organizations were operating well. Strong governing boards at both hospitals made it clear to their respective CEOs that their jobs were to manage operations. In spite of their differences, the two organizations amicably coexisted in the city of Richland, each successful in its own right.

All this was about to change as national for-profit hospital corporations were emerging as a force in healthcare. Indeed, one of these corporations, Continental Healthcare, began to purchase private, not-for-profit hospitals in Clay County. Continental had already purchased one of the smaller hospitals in the city of Richland and had also entered into negotiations with Suburban Medical Center. Both Trinity and Sutton Memorial were alarmed and fearful of losing their positions of prominence in Clay County. After much separate discussion, the governing board at each hospital arrived at the same conclusion: The hospital needed to partner with another organization to shore up its position in the community. As each organization sought an appropriate partner, it became clear that all they had was each other.

The governing boards of the two organizations took the lead in exploring the merger of Trinity and Sutton Memorial. The administrations of the two organizations were only minimally involved and, for the most part, remained focused on daily operations. Each governing board engaged the services of a consultant to explore the feasibility of the merger. Following the consultants' reports, both Trinity and Sutton Memorial decided a merger into a system was in each organization's best interests. At this point, the two governing boards met for their first face-to-face discussion, during which they decided to jointly engage the services of a nationally known consulting firm with experience in successfully implementing the mergers of healthcare organizations. The consulting firm's report clearly laid out enormous benefits, both present and future, that would accrue to both organizations once the merger was fully implemented. This report evolved into the only strategic plan used by the newly merged system and showed savings of millions of dollars from merging business operations and sharing expensive medical technology. The report also promised that the merger would increase bargaining power with health plans.

An initial step in the process was to determine the asset value of each organization. Trinity's assets were valued at $25 million more than those of Sutton Memorial. For the two organizations to enter into the merger as equal partners, Trinity placed $25 million into a newly created foundation for the merged system, named Richland River Valley Healthcare System (RRVHS), to use for healthcare programs in Clay County. Although it agreed to this resolution, the Sutton Memorial board was visibly annoyed with the results of the asset valuation. Its members were unaccustomed to being second best at anything.

As the implementation of the merger moved forward, both sides agreed that the RRVHS governing board would have 25 members: 12 from Trinity, 12 from Sutton Memorial, and the new RRVHS CEO. The RRVHS board would be responsible for strategic planning and financial oversight of the system. Sutton Memorial would appoint the first board chair for a two-year term. Trinity would then appoint the next board chair for a two-year term, and so on. As it turned out, the most powerful and influential members of each hospital board were appointed to the system board, while the hospital boards retained the less powerful members. The hospital governing boards would now be responsible for operations, credentialing, and facilities management at their respective organizations. The powerful RRVHS board decided that the hospital governing boards would no longer receive operating budgets or routine financial reports. The RRVHS board would provide financial oversight of both hospitals and would control the flow of financial information. Friction soon developed between the system board and the hospital boards, whose members became so frustrated at one point that the two hospital boards considered joint legal action against the system board.

The RRVHS board further decided that neither of the current hospital CEOs was capable of assuming the position of system CEO and hired an executive search firm to recruit an experienced system CEO. The RRVHS board, with powerful representatives from both hospitals, could not agree on an acceptable candidate to lead the newly merged entity. This dissension resulted in a lengthy and combative CEO search that left the new entity adrift with no management leadership for over a year.

Curtis Tower was finally hired as system CEO. During the recruitment process, Tower made it clear that the board needed to leave the management of the new system to him, and the search committee agreed to this condition. Soon after Tower assumed leadership responsibilities, however, he realized the board was either unwilling or unable to stay out of the management of the new system. The RRVHS board directed Tower to fire all the senior administrators at both hospitals and conduct a national search to replace them. By following this directive, Tower lost vital corporate memory at a time when it may have been needed most. The corporate cultures of both organizations were visibly shaken by this massive administrative turnover. Organizational values were questioned by the staffs of both hospitals, who became increasingly anxious in the uncertain environment.

Amid all this uncertainty, physicians in Clay County became a major influential force. Throughout the merger process, the hospitals' two medical staffs had been relegated to the sidelines. But a new opportunity presented itself in Richland. Physicians Partners Inc., a proprietary corporation that purchased and operated physician practices, began to buy physician practices in Richland. Now the RRVHS board and the two hospital boards had a common worry: What if their admitting physicians decided to admit elsewhere? A group of ten physicians who controlled most of the admissions, referrals, and outpatient ancillary services at both Trinity and Sutton Memorial approached board members at social gatherings with an idea. These physicians had lost their ability to leverage one hospital against the other with the creation of RRVHS. Now with Physician Partners Inc. rolling into town, the physicians had bargaining power once more. They suggested that RRVHS purchase their practices and asserted that through their personal connections to a renowned East Coast medical school, they could arrange for the establishment of an affiliated major medical clinic in Richland that would attract national and international patients. Such a clinic would secure the success of the new merger.

RRVHS entered into what proved to be a very lucrative arrangement for the physicians involved, and news of the agreement and the planned medical school–affiliated clinic disseminated rapidly throughout the medical community. Questions about who would control the clinic and, more important, who would be allowed to practice there were put to the RRVHS board. Dissension among the medical staff was palpable. Those physicians who continued to practice independently gave the RRVHS board an ultimatum: If plans for the clinic went forward, they would boycott both hospitals. The RRVHS board rejected the proposed affiliated clinic. The contract physicians became angry and resentful. The independent physicians remained distrustful and hostile. Throughout these discussions, negotiations, and agreements, the administrations of both hospitals had been absent.

Two years into the merger, RRVHS had yet to consolidate clinical services as recommended by the consultant's plan guiding implementation. The hospitals, four miles apart, were still duplicating all but business operations.

Equally troubling was the lack of medical staff consolidation. The differences in medical staff organization and structure at the two hospitals had proven to be significant barriers. Medical staff officers at Trinity were elected by the general medical staff, while medical staff officers at Sutton Memorial were appointed by the Sutton Memorial board. After much political maneuvering, it was agreed that consolidated medical staff officers would be elected, but the decision was just one more conten-tious issue between the two hospitals.

The administrative offices for the system were constructed in available space at Sutton Memorial, which further increased ill will between the hospitals. The members of the two hospital governing boards did not like each other, and more significant, their counterparts on the RRVHS board did not like each other either. The governing styles of the two hospitals were in conflict. Sutton Memorial took a corporate approach to healthcare delivery: Be innovative, operate efficiently, and practice good business management. Social status was important to its members. Trinity operated more like a public institution—process oriented and committed to care for all, regardless of ability to pay. Business operations were not its top priority, nor was the social status of its members.

The main barriers to the successful merger of the two organizations were the steadfast separation of all clinical services and disagreement over the allocation of capital resources for new programs and services. New clinical services to be based at one hospital or the other could never get past the planning stage. Administrative resources were spent, but no program materialized in return.

Frustrated and angry with the system, a high-profile group of surgeons began plans for a physician-owned surgicenter. At about this same time, amid falling patient volumes and problems with accounts receivable at both hospitals, a major donor withdrew her $72 million pledge to the cardiology program at Sutton Memo-rial on the grounds that the pledge was to Sutton and not to RRVHS.

Unable to consolidate clinical services and demoralized by the constant con-flict and financial woes, the RRVHS board finally agreed on something: to dissolve the merger. Within the first year following the dissolution of RRVHS, Continental Healthcare moved quickly to purchase both hospitals, which it now operates as separate healthcare facilities.

ETHICS ISSUES

Roles of governance and management: Were the roles of governance and man-agement being played out during the merger of Trinity and Sutton Memorial into RRVHS appropriate and consistent with the mission of the two hospitals? Were the actions of the principals involved in the best interests of patients and others served?

Fear-based action: Was the decision to pursue a merger based on a well-thought-out plan for the betterment of healthcare in the community? Or was it fear based and motivated by a desire to retain power and prestige?

Culture issues: Did the two hospital boards give appropriate consideration to the culture, values, and ethical standards guiding their respective organizations and how they might mesh in the newly merged system?

Failure to include medical staff: Was a successful merger possible without involving the physicians in its planning and implementation? Was clinical integration possible without physician leadership?

Stewardship of community resources: Did the two organizations have an ethical responsibility to use community resources prudently for the good of the community?

Ethical responsibilities to employees: Did the administrators and governing boards of the two hospitals, and later those of the merged system, have an ethical responsibility to adequately inform employees about—and involve them in—decisions that were being made that affected their employment, their healthcare, and their community? Were employees key stakeholders in these proceedings?

DISCUSSION

Roles of Governance and Management

The RRVHS case is like a very bad play where the actors don't know their lines or the roles they should be playing. The governing boards of the two institutions explored the possibility of a merger on their own instead of initiating joint discussions that included management and medical staff. A more inclusive approach might have identified potential obstacles to overcome. Neglecting to include management and the medical staff in all discussions and planning doomed the merger to failure. Following the merger agreement, the RRVHS governing board blurred its lines of authority and responsibility even more as it began to micromanage the system and withhold needed financial information from the governing boards of the two hospitals.

The American Hospital Association (AHA) is clear about board responsibilities and the difference between the board's policy-making responsibilities and management's operational responsibilities. The AHA's "Top Ten Principles and Practices of Great Boards" read in part as follows (AHA 2023b):

> Boards have an oversight function, but great boards govern—they don't try to run operations—explicitly or subtly. They are careful not to "get into the weeds" with overly detailed operational questions and micro-managing day-to-day decisions. . . . Governance—especially in large, complex organizations such as hospitals and health systems—is most effective when directors focus their work on higher-level strategic

choices, priorities, and future directions. Great boards create the space for great management to operate.

In simpler terms, the governing board's responsibility is to see the "why," whereas the "what" and "how" are management's job.

At RRVHS, administrative leadership should have played a major role in seeing that governing board members clearly understood their functions and responsibilities and had continuing education opportunities to keep abreast of changes in the field. Administrators also should have been active in the selection and engagement of the consultants to make certain that all drawbacks and barriers to the merger were explored along with the advantages and benefits. And finally, strong hospital leadership would have insisted on being an integral part, along with the medical staff, of all merger discussions and negotiations.

Had administrators from both hospitals been included in the merger discussions from the beginning, they could have ensured that the missions and values of their respective organizations were not compromised. Moreover, the participation of administrative and clinical representatives would have led to a broader and more balanced perspective on the situation. Because some board members inevitably lose their places at the table when a merger occurs, decisions made solely by the board may be skewed by individual board members' attempts to secure their positions.

Fear-Based Action

Although fear may be a great motivator, it rarely brings the success of a well-thought-out strategy and transitional plan based on community needs and mutually beneficial collaboration. The two organizations going into this merger had operated in isolation from each other for years. Neither knew anything about the other. The merger was like a marriage without a courtship. The consultants, if experienced in mergers, should have forewarned the organizations of the potential perils. Effective management, if involved, might have foreseen the difficulties. The governing boards, on the other hand, seemed too concerned about their own self-interests and power to recognize the problem.

Culture Issues

Healthcare managers know that the leadership of an organization is responsible for establishing the organization's culture. They know that a culture will accept or reject change, can create a negative or positive work environment, can promote teamwork or not, and can be ethical or not. Certainly, culture consists of behaviors and how business is conducted, but it also encompasses values and beliefs and reflects how members of governance, workforce, and management in an organization think and feel. Culture is a guiding philosophy about what is right and what is important. Organizations considering a merger tend to function best when their guiding philosophies are aligned.

Executive coach and former hospital CEO Larry Scanlan (2010) reminds us that "culture will eat strategy" and maintains that "unresolved culture conflicts can cripple or terminate a merger." Accordingly, he cautions leaders to have a solid understanding of their own organizational culture and to know when cultural differences between organizations make a successful merger unlikely.

Sutton Memorial and Trinity had very different cultures and value systems. Their differences seem not to have been given the consideration they deserved, especially at the board level. Power is a difficult thing to share, especially when values clash. Symbolism can become a source of friction if one of the hospitals in the merger is perceived to have such symbolic advantages as being the source of the new CEO, having more representatives on the board, being where the system offices are located, or controlling how publicity about the new system is crafted.

Although J. Daniel Beckham (2012), past chair of the board of directors of the American Marketing Association, agrees that culture is an important consideration when it comes to leadership and "there may be occasions when culture is well-positioned to eat strategy," he cautions that "a view of culture as fixed, omnipotent and sacred engenders passivity on the part of leaders." He challenges leaders to execute strategies that may overpower or change culture.

Regardless of their views on the primacy of culture, effective leaders are mindful of their organization's culture and the need to nurture it in ways that promote teamwork, collaboration, and organization-wide commitment to mission. Lack of respect for the influence of culture may result in careless and wasteful use of resources and failure to fulfill ethical responsibilities to communities served.

Failure to Include Medical Staff

The exclusion of key physicians and medical staff leaders from discussions about the feasibility of the RRVHS merger can only be described as ill-informed and misguided. Certainly, if the administrators of the two hospitals had been active participants in the discussions, they would have enlightened the boards about the need for physicians' insights, awareness of internal politics, and knowledge of the medical community, all of which are crucial to any clinical integration. Governing boards and administrators must never lose sight of the fact that healthcare is driven by physicians and that the success of a healthcare organization depends in large part on the quality and expertise of its clinical staff. It is foolhardy to believe that a successful merger is possible without planning and collaboration with the medical staff.

Stewardship of Community Resources

The failed RRVHS merger is an example of what typically happens when personal ambitions and goals take priority over an organization's mission and the stewardship of community resources. The hospital board's fiduciary responsibility is to protect its organization's assets and to act in good faith on behalf of the organization, not for personal benefit. The governing board members at RRVHS were not attentive to their stewardship of community resources or protection of the organization's assets. Struggles for power and control over an extended period wasted resources and raised the additional ethical question of what happens to patient care programs when time, energy, and capital are diverted elsewhere. The failure to eliminate duplication of services squandered the assets of both the health system and the community.

Ethical Responsibilities to Employees

The *Code of Ethics* of the American College of Healthcare Executives (ACHE 2022) is clear about a healthcare executive's ethical and professional responsibilities to employees. Maintaining a safe work environment that is conducive to ethical conduct, proper utilization of employees' skills and abilities, and freedom from harassment and discrimination are critical to providing high-quality and safe patient care. Poor communication with employees creates an environment of uncertainty, dissension, and mistrust. When management does not communicate appropriately, pseudoleaders do—often through rumor, innuendo, and false information. The anxiety and pessimism that result are inevitably reflected in exchanges with patients and coworkers.

Failure to recognize that employees are key stakeholders in the future of the merged organization ignores that the people who carry out the mission of patient care, whether directly or indirectly, are important contributors to the success of the organization. It also does not take into account that employees rely on the security of their employment and may be unable to relocate if they lose their jobs. Whereas administrators and board members may move on to other positions in other communities, employees are, for a variety of reasons, frequently locked into the community where they are employed.

Further contributing to the uncertain work environment at RRVHS is what appears to be the arbitrary firing of senior managers with the accompanying loss of corporate history, experience, and knowledge. Such upheaval fosters feelings that the organization lacks direction and that its leadership cannot be trusted. Were the fired managers treated fairly and ethically?

Many of these problems could have been avoided by implementing a well-thought-out employee communication strategy and plan aimed at acquiring employee input into the process and buy-in to the merger.

Lessons Learned

Although RRVHS is an example of a failed hospital merger, the lessons learned from this case are valuable to healthcare executives and governing boards who may, in the future, need to consider merging their healthcare organization with another. A clear rationale, a comprehensive feasibility study, and a well-thought-out implementation plan are essential to success.

Even after a merger is finalized, important work still needs to be done if the merger is to achieve the anticipated benefits. Peregrine and Nygren (2013) suggest eight follow-up steps that will ensure that the goals of the merger are realized:

1. Appoint a new leader who is qualified to achieve the vision.
2. Restructure departments and services to gain efficiency and avoid redundancy.
3. Name the new organization; roll out the image and branding initiative to create a shared identity.
4. Articulate the values and behaviors that will characterize the culture.
5. Make it clear to all that change must occur.
6. Focus on the strategic plan.
7. Honor post-closing agreements.
8. Communicate often.

A leadership team representative of governance, administration, and the medical staff will be needed to successfully complete the merger implementation.

A 2013 AHA study that analyzed the impact of hospital mergers found the number of mergers to be relatively small—only 316 mergers in six years (Stempniak 2013). However, as the Affordable Care Act was implemented and healthcare moved toward more efficient systems that coordinate care and emphasize cost savings and population health, it was a safe speculation that more mergers would occur. And that did, in fact, happen: Five years later, Kaufman Hall (2018) reported 115 hospital mergers and acquisitions in 2017, an increase of almost 13 percent over 2016 and the highest number of announced mergers and acquisitions since the consulting firm began monitoring them in 2000. Kaufman Hall called it a "transformative year for healthcare deal making" and noted that "intellectual capital, brand and presence, network infrastructure, risk-bearing capabilities, care continuum, clinical and business intelligence, consumerism, capital resources, and diversified operations represent the most frequently cited benefits of these transformative partnerships." For this reason, Kaufman Hall predicts the number of mergers and acquisitions will continue to rise. There is sufficient reason and little doubt that healthcare executives and their boards need to be cognizant of the potential pitfalls to avoid in these future transactions.

The COVID-19 pandemic put a damper on merger activity, and the recent past has not seen the number of hospital mergers increase at the rate seen before the pandemic. However, the sizes of hospital mergers keep growing, according to a Kaufman Hall report released in January 2023 (Hagland 2023). The report stated, "Four of the 17 announced transactions [for the fourth quarter of 2022] met our definition of 'mega merger,' in which the smaller party has annual revenues in excess of $1 billion, and a fifth had a smaller party with revenues in the $500 million to $1 billion range. This was the third consecutive quarter in 2022 in which the average size of the smaller party across all announced transactions exceeded $800 million. As a result, the average smaller party size for the entire year reached an historic high of $852 million, well above 2021's then-record size of $619 million" (Hagland 2023).

All predictions across the board are that the size of hospital mergers and acquisitions will continue to grow. As the AHA (2023a) observes:

> A range of partnerships, mergers and acquisitions enable hospitals to expand service offerings, broaden networks and access to specialists, improve quality and better serve patients where they live. . . . Mergers and acquisitions also are a vital tool that some health systems use to keep financially struggling hospitals open, averting bankruptcy or even closure. When hospitals become part of a health system, the continuum of care is strengthened for patients and the community, resulting in better care and decreased readmission rates.

REFERENCES

American College of Healthcare Executives (ACHE). 2022. *Code of Ethics*. As amended December 5. www.ache.org/about-ache/our-story/our-commitments/ethics/ache-code-of-ethics.

American Hospital Association (AHA). 2023a. "Fact Sheet: Hospital Mergers and Acquisitions Can Expand and Preserve Access to Care." Published March. www.aha.org/system/files/media/file/2023/03/FS-mergers-and-acquisitions.pdf.

———. 2023b. "The Top 10 Principles and Practices of Great Boards." Accessed October 27. https://trustees.aha.org/sites/default/files/trustees/Great-Boards-reprint-Top_Ten_Practices_of_Great_Boards.pdf.

Beckham, J. D. 2012. "Overestimating the Importance of Culture." *Hospitals & Health Networks Daily*, August 16.

Hagland, M. 2023. "Kaufman Hall: Sizes of Hospital Mergers Growing." Healthcare Innovation. Published January 12. www.hcinnovationgroup.com/finance-revenue-cycle/mergers-acquisitions/article/21292353/kaufman-hall-sizes-of-hospital-mergers-growing.

Kaufman Hall. 2018. "2017 in Review: The Year M&A Shook the Healthcare Landscape." Published January 26. www.kaufmanhall.com/ideas-resources/research-report/2017-review-year-ma-shook-healthcare-landscape.

Peregrine, M. W., and D. Nygren. 2013. "Merger's Closed: What's Next?" *Trustee* 66 (4): 13–14.

Scanlan, L. 2010. "Hospital Mergers: Pay Attention to Those Culture Issues." *Hospitals & Health Networks Daily*, August 16.

Stempniak, M. 2013. "New Study Analyzes Impact of Hospital Mergers." *Hospitals & Health Networks Daily*, June 3.

CHAPTER 11

When Patient Demands and Hospital Policies Collide: Hurley Medical Center

CASE STUDY

Hurley Medical Center, an inner-city hospital in a depressed area of the Midwest, made the front page of the local newspaper with the headline "Nurse's Lawsuit Draws Protestors." According to the article, a nurse claimed that the hospital granted a father's request that no Black nurses treat his baby, who was a patient in the hospital's neonatal intensive care unit (NICU). The nurse, who was Black, claimed that while she was working in the NICU, the child's father, who was White, asked to speak to her supervisor and allegedly rolled up his sleeve to reveal a tattoo believed to be a swastika. A White nurse was assigned to the baby, and a note was posted on the assignment clipboard: "No Black nurse to take care of baby."

The lawsuit alleges that on the following day, the hospital made a decision to grant the father's request. The hospital's CEO publicly denied that the request was granted. Protestors rallied outside the hospital, claiming discrimination, and the president of the National Action Network said the hospital's actions were "an atrocity and a reversal of times," as well as "a manifestation of institutional racism." He went on to say that "the National Action Network will be calling for . . . all federal, state, and local dollars allocated to Hurley . . . [to] have a major-league string attached that the staff and administrators go through sensitivity training so that those policies will not ever occur again." He went on to call the hospital's actions a "powder keg that could set off the city" and to say that it was "unreasonable to believe that the supervisor . . . still would be employed" by the hospital.

Two weeks after the lawsuit was filed, the newspaper reported that the case

---

Case study sources: Adapted from Adams (2013a, 2013b); Aldridge (2013); and Ridley (2013).

had been settled. While the details of the settlement were not made public, the hospital's CEO said, "We regret that our policies were not well enough understood and followed, causing the perception that Hurley condoned this conduct." She indicated that the incident would be used in future training sessions to prevent similar ones from happening again.

The political director of the National Action Network was quoted as saying, "We won't go away like a plaintiff in a lawsuit. We're here until the institutional practices of Hurley stop and they behave in a manner that's in the best interest of the community." The president of the state chapter of the National Action Network said about the hospital's leadership, "We would like to see that they make sure their staff is culturally competent. It needs to be very clear in their procedures and policies that this type of behavior warrants a reprimand."

ETHICS ISSUES

Patients' rights: Does a patient's bill of rights give patients—or, in the case of minors, parents and guardians—the right to select their caregivers in a health-care facility?

Patient safety: What actions can Hurley Medical Center take to ensure the safety and security of patients and parents in the NICU?

Ethical responsibilities to employees: What actions can be taken to ensure employee safety? What considerations must be given to avoid the development of a hostile work environment? Is discrimination a legitimate concern?

Adherence to hospital policies: Are hospital policies being followed? Are those policies well known to the employees?

Organizational implications: What are the organizational implications of the hospital's actions? How will they affect staff morale and perceptions of management? Public relations and community image? Medical staff referrals? Staff productivity?

Cultural competency: What is management's responsibility to promote cultural competency through education with respect to both the patient population and the workforce?

Community values: Does hospital administration have a responsibility to be aware of community values and how they may affect the organization and influence the outcome of management actions?

Legal implications: Is the hospital legally liable for discriminatory behavior by its employees? What about for a hostile work environment?

DISCUSSION

Chapter 1 notes that mistakes are often the result of the barrage of decisions that must be made by well-meaning managers who are pressed for time and strained by the demands of the job. Decisions are often made without the benefit of thoughtful reflection and the consultation of others that may be needed. Sufficient attention may not be given to the unintended consequences that may occur. The situation at Hurley may have been such a case.

Fault finding is easy for people who are not confronted with the stressful clinical demands of an intensive care unit and the human emotions inherent in life-threatening situations. To malign an entire institution and its policies and procedures without knowing all the facts can be a mistake. The only information available to the public in this case is in news reports about the initial incident and the comments and reactions that it elicited. Consequently, the discussion in this chapter is based on some assumptions and explores the issues that arise under those assumptions.

Chapter 2 discusses the interrelation of ethics and management and how the two cannot be separated when decisions are being made. The Hurley case involves an intersection of ethics, patient rights, and the law. A discussion of the resulting management challenges must take all three areas into consideration. Above all, this case presents a learning opportunity for all healthcare leaders because no organization is exempt from charges of discrimination based on race, age, sexual orientation, or other factors.

The incidence of requests for racially preferred caregivers in healthcare is much higher than commonly known. Law professor Kimani Paul-Emile (2012) calls it an "open secret," saying, "Patients routinely refuse or demand medical treatment based on the assigned physician's racial identity, and hospitals typically yield to patients' racial preferences. This widely practiced, if rarely acknowledged, phenomenon . . . poses a fundamental dilemma for law, medicine, and ethics." Paul-Emile concludes that although accommodating a patient's racial preferences appears to violate antidiscrimination laws, a conflict remains between "patient autonomy and accepted notions of racial equality." Others have called the accommodation of requests based on racial preferences a form of institutional racism (Aldridge 2013).

The *Code of Medical Ethics* of the American Medical Association (2023) prohibits physicians from refusing to treat patients on the basis of race, but no policy exists for handling race-based requests from patients. One University of Michigan study found that "a third of providers felt patients perceive better care from providers of shared demographics, with racial matching perceived as more important than gender or religion" (Padela et al. 2010). Some observers believe that requests for racial preferences are quietly honored and do not come to the attention of the public (Karoub 2013a).

In the barrage of published opinions that followed the Hurley incident, almost all the legal and medical experts who weighed in agreed that honoring racial preferences violates antidiscrimination laws and is morally wrong. One opinion stood out as more pragmatic than theoretical. Susan Goold, MD, a University of Michigan professor of internal medicine and public health, said, "In general, I don't think honoring prejudicial preferences . . . is morally justifiable . . . [but] there may be times when grudgingly acceding to a patient's strongly held preferences is morally OK" (Karoub 2013a). She indicated that in some cases, such as those involving rape or violence, honoring patients' racial preferences might be preferable to forcing caregivers on them who might exacerbate their health condition.

Clearly, this multidimensional problem has no simple answers. Managers must struggle with the legal and moral challenges of situations like that at Hurley while exercising caution not to compromise patient and employee safety and the integrity of the healthcare organization.

Patients' Rights

In 1973, the American Hospital Association (AHA) published "A Patient's Bill of Rights," which delineated a patient's rights and responsibilities when cared for by a healthcare organization (Bazemore 2016). The Joint Commission (2023) subsequently defined an accreditation standard requiring healthcare organizations to present patients with a copy of their rights, and hospitals throughout the nation soon adopted and distributed the AHA document.

The AHA revised its bill of rights in 1992, and many hospitals have developed their own list of patient rights and responsibilities and posted them online. Several states have enacted legislation requiring a patient's bill of rights; the attorney general's office in Michigan, where Hurley Medical Center is located, has posted the "Michigan Patient Rights and Responsibilities in State Licensed Facilities" on its website (State of Michigan Attorney General 2019). Hurley has dedicated a web page to patient rights and responsibilities (Hurley Medical Center 2023b), and it also has posted a nondiscrimination notice that begins as follows (Hurley Medical Center 2023a):

> **Discrimination Is Against the Law**
> Hurley Medical Center complies with applicable State and Federal civil rights laws.
> The hospital prohibits discrimination based on age, race, ethnicity, religion, culture,
> language, physical or mental disability, socioeconomic status, sex, sexual orientation,
> and gender identity or expression.

> Requests for specific caregivers will not be honored if those requests are based on race, color, disability, age, or national origin. Room accommodations will be assigned by the Admitting Office and House Director based on the clinical needs of the patient.

The AHA, state of Michigan, and Hurley documents do not grant patients, guardians, or family members the right to choose or reject an organization's assigned caregiver. The patient responsibilities listed on Hurley's website, however, do specify that patients must follow hospital rules and regulations and respect the rights of other patients and staff members. None of the many documents defining patient rights entitles patients or family members to dictate which healthcare staff are assigned to their care. In the opinion of Larry Dubin, a Michigan law professor, regarding the Hurley case, "The patient's father has the right to select the hospital to treat the child. The father does not have the right to exercise control over the hospital in discrimination of its employees" (Erb 2013).

Patient Safety

The primary concern of hospital staff must be the safety and well-being of the patients in their charge. Nurses are especially aware of their responsibility in this regard. In the Hurley case, the safety of the newborn in question and the safety of the other patients and parents in the NICU must be the top priority. Indeed, the hospital's CEO reported that the father's swastika tattoo "created anger and outrage in our staff" and that supervisors raised safety concerns (Karoub 2013b). Given those concerns, Hurley staff might have moved the conversation with the father to a quiet place outside the NICU, with a second staff member in attendance. Having a witness to the conversation could be helpful in the future, and a smaller audience might have tempered the father's demands.

The second person serving as witness could have been the administrator on call, the nursing supervisor, or the patient advocate, depending on the shift and time of day. That person could have informed the father that it is against both hospital policy and the law for the hospital to discriminate against its employees. The person conducting the meeting also could have emphasized the specialized expertise and training of the NICU staff and explained that the safety of his newborn would be ensured by having all NICU staff available to handle any problem that may have arisen.

If the father persisted in his request, the next step might be to refer him to his child's doctor or suggest that he consider transferring his infant to another hospital—under Hurley's patient's bill of rights, a patient, parent, or guardian has the right to choose a healthcare facility. The feasibility of a transfer would depend, however, on the condition of the newborn and the availability of an NICU at another location. If the charge nurse believed that the father's tone and demeanor suggested that the conversation could become heated, security could be alerted. However, caution must be exercised to avoid any action that may escalate hostility.

Ethical Responsibilities to Employees

Hospital management has ethical and legal responsibilities to ensure a safe working environment for all employees. In this case, moral and legal demands may conflict. Lance Gable, a law professor at Wayne State University, observed, "Maybe [the hospital's] explanation is an accurate description of what happened— the supervisor was scared of the father of this patient and made a decision that was ill advised. It might have been the right thing to do for the safety of the staff, and it still might be a violation of antidiscrimination laws" (Karoub 2013a). Indeed, the laws regarding workplace discrimination are clear. The safety of the nurse in this incident must be protected. Multiple phone and e-mail messages left for her through her attorney were not returned, so their content remains undetermined. She also had her listed phone number disconnected as a matter of caution (Karoub 2013a).

Management cannot ensure that caregivers will not encounter potentially volatile situations from time to time. Unfortunately, bigotry and prejudice cannot be eliminated. Management can and should, therefore, prepare employees with conflict management skills. Such training may be especially important for frontline caregivers and their supervisors, who regularly face emotionally charged situations. Management has a responsibility to equip staff to assess circumstances and know when to get help in defusing potentially volatile encounters.

Healthcare leaders must both abide by the law and ensure the safety of employees. They must take steps to create a nonhostile work environment that is secure and free from discrimination. As the Hurley case illustrates, this task can be difficult indeed. The ability to anticipate situations in which patient and family demands may conflict with hospital policies, and the foresight to prepare staff to deal with them effectively, are the marks of a superior manager.

Adherence to Hospital Policies

Hospitals must not only abide by government antidiscrimination laws but also establish internal antidiscrimination policies that apply to patients, clients, and employees. At Hurley, the decision to accede to the father's demands would appear to violate internal hospital policies, and, in fact, hospital officials admitted that it did (Karoub 2013a).

Educating employees about hospital policies is a daunting task. The orientation of new managers undoubtedly includes discussion of the organization's policy manuals, standard practices, mission, vision, and values. Disseminating that information throughout the employee ranks is difficult, however, and requires effective communication strategies, attention, and repetition. Case-based staff education and training can be especially useful in driving home the rationale and importance of hospital policies and chain-of-command reporting mechanisms. Employees need to know when and how to seek advice and help in the clarification and enforcement of policies. Just knowing a policy and being able to state it to a patient or a family member is not enough. Unless patients and families understand why a policy exists and how it benefits them, they will view it as just a bureaucratic barrier to something they want. The importance of having well-informed staff who are skilled at explaining policy cannot be overlooked.

Organizational Implications

Some unintended consequences of staff actions in the Hurley incident were immediate; others may be more long-term. The gathering of protestors outside the hospital, international media response, lawsuits, staff confusion, mistrust of management, and fear of unsafe working conditions all occurred immediately and required enormous amounts of legal, public relations, administrative, and staff time, energy, and dollars. The long-term effect of diverting those resources from patient care and other more beneficial activities cannot quickly be determined. The effect of the incident and its aftermath on the hospital's image and the community's trust cannot fully be measured. For example, will it affect physician referrals or patient admissions? Perhaps the most critical and immediate responsibility facing Hurley's administration is to repair and strengthen employee–management relationships, trust, and commitment to the regeneration of the hospital's image.

Cultural Competency

As the US population continues to become more culturally diverse, more and more organizations are devoting attention to training their employees in cultural competency. Accrediting and licensing agencies, marketing experts, business consultants, and lawyers all tout the organizational benefits of having a culturally competent workforce. In healthcare, the evidence suggests that patients' health status improves when they are cared for by culturally competent caregivers. Healthcare costs and liability may decrease as well.

Leaders must be culturally competent in managing their employees and provide employee education programs that foster respect for individual differences and awareness of actions that may be deemed discriminatory or illegal on the basis of race, gender, age, disability, national origin, or religion. For their part, employees need to be aware of actions that may be offensive to coworkers. For example, posting the note on the assignment board saying that no Black nurses were to care for the newborn at Hurley most likely humiliated the assigned nurse and other staff in the NICU. Cultivating staff sensitivity to the effect of such actions on coworkers' feelings can eliminate those behaviors and foster a more positive and productive work environment.

Better understanding and appreciation of individual differences can strengthen employee loyalty and commitment to organizational goals and success. Employees will feel more vested in the organization and more confident in their ability to handle potentially difficult situations.

Community Values

Experienced managers have learned that prevailing community values have a significant effect on an organization's public image and how its actions are judged. Those values may be heavily influenced by religion, socioeconomic status, politics, and the like. In a working-class community—especially one that is heavily unionized like Flint, Michigan, where Hurley is located—people will sympathize with workers and support their legal rights. Hospital administrators must therefore consider carefully the consequences of their actions and how they will play out in the community. When governing boards are representative of local demographics, board members will be quick to criticize actions that do not reflect community values.

Legal Implications

Several court decisions have addressed issues of discrimination similar to those at Hurley. A 2010 decision by the US Court of Appeals for the Seventh Circuit, for example, held that the federal Civil Rights Act prohibits nursing homes from making staffing decisions based on residents' racial preferences (Karoub 2013a). In that case, nursing assistants claimed that complying with residents' racial preferences created a hostile work environment for them. The court agreed, saying that the nursing home could have warned residents on admission that "discriminatory requests and/or harassment of employees would not be tolerated, informing employees of their right to complain about such conduct, and . . . discharging a racially hostile patient" (Starr and Murphy 2011). In this ruling, the court also found that hiring based on gender preference was permissible under Title VII.

In 2005, a federal lawsuit was filed in Pennsylvania by three Black employees of Abington Memorial Hospital who claimed that they were prevented from treating a pregnant White woman by her male partner, a member of a White supremacist group who used a racial slur. The hospital honored the man's request, citing fear for the safety of its employees. The case was settled out of court, and the hospital admitted no liability (Starr and Murphy 2011).

In yet another case, rather than go to court, a healthcare organization agreed to pay damages to the US Equal Employment Opportunity Commission and to implement policies and provide training to ensure that a patient's racial preferences are not honored over and above an employee's civil rights (Starr and Murphy 2011).

Whether lawsuits are won or lost, they are costly in terms of dollars, stress, time, and, most important, employee relations and public image.

REFERENCES

Adams, D. 2013a. "Flint Hurley Medical Center Lawsuit Settled; Nurse Glad It's a Learning Tool." *Flint Journal*, February 22.

————. 2013b. "Flint's Hurley Medical Center, Nurse, Settle 'No-Black-Nurses' Lawsuit." *Flint Journal*, February 22.

Aldridge, C. 2013. "Nurse's Lawsuit Draws Protesters." *Flint Journal*, February 19.

American Medical Association. 2023. "Prospective Patients." Opinion 1.1.2 of the AMA *Code of Medical Ethics*. Accessed September 25. www.ama-assn.org/delivering-care/ethics/prospective-patients.

Bazemore, N. 2016. "Here's Everything You Need to Know About the Patient's Bill of Rights." *Forbes*. Published March 21. www.forbes.com/sites/amino/2016/03/21/heres-everything-you-need-to-know-about-the-patients-bill-of-rights/.

Erb, R. 2013. "Nurse Sues After Hospital Grants Dad's Racial Request." *Detroit Free Press*, February 18.

Hurley Medical Center. 2023a. "Nondiscrimination Notice." Accessed September 25. www.hurleymc.com/nondiscrimination-notice/.

————. 2023b. "Patient Rights." Accessed September 25. www.hurleymc.com/patients-and-visitors/patient-rights/.

Joint Commission. 2023. *Comprehensive Accreditation Manual for Hospitals*. Oakbrook Terrace, IL: Joint Commission Resources.

Karoub, J. 2013a. "Lawsuits Highlight Challenge of Patients Who Refuse to See Doctors or Nurses of Different Race." *Associated Press*, February 22.

———. 2013b. "Race-Based Nursing Under Fire." *San Francisco Chronicle*, February 28.

Padela, A. I., S. M. Schneide, H. He, Z. Ali, and T. M. Richardson. 2010. "Patient Choice of Provider Type in the Emergency Department: Perceptions and Factors Relating to Accommodation of Requests for Care Providers." *Emergency Medicine Journal* 27 (6): 465–69.

Paul-Emile, K. 2012. "Patients' Racial Preferences and the Medical Culture of Accommodation." *UCLA Law Review* 60 (4): 462–504.

Ridley, G. 2013. "Nurse Sues Flint's Hurley Medical Center Over Claim She Was Barred from Treating Infant Because of Her Race." *Flint Journal*, February 18.

Starr, G. S., and P. J. Murphy. 2011. "Patient Choice Versus Employee Rights: Conflicting Obligations?" *Connecticut Law Tribune*, January 24.

State of Michigan Attorney General. 2019. "Michigan Patient Rights and Responsibilities in State Licensed Facilities." Accessed August 30. www.michigan.gov/ag/0,4534,7-359-82915_82919_82267_82302-447996--,00.html (content no longer available).

CHAPTER 12

"Baby Charlie" and End-of-Life Decisions

CASE STUDY

"Baby Charlie" died on July 28, 2017. His death made international news, much as his life did. Charlie's mother said that her son "had a greater impact on and touched more people in this world in his 11 months than many people do in a lifetime" (Bilefsky 2017). The dramatic events surrounding the end of Charlie's life captured the attention of people worldwide, including the pope and the president of the United States.

Charlie Gard was born in London, England, on August 4, 2016, and he appeared to be a healthy baby. In his first months, however, he failed to gain weight and was unable to lift his head or support himself as normal. On October 11, he was admitted to Great Ormond Street Hospital in London. There, he was diagnosed with mitochondrial DNA depletion syndrome—a rare, debilitating, and fatal genetic condition that left him on life support with irreversible brain damage for months. Soon, Charlie was unable to see, swallow, or move his arms or legs, and he showed no usual signs of brain activity, responsiveness to pain or pleasure, or crying. The medical team could not tell if Charlie was awake or asleep, and seizures became common. It was the "assessment of the medical team at Great Ormond Street Hospital that further treatment was futile and that palliative care should be pursued" (Hammond-Browning 2017, 462).

Charlie's parents, Chris Gard and Connie Yates, did not agree with this medical assessment, and they fought long and hard to control their son's life and, later, the terms of his death. What Charlie's parents wanted for him differed from what the medical team believed to be the right course of action, and a legal battle ensued, first in the British courts and eventually in the European Court of Human Rights. The European Court backed the hospital's opinion, "in part because experts said Charlie could be suffering" (Bilefsky 2017).

Much of the battle surrounded the parents' desire for Charlie to have an experimental treatment known as nucleoside therapy, which had not yet been tried on anyone with Charlie's diagnosis or debilitation. The parents had spoken with Dr. Michio Hirano, a neurologist at Columbia University Medical Center in New York, who said there was a "theoretical possibility" that the treatment could be of benefit to Charlie (Hammond-Browning 2017). Dr. Hirano indicated, however, that severe brain involvement was a contraindication to the use of nucleoside therapy.

The Great Ormond Street Hospital prepared a referral to the hospital's ethics committee to examine the ethical implications of using the experimental treatment. However, before the committee could meet, Charlie developed intermittent seizures and severe epileptic encephalopathy. The hospital's medical team decided that nucleoside was no longer a viable treatment option and would only serve to prolong Charlie's suffering (Hammond-Browning 2017).

The parents continued their fight by trying to take Charlie to the United States for nucleoside treatment. They used social media to seek funding and raised more than £1.3 million—the equivalent of more than $1.6 million. Funding for the treatment became a point of contention. The hospital insisted that funding was not the issue, but much of the public following the case was skeptical. In court, one medical expert testified that the United States and the United Kingdom had a difference in philosophy. She stated that, in the United States, any medical treatment will be attempted as long as funding is available, whereas her approach was centered on the best interests of the patient (Hammond-Browning 2017).

The court-appointed guardian for Charlie argued that nucleoside therapy was not in Charlie's best interest and that it was not a lifesaving treatment, but merely experimental. The judge agreed and ruled in favor of the hospital, declaring that the hospital could discontinue artificial ventilation and provide palliative care only (Hammond-Browning 2017). The parents then filed appeals.

In court, the lawyers for Great Ormond Street Hospital argued that Dr. Hirano had never examined Charlie and therefore did not have the benefit of his full medical record. Later, when Dr. Hirano traveled to London to examine Charlie, he determined that further treatment would be futile. The parents argued that the hospital had delayed the treatment until it was too late (Bilefsky 2017).

The experimental treatment was now out of the question, but the legal battle over the end of Charlie's life continued. The parents wanted to take Charlie home to die, but the hospital's medical team argued that the "risk of an unplanned and chaotic end to Charlie's life" while living at home was "unthinkable" (Bilefsky 2017). This heated and often acrimonious legal dispute was still ongoing when Baby Charlie died at the age of 11 months and 24 days. He had been on life support for the majority of his life (Bilefsky 2017).

As these emotional legal battles took place in the courts, heated debates spread widely over Facebook, Twitter, and other social media. Supporters of both the hospital's and the parents' viewpoints offered religious and political arguments, and experts in the fields of medicine, ethics, academia, research, and the law published their opinions. Past discussions of end-of-life decisions, assisted suicide, and death with dignity were resurrected, and parental rights and socialized medicine became renewed topics of political controversy. Pro-life advocates joined in the zealous fight. Crowds of protestors lined the streets outside of the hospital; some hospital staff even faced death threats (Bilefsky 2017). A powerful symbol for humanity, Baby Charlie Gard engendered significant, weighty questions—some of which society has yet to answer definitively.

ETHICS ISSUES

Patients' rights: Does a patient's bill of rights give patients—or, in the case of minors, parents and guardians—the right to select their treatment and make end-of-life decisions within a healthcare facility? Are extreme life-support measures more warranted for young people than for adults?

Experimental treatment: Can patients—or, in the case of minors, parents and guardians—demand and receive experimental treatment against the wishes of the medical team? Is it ethical for researchers to suggest the efficacy of experimental treatments that have not been proven to be beneficial in human subjects? Is it ethical to advance research objectives while offering false hope to people who are suffering?

Cultural competency: Should healthcare professionals respect and adhere to patients' and families' cultural traditions and religious beliefs about end-of-life decisions if those traditions and beliefs are in conflict with professional codes of conduct? How can healthcare professionals reconcile personal values with patient interest or values when a conflict occurs?

Management's role and responsibility: What is the ethical responsibility of management to uphold the healthcare organization's mission, values, and codes of conduct? What is management's ethical and financial responsibility to the public and the community served?

Organizational implications: Does the organization have the infrastructure in place to deal with major ethical decisions? What are the organizational implications of management actions related to end-of-life decisions for patients under its care—especially children? How will management actions be perceived by the public, and what impact might they have on community image and support?

Impact of the media: What is the impact of the media on healthcare services and delivery? On lifestyle choices and health? On public trust in healthcare institutions? How did media coverage of the Charlie Gard case influence events over the course of Charlie's hospitalization and treatment? Did it affect any outcomes?

Ethical responsibilities to employees: How will management actions affect staff morale, staff productivity, and staff perceptions of management? What is the ethical responsibility of management to provide a safe work environment for employees? To provide counseling and support for employees? To provide training in communication skills and conflict management?

Political implications: How do end-of-life decisions fuel the debate between right-to-die advocates and opponents? Between pro-life advocates and opponents? Do the events of this case contest or support the idea of universal healthcare?

Legal implications: What are the hospital's liability and course of action when patients—or, in the case of minors, parents or guardians—demand care or treatment that the medical team disagrees with and refuses to provide? Is the hospital legally liable for a hostile work environment when employees receive threats from the public? What is the hospital's liability when patients are given unproven experimental therapy?

DISCUSSION

Although the tragic events surrounding Baby Charlie took place in the United Kingdom, these same healthcare challenges occur in the United States. Medical decisions, human interactions, conflicting demands, and patient suffering test all healthcare professionals, regardless of the differences between the two nations' healthcare systems. Therefore, important lessons can be learned. This discussion will focus on circumstances relevant to the US healthcare system.

Patients' Rights

In the United States, patients have certain rights that are protected by federal or state law or guaranteed by healthcare organizations and accrediting and licensure agencies. These rights are often compiled into a document called a "patient's bill of rights," though the specific wording varies from one hospital to another (ABC Law Centers 2017).

A patient's bill of rights differs from a consent form. A consent form is a legal document signed by patients or legal guardians agreeing to undergo medical treatment. It indicates that people signing have been informed of the treatment, its risks, and its viable options and have decided to undergo the procedure. A patient's bill of rights guarantees that patients or legal guardians are provided with the necessary treatment information prior to giving their consent. Thus, a patient's bill of rights ensures that legally binding "informed consent" occurs (ABC Law Centers 2017). This issue is especially significant when treatment decisions are being considered during life-threatening situations or when the treatment is high risk or may produce severe adverse reactions.

Nowhere are treatment decisions more fraught with emotion, doubt, and controversy than during end-of-life discussions. Controversy over such decisions is common among family members or, as in the case of Baby Charlie, between family members and the medical team. And nowhere are these decisions more emotional and heart-wrenching than in cases involving children.

Healthcare professionals must be prepared for these decisions. They must be skilled communicators, able to ascertain that facts and realistic expectations of the patient's condition and prognosis have been made clear to the people responsible for end-of-life decisions. Healthcare management must work closely with medical and nursing staff to ensure that they provide accurate, understandable information to patients and are persuasive in advocating for the patients' best interests. All healthcare professionals must operate within the mission and values of the organization and within their own professional ethical codes of conduct. Doing so is a tall task. Sometimes, the demands of the patient—or, in the case of Baby Charlie, the parents—are irreconcilable with medical staff recommendations.

In such cases, patients and guardians need to be well informed of their rights. Respected healthcare organizations will refer patients or families struggling with these decisions to useful resources such as patient representatives, ethics committees, counseling services, and support groups. Some or all of these resources are available in most hospitals. These resources can be especially useful in explaining the patient's bill of rights to patients or guardians.

Do patients—or, in the case of minors, parents or guardians—have the right to select their treatment and make end-of-life decisions within a healthcare facility? A list of more than a dozen patient rights from The Joint Commission (2019) includes the rights to "make decisions about your care," to "refuse care," and to "be listened to by your caregiver." However, a hospital is not necessarily required to provide care that is determined to be not medically necessary or appropriate. Patients or their legal representatives must be actively involved in care decisions and should speak up about what they desire. Furthermore, nursing staff must advocate for the patient and make the patient's or guardian's desires known to the people in authority—even if those desires are in conflict with the personal or professional values and beliefs of the nursing staff.

Making certain that patients or their legal representatives are actively involved in the decision making about care and treatment is a serious responsibility for healthcare professionals—one that management also must be attentive to. Doctors and nurses have a legal obligation to ensure that patients or their legal representatives have been apprised of their rights and have received the necessary information to give informed consent before a course of treatment. If they fail to do so and the patient suffers as a result, the doctors and nurses may be guilty of medical malpractice, and they—and the healthcare facility—may be subject to litigation (ABC Law Centers 2017).

Experimental Treatment

The parents of Charlie Gard took legal action because they wanted the infant to receive experimental nucleoside therapy in the United States. When the case went to court, Charlie's court-appointed guardian argued that nucleoside therapy was not lifesaving, but rather "an experimental process with no real prospect of improving Charlie's condition or his quality of life" (Hammond-Browning 2017, 464). The parents' legal representative then asked the court "whether it would be worth giving it [nucleoside] a try on the basis that, without experimentation, medicine cannot advance" (Hammond-Browning 2017, 464). The judge responded that the legal test here "is what is in Charlie's best interests not what is in the best interests of medical experimentation" (Hammond-Browning 2017, 464).

The media helped fuel the debate by describing the therapy as "innovative," "radical," and "pioneering"—thus offering hope to the parents and encouraging them to continue their fight. Some researchers, however, suggested that such descriptions provided only false hope, serving to increase the suffering of both Charlie and his parents.

Others in the media debate focused on parental rights, pointing out that parents, understandably, would seek any treatment possible to save their child. Potentially germane to this debate was Dr. Hirano's position that the probability of benefit was "low but not zero" and that the existing damage to Charlie's brain could not be reversed (Hammond-Browning 2017, 463). Certainly, the medical evidence and the humanity of the principals in this tragedy challenge both ethical boundaries and objective analysis.

Yet another ethical question that surfaced during this case involves the provision of experimental treatment based solely on the availability of funding. Should experimental treatment be made available on demand if one has the funding to pay for it? Does the answer to this question depend on the anticipated treatment outcomes and the prognosis for patient improvement? The global media debate surrounding Baby Charlie generated divergent opinions: "On one side are those who hold that patients should be able to purchase whatever treatments they desire and can afford; on the other are those who maintain that governments must play a regulatory role in protecting patients from harm and that unproven therapies must meet a threshold of scientific validity before they are offered, regardless of the ability of the patient to pay" (Truog 2017). Some observers would argue that healthcare organizations have an ethical responsibility to allocate resources where they generate benefit.

Media coverage of the case implied that funding issues were preventing Charlie from receiving nucleoside treatment. However, Great Ormond Street Hospital insisted that funding was never an issue. The hospital pointed out that it had referred the issue to its ethics committee for approval and that the experimental treatment was considered, based on medical evidence, to be futile (Hammond-Browning 2017).

Typically, laws and policies related to healthcare research are in place to protect patients from being research subjects without their knowledge or consent. The American Hospital Association specifically states, "The patient has the right to consent to or decline to participate in proposed research studies or human experimentation or to have those studies fully explained before they consent. A patient who declines to participate in research or experimentation is still entitled to the most effective care that the hospital can otherwise provide" (Pecorino 2002). Hospitals establish institutional review boards to analyze the ethical implications of proposed research and to protect human subjects from harm or exploitation. Hospital ethics committees are charged with similar tasks.

Cultural Competency

In this case, Baby Charlie's parents sought the court's help in *demanding* experimental treatment for their son. In the United States, however, court referrals are more often made by the hospital when patients or guardians are *refusing* treatment that medical staff believe to be lifesaving. Refusal of treatment is typically based on cultural customs, religion, or political beliefs.

Hospitals and their staff have ethical and legal responsibilities to provide culturally competent care to their patients. However, these responsibilities do not require that all customs or beliefs be honored. Common sense tells us that patient or family requests that may be harmful to themselves, other patients, or staff do not require compliance. The same holds true for requests that may be illegal or unethical (see chapter 11 for analysis of one such case). The Joint Commission maintains that patients or their legal representatives have "a right to request or refuse treatment" but that hospitals are not required to provide care that is determined to be "medically inappropriate or unnecessary" (Hildebrand and Morrow 2016).

Hospitals and their staff must provide clear and accurate information about the patient's medical condition, treatment, and prognosis in a culturally competent manner that can be understood by patients or their legal representatives. According to Rice and Perry (2013, 82), "LEP [limited English proficiency] and disabled patients are granted the right to language assistance access by law. Healthcare facilities that participate in Medicare and Medicaid are legally bound to provide language assistance" as needed. The challenges of cultural competency confronting healthcare management are addressed in some detail in chapter 19.

Management's Role and Responsibility

Management, especially at the highest levels, determines a healthcare organization's culture. It determines what is encouraged, what is acceptable, what is punished, what is rewarded, and what is tolerated. A primary responsibility of management is to see that the culture of the workplace reflects the mission and values of the organization. Ethical decisions—especially the tough ones, such as those surrounding Baby Charlie—must be made within the framework of the mission and values.

Healthcare organizations exist for the sole purpose of providing healthcare for people in need. However, external pressures and demands can often interfere with managers' ability to focus on the needs and interests of the organization, its patients, and its employees. Successful leaders recognize that responding to the pressures and demands of the media and the public, in some instances, may not be in the best interests of patients or the organization as a whole. Distracting external pressures and the desire to put them quickly to rest must not prompt unsuitable management actions. Expediency should never take priority over ethics.

The management of a healthcare organization has a fiduciary responsibility, shared with the organization's governance, to ensure that the resources entrusted to the organization are used prudently and in areas where they are of benefit. This responsibility is a key concern when organizations are confronted with costly treatments that may produce little or no patient benefit. The use of nonmonetary resources such as human capital, time, and attention that may be diverted from other patients must also be a consideration.

Organizational Implications

End-of-life decisions, especially when children are involved, evoke strong emotional reactions from all who are involved—and also from many who are not personally involved. Dealing with this variety of stakeholders can test the capabilities and infrastructure of any healthcare organization.

The best interests of the patient must always be foremost. Necessary and appropriate care and medical equipment must be available. Trained, competent medical and nursing staff must be assigned. When a child is involved, the hospital's next priority must be the parents. Access to such resources as patient representatives, patient advocates, ethicists, ethics committees, counseling, and support groups should be available within the hospital or by referral. In cases where the patient's diagnosis is genetic or made while in utero, the hospital will have additional concerns. It should consider working with the medical staff to support prenatal care that includes genetic testing, counseling, and advance directives to better prepare parents for what may lie ahead for them and their child.

Typically, decisions about end-of-life treatment and alternatives are made in private by the people legally responsible, in concert with the medical team. Charlie's case, however, became highly public. Media coverage spanned the globe, the public passionately expressed opinions on both sides of the debate, and a heated controversy ensued. Although this case was extraordinary, all healthcare organizations should be prepared for situations in which news coverage and social media may threaten the organization's public image and the public's confidence in the institution. Having trained public relations staff and keeping a crisis communications plan in place can help protect against the dissemination of inaccurate, damaging information in the community and beyond.

Impact of the Media

Philosophers, historians, and social observers continue to examine the relationship of the media to society, seeking answers to the question "Does the media reflect society, or does society reflect the media?" University students are assigned papers on this very topic. Nowhere is the impact of the media more relevant than in the field of healthcare.

The empirical evidence suggests that popular media, especially television and social media, have significant influence over lifestyle choices and health outcomes. Businesses and marketers have honed their advertising craft to influence consumer behaviors and boost product sales. History shows that these efforts have worked profitably well across a wide variety of fields—often with troubling health implications. Advertisements from the 1800s lauded the benefits of such products as cocaine toothache drops and morphine syrup for infant teething (*Telegraph* 2012), and ads for lead-based paint were once widespread. Cigarette advertising long glamorized smoking, although controls on such advertising were enacted after a 1964 surgeon general's report highlighted smoking's health hazards (US Department of Health and Human Services 2014). Today's advertising is more sophisticated, but the goals remain the same. Advertising now recommends pharmaceuticals for seemingly every real or imagined human ailment, from headache to erectile dysfunction, and if you follow the data, it appears to be working. A correlation might even exist between the current opioid crisis and society's penchant for self-medicating, developed through advertising.

Another media issue commonly studied and debated involves the prevalence of violence on television and in video games and its relationship with violent crime, especially in schools. Yet another area of study focuses on the influence of social media on teen suicides and teen violence. Clinical psychologist Mary Pipher (2005, 66) describes the potentially problematic impact of the media on the lives of young people: "Parents wrongly assume that their daughters live in a world similar to the one they experienced as adolescents. They are dead wrong. Their daughters live in a media-drenched world flooded with junk values. As girls turn from their parents, they turn to this world for guidance about how to be an adult." Pipher says we are now seeing the first generations of young people socialized by the media. The Mayo Clinic (2022) reports studies showing that the risks for such negative effects as distraction, sleep disruption, depression and anxiety symptoms, and exposure to "bullying, rumor spreading, unrealistic views of other people's lives and peer pressure" increase for young people who use social media more frequently or for longer periods than for those with lower social media use.

The changing media landscape places a professional and moral responsibility on public health and healthcare professionals. These professionals must educate patients and families on current medical and scientific knowledge and disseminate information that promotes and supports good health. They may also have to counter competing messages that emerge from other sources.

The topic of childhood immunization—specifically, the debate over the rights of parents to refuse vaccinations for their children—has presented a media challenge with major public health implications. A number of highly visible media personalities have spoken out against immunizations, and growing antivaccine behaviors have contributed to epidemics in various parts of the world, including the United States. In 2019, a US outbreak of measles—a highly contagious, potentially deadly disease that had been declared eliminated from the country in 2000 (Centers for Disease Control and Prevention 2020)—intensified the political debate over government-mandated vaccinations. Opponents of mandated vaccinations argue that they violate personal freedoms, whereas supporters point out that unvaccinated children pose a public health risk. As of 2023, religious or personal belief exemptions from immunizations were allowed by law in all but five states (California, Connecticut, Maine, New York, and West Virginia), and efforts to eliminate such exemptions have been met with strong public resistance (National Vaccine Information Center 2023). Today's healthcare organizations have a moral responsibility to advocate for public health policies that protect the health and well-being of the communities they serve.

In the case of Baby Charlie, the media took a highly personal situation—a family's struggle with the emotionally fraught and tragic circumstances of a terminally ill child and end-of-life decisions—and turned it into an international news story and a matter of public debate. Many of the people who commented on the Gard family's court battle did so to promote a religious or political agenda; others may have simply been seeking attention. Nonetheless, the media impact was felt both by Charlie's family and by the medical team and staff of Great Ormond Street Hospital. The medical team had their medical judgment and ethics called into question, and some hospital staff received death threats. Protestors outside the hospital shouted menacing messages and harassed other families who were visiting their children there (Sky News 2017). Numerous critics argued that the British healthcare system was being cruel and uncaring. Some ideologues even blamed Charlie's parents for prolonging his life and possible suffering (Cepeda 2017). No one involved in the case went unscathed.

The power of the media was further illustrated in other ways—notably, through the more than $1.6 million raised over social media to fund experimental therapy for Charlie. In addition, some legal observers claimed that inaccurate US reporting about the situation "reinforced the parental refusal to accept this tragic situation" (Hammond-Browning 2017).

Ethical Responsibilities to Employees

Management has both an ethical and a legal requirement to provide a safe workplace for employees. The US Occupational Safety and Health Administration clearly states that employers are legally responsible for providing a work environment that is safe from illness or injury (US Department of Labor 2023). In addition, organizational codes of ethics and values statements nearly always recognize the organization's responsibility of "providing a safe and healthy work environment" (American College of Healthcare Executives 2022).

The emotionally charged, sometimes threatening environment that developed in and around Great Ormond Street Hospital presented significant management challenges. In addition to ensuring a work environment safe from immediate threats, management also had to be cognizant of how employee fear and stress could potentially affect employee well-being, patient care, and productivity. In cases of this nature, management has a responsibility to provide employee counseling, support, and other resources (including conflict management training) as needed to help mitigate the tension that employees will most certainly feel. Long-term hospitalizations, such as Charlie's, increase the probability that caregivers will closely bond with the patient and family. The emotional and psychological impact of a childhood illness can be especially strong for caregivers who are parents themselves.

Healthcare policy authority Donald Berwick (2011) urges healthcare professionals to follow two guiding principles in their management practice: (1) Remember the patient, and (2) help those who help others. Ultimately, caregivers are the ones who will determine a healthcare organization's success in meeting its mission.

Political and Legal Implications

The case of Charlie Gard raised a number of political and legal issues surrounding the role and financing of healthcare—issues similar to those currently being debated throughout the United States. Some liberals advocate Medicare for all, whereas some conservatives point to Baby Charlie as a "warning of the pitfalls of socialized medicine and the abrogation of parental rights" (Bilefsky 2017). In response to the latter argument, one anonymous internet user asked how young working-class parents with a baby who had a preexisting condition such as Charlie's would even pay for 11 months of hospital care in the United States.

Dr. Robert D. Truog of Harvard Medical School recognized that the Baby Charlie case had influenced the healthcare debate in the United States. Truog (2017) noted that some people have described US healthcare as "a money-driven system in which patients who have the means can pursue experimental treatments, even if the chances of success are slim." He also noted, however, that people cannot demand treatments in the United States that medical staff believe to be of no benefit, regardless of whether they can pay.

A key legal issue in this case surrounds the question of who has the authority to make end-of-life decisions. When doctors and parents do not agree, who prevails? When do parental rights override the medically recommended treatment? These important questions should be addressed long before an individual's end-of-life decisions are imminent, and the best way to do so is through advance directives. Physicians and healthcare professionals should therefore work to educate the public about the wisdom, advantages, and necessity of advance directives. Accurate, understandable literature about advance directives should be disseminated at physician offices, hospitals, urgent care facilities, outpatient clinics, public health programs, and other outlets.

A final thought on the various ethical issues entangled in the Baby Charlie case comes from an anonymous contributor to the social media debate (Bilefsky 2017, user comment):

The great German Philosopher G.W.F. Hegel once wrote: "Genuine tragedies in the world are not conflicts between right and wrong. They are conflicts between two rights." Charlie's parents cannot be vilified for fighting ferociously for his life, as we would expect any parents to do under ordinary circumstances. Nor can we consider his doctors evil for doing what they are ethically obligated to do, adhere to the Hippocratic aphorism, "first, do no harm." Both parties were trying to do the right thing, as they saw it. Failure to recognize this as a genuine human tragedy created by the circumstances of a very sick little boy and the prevailing limitations of science and medicine is the real ethical travesty. Charlie, his parents, and the doctors who attempted to protect him from unnecessary suffering, deserve only compassion. Attempting to exploit this situation for purely political purposes is the manifest presence of true evil in the world.

REFERENCES

ABC Law Centers. 2017. "What Is a Patient's Bill of Rights?" *Pregnancy* (blog). Published April 3. www.abclawcenters.com/blog/2017/04/03/what-is-a-patient-bill-of-rights/.

American College of Healthcare Executives (ACHE). 2022. *Code of Ethics*. As amended December 5. www.ache.org/about-ache/our-story/our-commitments/ethics/ache-code-of-ethics.

Berwick, D. 2011. "The Moral Test." Keynote address at Institute for Healthcare Improvement National Forum, Orlando, Florida, December 7.

Bilefsky, D. 2017. "Charlie Gard Dies, Leaving a Legacy of Thorny Ethics Questions." *New York Times*. Published July 28. www.nytimes.com/2017/07/28/world/europe/charlie-gard-dead.html.

Centers for Disease Control and Prevention. 2020. "Questions About Measles." Reviewed November 5. www.cdc.gov/measles/about/faqs.html.

Cepeda, E. J. 2017. "Infant's Death Not a Political Parable." *Albuquerque Journal*. Published August 5. www.abqjournal.com/1043658/infants-death-not-a-political-parable.html (content no longer available).

Hammond-Browning, N. 2017. "When Doctors and Parents Don't Agree: The Story of Charlie Gard." *Journal of Bioethics Inquiry* 14 (4): 461–68.

Hildebrand, P., and L. S. Morrow. 2016. "The Joint Commission: Patient Rights." Accessed November 21, 2019. http://3ohond29fxl43b8tjw115y91-wpengine.netdna-ssl.com/wp-content/uploads/Patient_Rights.pdf (content no longer available).

Joint Commission. 2019. *Speak Up: Know Your Rights*. Published August. www.jointcommission.org/-/media/tjc/documents/resources/speak-up/speak-ups/for-your-rights/speak-up-for-your-rights-85-x-11_.pdf.

Mayo Clinic. 2022. "Teens and Social Media Use: What's the Impact?" Published February 26. www.mayoclinic.org/healthy-lifestyle/tween-and-teen-health/in-depth/teens-and-social-media-use/art-20474437.

National Vaccine Information Center. 2023. "State Vaccine Laws and Exemptions." Accessed September 26. www.nvic.org/law-policy-state.

Pecorino, P. 2002. "The Patient's Bill of Rights: AHA." Accessed September 26, 2023. www.qcc.cuny.edu/SocialSciences/ppecorino/MEDICAL_ETHICS_TEXT/Chapter_6_Patient_Rights/Readings_The%20Patient_Bill_of_Rights.htm.

Pipher, M. 2005. *Reviving Ophelia: Saving the Selves of Adolescent Girls*. New York: Riverhead Trade.

Rice, J. A., and F. Perry. 2013. *Healthcare Leadership Excellence: Creating a Career of Impact*. Chicago: Health Administration Press.

Sky News. 2017. "Great Ormond Street Staff Receive Death Threats over Charlie Gard Case." Published July 23. https://news.sky.com/story/great-ormond-street-staff-receive-death-threats-over-charlie-gard-case-10957933.

Telegraph. 2012. "Cocaine Tooth Drops, Morphine Teething Syrup and Other Victorian Quack Cures." Published September 4. www.telegraph.co.uk/news/health/pictures/9519906/Cocaine-tooth-drops-morphine-teething-syrup-and-other-Victorian-quack-cures.html.

Truog, R. 2017. "The United Kingdom Sets Limits on Experimental Treatments: The Case of Charlie Gard." *JAMA*. Published September 19. https://jamanetwork.com/journals/jama/article-abstract/2645763.

US Department of Health and Human Services. 2014. *The Health Consequences of Smoking—50 Years of Progress. A Report of the Surgeon General*. Published January. www.ncbi.nlm.nih.gov/books/NBK179276/pdf/Bookshelf_NBK179276.pdf.

US Department of Labor. 2023. "Occupational Safety and Health Administration: Employer Responsibilities." Accessed September 26. www.osha.gov/as/opa/worker/employer-responsibility.html.

CHAPTER 13

Ethics and Management Lessons Learned from Hurricane Katrina: Memorial Medical Center

CASE STUDY

Hurricane Katrina ripped through New Orleans August 29–31, 2005, and yet it continues to haunt us. The lessons we can learn from it have remained timely as natural and human-created disasters continue to increase and the healthcare management responsibility to learn and better prepare for them continues.

Memorial Medical Center, an "esteemed community hospital" in New Orleans, Louisiana, was built in 1926 and known as Southern Baptist Hospital, until purchased in 1995 by Tenet Healthcare, a Texas-based for-profit organization. In addition to the healthcare provided by Memorial Medical Center, another healthcare company, LifeCare Hospital of New Orleans, was leasing the seventh floor at Memorial, where it separately operated a "hospital within a hospital" for critically ill patients, many of whom were on ventilators.

Memorial Medical Center is located three feet below sea level in hurricane-prone Louisiana. In spite of this, over the years, this Medical Center has served as a refuge during storms for people in the surrounding area. Early in the morning on August 29, 2005, Hurricane Katrina hit New Orleans and the city power to the Medical Center failed. At that time, about 2,000 people were housed within the Medical Center, including more than 200 patients and 600 Memorial employees. The rest were people who had sought shelter there.

Sources: Adapted from Encyclopaedia Britannica Online (2023); Fink (2009); Smith (2020).

On the morning of August 30, the poorly made federal levees, which bracket the drainage canals coursing through the city, were breached, and by afternoon, 20 percent of New Orleans was underwater. The mayor had ordered evacuation of the city the previous day, and an estimated 1.2 million people left ahead of the storm. Tens of thousands could not or would not leave and sought shelter in the New Orleans Convention Center or the Louisiana Superdome. By the evening of August 30, 80 percent of the city was underwater.

From shattered windows, Memorial staff could see the floodwaters rapidly advancing on the Medical Center, and panic set in. According to one report, "Memorial's main emergency power transfer switches were located only a few feet above ground level, leaving the electrical system vulnerable." Following Hurricane Ivan in 2004, Memorial's facilities personnel had reported that "it wouldn't take much water in height to disable the majority of the medical center." At that time, it was determined that "fixing the problem would be costly; a few less expensive improvements were made."

Memorial's nursing director was the designated "emergency incident commander," and she quickly consulted the 240-page Emergency Preparedness Plan to seek "guidance for dealing with a complete power failure and how to evacuate the hospital if the streets were flooded"—but no guidance was there. Meanwhile, Memorial administrative staff were desperately e-mailing colleagues at other Tenet hospitals outside New Orleans for help.

It quickly became clear to those physicians and nurses who remained at Memorial to care for patients that they needed to rapidly devise and implement an evacuation of the Medical Center if lives were to be saved. During their meeting, discussion promptly focused on how to triage patients for the evacuation. The Memorial physicians agreed that neonatal intensive care unit (NICU) patients, pregnant women, and critically ill adult ICU patients "should be the first evacuated." Then one of the physicians suggested that "all patients with a Do Not Resuscitate [DNR] Order should go last," and other physicians agreed. Physicians at this meeting did not later recall discussing this decision with LifeCare physicians.

Chaos reigned at LifeCare, whose corporate offices in Texas told its administrator that LifeCare patients and staff would be included in any Federal Emergency Management Agency (FEMA) evacuation of Memorial. LifeCare's administrator asked Memorial's administrators to include 52 LifeCare patients among those slated for evacuation and was told that permission for that would need to be granted by Memorial's Tenet corporate office in Texas.

In the afternoon of August 30, Coast Guard and private ambulance company helicopters landed on a "long-unused helipad atop of an eight-story parking garage adjacent to the hospital" and began evacuation of Memorial patients. With loss of power and elevators, patients needed to be "carried down flights of stairs, wheeled to the hospital wing where the last working elevator brought them to the second floor [and then] maneuvered onto a stretcher and passed through a roughly three-by-three-foot opening in the machine-room wall that offered a shortcut to the parking garage. Many patients were then placed in the back of a pick-up truck, which drove to the top of the garage and two flights of metal steps (that) led to the helipad."

As night approached and darkness fell on New Orleans, the looting began, with some looters shooting at rescuers. The helipad had little lighting and no guardrail, and the evacuation of patients had to stop for safety reasons. Memorial had 130 patients remaining, and LifeCare still had all 52 of its patients waiting, seven of them on ventilators.

Around 2:00 a.m. on August 31, Memorial's backup generators stopped and alarms went off as life support monitors and ventilators switched to limited battery reserves and then stopped completely. The Coast Guard indicated they could evacuate some LifeCare patients who were on life support, so volunteers who were manually bagging patients began carrying them down five flights of stairs in the dark. But some died before they could be evacuated. Exhausted and overwhelmed with grief, many staff cried as the chaplain prayed with them.

By daybreak on August 31, tap water had stopped flowing, the temperature had climbed above 100 degrees Fahrenheit, toilets were backed up, and the stench of sewage was noticeable. The doctors and nurses were frantically attempting to decide how to triage the remaining patients for evacuation. They had "little if any training in triage systems and were not guided by any triage protocol."

During this time, few helicopters were returning to evacuate patients, and as darkness approached once more, they stopped altogether. The triage discussion continued and physicians again suggested that patients with DNR orders be last to be evacuated. Heavy sedation of critically ill patients to relieve their pain and anxiety was also discussed by the physicians. On the afternoon of September 1, helicopters and boats finally returned to evacuate the hospital.

When the floodwaters had settled and the hurricane-damaged hospital closed, 45 dead bodies were discovered in the debris. Healthcare workers who remained at Memorial during Katrina claimed that a "well-regarded doctor and two highly respected nurses had hastened the deaths of some patients by injecting them with lethal doses of drugs."

Following investigation, nearly a year after Katrina, the Louisiana Department of Justice arrested the accused doctor and the nurses in connection with the deaths of four patients. The charges against the nurses were later dropped, and a New Orleans grand jury declined to indict the physician on second-degree murder charges.

Hurricane Katrina was the costliest natural disaster in US history and caused estimated damage of $186 billion. More than 1,800 people died in the hurricane and its aftermath, among them those who perished at Memorial Medical Center.

ETHICS ISSUES

Emergency preparedness planning: What does emergency preparedness planning include beyond writing a policy and developing a written policy manual? What is healthcare management's responsibility in emergency preparedness beyond delegating this planning responsibility to assigned staff? Will the Emergency Preparedness Plan prove to be effective in the event of an *unexpected* natural or human-created disaster? Are there strategies or processes or procedures that could make it more effective? Are staff and employees informed and sufficiently trained to know their roles and responsibilities in emergencies?

Management's responsibility in construction and maintenance of buildings: Does the responsibility for facility construction and maintenance fall solely under the authority and purview of engineering and construction management? Are these professionals solely responsible for meeting regulations and requirements that ensure the safe occupancy of the buildings? What about safe occupancy during disasters? What about safe emergency evacuation of buildings? What is management's responsibility for seeing that these requirements are anticipated and met in the construction and maintenance of buildings?

Management's responsibility for safe equipment storage and maintenance: What is management's responsibility for the safe storage and maintenance of healthcare equipment and technology? Is the delegation of this responsibility to biomedical engineering staff sufficient healthcare management action? Have the essential equipment and service needs that must be met for life support during a disaster been accounted for?

Management's responsibility for staff education and training in ethics and ethical conduct: Disasters challenge and test ethical boundaries. What is management's responsibility to provide resources that help staff to better meet ethical challenges? What does it mean to do the greatest good for the greatest number? Does the end justify the means? Which patients or clients get limited resources, and who decides? Where is the line between appropriate comfort care and "mercy killing"? How do we expect caregivers to act when their own lives or the lives of their families are at stake? How should caregivers reconcile their personal value systems with organizational codes of conduct? How do the professional and ethical codes of conduct such as "Do No Harm" fit in disasters such as Katrina? Does the Good Samaritan law apply in disasters? Should there be laws for the legal protection of healthcare workers who remain at great personal harm to care for patients during disasters? If so, of what substance?

Failure of federal, state, and local government agencies to mount an organized, coordinated response to Katrina: What is the legal and ethical responsibility of the federal, state, and local governments to plan and mount a coordinated and effective response to natural or human-created disasters within the United States? What is government's responsibility for the lifesaving rescue of its citizens who are victims of disasters and to the commitment of government resources toward their posttraumatic recovery? What is government's ethical responsibility to provide and maintain safe infrastructure for its citizens?

Environmental racism and discrimination based on socioeconomic class: Was there underlying racism within various governmental entities hampering any real humanitarian efforts to save the lives and property of the people of New Orleans? Would the disaster response and the rescue efforts have been characterized by less debate and more action if the population to be rescued were not black and poor?

Management's ethical responsibility to care for the caregivers: What is management's responsibility to provide care and resources to staff who survive disasters and suffer negative consequences as a result of their traumatic experience, especially to caregivers such as those who remained with patients at Memorial during Katrina? Has their experience had detrimental effects on their personal lives or on their professional careers (or both)? Does management have an ethical responsibility to plan and implement clinician wellness programs that address the health and well-being of its staff and employees? In all situations, but especially in the aftermath of disasters?

DISCUSSION

Emergency Preparedness Planning

This is not a chapter on emergency preparedness. That critically important instruction follows in chapter 28, "Ethics Issues in Healthcare Emergency Management." Carefully read that chapter. Current emergency management practice recommended for healthcare organizations follows the National Incident Management System and is structured around the following four phases of emergency management (Dobbs 2020):

1. Mitigation (prevention);
2. Preparedness (building capacity and resilience);
3. Response (mobilizing assets to stabilize the incident); and
4. Recovery (returning to a new normal).

Every healthcare manager needs to be aware of these recommendations and know what their organization has in place that is consistent with these recommendations.

Memorial Medical Center had an emergency preparedness plan, but when Katrina struck and the levees broke and the floods followed, the reality was very different from what had been planned for. We do not know the full extent of what was included in the Memorial Medical Center emergency preparedness plan or whether hospital staff, including physicians, had adequate training in the implementation of that plan. The chaos at Memorial Medical Center and the frantic debate over chain of command, triage of patients, and crisis standards of care during Katrina indicate that staff were not ready. Even if these elements were part of the plan and some staff training had occurred, there had not been sufficient education and training of the people left behind to implement the plan—and it also does not appear as though management had determined whether the building allowed for safe evacuation of patients and staff in the event of disaster.

A critical element of any emergency preparedness plan is to "identify the staff who will fill key response roles during an emergency event and ensure that these personnel are trained to function in those capacities and that they understand the ethical components of those roles" (Dobbs 2020). During Katrina, physicians, nurses, and the administrator all appeared to be acting independently and not always according to any agreed upon protocols related to such critical issues as disaster triage of patients and crisis standards of care. These critical questions were debated and actions taken that proved to be disastrous to the careers of some healthcare providers and deadly to some patients at Memorial.

The point here is that the "plan" *was* there at Memorial, but the plan and staff training were not sufficient to save the lives of 45 patients or the careers of some healthcare professionals.

Unfortunately, too often, healthcare managers throughout the healthcare system believe that having a plan or a policy on the shelf is the solution to any problem or preparation for any untoward event. But smart managers know that is not the case.

Former president and general Dwight D. Eisenhower has been quoted as saying, "Good planning without good working is nothing" (Hughes 2018). Regardless of the merit of the Memorial Center plan, it didn't work when Katrina struck New Orleans.

Management's Responsibility in Construction and Maintenance of Buildings

Memorial Medical Center was built in 1926 on one of the low points in New Orleans and three feet below sea level, as reported by physician-journalist Sherri Fink (2009).[1] Its age and location prompt the question of whether there had been any management discussion about relocating the Medical Center to higher ground and whether its current structure met all the required building codes and regulations that exist today.

Hurricane Katrina highlights the significant importance of a careful environmental assessment prior to any new construction or location of healthcare facilities. Such an assessment is critically significant in Louisiana. According to the National Weather Service, "some of the deadliest tropical storms and hurricanes to ever hit the United States have struck the Louisiana shoreline" (Roth 2010). In fact, according to the National Weather Service, "Katrina will likely be recorded as the worst natural disaster in the history of the United States" (Roth 2010). It has indeed been the costliest thus far (Encyclopaedia Britannica 2023).

With this history, it would appear that discussions about the safety and maintenance of the buildings and equipment and correction of any structural impediments to the emergency evacuation of patients and staff from the buildings would be routine discussions. It would certainly be essential to include inspection of evacuation routes as part of emergency preparedness, but clearly that did not happen at Memorial prior to Katrina.

We also do not know about the routine inspection and maintenance of the Memorial Medical Center buildings. But from the descriptions of the width of stairwells, the condition and access to the helipad, the poorly maintained roof that contained the helipad, and the extreme difficulty that staff had in the evacuation of patients, it appears that such inspections did not take place or that any needed improvements were deferred.

Although Katrina was an extreme case, these kinds of discussions and inspections should occur in all healthcare organizations and at the highest levels of management. The construction and maintenance of buildings and equipment constitute a safety issue for patients and employees. As such, it is a serious management responsibility that requires unremitting attention at all times and especially within the context of disasters.

The highly regarded CEO of a leading US medical center that was built decades ago on a floodplain was recently approached by the medical staff questioning whether the emergency department should be relocated from street level to a higher level in case of a flood. The CEO questioned the benefit of doing that since ambulances and other vehicles would not be able to access the flooded streets to get to the medical center. But these are exactly the kinds of discussions that management needs to have with clinicians prior to disasters so that problems can be anticipated and solved before disasters occur. During Katrina there *were* some people who traveled by boat to Memorial Hospital seeking medical care and refuge from the storm who were turned away, but they might not have been if sleep-deprived Memorial staff had not been struggling with rising floodwaters, no electricity, dying patients, and no further evacuation efforts in sight.

The point is that perhaps some of those seeking medical care during disasters *could* arrive at hospitals by boat and be cared for if life-threatening conditions, such as those at Memorial, had been anticipated and accounted for.

Healthcare management needs to be involved in decisions made in the planning and location of healthcare facilities, with special attention to an environmental assessment to determine predisposition toward disasters and the avoidance of those locations if at all possible. The planning, construction, and maintenance of all healthcare facilities must take into account and ensure that the physical entrance and egress of buildings make possible swift and easy evacuation if needed. The physical construction of all facilities must be conducive for the implementation of a well-developed emergency preparedness plan, but this is essential in planning for healthcare facilities. Katrina was a good example of the need for that.

Management's Responsibility for Safe Equipment Storage and Maintenance

Certainly, management has a responsibility to make sure that all medical equipment is maintained in safe condition for patient and staff use, but the maintenance and safe storage of nonmedical equipment may be overlooked as less important.

However, well-maintained and safely stored nonmedical equipment may prove to be lifesaving in a disaster. At Memorial Medical Center, management apparently did not give appropriate thought to the storage of emergency power transfer switches in a basement area that was susceptible to flooding, which left Memorial without the emergency power needed and essential for life support equipment when electrical power was lost.

The status and capability of communication equipment must also be routinely checked to make sure that it will remain functional in times of emergencies and that staff are adequately trained in its use. The communication problems that staff encountered during Katrina serve as a reminder that communication with external agencies and organizations is critical during disasters.

Management's Responsibilities to Employees and Staff

Healthcare managers must grapple with ethical dilemmas on a daily basis, but ethical decisions acquire significantly more importance and more public scrutiny when they must be made during disasters with limited time, resources, and consultation with other professionals. Never has this been more evident than in the public interest and media attention that have been given to the actions of the physicians and nurses who stayed behind with Memorial patients during Hurricane Katrina.

Much of what has been written about Hurricane Katrina focuses on the grand jury investigation into the cause of death in the 45 bodies found in Memorial following the hurricane and floodwaters that had stranded the Medical Center without power or water for five days. Some healthcare workers who remained at Memorial during this time claimed that a "well-regarded doctor and two highly respected nurses had hastened the deaths of some patients by injecting them with lethal doses of drugs" (Fink 2009). The New Orleans grand jury chose not to indict those charged. In the four years following Katrina, Anna Pou, the physician charged, "helped write and pass three laws in Louisiana offering immunity to health care workers from most civil lawsuits (except in cases of intentional misconduct) for their efforts in future mass casualty situations" (Fink 2009).

At the center of the grand jury investigation was the report that patients with "Do Not Resuscitate" orders on their charts were ones chosen for lethal doses of drugs that hastened their deaths. A closer look at the definition and intent of DNR orders is necessary and appropriate in this examination of what we can learn from Katrina.

According to the current National Library of Medicine definition, "A do-not-resuscitate order, or DNR order, is a medical order written by a doctor. It instructs health care providers not to do cardiopulmonary resuscitation (CPR) if a patient's breathing stops or if the patient's heart stops beating" (Vranick et al. 2022).

Whereas "advance directives may vary by state, all are designed to outline care preferences in the event one becomes incapacitated" (Vranick et al. 2022). Do not resuscitate does not mean do not treat and does not mean that all treatments are discontinued. Standard of care is not hindered by a DNR order (Vranick et al. 2022).

The National Library of Medicine goes on to say that "the goal is to educate the family and the patient that a DNR does not mean that the patient will have a poor quality of life—just the opposite. It is vital to assure the family that the patient will be made comfortable and any pain issues will be addressed" (Vranick et al. 2022).

Given this clear definition and rationale for DNR orders, it does not appear that hastening death by lethal injection is implied or intended as acceptable when a DNR order is signed.

We do not know whether any discussions about ethical or legal implications of "crisis standards of care" decisions took place in the emergency preparedness planning sessions at Memorial. But they should have, and, given the disagreement among the Memorial physicians during Katrina, it is doubtful that they did. Such discussions should have addressed the following legal and ethical questions:

- What are the local, state, or federal laws that must be part of the emergency preparedness planning discussions? For example, does the Good Samaritan law, which provides immunity from liability to a person attempting to help whose negligent administration of aid causes injury, have any application in disasters?
- What are the professional and ethical codes of conduct that apply in disasters?
- Where does "Do No Harm" fit in disasters such as Katrina?

Tough ethical questions need to be debated and agreed on in the emergency preparedness planning stages, not in the midst of a chaotic disaster, as was the case at Memorial during Katrina. Such questions include the following:

- What does it mean to do the greatest good for the greatest number?
- Does the end justify the means?
- Where is the line between appropriate comfort care and "mercy killing"?
- How do we expect caregivers to act when their own lives or the lives of their families are at stake?
- How should caregivers reconcile their personal value systems with organizational codes of conduct?

These kinds of questions must be debated and decisions made far in advance of disasters to clearly identify ethical and legal actions that can be taken when disasters occur. Policies, procedures, and training must leave no doubt about ethical and legal actions that can be taken. The mission and values of the organization must drive these policies, and consultation with attorneys, ethicists, clergy, and ethics committees may be required in their development.

Failure of Federal, State, and Local Government Agencies to Mount an Organized, Coordinated Response to Katrina

When reviewing the tragic events at Memorial Medical Center surrounding Katrina, it may be easy to overlook the fact that New Orleans was spared from a direct hit by the hurricane.

It was the breach of the poorly made federal levees which bracket the drainage canals coursing through the city that caused the death and destruction in New Orleans. As described in the case study, the levees were breached on the morning of August 29, 2005, and by afternoon, 20 percent of New Orleans was underwater. The mayor had ordered evacuation of the city the previous day and an estimated 1.2 million people had left ahead of the storm, but tens of thousands could not or would not leave and sought shelter in the New Orleans Convention Center or the Louisiana Superdome. By August 30, 80 percent of the city was underwater (Smith 2020).

With an estimated 30,000 people in the Superdome and 25,000 in the Convention Center and with temperatures over 90 degrees Fahrenheit, the storage of food and water, the absence of basic sanitation, and the omnipresent bacteria-rich floodwaters created a public health emergency. The local agencies that might have been able to help in this situation were underwater themselves. Helicopters were used to rescue many people, but many others were left to struggle to save themselves as the flooded city became more unsafe and looting began (Smith 2020).

The *New York Times* reported that on September 2, 2005, "as many still awaited rescue, and the death toll of more than 1,800 was still being tallied, *The Baltimore Sun* reported that the speaker of the U.S. House of Representatives, Dennis Hastert [R-IL], 'questioned the wisdom of spending billions to rebuild a city several feet below sea level.' It was a common sentiment at the time—also published in mainstream outlets like *Slate* and *The Washington Post*—that New Orleanians have never forgotten" (Smith 2020).

It wasn't until September 2 that an effective military presence was in place. And it wasn't until October 11 that the last of the floodwaters were pumped out of New Orleans. Decades after Katrina, the US Army Corps of Engineers acknowledged flaws in the construction of the levees (Smith 2020).

In the aftermath of Katrina, it was found that many parts of New Orleans were not formally listed as flood zones by the FEMA, so many homeowners had no flood insurance and no habitable homes remaining. Since then, New Orleans' flood protection system has been bolstered by $15 billion in federal funds, and the new improvements in the levees held during Hurricane Ida in 2021 (Encyclopaedia Britannica 2023).

But it's worthwhile to question why the levees weren't adequately constructed in the first place. Stephen Nelson, a professor emeritus of earth and environmental science at Tulane University and author of the seminal paper "Myths of Katrina: Field Notes From a Geoscientist" (Nelson 2015), has said that "the levees, properly built, easily 'could have been sufficient' for the storm surge. . . . But the Army Corps of Engineers failed to drive the steel pilings that hold levee panels together far enough into the earth" (Smith 2020).

In retrospect, we must also ask why it took the US government "roughly a week to put in place a thoroughly engaged rescue effort" in New Orleans. Where was the leadership needed to coordinate the federal, state, and local resources to help "the tens of thousands of people stuck without suitable shelter, food or water"? All levels of the US government seemed to be mired in political debate over the responsibility and funding for rescue efforts even as the death toll mounted (Smith 2020).

Environmental Racism and Discrimination Based on Socioeconomic Class

We must seriously consider whether some of this political discord may have been fueled by any underlying racism that may have existed among some politicians, their constituents, or within various governmental entities, hampering any real humanitarian efforts to save the lives and property of the people of New Orleans. We know that racial tensions and poverty existed in New Orleans prior to Katrina, so it is reasonable to consider whether these factors had any influence on rescue efforts during Katrina. Would the disaster response and the rescue efforts have been characterized by less debate and more action if the population to be rescued were not black and poor?

In 2000, the median Black income in the majority Black city of New Orleans was only $30,000. Huge numbers of the city's workers are employed in minimum wage jobs that support the tourism industry and pay $7.25 an hour. There was already a considerable shortage of affordable housing in New Orleans prior to Katrina, and most New Orleanians were and are renters (Smith 2020).

There were some observers who voiced dismay as to why residents didn't just evacuate from New Orleans when the evacuation was ordered by the mayor—never considering that many of those who stayed had no resources or means of transportation to evacuate—or that evacuation takes money that many residents did not have (Smith 2020).

We have long known that health disparities exist between Black and White populations. These disparities are well documented and evidence supported. "Being Black Is Bad for Your Health" was the theme of an op-ed published in *US News & World Report* in 2016 that acknowledged the links between racism and poor health in the United States (Lavisso-Mourey and Williams 2016). Upon reflection, it would appear that being Black and poor may also hinder one's chances for rescue during a disaster.

There is value and merit to think about Memorial and examine what happened there. Was there evidence of racism and discrimination in the government's rescue and response to Katrina? How does socioeconomic status impact government's disaster response?

According to a 2019 National Public Radio (NPR) investigative report, "How Federal Disaster Money Favors the Rich," socioeconomic status definitely matters: "Across the country, white Americans and those with more wealth often receive more federal dollars after a disaster than do minorities and those with less wealth. Federal aid isn't necessarily allocated to those who need it most; it's allocated according to cost-benefit calculations meant to minimize taxpayer risk" (Hersher and Benincasa 2019).

Management's Ethical Responsibility to Care for the Caregivers

In the aftermath of Katrina, much was publicized about the loss of life and property. More than 1,800 lives were lost, and Katrina was reported to be the costliest natural disaster in the history of the Unites States (Encyclopaedia Britannica 2023). Of the lives lost, much was written about the 45 dead found as the floodwaters receded from Memorial Medical Center. Much less has been written about the survivors of Katrina. Except for publicity surrounding the grand jury investigation into the cause of death in the 45 dead bodies found in Memorial Medical Center following the hurricane, little attention has been paid to the survivors.

Have there been significant indications of the negative impact of Katrina on the survivors of this traumatic experience, especially of those caregivers who remained at Memorial? Have they suffered survivor's guilt? Do they regret their actions or inactions related to the deaths of Memorial patients? No matter what their involvement may have been, is there a stigma attached to being present when the deaths were hastened of so many patients? Has this experience had any detrimental effects on the personal lives or on the professional careers of those healthcare providers who remained at Memorial and struggled to care for patients when evacuation efforts ceased and death was imminent?

In his memorable keynote address "The Moral Test," presented at the Institute for Healthcare Improvement in 2011, Don Berwick was exceptionally clear. Berwick challenges managers to "care for the caregivers . . . think first of the patients they serve and secondly of the caregivers caring for them." Berwick's admonition to healthcare managers is especially important and significant in our review of this case.[2] Healthcare management has an ethical responsibility to provide caregivers with resources and clinician wellness programs that promote and sustain the good health and resilience they need to care for others.

There are vast numbers of those who survived Katrina and suffered grief over the loss of family, friends, homes, jobs—in sum, their way of life. Are these not public health challenges that need to be addressed? What initiatives, efforts, and resources have been committed to the health and well-being of the survivors of these tragic events of Katrina? These *are* important public health issues that need attention following all disasters or the ill effects on the health of survivors may be present well into the future and place even greater stress on the US healthcare system. The COVID-19 pandemic has already shown that to be true.

Edward Buckles Jr., a Katrina survivor who was 13 years old at the time of the hurricane, recently produced a documentary film, *Katrina Babies* (Buckles 2022). The film examines the storm's reverberating effects on the children of New Orleans (St. Felix 2022). Buckles (2022) argues that the posttraumatic stress suffered by the children of New Orleans was not "inevitable" but was the result of government's inappropriate and "inhumane" response to Katrina and the New Orleans population.

Preparing for Human-Created Disasters and Gun Violence

Gun violence is another of the deadly "disasters" that challenge and threaten healthcare organizations and their workforce today. Gun violence in New Orleans during Katrina hampered evacuation efforts at Memorial Hospital and prompted some physicians to arm themselves out of fear of attack (Fink 2020).

The American Medical Association in 2016 declared gun violence a *public health crisis* (Leonard 2016). It subsequently adopted a strong, comprehensive, policy on gun violence and safety (Mole 2018). In 2022, the AMA adopted new, stronger policies and left no doubt that the AMA believes that physicians and healthcare professionals have a role and responsibility for advocacy in the prevention of dangers to the public health, including the dangers posed by gun violence (AMA 2022). The overwhelming AMA support of its 2022 additional recommendations followed "increases in the number of school shootings, inner-city gun violence and soaring suicide rates" (AMA 2022). Firearms account for roughly 40 percent of suicides, according to the latest CDC reports cited by the AMA (2022).

In May 2023, Georgia Governor Brian Kemp signed into law a hospital safety act, which followed the recommendations of a Georgia Senate Study Committee on Violence Against Healthcare Workers that had investigated a vicious attack by a patient on a nurse at Northeast Georgia Health System in 2021. The new law includes "criminal penalties for assaults against hospital workers and allows health care facilities in the state to create independent police forces" (Rayasam 2023). Tragically, just one day after the new law took effect, a shooting at a medical office building in Atlanta occurred that killed one person and injured four others.

According to the American Nurses Association, nearly 40 states have similar laws intended to protect healthcare workers from violence. According to federal data, "health care workers are five times as likely to experience violence as employees in other industries," and in 2022, the Centers for Medicare & Medicaid

Services (CMS) reported "the alarming rise of violence in health care settings" and recommended that "hospitals better identify patients who could pose a safety risk, increase staffing levels and improve training and education for staffers" (Rayasam 2023).

Currently there are few data to determine the effectiveness of any of the recent laws or programs that have been initiated to curb the violence in healthcare settings. Some observers fear the "unintended consequences" of legislation that promotes the presence of law enforcement in places where people receive medical care, arguing that it could further erode the public trust in the healthcare system and make some people more reluctant to seek the healthcare they need (Rayasam 2023).

While the effectiveness and the advisability of private policing of healthcare facilities in an attempt to curb gun violence may not as yet be determined, there is no doubt that other safety measures need to be put in place now.

The New Normal: Integration of Public Health and Healthcare Delivery

Deadly natural disasters, pandemics, and the escalation of gun violence and mass shootings have generated concern, awareness, and conversation about a "new normal" throughout the world.

The February 2023 death toll in Turkey and Syria from a devastating set of earthquakes passed 40,000 and continued to rise as more bodies were found (Englebrecht and Kirac 2023).

New York Times editor David Leonhardt recently reported that "the warming of the planet doesn't seem to have increased the *frequency* of hurricanes. But it has increased their *severity*, scientists say. Storms draw their energy from the ocean, and warmer water provides more energy. Warmer air, in turn, can carry more water, increasing rainfall and flooding " (Leonhardt 2020). This report predicts the potential of more and more serious injuries and deaths unless we are prepared.

This "new normal" presents unique challenges and vital responsibilities for our healthcare system. Certainly these responsibilities include emergency preparedness, ensuring a safe workplace, and caring for the sick and injured from disasters—and just as important, as Berwick reminds us, is caring for the caregivers so they have the resilience to care for others.

But additionally, we must not lose sight of the healthcare profession's essential role and responsibility in prevention, health education, policy, and research as it relates to the "new normal." The recent pandemic and some people's opposition to vaccination and to efforts to control the disease's spread have made it abundantly clear that there must be an integration of public health and healthcare delivery in order to make any real advances in the health of our society.

Through professional organizations and community engagement, healthcare professionals can take actions that help us better meet the challenges of the "new normal." They can identify disasters including gun violence to be the public health crisis that they are and develop public health research and education programs to address them. Through community engagement they can strengthen programs and initiatives that advocate for the disenfranchised and address health disparities. They can develop public education programs that help mitigate the negative impact of disasters, whether created by nature or humans.

While the triple-digit heat wave across the United States in the summer of 2023 fueled the political debates about climate change, it was a forceful call to action for healthcare organizations and their leadership. NPR reported that according to a new study by a team of international researchers from the World Weather Attribution, "climate change is not only making heat waves more common, it's also making them hotter" (Nuyen and Bhalero 2023). In the United States, heat kills more people in an average year than hurricanes, tornadoes, and floods combined. Victims of the heat have died of organ failure, cardiovascular collapse, heart attacks, and kidney failure as a result of dehydration (Nuyen and Bhalero 2023).

Jason Mitchell, a physician at Presbyterian Healthcare Services in Albuquerque, New Mexico, says that "the medical community will still be deeply concerned with the long-term impacts of climate change on health long after this current heat wave ends." In addition to heat-associated deaths and diseases, he notes that heat waves bring wildfires, dust storms, and air pollution that also increase severe respiratory diseases (Mitchell 2023). The strain on the healthcare system remains even as the temperatures fall.

A committee or "Green Team" of clinicians and staff was created at Presbyterian to focus on projects to make the organization a more environmentally responsible workplace. They asked, "What can we do in our hospitals and clinics to help reduce the impact of climate change?" and explored ways to reduce waste and optimize energy use. Significant to these efforts is a recent *Health Affairs* study that reported that the healthcare industry is responsible for 8 percent of national greenhouse gases in the United States (Mitchell 2023).

In addition to these initiatives, the Green Team is working to educate Presbyterian's workforce and the community on the health impacts of climate change and on health precautions to take to avoid heat exhaustion and the acute and chronic illnesses it produces. Presbyterian has also joined the National Academy of Medicine's Climate Action Collaborative for Decarbonizing Healthcare in the United States and has committed to advocate for efforts at the state level to reduce the impact of climate change (Mitchell 2023).

Lessons Learned

It is useful to contemplate "lessons learned" from Hurricane Katrina and to thoughtfully consider what Memorial Medical Center staff needed in place to help them make better decisions and save lives as they unselfishly stayed with patients while the hurricane ravaged on and threatened imminent death to all. Perhaps by examining these events, lessons can be learned to equip healthcare management to better prepare their organizations for the inevitable future disasters.

Healthcare managers have a responsibility to create a workplace environment that is safe, is nondiscriminatory, and provides employees with the resources and support they need to do their jobs. That responsibility is at the very core of management. That responsibility includes effective emergency preparedness, safe staffing levels, clinician wellness programs, and staff education and training that promotes a safe, ethical work environment. It also means paying attention to a lot of routine administrative duties that may seem boring and not as exciting as the latest technologies or innovations or medical advances. It's about preparing for the unexpected as well as the inevitable. It's about making decisions ahead of a crisis that will mitigate its negative impact on patients, staff, and the organization should a crisis occur—and then in the aftermath, reviewing and seeking ways to be better prepared for future such events. That has been the goal of this chapter—to examine what could be learned from Hurricane Katrina.

There is both an ethical responsibility and a professional opportunity here for healthcare managers to act in ways that better protect and greatly benefit the patients and the communities they serve.

NOTES

1. Significant gratitude is owed to physician-journalist Sherri Fink, MD, for her recording of the happenings of Hurricane Katrina. Much can be learned from her detailed, emotionally charged account of events as they occurred in the "The Deadly Choices At Memorial Hospital," published in the *New York Times* on August 25, 2009, and republished in the *New York Times Magazine* on November 25, 2020. Dr. Fink is also the author of the best-selling book *Five Days at Memorial: Life and Death in a Storm-Ravaged Hospital* (Fink 2013). As a physician, Dr. Fink is able to bring valuable medical insights into her accounts of the events of Katrina. Her book has been adapted for the TV miniseries *Five Days at Memorial* (2022) and vividly depicts the unsurmountable challenges faced and tragic decisions that were made by hospital staff left behind. It is instructive to read and view these resources to

fully understand and experience the fear, agony, and human costs to those who made these tragic decisions.

2. Don Berwick, MD, MPP, is former administrator of CMS, advocate for Single Payor System, and president and CEO of the Institute for Healthcare Improvement. He is the author of "Profiles in Leadership" videos.

REFERENCES

American Medical Association (AMA). 2022. "AMA Adopts New Policies on Firearm Violence." Press release, June 14. www.ama-assn.org/press-center/press-releases/ama-adopts-new-policies-firearm-violence.

Berwick, D. 2011. "The Moral Test." Keynote address at Institute for Healthcare Improvement National Forum, Orlando, Florida, December 7.

Buckles, E., Jr. 2022. *Katrina Babies*. New York: HBO Documentary Films. 85 min. Originally released August 24. Available through various streaming services with membership.

Dobbs, R. 2020. "Ethics Issues in Healthcare Emergency Management." In *Ethics and Management Dilemmas in Healthcare*, edited by F. Perry. Chicago: Health Administration Press.

Encyclopaedia Britannica Online. 2023. "Hurricane Katrina." Updated September 26. www.britannica.com/event/Hurricane-Katrina.

Engelbrecht, C., and N. Kirac. 2023. "Why Did a Turkish City Withstand the Quake When Others Crumbled?" *New York Times*, February 18, A4.

Fink, S. 2013. *Five Days at Memorial: Life and Death in a Storm-Ravaged Hospital*. New York: Crown.

———. 2009. "The Deadly Choices at Memorial." *New York Times*, August 25, MM28.

Five Days at Memorial. 2022. Apple TV+ miniseries, 6 hrs., 16 min. Originally released August 12.

Hersher, R., and R. Benincasa. 2019. "How Federal Disaster Money Favors the Rich." *All Things Considered*, NPR, March 5. Audio, 12 min. www.npr.org/2019/03/05/688786177/how-federal-disaster-money-favors-the-rich.

Hughes, K. 2018. "25 of the Best Planning Quotes." *Project Manager* (blog). Published October 4. www.projectmanager.com/blog/planning-quotes.

Lavisso-Mourey, R., and D. Williams. 2016. "Being Black Is Bad For Your Health." *Policy Dose* (blog), *US News & World Report*. Published April 14. www.usnews.

com/opinion/blogs/policy-dose/articles/2016-04-14/theres-a-huge-health-equity-gap-between-whites-and-minorities.

Leonard, K. 2016. "American Medical Association Calls Gun Violence a Public Health Crisis." *US News & World Report*. Published June 14. www.usnews.com/news/articles/2016-06-14/ama-calls-gun-violence-a-public-health-crisis.

Leonhardt, D. 2020. "The Morning." *New York Times*, August 27.

Mitchell, J. 2023. "Presbyterian Preparing for Health Impacts of Climate Change." *Albuquerque Journal*, July 26, A9.

Mole, B. 2018. "Fed-Up AMA Doctors Overwhelmingly Support Gun Restrictions in Sweeping Votes." Ars Technica. Published June 13. https://arstechnica.com/science/2018/06/angered-by-violence-ama-doctors-back-aggressive-gun-controls/.

Nelson, S. 2015. "Myths of Katrina: Field Notes from a Geoscientist." *Minnesota Review*, n.s., 85 (2015): 60–68. www2.tulane.edu/~sanelson/Katrina/Myths_of_Katrina.pdf.

Nuyen, S., and A. Bhalero. 2023. "Up First Briefing: Climate Worsens Heat Waves; Israel Protests; Emmet Till Monument." *Up First Newsletter*, NPR, July 25. Podcast, 13 min. www.npr.org/2023/07/25/1189907825/up-first-briefing-climate-worsens-heat-waves-israel-protests-emmett-till-monumen.

Rayasam, R. 2023. "Hospitals Create Police Forces to Stem Growing Violence Against Staff." *Shots: Health News from NPR*. Published May 15. www.npr.org/sections/health-shots/2023/05/15/1175889585/hospitals-create-police-forces-to-stem-growing-violence-against-staff.

Roth, D. 2010. *Louisiana Hurricane History*. Camp Springs, MD: National Weather Service. Modified January 13. www.weather.gov/media/lch/events/lahurricanehistory.pdf.

Smith, Talmon. 2020. "Remembering Katrina and Its Unlearned Lessons, 15 Years On." *New York Times*, August 21, SR10.

St. Felix, D. 2022. "How Many Generations of Katrina Babies Are There?" *New Yorker*, September 5.

Vranick, J., D. K. Sanghavi, K. D. Torp, and M. Stanton. 2022. *Do Not Resuscitate*. Treasure Island, FL: StatPearls Publishing. Updated September 26. www.ncbi.nlm.nih.gov/books/NBK470163/.

CHAPTER 14

C-Suite: Ethical Compass or Not?
St. Cecilia Medical Center

Robert S. Bonney

CASE STUDY

St. Cecilia Medical Center (SCMC) is located in the suburb of a West Coast city of more than one million people. It is a 350-bed community hospital in a growing part of the county. SCMC likewise has been growing to meet the community need. In addition to having the largest obstetrics program in the community, it is strong in cardiology, pediatrics, and general surgery.

Four years ago, at the urging of the medical staff, John Justice, the CEO for the last 25 years, fired the senior vice president of nursing and then hired Robert Henderson as the new chief nursing officer (CNO). The senior vice president for nursing had been the only female senior executive; with the hiring of Robert, the senior leadership staff at SCMC became entirely composed of men—specifically, White men. The reporting structure was adjusted so that nursing staff would report directly to Robert, who in turn would report to John. As CEO, John retained direct reporting responsibility for the heads of finance, human resources, and development.

The longtime chief financial officer (CFO), Jerry Hendrix, retired from SCMC three years later. The board of directors strongly recommended that the CEO engage a search firm to help recruit a highly qualified CFO who would add some diversity to the team. The search firm brought forward three candidates who met this criterion: Percy Williams, a Black man; Alice Anderson, a White woman; and Paul Chan, an Asian American man. In addition to John the CEO, all the senior executives interviewed all three candidates and provided feedback to the CEO. Both

Percy and Alice were highly qualified and had excellent references. Percy had an MBA degree in finance, with eight years as a CFO in a midsize hospital; Alice was a certified public accountant (CPA), with five years' experience as a CFO in a midsize teaching hospital. Both received high marks from the senior staff who interviewed them, but the overwhelming majority favored Alice. Everyone thought that Paul would not be a good fit for the team. Although John himself preferred Percy, the CEO decided it would be best for the cohesiveness of the team to hire Alice.

Alice was a strong CFO. She handled the refinancing of SCMC's debt with aplomb and strengthened the accounts receivable operation. The CEO gave her positive evaluations the first two years of her employment. In the third-year evaluation, however, he counseled her that her staff were complaining about her authoritative management style and told her that she needed to change. For example, John said, when he, the CEO, would call on financial staff with a question about a financial matter, Alice was always the one who responded. John was told that no one on her staff was permitted to give him answers to his questions. John told Alice that he wanted that stopped. There were questions the financial staff could answer without needing an intermediary, John said, and as the CEO, he needed answers and didn't always have time to wait for Alice's response. John cautioned Alice that her "micromanagement" was demoralizing to her staff.

Alice justified her actions, saying that she wanted to make sure that whatever information he received was correct. John told her she needed to trust her staff and when he went directly to one of her staff, it was with simple questions. John considered the matter closed.

But John's concerns lingered. He began to distrust Alice, wondering what, if anything, she was trying to hide. When Alice and John were reviewing the midyear financial statements, John asked what "cushions" existed at that time. Alice told him there was "around $500,000" available. This figure did not make sense to John, given his experience and the prior months' information. He later went to a finance staff member and asked the same question. The staff member said that she had given that information to Alice and he would have to get the information from Alice because that was Alice's policy. At the time, Alice was on vacation and unavailable for two weeks. John said he wanted the answer *now* and pressed the staff member to tell him what she had told Alice, whereupon he learned that there was an additional $2 million that Alice was saving "in case it was needed at the end of the year."

When Alice returned from vacation, John confronted her with this information. Alice admitted that she knew about the additional "cushion" but didn't think that John needed to know, believing that he would probably want to spend it before year end. If SCMC missed its budget target, there would be significantly smaller bonuses for the senior management. However, if they beat the target, there was a significant bonus upside (she didn't mention that it would also make her look good to the board). John was well aware of the implications regarding bonuses but believed he needed and had the right to know the correct information. John told Alice that he resented being lied to and had lost confidence in her; he gave her the choice to either resign or be fired. Alice said she would not resign and that if John fired her, she would seek the advice of her attorney on her subsequent actions.

SCMC is located in a state that recognizes *employment at will*, which, according to the Society for Human Resource Management (SHRM 2023), is "a legal doctrine which states that an employment relationship may be terminated by the employer or employee at any time and for any or no reason as long as no laws are violated." John terminated Alice's employment. Alice contacted an attorney who wanted to negotiate a settlement and avoid a lawsuit. Alice's demands included an 18-month severance package with monetary compensation plus SCMC paying her health insurance. In addition, Alice wanted John to write a strong letter of reference for her that she could use for future employment.

These demands infuriated John. The hospital's practice, on the rare occasions that a severance package was given, was to pay six months' salary plus one week for every year of service. John met with the senior vice president of human resources (SVP of HR) and the hospital's legal counsel to discuss his options. He told them that he initially had a feeling that Alice "might be trouble," but he hired her on the recommendation of his leadership team and the board. Now his gut feelings about her were coming to fruition. He told them he had worked hard to improve SCMC's reputation in the community and did not want it ruined with a lawsuit claiming sex discrimination, even if such claims were false. Both the SVP of HR and the legal counsel recommended against giving Alice the requested letter of reference. Instead, they suggested that John write a letter providing only dates of her employment, position she held, and a statement that she was not eligible for rehire at SCMC. However, John reluctantly told the SVP of HR to "give Alice what she wants and end this thing" and that he would sign the reference letter she wanted.

Following the departure of Alice, the CEO filled the CFO position with a highly qualified White man.

ETHICS ISSUES

Adherence to the organization's mission statement, ethical standards, and values statement: Are the actions of John consistent with the organization's mission statement, ethical standards, and values statement?

Adherence to professional code of ethical conduct: Are the actions here consistent with the codes of conduct published by professional organizations representing healthcare executives?

Legal implications: Are the actions of the CEO legal? Is there potential organizational liability based on the CEO's actions?

Justice and fairness: If the actions of John are legal, are they fair and just? Are Alice's demands fair and just? Was the CEO's decision fair and just to Percy, the candidate who was initially rejected?

Organizational implications: What are the organizational implications of John signing the demanded letter of reference for Alice? Of John hiring a White man to replace Alice? What effect, if any, does this situation have on other employees or departments within the organization?

Leadership responsibilities: Was John's conduct consistent with the role and responsibility inherent in the position of CEO of a healthcare organization?

Ethics committee: SCMC did not have an ethics committee in place to address nonclinical issues. Would one have helped in this situation?

DISCUSSION

Adherence to the Organization's Mission Statement, Ethical Standards, and Values Statement

What do the organization's mission statement, ethical standards, and values statement say regarding fostering a climate of diversity and inclusion? If doing so is part of the organization's stated position, what is the board's role in ensuring that this effort to foster a climate of diversity and inclusion happens?

John appears to be a patriarchal leader, wanting only men to be in leadership positions. Alice's concerns regarding gender discrimination may have been valid given John's hiring practices and whom he hired to replace her.

John took the easy route here and, in doing so, may have passed a problematic employee on to someone else. John also likely was not adhering to his organization's ethical standards by signing the outstanding letter of reference. The SVP of HR, on the other hand, demonstrated a strong commitment to his professional values (and likely the ethical standards of the organization) by recommending that John give Alice a strictly factual reference. In fact, many organizations have a policy stipulating that the only information the organization will give out regarding a former employee consists of dates of employment and position held; some organizations also include whether or not the employee is eligible for rehire.

Adherence to Professional Code of Ethical Conduct

The American College of Healthcare Executives (ACHE) *Code of Ethics*, as amended in December 2022, provides the following guidance under the section entitled "The Healthcare Executive's Responsibilities to the Profession of Healthcare Leadership" (ACHE 2022):

The healthcare executive shall: [. . .]

Conduct professional activities with honesty, integrity, respect, equity, fairness and good faith in a manner that will reflect well upon the profession.

Refrain from participating in any activity that demeans the credibility and dignity of the healthcare leadership profession.

Address situations in which they believe a healthcare executive is not adhering to the Code of Ethics.

In reviewing this criterion against the actions of the CEO in this case, an argument can be made that he did not conduct himself with honesty and integrity that would reflect well on the profession. John might even argue that by terminating Alice's employment and giving in to her demands, the greater good was served since the reputation of the organization was preserved and an underperforming employee was removed.

The ACHE *Code of Ethics* goes on to say in the section entitled "The Healthcare Executive's Responsibilities to the Organization" (ACHE 2022):

The healthcare executive shall, within the scope of his or her authority:

Be truthful in all forms of professional and organizational communication, and not disseminate information that is false, misleading or deceptive.

Evaluating the CEO's conduct against this criterion, an argument could be made that at the very least his reference was misleading because the CEO did not include some indication that he had some concerns regarding Alice's performance.

The section entitled "The Healthcare Executive's Responsibilities to Employees" states (ACHE 2022):

Healthcare executives have ethical and professional obligations to the employees they manage that encompass but are not limited to:

Ensuring a culture of inclusivity that seeks to prevent discrimination on the basis of race, ethnicity, religion, gender, sexual orientation, age and disability.

Evaluating the CEO's conduct against this criterion, one might conclude that the CEO did not support a culture of inclusivity that sought to prevent discrimination on the basis of gender, given that his senior leadership team is entirely composed of White men. The CEO likely would argue that the replacement for Alice was simply the best person for the job.

Finally, the section entitled "The Healthcare Executive's Responsibility to Report Violations of the Code" states (ACHE 2022):

> A member of ACHE who has reasonable grounds to believe that another member has violated this Code has a duty to communicate such facts to the ACHE Ethics Committee.

If members of the CEO's executive team learn of these events and the CEO's actions and are members of the ACHE, do they have an ethical obligation to report the CEO's actions to the ACHE Ethics Committee if the CEO is also a member? This is certainly a close call, as there are arguments and counterarguments to be made, but it needs to be considered.

Legal Implications

The CEO's requests for information from the financial staff were certainly legal and appropriate; but the CFO's withholding of the truth and her unwillingness to comply with the CEO's request to get information directly from her staff was inappropriate and wrong. It led to John's loss of confidence and trust in Alice and justified his termination of her employment. Because this case is occurring in an employment-at-will state, the CEO did not have to give a reason for the termination. If this situation had occurred in a non-employment-at-will state, the CEO still could have terminated the CFO's employment as *for cause*: she failed to follow a direct order from her supervisor, withheld important information, and in doing so misrepresented the then current financial position of the organization.

An interesting question would arise if later Alice were to be accused and found to have misused her position and embezzled funds from a subsequent employer. Could an argument be made that by giving such a glowing reference to the CFO, John the SCMC CEO is guilty of intentional misrepresentation? To prove such a claim, the harmed institution would have to show that there was (1) a misrepresentation of a material fact; (2) made with intent to deceive; and (3) causing justifiable reliance with resultant injury (*Guidry v. United States Tobacco Co.*, 1999). A lawsuit might allege that if the hospital seeking the reference had been aware of the circumstances surrounding Alice's departure from SCMC, it would not have hired her and thus would not have incurred the embezzlement.

A relevant real-life case exists, *Kadlec Medical Center v. Lakeview Anesthesia Associates* (2008), in which some anesthesia physicians wrote that an anesthesiologist in their group would be an asset to any anesthesia service and that he was an excellent physician, when they were aware that he had prior drug abuse issues. The recommended anesthesiologist later, while under the influence of the opioid pain medication Demerol, took actions that significantly harmed a patient, causing the hospital that employed him to pay more than $8 million to defend and settle the case. The anesthesiologists who provided the glowing letters of reference were found guilty of intentional misrepresentation.

Justice and Fairness

All the people in this case may have valid arguments as to why their actions or requests toward one another were fair and just. That is a difficult question—What is fair and just?—but one that must be explored in any ethical decision making. Another interesting question, however, is whether the CEO's decision was fair and just to Percy, the candidate who was initially rejected. One can argue that it was not. The overwhelming majority of the senior leaders who interviewed the candidates wanted Alice, and the CEO decided to choose Alice to maintain the cohesiveness of his team rather than hire the person he felt was best for the position: Percy. Another interesting question for which we will never know the real answer is: Did John favor Percy simply because he was male?

Organizational Implications

The actions of senior leadership are always under a microscope within any organization. Those actions demonstrate to the workforce the level of commitment to the words that are messaged. In this case, although the CFO's termination was justified, the subsequent actions send a message to the organization. Hiring a White man to a senior leadership team that is already composed entirely of White men sends the message that the organization does not value diversity and inclusion, even if that is a stated goal of the organization. The board of directors has a responsibility (through its finance committee chair) to, at the very least, discuss the implications and perceptions with the CEO regarding his selection as it relates to the organization's stated values.

The argument that the person selected was the best candidate could become the mantra of other departments when they are pushed to support the diversity and inclusion values of the organization. After all, if it is good for the CEO, then it must be acceptable for department heads or other senior leaders.

Assuming that some or all of the senior team members learn the facts around the severance agreement and letter of reference, John's desire to maintain cohesion might be in trouble. At the very least, his role modeling of expediency over ethics and values might lead to other situations wherein senior executives determine to follow expediency when a focus on values and ethics is called for.

Leadership Responsibilities

The CEO's actions have a significant impact on the corporate culture. In this case, not only did SCMC's mission and vision statements support diversity and inclusion, but the human resource policies also did. Yet the CEO's actions demonstrated that he did not believe these company documents applied to him. The message this sends to the organization is that these policies and statements are not really important, which can have a negative effect on staff morale, leading to turnover. Turnover can lead to inconsistent staffing and ultimately could negatively affect patient care. It could also lead to difficulty in recruiting staff who value diversity and inclusion.

The CEO's actions in this case may have created a sense among the senior staff that their opinion is not valued. This could be particularly true of the senior vice president for HR. At the very least, it sends a message to the SVP of HR that expediency in resolving human resource issues is a better choice than taking a firm position and risking a lawsuit, even if the situation calls for a firmer, more ethical position. Choosing expediency over ethics will undoubtedly have a negative impact on the corporate culture of the organization and promises to create problematic decisions in the future.

Ethics Committee

SCMC did not have an ethics committee in place to address nonclinical issues. Having one could have helped in this situation, although it is clear in this case that the CEO wanted to be in control, and thus it might not have mattered. Had there been one and the sense of the ethics committee was not to grant the CFO's request for a glowing reference and yet the CEO still did what he did, the committee might question its own value.

In fact, SCMC did not have an ethics committee to address nonclinical issues because the CEO did not want one. John preferred working with legal counsel on what was legal and determining for himself what he considered ethical or not. He likely did not think that outside advice regarding ethics was valuable. He may also have had concerns regarding confidentiality of the discussions around nonclinical ethical issues.

To be valuable, an ethics committee would need support from the highest level, and in this case it likely would not be there.

Taking nonclinical issues to an ethics committee is generally different than taking clinical issues to it. Clinical issues tend to be case specific. When dealing with nonclinical issues, if the discussion is around policy and not a specific case, it helps to better ensure confidentiality.

In this case, if there were an ethics committee that dealt with nonclinical issues, it might be asked what the policy should be when a subordinate is terminated for cause and what type of reference should be given if the organization is contacted for one. Numerous causes could be given, thereby ensuring the confidentiality of this particular case. For example, cause could be defined as too many medication errors, undisclosed conflict of interest, too many absences, or failure to follow a valid order of their supervisor. The committee could then discuss all of them and provide recommendation to human resources leadership. Regardless of the type of issue discussed by an ethics committee, it is critical that all members maintain absolute confidentiality about the discussion and recommendations.

REFERENCES

American College of Healthcare Executives (ACHE). 2022. *Code of Ethics*. As amended December 5. www.ache.org/about-ache/our-story/our-commitments/ethics/ache-code-of-ethics.

Guidry v. United States Tobacco Co. 1999. 188 F.3d 619, 627 (5th Cir. 1999).

Kadlec Medical Center v. Lakeview Anesthesia Associates. 2008. 527 F.3d 412 (5th Cir. 2008).

Society for Human Resource Management (SHRM). 2023. "HR Glossary: Employment at Will." Accessed September 29. www.shrm.org/resourcesandtools/tools-and-samples/hr-glossary/pages/employment-at-will.aspx.

CHAPTER 15

Legal Perspectives

Walter P. Griffin

Illegal actions may be unethical.
Unethical actions may be legal.
—Anonymous

ALTHOUGH THE GENERAL public may view *ethical lawyers* as an oxymoron, lawyers contending with healthcare issues must be aware of the ethical implications in addition to the legal ones. Unethical behavior may not be illegal per se, but the fine line between unethical and illegal is easily crossed. Lawyers are responsible for ensuring that their clients understand the differences between illegal actions and unethical ones.

As illustrated throughout this book, those differences are not always obvious. Lawyers learn through professional training and experience that court rulings establish the distinctions between illegal, unethical, and appropriate actions and that those distinctions are fluid and continually subject to change. A legal opinion provided by an attorney one day may be revised, reversed, or confirmed by a court of competent jurisdiction the next day. In the complex, multijurisdictional US legal system, lawyers must stay abreast of the latest court rulings and how those rulings might affect their clients. Timing is crucial. A court decision promulgated one year may be superseded by a new decision the next. That definitions of right and wrong can continually change seems improbable, and yet such changes can be seen throughout history.

PARADISE HILLS MEDICAL CENTER

The events at Paradise Hills Medical Center in chapter 3 illustrate a basic legal principle: Hospitals may be held responsible for the actions of their employees—in this case, a medical physicist whose miscalculations caused excessive levels of radiation to be administered to 22 oncology patients.

The legal and ethical questions are whether the institution has an obligation to notify the patients of the mistake, even though the results might not adversely affect the patients; whether the ordering physician should be informed of the mistake and allowed to decide if the patients should be notified; and whether hospital management could simply do nothing. From a legal point of view, the doctrine of fraudulent concealment is important. An institution or physician who withholds possibly detrimental medical information from a patient may establish the basis for a claim of fraudulent concealment. For example, a surgeon who knows that a sponge was left in a patient during surgery and does not tell the patient about the mistake has fraudulently concealed a fact on which a lawsuit could be formulated.

In the case of Paradise Hills Medical Center, each patient who received an excessive dose of radiation has a cause of action based on medical negligence. To fraudulently conceal the mistake would not only establish a separate cause of action but also indefinitely extend the statute of limitations that might otherwise bar legal action after a certain amount of time. Therefore, to conform with the law, the hospital should notify the patients. That notification would also satisfy ethical obligations.

However, one question remains: Who is responsible for notifying the patients—the institution or the ordering physician? The institution may discharge its legal obligations by notifying the ordering physician of the error, on the theory that the physician is acting as the outer ego of the patient; however, doing so might not fulfill the hospital's ethical responsibility. If an institution exists to benefit the public, it has a responsibility to be open and forthright. A lawyer's legal obligation can be discharged by informing the hospital's management that patients must be notified of the error through either direct communication with the patients or communication with the patients' physicians. The hospital's ethical responsibility might not be met, however, unless the hospital has direct contact with the patients. Whether a patient was actually harmed or whether the likelihood of future harm is very low is irrelevant.

QUAL PLUS HMO

In chapter 4, the governing board committee's position at Qual Plus HMO led to legal and ethical questions concerning the authority and action of the institution itself. A clear conflict of interest existed when a member of the governing board committee participated in decision making about bids for construction when that member had a financial interest in the outcome. The chief operating officer (COO), who had knowledge of the conflict, had a legal duty, based on his employment by a public corporation, to request that the member refrain from participation in construction-related committee matters and to inform the CEO of the conflict. In this case, he did object to the committee's motion that final bids be invited, and he did inform the CEO, who refused to discuss the committee's action.

Legally, the COO had discharged his duties. His lawyer would advise him to document the events and proceedings. From an ethical point of view, however, the CEO and the COO should have submitted the issue to Qual Plus's ethics committee or informed the governing board directly. The COO did attempt to present the issue informally to the ethics committee and was rebuffed. At that point, the COO should have formally requested the ethics committee to consider the issue, forcing a decision for or against his opinion. His ethical responsibility could have been discharged once that decision was made. If the ethics committee rejected the formal request and made no decision, an ethical argument could be made that the COO was required to communicate directly with the governing board. Although the CEO looked unfavorably on that approach, the COO might not have been protected from litigation had the board member's conflict of interest later become public knowledge. The COO must give top priority to performing the duties and responsibilities spelled out in his job description. By allowing a fraudulent bidding process to proceed, the CEO exposed himself to legal liability, and because the CEO acted as the outer ego of the health maintenance organization, the organization itself then became liable.

The appropriate method of addressing the conflict of interest would have been for the COO to formally request that the ethics committee look into the matter and resolve it. This case is a perfect example of the need for an ethics committee to facilitate the fair and impartial adjudication of internal ethical violations. The COO should not have retreated when his informal request was rejected. The COO was responsible for ensuring the integrity of the governing board committee's actions and had an ethical responsibility to expose any known conflicts of interest. Even if revealing the conflict might have put the COO's job in jeopardy, the governing board should have responded impartially. Once informed of the possible conflict of interest, the board had a legal responsibility to investigate the situation and decide how to deal with it. That decision, no matter what it was, would have shielded the COO if, at a later time, a third party had exposed the conflict of interest. To avoid his legal and ethical dilemma, the COO should have fully disclosed the conflict of interest to all levels of authority.

COMMUNITY MEDICAL CENTER

The situation at Community Medical Center in chapter 5 is filled with ambiguities. The lawyer listening to the CEO's description of his relationship with the postgraduate fellow could only wonder why the governing board would consider the CEO's actions detrimental to the institution. Although the CEO was imprudent in disclosing his personal feelings for the fellow and his assumptions about the future, he addressed the situation in a timely manner.

Because an employee–employer relationship had arguably not yet been established, the primary question remaining would be whether the CEO's decision was discriminatory because the fellow, as a woman, was a member of a protected class. From a legal perspective, if the CEO does not hire another person to fill the position that the fellow sought or declares that the organization no longer needs such a position, proving that he violated any statute or common law would be extremely difficult. Similarly, the fellow could not claim sexual harassment because she has no evidence of sexual contact or a hostile work environment. Moreover, the fellow does not appear to have voiced her disapproval of the CEO's covert or overt actions. In fact, from a legal perspective, a jury might be persuaded that the CEO's actions were actually intended to avoid the possibility of a future claim.

A more disturbing aspect of the case is the action of the governing board. Any decision the board made that might adversely affect the CEO's career could be legally actionable. Although the CEO is undoubtedly an at-will employee, various legal theories could be used to maintain a legal action against the institution for discharging the CEO under these circumstances. (For reference, an at-will employee is one who is employed at the discretion of the employer and may be discharged under any circumstances for any reason.)

UNIVERSITY HOSPITAL

In the University Hospital case in chapter 6, the basic principles are clear-cut, but the actions required by those principles are open to interpretation. A second-shift operating room (OR) supervisor, who had great respect for the attending trauma surgeon, faced a situation that forced her to choose between clear legal principles and strong personal loyalties. The applicable legal principles were that, as the second-shift OR supervisor, she had a legal duty both to stop an intoxicated trauma surgeon from performing surgery and to contact the second-call trauma surgeon if the original trauma surgeon did not arrive promptly to assist the resident in lifesaving surgery. In addition, in her managerial capacity, the OR supervisor may have had an ethical duty—to the community at large—to report the intoxication of a trauma surgeon to her superior.

Arguably, the OR supervisor also had a legal obligation to report the incident, because the hospital was responsible, on the theory of respondeat superior, for the actions of a trauma surgeon whom it supplied in an emergency situation. Whether the surgeon was an employee of the hospital or was acting as an independent agent does not make a difference.

Another issue is whether the supervisor had a responsibility to stop the resident from performing surgery. If the resident had a license to practice medicine in the state where University Hospital is located, the OR supervisor did not have a legal responsibility to stop the resident from performing surgery. However, she may have had legal responsibilities to notify the patient's relatives that life-threatening surgery was being performed by a resident, to obtain permission to proceed because the patient was unconscious and thus unable to consent, and to contact the second-call trauma surgeon because of both the delayed arrival and the inebriation of the original trauma surgeon. By obtaining consent from the patient's relatives and by notifying the second-call trauma surgeon, the supervisor would have discharged both her ethical and her legal obligations. By not doing so, she could have exposed the hospital to liability for allowing a resident to perform surgery, even if the action was justified in an emergency. She certainly exposed the hospital to liability for her failure as a supervisor to notify the second-call trauma surgeon when no supervising trauma surgeon was present. The hospital, in all likelihood, would not have been held responsible for the behavior of the intoxicated trauma surgeon because he did not perform the surgery—at least if the hospital was unaware of any previous episodes of intoxication.

This discussion assumes that the resident was licensed to practice medicine in the state where University Hospital is located and, therefore, did not violate licensing laws. It also presumes that a licensed resident can practice medicine and surgery under the statutes of the state. However, whether the resident was competent to perform the surgery creates legal exposure for University Hospital. From a legal standpoint, the question would be whether the resident, under the hospital's procedures and regulations, had privileges to perform surgery. From an ethical standpoint, an issue would be whether the patient's life-threatening condition demanded action even if the required privileges had not been extended to the resident. Clearly, the resident expected that an attending physician would be present to oversee the resident's performance of the surgery. The attending physician's presence would have been mandatory if the resident lacked the necessary privileges, but the ethical considerations would have remained the same. Ethically, the resident had to intervene.

The resident may have no personal liability because a life-threatening emergency demanded intervention with or without the extension of privileges or proof of competency. Nonetheless, the resident should have instructed the OR supervisor to contact the second-call trauma surgeon. And to ensure future patient safety, the resident should have informed the director of the residency program about the trauma surgeon's intoxication.

HILLSIDE COUNTY MEDICAL CENTER

Knowledge of the legal definition of *standard of care* as it applies to healthcare is essential to the analysis of the Hillside County Medical Center case in chapter 7. The term refers to the standard that a reasonable physician would adhere to when providing medical care in a given specialty under a certain set of circumstances and that other specialists in the same field would adhere to nationally. A similar standard applies to medical institutions, because their liability is created through their employee physicians, agent physicians, and other providers of medical care. Depending on the individual caregiver's expertise, either a professional standard or an ordinary negligence standard may be used, but the institution is still responsible for its employees.

A hospital's need to reduce its workforce because of economic difficulties or labor unrest is no defense for a breach of the standard of care. Legally, a reduction in workforce requires an equal reduction in the number of patients. The legal and ethical responsibilities of medical care providers are the same under these conditions. Legally, providers of medical care are required to follow the standard of care, and ethically they must give patients adequate care for their medical conditions. Simply stated, when too many patients have too few medical providers, the result is a breach in both ethics and the standard of care. "Do no harm" remains the legal and ethical basis for evaluating the actions of medical care providers.

METROPOLITAN COMMUNITY HOSPITAL

Metropolitan Community Hospital (MCH) in chapter 8 faces a problem common to hospitals throughout the United States: a shortage of nurses. The way the hospital reacts to the shortage could result in both ethical and legal complications detrimental to the hospital's mission.

MCH is located in an urban area that is perceived to have a high crime rate. As a result, potential nursing recruits often feel that employment at MCH could be risky. Other deterrents include tensions between physicians and nurses, the poor management style of the board, and the schism between US-born nurses and those born outside the United States. Although those issues are not legal in nature per se, each has the potential to escalate into a legal problem. For example, a patient could file a lawsuit claiming that, because of the shortage of nurses, they received inadequate care and suffered an unnecessary medical complication. If the nurse-to-patient ratio in MCH's medical/surgical unit is 1 to 12 and thus fails to meet the standard in the United States, the patient could have a basis for the claim. The plaintiff then would be required to prove a causal relationship (proximate cause) between the nursing shortage and the complication they experienced. The board and the chief nursing officer, in particular, need to focus on meeting the national standard for the nurse-to-patient ratio. Anything less creates a legal quagmire.

Another area of legal concern is the relationship between the physicians and nurses. The law is clear that an institution is responsible for its administrative staff when charges of harassment are levied. Most states have statutes directly related to the establishment of such a claim. The administration has a duty to educate its staff about the nature and ramifications of harassment and to implement measures to prevent it.

HEARTLAND HEALTHCARE SYSTEM

Information technology (IT) is at the heart of providing efficient and cost-saving healthcare. The creation of an interconnected medical information system—one that includes direct connections to the offices of private physicians and patient financial records—is a complex undertaking for any healthcare system. Unfortunately, at Heartland Healthcare System in chapter 9, the project became even more complex because of legal and ethical problems stemming from personal ambitions.

The system's new chief information officer (CIO) disregarded a reputable IT consulting firm's advice about upgrading its existing system and, with the CEO's approval, pursued his personal ambition to build an enterprise system that would be the envy of healthcare organizations throughout the Midwest. As he ventured into an area of healthcare for which he did not have the proper credentials, the CIO relied increasingly on the same independent contractor and refused to consider further evaluation by other IT vendors. Legally, failure to use a formal bid process to evaluate the system or to purchase equipment is highly unusual and likely to generate criticism. A formal bid process should always be the avenue for purchasing equipment and obtaining additional reviews.

The CEO and CIO in this case would most likely not be legally liable under these circumstances, but the possibility cannot be excluded. The CIO ignored resources at his fingertips, including input from accounting and nursing staff, which undoubtedly undermined the IT project's possibility of success. However, poor decisions are not the same as negligence. Actions would have to be far out of the norm for someone in their positions to be considered negligent.

RICHLAND RIVER VALLEY HEALTHCARE SYSTEM

In chapter 10, the merger between Trinity Medical Center and J. Blair Sutton Memorial Hospital brought together two organizations with distinct philosophies, boards, and cultures. Carrying out these types of mergers is difficult, and the formation of the Richland River Valley Healthcare System (RRVHS) was no exception. The attempt to blend such disparate organizations raised significant legal and ethical issues.

Each board of directors was bound to its own corporate culture and determined to maintain the philosophy and goals of its own institution. The two boards' duty to govern was not abrogated by the formation of a third board. Although power could legally be transferred to the merged board, the responsibilities for managing the hospital system still rested with the boards of the two institutions. Consequently, either the two hospitals' corporate cultures needed to be amalgamated or each board had to be allowed to continue to pursue its own interests.

Unfortunately, both boards abandoned their legitimate roles as governing bodies even though the establishment of the RRVHS board did not relieve them of board responsibility. That abandonment was obvious when the hospital boards allowed the RRVHS board to order the new CEO to fire the senior administrators of both hospitals, erasing vital corporate memory at a critical time. The boards also accepted the RRVHS board's decisions to assume financial oversight of both hospitals and to stop providing them with operating budgets and routine financial reports. As a result, the hospitals were deprived of the resources they needed for operations and growth. The RRVHS board's financial control also led to disagreements over the allocation of capital resources for new programs and services. A rivalry soon developed between the two hospitals over where new clinical services would be based.

Governing boards have legal and ethical responsibilities to maintain focus on their institutions' goals and culture and to take the actions necessary to ensure their institutions' ongoing soundness. The RRVHS merger failed in part because of a lack of attention by all three boards to the important role that corporate culture plays in every organization. An additional cause was the RRVHS board's unwillingness to provide the hospitals with the resources needed for the efficient and profitable delivery of healthcare.

HURLEY MEDICAL CENTER

The Hurley Medical Center case presents several legal issues. As events in the Hurley incident unfolded, several attorneys were interviewed, and their opinions were reported in the media. These legal perspectives are documented in the discussion in chapter 11.

The local newspaper headline "Nurse's Lawsuit Draws Protestors" was the culmination of several events that placed the hospital in a decision-making role that, based on the evidence, it may not have been prepared to take on. The primary legal issues are whether the hospital discriminated against an employee by relieving her from her duties because she was Black and whether the practice created a hostile work environment. The White father of a sick child had asked that no Black nurses or medical providers be allowed to care for his child.

Because the case was resolved prior to commencement of a trial, the claims concerning discrimination and a hostile work environment were not confirmed. However, the facts did establish that the actions of the hospital administration, in conceding to the demands of the child's father, were in fact discriminatory and did create a hostile work environment. The law is clear that the action described in this case is a violation of civil rights and that the hospital's decision is untenable. Further, the publicity stemming from the administration's actions, in and of itself, causes significant damage to the institution—especially given its location in the inner city of a large metropolitan area.

From the point of view of the hospital administration, it believed its primary role was to treat the patient by whatever means were appropriate, which included exchanging personnel for delivery of medical care. The administration's decision was also influenced, as it explained to the public, by a desire to avert possible physical harm to the employee in the wake of threatening behavior by the patient's father.

The patient's parent may have an inherent right to choose the institution that is going to provide care but does not have the inherent right to demand that certain personnel provide that care, unless the demand is substantiated based on the individual's medical training, experience, and presentation. The administration should not yield to demands made on racial profiling. Part of the responsibility of the administration is to educate patients and family members, through handbooks or other communications, that discriminatory demands will not be tolerated. A warning on admission is required.

From a legal perspective, an institution's failure to warn or to publicize to patients and families that discriminatory requests will be rejected may well be the basis for a claim when a discriminatory act occurs. The basis of the claim would be "failure to warn." Again, the question of injury would be for the jury.

The paramount concern is that the patient, if in an extreme condition, is treated. To provide treatment while avoiding a possible claim of discrimination and ensuring the safety of staff, the administration could have had security maintain a vigil of the threatening individual while care was delivered.

"BABY CHARLIE"

The legal issues surrounding the end-of-life decisions in the case of "Baby Charlie" in chapter 12 were litigated in the British courts and eventually the European Court of Human Rights. During each evidentiary session, the courts reaffirmed that the issue before them centered on "the best interests of the child" and that the term *best interests* should encompass medical care, emotional stability, and welfare. The best interests of the patient are the foremost concern—not the best interests of the parents, society, or medical providers.

From a legal perspective, the "best interests of the child" test is appropriate. Each court used this test as the basis for its opinion, rejecting trial by public opinion and declining to follow, without analysis, the directions of the parents.

In the United States, courts can intercede on petition by interested parties with respect to end-of-life decisions, and they may hear testimony from individuals, including medical providers, about the best interests of the patient. These decisions can be difficult and heartbreaking. In cases where the patients are children, the decisions are a nightmare for parents. For the adult population, individual states have allowed the use of medical directives—commonly called "living wills"—to direct end-of-life decisions based on the patient's stated desires. The medical directive would indicate under what medical conditions the patient would direct the end of life to occur; the directive is usually based on inability to sustain normal life activities and medical evidence that a condition will not allow survival. Unfortunately, in cases involving children, the court must be the arbiter if varying opinions exist.

In the case of Baby Charlie, the court appointed a guardian to determine whether nucleoside treatment in the United States, which was not available in the United Kingdom, was lifesaving or experimental. The guardian's opinion was that the treatment was not in the best interests of the child. Analysis by the various courts reinforced that the best interests of the child were the appropriate legal test.

MEMORIAL MEDICAL CENTER

Disasters always create chaos. Hurricane Katrina, which challenged staff at Memorial Medical Center in chapter 13, is no exception. Legal issues presented by this disaster are numerous. To focus, I will address two significant legal issues learned from Hurricane Katrina: (1) emergency planning and (2) care for patients.

Emergency Planning

A famous wartime general once stated that "all plans for battle are perfect until the first shot is fired." In this case, the first shot fired was the arrival of Hurricane Katrina.

In previous chapters, there have been discussions about preparation, documentation, and what instructions should be given to guide employees in a time of crisis. The problem presented here is that the magnitude of the crisis negates many reasonable and necessary written instructions to staff. The legal argument in defending civil claims of failure to follow the standard of care within the hospital pursuant to written instructions is that the disaster was of such magnitude that written instructions were meaningless.

A civil action against hospital personnel claiming that negligence was the cause of death of a patient could argue that rules and regulations, promulgated by the hospital, were violated. The counterargument is that under the circumstances presented in the Memorial Medical Center case, rules and regulations are irrelevant when water is surging into a hospital, no power is available, rescue efforts are futile, and staff members are not being supplied with the necessary instruments or medications for the required care. In other words, the argument would be "the staff was flying blind."

In a civil action, a jury would decide whether or not to take into consideration actions of individuals who it is claimed violated the general rules of care and whether that violation was a breach of the standard of care. Under these extreme conditions, a jury may be swayed by the defense.

As pertains to the alleged criminal actions of the hospital personnel, the adherence to preparation rules and regulations would have no bearing. It would only be an issue in a civil action for monetary damages.

Care for Patients

The more serious legal issue is the argument that the administration of medication caused the deaths of individuals during the four days of isolation at the institution. One physician was charged with second-degree murder by the district attorney in Orleans Parish. This charge requires a specific finding of "intent to kill" as part of the definition. Based on the evidence presented, a grand jury decided not to indict the physician for any of the deaths. Although there was evidence that the physician administered morphine to each of the patients, there was no evidence that the actions were from a specific intent to kill the patients. It is assumed the grand jury was swayed by the argument that the administration of morphine was for the comfort of those patients: The intent was to alleviate suffering, not to kill.

For an action of this type, second-degree murder, intent to perform the act to kill is a requirement. It is presumed that in this case, the grand jury could not, in good conscience, come to the conclusion that the physician's intent was to kill.

The issue of intent has been highlighted in other cases as well. In the *Court of Common Pleas, Franklin County Ohio, Case #19 CR02735, State of Ohio vs*

William S. Husel, an Ohio physician was acquitted in the deaths of 14 terminally ill patients who died after each was administered painkillers by the physician. It was the physician's position that the ordering and administration of the painkillers was not for the purpose of attempting to kill the patients but rather to provide comfort to them. The jury in this case found the physician not guilty on all 14 counts of murder in April 2022.

The issue of intent is controlling. The distinction between providing medical care and a claim of administration of medicine to kill always comes down to the intent of the person administering the medication.

PART III

Addressing Structural Issues That Affect Ethical Decision Making

CHAPTER 16

The Intersection of Governance, Management, and Ethics

Frankie Perry

CEOS ARE SOMETIMES reminded that they "serve at the pleasure of the board." Occasionally, this dynamic makes for a complicated relationship between governance and management. Ethical concerns often arise in interactions between management and the board, and the nature of the relationship can make healthcare managers reluctant to seek counsel when such dilemmas occur. CEOs and senior-level managers may find themselves confronted with conflicting moral demands when their personal integrity is challenged by the actions of board members or by the actions that board members request of them.

Unfortunately, some people will choose to serve on a board for the sake of "the perks and prestige—for what being on a hospital board [can] do for them and their friends" (Hofmann and Perry 2005, 183). They might see their appointment as an opportunity to enjoy the status and benefits of membership on a healthcare board while doing little more than attending a monthly meeting. Some board members may consider these benefits as payback for the use of their names and opinions; they may feel entitled to certain personal or business advantages. Such situations are more common than one might think, and they present personal challenges for managers. The actions taken or not taken in such a scenario can have a serious impact on the organization and the professional careers of all involved.

Conflict of interest remains a significant concern among governing board members, despite the prevalence of policies, disclosures, governance training, and protocols to address the issue. Often, board members are recruited and appointed because of their business acumen and their ties to the community. These same qualifications that make them valuable for organizational governance, however, can make conflicts of interest more likely to occur.

Chapter 4 details one such case at Qual Plus HMO. A board member was appointed to the building and grounds committee because his knowledge and skill in the construction industry were believed to be useful to the committee's deliberations. Such appointments are fairly typical and have generally been found to have merit. In this real-life case, however, the board member violated a legal bid process and manipulated it in such a way that he personally gained a financial advantage. The CEO chose to overlook the board member's actions; the results of that decision are described in the epilogue.

Chapter 10 presents the case of a merger of two community healthcare organizations, Trinity and Sutton Memorial, to form Richland River Value Healthcare System. The merger failed, but it might have succeeded if the two organizations' governing boards had understood their role and responsibility—and those of management—during merger discussions and planning. The epilogue describes consequences of that mistake—both to the healthcare organizations and to the community.

Conflicts between management and board members may surround the hiring of friends or family. Sometimes, a board member may ask that a friend or family member be hired by the healthcare organization, or even that a new position be created for that person. Such favoritism can have a significant impact on employee morale and a measurable effect on organizational productivity.

Chapter 5 describes a highly publicized case of employee backlash as a result of favoritism. The CEO of Beth Israel Deaconess Medical Center (BIDMC) in Boston was fined $50,000 by the hospital's board for "lapses in judgement" with regard to a personal relationship with a female employee he had been mentoring. An anonymous complaint, signed "concerned employees of BIDMC," described the inappropriate hiring and sexual relationship between the CEO and the hospital employee, and the board's reluctance to do more resulted in an investigation by the Massachusetts Office of the Attorney General. The effects of the scandal included damage to the organization's public image, the expenses associated with investigation of the allegations, and the eventual resignation of the CEO.

Not all cases involving the hiring of friends at the request of the board end up in the attorney general's office, but the unintended consequences can be damaging nonetheless. Consider the following case in which a board member requests that a "friend" be hired by the organization. The CEO complies and tells the human resources (HR) department to find a position for them. Once hired, the friend shares detailed information of HR transactions with the board member, causing other HR employees to begin isolating the friend and withholding information from them. In response, the friend claims prejudicial treatment. The friend says that the information they need to do their job is being withheld from them because of their relationship with the board member. The friend subsequently makes a claim of hostile work environment, and a labor attorney is called in to investigate. The attorney finds no criteria for hostile work environment but recommends discipline for several employees and the transfer of the complainant to another department. The attorney warns the board about inappropriate hiring requests and recommends that hiring practices be put in place that address the board's role in hiring recommendations and requests. The vice president for HR is fired for allowing this situation to escalate without appropriate management action.

Perhaps the most egregious example of governance overreach can be found in a reported case describing the actions of a board chair and the 12-member board of a healthcare organization currently under federal investigation. The board in this case is a self-perpetuating board with no term limits, and the process for appointment to the board is simple: A designated board committee submits recommendations for appointment to the full board for its approval. This process, however, was manipulated by the board chair, who saw an opportunity to fill the board with appointees who were obligated to him. Once he had his power base in place, he pushed for board approval of a bylaws change to extend compensation to board members and supplementary compensation to committee chairpersons. Committee chairpersons are appointed by the board chair, and appointments typically have gone to those board members who support the policies advocated by the board chair.

Are scenarios and actions such as those described here possible? What deterrents might help prevent these kinds of board and management actions? Where does the leadership accountability for a principled and moral organization rest? What management efforts and initiatives can promote and support ethical actions within the leadership and governance of a healthcare organization? I am reminded of a quote attributed to Oscar Wilde: "Morality, like art, means drawing the line somewhere."

The rest of this chapter will examine the roles, responsibilities, and authority of governance and management within the context of ethical questions.

DISCUSSION

by Paul B. Hofmann

This topic is easily broad enough to justify a separate book. For this discussion, I will simply highlight a variety of issues that merit more extensive examination and consideration. Because personal and professional values are intrinsic to any discussion of ethics, readers are encouraged to review chapter 17 of this book, titled "Deciding Values." In that chapter, Joan McIver Gibson provides a succinct description of key perspectives—legal, scientific, economic, social, aesthetic, and moral—along with exhibits that depict the sources of values and examples of values by type. Ultimately, the author notes, "Decisions made with integrity are comprehensive, coherent, and transparent."

The intersection between hospital management and governance has always been complex and challenging. Inevitably, many of the issues associated with this crucial relationship have significant ethical undertones or implications; occasionally, decisions are made without integrity. This chapter will discuss why ethical sensitivity to these issues is absolutely paramount for both board members and senior executives, particularly the CEO. The major challenges implicit in promoting and achieving an ethical culture will be explored, and recommendations will be proposed to help navigate the often-unpredictable waters that can compromise the board and the CEO.

People who are engaged in healthcare either as professionals or as board members are typically attracted to the field because of their altruistic instincts. They want to be of service and help others, and they want to be associated with like-minded people. Furthermore, they want to see the results of their efforts in quantifiable ways, such as the following:

- Improvements in community health status
- Lower healthcare cost per capita
- Reduced barriers to access
- High satisfaction scores from patients, employees, and physicians
- Few clinical errors, complications, and nosocomial infections
- Full compliance with Medicare core measures
- Increased cost-effectiveness of services provided
- Reduced race/ethnicity-related disparities in care and outcomes
- Performance recognition from state and national organizations

Questions for Exploring and Addressing Ethical Issues

No ethically sensitive individual goes to work or to a board meeting with the objective of *not* serving the organization, its patients, or the community as well as possible and in accordance with basic ethical principles. Twenty representative questions, however, can be used to explore where problems may occur and how they can be addressed. The community relies on the governing body and management to take seriously the ethical imperative of devoting constant attention to the provision of high-quality and safe patient care. The questions, therefore, begin with that crucial concern.

1. **Institutional vision, mission, and value statements are almost always eloquent and impressive, but why is there so often a disconnect between the rhetoric and the reality of organizational behavior?**

   My article "The Myth of Promise Keeping" suggests steps that should be taken to avoid the professional hypocrisy of creating public impressions unmatched by actual performance (Hofmann 2008). Trustees are responsible not only for their fiduciary duties but also, at least in part, for their hospital's moral compass (Hofmann 2014). Community residents cannot be fully aware of the competency of every physician and employee, so they rely on the board and management to ensure that the background, training, qualifications, and experience of every caregiver meet basic requirements. Each board member and executive should have full confidence in the care and treatment provided by every physician and employee.

2. **Why do we still see so many reports of preventable harm to patients?**

   Dr. John Eisenberg was a patient safety pioneer who served as director of the federal government's Agency for Healthcare Research and Quality prior to his death in 2002. The most prestigious annual awards that the National Quality Forum and The Joint Commission give to individuals and organizations for improving patient safety and healthcare quality are named in his honor. Dr. Eisenberg's son, filmmaker Mike Eisenberg, has carried on his father's legacy by producing a superb documentary, titled *To Err Is Human*, about the ethical and legal imperatives associated with medical errors—which now rank as the third leading cause of death in the United States, after heart disease and cancer (Finnegan 2019). According to journalist Joanne Finnegan, "The documentary tells the story of healthcare professionals working to increase patient safety and [to reduce the number of] patients harmed by medical errors" and includes interviews with healthcare leaders, footage of real-world safety-improvement efforts, and details of one family's story. She quotes Mike Eisenberg as saying that he recognizes that "while the vast majority of healthcare providers want to do the right thing, systems and processes often fail them. Human beings will make mistakes, but the healthcare industry can't allow doctors and other clinicians to make the same mistakes over and over again . . . with systems that fail to pick up errors and allow bad things to happen" (Finnegan 2019). The board's understanding of this challenge is essential for promoting and supporting system improvement.

3. **Why do governance and management assume that the development and dissemination of excellent policies ensure their effectiveness?**

   Correct policies are certainly essential, but the mere existence of appropriate policies can produce a false sense of organizational security, based on the belief that patients and staff will benefit simply by the policies' promulgation (Hofmann 2012). Abundant model policies have been designed to enhance high-quality, safe patient care and a positive work environment. However, for these policies to achieve their purpose, hospital trustees and executives must be confident that the following steps are taken:

- Intensive education is provided to ensure that staff members understand the policies and procedures, as well as the rationale for their application.
- Compliance is monitored to determine the frequency, type, source, causes, and possible patterns of noncompliance.
- Measures are taken to eliminate or minimize noncompliance, and these interventions are evaluated to confirm that they are successful.
- All policies and procedures are reviewed periodically, and revisions are made to keep them current and responsive to internal and external requirements.
- Hospital leadership should recognize that legitimate exceptions to policies may be made. Concurrently, nonpunitive and just cultures should encourage timely disclosure of policy violations, near misses, and actual clinical errors.

4. **Why are patients and families often not informed promptly when a clinical error occurs? Why are they not given a sincere apology, a commitment to provide timely reports of investigation results, and a description of preventive steps being taken to avoid recurrence?**
A number of key questions should be considered in developing a policy concerning clinical mistakes (Hofmann 2006b, 32):

- How should the organization's vision, mission and core values influence the disclosure of errors and the actions taken?
- How will the policy ensure that a patient-centered approach is promoted in dealing with errors?
- What constitutes a clinical error that should be disclosed?
- Are errors that have no measurable impact on patients addressed differently from those that do?
- What will be the roles of the nursing staff, risk management office, compliance office, human resources department, legal counsel, administration and public affairs office?
- What is the role of medical staff members?
- What should be communicated to patients and families when an error occurs, and who should be speaking with them?

- Under what circumstances does the organization communicate with other staff members, the governing body, outside regulators and the media?
- What information will be released, to whom and when? How are such communications handled?
- How will the organization deal with the individual(s) involved in the error in a blame-free and just culture?
- How will the organization address the system deficiencies that account for most mistakes?
- Is it necessary to provide a safe and anonymous means for staff members to report errors that have not been reported previously? And regardless of such steps, what is required to ensure retaliation will not be permitted or tolerated?
- What mechanisms have been developed to support proper involvement of patients and family, timely root cause analyses and other steps to reduce clinical mistakes?

In a subsequent article, I noted: "Too many hospitals take an instinctive deny-and-defend position when a clinical error occurs. Such an approach only heightens the risk of malpractice lawsuits and inhibits improvements in patient care" (Hofmann 2013).

5. **Why are some boards not receiving timely information about sentinel events that result in death or serious physical (e.g., loss of limb or function) or psychological injury?**

Jim Conway developed a governance quality-engagement diagnostic tool that identified 63 challenges that might hinder efforts to accelerate quality improvement. The challenges were placed in one of six categories based on "key drivers": (1) "set aims"; (2) "get data and hear stories"; (3) "establish and monitor system-level metrics"; (4) "change the environment, policies, and culture"; (5) "learn from others and each other"; and (6) "establish executive accountability" (Conway 2018). Certainly, the importance of each category is irrefutable. However, statistics on sentinel events are essentially patients with their tears wiped away; for a lasting, indelible impression to be made, these patients' actual stories must be told and heard. As powerful as data may be, individuals who remain invisible will be less likely to influence board members and senior management to address the challenges with the urgency they deserve.

6. **Why do some boards not learn of significant litigation against the organization until reading about it in the newspaper?**

As noted in a management ethics column, "despite impressions to the contrary, it is anger not greed that drives most malpractice lawsuits. Among other factors, this anger is usually driven by denials that a mistake occurred, the lack of timely disclosure and apology, a refusal to meet with a patient, family members or both to discuss an error, the unwillingness of the hospital, physicians and perhaps others responsible for the mistake to cooperate in providing a fair settlement, and a general sense that the organization was insensitive to the patient or family's needs" (Hofmann 2006a, 58–59). The column recommends that hospital CEOs provide a periodic report to the board on malpractice cases and their outcomes.

7. **Why are board members not invited more often to go on patient rounds at least two or three times annually?**
Hospital CEOs and other senior leaders find great value in regularly visiting patients and interacting with staff members on clinical units. Progressive hospitals plan for board members to do the same, usually one or two members at a time. The executives and board members normally speak with the head nurse or charge nurse in advance to determine which patients would be receptive to such visits. These personal encounters vividly remind the board of how its actions can directly affect the quality of patient care.

8. **Why is genuine patient/family-centered care not more prevalent?**
Recipients of the American Hospital Association's Quest for Quality Prize always excel in multiple areas. When asked to provide compelling evidence to demonstrate authentic patient/family-centered care, every successful applicant has provided both indisputable documentation and impressive testimony from patients and family members (during site visits) indicating that patient/family input has a direct influence on policies, procedures, and programs. Patients and families participate in rounds and in board, quality improvement, and other committees (Hofmann and Yates 2015).

9. **Why does the level of burnout and stress among healthcare professionals remain unacceptably high?**
This question is receiving much more consideration now than it has in the past. Expressing concern about the topic in a previous article, I wrote, "It is no exaggeration to suggest that hospitals can be unintentional incubators of intolerable stress" (Hofmann 2018, 294). I referenced emergency physician Natalie Newman (2018), who suggested that "it almost seems as if the medical industry is designed to destroy the very people who practice within it." The CEOs of ten of the nation's leading healthcare institutions have identified physician burnout as a public health crisis (Noseworthy et al. 2017).

One physician states (DocG 2018):

There is no question in my mind that physicians are victims of a health care system gone horribly wrong. It starts with medical school and residency. Doctors in training are exposed to sleep deprivation, physical, and emotional trauma from day one. We are harangued with unreasonable expectations, placed in a silo of silence and culpability, and shamed at almost any sign of weakness.

In "Physician and Nurse Well-Being: Seven Things Hospital Boards Should Know," Shanafelt and colleagues (2018) indicated that

- burnout is prevalent among healthcare professionals,
- their well-being affects the quality of care,
- such distress is financially costly,
- greater personal resilience is not the solution,
- different occupations and disciplines have unique needs,
- evidence and tactics are available to address the problem, and
- interventions work.

Governance and senior management are jointly responsible for creating and maintaining an organizational culture that promotes a healthy environment for staff as well as patients (Swensen and Mohta 2019). Every hospital conducts periodic employee and physician satisfaction surveys. CEOs must ensure that these surveys include questions related to burnout, and they should share the results with the governing body to illustrate how past and current interventions have affected stress levels.

10. **Why is disruptive behavior, including sexual harassment, often permitted among staff members who have more organizational power and authority?**

Without question, an organization's culture and values influence individual behavior, and regrettably, numerous examples exist of organizations tolerating unacceptable conduct (Hofmann 2004). The Joint Commission's July 2008 *Sentinel Event Alert* warned that "disruptive behavior can lead to medical errors, erode patient satisfaction, play a part in causing preventable adverse outcomes, raise the cost of patient care and increase clinician and staff turnover" (Sandrick 2009). In a previous article, I described the importance of having an effective policy to address disruptive behavior (Hofmann 2010c, 60):

Almost every healthcare organization has one or more physicians who occasionally are insensitive, volatile, rude, condescending or abusive in language or behavior. Typically, such behavior is widely known and often tolerated for a variety of reasons. This doctor's admissions could constitute a major share of the institution's revenue; he or she could be the only physician in a critical specialty; and/or the individual could be politically connected with close ties to elected officials, donors or board members.

For a painful and candid description of how female physicians often endure despicable behavior, "A Fight This Physician Didn't Ask For," by Quinn Bensi (2019), should be required reading for every board member and senior executive.

11. **Why are the well-publicized best demonstrated practices of exemplary organizations presented in seminars, webinars, and the literature but not replicated more quickly and extensively?**

No one disputes the continuing benefits of evidence-based medicine through the adoption of clinical guidelines, pathways, and protocols, which have produced improved outcomes and benefited innumerable patients. Nonetheless, the effort to capitalize on evidence-based management insights appears to be moving at a glacial pace.

There is no acceptable explanation for the failure of CEOs and other senior executives to emulate their administrative counterparts' successful practices and systems. "Failing to adopt documented best practices is ethically indefensible. We have an inherent fiduciary and moral responsibility to energetically pursue and implement improved management tools and techniques" (Hofmann 2010b, 48). Members of both the governing body and senior management should be aware of publications that have urged hospitals to capitalize on the expanding reservoir of resources to help facilitate performance improvement efforts.

12. **In determining compensation bonuses, why do some boards assign more weight to meeting or exceeding financial targets than to improving quality of care and patient satisfaction?**

Management and possibly other employees can have a portion of their compensation based on the institution's annual financial success, but metrics (both internal and external) related to clinical outcomes and patient satisfaction must also be taken into account. If core measures of organizational performance include optimal quality of care (as demonstrated by minimal adverse events, nosocomial infections, patient falls, readmissions within 30 days, and so on), patient satisfaction scores exceeding the national average, and improved community health status, then any financial incentives should be aligned much more heavily with these indicators.

13. **Why has too little effort been devoted to maximizing board and management diversity to ensure that the complexion of the institution's board, senior executive team, and medical staff leadership is comparable to that of its community?**

Cultural sensitivity alone is insufficient; it must also be accompanied by cultural competency. The continuing inequities and disparities in healthcare access and outcomes will be more likely to receive the attention they deserve if the racial and ethnic composition of the hospital's leadership in all areas mirrors the community it serves (Hofmann 2010a). Banks and Mazzenga (2015) make a persuasive case for why improving population health requires diverse governance. Also recommended is an excellent article by Schoonover (2018), who extensively explores ways to achieve health equity, with an emphasis on leadership diversity.

14. **Why are board agendas frequently created unilaterally by the CEO, and why are potentially controversial topics rarely included?**

    In too many hospitals, the CEO prepares the agenda with little or no participation by the board chair—conveniently, though not intentionally, holding the board hostage to the CEO's priorities and avoiding potentially contentious issues. Although this approach may make board meetings more predictable and less stressful for the CEO, it will not serve the institution well. I coauthored an article that had the intentionally provocative title "Tough Love: Ten Questions to Ask Your CEO," and each of its questions included a number of corollaries to encourage board members to be active rather than passive participants in the governance process (Hofmann and Jones 1999).

15. **Given that conflict-of-interest documents are completed annually as a matter of routine, why are actual conflicts often not disclosed when a vendor or physician attempts to persuade a trustee to support a contract or capital equipment purchase?**

    An attempt by an insurance broker, a banker, or a real estate broker to lobby a trustee is more likely in a smaller community, where fewer options are available, than in a larger community. Regardless of the community's size, however, a radiologist, a pathologist, or another physician who is a friend of a board member might lobby for approval of a purchase of an expensive piece of equipment.

    Invariably, the chief financial officer (CFO) and CEO will receive more requests than can be covered by the annual capital budget. Often, the requests will attempt to justify the potential purchase by casting it in a favorable light and citing higher volumes and lower operating costs than may be realistic. The challenge for the board is to analyze each request as thoroughly and objectively as possible. Trustees, therefore, must resist the temptation to advocate for—and, if necessary, recuse themselves from voting on—a proposed contract or expenditure that involves a conflict of interest.

    Both the board and management should have an appreciation for seven factors that complicate ethical decision making with regard to resource allocation: (1) inadequate funds, (2) strong opinions expressed by influential and politically powerful people, (3) severe time constraints, (4) conflicts of interest, (5) uncertainty about potential outcomes and unintentional consequences, (6) competing professional and personal values, and (7) possible negative impact on job security (Hofmann 2011).

16. **Why do some board members view a board appointment as recognition of their community prominence or financial donations and fail to fulfill their fiduciary obligations?**

Having high-profile public figures on the board should not be discouraged. However, a board appointment must provide a clear understanding of specific expectations, including the following:

- Attending board and committee meetings, as well as board retreats, consistently
- Demonstrating thorough familiarity with the content of agenda material prior to meetings
- Participating actively in board deliberations and using financial, legal, development, and other skill sets to benefit the organization
- Disclosing potential conflicts of interest and recusing oneself from participating in or voting on such issues
- Responding to periodic surveys pertaining to board performance in key areas
- Providing candid and constructive comments in response to the CEO's performance on an annual basis

17. **Why do some board members lack a clear understanding of the bifurcation of board and management responsibilities?**

The article "Board Oversight of Culture for High-Performing Hospitals" highlights the following comments from Lesley Rosenthal, general counsel of the Lincoln Center for the Performing Arts (Rabkin and Friedman 2019): "Good board members monitor, guide, and enable good management; they do not do it themselves." Rosenthal adds that "good governance includes forming strategic policies and goals; authorizing major transactions; overseeing viability of the organization's business model, integrity of its internal systems and controls, and accuracy of its financial statements; stewarding the organization's resources; mentoring senior management; and evaluating operations." Blouin (2018) writes specifically about how trustees can empower a healthy hospital culture.

Personally and professionally, board members may be tempted to expand their influence beyond fiduciary, strategic, and policy matters. For instance, a member might tell the CEO, either formally or informally, what should be done in dealing with an operational matter, such as a personnel decision. Nonetheless, unless the executive specifically asks for advice, such an intervention is often counterproductive; it could compromise the CEO's authority and accountability.

18. **Why has onboarding of new CEOs and trustees not been more common, rigorous, and effective?**

When MedShare was welcoming a new president and CEO in September 2011, the board vice chair (who had been a senior HCA Healthcare executive and former chair of the American College of Healthcare Executives) designed a formal process dedicated solely to maximizing her success. Subsequently, the president/CEO and the board officer coauthored an article describing the process and highlighting ten key components, recognizing some areas where they would have done things differently (Rentz and Evans 2019).

Coincidentally, in September of that same year, *Trustee* published an article titled "Set Up to Succeed," which stressed that a few key questions need to be asked to clarify expectations (Clarke and Barch 2013, 7):

- Is the board looking for sweeping changes in a short time span, or is there an understanding that changes will be gradual and phased in over a certain period?
- What agreements have been made on operational, financial, and organizational goals?
- What are the metrics for success for each of these goals?

Numerous publications have looked at why and how onboarding is critical to leadership effectiveness (Clarke and Mazzenga 2019). Shared values should be the focus of an early part of the conversation in recruiting and retaining high-performing senior executives (Hofmann 2006a). Ethical fitness should also be considered in the evaluation of potential board members.

19. **Why have institutions not been more proactive in addressing the social and economic determinants of health, such as nutrition, education, housing, employment, and poverty? What has prevented organizations from working collaboratively to improve community health status and population health?**

Even before the Affordable Care Act of 2010 required community health assessments for not-for-profit hospitals, many states stipulated that all such hospitals submit annual reports. In California, for example, legislation passed in 1994 required all private and not-for-profit hospitals to assume a social obligation to provide community benefits in the public interest, in exchange for their tax-exempt status. To qualify for tax-exempt status under that law, hospitals must do the following:

- Conduct a community needs assessment every three years
- Develop a community benefit plan in consultation with the community
- Annually submit a copy of the plan to the Office of Statewide Health Planning and Development

In "A Foundation for Improving Social Determinants of Health," Larson (2019) discusses why and how the board should be more engaged in this activity, with specific examples of what hospitals and health systems have accomplished when a concerted effort is made. She notes that "Today's potential donors want to address the root cause of poor health in their communities."

Cardinal Innovations Healthcare is an example of an organization that has recognized the unique needs of a distinct population. A large managed care organization serving people and families with intellectual or developmental disabilities, mental health issues, or substance use disorders in North Carolina, it "has reduced costs and improved member outcomes by focusing on housing" (Renfrow 2019).

20. **Why are ethical issues not discussed in board meetings more often?**
Both the American College of Healthcare Executives (ACHE) and the American Hospital Association (AHA) have long histories of encouraging greater sensitivity to ethical issues. ACHE (2023) has done so through its *Code of Ethics*, its distribution of ethics policy statements, its sponsorship of ethics-related seminars and courses, and the annual publication of its ethics self-assessment tool.

In June 1983, AHA established its Special Committee on Biomedical Ethics, with a charge "to identify the major biomedical ethical issues facing hospitals and to formulate guidelines to assist hospitals in developing institutional policies and processes for decision making on these issues" (Hofmann 1986, 169). Given two years to complete its charge, the committee responded with a sense of urgency. Hospitals throughout the country received guidelines for the organization, composition, and function of ethics committees in March 1984. They received a policy on the patient's choice of treatment options in March 1985.

The Joint Commission (2018) also maintains a focus on ethics. It requires that hospitals follow "a process that allows staff, patients, and families to address ethical issues or issues prone to conflict."

Even so, more attention still needs to be directed toward issues associated with organizational ethics (Hofmann 1997; Nelson 2008; see also chapter 25 in this book). At a minimum, CEOs should present an annual report on ethics committee activities, which typically include policy development and ethics consultations, along with staff and community educational programs. In addition, the board should have an appreciation for the institutional costs associated with ethics cases (Nelson and Weeks 2008). Even as organizations continually evaluate and strive to reduce clinical mistakes, their recognition of the financial and ethical costs associated with management mistakes tends to be insufficient (Hofmann 2002, 2003; Hofmann and Perry 2005).

The answers to these and other important questions are not simple or obvious. Nonetheless, they must be acknowledged and addressed. We can establish the foundation for a productive pursuit of these questions by examining what constitutes ethical behavior.

Elements of Ethical Behavior

Ethical behavior, both professionally and personally, has at least six fundamental elements (though, admittedly, several overlap):

1. Being ethically conscious, by having an appreciation of the ethical implications of your decisions and actions
2. Being ethically competent, by understanding the meaning of ethics and ethical principles
3. Being ethically committed to doing the right thing, particularly when not doing so is easy to rationalize
4. Being ethically courageous, by actually following one's convictions, not just knowing what should be done
5. Being ethically consistent, by avoiding a temptation to be morally neutral when the right course of action is unambiguous
6. Being ethically candid, by being a strong advocate for ethical behavior and serving as a clear role model

Compromise and negotiation are inevitably value laden. We must remain vigilant to avoid concessions that might be expedient but that betray organizational or personal integrity. All too often, otherwise ethical people seek to rationalize problematic actions (Hofmann 2016).

Most of the sources cited in this chapter contain specific recommendations to help create and sustain a high-reliability organization—one that improves the capacity of governance and senior management to deal with difficult questions productively and ethically. One superb resource is *Strengthening Ethical Wisdom: Tools for Transforming Your Health Care Organization*, written by Jack A. Gilbert (2007) for the American Hospital Association. A collection of Gilbert's "from-to's," shown in exhibit 16.1, provides valuable insights to guide improvement across various disciplines.

Exhibit 16.1: The "From-To's" of Ethical Governance

The disciplines of ethical governance exist to some degree in all organizations. They are not completely present or completely absent. Their condition can be thought to occur somewhere on a continuum. This table shows some of the "from-to's" of the disciplines and gives a sense for the "board mood" we want to minimize and the one we want to instill. The governance "from-to's" reflect the board's view of itself.

Discipline	From	To
Noble Purpose	The board's duty comes down to oversight of operating performance: "No profit, no mission."	Noble purpose is at the heart of our work as a board: "No mission, no profit."
	Vision, mission, and values are all important; but realistically the board cannot do its job and always be bound by them.	Our vision, mission, and values are the board's compass; whenever we stray from them, the board needs to refocus on them quickly.
	Board agendas stress the current condition of the organization and its immediate issues.	Board discussions always seek to assess the organization's progress towards realizing our vision, mission, and values.
Independent Engagement	The board agenda and focus are provided by the CEO.	The board agenda and focus are the result of a partnership reflecting the priorities of the board and the CEO.
	The board follows the CEO's recommendations with little if any debate.	The board makes sure it understands any issues for which the CEO is recommending action, and makes informed decisions.
	The board assumes that the CEO and the board would not be in their positions if they were not ethical.	The board conducts an annual evaluation that includes a close look at the ethics demonstrated by the CEO and the board.
	The board counts on the CEO to keep board members up to date with what they need to know.	The board directs a structured educational program to keep it abreast of current and future issues and trends in health care.
Ethical Culture (Mindfulness)	Board agendas are so crowded that I don't have time to reflect on what I am feeling.	As a board member, part of my duty is to be sensitive to when I feel something might be "off" ethically with a decision.

(continued)

Discipline	From	To
(Voice)	We go along with decisions even if there might be concerns; that is what it means to be a team.	Board meetings are designed so someone who has concerns can be heard, even if they do not have a lot of facts.
(Respect)	The board values members who think along the same lines.	Our board cultivates and encourages needed diversity of views and experience.
(Tenacity)	The board is what it is. We are lucky to get people to serve.	The board wants to excel at its duty; we are always looking for ways to improve our own effectiveness and the organization's ethics.
(Legacy)	The board is mostly focused on putting out fires and making whatever decisions are needed to get through immediate problems.	All board decisions, even those made to solve immediate, pressing issues, are made with the impact of any decision on the organization's noble purpose clearly in mind.
Ethical Succession	The board expects the CEO to give us fair notice if he or she plans to leave, hopefully with a recommendation for a successor.	The board has an emergency executive succession plan in place along with continuously updated successor selection criteria.
	As long as nothing comes to its attention, the board assumes the CEO is acting with integrity.	The board has a regular and objective CEO and executive evaluation process that probes the integrity of our leaders.
	The board starts looking for decent people willing to serve on the board a few months before they are needed.	The board has a member succession plan that maps the competencies needed to identify suitable candidates; planning for board replacements is at least a year out.

Source: Gilbert, Jack A. 2007. *Strengthening Ethical Wisdom: Tools for Transforming Your Health Care Organization.* Chicago: AHA Press. Reproduced with permission of the author.

Financial audits are not optional for our institutions, and management depends on the findings to stay informed about current or potential issues that require special attention. Ethics audits provide similar value, but they, surprisingly, are not yet common in hospitals and health systems. The time and effort to conduct such an audit are modest in comparison to its potential value (Hofmann 2019).

In 1995, an AHA organizational ethics task force worked with the Virginia-based Ethics Resource Center to develop an ethics audit consisting of 55 statements to be delivered as part of an anonymous and confidential staff survey (Hofmann 2019). Respondents would be asked if they strongly disagreed, disagreed, neither agreed nor disagreed, agreed, or strongly agreed with statements such as the following:

- All employees are treated fairly.
- Respect for employees is important in my organization's policies and practices.
- Organizational ethics are openly discussed within my organization.
- The system of discipline within my organization is fair for all staff.
- The standards at my organization are clear.
- I feel pressure to compromise the standards while performing my duties.
- I know I can freely approach any manager to ask a question about business ethics.
- My senior management acts in accordance with the organization's standards.

Surely, any institution would find the responses to these types of statements informative and useful.

As demonstrated by Gilbert's table in exhibit 16.1, governance and management have a shared interest in strengthening their ethical wisdom for the benefit of the organization, its patients, and the residents of their communities. All stakeholders must have confidence that they are being well served. The complex challenges facing our field will only increase, so board members and senior executives should take immediate action to structure sound answers to the questions posed in this chapter.

REFERENCES

American College of Healthcare Executives (ACHE). 2023. "Commitment to Ethics." Accessed October 2. www.ache.org/about-ache/our-story/our-commitments/ethics.

Banks, D., and J. Mazzenga. 2015. "Furthering Population Health Demands Diverse Governance." *Trustee*. Published November 9. www.trusteemag.com/articles/1019-

furthering-population-health-demands-diverse-governance (content no longer available).

Bensi, Q. 2019. "A Fight This Physician Didn't Ask For." *KevinMD* (blog). Published April 3. www.kevinmd.com/blog/2019/04/a-fight-this-physician-didnt-ask-for.html.

Blouin, A. S. 2018. "Empowering a Healthy Culture." *Trustee Insights*, American Hospital Association Trustee Services. Published November. https://trustees.aha.org/system/files/media/file/2019/04/TI_1118_culture_quality_blouin.pdf.

Clarke, B., and S. Barch. 2013. "Set Up to Succeed." *Trustee* 66 (8): 6–7.

Clarke, B., and J. Mazzenga. 2019. "Downloading Success: Beyond Downboarding." *Wharton Healthcare Quarterly* 8 (1): 16–17.

Conway, J. 2018. "Governance Leadership of Quality: Confronting Realities and Creating Tension for Change." *Trustee Insights*, American Hospital Association Trustee Services. Published July. https://trustees.aha.org/sites/default/files/TI_0718_Conway-quality-article.pdf.

DocG. 2018. "When Doctors Leave Medicine, Don't Blame the Victim." *KevinMD* (blog). Published October 14. www.kevinmd.com/blog/2018/10/when-doctors-leave-clinical-medicine-dont-blame-the-victim.html.

Finnegan, J. 2019. "A Son Carries on Father's Patient Safety Legacy with Documentary Film." *FierceHealthcare*. Published January 31. www.fiercehealthcare.com/practices/a-son-carries-father-s-patient-safety-legacy-documentary-film.

Gilbert, J. A. 2007. *Strengthening Ethical Wisdom: Tools for Transforming Your Health Care Organization*. Chicago: AHA Press.

Hofmann, P. B. 2019. "To Minimize Risk, Ethics Audits Are as Essential as Financial Audits." *Journal of Healthcare Management* 64 (2): 74–78.

———. 2018. "Stress Among Healthcare Professionals Calls Out for Attention." *Journal of Healthcare Management* 63 (5): 294–97.

———. 2016. "Exposing the Shadows of Compromise." *Healthcare Executive* 31 (5): 48–50.

———. 2014. "The Community's Conscience." *Trustee* 67 (8): 40–41.

———. 2013. "A Better Response to Clinical Errors." *Hospitals & Health Networks*. Published October 17. www.hhnmag.com/articles/5603-a-better-response-to-clinical-errors (content no longer available).

———. 2012. "The Myth of Comprehensive Policies." *Healthcare Executive* 27 (5): 50, 52.

———. 2011. "7 Factors Complicate Ethical Resource Allocation Decisions." *Healthcare Executive* 26 (3): 62–63.

———. 2010a. "Addressing Ethnic and Racial Disparities in Healthcare." *Healthcare Executive* 25 (5): 46–50.

———. 2010b. "The Ethics of Evidence-Based Management." *Healthcare Executive* 25 (1): 48–51.

———. 2010c. "Fulfilling Disruptive-Behavior Policy Objectives: Leaders Must Promptly Address Improper Clinician Behavior." *Healthcare Executive* 25 (3): 60–63.

———. 2008. "The Myth of Promise Keeping." *Healthcare Executive* 23 (5): 48–49.

———. 2006a. "The Executive's Role in Malpractice Cases." *Healthcare Executive* 23 (3): 58–59.

———. 2006b. "Responding to Clinical Mistakes." *Healthcare Executive* 21 (5): 32–33.

———. 2004. "Why Good People Behave Badly." *Healthcare Executive* 19 (2): 40–41.

———. 2003. "Management Mistakes in Healthcare: A Disturbing Silence." *Cambridge Quarterly of Healthcare Ethics* 12 (2): 201–2.

———. 2002. "Morally Managing Executive Mistakes." *Frontiers of Health Services Management* 18 (3): 3–27.

———. 1997. "Organizational Ethics: A New Mandate to Address Inescapable Challenges." *Surgical Services Management* 3 (8): 16–18.

———. 1986. "A Summary of Values in Conflict: Resolving Ethical Issues in Health Care." In *Making Choices: Ethics Issues for Health Care Professionals*, edited by E. Friedman, 169–74. Chicago: American Hospital Publishing.

Hofmann, P. B., and W. J. Jones. 1999. "Tough Love: Ten Questions to Ask Your CEO." *Trustee* 52 (9): 27–28.

Hofmann, P. B., and F. Perry (eds.). 2005. *Management Mistakes in Healthcare: Identification, Correction and Prevention*. Cambridge: Cambridge University Press.

Hofmann, P. B., and G. R. Yates. 2015. "The One Trait That Consistently High Performing Health Systems and Hospitals Share." *Hospitals & Health Networks*. Published September 21. www.hhnmag.com/articles/6553-the-one-trait-that-consistently-high-performing-health-systems-and-hospitals-share (content no longer available).

Joint Commission. 2018. "Revisions Related to EP Review Phase IV." Published August 22. www.jointcommission.org/assets/1/6/HAP_EP_Review_Prepub_LD_Jan2019.pdf (content no longer available).

Larson, L. 2019. "A Foundation for Improving Social Determinants of Health." *Trustee Insights*, American Hospital Association Trustee Services. Published March. https://trustees.aha.org/system/files/media/file/2019/04/TT_0319_larson_foundations.pdf.

Nelson, W. A. 2008. "Addressing Organizational Ethics." *Healthcare Executive* 23 (2): 43–46.

Nelson, W. A., and W. B. Weeks. 2008. "The Organizational Costs of Ethical Conflicts." *Journal of Healthcare Management* 53 (1): 41–52.

Newman, N. 2018. "What This Doctor Decided to Do About Physician Suicide." *KevinMD* (blog). Published March 28. www.kevinmd.com/blog/2018/03/doctor-decided-physician-suicide.html.

Noseworthy, J., J. Madara, D. Cosgrove, M. Edgeworth, E. Ellison, S. Krevans, P. Rothman, K. Sowers, S. Strongwater, D. Torchiana, and D. Harrison. 2017. "Physician Burnout Is a Public Health Crisis: A Message to Our Fellow Health Care CEOs." *Health Affairs* (blog). Published March 28. www.healthaffairs.org/do/10.1377/hblog20170328.059397/full/.

Rabkin, M. T., and S. Y. Friedman. 2019. "Board Oversight of Culture for High-Performing Hospitals." *Trustee Insights*, American Hospital Association Trustee Services. Published April. https://trustees.aha.org/system/files/media/file/2019/04/TT_0419_leadership-audit-rabkin.pdf.

Renfrow, J. 2019. "Cardinal Innovations Healthcare Lowers Costs, Boosts Outcomes Through Housing Program." *FierceHealthcare*. Published May 6. www.fiercehealthcare.com/payer/crisis-costs-drop-71-for-cardinal-members-moved-to-independent-housing.

Rentz, M., and C. Evans. 2013. "On-Boarding Your New CEO." *Georgia Nonprofit NOW*. Accessed August 13, 2019. www.gcn.org/articles/On-Boarding-Your-New-CEO (content no longer available).

Sandrick, K. 2009. "Disruptive Physicians: An Old Problem Comes Under New Scrutiny in an Era of Patient Safety." *Trustee* 62 (10): 8–12.

Schoonover, H. 2018. "Health Equity: Why It Matters and How to Achieve It." Health Catalyst. Published March 6. www.healthcatalyst.com/health-equity-why-it-matters-how-to-achieve-it.

Shanafelt, T. D., S. J. Swensen, J. Woody, J. Levin, and J. Lilie. 2018. "Physicians and Nurse Well-Being: Seven Things Hospital Boards Should Know." *Journal of Healthcare Management* 63 (6): 363–69.

Swensen, S. J., and N. S. Mohta. 2019. "Leadership Survey: Organizational Culture Is the Key to Better Health Care." *NEJM Catalyst*. Published April 4. https://catalyst.nejm.org/organizational-culture-better-health-care/ (content no longer available).

CHAPTER 17

Deciding Values

Joan McIver Gibson

Isolation is the worst possible counselor.
—Miguel de Unamuno, Spanish philosopher

DECISIONS WHETHER TO tell patients the "whole" story (including uncertainty, ambiguity, and bad news) to honor professional responsibility, to minimize legal liability, to provide safe and high-quality care, and to enhance programmatic and institutional financial health (not to mention survival) are values based. That is, they reflect what matters to the decision maker(s) in a given situation.

Indeed, we would be hard pressed to come up with any decision or issue (public, private, or professional) that is not at bottom defined by values—our beliefs about what is useful, important, worthwhile, or desirable. Certainly, the issues at Paradise Hills Medical Center (chapter 3) are defined by values. So how should healthcare executives, board members, and other managers, whose main "products" are decisions, apply this observation?

In a culture that still feels the effects of the nineteenth-century positivist separation of "fact" from "value," we find ourselves without a robust language or strategy for seeing, naming, and working with values. We are confident that as long as we are dealing with facts, we can make progress. And so we search for "hard" data to lead the way. In the Paradise Hills case, would a right decision become clear if we had more conclusive data on the adverse effects of the accidental radiation, or if hospital policy were clear-cut as to who the ultimate decision makers are, or if the hospital had an in-depth analysis of projected market share over the next five

---

This chapter describes a values-based decision-making process and tool developed by Joan McIver Gibson, PhD, and her colleague Mark Bennett, JD, of Decisions Resources Inc. The authors' book A Field Guide to Good Decisions: Values in Action *(2006) explains the entire process and includes cases and work tools.*

years? Probably not. The decision makers still must navigate a sea of conflicting interests and values.

As soon as someone raises the specter of a values discussion, however, many people fear a slide into the black hole of private, subjective, and interminable discussion. Such discussions are not helpful when things need to get done. This chapter introduces a process of values-based decision making for executives and managers in healthcare institutions. The process also is transferable to virtually every decision-making facet of life: professional, public, and private.

THEORY AND HISTORY

Are values really separable from facts? Do values enter decision making only when we specifically invite them in? Scientists and philosophers over the past half century have dropped the fact–value dichotomy as outmoded and unhelpful at best, and as wrong at worst. They observe that all reasoning—from the beginnings of language development through complex theory building—is the attempt to create, reflect on, and communicate meaning. Reasoning is the process of making meaning, or valuing. To label something as "factual" is to make a very strong claim about its importance, status, utility, and reliability—that is, about its value, a point made in the classic work by Polanyi and Prosch (1975).

How do we discern the values dimension of an issue or a decision? What vocabulary do we need for capturing values and crafting decisions that appropriately reflect those values? Expanding our understanding of the sources and types of values and their historical evolution in Western philosophy may help.

VALUES: SOURCES AND TYPES

Professions, organizational culture, law, religion, social customs, family, and personal experience communicate important values (see exhibit 17.1). What matters to us comes from the areas of strong influence in our lives. Consider the relative weight we place on these sources of interests and values. Sometimes, when faced with otherwise intractable conflicts among values, we make choices based on what we consider an influential source for values. For example, how should the CEO at Paradise Hills weigh the relative influences of professional, personal, and community values? Should values issuing from one of these sources override the values from the others?

Another related strategy is to recognize that decision makers project various roles and approach decisions on the basis of these roles. Cases present themselves differently depending on the disciplinary "lens" through which we view them. Our roles grow out of our professional, social, and personal identities and entail specific perspectives or lenses that refract according to the types of values important to a given discipline or role (exhibit 17.2). Consider the following perspectives:

- **Legal:** What does the law require?
- **Scientific:** Is the explanation comprehensive, coherent, and simple?
- **Economic:** Is this distribution of resources the best one available?

Exhibit 17.1: Sources of Values

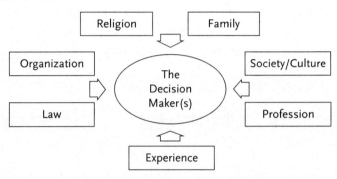

Exhibit 17.2: Examples of Values by Type

Economic	Context	Scientific
• Profitability • Efficiency • Frugality • Financial Security	We hold values that we use in making decisions. These values come from different sources. We have listed common values by type to assist you in identifying the values that you use in your work to make decisions. These types of values are not exclusive. For example, honesty is a religious value, a moral value, and a scientific value. We incorporate differing types of values to form our own unique set of personal values.	• Accuracy • Objectivity • Honesty • Knowledge
Aesthetic		**Legal**
• Beauty • Creativity • Simplicity • Elegance		• Justice • Equality • Freedom • Order
Personal	**Your Personal Values Related to Work**	**Social**
• Inner Harmony • Competence • Reliability • Happiness		• National Security • Cooperation • Responsibility • Loyalty

Religious	Institutional	Moral
• Charity • Sanctity of Life • Fidelity • Compassion	• Quality • Leadership • Teamwork	• Autonomy • Respect • Trustworthiness • Responsibility • Beneficence • Truth Telling • Integrity • Nonmaleficence • Justice/Fairness

- **Social:** Does this policy respect the values and traditions of our diverse community?
- **Aesthetic:** Do things fit together and run efficiently and smoothly?
- **Moral:** Is it the right thing to do?

This list is suggestive, not exhaustive, of the ways we unpack, label, and reorganize the variety of interests and values embedded in a single issue or decision.

Finally, history helps. In the United States, our contemporary set of values is a microcosm of more than 2,000 years of history. For example, reviewing the cumulative Western heritage, we see certain markers that signal different approaches to values. This tradition is but one of many cultural and historical strands that contribute to the American tapestry of values (see exhibit 17.3).

Exhibit 17.3: Major Historical Developments in Ethics

Historical Period	Major Ethical Tenet	Relevance to Us
Ancient Greece	Virtue	The "Character Counts!" movement *The Book of Virtues* by William Bennett
Christian Era	Sanctity of Life	Individual freedom as a political and moral principle, autonomy in decision making, civil rights
Renaissance/ Enlightenment	Scientific Morality	Abiding faith in the power of reason to discern right action and promote progress
Mid-20th Century	Principled Decision Making	Our rights and duties to each other and to society are the focus of ethics. Ethical principles are the standards for determining right action. Appeals to these principles are often used in public and political debate.
Late 20th Century	Context and Interdependence	Increasing emphasis on the impact of roles, relationships, and process in shaping the values that are present and operative when making good decisions.

In ancient Greece, virtue mattered most, at least to Plato and Aristotle (compare the Josephson Institute Center for Youth Ethics "Character Counts!" initiative; see Josephson Institute 2009). The question was "How do I personally cultivate virtuous character traits?"—that is, "Who should I be?" rather than "What should I do?" Plato and Aristotle believed that a morally good person with the right desires, motivations, or intentions is more likely to understand what should be done, more motivated to perform required acts, and more likely to form and act on moral ideals than someone without such virtuous traits.

At the beginning of the Christian era, two fundamental values were added: the sanctity of life and the importance of the individual person. Regardless of faith, the obligation to protect life and the intrinsic worth of persons as autonomous agents are values and imperatives that continue to drive American law and social policy.

During the Renaissance and Enlightenment, science, reason, and moral philosophy joined forces. The scientific values of simplicity, coherence, and comprehensiveness in explanation were extended to other disciplines (e.g., social theory, religion, art). These eras were characterized by a deep faith in the power of reason and the promise of progress, and morality was an important—perhaps the primary—object of rational inquiry. Faith in reason as the guide to right action continues, even (perhaps especially) as we lament its absence.

In the twentieth century, the application of reason to moral values became more systematized, even as it was separated from scientific and "factual" inquiry. Just as science, in one of its dimensions, is systematized explaining, so is moral philosophy (ethics) systematized valuing. One way moral philosophy is systematized is by extracting and abstracting from individual cases—those ever more general and encompassing reasons, standards, and justifications for what constitutes right actions. We call these most general and broadly applicable standards *principles*. This system of analysis and decision making took hold in medical ethics especially.

A principlist approach to valuing and ethics

- identifies the fundamental standards of right conduct, such as autonomy, respect for persons, beneficence, justice, truth telling, and professional responsibility and integrity;
- argues the moral importance of such standards; and
- applies each standard (where necessary) to a given situation.

How we justify these principles and the actions they support is important. Do we look to these standards themselves for self-evident value, or to their consequences? Is there something about respect for persons and telling the truth that is intrinsically valuable, regardless of the circumstances or outcomes? Or should we calculate the consequences and seek the greatest good for the greatest number of people? The former approach is a formalist approach, the latter utilitarian. They are not mutually exclusive, and both are helpful.

The task, however, is not simply and mechanistically to follow or apply certain principles (e.g., a code of ethics) to a given case, as one might follow a recipe, but rather to see how these standards help us understand and develop the moral dimension of a decision.

Toward the end of the twentieth century, as principlist ethics focused on formulating and impartially applying universally binding moral principles, contemporary philosophers began to observe that universal principles are inadequate for practical guidance—that abstract formulations and hypothetical cases that separate moral agents from the particularities and uniqueness of their individual lives and circumstances (and moral problems from social, historical, and contextual realities) are often less than helpful.

For example, telling the truth is important. Yet sometimes it is not clear what the truth is, or what meanings different "messengers" might communicate, or to what extent quality patient care and safety might be compromised if a program is shut down. Unique circumstances, players, and environment are moving targets to be reckoned with. Context matters.

VALUES-BASED DECISION MAKING: A CONTEXTUAL APPROACH

A contextual (not to be confused with relativistic) approach to values-based decision making accommodates general principles, uniqueness, and particular details by focusing on roles, relationships, and process. The elliptical diagram in exhibit 17.4 illustrates the approach. Features of the decision-making ellipse include the importance of context; the frames we and others bring to a situation; working with values by naming, clarifying, and weighing them; deciding on the basis of these values; and communicating the decision accurately and thoroughly along with the reasons behind it.

Context

Cases arise and decisions are made in specific contexts. Decision makers must see a case's full context, history, tradition, current conditions, and institutional values, as well as the specific people, roles, and relationships that are at work. They must promote values and argue for their relative weight. Any decision involving Paradise Hills Medical Center must consider its history and role in the community, the current business climate, the institution's role as a teaching hospital, and the

Exhibit 17.4: Decision-Making Ellipse

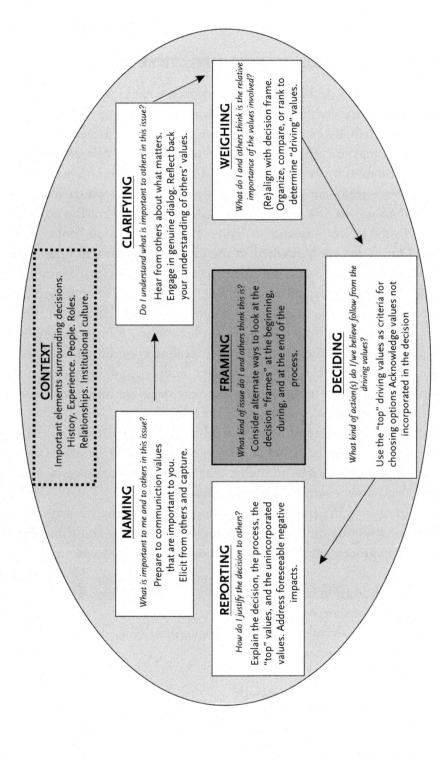

CONTEXT

Important elements surrounding decisions. History. Experience. People. Roles. Relationships. Institutional culture.

NAMING

What is important to me and to others in this issue?

Prepare to communiction values that are important to you. Elicit from others and capture.

CLARIFYING

Do I understand what is important to others in this issue?

Hear from others about what matters. Engage in genuine dialog. Reflect back your understanding of others' values.

WEIGHING

What do I and others think is the relative importance of the values involved?

(Re)align with decision frame. Organize, compare, or rank to determine "driving" values.

FRAMING

What kind of issue do I and others think this is?

Consider alternate ways to look at the decision "frames" at the beginning, during, and at the end of the process.

DECIDING

What kind of action(s) do I/we believe follow from the driving values?

Use the "top" driving values as criteria for choosing options Acknowledge values not incorporated in the decision

REPORTING

How do I justify the decision to others?

Explain the decision, the process, the "top" values, and the unincorporated values. Address foreseeable negative impacts.

various roles and relationships of the respective players (physicians, CEO, board members, community at large). Effective decision makers understand the influence of context and use it to their advantage.

Framing: What Kind of Issue Do I and Others Think This Is?

Each of us comes to any decision with a first take on what kind of issue is involved. We might initially consider the Paradise Hills case to be an issue of public relations; or perhaps one of liability exposure, institutional survival, or professional fiduciary responsibility; or maybe simply a matter of telling the truth. Different parties bring different initial frames to the decision (see exhibit 17.4). Frames are neither right nor wrong; they simply are. The Talmud (the source from which Jewish law is derived) reminds us that "we see the world not the way it is, but the way we are."

We need ways to simplify and structure all the information "noise" that surrounds us. Our brains are hardwired to use categorical frames to bound what is "in" (relevant, important) and "out" (irrelevant, less important). Frames usually exist outside our awareness and often remain untested and unexamined. Frames are not accessible for problem solving and decision making. Worse yet, they may impede our ability to see root causes of conflict. When frames are understood, appropriate, and flexible, they serve us well in dealing with difficult decisions and challenging situations. When they are hidden, unduly rigid, or based on flawed assumptions, they limit our ability to make wise decisions and may cause us to react to complex situations in an overly simplistic manner.

In decision making, frames determine who should participate; how the decision or question is formulated; what principles, values, and standards are applicable; what information is relevant; what is at stake; what the range of acceptable outcomes is; and how we should treat one another.

The main task of the framing step is to consider alternative ways to define the problem or structure the question, both at the beginning and throughout the decision-making process. Key framing questions include the following:

- What kind of decision is this?
- What assumptions are we making?
- What boundaries are we putting on this question?
- Who are the people involved?

Specific framing activities might include

- periodically stepping back during the decision process and asking if we have the question, issue, or problem framed well;

- consulting with possible stakeholders about ways to frame the issue;
- listing three to five ways to ask the question; and
- soliciting feedback from key people about the best way to approach the problem.

Naming and Clarifying: Do I Understand What Is Important to Me and to Others in This Issue?

The real brainstorming part of the process involves identifying the interests and values held by stakeholders. The goal of this step is to generate a comprehensive list of values described in everyday language, avoiding jargon. Questions that prompt useful values answers include the following:

- What really matters in this issue?
- What is important here that we need to consider?
- What do you think our duties and obligations are in this situation?
- What worries you about this issue?
- When we look back on this decision one year from now, how will we know we did the right thing?
- If your teenager were watching us make this decision and asked why we did it, what would you say to them?

In the Paradise Hills Medical Center case, answers to the question "What is important?" might include (1) that Paradise Hills protect its good reputation; (2) that quality care and patient safety remain paramount; (3) that past, current, and future patients and families be able to trust the healthcare professionals at Paradise Hills; (4) that the hospital enjoy a strong economic position in the local healthcare community; and (5) that physicians honor their fiduciary duties to patients.

As values are named, others need to understand what they mean to the holder. Frequently, our stated values are merely the visible tip of their much larger meaning. Listening well—not merely waiting to speak—is essential. Skills for avoiding "serial monologues" and creating dialogue include

- "reflecting back" one's understanding of someone's stated values;
- avoiding jargon by finding fresh ways to express values; and
- using the services of a facilitator to ensure a full, fair, and productive discussion.

When an individual's position is honored and allowed to take root in open dialogue, the health of the decision-making process is enhanced. Meanings are clarified, and participants feel they have been heard and may even be willing to let go of certain strong positions that might otherwise impede agreement. Even when full consensus is not possible or is not the goal, comprehensive naming and thorough clarification are necessary for decisions to last.

Weighing: What Do I and Others Think Is the Relative Importance of the Values Involved?

A comprehensive list of interests and values is usually too long to be fully and equally honored. For example, profit, fiduciary responsibility, quality and safety, public reputation, professional autonomy, organizational mission, and increased market share are not entirely compatible. The question thus becomes: If we cannot equally honor all these important interests, which are the most important? Put another way: If we do nothing else, we must make certain that _____ (fill in the value).

Values can be weighed and prioritized in several ways. Sometimes an "advocacy round" helps. Each participant speaks, briefly but strongly, to the value they think is most important. Other techniques include multiple voting, weighted multiple voting, and rank ordering. The rule of thumb is always to use a method that fits the situation. Patterns and agreement begin to emerge, at which point—and only at this point—decision options should be considered.

Deciding: What Kind of Action(s) Do I/We Believe Follow from the Driving Values?

This process is not meant to replace full-blown decision-making processes already in use. Rather, it highlights a dimension of decision making that is routinely overlooked in much decision-making theory and practice: the values base. At the point in any decision-making process where alternative options are generated and considered, each option should immediately be tested against the prioritized list of values. The goal is to develop a decision that is genuinely driven—not just "spun" or superficially rationalized—by the identified top values. The coherence between a decision and its stated reasons must be genuine.

Reporting: How Do I Justify the Decision to Others?

Decision makers may feel that they work through many of the steps described so far as a matter of course and that their decisions are strong and sound for that reason. Chances are, however, that the communication of their decisions and the reasons behind them leave something to be desired. People who deserve to know should be informed about the grounds for a decision. First, who actually made the decision? This information should not be communicated by leading with, "It was decided that . . ." How was the decision approached, and who was involved? What did the decision makers struggle with? What was most important in making the final decision? Finally, what is the decision?

Some decision makers prefer the "bottom line" approach, starting with the decision and working backward through the justifying reasons. Others prefer a more contextual or narrative approach that concludes with the decision. The components of a complete report are the same, however, and the common goal is to explain and justify the decision to stakeholders. Consider the two following Decision Summary Forms.

Form 1:
State the decision in direct, simple language. Be clear about who owns the decision.

(I/the executive committee have decided to _____.)

Describe the most important values that drove the decision.

(Ultimately, we believe that _____ and _____ had to drive our final choice.)

Directly address the downside of the decision—that is, what you do not like about it.

(There are some parts of this decision I do not like, such as _____.)

Describe applicable values that could not be honored, and indicate the reasoning behind your judgment that other values were more important in this situation. Address any negative effects of the decision on stakeholders. Pay particular attention to those who were not fully consulted in the decision process.

Form 2:
Describe how you approached the decision. Provide some brief highlights of the decision process—what steps you took, who was at the table, whom you consulted, and what level of time and effort was involved.

(Let me give you a sense of the road we took to get to this decision: _____.)

Be candid about the downside of the decision.

Describe applicable values that could not be honored. Address the negative effects of the decision on the stakeholder.

Describe (using everyday language) the values that drove the decision.
State the decision in direct, simple language. Be clear about who owns the decision.

CONCLUSION

Decisions made with integrity are comprehensive, coherent, and transparent (see exhibit 17.5). First, the decision maker has made a good-faith effort to consider the full range of interests and values (comprehensive). Second, the decision is logically grounded in the values considered to be the driving values—that is, the stated basis for the decision genuinely supports the decision (coherent). Third, the decision maker communicates the decision to those who deserve to hear it in a sincere, forthright manner. The decision maker is willing to stand up and be open and accountable to stakeholders by exposing the reasoning for the decision. Doing so requires a willingness to be tested, questioned, and judged by others (transparent).

This values-based decision-making process rests on certain important assumptions, observations, and hypotheses. All choices and decisions are driven by values—by what matters. Contemporary business approaches to ethics and integrity often focus on avoiding wrongdoing or lawbreaking. Many decisions, however, are not about right versus wrong but rather right versus right (competing "goods"). Decisions are effective and enduring when they are based on clearly identified values, are made efficiently, have the resources and support to be fully implemented, and produce positive results that significantly outweigh the negatives. Durable decisions usually follow thorough dialogue, consultation, and collaboration.

Exhibit 17.5: Triangle Representing Decisions Made with Integrity

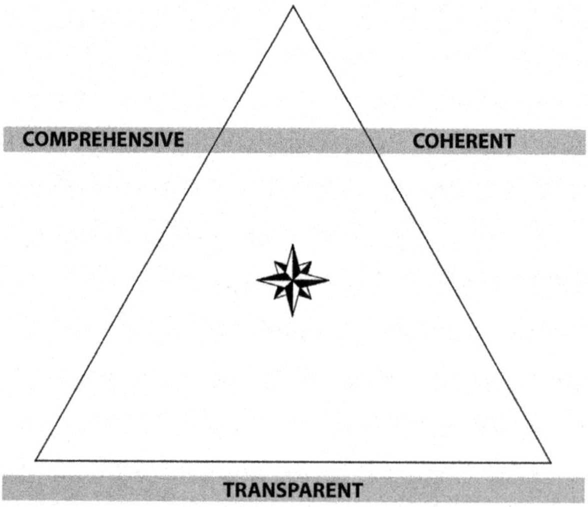

Source: Copyright 2014. Mark Bennett and Joan McIver Gibson. Permission granted to copy and use with attribution.

POSTSCRIPT

The following tool is useful for a "values analysis on the fly"—when time is short but values still must be considered.

1. *Come prepared to speak directly to the values dimension of the decision.*
   - If you know the issue ahead of time, ascertain what frame you bring and what values you think are most important, and be prepared to communicate them.
   - Encourage others to think ahead of time about their frames and values.
   - Create the expectation that this kind of "homework" will be done.
2. *Commit to an advocacy round.*
   - Ask everyone in the room to explain their frame and values.
   - Avoid jargon and encourage ordinary language that captures the values in context.
   - Listen well and check in with people as they explain their values.
   - Record the frames and values where everyone can see and refer to them.
   - Weigh these values for relative importance.
3. *Return to the values list as appropriate.*
   - As issues and options are explored, consider which values each choice honors.
   - Craft decisions that are genuinely driven by the values that are most important in the situation.
4. *Report your values-based decision.*
   - State the decision and name the values that drove it.
   - Acknowledge the values that could not be honored.
   - Explain values priorities.

REFERENCES

Gibson, J. M., and M. Bennett. 2006. *A Field Guide to Good Decisions: Values in Action.* Westport, CT: Praeger.

Josephson Institute. 2009. "Josephson Institute of Ethics Releases Study on High School Character and Adult Conduct: Character Study Reveals Predictors of Lying and Cheating." Press release, October 29. https://josephsoninstitute.org/surveys.

Polanyi, M., and H. Prosch. 1975. *Meaning.* Chicago: University of Chicago Press.

CHAPTER 18

The Ethics of Managing People

Frankie Perry

THE CASES AND ethical dilemmas presented in this book have one thing in common: They all deal with the interrelationships of people and the various values, special interests, and goals that each person brings to the workplace. That the cases involve conflicts, management, and ethical dilemmas should come as no surprise.

The cases presented are illustrative of the myriad interpersonal and professional relationships, diversity issues, external challenges, and management behaviors that predispose an organization to conflicts and ethical dilemmas. The case involving Paradise Hills Medical Center provides an example of the complex relationships that exist between physicians who deliver patient care and administrators who manage the delivery of that care. The Qual Plus HMO case examines the governing board's relationship with top management and probes whether top management does, literally, "serve at the pleasure of the board." Community Medical Center looks at the superior–subordinate relationship and the dynamic of professional power, and University Hospital explores professional relationships and the complexities of interaction with colleagues. Hillside County Medical Center demonstrates the importance of the relationships between management and unions and between management and the medical staff, especially in times of financial crisis. Metropolitan Community Hospital explores the dynamics of physician–nurse relationships and a culturally diverse workforce. Heartland Healthcare System looks at the causes and effects of a lack of interdisciplinary integration, whereas Richland River Valley Healthcare System shows what happens when the roles and responsibilities of governance and management are not clearly defined. Hurley Medical Center serves as a reminder to managers that they have ethical responsibilities to employees as well as to patients, some of which are guaranteed by law. The case of "Baby Charlie" presents the question of whether more effective interpersonal communications and support during a child's tragic illness might have kept the hospital and the child's family out of the courts. From Memorial Medical Center's experience during Hurricane Katrina, we learned that management must have a well-developed preparedness plan in place, staff well trained in how to implement it, and proven, operative clinician wellness programs that mitigate the negative aftereffects of disasters on the caregivers, all well in advance of a disaster. Most important, we learned that safely storing emergency electrical power equipment saves lives when it is needed by patients on life support. The COVID-19 pandemic highlighted the critical role and integration of public health and healthcare delivery and the major importance of information technology (IT) in crisis healthcare management and delivery.

All these cases highlight the importance of ethical practices and interpersonal relationships. Indeed, *management* can be defined as "the art of getting things done through people."

Healthcare managers often find the management of people to be the most difficult part of their jobs. Mastering skills in finance, planning, marketing, information systems, and the like is less difficult for most managers than dealing with the problems and conflicts that people introduce into the work environment. Complicating matters further is the diversity of today's workforce and the varying values, ethics, and cultural perspectives that employees bring to the job. The preponderance of clinicians and other health professionals introduces yet more ambiguities into this environment. Clinicians and professionals typically bring their own codes of conduct to the workplace, and they most often manifest their primary loyalty to their professions and the patients and clients they serve. Although commendable, this approach does not always translate to strong ethical practices in relationships with staff or colleagues. Dual lines of authority in the healthcare setting further complicate the role of the healthcare manager and their management of people. Unsurprisingly, healthcare managers often want to just get the job done without the time-consuming messiness of having to negotiate, motivate, coordinate, evaluate, delegate, educate, and communicate with people.

What does all of this have to do with ethics? Healthcare managers usually are acutely aware of their ethical responsibilities to patients, clients, the organization, and the community. For the most part, they know what business practices are considered ethical. Too often, however, they overlook their ethical responsibilities to the people they manage. They may give lip service to the concepts of justice, honesty, loyalty, and fairness but do not necessarily apply these concepts in their day-to-day management of the people who report to them.

Successful executives use practical strategies to reinforce and routinize ethical principles in the daily management of people. Ethical principles need to be integrated into management practices relating to management style, role modeling, and culture; recruitment and hiring practices; performance evaluations; conflicts in the workplace; team building; mentoring and staff development; employee communications; workforce diversity and inclusion; unions; firing practices; and the provision of references. These areas will provide the framework for this chapter.

Some readers may think, "This all has merit, but isn't this stuff the responsibility of human resources? Isn't my time better spent focusing on the financial viability and competitive advantage of the organization?" Smart managers know that, by ethically managing their people, they will be doing just that. Management must never lose sight of the fact that it is the people in the workforce who actually "deliver" the healthcare, and it is the people who ultimately fulfill the mission of the organization. A management consultant imparted this pure bit of wisdom: "With a bad boss, there are no good jobs. With a good boss, there are no bad jobs" (Dauten and O'Donnell 2019).

MANAGEMENT STYLE, ROLE MODELING, AND CULTURE

Healthcare managers at any level in the organization have control over a certain sphere of influence. Many managers would undoubtedly be surprised at how their personal management style and the ethical standards practiced in their area of responsibility (no matter how large or small) affect the organization as a whole.

The way employees within a department relate to other departments often determines whether projects are completed on time and within budget. The ways employees relate to one another within a department and with others throughout the organization set the tone for how employees relate to patients, clients, and customers. A departmental culture that encourages ethical behavior and civility among coworkers contributes greatly to a corporate culture that expects those same standards. Each manager must nurture such a culture in their sphere of influence. Although top management in an organization largely dictates the tenor and standards of the corporate culture, any department manager who abdicates responsibility in this matter is being naive and irresponsible.

In departments and programs with a strong ethical culture, managers have clearly defined expectations for the ethical conduct of their staff and serve visibly as role models of these prescribed standards. The effect of culture on ethical behavior must not be underestimated. A National Business Ethics Survey spanning more than ten years reported that "organizational culture was more influential in strengthening ethical behavior" than were ethics training, compliance programs, and the like (Gilbert 2013, 60). According to a more recent global survey by the Ethics and Compliance Initiative (ECI 2023), employees in cultures identified as "weak" were "much less likely to seek guidance from others when they were unsure of what ethical action to take"; they were also "less likely to state that they are prepared to handle situations that could lead to ethics violations."

The work environment helps create the organizational culture. Healthcare managers have an ethical obligation to create a safe work environment that fosters ethical behavior and is free from harassment and coercion—especially coercion to perform illegal or unethical acts. The work environment must also be free of discrimination of any kind. Management should ensure fair compensation for work done, equitable opportunity for advancement, and honest and fair performance appraisals and rewards, using the same standards for all employees. Consistency in the fair treatment of employees is both an ethical and a legal requirement.

Ethical healthcare managers are committed to the implementation of programs that assist employees in times of need and provide confidential mechanisms for the reporting of grievances. Leaders should be willing to confront difficult issues head-on—for instance, by providing treatment or referral in an instance of employee impairment or ensuring swift disciplinary action for a case of sexual harassment.

An especially troublesome problem is workplace negativity, which can be insidious, contagious, and extremely detrimental to the organization if not recognized and addressed early on. A negative working environment can lead to poor morale, high staff turnover, accidents, and—worst of all—medical errors and patient and family complaints. Topchik (2013) lists five causes of negativity in the workplace:

1. Poorly implemented change
2. Punishment of excellent performers (by giving them more work) and reward of poor performers (by giving them less)
3. Lack of a learning environment
4. Challenges to security or stability
5. Inappropriate motivational strategies

Most of these causes of negativity can be addressed through strong, effective employee communications and fair human resources practices.

When scarce resources threaten the fiscal viability of a healthcare organization, some executives look to workforce reduction as the only quick fix to the bottom line. Because hospitals are particularly labor-intensive organizations, downsizing may make financial sense; the ethical implications, however, warrant caution. The healthcare organization that achieves financial stability at the expense of its employees is not likely to enjoy long-term success. Employee burnout and unsafe patient care are significant risks. When legitimate workforce reductions are needed, as in the event of a merger, management's communications with employees should allow time for affected employees to adjust to new personal circumstances.

Furthermore, in times of financial crisis, an ethical healthcare executive will think twice before accepting a substantial bonus or salary increase in the face of massive employee layoffs. During the 2008 recession, a number of Wall Street executives faced criticism for taking bonuses while their companies went bankrupt. Asked whether ethics in the banking industry were worse today than in the past, economist Paul Volcker left no doubt: "[In the past] you didn't have these huge compensation practices, bonuses were not considered appropriate, people didn't raid each other for talent. . . . There has been a loss of discipline about what is right and natural and ethical" (Gelb 2012).

Renowned management consultant and author Peter Drucker has long cautioned against excessive executive compensation. He recommended that CEO salaries be no more than 20 times the salary of the company's average worker (Wartzman 2008); any more, he said, will undermine morale and make teamwork difficult. Some CEO salaries today are more than 300 times that of the average worker in the company. In the context of healthcare, CEO salaries should be evaluated in comparison to the average nurse in the organization. Drucker regarded excessive CEO compensation and bonuses during layoffs as "morally unforgivable" (Wartzman 2008).

Outsourcing is yet another practice that requires careful analysis, particularly if it is aimed at achieving cost savings through the use of "cheap labor," with low wages, no benefits, and poor working conditions. A number of US corporations have faced criticism for outsourcing jobs to overseas sweatshops, and their public image has suffered as a result.

Whether a healthcare executive practices participative management, continuous quality improvement, management by objectives, management by walking around, or whatever the latest trend is, the importance of honesty, justice, loyalty, and fair play does not change. As seasoned executives know, a manager most often uses a hybrid of styles. Some situations call for participation, others for a "benevolent dictator." Seasoned executives also know that managers must be adaptable, because not all employees respond alike to the same management style. Research has suggested that effective managers—those who get the results they want—have learned to use different styles strategically at different times.

Effective managers have a high level of emotional intelligence, which Goleman (2000, 80) defines as "the ability to manage ourselves and our relationships effectively." As described by Goleman, emotional intelligence "consists of four fundamental capabilities: self-awareness, self-management, social awareness, and social skill." Key elements of self-awareness include an understanding of your own emotions and their impact on others, an honest self-assessment of one's strengths and limitations, and a willingness to work at improvement. Key elements of self-management include self-control, consistent honesty and integrity, and adaptability to change. Key elements of social awareness include empathy, the ability to read the organization and navigate politics, and a service orientation. Key elements of social skill include the ability to develop and inspire others, communications and conflict management skills, and relationship-building expertise (Goleman 2000). In a National Public Radio (NPR 2014) interview, Goleman said that, although academic intelligence may predict the job you can get, emotional intelligence predicts the job you can hold. Given the large number of ethical violations that reflect hedonism, an emphasis on self-discipline might be wise.

Although the management styles used with each employee may vary, an ethical manager will make certain that performance expectations and appraisals, compensation, discipline, promotion, and educational opportunities are consistent across the board. Experienced managers know that favoritism, predictably, leads to staff dissension and a loss of respect and effectiveness for the manager. Above all, employees want to be treated fairly and honestly.

Equitable treatment can be especially challenging in situations that call for disciplinary action aimed at outstanding employees who are well liked by the manager. Disciplining such high performers is hard, but failing to do so adversely affects staff morale, productivity, and teamwork; ultimately, it lowers the bar for standards of conduct for all employees. Applying different standards to different employees may also set the stage for litigation, if inconsistent discipline is applied in similar situations.

Micromanagement should be avoided. If performance expectations are adequately explained and the necessary skills taught, managers can expect employees to function satisfactorily with appropriate supervision and accountability. If an employee is unable to perform, the manager may arrange for counseling or additional training; in some cases, a probationary period or reassignment to another position may be more appropriate. Micromanagement over an extended period can be detrimental to the employee and counterproductive for the manager. A micromanaged employee, knowing that the manager will be closely reviewing all aspects of their work, might lose interest in improving and abdicate responsibility for the work product. Over time, the employee might become a victim of learned helplessness and suffer an erosion of confidence, motivation, and productivity. The manager's productivity may suffer as well, as the time and effort they spend micromanaging could be better spent on other duties.

Personnel policies—whether corporate or departmental—should be constructive, not punitive. They should be developed with the goal of motivating all employees and improving work performance. They should not just be oriented toward poor performers, rule breaking, and disciplinary action.

Effective leaders insist on programs that reward accomplishments in line with organizational goals and that recognize individuals, teams, and the employee population as a whole. Enlightened leaders invest in the surveys and conversations to learn what recognition programs and celebrations have value among their employees (Perry 2012). Haden (2012) lists four rewards that are more powerful than money:

1. Asking employees for ideas on how to do their job better
2. Asking for help in solving a problem
3. Creating short-term, informal leadership roles to solve a problem
4. Teaming up—taking on a task or education session together

Although employees, clinicians, and management staff may be motivated by different things, three general truths about human nature remain constant (Perry 2012):

1. The workplace is a social setting. People want to enjoy work and to look forward to coming to the workplace each day.
2. Most people want to do a good job (those who do not should be fired or reassigned), and they want recognition, public or private, for a job well done.
3. People want their opinions about work to be solicited and valued.

Effective leaders motivate people to rise to their full potential and to the level of performance needed for organizational success. Bennis (1999, 189) states: "Management is getting people to do what needs to be done. Leadership is getting people to want to do what needs to be done."

Above all, a wise manager never underestimates the power of example. Ethical managers consistently practice the standards of conduct they expect employees to emulate. Employees and staff look to management to show what behavior is acceptable and what is valued. The actions that a manager takes or does not take on a day-to-day basis are considered the behavioral norm.

A wise physician healthcare executive made an astute observation about the redeeming value of professionalism, and it bears repeating here (Gomez 2018):

Professionalism is not a specific skill, nor is it granted when [one] graduates from medical school, a residency or fellowship, or a graduate program in healthcare administration. It does not mean dressing nicely, and it does not mean speaking in certain ways either. Rather, it is the amalgamation of personal characteristics, learned skills, experiences, and attitudes developed over a period of time that often eludes an exact definition—though often people say "they know it when they see it, they know it when they feel it, or they know it when they are in the presence of it."

Smart healthcare managers will thoughtfully choose as their personal role models those professionals they wish to emulate, and they will work toward that goal knowing that they in turn serve as role models for their staff. An authentic professional—one who embodies the desirable qualities of integrity, trustworthiness, and ethics—is the leader people will want to follow.

RECRUITMENT AND HIRING PRACTICES

Some of the most important decisions a manager will make involve employee hiring. Individuals drive the organization, create the culture, and determine whether the organization succeeds or fails. The task of hiring staff, therefore, needs to be taken extremely seriously. The cost of a bad hiring choice goes beyond just financial terms.

Getting the right people on board will make a manager's job and the achievement of organizational goals much easier. Collins (2001, 41) says that "executives who ignited the transformations from good to great [companies] did not first figure out where to drive the bus and then get people to take it there . . . they first got the right people on the bus (and the wrong people off the bus) and then figured out where to drive it." Inexperienced managers sometimes look to hire staff who are easy to control. Perhaps they are afraid to hire someone smarter than they are, lest they lose full authority. Experienced managers, however, know they need to fill key positions with bright individuals who bring needed skills, knowledge, and talents. Even more important, they seek out prospective recruits who possess integrity and strong character. Knowledge and skills are much easier to teach than integrity and character.

Managers often look for new employees who they believe will fit well in the organization and get along with others. Equally important is that the employees have a positive attitude about work and life in general. That kind of attitude will translate well into the employee's interactions with patients and with other departments in the organization. Positive employees of strong character contribute greatly to productivity, morale, and an ethical work environment.

Of course, a manager might not always be able to intuit or even observe all these attributes during an interview. For this reason, interviews, whenever appropriate, should be conducted by teams, and the teams should ask the candidates similar questions and allow them to answer expansively. Interviewers can present candidates with scenarios that include subtle ethical dilemmas and ask the candidates how they might respond. Many interviewers today favor these types of "experiential" questions, as opposed to the more traditional questions that a candidate might have practiced answers for. According to Hofmann (2017), such questions can provide insights into a candidate's "moral compass" and help determine the candidate's fit with the organizational culture.

Hofmann (2017, 48) suggests using such questions as the following:

- "What do you like most/least about your current position?"
- "Give me examples of two or three management mistakes you have made, and share what you learned from them."
- "Can you describe a couple of ethical dilemmas you have encountered and how you dealt with them?"

Mayer and Cates (2014, 197) state that "the hiring of a new employee may be the most expensive decision you ever make." Therefore, they believe "the central focus of hiring right [is] to check the qualities as closely as you check the qualifications" (Mayer and Cates 2014, 198). In differentiating between the two concepts, the authors explain that "qualifications" consist of such things as employment experience, education, credentials, computer skills, and intelligence, whereas "qualities" include honor, ethics, attitude, credibility, integrity, and customer skills. Mayer and Cates argue that managers must hire for customer service. Their recommended interview questions include the following (Mayer and Cates 2014, 197):

- "Have you ever had a patient who was really angry? How did you deal with that?"
- "When you have patients with unrealistic expectations, what do you say to them?"
- "If one of your direct reports tells you she has 'had it with all the complainers,' what advice do you give her?"

This kind of focus on customer service certainly makes sense in healthcare, where organizations exist to serve patients, clients, and communities.

When interviewing candidates, the hiring authority must pay attention to resumes and applications. Although the human resources staff may be primarily responsible for checking education, licensure, certifications, and the like, the managers responsible for hiring decisions must make sure that these qualifications have been verified. Attendance at a university does not mean that a degree was granted. A certification or license that has not been renewed may no longer be valid. A candidate's embellishment on a resume may be symptomatic of a major character flaw.

Russell and Greenspan (2005, 85–86) state that "hiring the right person to do the job is a challenge" but that "an even more difficult decision [is] to replace an existing staff member who is unable to do well the job that she was hired to do." They continue: "The biggest mistake managers consistently make is to recognize that they have the wrong person in a key position and fail to do something about it." Replacing an ineffective employee is especially difficult if the manager has strongly advocated for the employee or boosted salary and benefits as part of the recruitment effort. Hofmann (2017, 51) says that "the financial and nonfinancial costs of making a poor hiring decision are always higher than expected." Taking sufficient care in making a right hiring decision will serve management and the organization well.

When interviewing potential employees, the manager has an ethical responsibility to be honest and candid about the organization, its financial status (if appropriate), salary, benefits, job security, corporate culture, expectations of the position, and so forth. Employment is an implied contract, if not a written one, and neither party should experience any surprises. In the case of a top management position, the candidate may be relocating and making a substantial financial commitment for themself and their family. Withholding the fact that the position might be short term is unfair and dishonest, to say the least.

Another area of ethical ambiguity in recruitment involves salary inequities. A manager may offer a candidate a higher salary to join the organization than what the organization is paying an existing employee working in the same capacity. Often justified as a recruitment strategy, this practice raises questions of fairness, loyalty, and justice.

If qualified, existing employees should be allowed to apply for any promotion or other opening that occurs in the organization, and internal candidates should be given fair and equal consideration. If an internal candidate is not offered the available position, an explanation should be provided so that the person can identify performance areas to be strengthened or developed.

Pruitt (2017) states that hiring is "one of the more complex parts" of management and that "mis-hires" happen. He strongly favors probationary periods for just this reason. Pruitt stresses that management has a responsibility to ensure that new employees have clear expectations of the job and receive proper orientation and training in their new organizational environment. If problems persist even after the training, management may have to reconsider the hire. If the new hire is a good cultural fit for the organization but lacks the skills for the particular job, perhaps more training or a shift to a different position will help. But if neither of those options is appropriate, prolonging the new hire's departure is not fair to the organization or to the individual (Pruitt 2017).

Katz (2017) warns of some common hiring mistakes that can be costly both in the short term and in the long term:

- Hiring someone who may be brilliant but who lacks interpersonal skills can be detrimental to the team, as well as to patients or clients.
- Hiring people because they seem just like you rarely brings additional value to the organization.
- Valuing blind loyalty over trust can lead to situations where you can count on employees to do what they think you want them to do, but not necessarily to do the right thing.
- Replacing people too quickly might be tempting, but smart managers will take time to reassess the position to see if change is needed.
- Ignoring your intuitive feelings about a candidate is risky.

When in doubt, check references again, and ask others to interview the candidate. Be safe now rather than sorry later (Katz 2017).

A word about job descriptions is appropriate here. Unfortunately, job descriptions are often viewed as a necessary bureaucratic requirement when they can, in fact, be a valuable management tool. Job descriptions can be useful in recruiting and advertising for a position, and they can serve as helpful visual aids when hiring and interviewing candidates. They are beneficial and effective tools in appraising performance and, when necessary, in justifying termination of employment. They are also functional in helping to determine compensation. To accomplish these many tasks, job descriptions must be clear, accurate, and current, and they must reflect the values, mission, and goals of the organization. The responsibilities specified in the job description need to be measurable, so that managers can determine whether they have been met. Managers must carefully review and approve job descriptions; they should not just consider the descriptions a "hand me down" from human resources or delegate the responsibility elsewhere.

THE "GREAT RESIGNATION"

The recent COVID-19 pandemic has had a devastating impact on healthcare staffing, and the results are evident in its damaging toll on organizations, on employees, and—most alarming—on patients. Douglas Brown, president of UMass Memorial Community Hospitals, put it bluntly: "We're going through the worst staffing crisis in our history" (Schoenberg 2021). Healthcare management has an ethical responsibility to the patients they serve and to the workforce they manage to commit serious energy and resources to effectively deal with this crisis.

There are no simple answers for this alarming development. It is a complex issue that requires more than a few solutions. While some media accounts have placed blame for these staff shortages on vaccine mandates, many hospital officials say this staffing crisis is more the result of "burnout, retirements, a lack of traveling nurses, and high patient demand." Officials say they believe that the benefit of a vaccine mandate outweighs the cost in lost staff time to illness. They point to pandemic-associated burnout and a staffing model that did not account for large numbers of nurses being out sick and many nurses leaving the industry entirely or switching from hospital to agency work, where they can get more flexible shifts for higher pay, as causative factors of staff shortages. Not to be overlooked is that healthcare demand is extraordinarily high, both as a result of COVID-19 and because of patients who deferred care earlier in the pandemic and now are sicker (Schoenberg 2021).

In his article "How to Face the Great Resignation," physician Paul DeChant reports that since 2020, "18% of healthcare workers have quit their jobs and a number of surveys indicate anywhere from 20 to 50% of doctors and nurses are saying they're ready to quit within the next year" (DeChant 2023).

DeChant tells us we may be too quick to blame this "great resignation" on the pandemic. He argues that doctors and nurses are simply burned out and have been since long before the COVID-19 crisis. He attributes this burnout to the six drivers described by Christina Maslach, who developed the Maslach Burnout Inventory in 1981 (Maslach and Leiter 2021). The six drivers are the following (DeChant 2023):

1. **Insufficient Reward:** The ability to be in control and professional recognition
2. **Breakdown of Community:** Focus on computers rather than interaction with colleagues
3. **Absence of Fairness:** Discrimination based on gender, race, or country of origin
4. **Conflicting Values:** Personal values in conflict with organization's need to keep costs down or comply with insurance guidelines
5. **Work Overload:** Time-pressured environments with too much to do; information overload
6. **Lack of Control:** Loss of ability to make independent decisions

The COVID-19 pandemic exacerbated all six drivers to further increase burnout among physicians and nurses and develop what some observers have labeled "pandemic fatigue." Hospitals soon became overcrowded, and many reached capacities and had to convert ancillary space into patient units. Overworked physicians soon had to make morally challenging crisis-of-care decisions such as which patients would get limited life-support equipment. Patients in isolation were dying alone. Physicians and nurses were exposed to infection, especially when personal protective equipment became scarce. The healthcare environment soon became overstressed, and physicians and nurses became targets of criticism from unhappy patients or family members. Incidents of workplace violence occurred, and workplace safety became a frightening issue.

In addition to the pandemic-associated physical and mental fatigue experienced at work, healthcare workers often agonized about the health and safety of their families, especially about their young children homebound as the pandemic forced the closure of day care centers and schools.

As the pandemic raged and the work environment became more stressful, many baby boomers (people born between 1946 and 1964) who were near retirement age simply decided to retire earlier than they had planned. These early retirements exacerbated the preexisting staffing crisis.

To alleviate the longer-term staffing crisis, healthcare leadership needs to more closely examine the contributing causes of the crisis and develop better recruitment and retention strategies, as discussed in the sections that follow.

Short-Term Management Strategies

Management strategies to address and prevent the clinician burnout that fuels the staffing crisis are critical and must be multifaceted. Some strategies require little more than management paying attention to physicians and nurses and letting them know they are appreciated by being visible where they work and providing them with the support they need.

Many healthcare organizations are "throwing money at the staffing crisis" in an attempt to meet the patient demand and the great exodus of clinical staff. In their desperation to recruit nursing staff, many hospitals are offering flexible hours, signing bonuses, and payment for relocation expenses, which has sometimes resulted in a "bidding war" among hospitals. One retired nurse recently received two personalized recruitment e-mails the same day: one from her local hospital offering a $12,000 signing bonus, the other from a neighboring state offering a $75,000 signing bonus and relocation expenses. (The irony here is that this nurse is 88 years old.)

Other short-term management strategies include the use of travel nurses, but this strategy presents both an ethical and an economic dilemma for the hospital. While there is a compensation gap between hospital-employed and travel nurses, hospitals can ill afford to pay staff nurses the equivalent wage. For this reason, some staff nurses are resigning to opt for travel nursing, compounding the staff shortage at the institution they leave. Some healthcare systems are introducing their own internal travel agency programs in an attempt to combat the nursing shortage, recruit back their staff nurses, and reduce competition rates from external travel agencies (Chervoni-Knapp 2022).

Some healthcare organizations have also begun to offer retention bonuses to permanent nursing staff and incentive payments to healthcare professionals working in areas considered high risk, such as COVID-19 units (Chervoni-Knapp 2022).

Clinician Health and Wellness Programs

Other retention strategies require more planning and resources but promise greater long-term benefit to the organization. Initiatives such as clinician health and wellness programs that are explicitly designed for physicians and nurses can be highly effective in the recruitment and retention of physicians and nurses, improve the quality of patient care, and contribute to an ethical, productive organizational culture.

A prominent internal medicine physician at a university medical center was the personal physician to a large number of the medical staff. Recently, she found herself treating so many physicians for anxiety, depression, and physical symptoms of burnout in her private practice that she convinced the university to commit resources to a comprehensive physician health and wellness program that she helped design especially for physicians. Because it is physician driven, it has drawn wide participation by the medical staff.

One of the barriers to employee participation in employee wellness programs is the stigma attached with the admission that healthcare workers are unable to handle the stresses of the job without professional help. This is especially true in cases of mental wellness. Some state licensing laws require that healthcare professionals report all incidence of mental illness. As a result, many avoid seeking any treatment at all.

Trinity Health in Minot, North Dakota, has found a way to overcome this barrier. They found that digital therapeutics can be effective in providing confidential support to employees suffering from such mental health conditions as burnout fatigue, depression, and anxiety. Leadership knew they must address any stigma associated with mental health issues by speaking openly to their employees about this new technology and its easy access, confidentiality, and on-demand treatment value in addressing depression and problem drinking. It was also important that healthcare professionals, knowledgeable about the field, be made aware that digital therapeutics are held to the same regulatory standards as traditional medical treatments. To make it even more accessible, at Trinity, digital therapeutics are offered at no charge to all employees and their dependents. Employees have the option of signing up for digital therapeutics at home, using their personal e-mail to further ensure confidentiality. Although only limited data are available at this point, members of the Trinity leadership have received direct positive feedback from employee users of the program (Kutch 2022).

Other Innovative Strategies

As in all situations where management is attempting to solve a problem, the first step is to conduct a root cause analysis. In this staffing crisis, that means talking to clinical staff before the exit interview stage and finding out and modifying the job dissatisfiers to prevent staff decisions to resign. For example:

- It is no secret that physicians and nurses complain about time-consuming administrative duties that are not directly related to patient care imposed by inappropriate rules and regulations. Can these be modified or delegated elsewhere?
- Long hours, heavy patient caseloads, and physical and mental fatigue are real problems. Ideas for real solutions may come from the staff experiencing these problems. What about flex work—that is, part-time remote and part-time at work?
- Could childcare be offered for the children of physicians and nurses? Some hospital systems are committing sizable resources to build privately owned and operated childcare centers for their staff.
- How about partnering with educational institutions from high schools, community colleges, trade schools, and universities to promote and recruit candidates into healthcare careers? And offering internships and apprenticeship programs to students?
- Some existing staff may be interested in clinical training programs. If the organization offers tuition reimbursement for such programs, why not promote it? If it's not a current benefit, consider adding it?
- How about working with the US military to recruit their healthcare-trained personnel who are transitioning to civilian life?
- Many hospitals are expanding their use of physician assistants and advanced practice nurses to better support their medical staff and meet less critical patient needs. Would this be a viable option?

This is not the first healthcare staffing crisis in the United States. What can be learned from those in the past? A retired nurse recalls her experience during the 1950s nursing shortage. She was a young mother who opted to remain unemployed to care for her four young children. The local hospital called her repeatedly in an attempt to recruit her. Each time, she declined. Finally, when the hospital nursing office called and said she could work any shift she wanted on any patient unit she wanted, she responded, thinking it would be impossible, "How about 8:00 at night until 4:00 in the morning?" The hospital representative immediately replied, "Okay," and asked where she would like to work. She then told them she would work anywhere they needed her except pediatrics! She asked for those hours so she could put her children to bed and be home before they awoke; her husband would be home from work then and available to them overnight.

About this same time there was a national effort to train and license "practical nurses," and licensed practical nurses, or LPNs, became a vital staple in hospitals. Our retired nurse tells us that in the 1950s, many hospitals staffed entire patient care floors with LPNs, except for two registered nurses (RNs) in supervisory roles: the first RN as charge nurse and the second RN as medicine nurse.

During the 1950s physician shortage, to save time for the busiest of physicians, a medical transcriptionist accompanied the physician on rounds and took dictated notes as the physician examined the patient and then transcribed the notes on patients' charts for the physician to review. This program was especially popular with surgeons.

During the 1950s, the medical staff were directly involved in nurse recruitment and training. Physicians headed up many of the LPN training programs and actively participated in nurse recruitment. When our aforementioned retired nurse asked where the hospital got her name to call, she was told that a physician who had worked with her knew she had quit to have children.

Yet today's postpandemic staffing crisis is unsurpassed, owing to advances in medicine, technology, globalization, and new contagious organisms. This crisis is much more severe, so the solutions must be comprehensive and successful.

Healthcare management must take a leadership role in seeking out proven "best practices" in the recruitment and retention of their clinical staff. Through their professional organizations, they must advocate for community support to improve the working conditions of healthcare workers, and they must work with physicians and nurses to develop innovative solutions to the staffing crisis that will have benefits lasting well into the future.

PERFORMANCE EVALUATIONS

Ethical organizations give employees clear, accurate, and current job descriptions and a thorough explanation of what is expected from them in their position. In addition, the organizations provide employees with the resources they need to satisfactorily perform the job, including knowledge and skills development.

Ethical healthcare managers further ensure a working environment that properly uses the skills and abilities of each employee. Finally, ethical managers provide their employees with fair, honest, constructive performance evaluation on an ongoing basis—not just at an annual performance evaluation. In the parlance of educators, ethical managers need to take advantage of day-to-day "teaching moments" to help develop employee knowledge and skills and improve employee job performance. Holding back potentially constructive feedback and then "blindsiding" employees with criticism at an annual performance review is unfair.

So when did annual performance reviews become the norm? The idea originated with a Harvard professor in the 1930s and became more firmly established in the 1950s, when the federal Performance Rating Act mandated annual performance reviews for federal employees. Soon after, employee compensation became tied to these annual reviews (Suddath 2013).

At this point, annual performance reviews might seem firmly entrenched, but a number of business experts have criticized their many flaws and even recommended their complete abolition (Suddath 2013). Too often, they say, annual performance reviews criticize employees based on nebulous, unmeasurable characteristics, such as initiative or attitude, instead of just looking at the accomplishment of specific goals. Furthermore, critics argue that annual reviews are too infrequent and tend to evaluate employees on a curve that automatically labels some individuals as poor performers. Some critics even suggest that annual reviews are often used simply to produce documentation in support of firing an employee. Suddath (2013) reports: "A 1997 national survey by the Society for Human Resource Management found that only 5 percent of employees were satisfied (42 percent were dissatisfied) with their companies' review process. Even those who should be its champion—HR [human resources] departments—can barely muster enthusiasm. A 2010 Sibson Consulting study found that 58 percent of HR managers dislike their own review systems."

When conducted correctly and for the benefit of employees, performance evaluations have much merit. The teaching and development provided through regularly scheduled performance evaluations are an important part of the manager's role and responsibility to each employee. Some managers may procrastinate with this task because they feel uncomfortable discussing areas where the employee needs to improve. However, late performance evaluations—especially those that delay salary increases—will only make employees think that management is indifferent to their needs and places little value on their contributions. Delayed evaluations are also unfair to the employee, who may want prompt guidance on how to develop skills and improve performance. Most people want to do a good job and need clear direction about what is required and expected of them. Managers who assume that employees always know what is expected of them and how to do it may be doing themselves and their employees a disservice.

Managers who wish to nurture an ethical culture should reward ethical conduct and remedy questionable behaviors as part of the performance evaluation. The evaluation is also an opportunity for discussion of innovations and new ideas for problem solving. Most employees, regardless of their position, are interested in developing new skills and knowledge that can help further their careers. Smart managers will use performance reviews to create realistic growth plans that build on the employees' interests and expand their responsibilities. This practice can help foster a learning organization and cultivate a high-performance culture.

As mentioned earlier in this chapter, probationary periods for newly hired employees can benefit both the organization and the employee. Periodic performance reviews during the probationary period can help the employee to adjust and the manager to assess what training is needed. Probationary periods give the organization ample time to ensure that the new employee is working out and meeting the expectations of the job, and they give employees the opportunity to clarify what is expected and to ask for resources if needed.

Performance evaluations are a critical element of merit-based pay systems, also known as pay for performance, that are used at many organizations, especially those that practice management by objectives. Merit-based pay relies on a set of goals or objectives set by the employer, and the accomplishment of these goals serves as the basis for performance evaluation and compensation increases or bonuses.

Critics of merit-based pay often say that it "favors revenue generators" (Kumar 2015). They note that people working "behind the scenes" in an organization's cost centers (e.g., manufacturing, accounting, legal) create the foundation that makes revenue generation possible but rarely benefit to the same extent as those working "up front" to increase business revenue. Critics also say that merit-based pay "discriminates against the average worker" because, typically, people at the management level receive the bonuses for the work done by employees. Critics have also argued that using merit-based pay as the primary mechanism to motivate and reward employees "creates unhealthy competition" among coworkers (Kumar 2015). Not to be ignored is the resentment and distrust of management that can develop when employees receive small increases and the bosses receive large bonuses.

Pay for performance can prove to be an obstacle course if not appropriately implemented and managed. (The widely publicized scandal at Wells Fargo, described in the next section, highlights some of the potential risks.) Above all, the goal-setting process must be fair to the employee and beneficial to the organization. A company can have ambitious "stretch goals," but the goals must be attainable with effort. Some goals can emphasize the broader employee participation in organizational accomplishment, thereby promoting teamwork. Depending on the position of the employee, a mix of personal and organizational goals may be appropriate.

Finally, an ethical manager is aware that employees garner pay *for* work (i.e., salary) as well as pay *from* work (e.g., self-esteem, respect, a sense of contribution). Skilled managers seek to identify what activities provide gratification to each employee, and they attempt to distribute assignments accordingly. Although all employees must perform their fair share of less pleasant tasks, they will tackle those tasks with more enthusiasm if they know that gratifying assignments will come later.

The Wells Fargo Case

Around 2014, senior management at Wells Fargo learned that some employees at the company had been creating sham bank accounts and credit cards for their customers in an attempt to meet their demanding sales goals. The company soon initiated efforts to eliminate this illegal practice, instructing employees not to "create fake bank accounts in the name of unsuspecting clients" and firing employees found to be guilty of the practice (Corkery and Cowley 2016). Nonetheless, some three years after the first case, the practice continued. Former employees said the illegal activity continued to be a result of the exacting sales goals applied by Wells Fargo's management.

Wells Fargo executives maintained that the illegal activities were not the result of "a flawed incentive structure or an aggressive sales culture" and instead blamed employees for "misinterpreting" the goals (Corkery and Cowley 2016). Former employees disagreed, however, suggesting that the company had a "relentless push to meet sales goals that many considered unrealistic." Employees feared they would lose their jobs if they did not meet their sales goals, and they believed that the sales goals were not attainable in any legitimate way. Furthermore, employees resented the gross inequities in compensation that came as a result of the unreasonable goals. A series of YouTube videos expressed the prevailing cynicism among employees: "If [we] make those sales numbers each day, at the end of the month everybody in the branch will get a $5 gift card to McDonald's. The district manager will get a $10,000 cash bonus" (Corkery and Cowley 2016). Many speculated that management did not exercise due diligence in ferreting out and eliminating the illegal practices because of the personal financial rewards accrued to them as a result.

Once federal regulators moved in, the consequences were swift, harsh, and long term. Wells Fargo was found guilty of fraud. In 2016, it faced a

$185 million civil settlement, more than 5,300 employees were fired, and the CEO was forced to retire (Corkery and Cowley 2016). In 2018, Wells Fargo agreed to a $575 million settlement to all 50 US states for claims resulting from the 2016 exposure of its illegal activities (Levitt 2018). By 2019, federal regulators had 14 legal agreements restricting Wells Fargo activities, and the company once again faced the abrupt resignation of its CEO (Fitter and Cowley 2019).

Certainly, lessons can be learned here. In an ethical culture, the standards of ethical and legal conduct should be well known and practiced throughout the organization, from the top down. Any behavior that falls short of those standards should be reported and swiftly disciplined. Furthermore, the organization should have an infrastructure in place to support the ethical culture and to reward ethical behavior. At Wells Fargo, the predominant philosophy seems to have been that "the end justifies the means"; management oversight and accountability were insufficient to correct unethical and illegal behavior.

A key aspect of this case is the mismanagement of the merit-based payment system. To serve as an effective incentive, goals must be attainable and established in consultation with the employee. By all employee accounts, Wells Fargo met neither of those criteria.

MANAGING CONFLICT IN THE WORKPLACE

Conflict in the workplace is inevitable. As experienced managers know, some forms of conflict are valuable to the organization because they help identify problems and produce innovative solutions. Conflict is often related to workforce diversity. Having a variety of knowledge, experiences, values, attitudes, and viewpoints within an organization can lead to disagreements, but it also enhances problem solving. Diverse perspectives can help managers anticipate others' perceptions, as well as the possible unintended consequences of actions under consideration.

Some kinds of conflict, however, can be costly to the organization, whether in terms of employee absenteeism, turnover, productivity, morale, or the organization's reputation as a desirable place to work. Some conflicts can affect patient and client services, and others may even result in litigation. Tragically, in the extreme, conflict among coworkers can precipitate violence in the workplace. A manager may at times become engaged in conflict with coworkers, the boss, patients, clients, or others. More often, however, the manager will have to deal with conflicts among subordinates; managers typically will have the most control over this type of conflict.

The following management features and behaviors can help prevent unwanted conflict and bring about positive outcomes when conflict does occur:

- Clear policies and procedures
- Systems and structures for addressing employee concerns
- Diversity education to help employees understand and appreciate differences in communication or work styles
- Clear delegation of authority and accountability
- Conflict management training
- Informal employee events where employees can get to know one another
- Celebration of team accomplishments
- Performance evaluations that assess an employee's ability to function in a team
- Giving credit where it is due
- Fair and equitable compensation
- Role-modeling of acceptable behavior
- Codes of conduct for staff interactions
- Strong, two-way employee communications
- A hiring process that makes clear that teamwork is part of the job, perhaps through candidate interviews that present conflict scenarios or include such questions as the following:
  —Why did you leave your last job?
  —How did you get along with coworkers?
  —What kind of conflicts have you dealt with?
  —How did you deal with them?

In contrast, the following management behaviors tend to provoke conflicts among subordinates and should be avoided:

- Constant rule changing
- Playing the blame game
- Micromanaging
- Playing favorites
- Putting off addressing unsatisfactory job performance

Managers must also be keenly alert to employee behaviors that are often toxic to a well-functioning work environment; such behaviors should be addressed without delay. Problematic staff members include the following types:

- The condescending, self-righteous employee who must be right at all costs and resists any change unless it is the employee's own idea

- The capable employee who frequently undermines coworkers or the organization
- The naysayer who always has a reason why something will not work
- The dramatic employee who insists on making much ado about nothing
- The gossipmonger who thrives on others' or the organization's misfortunes

Negative employees who are otherwise competent must be made to recognize how their behaviors affect coworkers, damage team productivity, undermine professionalism, and detract from the good work the organization does. Often, these employees are not aware of how others perceive them. Failure to address toxic behaviors can cause significant damage to the corporate culture. Such behaviors can be contagious and, if left unchecked, become the accepted norm.

When conflict occurs, the manager should take a step back and determine whether the conflict is one that needs to be dealt with. Conflicts that disrupt the workplace or involve such issues as bullying, disrespect, sexual harassment, or a hostile work environment require immediate attention. However, not all conflicts need fixing; some will fix themselves. The manager should ask, "Does this conflict really matter? Is it temporary? Will it resolve itself? Do I really have any control over it?" The manager also needs to consider the appropriate level at which conflict resolution should take place. Sometimes, conflicts that should have been resolved at a supervisory level find their way to a higher manager. In such instances, the higher manager may offer advice to the supervisor but should resist personally dealing with the issue, instead returning it to the appropriate level for resolution.

A common characteristic of inexperienced managers is the tendency to avoid conflict altogether. Such a tendency can be dangerous, because the avoidance may give the impression that the manager condones the actions in question. If left unattended, minor conflicts can quickly turn into major ones. Equally dangerous behavior is jumping in too quickly to fix whatever problem might arise. Understandably, managers want things to run smoothly, and they want problems to be solved quickly. Nonetheless, sometimes a manager needs to allow employees the flexibility and freedom to solve the problem themselves.

When a manager determines that action is necessary to help manage a conflict, certain rules of engagement may be helpful. First, the manager should take time to think through how best to deal with the conflict, decide what they want to accomplish or gain by resolving the conflict, and get all the facts. Often, the truth lies somewhere between what one person believes to be true and what another person believes to be true. Once they have all the facts, the manager may wish to seek advice from a trusted colleague. If the conflict is process related, the manager should request a root cause analysis to identify and remedy any process breakdowns. When resolving a conflict between subordinates, the manager must

- remain objective and never take sides;
- address the issues, not the people;
- clarify the roles and responsibilities of those in conflict;
- be flexible and open to ideas;
- look for potential compromise; and
- show those in conflict how they will benefit by resolving the dispute.

After the conflict has been resolved, the manager must encourage those involved to move on and focus on goals.

Failure to recognize and effectively deal with friction in the workplace can heighten tension and stress; negatively affect patient and customer service; and consume time, energy, and resources that would be better put to other uses. In the extreme, it can generate allegations of a hostile work environment.

Rosenberg (2018) describes a number of management strategies for dealing with staff friction. Team-building activities can provide opportunities for coworkers to become better acquainted with one another's personalities. One manager has found success in assembling combative coworkers in a soccer team, to help them learn the benefits of teamwork. Others have found success by focusing on communication. Miscommunication is a common contributor to coworker conflict, particularly in the present era, when e-mail and texts often replace simple conversation. Often, misunderstandings and tension can be avoided if important or complex information is delivered in person or by phone, as opposed to newer technologies (Rosenberg 2018). Management should encourage good communication practices among staff and employees, and also use them itself. If initial strategies fail and staff discord becomes disruptive to the work environment, the manager may need to issue the ultimatum: If coworkers are unable to satisfactorily resolve their differences, they may be subject to transfers or termination of employment.

From time to time, healthcare workers may become involved in conflicts with patients and families. Such conflicts are often exacerbated by the stress experienced by patients and family members dealing with health concerns, as well as by the stress inherent in the day-to-day work of healthcare workers. When staff members are confronted with emotional patients or family members with unrealistic demands, I suggest that they start the conversation with a genuine "I'm sorry"— because, if nothing else, they truly are sorry that the patients or family members have to deal with the present situation. I recommend that they then continue with "Let's see if there is anything we can do about this. . . ." I caution against starting with "The policy is . . ."; such a statement can have the effect of throwing fuel on the fire for an emotionally distraught patient or family member. Calmly talking through the situation and making an effort to understand the rationale for a request can be helpful. Usually (though not always), if the people making the request feel that you are sincerely trying to help, they will feel reassured. Being a good listener is essential. Above all, people want to be heard and taken seriously, even if their requests or demands cannot be accommodated.

ADDRESSING VIOLENCE IN THE WORKPLACE

A webinar titled "Addressing Workplace Violence" was sponsored by the Agency for Healthcare Research and Quality (AHRQ) and presented by the National Action Alliance to Advance Patient Safety and the National Institute for Occupational Safety and Health (NIOSH) in 2023. The exceptionally high number of webinar participants and their engagement with this topic left little doubt of the healthcare management need and desire for knowledge and strategies that address violence in the healthcare workplace.

It was reported during the webinar that workplace violence in US healthcare resulted in 21 homicides and 32 suicides between 2003 and 2016. The majority of victims of violence were reported to be nurses and mental health workers (Menendez 2023). Although comprehensive data beyond those years are not yet available, all experience indicates that the COVID-19 pandemic greatly increased violence within the healthcare sector (Menendez 2023). The US Bureau of Labor Statistics (BLS 2020) stated that "studies indicate that 44% of nurses report experiencing physical violence and 68% report experiencing verbal abuse during the COVID-19 pandemic" and that "health care workers accounted for 73% of all nonfatal workplace injuries and illnesses due to violence in 2018."

These numbers are and should be alarming for an industry that seeks to comfort and cure human ills. Of special note is the number of *suicides* attributed to workplace violence. In response, the American Nurses Association in partnership with state nurses associations offers stress relief courses explicitly designed for nurses. In addition, they offer webinars, books, and articles and host complimentary online town halls on workplace violence (Michigan Nurses Association 2023). Clearly, it is to the healthcare organization's benefit for management to consider clinician wellness programs to be essential additions to employee benefits.

Research has identified hospitals and nursing residential care facilities as the most common healthcare locations to experience violence in the workplace. The most common perpetrators of violence were found to be patients or their family members or coworkers. These findings are predictable given the emotional and physical stress that these persons may be experiencing. It is also understandable given that these facilities, especially hospitals, typically have easy access, inadequate security, and insufficient staffing (Menendez 2023).

Important to note is that NIOSH (2014) defines *workplace violence* as "violent acts, (including physical assaults and threats of assaults) directed toward persons at work or on duty." Threats, verbal abuse, hostility, and harassment can cause significant psychological trauma and stress, even when no physical injury takes place, and may in some part account for reported suicides among healthcare workers. Regrettably, it is believed that incidents of workplace violence often go unreported because healthcare workers erroneously consider such incidents to be "part of the job." This attitude has contributed to underreporting and brings much-needed attention to this disparaging issue (Kerns 2023).

So, what are a number of proven strategies and best practices that can better equip healthcare managers to prevent violence within their organizations?

First and foremost, successfully preventing violence within one's organization requires a serious commitment from leadership of the healthcare organization. Governance and management must accept *safety* as a core value of the organization and commit the required time, attention, and resources to prevent violence and ensure that their organization is safe for patients and employees (Kerns 2023). Trinity Health, a national Catholic health system, has done just that and is a leader in workplace violence prevention. It has developed and implemented a number of effective practices in support of *safety* that are worthy of review.

Education is paramount in Trinity's approach to workplace violence prevention. In addition to its provision of comprehensive staff and employee education, Trinity has produced and widely distributed a staff booklet on *How to Implement and Sustain Best Practices in Violence Prevention* that helps staff learn preemptive strategies and identify persons who may become violent. Among Trinity's other practices are the following (Kerns 2023):

- A Patient Code of Conduct
- Real-time reporting of violent incidents that generates leadership and clinical support as well as security
- Data tracking
- A Canine Program using service dogs for de-escalation of events
- Gun violence prevention training
- Metal detectors in emergency departments
- Violence incident reporting to governance, leadership, and appropriate committees
- Signage indicating no violence or weapons allowed
- Limited access to buildings

Some of these initiatives require minimal time and costs to implement—for example, limiting access to the buildings and posting signage at entryways indicating no violence or weapons allowed. Employee uniforms and identification badges and visitor passes can be useful in identifying those who should have access to the healthcare facility. Since the implementation of Trinity's program of violence prevention, the system has seen decreases in lost days of work and worker's compensation claims (Kerns 2023).

In the high-stress healthcare environment, the perpetrators of violence are most often patients or family members. Nurses are most often the target of violence since they are ones caring for patients and communicating with families around the clock. Staff education and training in crisis intervention, conflict management, and emotional intelligence skills must be mandatory, recurrent, and effective. Case-based education using real-life cases of workplace violence to demonstrate prevention strategies can be most effective.

Addressing workplace violence proactively and assertively has other benefits as well. It helps the organization meet Occupational Safety and Health Administration requirements and Joint Commission standards for accreditation. It improves staff recruitment and retention. It enhances the public image of the healthcare organization as the safe and preferred system in which to work and to seek healthcare when needed.

Of particular significance is the ethical responsibility of healthcare managers to create a workplace environment that is safe and nondiscriminatory and that provides employees with the resources and support they need to do their jobs. That responsibility is at the very core of management. That responsibility is embedded in the professional codes of ethics and conduct for both healthcare managers and clinicians. That responsibility includes addressing and preventing violence in the healthcare workplace. The ACHE (2018) issued a policy statement on "Healthcare Executives' Role in Mitigating Workplace Violence" that urges healthcare executives to "lead efforts to ensure comprehensive violence prevention plans are in place for their facilities," to "raise awareness that workplace violence is a public health issue," and to "champion the planning and development of systems, processes and policies to intervene and mitigate incidents of violence within their workplace and communities."

TEAM BUILDING

Most managers spend considerable time talking about the importance of teamwork. Many even arrange team-building exercises or seminars for their employees, often led by high-priced consultants. Some managers, however, act in ways that sabotage the very teamwork they wish to achieve. Managers need to do more than ostensibly advocate teamwork and recognize its benefits; they need to model the behaviors that nurture it.

Managers can promote teamwork in small ways. Assigning teams to solve problems, recognizing team accomplishments, and simply providing opportunities for teamwork can streamline workflow, contribute to innovation and process improvement, and benefit morale. Managers must teach employees—particularly those who might lack team-oriented skills—how to participate in healthy debate, how to practice civil disagreement, and how to discuss controversial and not-so-controversial issues as a team, seeking acceptable resolutions to problems. Employees should be encouraged to think independently and express ideas freely; those employees who always agree with the boss contribute little to the discussion. Managers should reward team play so that employees place value on it, and they should structure action plans and reward systems to focus on teamwork in the achievement of articulated goals and organizational success.

Managers seeking to encourage teamwork must never show favoritism, and they must not allow employees to gossip, belittle coworkers, or make disparaging comments about others' work. Some employees might believe that making coworkers look bad makes them look better, but such thinking is mistaken. Remaining indifferent to negative comments is not enough; managers who do so silently acquiesce to the criticism. Instead, managers must articulate clearly that such behaviors are unacceptable and counterproductive.

Managers can also foster teamwork by ensuring equal "face time" and attention to all team members. Sometimes, a well-intentioned manager will adopt an open-door policy, only to find that one or two employees take advantage of unlimited access to the boss, to the detriment of the other team members. Reasonable and equitable access fosters teamwork and encourages more interaction among coworkers for problem resolution. Although most managers meet regularly with their individual direct reports, wise managers will convene periodic meetings with groups of department heads or division directors as well. An awareness of the current and future projects of each allows for collaboration and beneficial cross-pollination of ideas.

MENTORING AND STAFF DEVELOPMENT

Mentoring and staff development should not be regarded as just "nice things to do if you have the time." They should be built into the culture of an ethical organization.

Employees cannot be expected to meet the requirements of the job without the resources needed to accomplish the assigned tasks. Knowledge, skill, and guidance are just as critical as budgeted dollars. As more clinicians enter the management ranks, administrators must make sure these individuals are adequately prepared to achieve success in their new roles. This preparation may take the form of general management education or specific seminars on topics with which the clinician has little previous experience (e.g., staff performance evaluations, finance and budgeting). Time spent mentoring these new managers on the way things get done, the politics of the organization, and the chain of command is time well invested. Outstanding performers who are promoted to management may require special attention. Often, they have a tendency to micromanage their subordinates, because the subordinates have the same job the manager formerly had and did well.

On occasion, an employee who is a superstar in one aspect of their job (e.g., computer technology) may be deficient in another (e.g., customer service). If such an employee does not respond to training and counseling, managers have options. They can fire the employee, which might be the easiest course of action but not necessarily the best, or they can look for ways to build on the employee's expertise and use it to the organization's advantage. Reassignment may be a more ethical option for dealing with an employee who has something of value to contribute.

Clayton M. Christensen (2010), one of today's most influential business strategists, delivered an address called "How Will You Measure Your Life?" to the Harvard Business School class of 2010. His message bears repeating here:

> Management is the most noble of professions if it is practiced well. No other occupation offers as many ways to help others learn and grow, take responsibility and be recognized for achievement, and contribute to the success of a team. More and more MBA students come to school thinking that a career in business means buying, selling, and investing in companies. That's unfortunate. Doing deals doesn't yield the deep rewards that come from building people.

In his closing remarks, Christensen (2010) said, "I've concluded that the metric by which God will assess my life isn't dollars but the individual lives I have touched. . . . Don't worry about the level of prominence you have achieved; worry about the individuals you have helped become better people."

THE ETHICAL IMPORTANCE OF EMPLOYEE COMMUNICATIONS

The critical role that communications play in management, employee relations, organizational culture, and the achievement of organizational goals cannot be overstated. The role of communications is especially evident during events that threaten the status quo, people's job security, or the ongoing stability of the organization. Such events (e.g., new administrations, work reductions, layoffs, mergers, organizational acquisitions) have a personal effect on individual employees regardless of their place in the corporate hierarchy.

One of the chief causes of anxiety is uncertainty, and once people have information—good or bad—they can mobilize their personal resources to plan or take action. In times of change, ethical managers make sure that their employees and staff have as much information as they need. If management fails to provide adequate information, informal communication networks will likely fill the vacuum with rumor, speculation, and false conclusions. A negative work environment will likely result, and productivity will suffer. Managers may, justifiably, feel frustrated by having to repeat the same information several times to employees, but management is usually closer to the situations in question and has a better understanding of them. Employees will likely need time to process information and determine the effect it may have on them. Reinforcing the information can help build trust between the workforce and management.

"The medium is the message" is an oft-quoted admonition from Marshall McLuhan (1964, 9), a widely recognized expert on communication theory. He advanced the notion that the medium used for communication influences how the message is perceived—a notion highly relevant in the era of cyberspace. In many work settings, e-mail communications have become the norm. E-mails can convey information quickly and conveniently, saving considerable time; however, they can also lead to information overload, especially when an inordinate number of messages are mass copied and distributed. For important issues, alternative methods of communication should be considered.

Electronic communication is often not as effective as face-to-face communication. It does not convey the tone or tenor of a message and does not facilitate immediate response and dialogue. Without immediate response, points cannot be clarified, questions cannot be asked, and delivery cannot be adjusted to better convey the message's intent. Furthermore, the distance and anonymity inherent in many forms of electronic communication may entice people to say things they would not say face-to-face, or to say things with an unintended lack of civility that puts the recipient on the defensive. Even Steve Jobs, master of the digital universe, required his staff to have face-to-face meetings rather than electronic ones because he believed they fostered more creativity (Isaacson 2011).

In many electronic communications, the recipient might not know the actual identity of the sender but rather the computer of origin. Similarly, the sender might not have any assurance that the intended recipient has even received the message, unless the sender has requested confirmation. Particularly troublesome can be occasions when important information becomes lost in a barrage of messages or when a sensitive message unintentionally becomes part of a long chain of e-mails with many readers. The confidentiality of electronic communications is not guaranteed.

Ethical managers practice two-way communication with their employees. They seek employees' opinions and ideas, encourage civil disagreement and debate, and listen carefully. They seek to learn from employee comments rather than disregard them out of hand. Nancy M. Schlichting, former CEO of Henry Ford Health System in Detroit, had a habit to "attend new-employee orientation, give out my e-mail address, and tell employees to let me know if they have concerns about whether we are meeting our standards" (Rice and Perry 2013, 35). Ethical managers care what their employees think, and they work to develop employee communication strategies that build a community of shared values and commitment to organizational goals.

Beckham (2015) maintains that "clear communication defines leadership" and that "clarity requires specificity." Specificity will reduce the misdirection, wasted effort, confusion, and anxiety that ambiguity produces (Beckham 2015). Communications are human interactions, and words matter. If employees are to trust leaders, then leaders' actions must reflect their words. Successful leaders will choose their words wisely and thoughtfully, leaving no room for misinterpretation. The words will have clarity of meaning for the employee audience and allow for dialogue if further clarification is needed. Employees and staff should be left with no doubt about the actions they need to take as a result of the communication.

WORKFORCE DIVERSITY

Living with and managing diversity has become a central theme of the twenty-first century (Dunn 2021). Effective healthcare leaders develop strategies to recruit, motivate, retain, and mobilize a multicultural workforce to support the mission of the organization. They promote and support diversity initiatives oriented toward both their employees and their patient populations, and they strive to secure a workforce that is representative of the community's demographics. As Piper (2012, 16) writes, "For an organization to fulfill its social contract to provide high-quality, cost-effective, and safe healthcare, it must satisfy the needs and manage the expectations of those who directly deliver these services."

Diversity has many faces. In today's multicultural society, healthcare managers must be aware of ethnic, cultural, generational, and religious differences among employees, as well as differences in life experiences, economic status, sexual orientation, gender identity, and disability. In addition, multidisciplinary, multicultural healthcare professionals all bring their personal codes of conduct, values, and biases to the workplace (Rice and Perry 2013). Such a multitude of differences can pose a challenge to building a community of shared values.

Ethical management begins with the way one interacts with people, and understanding the perspective of others and the lenses through which they see the world greatly enhances these interactions' success. Cultural competency training is important not just in the care of patients; it also must be addressed in supervising, managing, and building relationships with employees. An ethical healthcare executive fosters inclusion and collaboration, avoids tokenism, expands networking and mentoring opportunities for minority managers, and eliminates structural barriers that prevent women and minorities from moving up the ranks. Above all, the ethical healthcare executive demonstrates, on a daily basis, the standards for acceptable conduct expected of all members of the workforce.

Ethical managers must ensure that human resources policies are fair and non-discriminatory and that respect is shown for cultural differences. Managers must never let personal prejudices or moral judgments influence their evaluation of an employee's job performance. Communications should consistently take into account cultural and generational differences to avoid misunderstandings. Some communications with younger employees, for instance, may need to be adjusted to accommodate their affinity for technology.

McNally (2017, 58) challenges healthcare managers to examine their organization's "generational competency." She reminds us that today's healthcare workforce comprises four generations of people who bring their own values, perspectives, and attitudes about work. Generational differences can bring innovation and new ideas to the workplace, but leadership must be open to new approaches. Leaders should look to foster collaboration among the generations, building on the strengths of each. For instance, whereas millennials may bring new ideas, baby boomers often have wisdom and corporate memory (McNally 2017). Managers must make certain that employees and staff of different generations have mutual respect and recognize their common goals. To ignore generational differences in expectations of supervision, work styles, and communication is to encourage conflict and misinterpretation of information.

Avoid age discrimination and the stereotyping of older workers as being "out of touch." Many older employees are not physically or mentally ready for retirement, and they can offer valuable experience and talent to the organization. In 2019, bipartisan legislation was introduced in Congress to better protect older workers from age discrimination "as strongly as people are protected against other types of discrimination" (Terrell 2019). According to a Transamerica Retirement Survey, "even employers that have diversity and inclusion policies typically don't include age as one of the characteristics they're trying to promote" (Weston 2019).

Any discussion of diversity and inclusion should devote some attention to the topic of unconscious bias. The Vanderbilt University Office of Equity, Diversity and Inclusion (2023) offers this foundational definition:

> Unconscious bias (or implicit bias) is often defined as prejudice or unsupported judgments in favor of or against one thing, person, or group as compared to another, in a way that is usually considered unfair. Many researchers suggest that unconscious bias occurs automatically as the brain makes quick judgments based on past experiences and background. As a result of unconscious biases, certain people benefit and other people are penalized. In contrast, deliberate prejudices are defined as conscious bias (or explicit bias). Although we all have biases, many unconscious biases tend to be exhibited toward minority groups based on factors such as class, gender, sexual orientation, race, ethnicity, nationality, religious beliefs, age, disability and more.

Authorities on unconscious bias suggest that it is a normal phenomenon, "as natural as breathing," that "allows us to navigate the world" (Glicksman 2016). As such, unconscious bias likely cannot be entirely eliminated, but its effects can be minimized. Many organizations have made unconscious bias a focus of their education and training around diversity and inclusion.

Unconscious bias is an especially serious concern in healthcare, given that it can affect treatment decisions, prescribed pain medications, diagnostic testing, and health outcomes (Glicksman 2016). It may also be evident in the ways that healthcare workers talk to patients and the kind and amount of information they share. Workers might, for instance, withhold certain information if they feel, as a result of unconscious bias, that a patient is not "smart" enough to understand it. Similarly, bias might lead workers to use a louder voice when speaking to an older patient, or to provide discharge instructions to an adult accompanying an older patient, rather than to the patient themself. Such behaviors can emanate from the unconscious bias of even the most well-intentioned healthcare professionals. Unconscious bias in healthcare is not limited to staff interactions with patients. It can also be found in the way professionals treat colleagues and subordinates, or in the way patients treat female or minority healthcare providers.

Managers need to understand unconscious bias and its effects on both patients and staff, and they need to commit resources to education and training to help minimize its harmful effects. A more comprehensive discussion of management's roles and responsibilities related to diversity can be found in chapter 19.

WORKING WITH UNIONS

This discussion is not intended to serve as a primer on labor relations, but a few observations about working with unions merit mention. Some managers fear losing all control when unions enter the picture, and working with unions certainly has its challenges. Nonetheless, valuable lessons can be learned from the experience.

Geographic areas with substantial union membership in industry or government also tend to have a strong union presence in healthcare. Hospitals are attractive targets for union organizers because they are often the largest employer in a municipality, they have jobs that cannot be moved offshore, and they are under constant pressure to reduce costs (Moore 2015).

RNs represent a significant percentage of unionized healthcare workers. Money is not the primary reason that nurses unionize; more typically, the nurses are motivated by the loss of control they feel as a result of staff reductions, other cost-saving measures, and the uncertainty of healthcare reform. Their union efforts focus largely on improving patient safety, increasing nurse staffing ratios, advocating for patients' rights, and having a stronger voice in public policy. Administrators should recognize the motives behind union activities, and they should not assume the nurses are simply driven by self-interest. In what has been called a "landmark deal on staffing," a nurses' union in New York City "reached an agreement with hospitals that sets minimum ratios of nurses to patients" (McGeehan 2019). Through negotiations, this union contract achieved what had not been possible through state legislation.

The key words in labor relations parlance are *negotiation* and *bargaining*. Successful negotiation requires that both parties understand what the other wants to achieve, why the organization exists, and how organizational success benefits both parties. Successful negotiations that arrive at fair contracts and that benefit the organization begin with trust and the ability of the two parties to find common ground. If either party enters into negotiations in an adversarial posture, the discussion will likely break down; it will become more of a power struggle than an attempt to reach agreement. Unions often see management as interlopers into an organization that the union's members have helped build. They may think that managers simply move up the career ladder and from one community to the next, whereas unions and their members are vested in their community long-term. Effective leaders work to dispel this perception of management, and they are attentive to the image and interpersonal skills of staff who represent management in negotiations.

Successful negotiations involve bargaining that produces safe working conditions and fair compensation for work done and that ensures both the short-term and long-term ability of the organization to fulfill its mission and obligation to the community. Management must be tough in negotiations, but always with the best interests of the organization guiding their decisions—especially on issues that might threaten the organization's long-term success. Concessions granted out of fear of a strike are not always in the best interests of the organization, the community, or even the union members themselves. Some automotive industry observers pointed out problems of this nature with General Motors: Management sacrificed the long-term viability of the corporation to avoid strikes and to enjoy short-term profits.

Working with unions has a number of aspects that many managers find burdensome and time-consuming—for instance, documentation of unsatisfactory performance and counseling, progressive discipline, timely performance evaluations, justification for firing, job descriptions that are current and consistent with assignments, and so forth. For inexperienced managers, however, these requirements may actually provide valuable direction for dealing fairly with employees—especially underperforming ones. Use of these guidelines when terminating employment for unsatisfactory performance can bring clarity and objectivity to the process, while also preventing litigation.

Healthcare executives who wish to avoid unionization need to heed the advice from Moore (2015): "The best way to avoid a union is to avoid giving employees incentive to organize in the first place." Treatment, not wages, is typically what motivates employees to unionize. In fact, contrary to popular belief, unions do not drive wages; the market does. According to experts, having an active problem-solving process through which employees can be heard and grievances resolved can go a long way toward avoiding unionization. Typically, a workforce that is treated with dignity and respect and rewarded fairly for a job well done does not feel the need for collective bargaining (Moore 2015).

The consistent practice of fair, equitable HR policies is likely the best way to avoid unionization—and potential legal trouble. Segal (2011) points out that an "employment at will" arrangement does not mean that employees can be terminated at whim, and he warns that a claim of unfair treatment can easily lead to litigation.

Managers in at-will employment organizations commonly make the following ten mistakes when dealing with problem employees (Segal 2011):

1. Failing to notify employees that their jobs are on the line
2. Failing to confirm the corrective action in writing
3. Failing to state that the final warning is, in fact, final

4. Focusing on the cause of performance problems, such as illness, depression, and so forth
5. Focusing on intent rather than outcome
6. Using labels rather than describing behaviors
7. Overstating the risks of retention
8. Ignoring the comparators
9. Delaying the inevitable
10. Failing to provide dignity and respect

When managers focus on what they assume to be the cause of a performance problem (e.g., illness, depression), they might inadvertently set the stage for a disability claim (Segal 2011). Focusing on an employee's intent is problematic because intent cannot be proven. Using general labels (e.g., the worker has a "bad attitude") typically does not indicate what exactly must change, and it may be interpreted as an expression of bias. Finally, inconsistent treatment of employees who display similar behavior can invite discrimination claims. Avoiding these and other mistakes is essential whether managers are working with unions or at organizations with employment at will.

When working with unions, managers should always remember that unions have a vested interest in the organization's fiscal viability; the key to effective negotiations is to find and appeal to that common ground. The prevailing wisdom of management consultants is to avoid unions if possible; however, if the union exists, managers should work seriously to establish and nurture a good relationship with its leadership (Moore 2015).

FIRING PRACTICES

Rarely does a manager relish the idea of firing an employee. However, when an employee is underperforming and appropriate remedial measures do not bring about improvement, not firing the employee is both unwise and unfair. It is unfair to coworkers who have to pick up the slack; to clients or others who are directly or indirectly affected by the poor performance; to the organization that is paying wages for unsatisfactory work; and to the manager who has to spend time and energy cleaning up after the poor work and trying to bring about a more satisfactory employment arrangement.

The organization may suffer in other ways as well. Tolerating poor performance lowers the bar for what is deemed acceptable, damages employee morale, and prevents the coalescence of the employee team. When top performers are forced to pick up the slack, they might question why they put in the effort to be good at their job when the reward is just more work. Such a situation can quickly erode the trust and respect the team has for the manager (O'Donnell 2017).

The firing of an employee should be carried out in a way that enables the employee to retain as much dignity and self-respect as possible. A clear explanation should be provided. Much has been written about firing practices, severance packages, liability protection, and the like. Although "what is done" is important, "how it is done" has ethical implications. Honesty, fairness, and respect must characterize the process. People who have been fired might not remember the exact words that were said, but they will always remember how the conversation made them feel.

PROVIDING REFERENCES

Often, managers receive requests from outside the organization for reference information about a former or current employee. The reference information provided, within the boundaries of the law and any applicable postemployment agreements, should be accurate, honest, and fair. If references are being sought regarding a current employee, as opposed to a former employee, managers must be equally fair and honest. If the employee is valuable to your organization, you may be reluctant to give a glowing recommendation; nevertheless, honesty must prevail.

Because of fear of litigation, some employers refuse to provide any information beyond the dates of employment and position held. To the people checking references, however, this reticence may imply, inaccurately, that the employee was fired, was asked to resign, or had an unsatisfactory performance. Honest responses to inquiries need not provide elaborate detail. Some questions are more appropriately answered by the former employees themselves—for example, "Why did this employee decide to seek other employment?" Answering based on personal assumptions is unwise; such questions should be referred to the employee.

When providing references, the manager generally focuses on the employee. However, the manager must also be fair to the reference checker, even though that person is usually a stranger. Ethics applies to all situations and to all relationships.

REFERENCES

American College of Healthcare Executives (ACHE). 2018. "Healthcare Executives' Role in Mitigating Workplace Violence." Policy statement. Approved by Board of Governors November 12. www.ache.org/about-ache/our-story/our-commitments/policy-statements/healthcare-executives-role-in-mitigating-workplace-violence.

Beckham, D. 2015. "How Clear Communication Defines Leadership." *Hospitals & Health Networks.* Published April 21. www.hhnmag.com/articles/3532-how-clear-communication-defines-leadership (content no longer available).

Bennis, W. 1999. *Managing People Is Like Herding Cats*. Provo, UT: Executive Excellence Publishing.

Chervoni-Knapp, T. 2022. "The Staffing Shortage Pandemic." *Journal of Radiology Nursing* 41 (2): 74–75. www.sciencedirect.com/science/article/pii/S1546084322000311.

Christensen, C. M. 2010. "How Will You Measure Your Life?" *Harvard Business Review*. Published July. http://hbr.org/2010/07/how-will-you-measure-your-life/ar/pr.

Collins, J. 2001. *Good to Great: Why Some Companies Make the Leap . . . and Others Don't*. New York: HarperCollins.

Corkery, M., and S. Cowley. 2016. "Wells Fargo Warned Workers Against Sham Accounts, but 'They Needed a Paycheck.'" *New York Times*, September 17, A1.

Dauten, D., and J. J. T. O'Donnell. 2019. "With a Bad Boss, There Are No Good Jobs." *Albuquerque Journal*, March 18, M7.

DeChant, P. 2023. "How to Face the Great Resignation in Healthcare." Vital WorkLife. Accessed July 1. https://info.vitalworklife.com/the-great-resignation-article.

Dunn, R. T. 2021. *Dunn and Haimann's Healthcare Management*, 11th ed. Chicago: Health Administration Press.

Ethics and Compliance Initiative (ECI). 2023. "Global View Ethics Outcomes: A Global View at How Stronger Ethics Cultures Have a Favorable Impact on Ethics Outcomes." Accessed October 10. www.ethics.org/knowledge-center/interactive-maps/.

Fitter, E. and S. Cowley. 2019. "Wells Fargo C.E.O. Could Be Banking's Worst Job: It's Open." *New York Times*, March 30, B1.

Gelb, L. H. 2012. "Oh, Those Greedy Bankers." *Newsweek*. Published September 17. www.newsweek.com/paul-volcker-greedy-bankers-ryan-plan-and-fed-64791.

Gilbert, J. 2013. "A Reflection on Everyday Ethics." *Healthcare Executive* 28 (1): 60–63.

Glicksman, E. 2016. "Unconscious Bias in Academic Medicine: Overcoming the Prejudices We Don't Know We Have." Association of American Medical Colleges. Published September 27. https://news.aamc.org/diversity/article/unconscious-bias/.

Goleman, D. 2000. "Leadership That Gets Results." *Harvard Business Review* 78 (2): 78–90.

Gomez, M. R. 2018. "Beginning, Middle, and End: The Redeeming Value of Professionalism." New Mexico Healthcare Executives newsletter, second quarter.

Haden, J. 2012. "4 Rewards That Are More Powerful Than Money." *Inc.* Published February 7. www.inc.com/jeff-haden/4-employee-rewards-that-are-more-powerful-than-money.html.

Hofmann, P. 2017. "Asking the Right Questions." *Healthcare Executive* 32 (5): 48–51.

Isaacson, W. 2011. *Steve Jobs.* New York: Simon and Schuster.

Katz, T. 2017. "Is That Candidate Really Great?" *Albuquerque Journal*, March 5, C10.

Kerns, T. 2023. "Becoming the Safest Health System in America." In webinar "Addressing Violence in the Workplace," presented by Agency for Healthcare Research and Quality (AHRQ), Chicago, June 27.

Kumar, S. 2015. "5 Reasons Merit-Based Pay Hurts Average Workers." *Fortune.* Published July 24. https://fortune.com/2015/07/24/5-reasons-merit-based-pay-hurts-average-workers/.

Kutch, J. M. 2022. "Focus on Employee Mental Wellness." *Healthcare Executive*, September/October, 36–37.

Levitt, H. 2018. "Wells Fargo to Pay States $575 Million Over Sales Practices." *Bloomberg.* Published December 28. www.bloomberg.com/news/articles/2018-12-28/wells-fargo-to-pay-575-million-to-states-over-sales-practices.

Maslach, C., and M. P. Leiter. 2021. "How to Measure Burnout Accurately and Ethically." *Harvard Business Review.* Published March 19. https://hbr.org/2021/03/how-to-measure-burnout-accurately-and-ethically.

Mayer, T. A., and R. J. Cates. 2014. *Leadership for Great Customer Service: Satisfied Employees, Satisfied Patients*, 2nd ed. Chicago: Health Administration Press.

McGeehan, P. 2019. "Facing Nurses' Strike, New York Hospitals Reach Landmark Deal on Staffing." *New York Times*, April 11, A25.

McLuhan, M. 1964. *Understanding Media: The Extensions of Man.* New York: McGraw-Hill.

McNally, K. 2017. "Leading a Multigenerational Workforce." *Healthcare Executive* 32 (1): 58–61.

Menendez, C. C. 2023. "Violence and Aggression in Healthcare Settings." In webinar "Addressing Violence in the Workplace," presented by Agency for Healthcare Research and Quality (AHRQ), Chicago, June 27.

Michigan Nurses Association. 2023. E-mail to author.

Moore, S. 2015. "As Unions Grow, Healthcare Execs Need to Know How to Handle Them." *Healthcare Finance.* Published July 9. www.healthcarefinancenews.com/news/unions-grow-healthcare-execs-need-know-how-handle-them.

National Institute for Occupational Safety and Health (NIOSH). 2014. "Violence Occupational Hazards in Hospitals." Reviewed June 6. www.cdc.gov/niosh/docs/2002-101/#What is workplace violence?

National Public Radio (NPR). 2014. "Transcript for Emotional Intelligence—Daniel Goleman." *To the Best of Our Knowledge* archive. Published March 2. http://archive.ttbook.org/book/emotional-intelligence-daniel-goleman (content no longer available).

O'Donnell, J. T. 2017. "My Boss Expects Me to Pick Up My Co-worker's Slack." *Inc.* Published March 6. www.inc.com/jt-odonnell/my-boss-expects-me-to-pick-up-my-coworkers-slack.html.

Perry, F. 2012. *Healthcare Leadership That Makes a Difference: Creating Your Legacy.* Self-study course. Chicago: Health Administration Press.

Piper, L. E. 2012. "Generation Y in Healthcare: Leading Millennials in an Era of Reform." *Frontiers of Health Services Management* 29 (1): 16–28.

Pruitt, J. 2017. "How Long Is Too Long with the Wrong Hire?" *Inc.* Published September 13. www.inc.com/jeff-pruitt/how-long-is-too-long-with-the-wrong-hire.html.

Rice, J., and F. Perry. 2013. *Healthcare Leadership Excellence: Creating a Career of Impact.* Chicago: Health Administration Press.

Rosenberg, J. 2018. "Smoothing Staff Friction Can Be Critical." *Albuquerque Journal*, October 22, 2.

Russell, J., and B. Greenspan. 2005. "Correcting and Preventing Management Mistakes." In *Management Mistakes in Healthcare: Identification, Correction and Prevention*, edited by P. B. Hofmann and F. Perry, 84–102. New York: Cambridge University Press.

Segal, J. A. 2011. "At Will but Still Armed." *Hospitals & Health Networks Daily.* Published March 24. www.hhnmag.com/articles/4713-at-will-but-still-armed (content no longer available).

Schoenberg, S. 2021."Vaccine Mandates Kick In as Hospitals Struggle with Staffing." *CommonWealth.* Published December 16. https://commonwealthmagazine.org/health-care/vaccine-mandates-kick-in-as-hospitals-struggle-with-staffing/.

Suddath, C. 2013. "Performance Reviews: Why Bother?" *Bloomberg.* Published November 7. www.bloomberg.com/news/articles/2013-11-07/the-annual-performance-review-worthless-corporate-ritual.

Terrell, K. 2019. "Legislation Introduced to Better Protect Older Workers." AARP. Published February 14. www.aarp.org/politics-society/advocacy/info-2019/bills-protect-older-workers.html.

Topchik, G. 2013. "Purging Workplace Negativity." American Society of Association Executives newsletter, January.

US Bureau of Labor Statistics (BLS). 2020. "Fact Sheet: Workplace Violence in Healthcare, 2018." Published April. www.bls.gov/iif/factsheets/workplace-violence-healthcare-2018.htm.

Vanderbilt University Office of Equity, Diversity and Inclusion. 2023. "Unconscious Bias." Accessed October 10. www.vanderbilt.edu/diversity/unconscious-bias/.

Wartzman, R. 2008. "Put a Cap on CEO Pay." *Bloomberg.* Published September 12. www.bloomberg.com/news/articles/2008-09-12/put-a-cap-on-ceo-paybusinessweek-business-news-stock-market-and-financial-advice.

Weston, L. 2019. "How to Stay Employed Past Retirement Age." *Albuquerque Journal,* June 1, B6.

CHAPTER 19

Management, Diversity, and Inclusion

James A. Rice and Frankie Perry

LIVING WITH AND managing demographic diversity has become a central theme of the twenty-first century (Dunn 2010, 490). As a nation, the United States is ill prepared to deal with the challenges that new demographic trends present. Nowhere is this lack of preparation more critical than in healthcare, where failure to understand and appropriately care for demographically diverse patients exacerbates health disparities, increases the morbidity and mortality of large segments of our population, and significantly drives up the costs of healthcare (Schulte 2010, 1). Failure to understand and motivate a cross-cultural workforce will increasingly thwart the achievement of organizational goals and, in the process, derail a leader's career effectiveness. Creating, embracing, and sustaining a culture of diversity is essential to the success of healthcare legacy leaders.

Healthcare executives can no longer think of diversity only in terms of race and gender. We live in a multicultural society and do business in a global economy. Indeed, the Institute of Medicine reported in 2004 that "the United States is rapidly transforming into one of the most racially and ethnically diverse nations in the world" (IOM 2004, 23). Clearly, "the diversity challenges confronting leaders today are unlike those of just a decade ago" (Dunn 2010, 489).

This chapter was originally published as "Managing Diversity" in Healthcare Leadership Excellence: Creating a Career of Impact *(Chicago: Health Administration Press, 2013). Used with permission. Although some references provided in this chapter may appear less than current, they have withstood the test of time and still hold true.*

But how is diversity today different from the diversity of the past, how do we currently define diversity, and what challenges does the "new diversity" present for healthcare leaders?

CHANGE IS COMPLEX AND ACCELERATING

Several changes in our society over the last decade carry major implications for healthcare. If healthcare leaders do not take them into consideration, their organizations' success, and their leadership legacy, will be suboptimized.

Demographics

Armada and Hubbard (2010, 4), citing data from the US Census Bureau, note that "48 of the 100 largest cities in the United States have minority-majorities. Five states—California, Texas, Hawaii, New Mexico, and Florida—also have minority-majorities and five other states, including New York, are expected to become minority-majority soon." Furthermore, they write, from now until 2050, more than 90 percent of the population growth in the United States is projected to be people of color. As of 2011, one in six Americans is Hispanic (Venegas 2011).

Immigration Patterns

Reflecting shifts in immigration patterns, most immigrants to the United States now arrive from Eastern Europe, India, China, Southeast Asia, Africa, Mexico, and South America. Not only are the language, religion, and culture of these immigrants significantly different from the predominantly Western European immigrants of the past, but their views of illness and Western medicine are often dissimilar as well (Armada and Hubbard 2010, 12).

Another shift related to immigration is the nature of newcomers' goals upon arriving in the United States: Rather than aiming to assimilate into the "melting pot," as did many immigrants of the past, today people now immigrating often strive to preserve and celebrate the unique culture and way of life of their diverse countries of origin.

Laws and Regulations

Specific laws, regulations, and accrediting standards are in place to ensure that diversity is honored and discrimination is eliminated. As in other areas of healthcare operations, legal and regulatory mandates for diversity bring increased complexity to healthcare management. Administrative attention must be given to ensure systematic, accurate patient data collection and that employee recruitment and hiring practices reflect the diversity of the patient population.

DRIVERS OF CHANGE

At one time, the human resources department was responsible for diversity initiatives, which were driven by equal employment opportunity laws and affirmative action practices and focused on race and gender to achieve a quota. Now, it is often clinicians who are driving the initiatives because of their concerns about misinterpreting diversity-related symptoms. For example, disease descriptions that are inaccurately understood can disrupt safety and quality of patient care (Armada and Hubbard 2010, 15).

Limited English Proficiency

Limited English proficiency (LEP) is now a prevalent-enough characteristic of the US population to have its own acronym. Twenty percent of US residents do not speak English at home; in some states, that figure is as high as 43 percent. These percentages do not include the 20 million individuals who are hearing impaired and use sign language or other means to communicate (Armada and Hubbard 2010, 9).

Sexual Orientation

Public conversations and political debate have brought the interests of openly lesbian, gay, bisexual, and transgender individuals to the forefront of demographic awareness. Indeed, the initialism LGBT is commonly recognized in management circles. This awareness is a significant driver of change in healthcare practices that will only increase in importance.

Global Economy

The US economy is wide open to global competition. This economic reality has in turn called attention to legal actions lodged against US-based multinational companies surrounding their failures to successfully integrate a diverse workforce. Healthcare is not immune to these failures. For example, the United Steelworkers union and the International Labor Rights Fund brought legal action against Coca-Cola alleging that Coca-Cola maintains relations with death squads to intimidate union leaders and repress trade union rights at its plants in Colombia. In another example, the National Labor Committee, *Businessweek*, and others have condemned Wal-Mart for sweatshop working conditions at its international factories. Wal-Mart's defense included that it conforms to local laws. But multicultural diversity brings differences in occupational safety and child labor laws, worker expectations, and business practices. US-based multinational organizations, including healthcare, must adhere to the laws and ethical standards of the United States.

Aging Workforce

The currently fragile economy and pending leadership shortages likely mean that many aging baby boomers will defer retirement and remain in C-suite positions, further increasing the generation gap between healthcare management and its workforce.

Increased Poverty

The socioeconomically disadvantaged experience a disproportionate burden of morbidity and mortality, and their numbers are increasing. Growing income inequalities will result in a rise in the numbers of uninsured and underinsured, who have less access to care.

Healthcare's Public Image

Healthcare organizations that fail to institute diversity initiatives may experience decreased patient satisfaction, lose market share, and risk future reimbursement. These predictions are especially valid if reimbursement becomes tied to patient satisfaction and outcomes (Armada and Hubbard 2010, 14).

International Medical Graduates

The number of international medical graduates (IMGs) working in the United States has been growing since 1981. Currently, more than 25 percent of US physicians are IMGs (Garman, Johnson, and Royer 2011), giving rise to potential cross-cultural conflicts among physicians, patients, and staff.

THE MANY FACES OF DIVERSITY

According to Armada and Hubbard (2010, 39), "diversity can be defined narrowly or broadly based on the unique attributes of a provider community and those stakeholders who are invested in the cultural, economic, and social life of an organization." The importance placed on diversity initiatives is directly related to the demographics of the population served.

As in the past, race and gender remain high on the diversity agenda, as they should. Women and people of color are most visibly underrepresented among minorities in healthcare management. In addition, today's multicultural society requires that leaders attend to several other groups on the diversity list. The implications for healthcare operations related to diversity among ethnic, cultural, generational, and religious groups as well as those with varied life experiences, economic status (including homelessness), sexual orientation, and disabilities are significant. Further complicating care delivery is the fact that an individual may be a member of more than one of these groups.

Finally, the healthcare environment is made more complex still by a multidisciplinary, multicultural healthcare workforce whose members bring their personal codes of conduct, values, and biases to the workplace.

All these diverse ingredients could be likened to a "demographic martini—shaken, not stirred." But this reference to James Bond films may be lost on readers of later generations and from non-Western cultures. And therein lies the dilemma. Leaders can no longer assume that everyone shares their standards, values, sense of humor, and ways of thinking. We do not all see the world through the same lens. This reality has a significant impact not only on patient access, treatment, and outcomes but also on the outcomes of a leader's efforts. Healthcare executives must manage diversity in ways that ensure safe, high-quality care for patients and maintain harmony and collaboration among diverse staff. Workforce effectiveness and leadership success demand a sharp focus on understanding and leading diverse groups, organizations, and communities.

Heightened recognition of diversity and the issues it introduces into the healthcare management environment informs leadership actions and career effectiveness. The various components of diversity are presented in the following section. (This discussion is not intended to be a comprehensive look at the characteristics of diverse groups or the issues surrounding them, as much has been written elsewhere in that regard.)

Race

Workforce
Racial minorities are still underrepresented in healthcare leadership positions. While it is accepted that leadership diversity should reflect that of the community being served, difficulties often arise in the recruitment and hiring of minorities. Healthcare leaders still grapple with the question of what factors should guide the hiring process: the qualifications and capabilities of the candidate, the

organization's goal for diversity in leadership, or the personal preference of the hiring authority (Garman, Johnson, and Royer 2011, 123)?

In addition, healthcare organizations often find they must compete with other industries for bright, promising minority candidates, in part because the healthcare sector has underinvested in leadership training programs. If healthcare leaders expect to strengthen the breadth and depth of minority leadership, they must commit more time and resources to minority leadership development and mentoring programs.

Minority candidates must be hired for what they bring to the organization. Their employment should further the ambitions and goals of both the candidate and the organization. Well-advised healthcare leaders avoid "tokenism," foster inclusiveness, and expand mentoring and networking opportunities for minority managers. A leader's legacy road map must be designed to guide her through challenging and, in some cases, uncharted waters.

Patients

"Research has found that minority populations have a higher level of mistrust of healthcare providers," according to Hofmann (2010). And with good reason. Evidence confirms that racial and ethnic disparities exist in healthcare. Minority professionals are less visible to patients during the healthcare experience, and physicians of color have not always been recruited or welcomed by organizations (Hofmann 2010).

Failure to recognize cultural differences among racial minorities further hinders competent patient care. Cordova, Beaudin, and Iwanabe (2010, 23) found that the "healthcare industry has no standardized requirements for [data] collection, categorization, or use." Healthcare leaders need to strongly advocate for these standards to further enhance culturally competent care. Assumptions that all Black people are African American, for example, are simply incorrect. Many members of the Black population are of Caribbean or South American descent with entirely different backgrounds and cultures than those of African Americans. Segments of the Black population may also differ in their religion and language. Similar assumptions regarding those categorized as Asian Americans/Pacific Islanders (who comprise 43 ethnic groups with 100 different languages) and Hispanics must be avoided (Cordova, Beaudin, and Iwanabe 2010, 36). The term *Hispanic* was introduced by the US Census Bureau in the 1980s as a way to categorize people connected to the Spanish language; it conveys no meaning regarding race or national origin. Hispanics may be Black or White and may originate from more than 20 countries.

Culture and Ethnicity

Legacy leaders appreciate that we live and work in a multicultural world. Dunn (2010, 490) states, "Culture is the sum total of one's way of living [and] includes values, beliefs, standards, language, thinking patterns, behavioral norms, communication styles, and other background and experience factors." All these influences guide an individual's decisions and actions. Failure to recognize this aspect of human nature by treating all people the same, known as "cultural blindness" (Dunn 2010, 490), is sure to damage a leader's legacy.

Data Collection

Data collection to measure diversity by both the US Census Bureau and healthcare organizations is unreliable. Cultural and ethnic categories are vague and general, variances in self-identification and reluctance of data collectors to verify their own assumptions increase inaccuracies, and data collection does not take country of origin into account. An Institute of Medicine (2000, 294) report assessing health communication strategies for diverse populations suggests that data collection for diversity should be reformulated as a sociocultural process. This approach would identify individuals specifically by culture, customs, and language rather than by skin color or continent of origin. Such a method makes sense, considering that one of the more significant barriers to culturally competent care is language.

Patients

Armada and Hubbard (2010, 3) write, "Cross-cultural healthcare involves three key issues: racial and ethnic disparities in quality of care provided in minority patients; cross-cultural value differences between immigrant patients and Western medical providers; and providing language assistance to limited and disabled persons." They contend that the goal of cultural competency training is to "create a healthcare system and workforce that are capable of delivering the highest quality of care to every patient regardless of race, ethnicity, culture, or language proficiency" (Armada and Hubbard 2010, 13). According to Cordova, Beaudin, and Iwanabe (2010, 20), the cultural competency of an organization can be measured by "its capacity to integrate principles and values of cultural competence into its policy, structure, attitudes, behaviors, and practices." How must healthcare leaders master these challenges as they earn, inspire, engage, and partner with followers?

LEP and disabled patients are guaranteed the right to language assistance access by law. Healthcare facilities that participate in Medicare and Medicaid are legally bound to provide language assistance. For guidance in ensuring compliance, hospitals and health systems may turn to The Joint Commission and the

National Quality Forum, which offer cultural competency standards for patients' access to language accommodation.

In addition to adhering to laws and regulations, providing language assistance makes good business sense. Hispanics, the largest minority in the United States, frequently choose hospitals on the basis of the level of language assistance provided. Providing language assistance reduces poor communication, medical errors, and healthcare costs. For example, costs escalate because physicians tend to order more diagnostic tests and hospital admissions when they cannot communicate adequately with the patient or family (Armada and Hubbard 2010, 9, 10).

Progressive healthcare organizations provide language accommodations. For example, Children's Hospital Los Angeles offers interpreters in 33 languages around the clock, pictorial communication materials for the illiterate, and a website in the languages of its community. Children's Hospital Central California added a telephone line for patients to access discharge instructions in three languages (Cordova, Beaudin, and Iwanabe 2010, 26–28).

Finally, ensuring that health communications with diverse patients and family members are clear and well understood is an ethical mandate. The guiding principles in the ethical treatment of patients include respecting an individual's autonomy, providing benefit, avoiding harm, and treating groups and individuals justly and equitably. These tenets cannot be fulfilled unless patients, families, and caregivers can communicate clearly (Institute of Medicine 2000, 305).

Workforce

The multicultural workforce brings its own set of considerations to the attention of healthcare leaders. As with patients, employees must be treated justly and equitably. And as with patients, communications must be clear and well understood if the work is to get done and the desired goals achieved.

Dunn (2010, 491) cites four challenges in managing multicultural teams of employees: differences in communication style, differences in attitudes toward hierarchy and authority, difficulty understanding accents and low-fluency speech, and conflicting norms for decision making. For example, people from non-Western cultures typically use indirect communication, prefer to communicate with those of the same culture, and discuss decisions at length, while individuals from Western cultural backgrounds tend to communicate directly, make decisions quickly, and not dwell on those decisions once they are made. These style differences can impede staff collaboration and harmony. Healthcare leaders must be able to mobilize and influence multicultural teams who may be very different from themselves to live the organization's mission and achieve its goals.

Gender

Despite the fact that large numbers of women complete university graduate programs in health services administration and many women serve in middle management healthcare positions, women continue to be underrepresented in senior leadership and governance positions.

The "glass ceiling," that invisible but real barrier to women rising to the highest ranks of management, persists as an obstacle to optimal organizational performance and talent development. Observers offer a variety of reasons for its persistence. Some claim that the image of leaders as male is deeply embedded in the American psyche. The fact that women have held high positions in other countries, such as Britain's Margaret Thatcher, India's Indira Gandhi, and Germany's Angela Merkel, suggests that this image issue is unique to the United States. Others say subtle and frustrating gender discrimination is at play. Still others contend the glass ceiling is a function of organizational structure, a systemic flaw that prevents women from rising to the top. Regardless of the reason, many healthcare organizations continue to forgo opportunities to benefit from a valuable female talent pool. Those led by enlightened leaders, on the other hand, seek out, mentor, and develop women leaders because they bring an important perspective and set of skills to the executive team. Modern legacy leaders make certain that their organizations provide equal compensation for women, afford equal access to information for effective decision making, and tolerate no sexual discrimination or harassment. They seek to eliminate structural barriers to the advancement of women managers, and they place women on teams and in positions where they may gain knowledge and experience needed to grow in their careers. Above all, legacy leaders trust and expect women executives to perform as successfully as their male counterparts do.

The Generation Divide

Patricia Crown, PhD, distinguished professor in the Department of Anthropology at the University of New Mexico, shared this experience regarding generation differences: In the past she would refer to the concentric circles on a record album to describe ancient pottery until her students asked, "What's a record album?"

How can leaders be effective if they cannot connect with their teams, staff, and communities, all of which are composed of members of several generations? More to the point, how can leaders achieve a career of impact if they suboptimize their engagement with followers by being inattentive to generational trends, knowledge, and ways of thinking?

Workforce

What once was the "generation gap" has become the "generation divide," a gulf that has been widened by new communication styles and technologies. The generations entering the workforce today prefer to text rather than talk, and they obtain information from an Internet search engine instead of the library. Communication within this generation is most often informal, direct, and grammatically incorrect. Its members interact less often through human contact and more often via avatars (virtual persons); they operate less with a workbook and more with Facebook. These employees are more concerned with social justice, the environment, and family life than are their parents.

Leaders need to consider new ways to motivate and effectively communicate with this younger generation of employees. Its ranks are accustomed to acting on their own inclinations, so new-employee orientation programs must include, and explain the rationale for, rules of employment, professional conduct, business communication, dress, punctuality, and teamwork. Incentive and reward programs need to be oriented to what younger employees consider important benefits and perquisites—which will not include seniority in the organization.

According to a study by the University of New Mexico's Anderson School of Management, 70 percent of employers surveyed face some intergenerational conflict in the workplace. Their response is not surprising when you consider that, for the first time in history, four generations of employees may be working together in their organizations (Quigley 2011). Especially in healthcare, which is characterized by a great breadth and depth of education and skills throughout the workforce, leaders are challenged to bring generations together to share goals and knowledge and to "play well with others." Legacy leaders intentionally assign intergenerational teams to work on projects or initiatives and encourage generations to appreciate the experiences and skills they can share with each other. Mentoring across diverse groups of mentees, while adding complexity to a leader's effectiveness, is also recommended to bridge the workforce generation divide.

Patients

Emerging generational differences in the patient population require healthcare leaders and their teams to adopt new ways of communicating with patients and new services to meet those patients' needs. Leaders must implement marketing strategies using social networking and peer pressure to attract young adult patients and influence their decision making. Members of this age group have a community and group mind-set and visit community centers, participate in "Mommy" groups, and arrange play dates for their kids. The younger generations of patients are less likely to develop relationships with their physicians and more likely to rely on the Internet for their health information, much of which is unregulated.

Healthcare leaders who develop Internet-accessible, current, reliable, and culturally appropriate health information for their communities will have a market edge.

As evidence of this trend, the *American Medical News* reported in late 2010 that 871 hospitals maintained more than 2,250 total social media sites, such as on Facebook and Twitter, to communicate with patients and physicians. Furthermore, hospitals are hiring staff specialists to manage social media and oversee their social media presence (Cook 2010).

The expanding older generations of patients present their own challenges, especially the growing numbers of people aged 85 or older. This group presents with the most complex health problems and social support needs. Healthcare leaders need to develop innovative programs and services to support healthy aging at home and reduce costly hospitalizations (Garman, Johnson, and Royer 2011, 34).

Whether in terms of patients or employees, regardless of the differences between generations, healthcare leaders should remember that all people want to be treated with dignity and respect and typically will respond in kind.

Multicultural Professionals

Under the best circumstances, healthcare leaders face challenges in bringing medical staff on board; physicians typically focus on individual patients and are reluctant to commit time to an organization and to expending effort that may not bring immediate results. To promote diversity among the professional ranks, we recommend encouraging physicians in management positions to champion the organization's diversity initiatives with their colleagues. For this approach to succeed, however, executives must make sure physician managers witness and communicate to their colleagues the value—to them and their patients—of supporting diversity and actively participating in cultural competency education. Physicians, nurses, and other professionals must see the clinical benefit and recognize that diversity education is a good use of their time and not just "a nice thing to do."

Once they have successfully recruited diverse professionals, healthcare leaders must be ready to overcome the next layer of challenges posed by a multicultural medical staff. With IMGs constituting more than 25 percent of physicians practicing in the United States (Garman, Johnson, and Royer 2011, 43), the cultural values and attitudes they bring to the healthcare environment sometimes interfere with their ability to relate appropriately to patients or to collaborate with nurses and other caregivers. This dissonance may be especially prevalent for those whose countries of origin have class distinctions or different attitudes about the role of women. Hofmann (2011) says that "compounding the growing challenge of effectively caring for our multicultural society is the largely ignored influence of patients who trigger moral judgments by physicians, nurses and other clinicians." Such judgments can influence patient communication, treatment, and outcomes, so physicians need to understand their biases and how they may affect patient care. Note, however, that, some African-American healthcare professionals may express resentment of the attention and accommodations given to newer immigrant patients because this same concern was not readily offered Black patients in the past (Armada and Hubbard 2010, 15). Thus, it behooves healthcare executives to attend to all the implications of their organization's diversity initiatives.

Physicians, for their part, must recognize the serious clinical issues associated with this new diversity. They need to understand not only the cultural differences surrounding death and dying, blood, transplants, mental health, and other potentially sensitive areas but also the diseases commonly seen in certain races and ethnic groups and those that are endemic to certain parts of the world. In addition, they must be able to interact effectively across cultures and work with interpreters (Armada and Hubbard 2010, 13–14).

Relationships between patients and caregivers significantly influence health outcomes, so it follows that diversity in the health professions that reflects the community improves patient satisfaction and compliance. However, the lack of availability of racially and ethnically diverse professionals to meet this need is problematic.

Current trends indicate that minority clinical professionals still face high barriers to entry into such segments as medicine, dentistry, and pharmacy (Cordova, Beaudin, and Iwanabe 2010, 22). Legacy leaders champion efforts to eliminate these barriers.

The medical profession in the United States recognizes the need for its physicians to adapt to a multicultural society. In 2004, the Association of American Medical Colleges began requiring medical schools to teach cross-cultural medicine. As of 2006, three states—California, New Jersey, and Washington—required training in cross-cultural medicine to be granted licensure (Armada and Hubbard 2010, 12).

Sexual Orientation

As mentioned earlier, LGBT individuals have seen a shift in awareness of their concerns and needs. Although the topic of sexual orientation may elicit strong responses from some individuals and groups in the healthcare workplace and tensions may arise between heterosexual and gay employees, LGBT patients and staff warrant the same considerations as those afforded all other groups. Healthcare leaders will need to address sensitive issues related to sexual orientation, about which conflicting viewpoints may be expressed. They must be able to set aside any personal biases, hone their conflict management skills, and sharpen those communication skills that ferret out and address underlying causes of conflict.

Religious Faith and Beliefs

Many healthcare organizations were founded by faith-based organizations and have historically served a predominantly Christian population. As the United States has transitioned to a multicultural society, other faiths and beliefs have entered the healthcare landscape. Interdenominational chapels adorned with the crucifix may be an architectural artifact. Just as prayer in schools has become a topic for debate, conversations about how and what spiritual comfort is provided for patients and families will undoubtedly occur. And as with sexual orientation, strong emotions will accompany these discussions. Among the questions that intentionally aware leaders address are: Will caregivers bring their prejudices and biases to the bedside? Will the growing Muslim population be treated with the same respect and dignity as are members of the Christian population? How will the different beliefs of the Mormon, Jew, Buddhist, Christian Scientist, and Confucian be honored? What about the agnostic? The atheist? As with other cultural differences, healthcare leaders must acquire sufficient knowledge and understanding of religions and beliefs to promote culturally competent care and to engender a productive and patient-centered workplace.

OPPORTUNITIES FOR HEALTHCARE LEADERS IN THE DIVERSITY ARENA

As a microcosm of the increasingly multicultural society, the US healthcare system must pay attention and respond to the needs of the new diversity of key stakeholders.

Governance and Leadership

Legacy leaders see opportunity in diversity. They harness their power to make diversity work to the advantage of the organization and the patients served. But they also must *value* diversity in the workplace—not just tolerate it, but truly appreciate it for the innovation it brings to the organization (Kouzes and Posner 1993, 95).

Grant (2010, 41) notes that "leadership representation, organizational culture, and organizational support of diversity are the most powerful change agents and should be the primary focus of diversity initiatives." In other words, diversity in the organization is leadership driven. Leadership must visibly support diversity initiatives and model them for the entire organization if the programs are to be taken seriously. The importance of diversity must be routinely included in leadership conversations. Legacy leaders champion advancement of diverse healthcare providers and managers and thereby promote organizational vitality.

As indicated earlier, the composition of leadership and the governing board should represent the community's demographic diversity. To achieve this representation, leaders must be proactive and persistent in recruiting minority members to serve in these roles. Governing boards must be held responsible to see that their membership appropriately reflects and is responsive to the community and should be encouraged to advance diversity initiatives within the organization. Cordova, Beaudin, and Iwanabe (2010, 21) write, "The importance of the governing body's role in ensuring quality of care is increasing as public reporting of quality data becomes more prevalent and providing culturally equitable care is a safety issue."

Workforce

Workforce diversity presents multiple challenges for healthcare leaders. Executives must recognize the game-changing nature of expanded diversity and mobilize people of many different cultures, languages, and values to enhance organizational performance by sharing knowledge and experiences and by valuing each other's perspectives. Leaders will direct these efforts toward finding common ground in the mission of the organization and in the achievement of its goals.

Deciding how to communicate with, motivate, mentor, evaluate, and reward employees of different cultures requires forethought. Images, humor, and words carry different meanings to different cultures. Managers must be educated in cultural awareness and sensitivity to effectively manage their employees, and professional staff and caregivers must be trained to provide culturally competent care. One advantage that diversity brings to an organization is the thoughtful dissent that can arise from multiple perspectives. It also enhances creativity, idea generation, productivity, and appreciation for the perceptions of others. Hesselbein and Shrader (2008, 348) recommend assigning accountability for building a richly diverse team to every person who directs the work of others.

The new diversity of the workforce brings a variety of value systems to the workplace. Legacy leaders ensure clarity about rules of professionalism, employment, and standards of ethical conduct within their organizations.

Furthermore, successful healthcare leaders recognize and celebrate the importance of the demographic composition of the workforce. Employees, including visible caregivers, should reflect and respect the population being served because that reflection will aid recruitment and retention: The organization becomes attractive to potential candidates, not to mention consumers of healthcare, when its workforce looks, sounds, and acts like them.

At a recent BridgeWorks conference, participants were advised to prepare for the coming worker shortage. Within seven years, the presenters projected, 30 million currently employed workers will be over the age of 55. To mitigate a potential leadership drain, healthcare organizations need to develop new leaders now from a multicultural generation, which comes with all the different values and ambitions discussed in this chapter (Lancaster and Stillman 2011). Successful legacy leaders have the vision to plan accordingly and recognize that, to be an employer of choice, their organizations must find a talented employee pool now and keep it in the future.

Patient Population

As implied through this chapter, healthcare leaders today must ensure that the multicultural patient population they serve receives culturally competent and safe care. According to Cordova, Beaudin, and Iwanabe (2010, 20), the cultural competency of an organization can be measured by "its capacity to integrate principles and values of cultural competence into its policy, structures, attitudes, behaviors, and practices." To accomplish this integration, effective legacy leaders adopt a systems approach to diversity and develop diversity initiatives as part of the strategic direction, including all facets of strategic planning and decision-making processes.

Healthcare executives must also make sure that the commitment to culturally competent care permeates the entire organization and the entire workforce (Cordova, Beaudin, and Iwanabe 2010, 23). Such widespread commitment requires ongoing staff education at all levels of the organization that is based on patient data and immigration patterns of the service area. Sharing knowledge derived from case studies and grand rounds works well in educating clinicians and is a key component to mentoring and developing managers.

THE BUSINESS CASE FOR DIVERSITY

Legacy leaders know their communities—not just their demographic patterns but also the people, with all their unique cultural needs and expectations, who populate those communities. To better understand the community, healthcare leaders need to build creative partnerships with civic organizations, schools, religious organizations, and cultural groups that represent it. Legacy leaders are not just observers; they are participants in efforts that affect the health and well-being of those they serve. Examples of such efforts include enlightened public policy, advocacy, health promotion activities, and dissemination of healthcare career information.

The American College of Healthcare Executives, American Hospital Association, Association of American Medical Colleges, Catholic Health Association of the United States, and National Association of Public Hospitals and Health Systems have joined to pursue the goal of eliminating health disparities and improving the quality of care for every patient. These organizations ask healthcare executives to fully embrace three key practices: increase the collection and use of race, ethnicity, and language preference data; increase cultural competency training; and increase diversity in governance and management.

In 2011, the Health Research & Educational Trust (HRET) and the Institute for Diversity in Health Management (IFD) published *Building a Culturally Competent Organization: The Quest for Equity in Health Care*. The publication presents the indisputable case for action on the diversity front. Of course, culturally competent healthcare can be advocated on the grounds that it is politically correct, socially correct, and ethically correct, but as minorities become an increasingly large proportion of the US population, cultural competency in healthcare becomes a business requirement and a clinical necessity as well. In fact, it can be said that the health and productivity of the nation depend on the ability of our healthcare organizations to deliver culturally competent care. HRET and IFD (2011, 2–3) identify seven tasks, with accompanying self-assessment questions, for healthcare leaders to move their organizations in the direction of representational diversity:

1. Collect race, ethnicity, and language preference
2. Identify and report disparities
3. Provide culturally and linguistically competent care
4. Develop culturally competent disease management programs
5. Increase diversity and minority workforce pipelines
6. Involve the community
7. Make cultural competency an institutional priority

The HRET/IFD report also reminds us that laws and regulations are in place that support culturally competent care. These include Title VI of the Civil Rights Act of 1964; the US Department of Health and Human Services National Standards on Culturally and Linguistically Appropriate Services; relevant Joint Commission accreditation standards; Executive Order 13166, "Improving Access to Services for Persons with Limited Language Proficiency"; and the 2010 Patient Protection and Affordable Care Act. Healthcare leaders must be knowledgeable about these laws and regulations and ensure that their organizations are in compliance (HRET and IFD 2011, 6).

Some states have also undertaken initiatives to move their healthcare organizations closer to diversity standards. The New Mexico Department of Health, in partnership with the Agency for Healthcare Research and Quality, is improving the New Mexico Hospital Inpatient Discharge Data to increase the quality, completeness, and reliability of the state's race and ethnicity data. All nonfederal hospitals across the state are implementing a standardized collection method based on the 1997 Office of Management and Budget Standards for the Classification of Federal Data on Race and Ethnicity and launching a program of extensive data collection for Native American tribal affiliates. This effort acknowledges the need for healthcare leaders to know their state and local populations and implement programs according to their makeup. New Mexico serves as a good example of how diversity affects healthcare delivery: Its Native American population is large and brings tribal differences to the healthcare arena that must be accommodated to ensure safe and effective care for the community.

THREE KEY ACTIONS TO HARDWIRE DIVERSITY INTO YOUR LEGACY ROAD MAP

Action 1: Be intentional about ensuring that leaders and trustees reflect the diversity of the community they serve. Commit to strategies for diversity recruitment and retention, and make certain that these efforts translate throughout the organization.

Action 2: Commit to learning about and understanding your multicultural patient population through personal immersion and community partnerships.

Action 3: Commit your organization to delivering culturally competent, safe patient care. Review and complete the HRET/IFD (2011) self-assessment questions, and use the feedback to implement programs that address organizational needs currently going unfulfilled. Research successful staff education and LEP programs in support of this legacy road map action step.

REFERENCES

Armada, A. A., and M. F. Hubbard. 2010. "Diversity in Healthcare: Time to Get REAL." *Frontiers of Health Services Management* 26 (3): 3–17.

Cook, B. 2010. "Hospitals' New Specialist: Social Media Manager." *American Medical News* (November): 8.

Cordova, R. D., C. L. Beaudin, and K. E. Iwanabe. 2010. "Addressing Diversity and Moving Toward Equity in Hospital Care." *Frontiers of Health Services Management* 26 (3): 19–34.

Dunn, R. T. 2010. *Dunn & Haimann's Healthcare Management*, 9th ed. Chicago: Health Administration Press.

Garman, A. N., T. J. Johnson, and T. C. Royer. 2011. *The Future of Healthcare: Global Trends Worth Watching*. Chicago: Health Administration Press.

Grant, S. 2010. "Diversity in Healthcare: Driven by Leadership." *Frontiers of Health Services Management* 26 (3): 41–44.

Health Research & Educational Trust (HRET) and Institute for Diversity in Health-care Management (IFD). 2011. *Building a Culturally Competent Organization: The Quest for Equity in Health Care*. Chicago: HRET.

Hesselbein, F., and A. Shrader. 2008. *Leader to Leader: Enduring Insights on Leadership*. San Francisco: Jossey-Bass.

Hofmann, P. B. 2011. "Culture Clashes and Moral Judgments." *Healthcare Executive* 26 (1): 52–55.

———. 2010. "Addressing Racial and Ethnic Disparities in Healthcare." *Healthcare Executive* 25 (5): 46–50.

Institute of Medicine (IOM). 2004. *In the Nation's Compelling Interest: Ensuring Diversity in the Health Care Workforce*. Washington, DC: National Academies Press.

———. 2000. *Toward a New Definition of Diversity*. Washington, DC: National Academies Press.

Kouzes, J. M., and B. Z. Posner. 1993. *Credibility: How Leaders Gain and Lose It, Why People Demand It*. San Francisco: Jossey-Bass.

Lancaster, L., and D. Stillman. 2011. "What a Difference a Generation Makes." Presentation at BridgeWorks Spring Conference, Chicago, March 7.

Quigley, W. 2011. "Working Through Differences." *Albuquerque Journal*, June 19, H1.

Schulte, M. F. 2010. "Diversity in Healthcare: Leading Toward Culturally Competent Care." *Frontiers of Health Services Management* 26 (3): 1.

Venegas, M. 2011. "Hispanics Must Use Growing Power Wisely." *Albuquerque Journal*, June 19, B3.

CHAPTER 20

Information Technology: Lasting Impact of Recent Pandemic Response Activities on Healthcare Management and Delivery

Pete Shelkin

IN SEPTEMBER 2019, a large US multihospital health system determined that it needed to make some significant improvements in how it leveraged and managed its information technology (IT) investment. Because the prior chief information officer (CIO) had recently left the organization, the CEO made the decision to first bring in an experienced interim CIO who could quickly assess what was needed to make improvements, craft a long-term strategy, and begin work on the most impactful "road map" items while the health system took the time needed in thoughtfully recruiting the long-term CIO.

The interim CIO arrived in late September, and by the end of January 2020, he had made some leadership changes within the IT department and was in the process of gaining approval for a long-term IT strategy. While the strategy was clearly beneficial, it would ultimately result in additional changes for the IT department, some of which were quite significant. February was an unsettling time for the 150 IT staff members—staff the CIO needed to keep engaged and focused for the organization to succeed. Then, over the course of March 2020, the world as everyone knew it changed dramatically with the onset of the COVID-19 pandemic.

Within a few weeks, the focus of the IT department shifted from preparing to update the technical infrastructure and application base to providing remote work capabilities to more than 15,000 staff members and repurposing dozens of clinical units across several hospitals. As if these challenges weren't big enough on their own, the urgency of the pandemic response dictated that these tasks, which would typically take weeks or months to perform, would need to be completed within a matter of days. Now, the 150 IT staff members who had "only" been worrying about their professional futures were being asked to complete these monumental tasks while also worrying about the health and safety of their families.

It helped that the technologies needed for remote work were not new to the health system. For instance, the tools needed to support remote workers—such as virtual private networks (VPNs), multi-factor authentication (MFA), and virtual workstations—were already in use and well known to the IT staff. The preexistence of the VPNs, MFA, and other virtual tools allowed the IT department to view the sudden need to vastly increase remote connectivity capacity and provide thousands of staff with secure workstations, laptops, and even some printers as more of a logistical challenge than a technical one.

However, logistics themselves are often complicated by crisis. With the entire country moving to a remote work model at the same time, telecom carriers and equipment suppliers were overwhelmed with requests for increasing capacity. Adding to the huge gulf between demand and supply was the fact that nearly all computing and network equipment relies in whole or in part on components manufactured and shipped from China. With China being the first country to begin shutting down during the COVID-19 pandemic, the United States was facing a backlog of equipment orders well before March 2020. Luckily, because one of the top priorities on the CIO's improvement plan was to upgrade the technical infrastructure, he had already been reaching out and building relationships with key vendor contacts, including local and regional executives at the telecom and network communication providers. He had also had similar calls with key suppliers of technical equipment such as network routers, servers, and workstations or laptops and was able to quickly escalate the health system's requests through the appropriate vendor channels.

An added challenge was the repurposing of existing inpatient units, most of which quickly became empty during the spring of 2020, and converting them to temporary intensive care and critical care units. On the heels of the successful rapid shift to remote administrative work, the CIO was aware that in the face of heightened expectations and a great sense of urgency, health system leadership needed to work together very closely to ensure that everyone understood what was practical to achieve in what time frame when it came to shifting the care delivery model. For example, whereas a computer could easily be moved from one location to another, a new care unit had to be "built" within the electronic health record for coding, charting, and even billing to take place. Trade-offs would be required, and leaders from all areas needed to be involved in making informed decisions, especially when it came to introducing changes to critical production information systems.

After examining and reviewing several options, the leadership team made their decisions on unit repurposing and remote care models, and all teams began a coordinated push to effect the changes as rapidly, and as safely, as possible.

As for providing outpatient services, many of the technologies needed for remote care were similar to those used for remote administrative work. However, shifting from on-site clinical consultations to remote consultations required much more coordination among IT, schedulers, billing and finance staff, on-site support staff, caregivers, and even facilities management. Patient technologies were also a factor because the health system needed to ensure that patients were able to securely interact with the health system and participate in remote visits using common home or consumer-grade computers, tablets, cell phones, and internet connections.

The CIO worked with clinical and administrative leaders to help practices shift from scheduling in-person appointments to providing telehealth appointments. IT staff quickly implemented the newly acquired technologies and updated billing systems as reimbursement practices were updated, while in a parallel effort the front office staff, caregivers, and revenue cycle staff were quickly trained in the use of new technologies. Within just a few weeks, the clinics were able to resume patient visits in a virtual manner and begin generating revenue again.

MANAGEMENT DILEMMAS PRESENTED

In the scenario presented in this chapter, the health system managed to avoid any ethical issues by working hard to stay true to the organization's values. However, many management dilemmas presented themselves, and without keeping a focus on values, the health system could have succumbed to many opportunities to move into ethical gray areas. Some of these issues included leverage, compliance, balance, and revenue and quality, as will be examined in the sections that follow.

Leverage

We read how the interim CIO had taken time during his first several weeks at the health system to reach out and speak directly with key vendor contacts, including local and regional executives. He had learned from experience that if an emergency situation ever demanded escalation on the part of a service provider, it was always easier if he already had people's names and numbers in his contact list and had already spoken with them under more pleasant circumstances. Then, as the health system began to discuss the option of having all nonfrontline clinical staff work from home, the CIO once again reached out and spoke directly with regional vice presidents at all suppliers and service providers to verify that the health system would be able to receive the equipment and services that it needed.

Although leveraging relationships is perfectly acceptable, ethics issues can come into play when, unlike the CIO in this chapter, one goes beyond simply knowing the right person to call or the fastest path through a complex process. One such gray area involves applying personal pressure, which in some instances can lead to threats of withholding business that would be unethical. Acts such as providing "gifts" or "favors" are clearly ethics violations.

In this chapter's scenario, the CIO was able to leverage national policy to get vendors to prioritize the needs of the health system in the face of extreme market demand. Most vendors understood that they were required by the US Department of Homeland Security to prioritize the needs of the Healthcare and Public Health Sector during a national health crisis, as outlined in the National Emergency Communications Plan (NECP) published by the Cybersecurity & Infrastructure Security Agency (CISA 2019). However, the CIO found that he needed to help one or two vendors understand how and when NECP directives applied and convince them to redirect shipments of equipment if necessary. With suppliers fully on board, the health system was able to successfully enable its more than 15,000 staff to work securely from home offices in less than one week's time.

Compliance

The vast increase in remote connectivity meant an equally vast increase in security exposure. However, the rapid pace at which the transition to remote work was conducted made it tempting to take shortcuts and set standards aside. To avoid increasing the risk of allowing a disruptive security event to occur, the CIO took care to remind his fellow administrators of how much more damaging it would be to suffer a cyberattack in the midst of the pandemic than it would be to take an extra day or to needed to ensure that standards were met. To this end, the cybersecurity team partnered with the human resources (HR), legal, and compliance teams to ensure that proper training, procedural, and technical controls were in place so that the health system would meet Health Information Portability and Accountability Act and other regulatory security requirements during the transition to remote work.

Balance

With the entire administrative workforce now working off-site, the CIO found that he had to lead a department of 150 staff using nothing but e-mail, messaging apps, and videoconferencing technology. He knew from experience that without some sort of structure—standards and guidelines—things tend to evolve on their own, and not always in the optimal direction. Being sensitive to the prevailing feeling in the world that "things were out of control," he asked for a handful of volunteers to create ad hoc multidepartmental work groups and develop guidelines for procedures such as how videoconference calls were to be handled (e.g., when cameras were to be on, off, or optional) now that all meetings were virtual. He also asked the department social committee, whose work was typically limited to planning the annual picnic and the holiday party, for help organizing regular online social activities to give staff some enjoyable social time in the midst of the ongoing crisis management activities. Recognizing that the IT staff were feeling even less control over their lives and futures with each passing week, he looked for as many opportunities as possible to allow them to exercise some level of control regardless of how trivial it might have seemed on the surface.

Revenue and Quality

Remote teleconsultation visits had been possible before the pandemic struck, but costs and the reluctance by all parties to give up the benefits of a face-to-face visit, as well as the slow pace of change related to reimbursement practices, historically kept telehealth technologies from becoming widely adopted. Once the pandemic struck and face-to-face visits were suddenly halted, telehealth technologies were just as suddenly regarded as a necessity. Although there was no question that the health system should provide telehealth visits as soon as possible, it was important to establish and adhere to quality targets: the sudden cessation of billable activities was driving all healthcare providers to find ways to generate revenue as soon as possible, but the health system needed to ensure that "mission" was seen as just as high a priority as "margin."

In addition to finding a way to provide outpatient consultations, the health system grappled with the question of when an "elective" procedure was no longer truly elective. Some procedures, such as cosmetic surgery, would always be considered elective, but others, such as spinal surgery needed to relive chronic pain, could only be delayed so long before the harm to the patient outweighed the benefit of isolation during a pandemic. With revenues all but halted, there was ample temptation for judgment calls to skew in the direction of scheduling more procedures. To ensure that proper decisions were made, an ad hoc medical committee made up of physician leaders and health system administrators was formed and charged with meeting daily to make individual decisions.

RELATED QUESTIONS TO CONSIDER

This chapter uses the example of a multihospital health system to review how technology was leveraged across the healthcare industry during the recent pandemic response and poses questions related to use of technology that will likely remain relevant long after the COVID-19 pandemic has been declared to be over. As a healthcare leader or a student aspiring to become one, consider how you would address the questions presented in the sections that follow.

Preparedness Toolkit

The CIO in this chapter's scenario understood not only the value of relationship building but also the laws and regulations that applied to managing a crisis despite the previous, commonly held belief that an extended global lockdown scenario was unlikely to ever unfold. Given all the competing demands on a leader's time, how can leaders best prepare for succeeding in a similar fashion if a similarly unlikely situation were to arise? Since no one person can be an expert in all areas, what relationships and information sources (both internal and external) can you leverage as part of your "preparedness toolkit"?

Crisis Management Process

Health system leaders in the example were able to work closely together and make tough decisions in a limited time frame and while under great pressure. One tool that the team had was a good crisis management process that they were able to follow and apply. Are there other policies and processes that could also prove beneficial if a similar situation were to occur? How might you best prepare yourself today for succeeding if you were to be responsible for managing a crisis situation in the future?

Staff Wellness

Despite their technical successes, the IT staff would have felt just as out of control over what was happening in the world as everyone else at the time, especially given that the team was already feeling unsettled before the pandemic struck. If you were to find yourself leading a large team during a time of great crisis, or even just great change, how might you create opportunities for your staff to sense that they have some areas where they can feel in control? How might you balance the need to keep staff fully engaged during a time of crisis with the need to provide them with the time and space to deal with personal and family matters? How might you also gauge staff's mental health and provide help for those who might need it? How might employee wellness programs evolve, given that it is acceptable for many jobs to be done remotely now?

With many people returning to offices, the remote work experience has permanently changed how we communicate with colleagues on a day-to-day basis. How have you adapted to managing social interaction, including celebrating success, now that many department meetings take place virtually?

Revenue Generation Opportunities

New technologies often mean new costs, which is why a solid business case tends to be required before approval is granted. Sometimes, however, technology is required as a temporary means of minimizing losses, as was the case when in-person visits were halted. In these instances, how can those technologies be leveraged to also drive revenue in ways that may not have been considered in the past?

Facilities and Infrastructure

With the need to reduce physical interaction, particularly in clinical spaces, while at the same time trying to maintain a healthy amount of social interaction, we've found that we need to redesign a lot of physical spaces in addition to using interactive technology. What can we do to develop and maintain a proactive edge in managing this balance as we plan new spaces in which to work and deliver healthcare services?

Productivity Metrics

With many administrative and support staff working remotely, the use of productivity metrics has become more relevant. Technologies have emerged that allow managers to monitor activity and productivity, but some of those technologies can border on the invasive. Still, with human nature being what it is, there will always be a few people who try to take advantage of a situation, such as the actual case of an IT help desk analyst who, when working from home, was found to be calling his own work phone number from his cell phone, setting his phones down, and taking a 45-minute break while the metrics appeared to show that he was handling a long call for IT assistance.

How can managers ensure that realistic yet challenging productivity targets are set and met, while at the same time avoid creating a draconian, intrusive, and punitive culture? How can staff be involved in shaping that culture so that everyone accepts what is realistically necessary as part of the trade-off that allows people the flexibility and benefits that they gain through remote work?

Recruitment and Retention

Now that people can, and do, take jobs anywhere in the country, regional pay grades based on local cost-of-living indexes are losing their relevance. While major metropolitan health systems with higher pay grades can attract candidates for remote positions from most locales, employers in rural areas may now find it harder to compete for qualified candidates. How might health systems adapt to this new reality? What changes do you see coming in recruitment and retention practices, and how might you guide those changes to be most beneficial for all involved?

In addition, the aging US workforce had already been posing challenges in terms of recruitment and retention, as any nurse manager will tell you. With technology enabling other parts of the healthcare workforce to become more mobile, the HR challenges are only increasing. At the same time, these very same technologies enable people to work more productively and efficiently, as well as to collaborate without physical bounds. How might we respond to these challenges and opportunities over the next few years, knowing that what we do today will have lasting impacts on how efficiently we can manage the healthcare delivery systems of the future?

Patient Migration

Now that patients can have virtual consultations with clinicians in very distant locations, how can providers keep patients from migrating? On the flip side, how might providers bring in new business from patients outside their traditional geographical market?

CONCLUSION: THE NEW NORMAL

During the years before the COVID-19 pandemic struck, IT departments in the United States had been slowly enabling health systems to increase mobility in their workforces. Then, in March 2020, IT groups were suddenly thrust center stage as they enabled institutions, regardless of size, to fully shift to remote work models in a matter of days. Although the pandemic disrupted day-to-day living, the technologies deployed and supported by IT groups allowed health systems to remain functional while the country was on an emergency lockdown.

Today, the health emergency has officially ended, but the ways in which we leveraged technology during the COVID-19 pandemic have brought about changes that are, for better or for worse, here to stay. Health system leaders now face challenges in managing the impact of changes in work processes, work culture, expectations (of staff, management, and patients), and even recruitment.

While the rapid pace of technology deployment allowed us to succeed in our work during 2020, it also meant that we did not have the luxury of thoughtfully planning for such significant changes. History has shown us that without careful guidance, ways of working will tend to take the path of least resistance, which is not necessarily the path to an optimal outcome. The challenge for today's healthcare leaders lies in answering the question of how to achieve "best" as opposed to simply "easiest."

Many crises come to an easily defined end: the smoke clears or the waters recede, and life works its way back to normal, albeit with some rebuilding often required along the way. Recovery from a pandemic may follow a similar pattern, but over a much longer time span wherein we see a gradual abatement of the pathogen along with a slow return to a life without emergency restrictions. Although pandemics are not new, the "return to normal" following the COVID-19 pandemic is different from historical postpandemic periods because of how we leveraged technology to keep us as functional as possible during the lockdown period. As the health system in this chapter's scenario came to learn, many of these technology-driven changes are creating a "new normal" that is here to stay.

REFERENCE

Cybersecurity & Infrastructure Security Agency (CISA). 2019. National Emergency Communications Plan. Published September. www.cisa.gov/sites/default/files/publications/19_0924_CISA_ECD-NECP-2019_1.pdf.

CHAPTER 21

Ethical Considerations and Challenges in Pandemics

Paul B. Hofmann

THE HUGE PERSONAL and financial costs associated with about 7 million global deaths attributed to COVID-19, as reported by the World Health Organization (WHO 2023)—including more than 1 million deaths in the United States, according to the Centers for Disease Control and Prevention (CDC 2023)—don't even begin to reflect the pain and suffering experienced by survivors and their families. For example, an article written by Hillis and colleagues in *JAMA Pediatrics* indicated that COVID-19 left 10.5 million children without parents or caregivers (Hillis et al. 2022). The total number of people of all ages enduring "long COVID" is undoubtedly high as well (Belluck 2023; Span 2023).

History tells us the bubonic plague ravaged Europe in the 1300s, killing more than 25 million people, or about two-thirds of the population at that time (Cleveland Clinic 2021), and then a more virulent strain occurred in the 1500s, followed by another at the end of the 1800s. The death rate was a striking 60 to 90 percent (Cleveland Clinic 2021). Fortunately, the eventual development of antibiotics prevented the subsequent devastation wrought by comparable diseases.

We know that the initial response to the COVID-19 pandemic was grossly inadequate, both in the United States and globally. Predictably, there have been innumerable critiques about why and how the recognition of such a major crisis could have been so poor. This chapter will examine what lessons should be considered, particularly from an ethical perspective, to position healthcare organizations to better serve our communities in the future. Most rational people reasonably assume that the key question is not *if* another pandemic will happen, but *when*.

COVID-RELATED ISSUES

"Lessons for Healthcare Executives and Other Leaders During COVID-19: Five Major Opportunities for Improvement" appeared in the *Journal of Ambulatory Care Management* (Hofmann 2021). In this article, I discussed why the following issues should have received much more attention, each of which has obvious ethical dimensions:

- Doing much better in mitigating burnout
- Acting expeditiously to protect staff from avoidable physical harm
- Not permitting patients to die alone
- Devoting insufficient attention to the disproportionate impact of the pandemic on those who historically have been compromised by racial disparities
- Having a plan in place for furloughing employees

It should be clear why each one of these issues has profound ethical implications. With reference to burnout, healthcare professionals predictably give higher priority to the needs of patients over their own needs. Even before the pandemic, they had to deal with stress, often associated with understaffing and a work culture in which no mistake was tolerated. Then consider the moral distress associated with insufficient equipment for increased patient volume during the pandemic leading to the need to withdraw a ventilator from one patient to save another with a better prognosis.

Regarding the importance of protecting staff from avoidable harm, the initial underappreciated scale of the COVID-19 crisis meant that some institutions of the government did not move quickly enough to acquire adequate supplies of personal protective equipment for healthcare workers, particularly nurses and other frontline caregivers at greatest risk of exposure to the deadly virus. One 46-page report indicated the consequence in its title: *Sins of Omission: How Government Failures to Track Covid-19 Data Have Led to More Than 1,700 Health Care Worker Deaths and Jeopardized Public Health* (National Nurses United 2020).

Because of restrictions on visitors for patients who were infected with COVID-19 during the early part of the pandemic before vaccines had been developed, four surgical residents affiliated with the University of Minnesota wrote "Not Dying Alone—Modern Compassionate Care in the Covid-19 Pandemic" for the *New England Journal of Medicine* (Wakham et al. 2020). They stated, "We believe that the U.S. health care system can do better. As telehealth and virtual meetings become the new normal, so can telecommunication between isolated patients and their families." In an article appearing in *FierceHealthcare*, the author noted that

Florida-based AdventHealth instituted video visits, but the health system took the additional step of providing about 1,000 Chromebook personal computers to patients who did not have their own devices (Reed 2020).

Crises typically worsen existing inequalities. In a blog posted by the Brookings Institution, the author stated that "African American communities are dying at significantly higher rates than others, and the full impact on marginalized communities probably won't be fully understood until the crisis is over. Racial inequality was baked into the recipe of the creation of the United States of America. Inequities in neighborhood resources and the healthcare system are manifestations of this recipe. And, when crises like the COVID-19 pandemic occur, inequalities are exacerbated rather than diminished" (Ray 2020). Two physicians have described an extensive educational program launched in 2017 at Brigham and Women's Hospital to combat institutional racism. Motivated by residents and the Black Lives Matter movement, a Department of Medicine Health Equity Committee was established to address health equity issues. The committee partnered with both a community health center, considered a leader in racial justice, and the highly regarded Institute for Healthcare Improvement, which had developed a learning collaborative to advance racial justice in healthcare. The physicians acknowledged that education at academic medical centers does not typically include issues of racism and racial inequity, so the community health center created a program called Adaptive Leaders for Racial Justice "to prepare clinicians to challenge the dominant beliefs about causes of and solutions to racial inequities in health" (Morse and Loscalzo 2020). After faculty members and residents from the health equity committee participated in the program, they "became leading voices for racial justice as well as formal and informal teachers on these issues" (Morse and Loscalzo 2020). Maulik Joshi, president and CEO of Meritus Health, has proposed a five-part action plan for the leadership of every healthcare organization, with precise target dates within a 12-month period to accomplish prescriptive objectives in four key dimensions: unconscious bias, disparities in care, racial and ethnic diversity in leadership, and social determinants of health. Notably, his final action requirement was that leaders "publicly commit to this one year of action as soon as possible" (Joshi 2020). An exemplary step was also taken by the University of California, Berkeley. It launched a new website, Racism and Health (2023), which aggregates data from more than 250 sociological and research studies at the university, as well as other institutions such as Stanford University, on how racism impacts health. The website "examines how cultural norms can promote racism and perpetuate negative health outcomes for minority populations" (Bay Area Global Health Alliance 2023).

When hospitals and health systems around the country had to cancel all elective medical and surgical procedures because of the pandemic, it was foreseeable that the workforce would have to be downsized. Nonetheless, too many leaders did not have a readily available plan that should have been in place for a long time, as I had recommended 24 years earlier in "The Ethics of Downsizing," published in the January/February 1996 issue of *Healthcare Executive*. Given that senior executives, including human resource officers, were facing multiple management challenges, it was inevitable that morale would fall in the midst of uncertainty about the number and type of personnel who were at risk of losing their income, including some who may have been infected by the virus. And yet the delay in developing a strategy and process meant that loyal employees did not know when and how they might be compromised further at a time of great anxiety both at work and at home.

In a remarkably comprehensive PowerPoint presentation shared with me on May 17, 2021, Dr. Margaret A. Liu, chair of the International Society for Vaccines Board, covered the following six topics (Liu 2021):

1. Information and decision making in the COVID era
2. State of the pandemic
3. Brief update about issues with different vaccines
4. Mutant strains
5. What activities you can/should do after you are immunized
6. How you make choices/decisions

During the pandemic, people in the United States and other countries were often overwhelmed with information, and it was not always reliable. Dr. Liu's impressive presentation is highlighted because it reminds us that we should consider the information's source. This is not to suggest that some people have hidden agendas but that their credentials should be considered before acting or not acting on reports.

ANALYSIS

Writing for *The Hill* on October 18, 2022, Alex Gangitano summarized the White House's national biodefense strategy to protect the United States from future pandemics and biological threats. The strategy for the next deadly pandemic calls for the United States to produce a test for a new pathogen within 12 hours of its discovery and enough vaccine to protect the nation within 130 days. A senior administration official was quoted by the author as saying, "We . . . know that the risk of another pandemic as bad or worse than COVID is a real threat" (Gangitano 2022). While this statement implicitly recognized that the previous administration greatly underestimated the seriousness of the epidemic, the rapidity with which it would spread, the magnitude of the crisis, and the eventual large death toll, most other countries were similarly unprepared.

The same day, *Reuters Fast Check* emphasized that COVID-19 vaccines were *not* linked to an 8,200 percent increase in child deaths in the past year. The incorrect assertion had been conveyed in a video by a man in a miliary uniform and was shared more than 2,300 times on Facebook, Instagram, and Twitter (Reuters 2022). The ethical ramifications of this type of misinformation are self-evident, but the actual consequences are immeasurable in terms regarding the number of people who may have been irreversibly harmed by not having been vaccinated.

"Errors in Converting Principles to Protocols: Where the Bioethics of U.S. Covid Vaccine Allocation Went Wrong" appeared in the highly respected *Hastings Center Report.* The criticism was very harsh. "The Centers for Disease Control and Prevention's Advisory Committee on Immunization Practices (ACIP) identified three fundamental ethical principles to guide the process: maximize benefits, promote justice, and mitigate health inequities," and the article's authors believed that none of these principles had been satisfied (Parker, Persad, and Peek 2022).

In January 2023, the news agency Reuters reported, "The world is 'dangerously unprepared' for future pandemics, the International Federation of the Red Cross and Red Crescent Societies (IFRC) say. . . . In its World Disasters Report 2022, the IFRC said 'all countries remain dangerously unprepared for future outbreaks' despite COVID-19 killing more people than any earthquake, drought or hurricane in history" (Reuters 2023). Echoing that concern, "An Even Deadlier Pandemic Could Soon Be Here" was the unsettling title of a February 3, 2023, opinion piece in the *New York Times.* The author warned, "Bird flu—known more formally as avian influenza—has long hovered on the horizons of scientists' fears. This pathogen, especially the H5N1 strain, hasn't often infected humans, but when it has, 56 percent of those known to have contracted it have died. Its inability to spread easily, if at all, from one person to another has kept it from causing a pandemic. But things are changing. The virus, which has long caused outbreaks among poultry, is infecting more and more migratory birds, allowing it to spread more widely, even to various mammals, raising the risk that a new variant could spread to and among people" (Tuifeki 2023).

As expected, the nation's public health response has been the subject of extensive criticism. A devastating critique in *Newsweek* was written by two physicians, one at Harvard and the other at Stanford. They asserted, "Our collective response to the COVID-19 pandemic constituted history's biggest public health mistake. We did not properly protect older high-risk Americans, while many ineffective COVID restrictions have generated long-term collateral public health damage that is now upon us. Both have yielded excess deaths. Public health crashed" (Kulldorff and Bhattachaya 2023).

Another article published in the *Washington Post* described why the United States will be even less prepared for another pandemic. "When the next pandemic sweeps the United States, . . . not even the president can force federal agencies to issue vaccination or testing mandates to thwart its march. Conservative and libertarian forces have defanged much of the nation's public health system through legislation and litigation. At least 30 states . . . have passed laws since 2020 that limit public health authority. . . . Health officials and governors in more than half the country are now restricted from issuing mask mandates, ordering school closures and imposing other protective measures or must seek permission from their state legislatures before renewing emergency orders" (Weber and Achenbach 2023).

Perhaps the most revealing postmortem analysis of how the pandemic spiraled out of control was published in a *New York Times Magazine* article on April 24, 2023. In "Dr. Fauci Looks Back: 'Something Clearly Went Wrong,'" the journalist who interviewed him at length included an ominous statement: "The month after Anthony Fauci retired as the four-decade head of the National Institute of Allergy and Infectious Diseases, barely half of Americans said they trusted the country's public-health institutions to manage a future pandemic" (Wallace-Wells 2023). Such a negative finding has broad ramifications for how US citizens will respond to recommendations and even when mandates are proposed. Compounding the problem is the fact that US public health departments have warned for decades that they are underfunded, a situation obviously exacerbated by the pandemic. Yes, state budgets are perennially unable to fund all valid requests, but what objective calculus can be used to weigh the ethical impact of low funding and human suffering?

On May 11, 2023, another *New York Times* article stated, "A lot went wrong during the coronavirus pandemic as the virus tore through a polarized nation and public health leaders, policymakers and elected officials struggled to respond. Chronic underinvestment in public health at the federal, state, and local levels only made things worse. All told, more than 1.1 million people have died of Covid-19 in the United States, and more than 1,000 are still dying each week" (Stolberg and Weiland 2023). It is difficult to imagine a more stinging ethical indictment of the country's lack of preparation and insufficient mitigation.

EVOLUTION OF THE PANDEMIC

For those interested in learning how the pandemic evolved, the CDC has created a detailed timeline identifying key dates beginning on December 12, 2019, through July 8, 2022. After reviewing hundreds of dates, I felt that all the following events had serious ethical undertones (CDC 2023):

- May 18, 2020: "Navajo Nation now has the highest infection rate per capita in the U.S."
- June 29, 2020: "Despite its development and clinical trials being supported by as much as $6.5 billion in public funds, Gilead Sciences sets the price of Remdesivir, an anti-viral used to treat COVID-19 that can shorten hospital stays and reduce the need for mechanical ventilation, at $3,120 for one typical treatment course ($520 per vial) for insured patients in the U.S."
- July 14, 2020: "Florida, Texas, Oklahoma, Mississippi, North Carolina, South Carolina, and Georgia have both the greatest percentage of adults who are currently uninsured and the highest numbers of new COVID-19 cases."
- October 6, 2020: "Food insecurity in the U.S. reaches 52 million people due to the COVID-19 pandemic—17 million more people than pre-pandemic numbers."
- April 8, 2021: "CDC announces $2.25 billion in spending over two years to address COVID-19 related health disparities for people living in rural areas and racial and ethnic minority groups."
- October 7, 2021: "More than 140,000 children in the U.S. have lost their primary or secondary caregiver to the COVID-19 pandemic. One of every 168 American Indian and Alaska Native children, 1 of every 310 Black children, 1 of every 412 non-White Hispanic children, 1 of every 612 Asian children, and 1 of every 753 White children have now experienced orphanhood or the death of caregivers."
- January 17, 2022: "The American Civil Liberties Union (ACLU) sues an Arkansas jail on behalf of detainees who reported COVID-19 like symptoms and say they were unknowingly given ivermectin and hydroxychloroquine, two drugs that CDC does not recommend for the treatment of COVID-19."
- March 31, 2022: "CDC releases data from the Adolescent Behaviors and Experiences Survey (ABES) showing that from January 2021–June 2021 among high-school aged adolescents: 44% report feeling persistently sad or hopeless; 55% report emotional abuse in the home; 11% report physical abuse in the home; and 29% report job loss by an adult in the home. Lesbian, gay, bisexual, and female youth reported the poorest overall mental health, the most emotional abuse by a parent or caregiver, and attempted suicide more than their peers during the COVID-19 pandemic."
- May 10, 2022: "During the COVID-19 pandemic, there has been a 35% increase in the firearm homicide rate, resulting in the highest firearm homicide rate in more than 25 years. Firearm homicide rates are the highest among males, adolescents, young adults, and non-Hispanic Black and non-Hispanic American Indian and Alaska Native people. Rates of firearm

suicide remained high, increasing most notably among American Indian and Alaska Native males ages 10–44, and are highest in rural areas."

- May 16, 2022: "Researchers from Brown University School of Public Health, Brigham and Women's Hospital, and Harvard T. H. Chan School of Public Health, estimate that approximately 50% of COVID-19 deaths in the U.S. were vaccine-preventable deaths."
- June 2, 2022: "A Kaiser Foundation study tested three widespread false statements about COVID-19 vaccines: 'pregnant women should not get the COVID-19 vaccine; it is unsafe for women who are breastfeeding to get a COVID-19 vaccine; and the COVID-19 vaccines have been shown to cause infertility.' Vaccine misinformation is so pervasive that about six in ten U.S. adults and seven in ten women who are pregnant or planning to become pregnant either believed or were unsure about at least one of these false statements."

Not surprisingly, 2023 continued to reflect ongoing confirmation that other ethical challenges were associated with the pandemic. An alarming report appeared in *Becker's Hospital Review*. It stated that "2022 was the worst year on record for acts of violence against healthcare facilities and personnel on the global level, according to a new report from the Safeguarding Health in Conflict Coalition. The coalition documented 1,989 incidents of violence against or obstruction of healthcare in conflicts and situations of political unrest in 32 countries and territories, a 45 percent increase compared to 2021 and the highest annual number of incidents that the coalition has recorded since it began tracking such violence. The coalition notes that the annual tally is likely an undercount. Violence included the deliberate targeting of health facilities with explosive weapons; destroying and looting hospitals and clinics; killing, kidnapping and threatening health workers; and the deliberate obstruction of patients' access to healthcare" (Gamble 2023).

STEPS FOR THE FUTURE

Given the likelihood we will eventually have to confront another pandemic or similar crisis in the future, what logical steps can be taken to capitalize on previous lessons learned to minimize the ethical burdens placed on our organizations and communities? Such steps should be apparent from what has been written in this chapter, but nevertheless they deserve emphasis.

1. The White House's national biodefense strategy to protect the United States from future pandemics and biological threats should receive the priority it

deserves, especially when a senior administration official states, as mentioned previously, "We . . . know that the risk of another pandemic as bad or worse than COVID is a real threat."

2. State and local public health department budgets should receive adequate funding so that they will be positioned to be more responsive to the next pandemic.

3. Our health systems and hospitals can and should be better prepared, and they can do so by learning from those whose creative initiatives improved care for patients and their families, as well as by supporting the essential needs of staff members.

4. The well-documented inequities and disparities in access and clinical outcomes among racial and ethnic minorities and the LGBTQ community will not be reduced quickly, but the appointment of diversity, equity, inclusion, and belonging officers demonstrates that more health systems and hospitals recognize the significance of these concerns.

5. Whether it is called misinformation or disinformation, its prevalence has compromised the provision of vaccinations to people who needed them, and our institutions should be actively involved in combating such deceptions.

6. No one would deny that any violence against healthcare personnel and facilities is intolerable, so the crucial questions focus on what more can be done to prevent it and which organizations have had the greatest success in preventing or at least minimizing this violence.

While predicting the future is perilous, every indicator suggests that another pandemic is likely. Our ethical imperative is to take individual and collective leadership actions to lessen its pain and suffering.

REFERENCES

Bay Area Global Health Alliance. 2023. *Global Health Connections*, October. E-mail newsletter received by author.

Belluck, P. 2023. "Who Is Most at Risk for Long Covid?" *New York Times*, March 24, A20.

Centers for Disease Control and Prevention (CDC). 2023. "CDC Museum COVID-19 Timeline." David J. Senser CDC Museum in Association with the Smithsonian Institution. Reviewed March 13. www.cdc.gov/museum/timeline/covid19.html.

Cleveland Clinic. 2021. "Bubonic Plague." Reviewed June 17. https://my.clevelandclinic.org/health/diseases/21590-bubonic-plague.

Gamble, M. 2023. "A Disturbing Year for Violence Against Global Healthcare." *Becker's Hospital Review*. Published June 12. www.beckershospitalreview.com/workforce/a-disturbing-year-for-violence-against-global-healthcare.html.

Gangitano, A. 2022. "Biden's Biodefense Strategy Aims to Combat Future Epidemics." *The Hill*. Published October 18. https://thehill.com/homenews/administration/3693368-bidens-biodefense-strategy-aims-to-combat-future-pandemics/.

Hillis, S., P. Ntwali n'Konzi, W. Msemburi, L. Cluver, A. Villaveces, S. Flaxman, and H. J. T. Unwin. 2022. "Orphanhood and Caregiver Loss Among Children Based on New Global Excess COVID-19 Death Estimates." *JAMA Pediatrics* 176 (11): 1145–48. https://doi.org/10.1001/jamapediatrics.2022.3157.

Hofmann, P. B. 2021. "Lessons for Healthcare Executives and Other Leaders During COVID-19: Five Major Opportunities for Improvement." *Journal of Ambulatory Care Management* 44 (1): 66–70.

———. 1996. "The Ethics of Downsizing." *Healthcare Executive*, January/February.

Joshi, M. 2020. "Hundreds of Days of Action as a Start to Address Hundreds of Years of Inequity." NEJM Catalyst: Innovations in Care Delivery. Published July 13. https://catalyst.nejm.org/doi/full/10.1056/CAT.20.0362.

Kulldorff, M., and J. Bhattacharya. 2023. "We Need a COVID Commission." *Newsweek*. Published February 22. www.newsweek.com/we-need-covid-commission-opinion-1782857.

Liu, M. A. 2021. "How to Think About and Make Personal Decisions About Activities in the May 2021 COVID-19 Era." PowerPoint presentation to author, May 17.

Morse, M., and J. Loscalzo. 2020. "Creating Real Change at Academic Medical Centers—How Social Movements Can Be Timely Catalysts." *New England Journal of Medicine* 383 (3): 199–201. https://doi.org/10.1056/NEJMp2002502.

National Nurses United. 2020. *Sins of Omission: How Government Failures to Track Covid-19 Data Have Led to More Than 1,700 Health Care Worker Deaths and Jeopardized Public Health*. Published September. www.nationalnursesunited.org/sites/default/files/nnu/documents/0920_Covid19_SinsOfOmission_Data_Report.pdf.

Parker, W. F., G. Persad, and M. E. Peek. 2022. "Errors in Converting Principles to Protocols: Where the Bioethics of U.S. Covid Vaccine Allocation Went Wrong." *Hastings Center Report*, October 13.

Racism and Health. 2023. "Racism Harms Health." University of California, Berkeley. Accessed October 16. https://racismharmshealth.berkeley.edu.

Ray, R. 2020. "Bad Apples Come from Rotten Trees in Policing." *Brookings* (blog), Brookings Institution. Published May 30. www.brookings.edu/articles/bad-apples-come-from-rotten-trees-in-policing/.

Reed, T. 2020. "COVID-19 Special Report: Lessons in Combining Compassion with Technology." *FierceHealthcare*. Published July 27. www.fiercehealthcare.com/hospitals/covid-19-special-report-lessons-combining-compassion-technology.

Reuters. 2023. "All Countries 'Dangerously Unprepared' for Future Pandemics, Says IFRC." Published January 30. www.reuters.com/business/healthcare-pharmaceuticals/all-countries-dangerously-unprepared-future-pandemics-says-ifrc-2023-01-30/.

———. 2022. "Fact Check: COVID-19 Vaccines Not Linked to 8,200% Increase in Child Deaths in Past Year, as Claimed in Online Video." Published October 19. www.reuters.com/article/factcheck.

Span, P. 2023. "Long Covid Poses Special Challenges for Seniors." *New York Times*, September 5, D3.

Stolberg, S., and N. B. Weiland. 2023. "Experts See Lessons for Next Pandemic as Covid Emergency Comes to an End." *New York Times*, May 11, A15.

Tuifeki, Z. 2023. "An Even Deadlier Pandemic Could Soon Be Here." *New York Times*, February 3, SR8.

Wakham, G. K., J. R. Montgomery, B. E. Biesterveld, C. S. Brown. 2020. "Not Dying Alone—Modern Compassionate Care in the Covid-19 Pandemic." *New England Journal of Medicine* 382 (24): e88. https://doi.org/10.1056/NEJMp2007781.

Wallace-Wells, D. 2023. "Dr. Fauci Looks Back: 'Something Clearly Went Wrong.'" *New York Times Magazine*, April 24, MM36.

Weber, L., and J. Achenbach. 2023. "Covid Backlash Hobbles Public Health and Future Pandemic Response: Lawsuits and Legislation Have Stripped Public Health Officials of Their Powers in Three Years." *Washington Post*, March 8.

World Health Organization (WHO). 2023. "Coronavirus Disease (COVID-19)." Fact sheet. Published August 9. www.who.int/news-room/fact-sheets/detail/coronavirus-disease-(covid-19).

CHAPTER 22

The Critical Role and Integration of Public Health Within the Healthcare Delivery System

Tracie C. Collins

THIS CHAPTER WILL explore the need and obstacles within the US healthcare system for better integration of public health and the current healthcare delivery system that were identified during the COVID-19 pandemic. It will examine lessons learned during this pandemic and identify initiatives that support more effective systemwide collaboration to address problem areas, such as data collection that is required by law and often done ineffectively and manually.

In late 2019, the first cases of human infection with what the World Health Organization (WHO 2023a) identified as the SARS-CoV-2 coronavirus emerged. Infections caused by this novel (new) coronavirus are noted as COVID-19, a shorthand for "coronavirus disease 2019," with *CO* standing for *corona*, *VI* for *virus*, *D* for *disease*, and 19 for the year the outbreak was first recognized (Kaplan 2020). We now have more clarity about the virus, but in the early months of the infections, those of us in public health leadership roles were quickly learning so much and preparing to keep communities safe.

COVID-19 negatively impacted many lives, evolving into a worldwide health emergency. Globally, by October 2023, there had been more than 771 million known cases, with nearly 7 million deaths (WHO 2023b). In the United States, there had been more than 103 million known cases, with approximately 1.1 million deaths (WHO 2023c). The number of actual cases is grossly underestimated given the use of home testing without required reporting of results.

COVID-19 disproportionally impacted communities of color (Graham 2021). Black and Latinx populations were four to nine times more likely to experience COVID-19 than non-Latinx Whites in communities that were noted for having high caseloads. Indigenous communities were severely impacted by COVID-19, with more cases and much higher rates of death as compared with non-Latinx White communities.

Concurrent with the pandemic were horrific acts of social injustice at the hands of police officers. We witnessed the unjustified no-knock warrant at the home of Breonna Taylor leading to her shooting death. We witnessed the homicide of George Floyd by officers' excessive use of force as Floyd cried out for his mom with his dying breath. We also witnessed an officer's use of a firearm instead of the intended stun gun leading to the death of Daunte Wright, with a questionable explanation as to why he had been stopped by police. These three incidents in which Black people lost their lives as a result of police actions are just a few of the many devastating outcomes in communities of color at the hands of law enforcement, which raises the questions of whether "serving and protecting" are reserved for nonminorities.

LINK BETWEEN RACISM AND HEALTH INEQUITIES

The trauma from the aforementioned events and others is an extension of many years of structural racism. *Structural racism* is a system driven by structures, policies, practices, and norms that work in concert to perpetuate inequities by race/ethnicity that affect multiple generations (Krieger 2014). Structural racism negatively impacts the *social determinants of health* including housing, transportation, education, income, access to nutrient-dense foods, and access to healthcare. There is a clear link between structural racism and the devastation from COVID-19 among communities of color (Grills et al. 2022). A few examples include residing in multigenerational homes that don't allow for social distancing or isolation, employment requiring physical interaction with the public and therefore an increased risk for exposure, and lack of running water limiting handwashing. Further, preexisting chronic conditions combined with environmental and socioeconomic inequities amplified the poor outcomes from COVID for traditionally marginalized communities.

The thread underlying structural racism in the United States is settler colonialism (Saito 2020). Settler colonialism is more than identifying resources and labor to support the settlers' homelands. Unfortunately, colonialism includes people of European origin establishing policies and practices to eliminate Indigenous Peoples while taking their land. In addition to ravaging the land and lives of Indigenous Peoples, there was the capture of Africans from their homelands for the purpose of enslavement as a workforce to generate a profit on the stolen land (Rowe and Tuck 2016). Settler colonialism also created the label of *migrants*, which allowed for utilizing these "Other" communities (e.g., Mexicans) for labor when it was profitable while deporting such communities when the labor needs ended.

Structural racism is the foundation of historical trauma. *Historical trauma* stems from one or more events systemically conferred on a group of people with a common identity leading to disadvantages that greatly hinder a group's ability to move beyond some barriers (e.g., lower socioeconomic status). Examples of historical trauma include forced relocation, slavery, Native American boarding schools, racial violence, and medical experimentation. Such events can eradicate culture, language, self-worth, and independence. In the movie *The Help* (Taylor 2011), we see generations of Black women who are domestics, or household "help," for non-Latinx White women. These Black women receive limited pay and live in poverty; many have limited education and often include their teenage children in their work. The additional family income generated from their children comes at the expense of limiting the child's education, which can affect multiple generations. Some of the domestics in the movie are asked to assist a young White woman, a recent college graduate, in her effort to write a book about their experiences. The writing process allows many of the Black women to release frustrations and share their common experiences as domestics. The book is published, and it becomes a must-read among the White women in the community. Some of the Black women who are domestics receive a substantial paycheck as well as confidence to write more books. Their ability to write more books that will generate more money is an example of potentially breaking the cycle of poverty. The movie is based on the best-selling debut novel by Kathryn Stockett (2009), a non-Latinx White woman born and raised in Mississippi.

Race, ethnicity, and worker status have been clearly linked to COVID-related health inequities. The disproportionate representation of persons of color as essential workers increased the risk for exposure to COVID-19. According to the US Census Bureau (2020), people of Hispanic origin represent approximately 19 percent of the US population but constitute 28 percent of essential workers in the food and agriculture industry and 40 percent of workers in commercial and service groups. In survey data from work conducted by Grills and colleagues (2022), more than 67 percent of Latinx essential workers reported that they or someone in their household had to continue working despite having been in close contact with people who were potentially COVID positive; also, 40 percent reported receiving inadequate medical care during the pandemic, and 28 percent indicated that they or another household member were unable to access medical care for chronic conditions.

HOPE, COMMUNITY ENGAGEMENT, AND RESILIENCE

With the devastating impact of COVID among many US communities, there was great hope once an approved vaccine became available in the United States. Yet this hope was diminished in part because of vaccine hesitancy. COVID-19 vaccine hesitancy has been pervasive among many communities. For rural communities in which Christian ideology is pervasive, fear and mistrust of the US government fueled concerns about the vaccine. Among Blacks, mistrust of the healthcare system and fear of experimentation have been driving factors for vaccine hesitancy. One example of historical trauma that contributed to such mistrust is the Tuskegee Experiment in which for 40 years, from 1932 to 1972, the US Public Health Service (PHS) conducted an experiment on a group of African American men who suffered from syphilis. The PHS, which compelled the men with the prospect of free medical care and meals, withheld treatment and did not reveal the true purpose of the experiment: to study the long-term effects of untreated syphilis. As a result, hundreds of the men suffered debilitation and death that could have been prevented (Washington 2007). Additionally, there are instances throughout US history wherein medical schools disproportionately used Black subjects in clinical trials and live surgical demonstrations.

During my time as New Mexico Secretary of Health during the COVID-19 vaccine rollout, I held many press conferences and town halls to address the COVID-19 vaccine hesitancy. Many diverse communities had concerns about vaccine safety and which vaccines were the best. Among Black communities within New Mexico, there was fear that the US vaccines made available within Black communities would be inferior to those made available to communities with a higher proportion of non-Latinx Whites. Addressing these concerns required clear presentation of quality data, cultural sensitivity, and sharing the voices of community champions who were vaccinated. Distinct from following misinformation or advocating for the use of unproven drugs (e.g., Ivermectin), communities of color more often wanted to avoid the use of drugs unless it was absolutely clear that they were efficacious.

As we think of marginalized communities, it is so important that we recognize the value of community engagement and abundance of resilience. As noted by Grills and colleagues (2022), navigating the pandemic and its trauma required relationships, or "communalism." It also required, music, spirituality, a belief in eternity (another life after one dies), reverence for ancestors, and prayer. Many community members relied on spending quality time with family, virtual interactions with other family as well as friends, and remote attendance at church to survive the early phases of the pandemic. Such community engagement and resilience can inform the integration of public health and healthcare delivery. Specifically, as we consider the value of community health workers (CHWs) who are on the ground within communities, they can leverage community engagement and potential resilience to help with prevention, health promotion, and health systems.

US spending priorities are not aligned with upstream factors, or population-level socioeconomics, but more focused on downstream factors, or individual interventions. In Thomas Frieden's health impact pyramid (Frieden 2010), he highlights an array of factors that determine a population's health (McCullough, Eisen-Cohen, and Lott 2020). At the base of the pyramid are socioeconomic factors, and at the top are individual interventions including counseling and education (see exhibit 22.1).

There is substantial misalignment of spending, with fewer dollars invested in the population health impact at the base of the pyramid versus many dollars used for individual healthcare services at the top of the pyramid. According to the Centers for Medicare & Medicaid Services (CMS 2023), the US national health expenditure grew 2.7 percent in 2021, to $4.3 trillion. Based on 2014 dollars, per capita public health expenditures peaked at $281 in 2008, falling 9.3 percent to $255 in 2014. Public health's share of total health expenditures rose from 1.36 percent in 1960 to a high of 3.18 percent in 2002 (when spending briefly surged following the terrorist attacks of September 11, 2001). By 2014, there was a decline of 17 percent (Himmelstein and Woolhandler 2016). Maintaining public health's share of total health spending at its peak 2002 level would have required an increase of $247.8 billion between 2015 and 2023.

Exhibit 22.1: Health Impact Pyramid

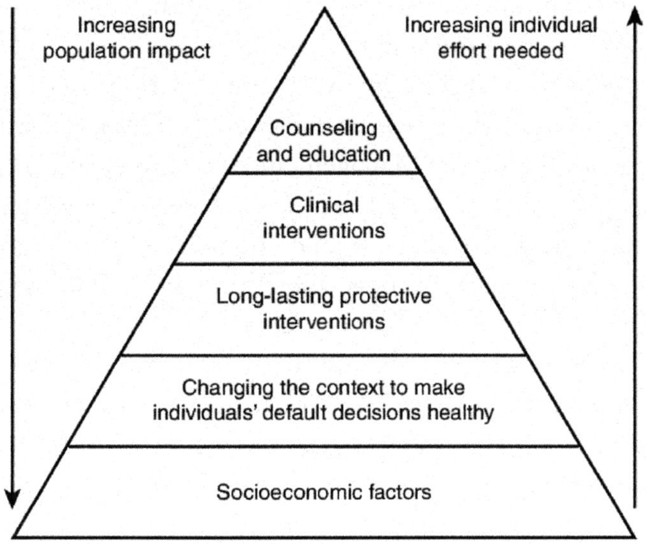

Source: Frieden (2010). Reprinted with permission.

PANDEMIC RELIEF EFFORTS

Beginning in 2020, the federal government provided funds of approximately $5 trillion to support the US economy during the earlier phases of the COVID-19 pandemic. As reported in the *New York Times* (Parlapiano et al. 2022), of that $5 trillion, nearly $482 billion was used in healthcare, including vaccine development ($45 billion), vaccines and treatments ($64 billion), testing, monitoring, and research ($46 billion), grants to healthcare providers ($156 billion), support for health agencies ($12 billion), Medicaid coverage ($56 billion), Medicaid changes ($38 billion), Consolidated Omnibus Budget Reconciliation Act coverage ($18 billion), waiving of some cost sharing ($13 billion), expansion of Affordable Care Act subsidies ($22 billion), and other healthcare-related relief measures ($11 billion). Funds were used to help hospitals remain financially viable given the tremendous loss in revenue from halting elective procedures and reduced use by patients seeking other care. The American Rescue Plan expanded health insurance subsidies under the Affordable Care Act for two years (Parlapiano et al. 2022).

The surplus of funds during the pandemic to support health, including public health, was helpful in the short term. Unfortunately, the health inequities and the need for an appropriate distribution of funds for both public health and healthcare delivery are long-term issues. Public health agencies worked closely with hospitals during the pandemic to prevent an overwhelming influx of emergency department visits and hospitalizations. Public health practitioners worked many long hours to help communities understand the need for social distancing, handwashing, and the use of masks to prevent the spread of the virus. Public health and healthcare delivery committees were formed around the country to operationalize the steps necessary to keep communities safe.

As vaccines became available, many hospitals partnered with public health to set up vaccine clinics and mass vaccination events. Also, in New Mexico as in many states, Federal Emergency Management Assistance was available to provide mobile vaccine units. At the New Mexico Department of Health, we utilized an Incident Command Structure (ICS) to operationalize vaccine rollout. This structure is used for efficiency, effectiveness, and equity. It includes stakeholders (e.g., governor's office), a joint information center, unified command, command staff, and general staff (i.e., operations, planning, logistics, and finance).

Key stakeholders within the ICS included the governor's office and cabinet members as well as a joint information center. The general staff included operations, planning, logistics, and finance. Each of these four groups of staff met at least once daily but often multiple times daily during the first phase of the vaccine rollout; during this phase, there were two shots for Pfizer or Moderna and one shot for Johnson & Johnson. In addition to the ICS, there was a Medical

Advisory Team that met weekly, including some weekends, which included healthcare providers and public health practitioners around New Mexico. Having all parties at one table to discuss the current and future needs of the state in regard to COVID-19 is something that needs to continue beyond the pandemic.

COVID-19 was also devastating to adults aged 65 or older. By 2030, the US population will likely have a larger percentage of people aged 65 or older than those aged 5 or younger. Addressing the needs of older adults will require a strong integration of public health and healthcare delivery. One key component of this integration is the strategic use of community health workers or frontline public health workers who are trusted members within their communities and have a clear understanding of the community they serve. As described by the American Public Health Association (APHA 2023), CHWs are liaisons between public health, the community, and healthcare settings. They can support patients in addressing unmet needs that increase the risk for poor health and adverse health outcomes.

An important component of the work of CHWs is addressing the social determinants or social determination of health—the conditions in which people are born, grow, live, work, and age, as shaped by the distribution of money, power, and resources at global, national, and local levels—which drive health and health outcomes (Kangovi et al. 2020). Prior work has clearly demonstrated the efficacy of CHW interventions to improve chronic disease control, behavioral health, and quality of care. In a return on investment analysis for one CHW intervention conduced in Pennsylvania, Kangovi and colleagues (2020) demonstrated that for every dollar invested in the CHW intervention, there was a return of nearly $2.50 to an average Medicaid payer within the fiscal year.

IMPROVING HEALTH OUTCOMES

To improve health outcomes for our most vulnerable populations, including older adults, we must address healthcare and public health workforce shortages, strengthen and innovate public health infrastructure, eliminate health inequities, utilize technology that reaches all communities, and identify ways to help seniors age at home. We also must engage in efforts to address the issue of misinformation that can hamper many of these other efforts for improvement.

To address US workforce shortages, the Health Resources and Services Administration as well as the Centers for Medicare & Medicaid Services must provide funding to support the recruitment and retention of diverse and highly qualified workers across settings including public health and healthcare delivery. Recruitment and retention incentives may include housing subsidies, transportation, training scholarships, and loan repayment.

To strengthen and innovate the US public health infrastructure, substantial and long-term funding is needed to support activities conducted at all levels, including federal, state, and tribal agencies. Further, funding for hospitals should be extended to include public health agencies. Support should be provided for innovative and high-quality data infrastructure that allows for efficient exchange of information across public health, laboratories, and healthcare delivery settings.

To eliminate health inequities, support is needed to convene an interdisciplinary committee to strategically plan and operationalize actions to address economic and structural barriers that hinder the achievement of ideal health for all US residents. The interdisciplinary committee should include representation from state and federal agencies as well as community leaders—persons not self-appointed but acknowledged as leaders by their respective communities. For efficient healthcare delivery, federal leaders should determine the optimal balance between face-to-face and remote care. Further, policies should be implemented to support telehealth, both for the patient (telemedicine) and for access to specialists as part of training (teleconsultation).

Specific to long-term services, innovation is needed to expand services in the United States beyond nursing homes to support aging at home, or "aging in place," and to provide appropriate community-based services offered at a minimal cost to older adults.

A major issue that the COVID-19 pandemic ignited was misinformation, thereby underscoring the urgent need for public health and healthcare delivery to synergize to address this challenge. Throughout the pandemic, there were theories put forth around the use of certain drugs (including medications to treat rheumatoid arthritis or parasites) as well as the very unfortunate recommendation by a prominent political leader to ingest cleaning agents. There was either no information to support use of those drugs to treat COVID-19 or serious risk of harm from use or ingestion of those substances—or both. Yet some people nevertheless acted on this misinformation and consequently incurred injury or death.

Other misinformation led to the perspective that COVID-19 vaccines were dangerous and even the misperception that the virus itself was not real. Whereas any vaccine or medication has side effects, overwhelmingly the vaccines produced by Pfizer and Moderna were highly efficacious and carried limited serious side effects. As millions of people throughout the world lost their lives to COVID-19, it became evident to anyone who was not mired in denial that the virus is real. Some of the people who succumbed to these types of misinformation chose to forgo vaccination and then ended up suffering greatly or dying after they contracted the disease.

To help reduce such preventable adverse outcomes, messaging is needed from public health practitioners and health professionals as well as community leaders that is culturally, ideologically, and geographically tailored to the community served. Undoing the effects of misinformation warrants meeting communities with an open mind, facts, compassion, and knowledge exchange as well as addressing both health literacy and media literacy. Partnering with community members to create valid messaging is an important component of addressing misinformation. There is also value in providing support to diverse communities on how to interpret and fact-find to better understand postings on social media.

Public health practitioners and other providers must work together with a strategic plan to address misinformation nationally and globally. We must involve Congress and other leaders at the state and local levels to hold accountable people who spread information for which there is poor-quality or no evidence.

REFERENCES

American Public Health Association (APHA). 2023. "Community Health Workers." Accessed December 1. www.apha.org/apha-communities/member-sections/community-health-workers.

Centers for Medicare & Medicaid Services (CMS). 2023. "NHE Fact Sheet: Historical NHE, 2021." Modified September 6. www.cms.gov/data-research/statistics-trends-and-reports/national-health-expenditure-data/nhe-fact-sheet.

Frieden, T. R. 2010. "A Framework for Public Health Action: The Health Impact Pyramid." *American Journal of Public Health* 100 (4): 590–95.

Graham, G. 2021. "Addressing the Disproportionate Impact of COVID-19 on Communities of Color." *Journal of Racial & Ethnic Health Disparities* 8 (2): 280–82.

Grills, C., F. L. Carlos Chavez, A. Saw, K. L. Walters, K. Burlew, S. M. Randolph Cunningham, C. Capelio Rosario, R. Samoa, and H. Jackson-Lowman. 2022. "Applying Culturalist Methodologies to Discern COVID-19's Impact on Communities of Color." *Journal of Community Psychology* 51 (6) 2331–54. https://doi.org/10.1002/jcop.22802.

Himmelstein, D. U., and S. Woolhandler. 2016. "Public Health's Falling Share of US Health Spending." *American Journal of Public Health* 106 (1): 56–57.

Kangovi, S., N. Mitra, D. Grande, J. A. Long, and D. A. Asch. 2020. *Health Affairs* 39 (2): 207–13.

Kaplan, K. 2020. "What does COVID-19 Stand for Anyway?" *Los Angeles Times*. Published March 27. www.latimes.com/science/story/2020-03-27/what-does-covid-19-stand-for.

Krieger, N. 2014. "Discrimination and Health Inequities." *International Journal of Health Services* 44 (4): 643–710.

McCullough, J. M., E. Eisen-Cohen, and B. Lott. 2020. "Barriers and Facilitators to Intraorganizational Collaboration in Public Health: Relational Coordination Across Public Health Services Targeting Individuals and Populations." *Health Care Management Review* 45 (1): 60–72.

Parlapiano, A., D. B. Solomon, M. Ngo, and S. Cowley. 2022. "Where $5 Trillion in Pandemic Stimulus Money Went." *New York Times*, A19.

Rowe, A. C., and E. Tuck. 2016. "Settler Colonialism and Cultural Studies." *Cultural Studies/Critical Methodologies* 17 (1): 3–13.

Saito, N. T. 2020. *Settler Colonialism, Race and the Law: Why Structural Racism Persists.* New York: New York University Press.

Stockett, K. 2009. *The Help.* New York: G. P. Putnam's Sons.

Taylor, T., dir. 2011. *The Help.* Universal City, CA: Dreamworks.

United States Census Bureau. 2022. "2020 Census." Revised November 29. www.census.gov/programs-surveys/decennial-census/decade/2020/2020-census-main.html.

Washington, H. 2007. *Medical Apartheid: The Dark History of Medical Experimentation on Black Americans from Colonial Times to the Present.* New York: Doubleday.

World Health Organization (WHO). 2023a. "Coronavirus Disease (COVID-19)." Fact sheet. Published August 9. www.who.int/news-room/fact-sheets/detail/coronavirus-disease-(covid-19).

———. 2023b. "Global Situation." Updated October 4. https://covid19.who.int/.

———. 2023c. "United States of America Situation." Updated October 4. https://covid19.who.int/region/amro/country/us.

CHAPTER 23

Increasing the Capacity for Innovation in Healthcare Management

Howard J. Gershon

Innovation distinguishes between
a leader and a follower.
—Steve Jobs

THROUGHOUT THE PAST several decades, politicians and pundits have argued that the United States' healthcare delivery system is not sustainable in its current form. Despite our efforts to improve, we are seeing continuing cost increases, less-than-optimal health outcomes, and growing demand and consumerism—collectively, a "perfect storm" calling for a major systemic transformation (Abendshein 2019). To paraphrase from Albert Einstein, doing the same thing over and over and expecting a different result is the definition of *insanity*. So how do we find new ways of doing things that will facilitate the necessary transformation of our healthcare system? The key is innovation. Our ability to embrace innovation was challenged dramatically during the COVID-19 pandemic, which required that the entire US healthcare system quickly adapt to a changed environment. From the rapid development of vaccines to the setup of temporary morgues, new ways of thinking and demonstrations of creativity were hallmarks of innovation.

TYPES OF INNOVATION

Merriam-Webster (2023) defines *innovation* simply as "the introduction of something new." When thinking about innovation, people often focus on radical or disruptive innovations, such as Apple's development of the iPhone. *Disruptive innovation* is a term coined by Clayton Christensen, a professor at the Harvard Business School. It refers to the introduction into an established industry of a product or service that performs better and, generally, at a lower cost than existing offerings, thereby displacing the leaders in that particular market space and transforming the industry (Christensen 1997). Examples include online retailing, which has had a dramatic impact on brick-and-mortar stores, and retail clinics such as those offered by CVS, which are now challenging our traditional approach to primary care.

Another type of innovation, at the opposite end of the innovation spectrum, is *efficiency innovation*. Efficiency innovations focus on improving existing conditions through more minor adjustments, and they occur almost daily in healthcare organizations, often as the result of "work-arounds." Examples may include changing hours of operation to expand service accessibility, centralizing appointment scheduling to improve user convenience, standardizing reports and order sets, or developing more robust case management programs to ensure appropriate handoffs and care transitions for patients.

Evolutionary innovation occupies the space between the disruptive and efficiency approaches. Evolution typically involves a gradual change or metamorphosis that results in ideas that are distinctly new and better. For example, automated teller machines have changed the way banks service their customers, and the growing use of virtual visits has changed the practice of many healthcare providers. Similarly, e-learning has given rise to a whole new way of educating and training healthcare practitioners.

Several innovation experts, including Christensen, have argued that the United States is spending too much time on efficiency innovations (Nisen 2012). Meanwhile, disruptive innovations tend to be few and far between. To achieve the transformation that our health system needs, most organizations will likely need to pay considerable attention to evolutionary innovation.

CURRENT INITIATIVES

The current emphasis on innovation has resulted in two key initiatives among healthcare organizations: (1) the development of innovation centers and (2) the establishment of the position of chief innovation officer.

One of the first innovation centers in the United States was the Kaiser Permanente Garfield Innovation Center (2023), named after Kaiser Permanente's founding physician, Sidney Garfield. It claims to be the largest center of its type, exploring new care solutions through hands-on simulations, quick prototyping, and technology testing. Successful initiatives from the Garfield Innovation Center typically evolve into pilot programs in Kaiser Permanente medical centers, clinics, and offices across the nation. Examples have included KP MedRite, a step-by-step workflow designed to avoid medication errors, and the Interactive Patient Care System, a screen-based hub in patient rooms that facilitates communication with the care team.

Similar centers have been established by more than 50 other pioneering organizations, including Memorial Health System in South Bend, Indiana; Northwestern Memorial in Chicago; Vanderbilt University Medical Center in Nashville, Tennessee; Geisinger Health System in Danville, Pennsylvania; Mayo Clinic in Rochester, Minnesota; and Ascension Health in St. Louis, Missouri. Although each of these centers is unique, common elements include simulation laboratories, room mock-ups, coworking spaces, classrooms, meeting rooms, and 3D printers.

Some organizations, such as Children's Hospital Los Angeles (2023), have partnered with universities to facilitate access to grant funding. Others have affiliated with manufacturers and serve as testing grounds for new products and technologies. Several organizations have sought to translate research and innovation from within the health system into products that have commercial value. For example, Cleveland Clinic Innovations (2023), founded in 2000, has supported thousands of innovations that have resulted in hundreds of patents and licenses.

Even more organizations have established the position of chief innovation officer. Though it first took hold in large businesses in other sectors, the position has become a fast-growing addition to the healthcare C-suite. Since 2018, a professional organization, the Healthcare Innovators Professional Society (HIPS), has provided a forum and supportive community for professionals in the role of chief innovation officer (or chief transformation officer) at healthcare organizations (HIPS 2023).

The chief innovation officer often reports directly to the organization's chief executive officer. Individuals occupying such positions come from a variety of backgrounds, both within and outside healthcare, and must possess excellent interpersonal skills. They are responsible not only for developing ideas to help their organizations thrive but also for communicating and implementing those ideas, establishing collaborative relationships, and encouraging change. Chief innovation officers should have strong analytical abilities to help them determine current and future needs, understand industry trends, and know how the organization can differentiate itself. Other skills and abilities include the following:

- An inquisitive and creative mind
- An ability to self-direct while also leading and working with a team of creative individuals
- Superior research and analytical skills to track and predict trends

- Strong business knowledge and comprehensive understanding of various business practices
- A willingness to take calculated risks and manage expectations of both internal teams and potential and existing customers

Chief innovation officers are typically responsible for managing the process of innovation and change management by developing goals, collecting and nurturing ideas from within their organizations, training and educating associates, tracking technology, and managing new business ventures. However, the most important assignment for many of these individuals is facilitating a culture that supports innovation. As is often noted, culture eats strategy for lunch!

A CULTURE OF INNOVATION

So, how does an organization develop a culture of innovation, one that builds on the traditions of the past but allows associates to "let go of what was in favor of what can be" (Radick 2019, 31)? In her popular book *The Seeds of Innovation*, Elaine Dundon (2002) discusses three critical components that are necessary to create that culture. First, the organization must encourage creativity among its associates. Second, this creativity must be channeled so that it creates value. And third, associates must be provided with the tools and techniques to facilitate change within the organization. Each of these components is discussed in greater detail in the following sections.

Encouraging Creativity

The artist Pablo Picasso once noted, "Every child is an artist. The problem is how to remain an artist once he grows up" (*Forbes* 2023). As healthcare professionals, we typically experience years of training that embed in us rules and patterns that tend to stifle our ability to be creative. Furthermore, given the field's heavily regulated nature, we are often required to do things in a prescribed fashion, with a focus on standardizing processes and minimizing variations. Often, however, variations are what lead to innovations. If creativity is really about finding new connections, then everyone should seek to retain it. So how do we encourage creativity?

Creative folks tend to be collaborative, so organizations can encourage creativity by providing opportunities for teamwork. Often, assembling teams of people with different backgrounds and skill sets will generate surprising results. A few years ago, the finance team at one healthcare system was struggling with a revenue cycle issue. When the organization's leadership created a cross-functional task force with associates from several other departments, including home care, nursing, and ambulatory services, a novel solution to the problem quickly emerged.

Creative individuals also exhibit a considerable amount of curiosity, so encouraging questions of *why, what,* and *what if* is essential. Years ago, as an administrative resident with no previous experience in hospital operations, I was able to use my "student" status to ask a lot of *why* questions. Why was the cafeteria closed when the night shift was breaking for "lunch"? Why did an outpatient have to register separately for a laboratory test and an X-ray? Why was outpatient physical therapy located on the fifth floor of the main hospital building when many of the patients who needed that service had difficulty just getting from the parking lot into the hospital? An environment that encourages these kinds of questions from associates is essential for fostering innovation.

Another trait of creative individuals is the understanding of the various alternatives that often exist. How do we encourage the exploration of alternatives? Oftentimes, alternatives are at our fingertips if we simply reimagine the situation. For example, when thinking about customer service issues, why not approach them from the perspective of Nordstrom or some other icon of customer satisfaction? When evaluating potential sites for a new primary care office, how about looking at the criteria Starbucks uses for store locations? Several health systems have had significant success adopting methodologies from Toyota to redesign their processes. Similarly, many improvements in surgical suite performance have resulted from the adoption of the checklist approach used by airline pilots. Many lessons can be found outside traditional healthcare settings, if we only look for them.

Creative individuals are also persistent, meaning they will not give up easily. However, they still need ongoing encouragement and feedback. Creativity can be encouraged through the simplest form of associate engagement, the good old suggestion box, as well as from bonus and financial incentive programs that reward associates for ideas that result in measurable improvements. Consider the possibility of just giving staff protected time, support, and training to pursue projects of their own choosing.

Establishing Value

Although creativity is essential to innovation initiatives, it is only a starting point; we must also ensure that the ideas have value. Most organizations have significantly more ideas and opportunities than resources available to pursue them. As we strive to be creative in problem solving, we must ensure that potential solutions are grounded in data and considered based on careful research.

Some ideas are simply bad ideas. Remember the Apple Newton? Developed in 1993 as a forerunner to the iPad, it had huge research and development costs (estimated at over a billion dollars), was rushed to market, and failed miserably. Similarly, a few of us might also be old enough to remember the Ford Edsel. Hyped as the "car of the future" when it was unveiled in 1957, it never attracted many buyers.

If you have been encouraging and supporting creativity among your associates, you are likely to get a mix of good and not-so-good ideas. How do you sort the winners from the losers and focus your resources on the ideas that have the best opportunity to advance the organization? For starters, make sure you have an overall context that originates with the organization's mission, vision, and strategic plan. In many industries, research and development (i.e., innovation) functions are clearly articulated in board-level policies, and priority areas for investigation are identified by an established set of screens. How does a potential idea contribute to the organization's value proposition? What is the fit with the organization's strategic priorities? Is there a potential payback? Will it have unintended consequences? Addressing these questions will help you focus your investigations.

Another important consideration is clarity regarding the problem to be solved. Consider, for instance, this widely shared (yet fictional) story about scientists from the National Aeronautics and Space Administration (NASA) during the 1960s. According to the myth, the scientists recognized that pens could not function in space, and they needed to figure out a way for astronauts to write things down. NASA then devoted years of work and millions of taxpayer dollars to develop a pen that could put ink to paper without gravity. Meanwhile, the scientists' Soviet counterparts simply handed their cosmonauts pencils (Curtin 2006). So, what was really the problem the NASA scientists were trying to resolve?

Healthcare is full of instances where responses have been proposed even though the problem to be solved has not been clearly identified. A few years ago, a major academic medical center was considering a multimillion-dollar renovation of its obstetrical facilities. The center was concerned about a decline in utilization and assumed that the decline was a result of the facilities being outdated. Before committing to the project, however, senior management tested that assumption with a series of focus groups with women of childbearing age. Surprisingly, the focus group revealed that the declining utilization had little to do with the facilities and was largely attributable to the fact that the center was no longer "in network" with several of the area's leading health insurance plans. Ultimately, the center did proceed with a capital improvement plan, but it was significantly scaled back.

Similar concerns apply when considering situations such as "no-show" rates in outpatient services. Is the fact that someone misses an appointment attributable to insurance constraints, hours of operation, transportation issues, or one of a dozen other potential causes? How about increases in emergency department visits? Are they attributable to the lack of primary care in the area or other factors? Innovative ideas are only helpful when the problem to be solved is clearly defined.

Although *value* has become a buzzword in healthcare, defining it remains a significant challenge for many organizations. Typically, value is in the eyes of the beholder. Value to patients and their families will be different from value to payers, which in turn will be different from value to providers. And what constitutes value will change over time based on how your constituents change. The things that are important to physicians who have recently graduated will be different from those that are important to physicians in the later stages of practice—and, furthermore, what is important to both will change in response to new or different reimbursement mechanisms.

Assessing the value of an innovation initiative requires that we look toward the future and consider how and when our operating environment is likely to change. As is often said, timing is everything! Remember the internet search engine Ask Jeeves? It included many of the techniques that would later make their way into Google, including semantic search (i.e., understanding queries in natural language) and even ranking of web pages by hyperlinks (often regarded as Google's "secret sauce"). Ask Jeeves was popular for about a year but ultimately failed, likely because it launched too early given the technological limitations of the time. How many organizations do you know that wound up on the "bleeding edge" rather than the leading edge?

Conversely, many organizations run the risk of corporate inertia, which occurs when an established company remains rigid in its thinking and actions rather than being open to changing industry and company dynamics. Company leaders can easily become complacent when things are going well, but inertia will eventually cause a loss of competitive advantage—and potentially even failure. Kodak, for instance, was in a position of leadership in the photography industry for a long time but ultimately could not escape its own inertia. Kodak invented some of the first digital camera technology in 1975—some 15 to 20 years before digital photography became popular among mainstream consumers. However, the appeal of continued investment in its profitable film division prevented Kodak from fully pursuing this riskier or more innovative direction, and it did not move fast enough to beat its digital competitors to market.

How many healthcare organizations can you think of that are no longer with us? How many of them are gone because they failed to change their business model or because they made a change too late? Some observers would argue that many of our nation's community hospitals and rural hospitals are likely to suffer this fate if they do not act soon.

Facilitating Change

Even if an idea is highly creative and offers a strong case for value, it will be useless if it does not ever come to fruition. Becoming an innovative organization requires change, and change is often difficult to accept, much less implement.

In his seminal book *The Fifth Discipline: The Art and Practice of the Learning Organization*, Peter Senge (1990) relates the story of the boiling frog. According to the story, if you place a frog in a pot of boiling water, it will immediately try to jump out. However, if you put the frog in a pot of water at room temperature, it will stay put. If you gradually turn up the temperature of the pot of water, something interesting happens. As the temperature climbs toward 80 degrees Fahrenheit, the frog will likely do nothing; perhaps it may even show signs of joy or relaxation. But as the temperature continues to increase, the frog will become groggier and weaker. As the water reaches the boiling point, the frog, unable to climb out, will sit in the pot and boil. The explanation for this behavior is that the frog is accustomed to reacting to sudden changes in its environment, not to slow, gradual changes. So how do we ensure that our organizations stay in tune with gradual changes and are not caught off guard when their operating environment transforms?

The management literature is replete with approaches and methodologies to support change management. Common elements include the following:

- *Eliminate excuses.* Overcome the tendency to say, "We've always done it this way," or "That's a great idea, but it won't work here." Eliminate *can't, won't,* and *yeah but* from your organizational vocabulary.
- *Accelerate the decision-making process.* Healthcare organizations tend to be hierarchical bureaucracies. Consider removing structural layers and granting decision-making rights to more associates.
- *Identify informal leaders.* You can find effective change leaders throughout your organization; they do not necessarily follow the traditional company hierarchy. To lead change, you need to bring together a coalition of influential people whose power comes from a variety of sources, including job title, status, expertise, and political importance.
- *Remove obstacles.* Often, people resist change because they fear failure. Staff need to know that failing is acceptable within certain parameters and that risk taking is not a career-ending activity.
- *Pursue short-term wins.* You are not going to transform your organization overnight. Look for "low-hanging fruit," and attack those situations with innovative initiatives early on. Once you have some early wins, you can more easily build on those successes.

- *Celebrate.* Staff dissatisfaction and burnout are common, and people too often focus on the negative aspects of individual and organizational performance. Celebrations are essential for supporting continued change.

Ethical Issues

Clearly, innovation will be fundamental to improving the US healthcare delivery system. However, as we implement new innovations and adopt new ways of doing things, we still must operate within a set of ethical boundaries. Many hospitals—particularly academic and teaching institutions—have institutional review boards that address the use of new technologies and procedures and develop policies covering such issues as informed consent, right to privacy, and protections from harm. Nonetheless, challenges remain.

Innovation is responsible for most advances in the field of surgery, and new approaches to clinical problems have contributed to decreased morbidity, decreased mortality, and improved patient outcomes. However, not all innovations are successful, and not all result in improved patient care. The ethical dilemma lies in the uncertainty of whether a particular innovation will prove to be a good thing. By its very nature, innovation introduces uncertainty, which may involve potential risks to patient safety.

Innovative developments also raise ethical issues related to cost and resource distribution. These issues have attracted widespread attention, particularly as they relate to the development of new and improved pharmaceuticals. For example, discussions about the cost and appropriate reimbursement for CAR T-cell cancer therapy have raised questions about what is in the best interest of the patient and what is more focused on the scientific or financial rewards of success. Similar questions have revolved around procedural and technological advances, such as the advent of computer-assisted surgery or stem cell and proton therapies. The way in which one values healing and life itself can result in significant ethical dilemmas.

Innovative approaches to the promotion of healthcare services can also raise ethical issues. For instance, airline magazines might include advertisements for the "best plastic surgeons" or the "best orthopedic surgeons," and hospital campuses might fly banners claiming that they are the "best orthopedic hospital" or "number-one ranked heart center." These "best" claims often have a questionable basis, and some push the boundaries of truth in advertising. When employing innovative strategies, organizations should remain scrupulously honest in their advertising.

Finally, some innovative efforts may have unintended consequences that carry ethical implications. For instance, an organization might introduce a billboard that shows the wait time in a nearby emergency department or provide similar information through a website or phone app, with the aim of providing a higher level of customer service. That information, however, might have the unintended consequence of steering patients to treatment settings other than those most appropriate for their particular needs. Once again, questions of cost and resource distribution come into play.

CONCLUSION

Clearly, the US healthcare delivery system is undergoing a major transformation, and innovation will be critical to its success. To capitalize on this opportunity, healthcare organizations will be challenged to shift from a rules-driven, hierarchical organizational culture to an environment that values creativity, experimentation, and risk taking, while also respecting the ethical boundaries inherent in matters of people's health and well-being.

REFERENCES

Abendshein, J. 2019. *Health Care in the Next Curve: Transforming a Dysfunctional Industry*. New York: Taylor & Francis Group.

Children's Hospital Los Angeles. 2023. "About Children's Hospital Los Angeles." Accessed October 21. www.chla.org/about-childrens-hospital-los-angeles.

Christensen, C. M. 1997. *The Innovator's Dilemma: When New Technologies Cause Great Firms to Fail*. Boston: Harvard Business Review Press.

Cleveland Clinic Innovations. 2023. "About Us." Accessed October 21. https://my.clevelandclinic.org/innovations/about.

Curtin, C. 2006. "Fact or Fiction?: NASA Spent Millions to Develop a Pen That Would Write in Space, Whereas the Soviet Cosmonauts Used a Pencil." *Scientific American*. Published December 20. www.scientificamerican.com/article/fact-or-fiction-nasa-spen/.

Dundon, E. 2002. *The Seeds of Innovation: Cultivating the Synergy That Fosters New Ideas*. New York: AMACOM.

Forbes. 2023. "Quotes: Thoughts on the Business of Life." Accessed October 21. www.forbes.com/quotes/7314/.

Healthcare Innovators Professional Society (HIPS). 2023. "Helping Healthcare Transformers Transform." Accessed October 21. https://hips.healthcare/.

Kaiser Permanente Garfield Innovation Center. 2023. "About Us." Accessed October 21. https://garfieldcenter.kaiserpermanente.org/about-us/.

Merriam-Webster. 2023. "Innovation." *Merriam-Webster.com Dictionary*. Accessed October 21. www.merriam-webster.com/dictionary/innovation.

Nisen, M. 2012. "Clay Christensen: Our Obsession with Efficiency is Killing Innovation." *Business Insider*. Published December 12. www.businessinsider.com/clay-christensen-our-obsession-with-efficiency-is-killing-innovation-2012-12.

Radick, L. 2019. "Insights on Innovation: An Interview with Congress Opening Session Speaker Josh Linkner." *Healthcare Executive* 34 (1): 29–34.

Senge, P. 1990. *The Fifth Discipline: The Art and Practice of the Learning Organization*. New York: Doubleday/Currency.

CHAPTER 24

Ethics Issues in Managed Care

Richard H. Rubin

THE FIELD OF medical ethics has become increasingly important in both medical education and clinical practice. The expanding role of medical ethics has manifested itself in the escalating number of books and journal articles on this topic, in the percentage of medical schools that now include training in medical ethics as part of the standard curriculum, and in the growing number of hospitals nationwide where ethics committees meet regularly to resolve perceived ethical dilemmas.

Managed care has evolved to become a major factor in the delivery of healthcare in the United States. Although the term *managed care* refers to a rather heterogeneous group of institutions, a feature common to all managed care organizations (MCOs) is a systematic approach to controlling what has been a progressive escalation in healthcare costs in the United States since the 1970s.

The increasing prominence of both medical ethics and managed care has resulted in a number of well-publicized collisions, if not a head-on crash, between the two. The reason the two have collided has largely been their different perspectives of the moral universe and the social good. Medical ethics, undoubtedly influenced by the twentieth-century civil rights and consumer rights movements, has placed great emphasis on patient autonomy—the notion that every patient has a right to be treated with respect and dignity as well as to make all decisions related to their healthcare (the goal being an "optimal outcome" as defined by the fully informed individual patient). Thus, the focus has been on the primacy of the individual patient and the responsibility of physicians to be advocates for their individual patients.

Managed care, on the other hand, has clearly concerned itself with not only the health of individual patients but also the collective health of a defined population—namely, the MCO's membership or so-called medical commons. The question of what should take precedence in the physician's mind—the individual patient or the collective medical commons—is at the crux of many disagreements between physicians and MCO managers. These often-wrenching ethical dilemmas have been complicated by the addition of still another element into the equation—the fact that the majority of MCOs are now of the for-profit variety, with a fiduciary responsibility to their shareholders.

Some observers have proposed that the potential for conflict among these various constituencies (individual patients, the medical commons, and shareholders) make the for-profit MCO model so ethically suspect as to have no rightful place in the US healthcare system. Others, meanwhile, contend that the currently dominant for-profit model is the most realistic and efficient means of achieving managed care's most overarching goal—namely, to exercise some semblance of ongoing control over the nation's healthcare costs.

While this debate rages on, physicians and managers in the managed care setting continue to face ethical challenges in their day-to-day work lives. This chapter reviews some of these commonly faced ethical dilemmas and offers useful and practical guidelines for both physicians and managers. It also aims to provide both physicians and managers with some appreciation of the issues faced by their counterparts and to help each group gain a better understanding of the other's thinking and perspective.

This chapter addresses seven questions:

1. What are the relevant principles of medical ethics?
2. What are the relevant principles of business ethics?
3. What ethics issues are commonly faced by physicians practicing in a managed care setting?
4. What ethics issues are commonly faced by managers in the managed care setting?
5. What are the legal ramifications for both physicians and managers in the managed care setting?
6. What ethical guidelines can be offered to physicians practicing in a managed care setting?
7. What ethical guidelines can be offered to managers in the managed care setting?

RELEVANT PRINCIPLES OF MEDICAL ETHICS

The task of medical ethics is to analyze and optimally resolve ethical dilemmas that arise in medical practice and biomedical research. Medical ethics is not a static, rigid entity; on the contrary, disagreements among acknowledged experts are common. Much of medical ethics has concerned itself with end-of-life issues and medical decision making in the case of incapacitated patients. Focusing on the issue at hand, however, the following six principles of medical ethics have special relevance to managed care:

1. *Autonomy.* Autonomy refers to (1) a person's right to be fully informed of all pertinent information related to their healthcare, and (2) a person's additional right, after being so informed, to choose among or to refuse the available treatment options. Autonomy also implies a respect for the dignity and intrinsic worth of each individual person.
2. *Beneficence.* Beneficence is the commitment to "do good." It usually refers to the physician's obligation to work for optimal health outcomes for individual patients (although what constitutes an "optimal outcome" in a given situation is a decision that the competent, informed patient will help the physician determine).
3. *Nonmaleficence.* The flip side of beneficence is nonmaleficence—the commitment to "do no harm."
4. *Fidelity.* Fidelity is the notion that the physician should be faithful and loyal to the individual patient. It implies that the physician will, if necessary, subordinate their own interests to serve the patient's interests.
5. *Veracity.* Veracity, or truth telling, refers to the physician's responsibility to be truthful to the individual patient, avoiding deception and disclosing to the patient all information relevant to the patient's health.
6. *Justice.* In the realm of healthcare, justice implies that all patients should be treated fairly, without regard to their race, ethnic background, socioeconomic status, educational level, or other factors. *Distributive justice* refers to the related notion that the allocation of limited healthcare resources should be determined on a fair and equitable basis.

All six principles represent values that most thoughtful members of society would regard as worthwhile. However, even a brief consideration of the principles reveals how two or more of them could easily come into conflict and how two ethically astute physicians might differ in their viewpoints. For example, although practicing physicians typically think in terms of their responsibility to individual patients (including honoring the autonomy of individual patients), a public health physician entrusted to ensure the well-being of a wider community would likely view distributive justice as an overriding ethical principle. The difference in perspective between the practicing physician and the public health physician reflects, in large measure, the parties that each regards as the major stakeholders affected by their decisions. In the case of the practicing physician, the major stakeholders are the individual patients the physician sees on a day-to-day basis. For the public health physician, the major stakeholders are the members of the community as a whole. In the real world of medical practice, ethical principles thus commonly come into conflict, with one's perspective typically determining which ethical principle one views as paramount in a given situation. The same situation is true whether the different perspectives are held by two physicians or a physician and a managed care executive.

RELEVANT PRINCIPLES OF BUSINESS ETHICS

Like medical ethics, business ethics is an example of what has been termed *applied ethics*—that is, ethics applied to a specific profession or occupation. Also like medical ethics, business ethics is a dynamic field where disagreement among acknowledged experts is commonplace. This disagreement may even extend to fundamental issues, such as what the goal of a business should be.

Many observers would contend that the obvious goal of any business enterprise is to be as financially successful as possible. If the business enterprise is a publicly traded company, a related goal would be to maximize profits for shareholders. Under this model, the guiding ethical principle for corporate leadership would be, first and foremost, to reward its investors—those who have risked their own capital in the company's interest. To take this line of reasoning one step further, any deviation from the investor-first principle might well be viewed as unethical, especially if it ran contrary to what shareholders were led to believe.

Others would contend, however, that investors represent only one group of stakeholders that the corporate leadership needs to consider when making decisions. In this view (the second model), the needs of other stakeholders are also a rightful part of the equation. Such noninvestor stakeholders include consumers, business partners, and employees. This so-called stakeholder model of business ethics is obviously more complex than the investor-first model and is one that many US businesses are now espousing.

In a third model, the corporate leadership might decide that the business enterprise should take on the additional role of enhancing the social good and allocate a percentage of its resources for that purpose. A number of US companies have followed this route, although they are hardly in the majority.

The three models described here illustrate the wide spectrum of thinking in business ethics. A major question in managed care, especially the for-profit model of managed care, has been whether healthcare should be considered just another business. The Woodstock Theological Center, a nonprofit research institute at Georgetown University, convened a diverse group of executives, healthcare professionals, and ethicists to develop a consensus statement of ethical principles pertinent to the business aspects of healthcare. The Woodstock participants formulated the following six core principles, which are still valid today (Woodstock Theological Center 1995):

1. *Compassion and respect for human dignity.* The Woodstock group affirmed that patient care is the primary goal and responsibility of healthcare enterprises. Furthermore, the group declared it would be unethical for healthcare providers to exploit the vulnerability of patients to enhance the organization's or a professional's income or profits.
2. *Commitment to professional competence.* All healthcare professionals, including physicians, nurses, and healthcare executives, have an ethical duty to continue their educational efforts and enhance their competence.
3. *Commitment to a spirit of service.* Healthcare professionals have a responsibility both to the community they serve and to individual patients. This responsibility extends to providing uncompensated or undercompensated care to the poor and needy.
4. *Honesty.* Healthcare professionals and executives have a responsibility to be truthful in their interactions, including their interactions with each other and with patients and families. Medical records should also reflect this commitment to truthfulness and accuracy.
5. *Confidentiality.* Information pertaining to a patient should be shared only with the express permission of the patient or legal guardian, except as required by law.
6. *Good stewardship and careful administration.* Healthcare professionals have an obligation to use health resources wisely, carefully weighing the relative costs and benefits of the available treatment options.

The similarities between the principles of medical ethics listed earlier and the Woodstock compendium of ethical principles for those in the business of healthcare are noteworthy but not surprising. "Compassion and respect for human dignity," for example, clearly resonates with the principles of patient autonomy, beneficence, and nonmaleficence. In addition, the principles of "commitment to a spirit of service" and "good stewardship and careful administration" both relate to the notion of distributive justice. Finally, the potential for conflict between several of the principles of medical ethics cited previously mirrors a similar potential for conflict in the Woodstock group's core principles. In the setting of limited healthcare resources and market competition, for example, can the "provision of uncompensated or undercompensated healthcare to the poor and needy" realistically coexist with "good stewardship and careful administration"?

ETHICS ISSUES FACED BY PHYSICIANS PRACTICING IN THE MANAGED CARE SETTING

Before examining ethical dilemmas faced by physicians in the setting of managed care, a brief discussion of ethics issues faced by physicians in the pre–managed care (fee-for-service) era might be beneficial. Otherwise, the reader might get the erroneous impression that ethical dilemmas for physicians only arose when managed care came on the scene.

As its name implies, in the fee-for-service model of healthcare delivery, physicians were paid a specific fee for performing a specific service, whether that service was an annual physical examination or bypass surgery. Although some older physicians might hark back to the fee-for-service era as "the good old days," it was not free of ethical quandaries. For example, distributive justice was a major (if perhaps inadequately considered) problem, as the indigent and uninsured frequently could not afford the physician's fee and, except for charity care, were essentially shut out of the system. In addition, the physician's fidelity to the patient may sometimes have been compromised in a system where physicians were financially rewarded for providing services that might have been of questionable or only marginal benefit to the patient. Physicians' veracity (truth telling) may also have been less than optimal in the fee-for-service system if, for example, the physician just happened to be a part owner of the laboratory to which patients were referred for tests. Finally, in retrospect, nonmaleficence (the obligation to do no harm) may not have been observed as much as one would hope; one wonders how many patients in the fee-for-service system were ultimately harmed by procedures that were recommended for questionable or marginal reasons by physicians and surgeons who benefited financially from performing as many of those procedures as possible.

Unfortunately, ethical dilemmas for physicians appear to be no less common (and, some would argue, are even more common) in the setting of managed care. Many of these ethical quandaries are related to one fundamental question: In the managed care system, where should the physician's loyalty ultimately lie—with the individual patient, the medical commons, or the MCO itself? This fundamental question branches out into a number of others:

- Should the physician engage in the rationing of healthcare at the bedside of an individual patient?
- How should the physician respond when they believe that the patient requires the specific expertise of a consultant not on the MCO's panel of consultants?

- Under what circumstances should the physician prescribe medications not on the MCO's formulary—medications that might well be more expensive than those listed on the MCO's formulary?
- How much information related to diagnostic and therapeutic options should the physician disclose to the patient?
- How forcefully should the physician "fight" the MCO when the MCO makes a patient care–related decision with which the physician disagrees?

Rationing Care at the Bedside

A topic of ongoing—and often heated—discussion among medical ethicists is whether physicians should ration care at the bedside of an individual patient. Some observers would argue that a "new ethic" requires that the physician's level of concern about the medical commons be so pervasive as to influence the physician's recommendations to individual patients. Others, however, contend that to act in this manner undermines the very foundation of the patient–physician relationship—that is, the patient's expectation that the physician is the patient's advocate, recommending those diagnostic studies and therapeutic interventions that the physician believes are in the patient's best interest. After all, how can the patient trust the physician to give proper care if the physician is thinking primarily about the welfare of the medical commons? One view is that physicians should not engage in rationing healthcare at the bedside of individual patients because it violates the physicians' ethical responsibility of fidelity, an ethical responsibility that patients have rightfully come to regard as an underlying premise of the entire patient–physician relationship.

However, physicians should acknowledge the reality that healthcare resources are finite. Physicians can reasonably do so in at least three ways without violating the trust their individual patients have placed in them. First, physicians need to recognize that there is no ethical obligation to provide clearly useless or futile care, whether it is prescribing antibiotics for a viral illness or extending the life of a terminally ill patient with prolonged ventilator care. Second, all things being equal, physicians should prescribe the least costly among effective therapies. Why choose a more expensive quinolone antibiotic for an uncomplicated urinary tract infection, for example, when the inexpensive antibiotic trimethoprim-sulfamethoxazole will treat the infection just as well? Finally, the question of how best to enhance the well-being of the medical commons in an environment of limited healthcare resources is clearly a profound and entirely legitimate concern. This issue, and the related matter of priority setting, should be addressed in an ongoing, transparent, and careful manner at the MCO's highest policymaking level, with thoughtful input from physicians as well as from the MCO's membership.

Choice of Consultants

A common question that arises for primary care physicians in the managed care setting is whether a specialty consultant on the MCO's panel is the optimal consultant for a given patient's clinical condition. The following two cases illustrate such issues in everyday practice.

> *Case 1:* A 50-year-old MCO patient with an inguinal (groin) hernia asked their primary care physician to refer them to a surgeon in Canada who they heard had developed a new technique for hernia surgery.

> *Case 2:* A 74-year-old MCO patient with hearing loss and vertigo was diagnosed as having an acoustic neuroma, a relatively rare tumor of the acoustic (ear) nerve. Even though the MCO had contracted with a local neurosurgeon to handle all of the plan's neurosurgical procedures, the MCO's consulting neurologist advised the primary care physician to refer the patient to a nearby tertiary care medical center because the center had much more experience with the required neurosurgical procedure.

In Case 1, the primary care physician did not agree to the patient's request to be referred to the surgeon in Canada because the physician knew that the MCO's general surgeon was experienced in performing herniorrhaphy (hernia surgery) and that a high-quality outcome could be anticipated if the MCO's surgeon performed the operation.

In Case 2, however, the physician decided to refer the patient to the tertiary care center for the more specialized type of operation the patient needed. The MCO did not approve this referral at first, but after a series of appeals by the patient, the primary care physician, and the consulting neurologist (and after the patient informed the MCO that they had hired an attorney to ensure that their interests were safeguarded), the MCO reversed its initial decision. The patient subsequently underwent successful surgery at the tertiary care center.

If the physician has good reason to believe that the patient requires special expertise for appropriate care management, then the physician has an obligation to pursue the necessary out-of-plan referral with the MCO's administration.

Nonformulary Prescriptions

In many respects, the issue of prescribing nonformulary medications is analogous to the situation just discussed—namely, referring the patient to a consultant not on the MCO panel. If the physician is convinced that a nonformulary drug is superior to its counterpart on the MCO's formulary, then the physician should serve as the patient's advocate and prescribe the nonformulary medication, explaining to the MCO's pharmacists and administration why they made that choice. In addition, physicians should work with the MCO's pharmacy committee to modify the MCO's formulary when they believe such action is in the best interest of patient care.

Disclosure of Information

Physicians should adhere to the ethical principle of veracity (truth telling), disclosing to the patient all information pertinent to the patient's care. This information includes all relevant diagnostic and therapeutic options, because an informed healthcare decision on the patient's part is impossible if such information is withheld. Physicians should also disclose to the patient all relevant financial arrangements between themselves and the MCO because patients have a right to know about possible conflicts of interest, especially if such conflicts of interest could affect the care they receive.

In addition to their obligation to communicate in a truthful manner with patients and families, physicians also have an obligation to communicate truthfully with MCOs. Physicians should not try to "game the system" by providing MCOs with inaccurate or incomplete information, even when their rationale for doing so is to assist the patient in obtaining MCO approval for requested consultations, prescriptions, or other services.

Challenging the MCO's Decisions

Several of the scenarios mentioned can place the physician in the position of challenging decisions that the MCO makes. Without a doubt, this position can be uncomfortable for the physician—that is, being between the "rock" of fulfilling one's ethical responsibilities to the patient and the "hard place" of a potentially adversarial relationship with the MCO. The latter possibility is hardly a trivial issue. If the physician is a salaried employee of a staff model MCO, for example, the MCO could conceivably fire them for "not being a team player." In the more common situation, where the physician enters into contracts with a number of

MCOs to ensure an adequate volume of patients, the MCO could decide to terminate its contract with the physician. Depending on the precise wording of the MCO–physician contract, such termination (known in the trade as "deselection") can often be accomplished with minimal notice and without explanation or due process. Physicians routinely walk a tightrope in the managed care setting, one that might cause them to be less than forceful in their patient advocacy role.

Financial Incentives and Disincentives

In addition to the threat of deselection, MCOs use another instrument to influence physician behavior. Most MCO–physician contracts feature clauses outlining financial incentives, financial disincentives, or both. Financial incentives and disincentives are meant to engage the physician (or physician group) more actively in the MCO's cost-containment efforts by using a "carrot or stick" approach. Successful cost-containment efforts over the contractual term will result in the physician (or physician group) receiving a monetary bonus, whereas incurring excessive patient costs will result in money being withheld (usually in escrow). If financial incentives and disincentives are modest or are based on the performance of a sizable group of physicians, physicians will likely not be influenced by these arrangements when caring for individual patients. When the financial incentive or disincentive is significant and based on the performance of an individual physician or a small group of physicians, however, the physician's financial interest may be pitted against the patient's interest in a direct and disturbing way, raising the suspicion, if not the reality, of physician misbehavior if the patient believes that the care provided is somehow being compromised.

Pay for Performance

Since the beginning of the twenty-first century, the term *pay for performance* (P4P) has been used increasingly by healthcare policy analysts and in the medical literature (Doran et al. 2006; Ryan and Blustein 2012). As the phrase suggests, P4P involves a financial incentive for assiduously following a set of recommended clinical guidelines or, even better, achieving optimal patient outcomes. P4P can be applied either at the macro level (to hospitals or groups of physicians) or at the micro level (to individual physicians). A number of ethics issues have also been raised about P4P, especially as it pertains to individual physicians and so-called targeted outcomes (e.g., average level of blood sugar control in a physician's panel of patients with diabetes). For example, will a physician's MCO profile be enhanced (and a financial incentive gained) if the physician "fires" sicker or more challenging patients—the very patients, arguably, who need help the most?

ETHICS ISSUES FACED BY MCO MANAGERS

MCO executives also face a variety of ongoing ethical challenges. Some of these ethical dilemmas are similar to those faced by physicians, whereas others are different.

Persuasive Advertising and Selective Marketing

Veracity is usually not uppermost in the minds of those who produce radio, television, internet, or print media advertisements. The entire point of advertising, after all, is to present the product in the best possible light, and if some less-than-flattering details are left out in the process, that is to be expected. Unfortunately, in the case of MCOs, deceptive advertising can result in the prospective MCO member being misled—for example, when an ad implies that MCO members can see whichever specialist they please. The primary care physician is left with the responsibility of educating the new MCO member on how the plan actually works, including the fact that the "gatekeeping" primary care physician first has to make specialty referrals and the MCO member is usually restricted to seeing those consultants on the MCO's panel.

An issue closely related to advertising is marketing. From a bottom-line business perspective, a younger, healthier member is preferable to an older, sicker one. Some MCOs have been known to direct their marketing efforts to effectively exclude those members of the community who are most frail or infirm—for example, by holding sign-ups for seniors at dances or movie screenings, events unlikely to be attended by the bedridden, the housebound, or those requiring walkers or wheelchairs. Such selective marketing aimed at attracting the healthiest (and least costly) prospective members is like "cherry picking."

Although advertising that is less than fully truthful and marketing that is selective might be accepted behavior in other businesses, ethical healthcare organizations should refrain from engaging in such practices.

Disclosure of Information

Honesty should be the rule for MCOs, not only when dealing with prospective members but also when dealing with those already enrolled in the plan. Patients have a right to be informed of all pertinent diagnostic and therapeutic options related to their healthcare and of all financial arrangements between the MCO and its physicians (including incentives and disincentives) that could potentially affect that care. "Gag rules," whereby physicians are instructed to withhold such information from patients, should be prohibited.

Financial Incentives and Disincentives

For MCOs (and physicians) to simply disclose information pertaining to financial incentives and disincentives is not enough. From an ethical standpoint, such incentives and disincentives must be based on the performance of a sizable group of physicians and not be of such magnitude as to place the physician's personal financial interests in direct conflict with the interests of individual patients.

Ensuring Quality

Although each individual healthcare professional has a duty to maintain a high level of expertise and competence, the MCO is responsible for making sure that its members are receiving high-caliber medical care. From an organizational standpoint, high-quality care can be accomplished in several ways:

- Contracting only with well-trained and suitably credentialed primary care physicians and specialty consultants who are highly regarded in the local or regional medical community
- Working with physicians to establish diagnostic and therapeutic guidelines that are evidence based, especially for commonly encountered conditions
- Soliciting thoughtful physician and pharmacist input when developing the MCO's drug formulary, with a periodic review process to keep the formulary up-to-date
- Providing performance-based feedback to physicians through a carefully conducted and accurate profiling system and soliciting physician input in the profiling process
- Using patient satisfaction measures as an additional means to evaluate physician performance

Appeal Procedures

Either patients or physicians, acting in good faith, may on occasion disagree with the MCO's decisions, especially those related to patient care issues. MCOs need to have a clearly outlined appeal procedure in place. This appeal protocol should be logical, reasonable, and fair and should not be biased against individual patients. These qualities are especially important when questions arise as to whether a particular innovative or experimental therapy is covered by the MCO because medicine is an ever-changing field. In addition, the MCO must clearly state that it will never act in a punitive fashion or take retribution against either patients or physicians who challenge the MCO's decisions or who otherwise participate in the appeal process.

Confidentiality

Like any other healthcare organization, MCOs need to have systems in place to carefully protect patient confidentiality. This includes adherence to the provisions of the Health Insurance Portability and Accountability Act.

Allocation of Resources

Because healthcare resources are finite and MCOs must remain economically competitive in a market economy, priorities in allocating healthcare resources need to be established. MCOs should make these allocation decisions in an open manner, with input from physicians and the MCO's members.

Fostering the Social Good

Because of the predominance of the for-profit MCO model, the US healthcare system has had difficulty financing several domains that may be considered under the general heading of "the social good." These include (1) medical education and the training of future healthcare professionals; (2) biomedical research; and (3) the care of the uninsured, who in early 2023 numbered about 25 million, according to a report released by the National Center for Health Statistics (Cohen and Martinez 2023; Tsai 2023). What role should MCOs (including for-profit MCOs) play in addressing such social concerns? The responsibility of healthcare organizations to promote the social good is not merely an issue raised by "ivory tower" ethicists. The *Code of Ethics* of the American College of Healthcare Executives (ACHE 2022), for example, says:

> The healthcare executive shall: Work to identify and . . . meet the health needs of the community[;] . . . promote an understanding of the social determinants of health and encourage initiatives to address factors influencing them . . . while applying short- and long-term assessments to leadership decisions affecting both community and society[;] . . . [and] support access to healthcare services to all people, particularly the underserved and disenfranchised.

LEGAL RAMIFICATIONS FOR PHYSICIANS AND MANAGERS IN THE MANAGED CARE SETTING

Ideally, ethical guidelines should suffice in causing physicians and MCO managers alike to do the right thing. However, inappropriate behavior sometimes crosses a line and becomes not only ethically suspect but also legally negligent.

A landmark and still very illustrative case in the annals of managed care case law is *Wickline v. State of California* (1986). Lois Wickline was admitted to a hospital in California in the late 1970s for a peripheral vascular procedure. Following that procedure, her physicians recommended an additional eight days in the hospital for postprocedure care and observation. Wickline's insurer was Medi-Cal (California's Medicaid program), which denied her physicians' request for eight days of additional hospitalization, approving a four-day stay instead. At the end of four days, Wickline was discharged. She subsequently developed complications that necessitated readmission and eventual amputation of her leg. Wickline did not sue her physicians, whom she regarded as her advocates, but rather Medi-Cal, whom she blamed for the abbreviated initial hospital stay. In a lower court, Wickline won her suit and was awarded several hundred thousand dollars. Medi-Cal appealed that decision, however, and in a 1986 ruling the appellate court reversed the lower court's decision. The ruling of the appellate court was noteworthy in two respects:

> Third-party payers . . . can be held legally accountable when medically inappropriate decisions result from defects in the design or implementation of cost containment mechanisms as, for example, when appeals made on a patient's behalf for medical . . . care are arbitrarily ignored or unreasonably disregarded or overridden.

> However, a physician who complies without protest with the limitations imposed by a third-party payer, when his medical judgment dictates otherwise, cannot avoid his ultimate responsibility for his patient's care. He cannot point to the healthcare payer as the liability scapegoat when the consequences of his own . . . medical decisions go sour.

The first paragraph indicates that a third-party payer—whether an MCO or a government program such as Medicaid—could be sued if its cost-containment policy resulted in medical harm, especially if the treating physician's legitimate objections were arbitrarily ignored or overridden. The second paragraph is clearly aimed at physicians working in managed care settings and emphasizes that the physician's ultimate obligation is to the individual patient and not passive acceptance of the third-party payer's cost-containment policies.

Since *Wickline v. California*, a number of other cases (e.g., *Boyd v. Einstein, Hand v. Tavera, Fox v. Health Net of California*) have involved the legal liability of physicians in the managed care setting or the legal liability of MCOs (Gosfield 1995; Moskowitz 1998). Although each of these cases is different from *Wickline v. California*, the common theme is that adverse patient outcomes resulting from cost-containment policies can place both the physician and the MCO at legal risk. MCO executives also need to be aware of yet another case, *McClellan v. Health Maintenance Organization of Pennsylvania* (1995), in which the court ruled that the MCO in question had an obligation to select and retain only competent physicians.

Notably, despite the cases cited here, MCOs have been relatively protected from lawsuits in state courts for medical negligence because of the 1974 Employee Retirement Income Security Act (ERISA). The purpose of ERISA was to prohibit state regulation of employee pension plans and other employee benefit plans, including health benefit plans. Because most Americans in MCOs are enrolled through their employer, ERISA has effectively barred most MCO enrollees from suing their MCO for medical negligence in state courts (although it has not prevented patients from suing their MCO physicians in state courts). In their decisions in the cases of *Pegram v. Herdrich* (2000), *Aetna Health Inc. v. Davila* (2004), and *Cigna Healthcare of Texas Inc. v. Calad* (2004), the US Supreme Court ruled to uphold ERISA, continuing MCOs' immunity from medical liability, at least in many of the situations commonly encountered. The issue of whether ERISA should be overturned or amended remains the subject of ongoing and intense political debate.

ETHICAL GUIDELINES FOR PHYSICIANS PRACTICING IN THE MANAGED CARE SETTING

Physicians practicing in the managed care setting should consider the following recommendations:

- The physician–patient relationship is the cornerstone of the practice of medicine, and physicians should view their primary obligation as the provision of humane, high-quality care to their individual patients.
- Physicians are not obligated to provide care that is clearly useless. In addition, physicians have a responsibility to choose among the least costly of effective therapies.
- Any decisions regarding the allocation of healthcare resources should be made on a broad, policymaking level and not at the bedside of individual patients. Physicians have a responsibility to participate in these resource

allocation decisions, bearing in mind the ethical principle of distributive justice.

- Physicians should be truthful in their dealings with patients and families. All information that might affect patient care should be disclosed, including (1) relevant diagnostic and therapeutic options and (2) all physician–MCO financial relationships that might affect patient care.
- Physicians should be truthful in their dealings with MCO management and refrain from attempts to game the system.
- Any financial incentives and disincentives should be limited in magnitude and ideally should be based on the performance of a sizable group of physicians rather than that of a single physician or a small group of physicians. The physician's personal interests should never result in the withholding of care that is medically necessary or medically advisable.
- Physicians have an obligation to maintain their professional competence and seek appropriate consultation for patient care issues outside their realm of expertise.
- Physicians should serve as advocates for a system of healthcare that (1) is based on humaneness, high-quality care, and optimal outcomes for patients and (2) does not place restrictions on access to medical care that is necessary or advisable.

ETHICAL GUIDELINES FOR MCO MANAGERS

In many respects, recommendations for MCO managers parallel those made for MCO physicians. For example, recommendations regarding truth telling, the fair and equitable allocation of healthcare resources, and limitations on financial incentives and disincentives are germane to both physicians and MCO executives. Additional recommendations for MCO managers include the following:

- Refrain from engaging in misleading advertising or selective marketing, no matter how great the temptation.
- Establish and maintain systems within the MCO that aim to protect patient confidentiality.
- Ensure high-quality patient care by (1) selecting and retaining only high-caliber healthcare professionals, (2) working with physicians to establish diagnostic and therapeutics guidelines that are evidence based, and (3) providing performance-based feedback to physicians that is meaningful and accurate.
- Establish appeal procedures that are fair and free of punitive overtones.

- Consider carefully how the organization might contribute to the social good, including medical education, medical research, and care of the indigent or uninsured.

A BLUEPRINT FOR THE FUTURE: THE TAVISTOCK PRINCIPLES

Although this chapter's ethical recommendations to physicians and those to MCO managers overlap considerably, a common perception is that each constituency in the healthcare universe (physicians, MCO executives, or others) tends to view healthcare issues through its own particular lens, hampering meaningful discussion and interdisciplinary cooperation.

In 1999, a group of interested parties, including physicians, nurses, healthcare executives, economists, and ethicists, convened to develop a set of mutually agreed-on ethical principles. Called the Tavistock Group because they initially met near Tavistock Square in London, these parties proposed the following seven principles (Davidoff 2000):

1. *Rights.* People have a right to health and healthcare.
2. *Balance.* Care of individual patients is central, but the health of populations should also be our concern.
3. *Comprehensiveness.* In addition to treating illness, we have an obligation to ease suffering, minimize disability, prevent disease, and promote health.
4. *Cooperation.* Healthcare succeeds only if we cooperate with those we serve, with each other, and with those in other sectors.
5. *Improvement.* Improving healthcare is a serious and continuing responsibility.
6. *Safety.* Do no harm.
7. *Openness.* Being open, honest, and trustworthy is vital in healthcare.

The Tavistock principles are similar in spirit to the principles outlined by the Woodstock group nearly a decade earlier. The tone of shared values and productive cooperation embodied in both sets of principles may one day replace the rancor and divisiveness that has all too often characterized discussion of the US healthcare system. Only time will tell if the for-profit MCO model will be able to adhere to these principles while simultaneously generating the level of profits that investors in other businesses typically expect. Healthcare reform and the political controversy surrounding it have introduced an additional measure of uncertainty to the current US healthcare system. However, no matter what model of healthcare delivery prevails in the future, healthcare professionals of all stripes and at every level must make sure that the ethical underpinnings of patient care are honored.

REFERENCES

Aetna Health Inc. v. Davila (2000). 530 U.S. 200 (2004).

American College of Healthcare Executives (ACHE). 2022. *Code of Ethics*. Updated December 5. www.ache.org/about-ache/our-story/our-commitments/ethics/ache-code-of-ethics.

Cigna Healthcare of Texas Inc. v. Calad. 2004. 540 U.S. 981 (2004).

Cohen, R. A., and M. E. Martinez. 2023. *Health Insurance Coverage: Early Release of Quarterly Estimates from the National Health Interview Survey, January 2022– March 2023*. National Center for Health Statistics. Published August. www.cdc.gov/nchs/data/nhis/earlyrelease/Quarterly_Estimates_2023_Q11.pdf.

Davidoff, F. 2000. "Changing the Subject: Ethical Principles for Everyone in Healthcare." *Annals of Internal Medicine* 133 (5): 386–89.

Doran, T., C. Fullwood, H. Gravelle, D. Reeves, E. Kontopantelis, U. Hiroeh, and M. Roland. 2006. "Pay-for-Performance Programs in Family Practices in the United Kingdom." *New England Journal of Medicine* 355 (4): 375–84.

Gosfield, A. G. 1995. "The Legal Subtext of the Managed Care Environment: A Practitioner's Perspective." *Journal of Law, Medicine & Ethics* 23 (3): 230–35.

McClellan v. Health Maintenance Organization of Pennsylvania. 1995. 442 Pa.Super. 504 (1995).

Moskowitz, E. H. 1998. "Medical Responsibility and Legal Liability in Managed Care." *Journal of the American Geriatrics Society* 46 (3): 373–77.

Pegram v. Herdrich. 2000. 530 U.S. 211 (2000).

Ryan, A., and J. Blustein. 2012. "Making the Best of Hospital Pay for Performance." *New England Journal of Medicine* 366 (17): 1557–59.

Tsai, B. 2023. "U.S. Uninsured Rate Hits Record Low in First Quarter of 2023." *NCHS: A Blog for the National Center for Health Statistics*, Centers for Disease Control and Prevention. Published August 3. https://blogs.cdc.gov/nchs/2023/08/03/7434/.

Wickline v. State of California. 1986. 192 Cal.App.3d 1630 (1986).

Woodstock Theological Center. 1995. *Ethical Considerations for the Business Aspects of Healthcare*. Washington, DC: Georgetown University Press.

CHAPTER 25

Evaluating Healthcare Ethics Committees

Rebecca A. Dobbs

THE HEALTHCARE SYSTEM in the United States continues to undergo radical changes in its structure, delivery and financing of services, and role in society. The current environment is characterized by an increased awareness of patient rights and responsibilities, increased treatment options, significant advances in biomedical technology, higher costs, and the powerful influence of insurers in healthcare delivery and decision making. The era is characterized by broad changes in not only the mechanics of healthcare delivery and financing but also social values and public expectations. Newly raised ethical concerns stemming from resource allocation issues (e.g., rationing of care), scientific and technological advancements (e.g., human genetics), moral duplicity (e.g., assisted suicide), evolving financial arrangements (e.g., conflicts of interest, the Affordable Care Act), and increased attention to quality and accountability (e.g., new quality measures and performance standards from the Centers for Medicare & Medicaid Services) pose new challenges for healthcare institutions and professionals.

In March 2010, the Affordable Care Act and its amendment, the Health Care and Education Reconciliation Act, were signed into law, further affecting healthcare reform in federal and state programs (e.g., Medicare and Medicaid). Healthcare organizations will be challenged to transform into entities that provide high-quality care and services to a growing population amid increasing fiscal constraints. These challenges underscore the importance of a formalized, comprehensive ethics program to deal with an ever-changing healthcare delivery system, evolving societal expectations, and their effect on professional behavior.

Many healthcare organizations have already recognized the need for a comprehensive ethics program. Historically, such programs have taken a variety of forms. Some healthcare organizations have chosen to use individual ethics consultants or bioethicists, some have written extensive ethics policies and procedures to be carried out by existing organizational committees or entities, and still others have formed ethics committees dedicated to the task of dealing with ethics issues as they arise. Some organizations have created positions for ethics officers or compliance officers to monitor the organizations' adherence to ethical standards.

Few organizations, however, have ventured into the realm of a fully integrated healthcare ethics program—one that monitors the ethical climate of the organization, proactively addresses potential ethics issues, aggressively manages ethical discourse in both the clinical and the organizational context, critically evaluates the overall effectiveness of program activities, and takes action to change the organization's ethical culture and processes. Efforts to create an integrated ethics program so far have primarily entailed the merging of existing organizational areas (e.g., compliance, accreditation, quality assurance, risk management, clinical ethics) under a single title. Until a fully integrated healthcare ethics program matures enough to meet the growing ethical needs of healthcare organizations, the healthcare ethics committee (HEC) remains the primary vehicle for fielding ethics issues in healthcare organizations.

Historically, HECs have been oriented toward acute care, but they are increasingly being presented with primary care and outpatient issues that further blur the distinction between bedside (clinical) and boardroom (organizational) ethics. Hence, HECs may be called on to respond to an increasing number of organizational ethics concerns that cannot be disentangled from purely clinical ones.

HECs have a powerful influence on healthcare decision making. Although formalized requirements for performance assessment and improvement have not been extended to HEC functions and processes, and no widely publicized or accepted performance standards exist to guide HEC activities, an increased level of scrutiny and accountability with respect to HEC composition, management, and functions can still be expected.

HEC FUNCTIONS

In 1986, the American Hospital Association published a *Handbook for Hospital Ethics Committees*, in which it defined three main HEC functions: education, policy development, and case consultation. These three functions remain the primary focus of HECs in the United States and internationally (Hester and Schonfeld 2012; Hajibabaee et al. 2016; Ross et al. 1993).

Education

The HEC's education function serves three principal audiences: the ethics committee itself, the organization's staff, and the community at large. Education of ethics committee members is widely accepted as a priority. Educational initiatives frequently focus on medicolegal issues, ethical theories and principles, the application of these theories and principles to ethics policy development and ethics review and consultation, committee functions and obligations, group processes, and communication skills. Educational goals may vary depending on the HEC's mission and objectives, committee member needs, organizational setting, and available resources.

Ethics education provided within the organization often focuses on improving staff's understanding of general bioethical and medicolegal issues as they relate to medical treatment and patient care activities. Topics may include current issues in bioethics and the organization's institutional policies and procedures. According to Hester and Schonfeld (2012), such initiatives can prevent issues arising from lack of awareness and thereby increase the HEC's visibility and credibility. Community education efforts focus on stakeholders beyond the confines of institutional boundaries. Educational needs in the community can be addressed by providing local workshops on selected topics, conducting focus groups to share information and solicit input for policy development and revision, working with university faculty on curriculum development, working with legislators to develop new legislation, and testifying before legislative bodies. The success of community education depends largely on adequately identifying the needs and interests of the target audience and planning educational opportunities accordingly (Ross et al. 1993).

Policy Development

The second HEC function encompasses those committee activities related to the development, implementation, review, revision, and compliance assessment of ethics policies and guidelines. *Ethics policies* establish standards or define ethical boundaries within which specific activities must occur, whereas *ethics guidelines* are more flexible and less prescriptive. Guidelines simply suggest options in or alternatives to a given ethical situation. The level of HEC involvement in the policy development function varies among healthcare organizations. Some HECs are directly involved in ethics policy and guideline activities, whereas others take on a more consultative role. Most HECs write policies and guidelines concerning well-documented topics for which broad societal consensus exists; some HECs, however, venture into relatively uncharted waters by developing policies and guidelines concerning clinical issues such as organ transplant recipient criteria and organizational issues such as resource allocation during public health emergencies (most recently the COVID-19 pandemic) and disasters. The degree of HEC involvement in ethics policy development is determined largely by organizational culture, the composition and maturity of the committee, and its role in the organization and community. According to Hester and Schonfeld (2012), developing reasonably clear guidelines and policies can assist in decision making and thereby prevent some ethical issues from arising.

Case Consultation

Ethics reviews and consultations are performed primarily to assist healthcare professionals, patients, and families or surrogates in sorting out treatment options, making informed decisions, or resolving conflicts. An *ethics review* is generally performed retrospectively to analyze a situation about which an ethical concern or issue has been raised. An ethics review performed in this manner can have a positive effect on future situations presenting a similar issue, but its timing prevents it from having any effect on the situation being studied. An ethics review can also be performed proactively in a hypothetical setting, which can help HECs and organizations work through ethical dilemmas before they occur. An ethics review can also provide useful inputs to the development, review, and revision of ethics policies and guidelines. An *ethics consultation*, on the other hand, generally refers to the analysis of a current ethical concern or issue by the parties involved to resolve the ethical dilemma (Ross et al. 1993). An ethics consultation can be performed by the full committee, a consultation team, or an individual consultant. Hester and Schonfeld (2012) point out that the type of consult employed will be determined by the nature of the ethical issue and the resources of the HEC, as well as its scope within the organization.

An HEC can choose from among a variety of models (medical, legal, or educational) to guide an ethics review or consultation. The medical model emphasizes the medical expertise of physicians, nurses, and usually a chaplain in addressing clinical matters. The legal model treats the ethics review or consultation as a type of hearing, in which input is sought from the parties involved and attention is given to issues of due process. The educational model employs a multidisciplinary approach to explore the various ethical dimensions of a given situation. Selection of an appropriate model for an ethics review or consultation is based largely on the specific ethics issue and the special concerns of the people involved (Ross et al. 1993).

Administration and Management

To the three widely accepted HEC functions, Dobbs (2000) added a fourth function—HEC administration and management. This function addresses activities related to infrastructure, strategic planning, the committee's composition and role in the organization, committee membership criteria, resource allocation, and performance evaluation. HECs across the country, as well as internationally, differ significantly in mission, structure, organizational role, scope of activities, and formality of internal processes. Therefore, among the recognized HEC functions, the administration and management function is likely the most widely varied—in part because little has been written about the topic.

Despite the scarcity of published data on evaluation strategies or performance standards and criteria, HEC evaluation is necessary, in part, to enhance HEC credibility and to justify the commitment of increasingly scarce institutional resources. Information obtained from the HEC evaluation process can be used to

- identify areas for improvement,
- prioritize improvement activities,
- assist in the strategic planning process,
- plan resource requirements,
- provide baseline data for future evaluation and benchmarking activities, and
- document activities for internal management reviews and external accreditation surveys.

HEC EVALUATION STRATEGIES

Although many observers agree that critical evaluation of HEC processes demonstrates an organization's commitment to high-quality healthcare and attention to societal needs and concerns, no consensus has yet been reached about which approach is most suitable for conducting such an evaluation. Evaluation strategies commonly used to assess healthcare functions or programs include program evaluation, internal evaluation, and self-assessment. Program evaluation provides a highly structured analysis of program elements and activities by an external source. Internal evaluation provides an organizational perspective of a program's interrelated components and functions as measured by other members in the organization. Self-assessment provides an intimate evaluation of a program by those who are directly responsible for its planning, execution, and management. Whichever method is selected, Nelson and Elliott (2012) suggest that the evaluation process include a review of expectations concerning the committee's functions, its structure (particularly membership), access to the committee, the consultation process and outcomes, and overall committee efficiency.

Program Evaluation

Program evaluation is a process for determining the value or effectiveness of a program or program elements. It is typically classified as *formative* (process oriented) or *summative* (outcome oriented), depending on the type of information produced and how that information is used.

Formative evaluation assesses the process by which the program conducts its activities, with the aim of improving the program and its management. A formative approach has certain advantages: (1) Practitioners can develop performance standards and assessment criteria relatively easily, and (2) even when not fully validated, the standards and criteria can serve as interim measures of acceptable performance. The main disadvantage to a formative approach is that it may actually encourage dogmatism and perpetuate potential errors in what is determined to be acceptable performance (Donabedian 1980).

Summative evaluation focuses on the long-term effects of a program—its end product, how well it is functioning, and whether it has had any effect on given performance indicators. A summative approach also has certain advantages: It (1) discourages dogmatism, (2) reflects the contributions of all practitioners, and (3) provides a more direct assessment of the practitioner–customer relationship when customer satisfaction measures are included. Disadvantages of the summative approach include (1) the difficulty practitioners experience in specifying outcomes of optimal performance, (2) the ethics issue associated with waiting for adverse outcome trends to emerge before taking action, and (3) the challenge of drawing pertinent conclusions when outcomes are assessed without evaluating the related processes (Donabedian 1980).

Program evaluation is an integrated process of collecting and analyzing data using various scientific methods to determine the relevance, progress, efficiency, effectiveness, and impact of program activities. Five approaches to program evaluation are widely accepted:

1. *Monitoring* is concerned with program progress and improvement and involves the comparison of program expectations with actual results. Even though monitoring may be viewed as mundane or nonscientific, it is particularly important for formative evaluation and critical to the evaluation of progress and continuous improvement.

2. *Case studies* rely more on the ingenuity, insight, and experience of the researcher than on rigorous sampling and statistical techniques. Even though they are primarily qualitative in nature, case studies frequently employ a variety of quantitative data collection and analysis techniques.

3. *Survey research* has become a common evaluation strategy, particularly in the summative evaluation of programs. Surveys are generally either descriptive or analytic in nature. Descriptive surveys are used to produce an accurate depiction of a phenomenon being studied by describing a problem that requires some type of program activity, describing the program from the perspective of providers or participants, or describing the program's results from the perspective of the providers or participants. Analytic surveys are used to describe relationships between various aspects of a phenomenon. They can determine whether participants with different characteristics view a program more or less favorably or whether the program has some differential effect on participants who have certain characteristics.

4. *Trend analysis* is an evaluation strategy for examining tendencies in performance indicators over time. It can be done in conjunction with monitoring to determine whether the introduction of a particular program has a causal connection to changes in the condition that the program was established to influence.

5. *Experimental design* is the most powerful program evaluation approach. It can be a complex undertaking even though the basic pattern is relatively simple: The state of a system is observed at a given point in time, an experimental variable is introduced, and the state of the system is observed again to determine the effect of the variable on the system. Though some experimental designs may be too complex for healthcare settings, designs that appear to be feasible and appropriate include pretest and posttest, pretest and posttest with a control or comparison group, multiple group pretest and posttest, and posttest only.

The selection of an evaluation approach does not dictate the use of the formative approach or the summative approach exclusively. Rather, a well-designed program evaluation may require a combination of approaches reflecting the nature of the information to be obtained and other requirements of the situation.

Internal Evaluation

Another evaluation strategy applicable to healthcare settings is internal evaluation. Performed by members of the group or organization under study, internal evaluation examines the organization as a set of interrelated components and functions. Data obtained from internal evaluation activities can assist the healthcare organization in

- preparing for compliance or accreditation reviews,
- meeting internal or external reporting requirements,
- identifying and documenting client or customer needs,
- describing programs and services,
- identifying program strengths and weaknesses,
- establishing program priorities,
- planning budgets,
- obtaining and maintaining financial support, and
- relating to external customer groups.

Self-Assessment

Social values today call for interdisciplinary team building, trust, responsibility, and accountability in healthcare organizations. Self-assessment is a process by which a healthcare organization, or an entity within the organization, evaluates itself to systematically monitor performance against established standards. The primary steps of the self-assessment process are the following:

1. Set recognized standards.
2. Rate the standards.
3. Make changes necessary to satisfy the standards.
4. Confirm achievement of the standards by external evaluators.

Self-assessment can be used to evaluate compliance, effectiveness, or performance. Compliance self-assessments are generally performed on a routine, periodic basis in anticipation of an upcoming external evaluation, such as an accreditation review or licensing board visit. Effectiveness self-assessments are often performed to identify system improvement opportunities. Performance self-assessments are differentiated from the other two by their direct observation and evaluation of a process or an activity.

Even though a self-assessment may provide the organization with information about its strengths and weaknesses, it does not render a prioritization of improvement actions. The organization needs to review and prioritize improvement actions on the basis of its mission, goals and objectives, resources, and desired level of performance.

Self-assessment provides a snapshot of how well the organization meets stated requirements, establishes methods of program delivery that meet high professional standards, and monitors the quality of its services. The selection of standards for assessing HEC performance is an important, but often difficult, decision that an organization must make. Performance standards fall into three categories (Donabedian 1980):

1. *Outcome standards* measure specific characteristics of services that an organization provides, define both desirable and undesirable results, and can be used to benchmark performance. Even though outcomes are the typical indicators of organizational effectiveness, they can present problems in interpretation. For example, outcomes reflect not only work performance but also the application of technology and other characteristics of the organization's internal and external environments. Thus, knowledge about causes and effects can be considered relatively complete only when the organization can control its environment. In healthcare ethics, many factors beyond the HEC's locus of control (e.g., legislation, organizational policies, social norms, cultural influences, individual preferences) can have a significant impact on the services being provided and outcomes produced. Outcome measures associated with HEC functions (particularly ethics review and consultation) tend to be controversial because of the broad range of ethical resolutions and the lack of consensus on any single best one.

2. *Process standards* specify how an organization's performance capabilities are operationalized. Clearly defined processes reduce process variation, leading to more predictable outcomes. Even so, full compliance with process standards is not expected because a certain degree of variation may be justifiable in certain situations. Process measures assess the quantity or quality of organizational activities with respect to effort rather than effect or achievement. Compared with other measures of organizational performance, process measures may be more valid because they directly assess performance values. However, they assess conformity to a given standard, not the adequacy or correctness of the standard. Surveys, interviews, direct observations, and documentation reviews can be used effectively to evaluate HEC functions from a process perspective.

3. *Structure standards* define the rules under which the organization is governed and services are rendered. They are the absolutes of the organization and cannot be situationally modified. Structure standards assess the organization's capacity to perform effectively, and they are based on relatively stable organizational features or individual characteristics presumed to have an impact on organizational effectiveness (e.g., accreditation rating; professional staff licensure; available tools and technology; human, physical, and financial resources). Structure standards are especially useful in the planning,

design, and implementation of healthcare programs. However, structure is relevant only to the extent that it can increase or decrease the probability of good performance. Appropriate structural measures of HEC functions include identifying the presence of (a) mechanisms for conducting ethics consultation, formulating ethics policies, and communicating information to patients and surrogates; (b) written policies; (c) library holdings on ethics subjects; (d) budget allocations and personnel to support education; and (e) ongoing ethics assessment.

Donabedian (1980) suggests the following ordering of these performance measures based on fundamental functional relationships between them: structure $\rightarrow$ process $\rightarrow$ outcome. In essence, structure (prerequisites, organization, resources) affects process (content, configuration, rendering of services), which affects outcomes (end product, effects of services provided).

As an evaluation strategy, self-assessment is the most desirable because it is executed by the people who are most knowledgeable and who have the highest degree of control over healthcare ethics programs—HEC chairs and members. Self-assessment incorporates the most beneficial elements of program evaluation (formalized structure) and internal evaluation (organizational focus) to provide a comprehensive analysis of HEC functions.

PRACTICAL APPLICATION

If HECs are to be recognized as credible components of the healthcare system, organizations must be willing to evaluate performance, document success, identify opportunities for improvement, and ensure customer satisfaction. When properly planned and executed, almost any evaluation approach can be used effectively to assess HECs. The common elements of successful evaluation endeavors are objectivity, management support, an ability and willingness to change, and a commitment to improvement. Practical tips for the various steps of an HEC evaluation include the following:

1. *Discuss the proposed evaluation activity as a committee.* Get the group's support and commitment, and seek volunteers to champion major tasks.
2. *Secure management support.* Identify the necessary organizational resources, and seek additional funding if needed.
3. *Design the evaluation effort.* Delineate clearly its purpose and scope. Will it be a comprehensive evaluation or will it focus on a specific HEC function or process? What evaluation approach (or combination of approaches) will

be used? What key questions does the committee want to answer? Develop an evaluation timeline.

4. *Conduct the evaluation.* Because most HEC members are volunteers, time constraints will likely preclude having the entire committee participate in the evaluation. Consider identifying a small number of committee members who are interested in participating. Schedule appropriate time for the evaluation. The assessment of a major function or process can take several hours, but the actual time frame will depend on the scope and depth of the evaluation, the selection of participants, and their knowledge of the committee's historical background and current functions. Consider scheduling separate sessions for each functional area or process being assessed.

5. *Analyze the data.* The evaluation is intended to give the committee an opportunity to reflect on its activities and to generate topics for further discussion and consideration. If performance standards were developed, the committee does not yet need to perform at the level at which the standards were written. Performance standards provide a benchmark against which the committee's current level of development can be measured to plan improvement activities. Do not hesitate to seek an external interpretation of the data.

6. *Share the evaluation findings with the committee.* Review and discuss the findings with committee members.

7. *Document the findings.* Record the evaluation participants and processes used. Maintain evaluation files for other uses (e.g., historical records, benchmarking progress, accreditation surveys, budget preparation).

8. *Report the findings.* Decide what will be reported. Will it be major findings, data and results, alternatives, or recommendations? Determine in what format the findings will be reported. Should they be in a formal written report, an executive summary, an oral briefing with charts, a newsletter or journal article, or a group discussion? Decide how widely evaluation findings will be distributed. Who are the intended users, and who else could benefit from the data being generated?

9. *Take action on the findings.* Develop an action plan and timeline to address the findings. Prioritize activities, and seek volunteers to champion major tasks. Track action items, and provide regular progress reports to the committee. Keep management informed on progress, as required. Seek additional resources as needed.

10. *Start planning the next HEC evaluation.* Revising the process and instruments used for the most recent evaluation while critical comments are still fresh will make the next evaluation flow more smoothly.

REFERENCES

Dobbs, R. A. 2000. "Self-Assessment of Hospital Ethics Committees in New Mexico: A Study in Process Improvement." PhD diss., Walden University, Minneapolis.

Donabedian, A. 1980. *Explorations in Quality Assessment and Monitoring: The Definition of Quality and Approaches to Its Assessment, Volume 1.* Chicago: Health Administration Press.

Hajibabaee, F., S. Joolaee, M. A. Cheraghi, P. Salari, and P. Rodney. 2016. "Hospital/ Clinical Ethics Committees' Notion: An Overview." *Journal of Medical Ethics and History of Medicine* 9: 17.

Hester, D. M., and T. Schonfeld (eds.). 2012. *Guidance for Healthcare Ethics Committees.* Cambridge: Cambridge University Press.

Nelson, W. A., and B. A. Elliott. 2012. *Critical Access Hospital Ethics Committee Resource Guide.* Dartmouth College. Accessed October 26, 2023. https://geiselmed. dartmouth.edu/cfm/wp-content/uploads/sites/97/2022/04/cah_guide.pdf.

Ross, J. W., J. W. Glaser, D. Rasinski-Gregory, J. M. Gibson, and C. Bayley. 1993. *Health Care Ethics Committees: The Next Generation.* Chicago: American Hospital Publishing.

CHAPTER 26

Prevention and Treatment of Substance Use Disorders Among Healthcare Professionals

J. Mitchell Simson

HEALTHCARE MANAGERS MUST be able to identify an impaired healthcare professional and understand what assessment, intervention, and treatment entail. Although the *Code of Medical Ethics* of the American Medical Association (AMA) discusses physician impairment at length (AMA 2023), the number of impaired physicians reported by colleagues appears to be much lower than the estimated number of physicians who become impaired (DesRoches et al. 2010).

Before this issue can be examined, however, relevant terminology must be defined. *Impairment* is "the inability to practice medicine with reasonable skill and safety to patients by reason of physical or mental illness, including deterioration through the aging process, the loss of motor skills or the excessive use or abuse of drugs, including alcohol" (AMA 1992). *Addiction* is "a treatable, chronic medical disease involving complex interactions among brain circuits, genetics, the environment, and an individual's life experiences. People with addiction use substances or engage in behaviors that become compulsive and often continue despite harmful consequences" (American Society of Addiction Medicine 2019).

The fifth edition of the *Diagnostic and Statistical Manual* (DSM-5), published in May 2013, combined the previous diagnoses of *substance abuse* and *substance dependence* into a single overarching diagnosis—*substance use disorder* (American Psychiatric Association 2013). The severity of the disorder is now graded according to the number of criteria the individual meets. If the individual meets none or only one criterion, no diagnosis is made; if two or three, the diagnosis is mild; if four or five, moderate; if six or more, severe.

For example, the 11 criteria of an alcohol use disorder are:

1. Missing work or school because of alcohol use
2. Drinking in hazardous situations
3. Drinking despite social or personal problems
4. Craving alcohol
5. Development of tolerance
6. Withdrawals when cutting down or trying to quit
7. Drinking more than intended
8. Inability to successfully quit
9. Increase in alcohol-seeking behavior
10. Interference with important activities
11. Continued use despite health problems

THE IMPAIRED HEALTHCARE PROFESSIONAL

To help readers identify the healthcare professional impaired by a substance use disorder, the general characteristics of physicians with substance use disorders are described here (based on studies undertaken from the 1990s on into the twenty-first century). Although the exact prevalence of substance use disorders among physicians is unknown, one survey of nearly 2,000 physicians in Denmark found that 18.9 percent self-reported risky alcohol use and 3 percent self-reported risky drug use (Sørensen et al. 2015). If these findings are extrapolated to the approximately 1 million professionally active physicians in the United States (Michas 2021), then approximately 189,000 physicians abuse alcohol and 30,000 abuse other drugs.

The age at first presentation for treatment of addiction is bimodal: Physicians in training and in early practice constitute the first wave, and physicians in mid- to late career constitute the second (Ries et al. 2014). From 1998 to 2007, the average age of physicians entering addiction treatment increased from 42.5 years to 48.0 years. More men enter treatment than women, in a ratio of between 6 and 10 to 1, which contrasts with a male-to-female physician ratio of only 3 to 1 (McGovern et al. 1998; Wunsch et al. 2007). Female physicians in treatment tend to be younger (average age 39.9 years versus 43.7 for males), have more medical and psychiatric comorbidity, and are more likely to use sedatives or hypnotics than male physicians (Wunsch et al. 2007). Women are more likely than men to have suicidal ideation and more likely to have attempted suicide either under or not under the influence of alcohol or other drugs. Addiction does not appear to account for any gender difference in employment problems or legal problems (Wunsch et al. 2007).

Many studies have examined the specialties of physicians receiving care in addiction treatment centers. Psychiatry, emergency medicine, anesthesiology, and family medicine predominate (Ries et al. 2014). An interesting correlation is that physicians in all specialties except psychiatry self-report higher levels of burnout (Shanafelt et al. 2012).

At the top of the list of drugs that are abused by physicians (and by the general population) is alcohol. A more recent study has confirmed previous findings that 12.9 percent of male physicians and 21.4 percent of female physicians meet diagnostic criteria for alcohol abuse or dependence (Oreskovich et al. 2015). Factors independently associated with an alcohol use disorder are younger age, fewer hours worked, female gender, dissatisfaction in a relationship with a spouse or partner, not having children, and practicing any specialty other than internal medicine. In the general population, heavy drinking decreases with age, but among physicians, it increases with age (McAuliffe et al. 1991). An alcohol use disorder is associated with burnout, depression, suicidal ideation, lower quality of life, lower career satisfaction, and medical errors.

One study of Estonian physicians found that 12 percent of male physicians and 5 percent of female physicians smoke daily (Põld and Pärna 2017)—numbers that are probably similar to those in the United States. Surgeons and emergency medicine physicians smoke more than other physicians do, but overall, physician tobacco use is decreasing (Buhl et al. 2011; Mangus, Hawkins, and Miller 1998). Cocaine use seems to be higher among physicians in surgical specialties who have medical access to it (ear, nose, and throat; plastics; head and neck surgery; ophthalmology) and among emergency medicine physicians. The national plague of opioid abuse is reflected in physician use: Opioids are the second most common drug that physicians abuse. Family medicine and obstetrics/gynecology physicians tend to abuse oral opioids, while anesthesiologists use the highly potent opioid injectables (Seppala and Berge 2010). Anesthesiologists also abuse other injectables to which they have access, such as ketamine and propofol (Bryson and Silverstein 2008). Marijuana abuse seems more prevalent in emergency medicine, family medicine, and anesthesiology. Psychiatrists report a higher frequency of unsupervised benzodiazepine misuse (Hughes et al. 1992).

A study of emergency medicine physicians in physician health programs (PHPs) indicated that about half enrolled because of alcohol-related problems, and more than a third enrolled because of opioid use (Rose, Campbell, and Skipper 2014). Among all physicians entering treatment, alcohol is the primary problematic substance, remaining fairly stable over decades at 44–50 percent. Opioids, which have long been available to physicians through drug sales representative samples, self-prescribing, and diversion from the workplace, account for 33–37 percent of admissions. Stimulant use accounts for 8–16 percent and sedatives for about 4 percent of admissions. About 50 percent of physicians use more than one substance, and intravenous substance use has climbed to about 14 percent (DuPont et al. 2009; Rose et al. 2017).

Many other risk factors for physician addiction have been studied since the 1960s. Physicians have the same genetic predisposition as the general population (i.e., a family history of drug or alcohol dependence). Personality disorders have also been postulated as increasing the risk of drug use and abuse. One study that examined the role of personality disorders on physicians' rates of sobriety in the first two years following treatment did not find a significant relationship between personality and substance abuse (Angres, Bologeorges, and Chou 2013). Other studies examined "personality types" such as sensation seeking (McAuliffe, Rohman, and Wechsler 1984), perfectionist (Bissell and Jones 1976), compulsive (Udell 1984), and introverted and introspective (Yufit, Pollock, and Wasserman 1969; Zeldow and Daugherty 1991). Physicians' work may, arguably, benefit from introspection and a certain amount of compulsivity. Physicians and other healthcare professionals are not immune to other medical, psychiatric, and emotional comorbidities that can include depression, bipolar disorder, anxiety, chronic pain, and posttraumatic stress disorder.

Research since the 1980s shows an increase in physician burnout. In surgeons who self-reported a major surgical error, the only factors that were independently associated with their perception of the cause of the error were burnout and depression (Shanafelt et al. 2010). To date, most efforts to reduce surgical errors have looked at systems errors that can be corrected by applying quality improvement matrixes, but individual factors such as burnout and depression need to be more fully identified and remedied. Despite evidence that self-disclosure of errors reduces medical liability, many physicians do not feel supported by their healthcare organization in disclosing errors.

IDENTIFYING AND REPORTING THE IMPAIRED HEALTHCARE PROFESSIONAL

How does a healthcare manager identify the impaired health professional? Sometimes they self-identify ("self-ID") after seeking treatment for their addiction on their own. Sometimes they "self-OD," as when an anesthesiologist is found unconscious from a sufentanyl overdose or an internist is hospitalized with acute pancreatitis resulting from alcoholism. Not uncommonly, the work site sees a behavioral change that is typically first reported by ancillary staff—rounding at irregular hours, irritability and explosive behavior toward support staff and colleagues, falling asleep on the job or between shifts, alcohol on the breath at work, disheveled appearance, glassy eyes or small pupils, intoxication without alcohol odor, frequent bathroom breaks or unexplained absences, significant weight gain or loss, depression, forgetfulness, a drop in productivity, frequent job changes, and so forth. Sometimes, if the work site is the source of the abused drug via samples or diversion, the physician works additional shifts to increase access to that drug. Thus, the physician might mask their drug abuse by hiding their behavioral change in a cloak of increased productivity. Yet incomplete charting or repeated errors in paperwork may occur, indicating a possible addiction (Addiction Center 2023).

Dealing with an impaired colleague is a difficult and emotionally charged job for physician leaders and hospital administrators, who often have little training on how to handle such a situation (Seppala and Berge 2010). Regarding the hospital's ethical responsibilities in assisting impaired physicians, Darr (1991) states:

> Two themes must describe the context of the hospital's relationship with physicians: the primacy of the patient, and the trustees and managers as moral agents. The personal ethic of each trustee and manager, within the context of the hospital's organizational philosophy, provides a moral framework for the relationships among patients, physicians, employees, organization, and community. Managers especially are not, and cannot be morally neutral technocrats. Rather, trustees and managers morally affect and are morally affected by decisions made and actions taken. This means decision making is not value-free: there is a moral dimension to the decision's effect on its environment and all persons touched by it. Primarily, meeting the hospital's ethical responsibility to impaired physicians requires an inquiring mind and attention to detail. Those involved must ask whether the specific action contemplated violates the principles of respect for persons, beneficence, nonmaleficence, and justice.

Similarly, physicians have an ethical duty to report impairment in colleagues. According to the American Medical Association (2011):

> Physicians have an ethical obligation to report impaired, incompetent, and/or unethical colleagues in accordance with the legal requirements in each state and assisted by the following guidelines. . . . Physicians' responsibilities to colleagues who are impaired by a condition that interferes with their ability to engage safely in professional activities include timely intervention to ensure that these colleagues cease practicing and receive appropriate assistance from a physician health program.

Nevertheless, not all physicians aware of an impaired colleague will report that person to the appropriate authority. According to one study, only 64 percent of 1,891 surveyed physicians completely agreed that all instances of impairment or incompetence should be reported (DesRoches et al. 2010). Reporting was significantly correlated with the type of practice organization: 76 percent of physicians practicing in hospitals and 77 percent of those in medical schools or universities reported an impaired or incompetent colleague to a relevant authority, whereas only 44 percent of physicians in solo or two-person practices did so. The reasons for failing to report an impaired or incompetent colleague included the following (DesRoches et al. 2010):

- "Thought someone else was taking care of it" (19 percent)
- "Believed nothing would happen as a result of the report" (15 percent)
- "Fear of retribution" (12 percent)
- "Believed it was not your responsibility" (10 percent)
- "Believed the person would be excessively punished" (9 percent)
- "Did not know how to report" (8 percent)
- "Believed it could easily happen to you" (8 percent)

Despite legal, ethical, and moral considerations to report impairment, a "culture of resistance to 'whistle blowing'" still exists (Scarpello 2012).

TREATMENT OF THE IMPAIRED HEALTHCARE PROFESSIONAL

Once a healthcare professional is identified as having some type of performance problem, a comprehensive assessment should be performed even if the physician resists. Multidisciplinary assessments can be conducted through PHPs or as an outpatient evaluation undertaken over several days at a treatment program for health professionals. Such assessments typically include a full medical and psychological evaluation, neuropsychological testing, and drug testing (Ries et al. 2014). Most states have PHPs, which can be independent businesses, offices of state medical societies, or operated by state medical licensing boards (Gunderman and Grogan 2012). PHPs typically monitor physicians after they have completed their initial inpatient or outpatient treatment for the substance use disorder. Monitoring involves random drug testing (usually through urine samples but sometimes blood or hair); accessing or providing individual or group counseling; and interfacing with state medical boards, hospital PHPs, and credentialing committees.

The outlook for physicians who agree to intensive treatment and monitoring is good (Addiction Center 2023). A study of 16 PHPs found that over the study period of five to seven years, 78 percent of addicted physicians were continuously abstinent and more than 90 percent were still practicing medicine (McLellan, Skipper, and Campbell 2008). Similar high rates of success have been reported by hospital impaired-physician committees (Schwartz et al. 1995) and PHPs (Buhl et al. 2011) and among emergency medicine physicians (Rose, Campbell, and Skipper 2014).

With the advent of the patient-centered medical home and the increasing burden of electronic medical record requirements, even more stresses are placed on primary care health providers. Increasing levels of stress coupled with a heavier workload may lead to a feeling of lack of control over one's practice life and a loss of meaning, both strongly associated with burnout. However, an intensive educational program in mindfulness, communication, and self-awareness can improve physicians' feelings of well-being and attitudes associated with patient-centered care (Krasner et al. 2009). A proactive approach to reduce psychological distress can reduce burnout before it leads to personal or professional impairment.

CONCLUSION

The tasks set before the healthcare manager to identify and intervene with impaired physicians are complex. The organizational culture needs to be one that encourages confidential reporting of impairment and incompetence, and a clear procedure needs to be provided to staff and physicians for reporting impairment and incompetence confidentially without fear of retribution. Ongoing education about successful treatment of addictive disorders should be provided to staff and to physicians so that they do not shirk their legal and ethical duties to report concerns about impairment. Hospitals also should support research and educational programs for their medical staff and for those in the community who may not understand how to confidentially report concerns about impaired colleagues. Finally, active programs should be in place to identify sources and reduce levels of stress, depression, and burnout among all staff.

REFERENCES

Addiction Center. 2023. "Addiction in Medical Professionals." Updated April 13. www.addictioncenter.com/addiction/medical-professionals/.

American Medical Association (AMA). 2023. "Reporting Incompetent or Unethical Behaviors by Colleagues." Opinion 9.4.2 of the AMA *Code of Medical Ethics*. Accessed October 22. www.ama-assn.org/delivering-care/reporting-incompetent-or-unethical-behaviors-colleagues.

———. 2011. "AMA Code of Medical Ethics' Opinions on Physicians' Health and Conduct: Opinion 9.031—Reporting Impaired, Incompetent, or Unethical Colleagues." *AMA Journal of Ethics*. Published October. https://journalofethics.

ama-assn.org/article/ama-code-medical-ethics-opinions-physicians-health-and-conduct/2011-10.

————. 1992. "Reporting Impaired, Incompetent, or Unethical Colleagues." Report of the AMA Council on Ethical and Judicial Affairs. *Journal of the Mississippi State Medical Association* 33 (5): 176–77.

American Psychiatric Association. 2013. *Diagnostic and Statistical Manual of Mental Disorders*, 5th ed. (DSM-5). Arlington, VA: American Psychiatric Publishing.

American Society of Addiction Medicine. 2019. "Definition of Addiction." Updated September 15. www.asam.org/quality-care/definition-of-addiction.

Angres, D., S. Bologeorges, and J. Chou. 2013. "A Two Year Longitudinal Outcome Study of Addicted Health Care Professionals: An Investigation of the Role of Personality Variables." *Substance Abuse* 7: 49–60.

Bissell, L., and R. W. Jones. 1976. "The Alcoholic Physician: A Survey." *American Journal of Psychiatry* 133 (10): 1142–46.

Bryson, E. O., and J. H. Silverstein. 2008. "Addiction and Substance Abuse in Anesthesiology." *Anesthesiology* 109 (5): 905–17.

Buhl, A., M. R. Oreskovich, C. W. Meredith, M. D. Campbell, and R. L. Dupont. 2011. "Prognosis for the Recovery of Surgeons from Chemical Dependency: A 5-Year Outcome Study." *Archives of Surgery* 146 (11): 1286–91.

Darr, K. 1991. "Hospital's Ethical Responsibilities: Assisting the Impaired Physician." *Hospital Topics* 69 (1): 4–7.

DesRoches, C. M., S. R. Rao, J. A. Fromson, R. J. Birnbaum, L. Iezzoni, C. Vogeli, and E. G. Campbell. 2010. "Physicians' Perceptions, Preparedness for Reporting, and Experiences Related to Impaired and Incompetent Colleagues." *Journal of the American Medical Association* 304 (2): 187–93.

DuPont, R. L., A. T. McLellan, W. L. White, L. J. Merlo, and M. S. Gold. 2009. "Setting the Standard for Recovery: Physicians' Health Programs." *Journal of Substance Abuse Treatment* 36 (2): 159–71.

Gunderman, R. B., and K. Grogan. 2012. "Physician Impairment and Professionalism." *American Journal of Roentgenology* 199 (5): W543–W544.

Hughes, P. H., D. C. Baldwin, D. V. Sheehan, S. Conard, and C. L. Storr. 1992. "Resident Physician Substance Use by Specialty." *American Journal of Psychiatry* 149 (10): 1348–54.

Krasner, M. S., R. M. Epstein, H. Beckman, A. L. Suchman, B. Chapman, C. J. Mooney, and T. E. Quill. 2009. "Association of an Educational Program in

Mindful Communication with Burnout, Empathy, and Attitudes Among Primary Care Physicians." *Journal of the American Medical Association* 302 (12): 1284–93.

Mangus, R. S., C. E. Hawkins, and M. J. Miller. 1998. "Tobacco and Alcohol Use Among 1996 Medical School Graduates." *Journal of the American Medical Association* 280 (13): 1192–93.

McAuliffe, W. E., M. Rohman, P. Breer, G. Wyshak, S. Santangelo, and E. Magnuson. 1991. "Alcohol Use and Abuse in Random Samples of Physicians and Medical Students." *American Journal of Public Health* 81 (2): 177–81.

McAuliffe, W. E., M. Rohman, and H. Wechsler. 1984. "Alcohol, Substance Use, and Other Risk-Factors of Impairment in a Sample of Physicians-in-Training." *Advances in Alcohol & Substance Abuse* 4 (2): 67–87.

McGovern, M. P., D. H. Angres, N. D. Uziel-Miller, and S. Leon. 1998. "Female Physicians and Substance Abuse: Comparisons with Male Physicians Presenting for Assessment." *Journal of Substance Abuse Treatment* 15 (6): 525–33.

McLellan, A. T., G. S. Skipper, and M. Campbell. 2008. "Five Year Outcomes in a Cohort Study of Physicians Treated for Substance Use Disorders in the United States." *British Medical Journal* 337: a2038.

Michas, Frédéric. 2021. "US Physicians—Statistics and Facts." Statista. Published October 19. www.statista.com/topics/1244/physicians/.

Oreskovich, M. R., T. Shanafelt, L. N. Dyrbye, L. Tan, W. Sotile, D. Satele, C. P. West, J. Sloan, and S. Boone. 2015. "The Prevalence of Substance Use Disorders in American Physicians." *American Journal on Addictions* 24 (1): 30–38.

Põld, M., and K. Pärna. 2017. "Smoking Prevalence and Attitudes Towards Smoking Among Estonian Physicians: Results from Cross-Sectional Studies in 2002 and 2014." *BMJ Open* 7 (11): e017197.

Ries, R. K., D. A. Fiellin, S. C. Miller, and R. Saitz. 2014. *Principles of Addiction Medicine*, 4th ed. Philadelphia, PA: Lippincott Williams & Wilkins.

Rose, J. S., M. Campbell, and G. Skipper. 2014. "Prognosis for Emergency Physician with Substance Abuse Recovery: 5-Year Outcome Study." *Western Journal of Emergency Medicine* 15 (1): 20–25.

Rose, J. S., M. D. Campbell, P. Yellowlees, G. E. Skipper, and R. L. DuPont. 2017. "Family Medicine Physicians with Substance Use Disorder: A 5-Year Outcome Study." *Journal of Addiction Medicine* 11 (2): 93–97.

Scarpello, J. 2012. "Dysfunctional Doctors—Will Revalidation Help?" *Clinical Medicine* 12 (2): 111–13.

Schwartz, R. P., R. K. White, D. R. McDuff, and J. L. Johnson. 1995. "Four Years' Experience of a Hospital's Impaired Physician Committee." *Journal of Addictive Diseases* 14 (2): 13–21.

Seppala, M. D., and K. H. Berge. 2010. "The Addicted Physician: A Rational Response to an Irrational Disease." *Minnesota Medicine* 93 (2): 46–49.

Shanafelt, T. D., C. M. Balch, G. Bechamps, T. Russell, L. Dyrbey, D. Satele, P. Collicott, P. J. Novotny, J. Sloan, and J. Freischlag. 2010. "Burnout and Medical Errors Among American Surgeons." *Annals of Surgery* 251 (6): 995–1000.

Shanafelt, T. D., S. Boone, L. Tan, L. N. Dyrbye, W. Sotile, D. Satele, C. P. West, J. Sloan, and M. R. Oreskovich. 2012. "Burnout and Satisfaction with Work–Life Balance Among US Physicians Relative to the General US Population." *Archives of Internal Medicine* 172 (18): 1377–85.

Sørensen, J. K., A. F. Pedersen, N. H. Bruun, B. Christensen, and P. Vedsted. 2015. "Alcohol and Drug Use Among Danish Physicians. A Nationwide Cross-Sectional Study in 2014." *Danish Medical Journal* 62 (9): A5132.

Udell, M. M. 1984. "Chemical Abuse/Dependence: Physicians' Occupational Hazard." *Journal of the Medical Association of Georgia* 73 (11): 775–78.

Wunsch, M. J., J. S. Knisely, K. L. Cropsey, E. D. Campbell, and S. H. Scholl. 2007. "Women Physicians and Addiction." *Journal of Addictive Diseases* 26 (2): 35–43.

Yufit, R. I., G. H. Pollock, and E. Wasserman. 1969. "Medical Specialty Choice and Personality." *Archives of General Psychiatry* 20 (1): 89–99.

Zeldow, P. B., and S. R. Daugherty. 1991. "Personality Profiles and Specialty Choices of Students from Two Medical School Classes." *Academic Medicine: Journal of the Association of American Medical Colleges* 66 (5): 283–87.

CHAPTER 27

Ethics Issues in Graduate Medical Education

C. Rod Pattan

Ethics often does not provide definitive answers—they do, though, limn general principles to clarify our thinking.
—Dr. Richard McMurray

THAT THE COMPLEX and continually evolving impartation of graduate medical education presents ethical issues is not surprising. Many of the procedures expected, and accepted, as part of postgraduate medical training (long clinical hours, lack of autonomy, low wages for services provided, etc.) have long been among the "dirty secrets" of medicine that escaped open scrutiny. Changes in medical training and in the delivery of medical care, however, have forced responsive changes to medical education structures and oversight. These ongoing changes make it apropos to revisit some of the ethical considerations germane to this endeavor.

Post–medical school training (residency, fellowship, or both) is by nature conflicted, often bordering on schizophrenic. Trainees are expected to fill dual, often incompatible roles. They are expected to provide clinical service, to patients of the organization training them, for which they receive a stipend or

---

The late physician Dick McMurray (1922–2018), to whom this chapter is dedicated, was a tireless advocate for graduate medical education and for the ethical exploration of issues throughout medicine. For five years, late in his career, he chaired the American Medical Association's Committee on Ethical and Judicial Affairs. He brought a worldliness, warmth, and humor to that position and influenced many people in that role. He had a marvelous gift for seriously discussing ethics and morality while remaining completely innocent of sanctimony. His sane and sensible counsel was missed during the revision of this submission.

salary, and they are concurrently expected to further their education through didactic courses, self-study, and apprenticeship collaboration with experienced faculty members. Finding the appropriate balance for these divergent functions is a challenge and requires significant individualization based on program characteristics and trainee talents and skills. These conflicting roles, and the variability in training opportunities from site to site, create a fertile environment for ethical dilemmas to arise.

Medical services and the businesses supporting them have expanded to the point that in 2021 they accounted for 18.3 percent of the United States gross domestic product (GDP), according to the Centers for Medicare & Medicaid Services (CMS 2023). As a result, the need for clinical providers has increased, and the training of clinicians in graduate medical education has burgeoned. From 2002 to 2022, the number of students enrolled in an accredited US medical school increased by greater than 50 percent, as reported by the Association of American Medical Colleges (AAMC 2022). Medical schools and teaching hospitals affiliated with them account for an estimated $728 billion toward US GDP. They account for 7.1 million jobs—approximately 5 percent of all US employees—and $488 billion in labor income (AAMC 2022). Medicine and medical education expand along with, and in many ways ahead of, the expanding US economy.

Commensurate expansion has occurred in the post–medical school training. The number of first-year residency (PGY-1) positions in the United States has nearly doubled since the turn of the twenty-first century, as reported by the National Resident Matching Program (NRMP 2022). In 2000, 20,598 PGY-1 positions were on offer in the match; by 2022, this number had increased to 36,277 (NMRP 2022). The funding for these positions is based mainly on federal support through the Medicare program. In 2015, Medicare contributed more than $10 billion, accounting for two-thirds of total funding toward the support of residency training (Heisler et al. 2018)—an average in excess of $100,000 per resident annually. This money is parceled out through a byzantine solicitation program that creates significant discrepancies in per resident funding between programs. This federal support has been threatened multiple times in the past, thus we cannot blithely assume that the government largesse will continue without modification (Inglehart 2011).

These evolutions have restyled the canvas on which medical clinicians have historically learned their art. In the 1970s, the vast majority of residents received their training and provided their services in university programs, large referral centers where diverse clinical experiences were all but assured and where resources, in both personnel and equipment, were guaranteed. Slowly—and with increasing pace since the 1990s—this model has mutated so that much resident education and experience now comes from training programs based in community hospitals.

These changes have created the potential for marked variability in trainees' experience, based on the geographic location or size of the institution at which they train. These variations may in turn affect the skills and abilities of residents at graduation, relative to their peers in other programs. The following case illustrates the type of ethical dilemma such circumstances can, and increasingly do, create.

CASE 1

Residents graduating from your program are failing to obtain desired faculty positions because of a relative paucity of robotic surgery experience offered by the program. Your organization's budget cannot support the acquisition of its own robot, and the idea of paying for residents to gain this experience at an outside institution has been met with resistance (again, cost prohibitive). Does the program have an ethical responsibility to ensure more than the minimum necessary experience to meet graduation requirements so as to maximize the employability of its graduates?

This case touches on several ethical principles that have evolved in the healthcare field over time. The American Medical American (AMA) published its first code of medical ethics in 1847, the same year as the association's inception (AMA 2023a). Today, the AMA Council on Ethical and Judicial Affairs (CEJA)—comprising seven physicians, one resident or fellow, and one medical student—is responsible for updating the code of ethics periodically. The contents of the code, consistent with previous additions, make no specific mention of ethics in regard to graduate medical education.

The field of bioethics, the foundation from which most of our medical ethical decisions are based, only emerged in the 1960s. This emergence was in response to the identification of multiple instances in which medical care was used in ways antithetical to the AMA's code (e.g., World War II–era medical experiments, the Tuskegee Syphilis Study, the Willowbrook State School for Children's hepatitis study, the Chester Southem live cancer cells study at Sloan-Kettering Institute). Several institutes dedicated to medical ethics were soon established, and the national commission for the protection of human subjects of biomedical and behavioral research issued its *Belmont Report* in 1979. The report delineated three basic principles upon which medical ethics were underpinned: (1) respect for persons, (2) beneficence, and (3) justice (US Department of Health, Education and Welfare 1979).

In short order, these principles were modified into the set of four ethical principles that have guided ethical committees since the 1980s:

1. autonomy,
2. beneficence,
3. nonmaleficence, and
4. justice.

As American medicine continued to evolve and new treatment and management options for disease became available, this set of ethical principles expanded further. It now includes the first four as well as three more:

5. honesty (also known as truthfulness or veracity),
6. fidelity, and
7. the right to know.

These seven principles appropriately addressed the behaviors that should be considered acceptable when dealing with vulnerable patients seeking medical care and expertise. Nothing in them, however, is directed toward graduate medical education and behavior toward trainees. We are left to infer that the principles apply there as well. The lack of a clear link between the principles and graduate medical education is unfortunate, and it is probably the reason that external actors have felt the need to interject their authority in the graduate medical education process to ensure the safety of patients as well as residents (e.g., as with New York's work hour restrictions for residents in training, known as the Libby Zion Law [New York State 2018]).

CEJA has recently promulgated an opinion on ethics with regard to resident physician training, reaffirming that residents have a dual role as trainees and care-givers (AMA 2023b). The opinion emphasizes the following issues with regard to resident physician training: (1) adequate clinical oversight and graduated responsibility, (2) honesty in patient interaction, (3) patient's autonomy to refuse trainee care, (4) quality improvement participation, (5) self-monitoring of health and alertness for examples of fatigue, and (6) patient primacy and conflict resolution. As far as providing explicit guidance to help institutions ensure both adequate and safe training of residents, however, the document is thin gruel. It lacks specific protective suggestions addressing the well-being of trainees who are providing valuable (and relatively inexpensive) clinical services while learning.

With this meager template to follow, let us return to our hypothetical case. If we use the seven principles previously delineated to analyze the situation, we can easily generate more in the way of further questions than definitive answers. This is common to ethical analyses.

Remember, we have residents who are meeting the basic criteria to graduate but who are not receiving the extensive experience required, or preferred, by prestigious organizations looking to hire a new graduate. The following is a list of questions we might generate based on the ethical principles:

- **Autonomy:** Should residents in training, like patients under our care, have the autonomy to control the aspects of their training they want to emphasize? Or the corollary: Do all residents in a program need to have indistinguishable experiences?
- **Beneficence:** Is a program obligated to tailor experiences to meet a resident's plan for future practice?
- **Nonmaleficence:** Does a program have a damaging effect on residents in training if it does not ensure a robust experience in all aspects of their chosen specialty?
- **Justice:** Is it just for a resident, after providing years of clinical service to an organization, to graduate with limited options for subsequent employment?
- **Honesty:** Is a program responsible for the clear communication of graduate's experiences, abilities, skills, and characteristics to future employers or medical staff? How detailed and objective do these communications need to be?
- **Fidelity:** Is a program remiss, or culpable, if its graduates are unprepared for any clinical eventuality common to their specialty?
- **Right to know:** Do resident applicants have the right to know the historical success, or lack thereof, for previous graduates of the program in obtaining their first choice of postgraduate employment?

This type of analysis can easily become circular in nature, as several principles have obvious overlap and commonality. It also does not directly address inherent resource limitations, which all training programs face and which will likely be more constraining in the future. This analysis, however, can allow an organization to thoughtfully determine its own principles with regard to the training of its residents.

The next case presents another ethical dilemma, this one dealing with recruitment of residents.

CASE 2

The residency director at a community hospital–based program, where the faculty consist almost exclusively of physicians in private practice groups, is asked by a faculty member to give priority to an applicant of a specific religious and cultural background. The request is based on the member's belief that this applicant will remain in the area after training and bolster the services desired by a large minority community, of which this faculty member is a prominent leader.

With multiple nuanced permutations, such requests are a relatively common occurrence in today's graduate medication education environment. The question, from an ethical standpoint, is whether consideration of this type is proper and whether the ends they are intended to achieve justify the means through which they come to fruition. Using our established principles, the following are some questions that need to be considered:

- **Beneficence:** The faculty members' plan might be beneficial to the individual trainee and later to the segment of the community desiring the trainee's services; however, it might cause a more qualified candidate to be denied a spot in the training program. Is this trade-off ethical?
- **Nonmaleficence:** The proposed plan might not cause overt damage to others, but is it ethically acceptable if another qualified applicant is denied?
- **Justice:** Limited positions are available in each specialty and each program. Is it just to prioritize candidates based on potential advantage to the program or the community, or should all positions be awarded as a purely meritocratic exercise?
- **Honesty:** Is the process transparent, with all involved or affected parties being informed of the decision process and the goals of the plan?
- **Fidelity:** Is the potentially prioritized candidate bound to remain in the community upon the completion of training? Does this assumption need to be codified prior to execution?
- **Right to know:** Who has the right to know the rationale and details of the plan? Should the final decision be reached by consensus, majority or plurality, or director conclusion?

Each residency program clinically serves a specific population of patients, and these populations have varying degrees of homogeneity or diversity. Although a population group may benefit from having clinical providers of a similar ethnic or religious affiliation, it is less clear whether the manipulation of the residency match process to achieve a specific cohort is ethically appropriate or clinically beneficial. An additional concern involves a precedent that could be established by this plan. If the plan is carried out, will other groups subsequently try to champion select candidates who may or may not be the most qualified?

The next case addresses is another demographic issue that is frequently evaluated for manipulation.

CASE 3

For several years, a residency program has had a resident cohort that is exclusively of one gender (biologic sex). Faculty members of the other gender have strongly urged that recruiting efforts for future classes focus on identifying candidates of the unrepresented gender. (This case is presented within a traditional male/female binary framework, as used for statistical calculations; nonbinary gender identity is not addressed.)

The gender demographics of medical training have undergone a sea change since the 1970s. What was once a male-dominated profession now boasts significantly improved gender parity. In 2018, 52.6 percent of medical school graduates were male and 47.4 percent were female. By 2022, these numbers had essentially reversed, with 46.3 percent male and 53.7 percent female (AAMC 2022).

However, despite the trend at the medical school level, significant gender imbalances persist in certain specialties. Studies between 2012 and 2022 have consistently shown that 85 percent of residents in obstetrics and gynecology programs were female, whereas 86 percent of orthopedic surgery residents were male (AAMC 2022; O'Connor 2012; Vassar 2015). Similarly, 75 percent of pediatric residents were female, whereas 73 percent of radiology and 78 percent of neurosurgery residents were male (AAMC 2022; Vassar 2015). With such large disparities, some programs might have cohorts in which their trainees are all the same gender.

Many factors go into medical school graduates' specialty selections. According to a survey of residencies across nine medical and surgical specialties, geography was the issue most frequently cited as having an impact on the quality of resident experience, followed by clinical training, and experience with colleagues (Dulmage et al. 2018). Other sources have cited gender ratios as an important factor in medical student selection of specialty and institutional site (O'Connor 2012). What amount of effort, if any, should be exerted toward having the gender ratios within a specialty approach, or equal, those seen in medical school admission and graduation? Returning to our ethical principles, the following questions could be posited:

- **Autonomy:** Should graduating medical students be able to choose a training program with gender composition as a consideration, or should all programs be incentivized to mirror the gender equity that has been achieved by medical schools?
- **Beneficence:** Who, if anyone, is positively or negatively affected by making residency programs gender equitable?

- **Nonmaleficence:** Who, if anyone, is harmed by having residency programs remain gender disparate? As corollary, who, if anyone, is harmed by striving to make them gender equitable?
- **Justice:** Given that significant public financial resources (i.e., tax dollars) are funneled to graduate medical education programs, are the programs required to do everything possible to achieve gender equity in their training cohorts?
- **Honesty:** Do qualified applicants need to be informed if their candidacy could be affected by a desire to achieve a specific gender ratio with a program?

As is common in ethical conundrums, this case involves a conflict between the various principles of ethics. Clearly, prioritizing autonomy over justice, or vice versa, could sway the outcome in a predictable manner. Without new legislation or revised guidance from the American Council on Graduate Medical Education (ACGME) or the Residency Review Committee, these decisions and prioritizations will continue to be prosecuted at the individual institutional site.

The first three cases in this chapter have focused on ethical issues that pertain, to a great degree, to the recruitment or selection of residents. Additional ethical considerations manifest once residents have matriculated into a program. Examples may involve evaluation of performance, disciplinary action for poor performance or behavior, and graduate references.

CASE 4

A first-year resident scores below the second percentile on the annual in-service examination for the specialty. The program determines that an academic remediation plan must be developed and instituted and that objective measurements of improvement must be demonstrated for the resident to be retained. What role, if any, should the resident play in developing the remediation plan?

Although annual in-service exams are imperfect predictors of subsequent board performance, clinical skill, or technical expertise, they do allow for an objective academic assessment of a resident relative to their peers. Scores at the level described in this case would be a significant concern to any program director, and they should also be a clarion call for the resident involved. Overcoming this degree of deficiency is exceedingly difficult. Often, mobilizing resources to shore up one individual's deficiencies detracts from the attention available to other, more academically prosperous trainees. Such a situation may also create the perception or even the reality that other trainees are shouldering more of the clinical burden, subsequently leading to morale issues throughout the program. Development of a remediation program requires thoughtful consideration of these and other ethical issues:

- **Autonomy:** How much input should the deficient resident have in developing the remediation program? Should the resident be able to choose which type of assessment to undergo (e.g., intelligence testing, neuropsychological testing, sleep disorder testing)? Should the resident's identified learning style preference be considered in developing the remediation program?
- **Beneficence:** What efforts, if any, should be made to assist the resident in finding another program in which to transfer, either in the same specialty or a different one? If the resident desires a transfer, what degree of transparency needs to be present in briefing the receiving program about the resident?
- **Nonmaleficence:** What, if any, increased oversight should be in place for this resident to prevent avoidable patient harm? What monitoring needs to be done to ensure that other trainees are not adversely affected by this individual resident's need for more intense faculty scrutiny?
- **Justice:** The resident has invested considerable time, and likely taken on significant financial debt, to complete medical school. The program also has financial burdens that can be affected by remedial projects. What is a reasonable timeline for the resident to demonstrate progress toward acceptable performance? What financial burden, if any, should the resident bear in executing the remediation program?
- **Honesty and the right to know:** What, if any, information should be shared with faculty and other trainees about the resident's need for remediation?
- **Fidelity:** If the resident narrowly fails to meet predetermined improvement measures, should extension of the remediation be considered or offered?

Resident failure, whether during training or during the board examination process following graduation, can have lasting negative effects on both the resident and the program. Great care needs to be taken in assessing the causes of underperformance, as well as in developing and implementing remediation programs. Financial considerations must be taken into account on both sides, and the emotional concerns of both the affected resident and others in the program, who might feel neglected or overburdened, need to be addressed. Careful, unbiased monitoring of all involved is critical for saving a resident from academic failure. The structure of residency training programs is supposed to ensure such monitoring through a Clinical Competency Committee, a construction mandated by the ACGME as part of the *Common Program Requirements* for all residency training programs. The intent of this committee is to ensure that each resident receives semiannual feedback on their performance in a formal manner and that this feedback constitutes consensus comment from a representative sample of experienced faculty (ACGME 2023).

Failures that occur during residency training are a challenge, both to identify and to rectify. Failures can also occur after a resident has completed the training program. Two common examples are illustrated in the next case.

CASE 5

After graduating, a former resident, despite having performed acceptably on academic assessment during training, fails the board examination. Shortly after receiving the failure notice, the physician is the primary provider in a case resulting in an unexpected patient death for which the doctor is found to have deviated from the criteria for standard of care. The medical system that employs the physician informs the program director that it plans to bring suit against the training institution for failure to adequately train this physician.

All residents, prior to being allowed to practice in unsupervised settings, must demonstrate cognitive competence in assessing, diagnosing, and properly treating patients. Residents in procedure-based specialties must also demonstrate technical competence in the safe execution of the procedures they will be expected to perform. Once residents leave the training program, the program's only control over them is through communication with the medical staff in the hospital organizations where they ply their trade. It has become increasingly important that objective data and reliable affirmations of competence accompany graduates to their new place of practice. The sharing of such information is imperative, not only to protect the patients for whom the graduate will be providing care but also to protect the program from liability if the physician were to deviate from established standards of care.

Our list of ethical principles raises the following considerations:

- **Autonomy:** As a bioethical principle, autonomy is applied to patients making decisions about their care; it does not grant physicians the right to exercise their own autonomy over that of the patient. The AMA Code of Medical Ethics clearly states in its Principles of Medical Ethics: "VIII. A physician shall, while caring for a patient, regard responsibility to the patient as paramount" (AMA 2001). Although broad autonomy is granted in establishing practice type and structure, as well as deciding what patients a physician will or will not care for, deviation from practice standards is not an acceptable form of autonomy. Residency and fellowship programs should clearly communicate with graduates, and the organization to employ them, what, if any, limitations on their practice should be considered based on their performance or experience while in training.

- **Beneficence:** Despite the struggles the former resident has encountered since graduation, this individual still a part of the program—even if only in a historical sense. Continued support of the newly practicing physician, to the degree appropriate, should be part and parcel of the program's responsibility. Even if it simply functions as a sounding board for the physician, the expression of support can help smooth the rugged path the physician is navigating.

- **Nonmaleficence:** Should behavioral or interpersonal challenges during the physician's training be shared with future employees if they are not specifically solicited? Emotional or interpersonal biases must not be the basis for reporting such issues. Patient safety needs to remain paramount in all such considerations. The sharing of concerns about an individual's interpersonal behavior should be done judiciously and with care to avoid transference of other's biases. During a professional crisis—such as the one this physician is experiencing—the program needs to thoughtfully balance the support given its former charge with a need to provide honest information to the individual's new employer and medical staff.

- **Justice:** Due process is the right of the patient, or the patient's family, the new medical staff, and the physician involved. All have significant stakes in a just assessment and resolution of these unfortunate events. The program should cooperate in every way possible with both the former resident and the medical staff at the physician's new place of practice. The information shared should be, to the extent possible, objective in nature and free of personal bias.

- **Honesty:** Is it acceptable for a program to be protective of a former resident's fledgling career? Is it acceptable to withhold information that might damage that career and might reflect negatively on the program? Typically, highly specific requests for information and documents are tendered in these kinds of circumstances, and compliance with such requests is always prudent. Offering comprehensive facts initially is preferable to having damaging information revealed later on. The organization should behave with utmost transparency throughout the process.

- **Right to know:** Should this former resident's struggles be shared with faculty, current residents, or hospital administration?

Every crisis is a potential opportunity. In this scenario, the problems plaguing this resident could provide a learning opportunity for others and occasion for critical analysis of program performance. These laudable goals of learning and improvement can be pursued without identifying, or especially disparaging, the individual involved. Legitimate sharing of information to teach and advance program quality improvement initiatives is appropriate; personalizing the information is not.

This case demonstrates a dreaded scenario for any physician, as well as for any program that trains physicians. To ensure that the program's structure is not contributing to a trainee's struggles or failures, each residency program director is responsible for appointing a Program Evaluation Committee, composed of faculty and residents, whose role is to monitor program goals and the success in meeting them. Objective evaluation of the program, its faculty, and the residents is required to be submitted in report form annually to the designated institutional official of the residency's sponsoring organization. As part of the ten-year cycle of accreditation, this committee must help produce a Self-Study for review by accrediting reviewers (ACGME 2023).

One hopes that the overriding goal of every training program is that its graduates are safe, effective providers ready to experience success in their careers. Probably no single factor in this hoped-for success is more important than high-quality, committed faculty members who model clinical excellence and professional behavior. Unfortunately, because faculties consist of fallible humans, this ideal is not always realized, with ethical conundrums the result. The next case presented for consideration revolves around faculty oversight.

CASE 6

A subspecialty division of the department has become increasingly important to the success of the residency program and the department. The division was recently expanded from one to two physicians, and significant rancor has developed between the two. The discord is largely from a perception by the newer physician that division staff is funneling preferred cases to the senior physician. The conflict has spilled into the program, with both physicians marshaling allies to support their position. Residents feel trapped and perceive disparate treatment depending on their perceived allegiance.

As financing of graduate medical education has become more tenuous and less assured, the financial performance of faculty takes on greater importance. The resulting performance pressure can diminish the time and energy devoted to trainees' academic needs and can lead to competitive conflicts among faculty members, both within and across divisions. The director and administration must monitor these conflicts and manage them to ensure that the training program remains functional. Our template of ethical principles provides ample fodder for consideration:

- **Autonomy:** Should the senior division member be allowed to dictate case distribution for the division? While the loss of personal autonomy can be considered a lamentable development of modern medicine, graduate education must be approached as a team endeavor. Faculty members in the residency training program are part of the team committed to the training of other professionals, and as such, they should not expect unchecked autonomy. Individuals' personal agendas need to be subsumed by the larger group's curricular priorities. The ACGME highlights professionalism as a basic competency; it is a behavior that all faculty members are expected to model for residents in training.
- **Beneficence:** Should the senior member of the division be expected to randomly split patients referred to the section? Should the new department member have financial subsidies to help in building a financially viable practice?
- **Nonmaleficence:** Should the senior member of the division be made to suffer financial embarrassment for the trade-off of decreased teaching and call responsibilities?
- **Justice:** Assume that the new physician faculty hire has a skill previously unknown to this community and that supporting the skill will engender significant costs for capital improvements. Where should the budgetary support for the new equipment come from? Given that all units face limited resources and budgetary constraints, what divisions or other departments should be expected to sacrifice their own capital improvements to support this one?
- **Honesty and fidelity:** If other divisions or departments are asked to sacrifice part of their support now, with the promise of recompense in subsequent years, is this arrangement codified and monitored for later adjustment?
- **Right to know:** Do the patients assigned to the senior member of the department need to be informed that a less invasive approach to their potential surgery may be available through another provider? Do all members of the department deserve to know the precise cost inherent in supporting this new surgical technology?

Interpersonal conflict is a frequent cause—maybe the most frequent cause—of ethical dilemmas in graduate medical education. The mandated Program Evaluation Committee should have a lead role in the oversight of these issues. Because of overlapping interests, this self-policing often can't be realized. Programs would therefore be well served to have, as part of the educational curriculum, training in conflict resolution. Many organizations have mediators on staff who are effective in training and small group interventions. A number of organizations also offer services in this regard and are tailored toward the medical profession (e.g., TeamSTEPPS, Arbinger Institute, HCPro). Liberal use of expert consultants of this type should be encouraged.

RESEARCH

No discussion of ethics in graduate medical education would be complete without some attention to clinical research. In this realm, ethical considerations are of paramount importance and need to be thoughtfully navigated.

In regard to research, the following three areas have been found to account for the vast majority of ethical dilemmas:

1. Safety and consent of study participants
2. Conflicts of interest
3. Intellectual integrity

Patients participating in research studies deserve to know that the research they participate in is legitimate, appropriate, and as safe as possible, as stipulated by the World Medical Association (WMA) Declaration of Helsinki (WMA 2022) and the Nuremburg Code (UNC Research 2023). They deserve to know that their personal information will be kept confidential and that they will be informed about all risks and alternatives available. Finally, they need to know that they can remove themselves from participation at any time without explanation. Institutional review boards (IRBs) are required for any organization that undertakes research on human subjects. Ensuring that IRBs are functional and accountable is a responsibility of every training program prior to allowing faculty or trainees to participate in research activities.

Conflicts of interest and matters of intellectual integrity tend to be less closely regulated and monitored. Recent studies have questioned whether pressure to publish research or gain funding through grants may be creating an environment wherein research is becoming less beneficial and efficient (Thompson 2023). These analyses seem to indicate that researchers are gravitating toward safer research projects that are more likely to generate publication than any meaningful addition to the body of scientific knowledge. Thompson (2023) refers to this as "the crappy paper" problem, positing that the incentives to publish have created a culture where little new scientific knowledge is being created. He presents what he calls the Consolidation-Disruption Index, whereby many papers now have so little relevance that they are rarely, if ever, cited by other authors (Thompson 2023).

These are ethical issues that graduate medical education programs should be cognizant of and strive to avoid. Publishing meaningless articles to pad a resume is a form of intellectual dishonesty that does little or nothing to advance the profession. There are multiple techniques that can be employed to avoid this temptation, and each program should monitor its output for societal value and not individual career advancement via padding of publication lists. The recognition that grants are public subsidies and that their misuse can be viewed as a type of theft should be a measure of any grant submission. Graduate medical education programs should regularly assess their incentive systems to ensure that faculty are not encouraged to pursue these lines of behavior.

As funding for graduate medical education becomes less certain, collaboration with partners in medical industry will almost certainly increase. Much has been written concerning the potential influence of industry on the quality and the legitimacy of research. Client program directors and research staff engaged in externally funded endeavors must be vigilant to ensure the safety, accuracy, and legitimacy of study designs and results. The prospect of financial gain should not influence a clinical investigator's methods (Cosgrove 2013).

Intellectual integrity is an area of research that always deserves close scrutiny. Control of and confirmation of data, authorship, and locations for publication can all influence the integrity of the study. Data need to be carefully and completely analyzed, with scrupulous avoidance of selective use of data to support a desired outcome. Failing to do so diminishes the scientific endeavor to one of base advocacy. There are numerous contemporary examples of poorly vetted or inadequately peer-reviewed publications leading to public and media confusion about scientific findings (e.g., vaccines and autism, progesterone preventing preterm delivery, COVID-19 prevention and therapeutics). These cases inconsistently result in censure of the researchers involved. They also can result in unwanted reputational damage to the institutions employing those researchers. Most important, though, they erode public trust in medicine and the scientific method.

Teaching programs and the corporate world have mutual reasons to work together in research. Such a collaboration can net resources for the program, create opportunities for residents to pursue individual interests, advance medical knowledge, and lead to new diagnostic and treatment modalities. However, this type of collaboration has risk, and directors would be wise to ensure that appropriate policy guidelines are in place to keep research consistent with articulated standards. Accessible public disclosure, down to the individual physician level, has been shown to increase patient confidence that industry relationships are not affecting their treatment (Mendivil 2012). Organizational transparency of research activities should therefore be encouraged.

Increasing globalization has also produced new ethical issues in medical research and clinical trials. In part because of the cost and time that intensive compliance documentation require, some medical industry leaders are outsourcing clinical trials to contract research organizations (CROs). The CROs can be commercial or academic, and they often perform their studies in developing countries, such as China or India (Mendivil 2012). The choice of these countries is deliberate. Both China and India offer large populations with widespread, crushing poverty. In some cases, payment for participation in a study may be a participant's only source of income. Opportunities for abuse or misuse in these circumstances are obviously abundant, and the paucity of regulatory infrastructure in these countries allows for little local oversight. The WMA Declaration of Helsinki clearly states that potential subjects for medical research must be adequately informed about all potential risks, expected benefits, and goals of the study; furthermore, they must know that they have the right to deny participation or withdraw from the study at any time (WMA 2022).

As for-profit organizations, CROs may be tempted to use shortcuts to meet the sponsoring institution's needs at prices acceptable to them. It remains the express responsibility of the sponsoring institution to ensure that research, even that farmed about via contract, meets today's ethical standards.

REFERENCES

Accreditation Council for Graduate Medical Education (ACGME). 2023. *ACGME Common Program Requirements*, Chicago: ACGME.

American Medical Association (AMA). 2023a. "Code of Medical Ethics." Accessed October 17. https://code-medical-ethics.ama-assn.org/.www.ama-assn.org/topics/ams-code-medical-ethics.

———. 2023b. "Resident and Fellow Physicians' Involvement in Patient Care." Accessed October 17. https://code-medical-ethics.ama-assn.org/ethics-opinions/resident-fellow-physicians-involvement-patient-care.

———. 2001. "AMA Principles of Medical Ethics." Revised June. https://code-medical-ethics.ama-assn.org/principles.

Association of American Medical Colleges (AAMC). 2022. "Nation's Medical School Increased Enrollment." News release, May. www.aamc.org/newsroom/newsreleases/ enrollment survey (content no longer available).

Centers for Medicare & Medicaid Services (CMS). 2023. "National Health Expenditure Data: Historical." Modified September 6. www.cms.gov/data-research/statistics-trends-and-reports/national-health-expenditure-data/historical.

Cosgrove, T. 2013. *Transparency: A Patient's Right to Know.* Commentary, Institute of Medicine. Published May 17. https://nam.edu/wp-content/uploads/2015/06/ RighttoKnow.pdf.

Dulmage, B. O., L. Akintilo, L. J. Welty, M. M. Davis, M. Colavincenzo, and S. Xu. 2018. "A Qualitative, Cross-Sectional Study of Positive and Negative Comments of Residency Programs Across Nine Surgical and Medical Specialties." *American Journal of Medicine* 131 (9): 1130–34.

Heisler, E. J., B. H. P. Mendez, A. Mitchell, S. V. Panangala, and M. A. Villagrana. 2018. *Federal Support for Graduate Medical Education: An Overview.* Congressional Research Service. Published December 27. https://fas.org/spg/crs/misc/R44376.pdf (content no longer available).

Iglehart, J. K. 2011. "The Uncertain Future of Medicare and Graduate Medical Education." *New England Journal of Medicine* 365 (14): 1340–45.

Mendivil, L. 2012. "Ethical Implications: Outsourcing of Clinical Trials by Pharmaceutical Companies." University of Arizona Student research. Accessed October 17, 2023. www.yumpu.com/en/document/read/18040647/luis-mendivil-ethical-implications-outsourcing-of clinical-trials-by-.

National Resident Matching Program (NRMP). 2022. *Results and Data: 2022 Main Residency Match.* Published May. www.nrmp.org/wp-content/ uploads/2022/11/2022-Main-Match-Results-and-Data-Final-Revised.pdf.

New York State. 2018. "Section 405.4— Medical Staff." Published November 14. https://regs.health.ny.gov/contentsection-4054-medical-staff (content no longer available).

O'Connor, M. I. 2012. "Orthopedic Surgery: Women on the Rise in a Male-Dominated Field." *HuffPost* (blog). Published August 2. www.huffpost.com/entry/ orthopedic-surgery-women_b_1726145.

Thompson, D. 2023. "The Consolidation-Disruption Index Is Alarming: Science Has a Crummy Paper Problem." *Atlantic*, January 11.

UNC Research. 2023. "Nuremberg Code." University of North Carolina at Chapel Hill. Accessed October 18. https://research.unc.edu/human-research-ethics/ resources/ccm3_019064/.

US Department of Health, Education, and Welfare. 1979. *The Belmont Report: Ethical Principles and Guidelines for the Protection of Human Subjects of Research.* Published April 18. www.hhs.gov/ohrp/regulations-and-policy/belmont-report/read-the-belmont-report/index.html.

Vassar, L. 2015. "How Medical Specialties Vary by Gender." American Medical Association. Published February 18. www.ama-assn.org/medical-students/specialty-profiles/how-medical-specialties-vary-gender.

World Medical Association (WMA). 2022. "WMA Declaration of Helsinki—Ethical Principles for Medical Research Involving Human Subjects." Updated September 6. www.wma.net/politics-post/wma-declaration-of-helsinki-ethical-principles-for-medical-research-involving-human-subjects/.

CHAPTER 28

Ethics Issues in Healthcare Emergency Management

Rebecca A. Dobbs

SINCE 2013, THE Federal Emergency Management Agency (FEMA 2023) has issued more than 1,300 disaster declarations in the United States for such events as severe weather (e.g., tornados, typhoons, hurricanes, straight-line wind, winter storms), flooding, wildfires, landslides, mudslides, earthquakes, tsunamis, volcanic eruptions, building collapse, pandemic, contaminated water (Michigan), chemical spills, and terrorism or violence (e.g., Boston Marathon bombing, Nashville bombing, attempted disruption of Joe Biden's presidential inauguration). Many of these events led to forced evacuations, mass casualties, access and service disruptions, and workforce safety and security concerns, stressing an already strained US healthcare system at the national, regional, and local levels.

In addition to addressing the more typical natural and technological hazards, the US healthcare system has seen a marked increase in human-made hazards, particularly shootings and workplace violence. According to data from Gao and Adashi (2023) and Kelen and colleagues (2012), hospital shootings are rare but have increased in the twenty-first century; they rose from a few in 2000 to more than 20 in 2015 (Ducharme 2018). Attacks on healthcare workers, both physical and verbal, spiked during the COVID-19 pandemic amid understaffed medical facilities, restricted access for family members, increased substance abuse, and an overall lack of available mental health services (Campisi 2023). Such events serve as a stark reminder that the healthcare system is vulnerable to a variety of risks. Comprehensive emergency preparedness, therefore, must include deliberate planning for mitigation, response, and recovery activities with appropriate attention to ethical concerns.

In February 2003, the White House issued Homeland Security Presidential Directive 5, which directed the US Department of Homeland Security to develop and administer a single comprehensive system for preventing, preparing for, responding to, and recovering from a domestic event of any size or complexity. As a result, contingency-based planning was replaced with the National Incident Management System—an all-hazards approach intended to improve coordination and cooperation among entities at all levels, including federal, state, local, tribal, private sector, and nongovernment organizations. Current emergency management practice in the healthcare arena follows these nationally recognized principles and is structured around the four phases of emergency management:

1. Mitigation (preventing or reducing the impact)
2. Preparedness (building capacity and resilience)
3. Response (mobilizing assets to stabilize the incident)
4. Recovery (returning to a new normal)

For the purposes of this chapter, an *emergency* is defined as any hazard resulting in an incident that causes a disruption in normal operations. Hazards are classified as natural (e.g., weather, naturally occurring disease), technological (e.g., utility failure, transportation accident), or human-made (e.g., active shooter, workplace violence, labor strike). An emergency can significantly disrupt a healthcare organization's ability to provide care or services; compromise the environment of care; or result in a sudden, radically changed or increased demand for services. A *disaster* generally refers to an emergency resulting in large-scale or widespread damage or destruction; numerous casualties or fatalities; drastic change to the environment; or marked degradation of the economic, social, and cultural aspects of life.

Ethical concerns can arise during an emergency of any cause, size, or complexity. Healthcare practitioners must work closely with emergency management planners and coordinators to ensure that a mechanism is in place to proactively identify and adequately address potential ethical issues during all phases of emergency management. Understanding how ethical values can be integrated into the emergency management paradigm will help with this process.

ETHICAL DECISION MAKING DURING A CRISIS

Based on experiences from the severe acute respiratory syndrome (SARS) pandemic of 2003, the University of Toronto Joint Centre for Bioethics (2005) developed ten substantive values and five process values to guide ethical decision making during a crisis. Even though these values were defined specifically for a pandemic influenza outbreak, they remain relevant and could easily serve as an ethical framework in planning for any healthcare emergency.

The ten substantive values, summarized from the University of Toronto Joint Centre for Bioethics (2005) report, are as follows:

1. *Individual liberty.* Restrictions to individual liberty should be proportional, necessary, and relevant; employ the least restrictive means; and be applied equitably.
2. *Protection of the public from harm.* Required actions that impinge on individual liberty should assess the imperative for compliance, provide incentives for compliance, and establish review mechanisms.
3. *Proportionality.* Actions that restrict individual liberty should not exceed what is necessary to address the actual risk or critical needs of the community.
4. *Privacy.* Overriding individual privacy may be necessary during an emergency to protect the public from serious harm.
5. *Duty to provide care.* Healthcare professionals must weigh their duty to provide care against obligations to their own health and that of their families.
6. *Reciprocity.* Society has a duty to support people taking extraordinary measures for the public good and take steps to minimize disproportionate burdens.
7. *Equity.* During an emergency, care normally available to all patients on an equal basis may need to be curtailed or deferred.
8. *Trust.* Confidence in decisions being made requires transparency and thoughtful communication to all stakeholders.
9. *Solidarity.* Collaboration and a shared vision are essential in and among the various healthcare entities.
10. *Stewardship.* Resource decisions are intended to achieve the best patient and public health outcomes given the situation.

The five process values, summarized from the University of Toronto Joint Centre for Bioethics (2005) report, are as follows:

1. *Reasonable.* Credible, accountable people must be able to provide the rationale for actions taken.
2. *Open and transparent.* The decision-making process must be publicly accessible and open to scrutiny.
3. *Inclusive.* Stakeholders should be involved in the decision-making process.
4. *Responsive.* New information should be incorporated into the decision-making process with a mechanism to address disputes and complaints.
5. *Accountable.* Decision makers are held accountable for their actions and inactions.

Emergency planners, policymakers, and healthcare professionals have posed numerous questions regarding the ethics and standards that apply to care decisions and care delivery during unusual or extreme circumstances. Some of the more prominent questions pertain to the duty of healthcare workers to respond during an event, disaster triage, the allocation of scarce medical resources, and crisis standards of care.

Duty of Healthcare Workers to Respond

According to a report from the Institute of Medicine (IOM 2012), healthcare professionals have an obligation to provide care during an emergency or disaster and must be able to adjust from individual-based to population-based care strategies as dictated by the situation. Likewise, healthcare organizations have a reciprocal obligation to protect healthcare workers (e.g., safety, security, liability) and to provide support mechanisms to enable workers to meet personal needs (e.g., dependent care, mental health) while carrying out their professional responsibilities.

The American Nurses Association (ANA 2017) reports that registered nurses "have consistently [been] shown to be reliable responders, and their compassionate nature typically compels them to respond to those in need, even when it puts their own safety or well-being at risk." However, emergency plans, policies, and staff training need to reflect organizational expectations, and resources need to be made available to support worker compliance. A 2010 story about 11 nurses and 5 staffers being fired from a Washington, DC, hospital for not reporting to work following back-to-back snowstorms highlights the need to identify and discuss such issues (Francis 2010).

According to a survey by Jacobs and Burns (2017), 39 percent of laypeople and 27 percent of healthcare professionals indicated that physicians and nurses should accept a high or very high degree of personal risk in caring for patients who cannot get out of harm's way. Ongoing questions about the duty of healthcare workers to respond to emergencies include the following:

- How can workers travel safely to work locations?
- Could a risk of exposure to disease or dangerous elements bring harm to the worker or family members?
- Is physical security adequate at the work location?
- What if the worker's family members or dependents need assistance?
- Is a practitioner's license protected when working outside the normal work area or specialty?
- Is the healthcare worker legally bound to respond?

- Are worker's compensation or other benefits available while providing emergency response services?
- What are the legal ramifications of not being able to provide adequate care because of limited resources?

The ANA (2017) contends that these concerns and other unanswered questions represent a gap in the nation's disaster preparedness and response systems. The ANA has therefore partnered with government groups, nongovernment organizations, and employers to promote policies and laws that enable healthcare workers to respond confidently to disasters so that the needs of the American public can be met.

In 2006, the Uniform Emergency Volunteer Health Practitioners Act was enacted to streamline the deployment of licensed healthcare workers to areas of declared emergency and to provide certain legal protections (American College of Surgeons 2023). The act allows state governments, during a declared emergency, to give reciprocity to other states' licensees so that covered individuals may provide emergency health services without meeting the licensing requirements of the state where the emergency was declared. Today, there are 41 states and two US territories that have passed legislation to enable licensed nurses to practice across state lines. Healthcare professionals can also register either in advance or during an emergency using the federally funded Emergency System for Advance Registration of Volunteer Health Professionals or Medical Reserve Corps programs.

Going forward, concerted efforts by federal and state governments, state agencies, and healthcare organizations are essential to resolving issues related to emergency preparedness and response. According to the ANA (2017), the role of the federal government should be to establish "the vision for seamless, coordinated, safe response efforts"; state legislatures, planners, policymakers, and response agencies should create "non-punitive environments that enhance [healthcare workers'] efficiency and capacity to provide ethical care in response efforts"; and employers should ensure that emergency plans "meet the medical needs of the community" while protecting healthcare workers and volunteers.

Disaster Triage and the Allocation of Scarce Medical Resources

Disaster triage may be used to ration or reallocate limited resources when healthcare providers cannot meet all care needs or provide care equitably. To be medically acceptable and ethically defensible, disaster triage protocols need to be developed in advance of emergencies to support provider decision making, to create other forms of care for patients, and to anticipate the ensuing behavioral health needs of healthcare professionals (ANA 2008).

The process of developing disaster triage protocols should be transparent and open. Numerous stakeholders (including healthcare providers and members of the public) should assist in identifying, clarifying, and prioritizing ethical values to ensure the fairness of critical medical decisions that may need to be made quickly. Disaster triage protocols must be used consistently to ensure ongoing public trust and cooperation.

Many healthcare professionals who are trained to provide unconstrained emergency care for all patients may find the use of disaster triage protocols and the allocation of scarce medical resources to be distressing. Therefore, healthcare professionals must receive appropriate training for situations in which they may be called on to provide care only to those people who are likely to recover as a result of receiving that care (ANA 2008).

Scarce medical resources may include physical items (e.g., medical equipment and supplies, pharmaceuticals), services (e.g., diagnostics, treatments, nursing care, palliative care), and healthcare personnel (e.g., physicians, nurses, lab technicians, other essential workers in healthcare settings). During a major emergency, the allocation of such resources may need to change to support the needs of the situation. Making the right decisions about the allocation of scarce resources will be instrumental to healthcare system survivability and optimal functioning; ultimately, it may contribute to many lives saved (Phillips, Knebel, and Johnson 2009).

Large-scale emergencies can quickly deplete the resources of healthcare entities and jurisdictions, and response activities often require the movement of people and resources from various locations to the places where they are needed most. However, until an emergency is officially declared, legal and fiscal limitations may hinder the sharing of resources by the entities that possess them with those that need them. An emergency declaration may authorize interjurisdictional coordination efforts or suspend laws that interfere with such coordination. Examples of existing interjurisdictional legal coordination include the following:

- *Nations.* Through a Memorandum of Understanding (The Compact), and in support of Resolution 23-5 of Conference of New England Governors and Eastern Canadian Premiers, since 1998 the International Emergency Management Group (IEMG) has supported the process of planning, mutual cooperation, and emergency-related exercises, testing, and other training activities in the United States and Canada (IEMG 2023).
- *States.* The Emergency Management Assistance Compact (EMAC) is a state-to-state mutual aid system in the United States that provides automatic license reciprocity to volunteer health providers deployed from other states, immunity from civil liability for harm to patients, and access to state worker's compensation benefits (EMAC 1996).

- *Local governments.* In place since 2004, the Illinois Public Health Mutual Aid System agreement provides for assistance in the form of personnel, equipment, supplies, and services between local health departments (Illinois Department of Public Health 2004). Many other states follow a similar model.
- *Healthcare coalitions.* Healthcare coalitions, such as the Northern Virginia Hospital Alliance, exist in many locales to "coordinate emergency preparedness, response, and recovery activities for the member hospital and healthcare systems in cooperation with local, regional, state, and federal response partners" (Cause IQ 2023). Such healthcare coalitions can foster interagency or interfacility communications during emergencies; manage bed and medical surge capabilities; and coordinate the location and sharing of medical resources. Other coalitions, such as the Managed Emergency Surge for Healthcare (MESH) Coalition in Indiana, provide not only preparedness and planning services but also education, training, and exercise programs; healthcare intelligence services; and regulatory and policy analysis (MESH 2023).

Formal (written) coordination agreements facilitate emergency planning processes and training, mutual cooperation, and the real-time exchange of resources during emergencies under prespecified conditions. Although they do not address specific ethical issues associated with emergency declarations and the deployment of medical resources during an emergency, they do support ethics principles by providing a mechanism for the identification and sharing of resources in a transparent, inclusive, and responsive fashion.

Crisis Standards of Care

A *standard of care* is a legal definition that reflects the level and type of care that a reasonably competent and prudent healthcare professional would provide under a certain set of circumstances. *Crisis standards of care* (CSCs) guide decision making designed to achieve the best outcome for a group of patients rather than focusing on an individual patient. Examples of events that may cause such a shift in the provision of care include the following:

- A complete loss or severe disruption of essential services (e.g., power, water, medical gases, supply chain)
- A loss of infrastructure (e.g., facilities, medical informatics)
- A personnel shortage resulting from transportation issues, worker or worker's family illness or injury, or unwillingness to report to work

- A large number of people affected by an emergency
- A sudden increase in the number of patients in marked excess of capacity or severity of illness/injury
- The required relocation of care services to an alternate facility not equipped for patient care

According to the *Rapid Expert Consultation on Crisis Standards of Care for the COVID-19 Pandemic* published by the National Academies of Sciences, Engineering, and Medicine (NASEM 2020), an organization's ability to handle a significant increase in demand for services falls into one of three following basic categories of surge capacity, depending on the magnitude of the incident:

- *Conventional.* Facility space, staff, and supplies required are consistent with normal operations within the organization.
- *Contingency.* Facility space, staff, and supplies required begin to exceed supply, but the care provided is functionally equivalent to that provided during conventional operations, recognizing that some adjustments to usual care are necessary.
- *Crisis.* Resources are so depleted that functional equivalent care is no longer possible.

As the imbalance increases between resource availability and demand, the provision of healthcare services moves from conventional through contingency to crisis as the capacity at each level is maximized. Consequences can be severe if changes in care practices are not undertaken when appropriate to mitigate loss of life or the exposure of patients and staff to unreasonable risks.

The following five key elements should form the basis for CSC planning (NASEM 2020):

1. A strong ethical grounding that enables a process deemed equitable based on its transparency, consistency, proportionality, and accountability
2. Integrated and ongoing community and provider engagement, education, and communication to ensure the legitimacy of the process and the resulting standards
3. Legal considerations that inform CSCs and create incentives for protecting health and respecting individual rights
4. Clear indicators, triggers, lines of responsibility, and the situational awareness to know when and how CSCs should be deployed
5. Evidence-based clinical processes and operations that evolve as evidence accrues

Although health and medical professionals who are closest to an event may make decisions that trigger the move to CSCs, policies that support the move to those standards (e.g., professional scope of care, hospital licensure, liability protections) must be implemented by the highest levels of authority. A formal emergency declaration may activate certain statutory, professional, or regulatory provisions that provide legal protections. However, changes in care patterns may be necessary before such a declaration is made. In either case, the public must be informed about resource allocation, patient relocation, and other decisions that may lead to crisis standards of care. Such communications should be coordinated with the appropriate public information structures at the local level.

Extreme conditions may arise with or without warning as a result of a variety of hazards—natural, technological, or human-made—to which healthcare organizations are exposed. The entire healthcare workforce has a professional and ethical responsibility to be ready and willing to adapt and provide essential care under any condition. This responsibility can be better met if healthcare leaders and professionals consider relevant ethics issues in advance, address them in the planning process, prepare staff at all levels, and remain committed to delivering the best care possible regardless of the circumstances.

ALL-HAZARDS APPROACH

The all-hazards approach to emergency management does not literally involve preparing for all hazards. Rather, it provides a general framework to address any type of disaster that might occur. Hazards are generally categorized into three types: natural, technological, and human-made. Natural events are the result of forces occurring in nature or the environment (e.g., naturally occurring disease outbreak, flood, severe weather, earthquake). Technological events are the result of accidents or failures involving processes or systems (e.g., transportation, utilities, telecommunications). Human-made events are those intentionally caused by human intervention (e.g., active shooter, workplace violence, terrorism, labor strike, bomb threat).

PHASES OF EMERGENCY MANAGEMENT

The four generally recognized phases of emergency management are mitigation, preparedness, response, and recovery. Activities in each phase contribute to the healthcare organization's overall resilience—its ability to prepare for, respond to, and recover from an event of any size or complexity. Ethical dilemmas can occur at any point in the emergency management cycle. Therefore, a thoughtful application of ethics principles in each phase can help ensure that ethical challenges are identified and appropriate courses of action are developed and implemented before an emergency occurs.

Mitigation

Mitigation measures are activities that eliminate the hazard, reduce the likelihood of its occurrence, or reduce its damaging effects. Administering immunizations, hardening facilities, and purchasing flood insurance are examples of mitigation activities.

The cornerstone of the mitigation phase is the hazard vulnerability analysis (HVA). The HVA is conducted to identify

- potential hazards that could affect the demand for healthcare services or an organization's ability to provide services,
- the likelihood of the hazard occurring,
- the consequences of the hazard occurring,
- the current level of preparedness for the hazard, and
- areas where the healthcare organization may be vulnerable.

The HVA serves as the basis for developing emergency plans and procedures, conducting training and exercises, budgeting for and acquiring resources and assets, establishing external support agreements, and prioritizing mitigation and preparedness activities.

Much as an HVA examines potential natural, technological, and human-made hazards and the organization's vulnerability to them, an "ethics vulnerability analysis" enables the organization to identify potential ethical issues as well as the consequences of not taking action to mitigate them. A thorough assessment of a healthcare organization's ethics vulnerabilities in the mitigation phase is instrumental to developing plans, policies, and procedures for eliminating or lessening their impact during an emergency.

Ethics principles can be applied in the mitigation phase through the following activities:

- Conduct ethics and legal audits of all emergency plans, plan annexes, policies, procedures, guidelines, standards of care, treatment protocols, key processes (e.g., triage, admission, discharge, allocation of scarce resources, security protocols), and external support agreements (e.g., contracts or memoranda of agreement with vendors, other healthcare entities, public agencies such as law enforcement or public health) to identify areas requiring clarification or revision to address ethical and legal concerns. Some of these, particularly processes or external support agreements, may currently be informal or unwritten, in which case the organization should strongly consider formalizing them by committing them to written form, reviewing them annually, and updating them as needed.

- Invite an ethics consultant or a member of the organization's ethics committee (or its equivalent) to be a standing member of the emergency management committee (or its equivalent). Having this person available during discussions of the HVA, proposed mitigation activities, and program review processes will ensure that ethics issues and concerns are identified before the planning process even begins.

- Mitigation activities (e.g., vaccination programs, quarantine, planned evacuation, interfacility transfers, security processes) should have clearly defined and realistic goals, especially when they infringe on liberty, autonomy, or individual rights. Planners should work closely with stakeholder groups to explain the rationale for mitigation activities and strive to reach consensus on the least intrusive yet still effective courses of action.

- Assess all employees (e.g., housekeeping, maintenance, dietary), not just healthcare practitioners, to determine their ability and willingness to respond to certain types of emergencies (e.g., hurricane, epidemic, radiological incident). Some employees might be unable to respond during an emergency because of family commitments (e.g., single parent with small children, caregiver for an older relative or dependent). Others may hesitate to respond out of fear for their personal safety. Determine what factors (e.g., personal and patient safety concerns, fear of liability, family obligations) would limit their participation. Identify issues that require input and guidance from internal entities (e.g., legal department, risk management) as well as external entities (e.g., professional licensing boards, insurers, accreditation bodies). Misconceptions about policies related to personal protective measures, disaster triage, allocation of scarce medical resources, or crisis standards of care could be resolved through additional training or by clarifying procedures during the preparedness phase. This information will be crucial in developing effective response plans and training initiatives.

Preparedness

Preparedness activities are designed to build and sustain capacity and capabilities by readying the organization and staff for response and recovery operations. Preparedness activities include planning, developing policies and procedures, stockpiling resources, conducting role-appropriate training for all staff, and testing capabilities through drills and exercises. Preparedness activities are defined and prioritized on the basis of hazards and vulnerabilities identified in the organization's HVA.

In the United States, cultural individualism and ethical systems that stress autonomy and civil liberties may directly affect the healthcare organization's ability to develop ethically acceptable emergency plans and procedures. Some directives may be perceived as inherently paternalistic and therefore need to be fully explained and justified to stakeholders and the public. Consequently, the ethical acceptability of an emergency plan is a function of both its content and the process by which it was developed, debated, and ultimately approved. When properly executed, preparedness activities can actually become a form of social contract to which stakeholders have given their implied informed consent.

Jennings and Arras (2008) offer seven ethical goals to guide the development, review, revision, and implementation of emergency preparedness plans:

1. *Harm reduction and benefit promotion.* Emergency preparedness planning and response activities should protect public safety, health, and well-being. They should minimize death, injury, disease, disability, and suffering during an emergency and afterward.
2. *Equal liberty and human rights.* Preparedness and response activities should be designed so that they respect the equal liberty, autonomy, and dignity of all people.
3. *Distributive justice.* Preparedness and response activities should be conducted in such a way that the benefits and burdens imposed on the population by the emergency and by the need to cope with its effects are shared uniformly and fairly.
4. *Public accountability.* Preparedness and response activities should be based on decision-making processes that are inclusive and transparent and that sustain public trust.
5. *Strength and safety of communities.* Preparedness and response activities should strive to develop hazard-resistant and resilient communities in the long term. Such communities have robust internal support systems; have networks of mutual assistance and solidarity; and maintain sustainable and risk-mitigating relationships with local ecosystems and the natural environment.
6. *Public health professionalism.* Preparedness and response activities should recognize the special obligations of various healthcare professionals and promote their competency, as well as coordination among them.
7. *Responsible civic response.* Preparedness and response activities should promote a sense of personal responsibility and citizenship.

These goals can be used to formulate answers to various ethical questions that may likely arise during the planning process, such as the following:

- Who and what should be protected and to what level?
- How are budgets and planning priorities established?
- In what order should patients be evacuated?
- Which staff should remain behind with those who cannot be moved?
- In what situations should healthcare workers be allowed to choose between saving their own lives or assisting their patients?
- When and under what circumstances should therapeutic efforts be stopped and shifted to palliative care to conserve scarce medical resources?

Emergency planning is an imperfect process. Unexpected events will occur, system failures will happen, and those with operational responsibility will be forced to make on-the-spot decisions requiring ethical judgments. Ethical considerations need to be explicit during the planning process so that, when those decisions must be made, they are consistent with the spirit of the ethical judgments that guided the planning process.

According to Jennings and Arras (2008), the application of ethics principles in the preparedness phase can be accomplished through the following activities:

- Actively engage the ethics representative during the planning process. Obtain an ethical perspective as plans, procedures, and external support agreements are being developed or revised. Seek guidance on resolving ethical conflicts.
- Identify the staff members who will fill key response roles during an emergency. Ensure that these personnel are trained to function in those capacities and that they understand the ethical components of those roles.
- Identify individuals and groups (e.g., older adults, people with disabilities, those who are medically underserved) who are particularly susceptible to harm or injustice during emergencies to ensure that their needs will be addressed.
- Emergency Operations Plans (EOPs) typically comprise a base plan followed by a series of incident annexes, support annexes, and resource annexes. Develop a support annex to the EOP that describes the decision-making process for the allocation of scarce medical resources and implementation of crisis standards of care:
  —Identify and describe the relevant ethical constructs. Be clear about how *disaster ethics*, which emphasize broader goals such as the fair distribution of limited resources, differ from *clinical ethics*, which emphasize protecting the rights of individual patients.

—Identify which triggers will activate the annex.

—Describe how the annex will work in practice.

—Describe the processes for withholding or withdrawing scarce resources (e.g., mechanical ventilators, intravenous fluids, medications) from a patient when clinicians determine that another patient is more likely to benefit from the resource.

—Describe how existing resources will be fairly distributed during an emergency.

—Justify why priority access to scarce resources may be provided to certain individuals or groups.

—Document who was involved in developing the annex and the process used.

—Describe how the annex will be reviewed and revised. Make the annex available for public review and comment.

- Provide role-specific ethics training (both initial and refresher training) for *all* employees. Leadership, managers, planners, and members of the incident management team will require a broad exposure to ethical principles and required actions, whereas healthcare practitioners will benefit from training that focuses primarily on clinical care issues. Even administrative and housekeeping personnel need a general understanding of planned response actions and the rationale behind them. Look for opportunities to incorporate ethics training into existing training offerings.

- Test the ethics components of emergency plans and procedures during periodic drills and exercises. Identify and document ethics questions and issues that arise so that plans and procedures can be clarified before they are needed for an actual emergency. Provide follow-up training on any changes made as a result of this process.

- Develop a mechanism for ongoing monitoring of the use of authority and power during the response phase. Experience shows that solidarity and self-sacrifice often give way to disillusionment, recrimination, and litigation in the aftermath of an emergency or disaster.

Response

Response activities address the immediate, near-term effects of the emergency. Response is the act of putting preparedness plans into action by mobilizing resources to save lives, stabilize the incident, and prevent further property damage or loss of assets.

The application of ethics principles in the response phase can be accomplished through the following activities (Jennings and Arras 2008):

- Monitor the use of authority and power to ensure that they are not abused and that paternalistic or coercive measures are justified under the circumstances.
- Maintain transparency in communications with the public:
  —Acknowledge uncertainty.
  —Provide follow-up information as it becomes available.
  —Advise patience and flexibility.
  —Admit mistakes and move on.
  —Provide guidance that can realistically be acted on.
- When selecting individuals for key response roles or deployment, ensure that the process is orderly, transparent, and fair and that it prevents undue family burden and personal hardship. If an individual believes an assignment is inappropriate or has been wrongly motivated, an expedient and confidential review and appeals process should be undertaken.

Successful emergency or disaster response requires coordination and integration across all stakeholder groups, including state and local governments, emergency management services, public health agencies, hospitals, outpatient settings, and home health. Integration of response activities among the various agencies at the federal, state, and local levels is important. A foundation of strong ethical obligations (i.e., values that do not change even when resources are scarce), appropriate legal authorities, and a regulatory environment that allows for shifts in expectations for the best possible care based on a particular context is crucial for success (IOM 2012).

Recovery

Recovery activities are designed to return the healthcare organization to the condition it was in before the emergency or disaster by restoring systems critical to the provision of care, treatment, and services. Recovery actions include compiling documentation of the emergency or disaster, conducting a critique of response activities, preparing an after-action report, identifying corrective actions, developing an improvement plan, performing critical incident stress debriefing, replenishing supplies, repairing or replacing equipment, addressing physical plant issues, reviewing and revising the Emergency Operations Plan (and related documents), and training or retraining personnel as necessary.

The decision to restore care or services disrupted during an emergency should take into account the needs of the population now being served as well as the resources available to resume operations. A phased approach to resuming services—one that allows personnel mobilized during the response phase to attend to personal or family needs before returning to the assignments and shift rotations they had before the emergency—may be necessary. All staff (including volunteers) who participated in the emergency response, regardless of their role, have an obligation to participate in the evaluation of the response to help identify what worked well and what needs to be improved.

The application of ethics principles in the recovery phase can be accomplished through the following activities:

- Identify ethics issues and concerns during the post-emergency critique and document findings and corrective actions in the after-action report.
- Invite the organization's ethics consultant or a member of the ethics committee (or its equivalent) to participate in postemergency critique and evaluation activities.
- Review findings and observations of an ethical nature with the appropriate organizational entities (e.g., leadership, relevant committees, medical staff, department heads).
- Provide a forum for the discussion of ethics issues with all staff and relevant stakeholders.
- Review and revise the Emergency Operations Plan, plan annexes, policies, procedures, external support agreements, and training materials to incorporate improvements to the ethical aspects of the emergency response.
- Ensure that revised training materials reinforce ethical constructs or reflect changes in processes of an ethical nature.
- Test revised processes during drills and exercises to determine whether ethics issues and concerns have been adequately addressed and mitigated.
- Provide postemergency medical follow-up to personnel who were exposed to harmful agents or were injured during the emergency response.
- Provide access to behavioral health support for all personnel affected by the emergency, regardless of whether they were directly involved in response activities.
- Repatriate staff and patients who may have been displaced as a result of evacuation or service disruption; use processes that minimize further disruptions and stress to personnel.

SUMMARY

Ethical values, though widely shared in American culture, are neither simple nor consistent. Although we can easily invoke the notion of the greatest good, attempting to do the greatest good while also providing universal assistance is a complex task that requires judgment and compromise. The inclusion of deliberate ethics planning as part of the emergency management construct provides a mechanism for identifying and resolving ethical issues that healthcare professionals face during emergencies and disasters—such as the duty to respond, allocation of scarce resources, and crisis standards of care—and supports their professional concerns as well as the needs of the communities they serve.

REFERENCES

American College of Surgeons. 2023. "Uniform Emergency Volunteer Health Practitioners Act." Accessed November 3. www.facs.org/advocacy/state-legislation/uniform-emergency-volunteer-health-practitioners-act/.

American Nurses Association (ANA). 2017. *Who Will Be There? Ethics, the Law, and a Nurse's Duty to Respond in a Disaster.* Issue Brief. Accessed November 3, 2023. www.nursingworld.org/~4af058/globalassets/docs/ana/ethics/who-will-be-there_disaster-preparedness_2017.pdf.

———. 2008. *Adapting Standards of Care Under Extreme Conditions: Guidance for Professionals During Disasters, Pandemics, and Other Extreme Emergencies.* Published March. www.nursingworld.org/~4ade15/globalassets/docs/ana/ascec_whitepaper031008final.pdf.

Campisi, J. 2023. "Attacks on Health Care Workers Raise Concerns." Business Insurance. Published September 1. www.businessinsurance.com/article/20230901/NEWS08/912359414/Attacks-on-health-care-workers-raise-concerns.

Cause IQ. 2023. "Northern Virginia Hospital Alliance (NVHA)." Accessed November 3. www.causeiq.com/organizations/northern-virginia-hospital-alliance,300128207/.

Ducharme, J. 2018. "Doctors and Nurses Treat Gunshot Wounds All the Time. Now They're Preparing for Active Shootings at Their Own Hospitals." *Time.* Published November 28. http://time.com/5463358/hospitals-active-shooter-drills.

Emergency Management Assistance Compact (EMAC). 1996. "EMAC Legislation." Approved October 19. www.emacweb.org/index.php/learn-about-emac/emac-legislation.

Federal Emergency Management Agency (FEMA). 2023. "Declared Disasters 2013-2023." Accessed November 3. www.fema.gov/disaster/declarations.

Francis, E. 2010. "D.C. Hospital Fires Employees for Missing Work During Storms." Published March 1. https://wamu.org/story/10/03/01/dc_hospital_fires_employees_for_missing_work_during_storms/.

Gao, H., and E. Adashi. 2023. *An Analysis of Active Shooters in the Hospital Setting, 2000–2015*. Alpert School of Medicine, Brown University. Accessed November 3. https://repository.library.brown.edu/studio/item/bdr%3A581443/PDF/.

Illinois Department of Public Health. 2004. *Intergovernmental Mutual Aid Agreement for the Establishment of the Illinois Public Health Mutual Aid System (IPHMAS)*. Published June 4. https://dph.illinois.gov/content/dam/soi/en/web/idph/files/publications/iphmas-specimen-agreement-between-local-health-departments-2004-041816.pdf.

Institute of Medicine (IOM). 2012. *Crisis Standards of Care: A Systems Framework for Catastrophic Disaster Response*. Vol. 1, *Introduction and CSC Framework*. Washington, DC: National Academies Press.

International Emergency Management Group (IEMG). 2023. *International Emergency Management Assistance Memorandum of Understanding*. Accessed November 3. https://cap-cpma.ca/wp-content/uploads/2019/08/EMO-MOU-English-3.pdf.

Jacobs, L. M., and K. J. Burns. 2017. "The Hartford Consensus: Survey of the Public and Healthcare Professionals on Active Shooter Events in Hospitals." *Journal of the American College of Surgeons* 225 (3): 435–42.

Jennings, B., and J. Arras. 2008. "Ethical Guidance for Public Health Emergency Preparedness and Response: Highlighting Ethics and Values in a Vital Public Health Service." White paper prepared for the Ethics Subcommittee, Advisory Committee to the Director, Centers for Disease Control and Prevention. Published October 30. https://stacks.cdc.gov/view/cdc/44130.

Kelen, G. D., C. L. Catlett, J. G. Kubit, and Y. H. Hsieh. 2012. "Hospital-Based Shootings in the United States: 2000 to 2011." *Annals of Emergency Medicine* 60 (6): 790–98.

Managed Emergency Surge for Healthcare (MESH). 2023. "About MESH." Accessed November 3. www.meshcoalition.org/about.

National Academies of Sciences, Engineering, and Medicine (NASEM). 2020. *Rapid Expert Consultation on Crisis Standards of Care for the COVID-19 Pandemic (March 28, 2020)*. Washington, DC: National Academies Press.

Phillips, S. J., A. Knebel, and K. J. Johnson (eds.). 2009. *Mass Medical Care with Scarce Resources: The Essentials*. Rockville, MD: Agency for Healthcare Research and Quality.

University of Toronto Joint Centre for Bioethics. 2005. *Stand on Guard for Thee: Ethical Considerations in Preparedness Planning for Pandemic Influenza*. Report of the Pandemic Influenza Working Group. Published November. http://jcb.utoronto.ca/people/documents/upshur_stand_guard.pdf.

Follow-Up on the Cases

ALTHOUGH THE CASES presented in this book have been taken from the headlines and for the most part fictionalized, even fiction has an ending. My favorite reading as a child was *What Happened Then Stories*, and the following is what actually happened or a fictional account of what most likely happened in these cases.

Recall that each of these cases is characterized by ambiguities and intertwining ethical issues, so the resolution (or lack of resolution) may have an impact on several people and programs in an organization or in the community in which that organization is located.

A healthcare manager is confronted with ethical dilemmas every day. Most of the time, the manager makes the right decisions unconsciously and "does the right thing." For the most part, those involved in healthcare are decent, moral individuals who are attracted to the healthcare field because they wish to contribute something positive to society. Nevertheless, they occasionally make errors in judgment, detrimental decisions, and unintentional mistakes. More often than not, mistakes are the result of the barrage of decisions that must be made by managers who are pressed for time and strained by the demands of the job. Decisions are frequently made without the benefit of thoughtful reflection or consultation with others.

The cases in this book are intended to remind healthcare managers of the untoward consequences of hasty decisions that do not consider all the ethical dimensions involved.

PARADISE HILLS MEDICAL CENTER

The matter of the radiation overdose given to 22 oncology patients was referred to the medical center's ethics committee. Following deliberations, the committee recommended that the patients affected be informed about the errors and monitored closely for adverse effects. The medical staff and administration reviewed the committee's recommendation, but the administration decided not to follow it, maintaining that it was under no obligation to do so because the ethics committee was only advisory in nature. After review, the governing board concurred. Its decision was based on a fear of litigation and the bad publicity that was certain to follow if knowledge of the errors became public. Consequently, the patients involved were not informed about the errors. Four of the patients suffered adverse effects, the most serious of which were radiation burns.

Three months later, one of the patients learned about the errors and filed a lawsuit against the hospital for fraudulent concealment. Because the reason for the lawsuit was fraud and not malpractice, the hospital's malpractice insurance did not provide coverage. The case was settled out of court for $300,000. The lawsuit and settlement received broad news coverage both on television and in the local newspapers. As the other patients involved became aware of the incident, only a few chose to file lawsuits and settled out of court for similar amounts. The hospital considered itself lucky.

The aftermath of this experience was characterized by tension among the staff, who disagreed among themselves about how this case should have been handled. The nurses in the oncology program adamantly believed that the patients should have been told immediately about the accidental overdoses. In fact, some staff members speculated that one of the nurses had informed the first patient about the errors. A prestigious oncology medical group practice, uncomfortable with all the publicity and the inquiries from patients about the medical center's capabilities, began to disassociate itself from Paradise Hills Medical Center and to refer patients to a competing facility. Relationships between some primary care physicians and oncologists remained strained. The oncology program suffered a moderate decline in census. Some members of the governing board felt they had been misled by the hospital's administration. A general sense of mistrust was palpable throughout the medical center, and employees and hospital staff were chagrined that they had to defend the medical center to friends and family who were shocked by the disclosure.

QUALPLUS HMO

Jim decided to play the game and followed the lead of his boss and the governing board. "Final" bids were requested, and the contract was awarded to Acme Construction.

Still, Jim's relationships with Brent and with the board members who had served on the facilities committee were strained. Brent began to micromanage

Jim's operations, and some of Jim's responsibilities were assigned to other staff. Jim was especially offended when Brent gave oversight of the construction project to one of his coworkers.

More and more, Jim felt marginalized. His invitations to golf were declined. He began to feel slighted at social functions as well. Even Jim's wife mentioned that Brent and his wife seemed particularly cool lately.

Most of all, Jim was uncomfortable with himself. He was being eased out of the organization even though he had done what they wanted. Now he wished he had stood by his principles—and resigned, if necessary. At least he would still have his self-respect.

COMMUNITY MEDICAL CENTER

John never fully recovered from the incident at Community Medical Center. He was bitter because he believed that the board had treated him unfairly. He insisted he had done nothing wrong, but he believed the board was more interested in appearances than fact. They did not ask for his resignation, but John knew that he had lost credibility with them. His wife felt humiliated by his behavior and asked for a separation until things blew over. His children were openly disdainful of him. The general consensus among his colleagues, even those who liked him, was that he had been unbelievably careless.

The postgraduate fellow sought legal counsel and was told that she probably had grounds for litigation because the position was not offered to her on the basis of her gender. However, she decided not to pursue litigation. She had no difficulty finding another responsible position. Unfortunately, her experience at Community Medical Center loomed like a shadow over her. The word was that she had threatened sexual harassment charges. Male colleagues behaved professionally toward her but kept their distance. The senior executives limited the amount of time they spent with her. She knew she had done nothing wrong, but she also believed that her experience at Community Medical Center had hurt her career.

Some of the hospital staff congratulated themselves for knowing something was going on and imagined the most sordid of affairs. John's defenders were quick to label the postgraduate fellow as a seductress, noting that no one can trust anyone that young, attractive, and ambitious.

The incident was never made public, but word got around. The gossip was about marital infidelity. Two board members who had been among John's early supporters suggested that John might want to start looking for another position. They were apologetic but noted that the small, family-oriented community in which Community Medical Center was located was not very tolerant. They mentioned that another board member had even suggested that John's judgment was impaired and that he could not be trusted to make appropriate decisions in the future. John was baffled by the board's lack of compassion and support.

UNIVERSITY HOSPITAL

As expected, that afternoon the newspaper reported that a resident-in-training had performed unsupervised emergency surgery at University Hospital. The reporter had interviewed the patient and his family, who said that they were completely satisfied with the care they had received and that they had no intention of criticizing University Hospital or seeking legal remedy.

The hospital staff were relieved, as were the medical staff, the surgery residency program director, the resident physician, and Dr. Spalding.

Jan was reprimanded for not calling in the surgeon on second call and for not reporting Dr. Spalding's impairment. She was found lax in her responsibility for the safe care of the patient.

Dr. Truman was reprimanded for not ordering that the surgeon on second call be notified and for not asking that the surgery residency program director be notified about the absence of an attending physician.

Following disciplinary review, Dr. Spalding had his surgical privileges suspended until he provided evidence to the credentialing committee that he had sought treatment for his drinking problem.

The publicity about the incident did not appear to harm the hospital's image. On the contrary, many thought that the patient's favorable testimonial actually helped public relations.

HILLSIDE COUNTY MEDICAL CENTER

In analyzing Hillside's overall financial situation, the CEO determined that the medical center's financial challenges had to be addressed in a manner that would ensure its long-term survivability and success. He believed that accomplishing this task would require a collaborative effort involving the input and engagement of key stakeholders, such as medical staff and union leadership. In addition, he knew that the mission of the organization could not be compromised.

Accordingly, a medical staff advisory board was established. The initial responsibility of this medical advisory group (MAG) was to identify the most appropriate way to deal with the financial challenges that Hillside currently faced. The

MAG identified opportunities for program and cost reductions, as well as new opportunities for financial expansion. Issues such as length of stay were recognized as key opportunities for reducing operational costs. It was agreed that the MAG would continue to meet on a quarterly basis to define and develop collaborative opportunities.

At the same time, meetings were held with key union leaders to seek their input and assistance in identifying opportunities for cost reductions. Through this collaboration, significant and valuable suggestions were incorporated into the cost-reduction process. Not only was the outcome more successful, but everyone involved also gained a better understanding of the challenges that the organization faced.

This initial success did not guarantee that Hillside's financial obstacles were permanently overcome. However, it proved that Hillside was capable of addressing these concerns in a collaborative manner. In the long run, collaboration was key to achieving significant cost reductions.

METROPOLITAN COMMUNITY HOSPITAL

Frustrated with the lack of attention to their concerns, the nursing staff at Metropolitan began serious discussions about unionizing so that they could speak with an organized voice. The debate and dissension among the nursing staff about the desirability of this action soon spilled over into the community and made its way to the hospital's board.

The board put Eugene's feet to the fire and demanded that he quickly handle the situation before it got worse. Eugene asked Jane to resign and appointed a strong search committee that had nursing and medical staff representation. The search committee's mandate was to recruit a competent and innovative CNO as quickly as possible. The committee was successful.

The new CNO made rapid progress toward stabilizing the nursing workforce. Even retention improved. Eugene was beginning to relax when yet another staff conflict required his attention. The new CNO and the COO, Carter Sims, adamantly disagreed about whether and how the physicians' disruptive behavior should be addressed. The CNO argued that such behavior was unacceptable and that action needed to be taken immediately. Carter believed that the CNO was overreacting and argued that the medical staff were not within her purview. Eugene agreed with the CNO and knew the time had come to consider replacing Carter with a COO who could see the big picture and collaborate as part of a functional senior team. Eugene had become so far removed from operations that he knew this task was not going to be easy.

HEARTLAND HEALTHCARE SYSTEM

Richard had been Heartland's CEO for more than 15 years and was widely credited with the success of the system. The board and the community had great confidence in his character and abilities. Richard was able to capitalize on their confidence and goodwill. He candidly admitted his hiring mistake and moved quickly to replace Jack as CIO and to terminate Alan's employment. He appointed a multidisciplinary search committee, chaired by the chief operating officer, to whom the new CIO would report, and engaged the services of a nationally recognized search consultant to find a new CIO—preferably one with healthcare experience.

The board supported Richard in his efforts, and he assured the board members that once the new CIO was in place, they would receive regular reports on the objectives, metrics, and progress of information technology at Heartland. The staff at Heartland were enthusiastic about these efforts and pledged to support the incoming CIO. A year later, real IT progress had been made.

RICHLAND RIVER VALLEY HEALTHCARE SYSTEM

Within the first year following the dissolution of the Richland River Valley Healthcare System (RRVHS), Continental Healthcare moved quickly to purchase both Trinity and Sutton Memorial, which Continental now operates as separate healthcare facilities under its national for-profit healthcare corporation.

Not wanting to labor under corporate direction and frustrated with mismanagement, a large group of prominent, highly regarded physicians in Clay County formed a physician-owned medical group practice—Richland Health Partners (RHP)—to provide primary and specialty care, urgent care, and hospital care. Continental negotiated with RHP for hospital care, and all seemed well for two years. However, the physicians were never really comfortable with the arrangement, feeling they had relinquished control and any ability to influence the delivery of healthcare in Richland. When the contracts came up for renewal, negotiations failed, the contracts were terminated, and Continental informed the physicians that they could no longer treat patients at Continental's facilities. This outcome caused much alarm in the community and prompted lawsuits between Continental and RHP.

Employees at Trinity and Sutton Memorial likewise continued to experience turmoil. When Continental took over, it implemented staff reductions to trim costs at both hospitals. Uncertainty and dissension between the medical staff and administration exacerbated the staff's mistrust of the new management. The unions at Trinity were about to enter into contract talks with Continental and feared the worst. Few of the original board members were retained. Both they and those who resigned lost the respect of the community, which felt its hospitals had been "sold out."

HURLEY MEDICAL CENTER

The lawsuit against Hurley Medical Center alleging racial discrimination was filed in January 2013 and was settled out of court in February 2013. The newspaper story about the settlement carried the headline "Flint Hurley Medical Center Lawsuit Settled; Nurse Glad It's a Learning Tool." Although details of the settlement were not disclosed, it was said to have been "amicably resolved" (Adams 2013). Indeed, the president and CEO of the hospital made the announcement with the plaintiffs alongside. The president said that the incident would be used in training at the hospital to prevent similar incidents from happening in the future.

The National Action Network announced that it still planned to protest outside the hospital. The political director for the Michigan chapter of the group said, "We're challenging the institution of racism that manifested itself when staff and management followed the directives of a guy that may be a Nazi" (Adams 2013). The group asked for a meeting with hospital officials.

News coverage of the event continued throughout national media. Ten days after the lawsuit was settled, the nurse involved in the incident was interviewed on ABC-TV by Katie Couric, who was later quoted as saying she believed the nurse took appropriate action in the case (Ridley 2013).

On September, 26, 2013, the US Equal Employment Opportunity Commission (EEOC) issued a press release announcing that "Hurley Medical Center in Genesee County, Mich., has agreed to settle a race discrimination charge filed against it with the U.S. Equal Employment Opportunity Commission" (EEOC 2013). In its press release, the EEOC made clear that "assignment of employees based on customer racial preferences violates Title VII of the Civil Rights Act of 1964" (EEOC 2013). The EEOC agreement with Hurley Medical Center includes the following (EEOC 2013):

> As part of a five-year collaborative agreement, Hurley Medical Center is partnering with EEOC on a variety of programs and initiatives aimed at educating and developing youth from Flint and the surrounding Genesee County community. Hurley and the EEOC will team up on a variety of internal programs at the medical center that are focused on workforce development involving the youth in the community. This will include increasing the number of high school career day sessions offered at Hurley, where EEOC staff will participate as speakers for each session.

In addition, as part of ongoing leadership development and education of the work-force, the EEOC will conduct non-discrimination training for the management staff of the hospital annually. As part of Hurley's commitment to diversity and inclusion, the EEOC will also meet with the Hurley Diversity and Inclusion Council annually to hear the council's accomplishments and to offer advice that will assist in furthering the efforts of the council.

The widespread media coverage of this case generated much public interest and conversation—so much so that, in 2016, it inspired *New York Times* best-selling author Jodi Picoult to publish her popular novel *Small Great Things*. In the author's note at the end of the book, Picoult says that she had always wanted to write about racism but had never felt capable of doing so. "Then," she says, "I read a news story about an African American nurse in Flint, Michigan . . . [and] I realized I had to write this book" (Picoult 2016). Her novel captures the real-life events at Hurley Medical Center, re-creating the same circumstances in fiction. Picoult says she believes that writing the novel "was the right thing to do" and hopes that it will generate more discussion about institutional racism in the United States.

BABY CHARLIE GARD

Baby Charlie Gard died on July 28, 2017, but his memory lives on through the Charlie Gard Foundation, founded by his parents, Chris Gard and Connie Yates. In their words (Charlie Gard Foundation 2023b):

> Out of this tragic situation we have decided to create The Charlie Gard Foundation with the money raised from Charlie's campaign. The foundation aims to become one of the UK's leading charities dedicated to fighting mitochondrial disease, and we hope we can deliver on this promise to ensure we honour Charlie's legacy. Charlie has already changed the world, and his legacy will continue to follow in those tiny, but mighty, footsteps.

Officially launched on June 1, 2018, the foundation boasted 400,000 worldwide supporters, 84,000 donations, and £1.3 million raised in just two months. Following Charlie's death, his parents spent several months developing draft legislation for "Charlie's Law," which was brought before the British Parliament in an effort to spare other families from courtroom clashes with medical teams over treatment decisions. The foundation has a website and a Facebook page through which it publicizes fund-raising events and allows other parents facing similar challenges to share their experiences (Charlie Gard Foundation 2023a, 2023b).

MEMORIAL MEDICAL CENTER

Memorial Medical Center remained closed after Hurricane Katrina until 2006, when it was sold to Ochsner Baptist Health System and renamed Ochsner Baptist Medical Center in honor of its original roots.

In 2015, CNBC reported that the Ochsner Baptist Health System invested well over $100 million in renovating the Katrina-damaged Memorial Medical Center. Huge resources were invested in "moving the building's emergency backup systems well above the highwater mark from Katrina, including a massive generator that is able to run all of the hospital's systems. In addition, water and fuel pipelines have been installed to make sure the generator can keep running" (Coombs 2015). The new hospital owners also invested in a "fleet of rescue boats and staffers who undergo water rescue training" to facilitate the evacuation of patients in floods (Coombs 2015). Most of the hospital has been renovated except for the building that includes the original main entrance to Memorial. That part was still abandoned and almost untouched as of January 2023.

Following the Louisiana grand jury's decision not to indict Dr. Anna Pou for any wrongdoing during Katrina, the charges against her were expunged and the state of Louisiana agreed to pay Pou's legal fees. Pou returned to practicing medicine as an otolaryngology surgeon in 2007. She continues to lecture on medicine, ethics, and disaster preparedness.

CONCLUSION

As these sequels demonstrate, there are few winners after a breach of ethical conduct. Typically, the problems that result touch more than a few lives. For this reason and others, healthcare executives would be wise to put organizational mechanisms in place that help staff make sound ethical decisions to begin with. In the matter of ethics, as in other matters, preventing problems requires less time and energy, is less costly, and is certainly more rewarding.

REFERENCES

Adams, D. 2013. "Flint Hurley Medical Center Lawsuit Settled; Nurse Glad It's a Learning Tool." *Flint Journal*, February 22.

Charlie Gard Foundation. 2023a. "The Charlie Gard Foundation." Facebook. Accessed October 3. www.facebook.com/charliegardfoundation.

———. 2023b. "Charlie's Story." Accessed October 3. https://thecharliegardfoundation.org/about/charlies-story/.

Coombs, B. 2015."Ochsner: Hospital Powerhouse Forged in the Wake of Katrina."
    CNBC. Published August 27. www.cnbc.com/2015/08/26/ochsner-hospital-power-
    house-forged-in-the-wake-of-katrina.html.

Picoult, J. 2016. *Small Great Things*. New York: Ballantine Books.

Ridley, G. 2013. "Nurse Sues Flint's Hurley Medical Center over Claim She Was
    Barred from Treating Infant Because of Her Race." *Flint Journal*, February 18.

US Equal Employment Opportunity Commission (EEOC). 2013. "Hurley Medical
    Center Agrees to Settle Race Discrimination Case." Press release, September 26.
    www.eeoc.gov/newsroom/hurley-medical-center-agrees-settle-eeoc-race-discrimina-
    tion-case.

American College of Healthcare Executives Ethics Self-Assessment

PURPOSE OF THE ETHICS SELF-ASSESSMENT

Members of the American College of Healthcare Executives agree, as a condition of membership, to abide by ACHE's *Code of Ethics*. The *Code* provides an overall standard of conduct and includes specific standards of ethical behavior to guide healthcare executives in their professional relationships.

Based on the *Code of Ethics*, the Ethics Self-Assessment is intended for your personal use to assist you in thinking about your ethics-related leadership and actions. It should not be returned to ACHE nor should it be used as a tool for evaluating the ethical behavior of others.

The Ethics Self-Assessment can help you identify those areas in which you are on strong ethical ground; areas that you may wish to examine the basis for your responses; and opportunities for further reflection. The Ethics Self-Assessment does not have a scoring mechanism, as we do not believe that ethical behavior can or should be quantified.

HOW TO USE THIS SELF-ASSESSMENT

We hope you find this self-assessment thought-provoking and useful as a part of your reflection on applying the ACHE Code of Ethics to your everyday activities. You are to be commended for taking time out of your busy schedule to complete it. Once you have finished the self-assessment, it is suggested that you review your responses, noting which questions you answered "usually," "occasionally" and "almost never." You may find that in some cases an answer of "usually" is

Source: Reprinted with permission of the American College of Healthcare Executives.

satisfactory, but in other cases, such as when answering a question about protecting staff's well-being, an answer of "usually" may raise an ethical red flag.

We are confident that you will uncover few red flags where your responses are not compatible with the ACHE *Code of Ethics*. For those you may discover, you should use this as an opportunity to enhance your ethical practice and leadership by developing a specific action plan. For example, you may have noted in the self-assessment that you have not used your organization's ethics mechanism to assist you in addressing challenging ethical conflicts. As a result of this insight you might meet with the chair of the ethics committee to better understand the committee's functions, including case consultation activities and how you might access this resource when future ethical conflicts arise.

We also want you to consider ACHE as a resource when you and your management team are confronted with difficult ethical dilemmas. Access the Ethics Toolkit, a group of practical resources that will help you understand how to integrate ethics into your organization, at ache.org/EthicsToolkit. In addition, you can refer to our regular "Healthcare Management Ethics" column in *Healthcare Executive* magazine.

Please check one answer for each of the following questions.
Almost Never/Occasionally/Usually/Always/Not Applicable

I. Leadership

I take courageous, consistent and appropriate management actions to overcome barriers to achieving my organization's mission.

Almost Never	Occasionally	Usually	Always	N/A
☐	☐	☐	☐	☐

I place community/patient benefit over my personal gain.

Almost Never	Occasionally	Usually	Always	N/A
☐	☐	☐	☐	☐

I strive to be a role model for ethical behavior.

Almost Never	Occasionally	Usually	Always	N/A
☐	☐	☐	☐	☐

I work to ensure that decisions about access to care are based primarily on medical necessity, not only on the ability to pay.

Almost Never	Occasionally	Usually	Always	N/A
☐	☐	☐	☐	☐

My statements and actions are consistent with professional ethical standards, including the ACHE *Code of Ethics*.

Almost Never	Occasionally	Usually	Always	N/A
☐	☐	☐	☐	☐

My statements and actions are honest even when circumstances would allow me to confuse the issues.

Almost Never	Occasionally	Usually	Always	N/A
☐	☐	☐	☐	☐

I advocate ethical decision making by the board, management team and medical staff.

Almost Never	Occasionally	Usually	Always	N/A
☐	☐	☐	☐	☐

Source: Reprinted with permission of the American College of Healthcare Executives.

I use an ethical approach to conflict resolution.

Almost Never	Occasionally	Usually	Always	N/A
☐	☐	☐	☐	☐

I initiate and encourage discussion of the ethical aspects of management/financial issues.

Almost Never	Occasionally	Usually	Always	N/A
☐	☐	☐	☐	☐

I initiate and promote discussion of controversial issues affecting community/patient health (e.g., domestic and community violence and decisions near the end of life).

Almost Never	Occasionally	Usually	Always	N/A
☐	☐	☐	☐	☐

I promptly and candidly explain to internal and external stakeholders negative economic trends and encourage appropriate action.

Almost Never	Occasionally	Usually	Always	N/A
☐	☐	☐	☐	☐

I use my authority solely to fulfill my responsibilities and not for self-interest or to further the interests of family, friends or associates.

Almost Never	Occasionally	Usually	Always	N/A
☐	☐	☐	☐	☐

When an ethical conflict confronts my organization or me, I am successful in finding an effective resolution process and ensure it is followed.

Almost Never	Occasionally	Usually	Always	N/A
☐	☐	☐	☐	☐

I demonstrate respect for my colleagues, superiors and staff.

Almost Never	Occasionally	Usually	Always	N/A
☐	☐	☐	☐	☐

I demonstrate my organization's vision, mission and value statements in my actions.

Almost Never	Occasionally	Usually	Always	N/A
☐	☐	☐	☐	☐

Source: Reprinted with permission of the American College of Healthcare Executives.

I make timely decisions rather than delaying them to avoid difficult or politically risky choices.

Almost Never	Occasionally	Usually	Always	N/A
☐	☐	☐	☐	☐

I seek the advice of the ethics committee when making ethically challenging decisions.

Almost Never	Occasionally	Usually	Always	N/A
☐	☐	☐	☐	☐

My personal expense reports are accurate and are only billed to a single organization.

Almost Never	Occasionally	Usually	Always	N/A
☐	☐	☐	☐	☐

I openly support establishing and monitoring internal mechanisms (e.g., an ethics committee or program) to support ethical decision making.

Almost Never	Occasionally	Usually	Always	N/A
☐	☐	☐	☐	☐

I thoughtfully consider decisions when making a promise on behalf of the organization to a person or a group of people.

Almost Never	Occasionally	Usually	Always	N/A
☐	☐	☐	☐	☐

I take responsibility for understanding workplace violence and take steps to eliminate it.

Almost Never	Occasionally	Usually	Always	N/A
☐	☐	☐	☐	☐

II. Relationships
Community

I promote community health status improvement as a guiding goal of my organization and as a cornerstone of my efforts on behalf of my organization.

Almost Never	Occasionally	Usually	Always	N/A
☐	☐	☐	☐	☐

Source: Reprinted with permission of the American College of Healthcare Executives.

I personally devote time to developing solutions to community health problems.

Almost Never	Occasionally	Usually	Always	N/A
❏	❏	❏	❏	❏

I participate in and encourage my management team to devote personal time to community service.

Almost Never	Occasionally	Usually	Always	N/A
❏	❏	❏	❏	❏

I engage in collaborative efforts with healthcare organizations, businesses, elected officials and others to improve the community's well-being.

Almost Never	Occasionally	Usually	Always	N/A
❏	❏	❏	❏	❏

I seek to identify, understand and eliminate health disparities in my community.

Almost Never	Occasionally	Usually	Always	N/A
❏	❏	❏	❏	❏

I seek to understand and identify the social determinants of health in my community.

Almost Never	Occasionally	Usually	Always	N/A
❏	❏	❏	❏	❏

Patients and Their Families

I use a patient- and family-centered approach to patient care.

Almost Never	Occasionally	Usually	Always	N/A
❏	❏	❏	❏	❏

I am a patient advocate on both clinical and financial matters.

Almost Never	Occasionally	Usually	Always	N/A
❏	❏	❏	❏	❏

I ensure equitable treatment of patients regardless of socio-economic group or payor category.

Almost Never	Occasionally	Usually	Always	N/A
❏	❏	❏	❏	❏

Source: Reprinted with permission of the American College of Healthcare Executives.

I respect the practices and customs of a diverse patient population while maintaining the organization's mission.

Almost Never	Occasionally	Usually	Always	N/A
☐	☐	☐	☐	☐

I demonstrate through organizational policies and personal actions that overtreatment and undertreatment of patients are unacceptable.

Almost Never	Occasionally	Usually	Always	N/A
☐	☐	☐	☐	☐

I protect patients' rights to autonomy, clinical efficacy, and full information about their illnesses, treatment options, and related costs.

Almost Never	Occasionally	Usually	Always	N/A
☐	☐	☐	☐	☐

I promote a patient's right to privacy, including medical record confidentiality, and do not tolerate breaches of this confidentiality.

Almost Never	Occasionally	Usually	Always	N/A
☐	☐	☐	☐	☐

I am committed to eliminating harm in the workplace.

Almost Never	Occasionally	Usually	Always	N/A
☐	☐	☐	☐	☐

I am committed to helping address affordability challenges in healthcare.

Almost Never	Occasionally	Usually	Always	N/A
☐	☐	☐	☐	☐

Board

I have a routine system in place for board members to make full disclosure and reveal potential conflicts of interest.

Almost Never	Occasionally	Usually	Always	N/A
☐	☐	☐	☐	☐

Source: Reprinted with permission of the American College of Healthcare Executives.

I ensure that reports to the board, my own or others', appropriately convey risks of decisions or proposed projects.

Almost Never	Occasionally	Usually	Always	N/A
☐	☐	☐	☐	☐

I work to keep the board focused on ethical issues of importance to the organization, community and other stakeholders.

Almost Never	Occasionally	Usually	Always	N/A
☐	☐	☐	☐	☐

I keep the board appropriately informed of patient safety and quality indicators.

Almost Never	Occasionally	Usually	Always	N/A
☐	☐	☐	☐	☐

I promote board discussion of resource allocation issues, particularly those where organizational and community interests may appear to be incompatible.

Almost Never	Occasionally	Usually	Always	N/A
☐	☐	☐	☐	☐

I keep the board appropriately informed about issues of alleged financial malfeasance, clinical malpractice and potential litigious situations involving employees.

Almost Never	Occasionally	Usually	Always	N/A
☐	☐	☐	☐	☐

Colleagues and Staff

I foster discussions about ethical concerns when they arise.

Almost Never	Occasionally	Usually	Always	N/A
☐	☐	☐	☐	☐

I maintain confidences entrusted to me.

Almost Never	Occasionally	Usually	Always	N/A
☐	☐	☐	☐	☐

Source: Reprinted with permission of the American College of Healthcare Executives.

I demonstrate through personal actions and organizational policies zero tolerance for any form of staff harassment.

Almost Never	Occasionally	Usually	Always	N/A
☐	☐	☐	☐	☐

I encourage discussions about and advocate for the implementation of the organization's code of ethics and value statements.

Almost Never	Occasionally	Usually	Always	N/A
☐	☐	☐	☐	☐

I fulfill the promises I make.

Almost Never	Occasionally	Usually	Always	N/A
☐	☐	☐	☐	☐

I am respectful of views different from mine.

Almost Never	Occasionally	Usually	Always	N/A
☐	☐	☐	☐	☐

I am respectful of individuals who differ from me in ethnicity, gender, education or job position.

Almost Never	Occasionally	Usually	Always	N/A
☐	☐	☐	☐	☐

I convey negative news promptly and openly, not allowing employees or others to be misled.

Almost Never	Occasionally	Usually	Always	N/A
☐	☐	☐	☐	☐

I expect and hold staff accountable for adherence to our organization's ethical standards (e.g., performance reviews).

Almost Never	Occasionally	Usually	Always	N/A
☐	☐	☐	☐	☐

I demonstrate that incompetent supervision is not tolerated and make timely decisions regarding marginally performing managers.

Almost Never	Occasionally	Usually	Always	N/A
☐	☐	☐	☐	☐

Source: Reprinted with permission of the American College of Healthcare Executives.

I ensure adherence to ethics-related policies and practices affecting patients and staff.

Almost Never	Occasionally	Usually	Always	N/A
☐	☐	☐	☐	☐

I am sensitive to employees who have ethical concerns and facilitate resolution of these concerns.

Almost Never	Occasionally	Usually	Always	N/A
☐	☐	☐	☐	☐

I encourage the use of organizational mechanisms (e.g., an ethics committee or program) and other ethics resources to address ethical issues.

Almost Never	Occasionally	Usually	Always	N/A
☐	☐	☐	☐	☐

I act quickly and decisively when employees are not treated fairly in their relationships with other employees.

Almost Never	Occasionally	Usually	Always	N/A
☐	☐	☐	☐	☐

I assign staff only to official duties and do not ask them to assist me with work on behalf of my family, friends or associates.

Almost Never	Occasionally	Usually	Always	N/A
☐	☐	☐	☐	☐

I hold all staff and clinical/business partners accountable for compliance with professional standards, including ethical behavior.

Almost Never	Occasionally	Usually	Always	N/A
☐	☐	☐	☐	☐

I am sensitive to the stress of the healthcare workforce (including physicians and other clinicians), and take steps to address personal wellness and professional fulfillment, such as incorporating these issues in employee and physician satisfaction/engagement surveys.

Almost Never	Occasionally	Usually	Always	N/A
☐	☐	☐	☐	☐

Source: Reprinted with permission of the American College of Healthcare Executives.

I take steps to understand my workforce as it relates to safety, stress and burnout, and consider the impact of those who are in positions of authority (including executives and physicians).

Almost Never	Occasionally	Usually	Always	N/A
☐	☐	☐	☐	☐

Clinicians

When problems arise with clinical care, I ensure that the problems receive prompt attention and resolution by the responsible parties.

Almost Never	Occasionally	Usually	Always	N/A
☐	☐	☐	☐	☐

I insist that my organization's clinical practice guidelines are consistent with our vision, mission, value statements and ethical standards of practice.

Almost Never	Occasionally	Usually	Always	N/A
☐	☐	☐	☐	☐

When practice variations in care suggest quality of care is at stake, I encourage timely actions that serve patients' interests.

Almost Never	Occasionally	Usually	Always	N/A
☐	☐	☐	☐	☐

I insist that participating clinicians and staff live up to the terms of managed care contracts.

Almost Never	Occasionally	Usually	Always	N/A
☐	☐	☐	☐	☐

I encourage clinicians to access ethics resources when ethical conflicts occur.

Almost Never	Occasionally	Usually	Always	N/A
☐	☐	☐	☐	☐

I encourage resource allocation that is equitable, is based on clinical needs and appropriately balances patient needs and organizational/clinical resources.

Almost Never	Occasionally	Usually	Always	N/A
☐	☐	☐	☐	☐

Source: Reprinted with permission of the American College of Healthcare Executives.

I expeditiously and forthrightly deal with impaired clinicians and take necessary action when I believe a clinician is not competent to perform his/her clinical duties.

Almost Never	Occasionally	Usually	Always	N/A
☐	☐	☐	☐	☐

I expect and hold clinicians accountable for adhering to their professional and the organization's ethical practices.

Almost Never	Occasionally	Usually	Always	N/A
☐	☐	☐	☐	☐

Buyers, Payors and Suppliers

I negotiate and expect my management team to negotiate in good faith.

Almost Never	Occasionally	Usually	Always	N/A
☐	☐	☐	☐	☐

I am mindful of the importance of avoiding even the appearance of wrongdoing, conflict of interest, or interference with free competition.

Almost Never	Occasionally	Usually	Always	N/A
☐	☐	☐	☐	☐

I personally disclose and expect board members, staff members and clinicians to disclose any possible conflicts of interests before pursuing or entering into relationships with potential business partners.

Almost Never	Occasionally	Usually	Always	N/A
☐	☐	☐	☐	☐

I promote familiarity and compliance with organizational policies governing relationships with buyers, payors and suppliers.

Almost Never	Occasionally	Usually	Always	N/A
☐	☐	☐	☐	☐

I set an example for others in my organization by not accepting personal gifts from suppliers.

Almost Never	Occasionally	Usually	Always	N/A
☐	☐	☐	☐	☐

Source: Reprinted with permission of the American College of Healthcare Executives.

After you've completed the self-assessment:

Now that you have finished the self-assessment, you will want to review your responses, noting which questions you answered "usually," "occasionally," and "almost never." You may find that in some cases, an answer of "usually" is satisfactory, but in other cases, such as when answering a question about protecting staff's well-being, an answer of "usually" may raise an "ethical red flag." You will note that the instrument does not have a scoring mechanism; this is intentional. We do not believe that ethical behavior can or should be quantified.

We are confident that you will uncover few red flags and that if you do, you will willingly and appropriately address them. We also want you to consider your professional society as an additional resource when you and your management teams are confronted with difficult ethical dilemmas. You should find our regular "Healthcare Management Ethics" column in *Healthcare Executive* magazine a useful resource as well as ACHE's *Ethical Policy Statements*. In addition, you may wish to refer to the Ethics Bibliography, which we have compiled for your use. Finally, you may want to consider attending our annual ethics seminar.

Source: Reprinted with permission of the American College of Healthcare Executives.

American College of Healthcare Executives
*Code of Ethics**

PREAMBLE

The purpose of the *Code of Ethics* of the American College of Healthcare Executives is to serve as a standard of conduct for members. It contains standards of ethical behavior for healthcare executives in their professional relationships. These relationships include colleagues, patients or others served; members of the healthcare executive's organization and other organizations; the community; and society as a whole.

The *Code of Ethics* also incorporates standards of ethical behavior governing individual behavior, particularly when that conduct directly relates to the role and identity of the healthcare executive.

The fundamental objectives of the healthcare leadership profession are to maintain or enhance the overall quality of life, dignity and well-being of every individual needing healthcare service, and to create an equitable, accessible, effective, safe and efficient healthcare system.

Healthcare executives have an obligation to act in ways that will merit the trust, confidence and respect of healthcare professionals, staff and the general public. Therefore, healthcare executives should lead lives that embody an exemplary system of values and ethics.

In fulfilling their commitments and obligations to patients and others served, healthcare executives function as moral advocates and models. Since every leadership decision affects the health and well-being of both individuals and communities, healthcare executives must carefully evaluate the possible outcomes of

---

* As amended by the Board of Governors on December 5, 2023.
Source: Reprinted with permission of the American College of Healthcare Executives.

their decisions. In organizations that deliver health services, they must work to safeguard and foster the rights, interests and prerogatives of all patients and others served.

The role of moral advocate requires that healthcare executives take actions necessary to promote such rights, interests and prerogatives. Paying attention to the potential disparities of care that exist in their community is a fundamental part of their leadership role.

Being a model means that decisions and actions will reflect personal integrity and ethical leadership that others will seek to emulate.

I. THE HEALTHCARE EXECUTIVE'S RESPONSIBILITIES TO THE PROFESSION OF HEALTHCARE LEADERSHIP

The healthcare executive shall:

A. Uphold the *Code of Ethics*, mission and values of the American College of Healthcare Executives.

B. Conduct professional activities with honesty, integrity, respect, equity, fairness and good faith in a manner that will reflect well upon the profession.

C. Comply with all laws and regulations pertaining to healthcare leadership in the jurisdictions in which the healthcare executive is located or conducts professional activities.

D. Maintain competence and proficiency in healthcare leadership by implementing a personal program of assessment and continuing professional education.

E. Never intentionally exploit professional relationships for personal gain.

F. Disclose—and and when required or determined by a board review of the executives' disclosure, avoid—financial and other conflicts of interest.

G. Use this Code to further the interests of the profession and not for self-serving reasons.

H. Respect professional confidences and protect sensitive information and communications.

I. Enhance the dignity and image of the healthcare leadership profession through positive public information programs.

J. Refrain from participating in any activity that demeans the credibility and dignity of the healthcare leadership profession.

Source: Reprinted with permission of the American College of Healthcare Executives.

K. Address situations in which they believe a healthcare executive is not adhering to the *Code of Ethics*.

II. THE HEALTHCARE EXECUTIVE'S RESPONSIBILITIES TO PATIENTS OR OTHERS SERVED

The healthcare executive shall, within the scope of his or her authority:

A. Work to ensure the existence of a culture of respect, equity and dignity.

B. Build trust with all patients and their families, as well as with all members of the community.

C. Work to ensure the existence of a process to evaluate the safety, value, quality and equity of care or service rendered.

D. Work to ensure fair and equitable processes pertaining to patients' financial matters.

E. Work to establish safeguards that will not allow discriminatory organizational practices to exist.

F. Work to ensure the care team is representative of the patients and communities it serves, which can help improve health outcomes.

G. Work to ensure the existence of a process that will advise patients and others served clearly and truthfully of the rights, opportunities, responsibilities and risks regarding available health services.

H. Work to ensure there is a process in place to facilitate the resolution of conflicts that may arise when the personal values of patients and their families differ from those of employees and other providers of care.

I. Demonstrate zero tolerance for any abuse of power that compromises patients and others served.

J. Work to provide a process that ensures the autonomy and self-determination of patients and others served.

K. Work to ensure the existence of procedures that will safeguard the confidentiality and privacy of patients and others served.

L. Work to ensure the existence of an ongoing process and procedures to review, develop and consistently implement evidence-based clinical practices throughout the organization.

Source: Reprinted with permission of the American College of Healthcare Executives.

III. THE HEALTHCARE EXECUTIVE'S RESPONSIBILITIES TO THE ORGANIZATION

The healthcare executive shall, within the scope of his or her authority:

A. Lead the organization in prioritizing patient care above other considerations.

B. Provide healthcare services consistent with available resources and, when there are limited resources, work to ensure the existence of a resource allocation process that reflects the ethical considerations of fairness, equity and transparency.

C. Conduct both competitive and cooperative activities in ways that improve community health services.

D. Lead the organization in the use and improvement of standards of management, ethical leadership and sound business practices.

E. Respect the customs, beliefs and practices of patients or others served, consistent with the organization's philosophy.

F. Be truthful in all forms of professional and organizational communication, and not disseminate information that is false, misleading or deceptive.

G. Report negative financial and other information promptly and accurately, and initiate appropriate action.

H. Prevent fraud, abuse and aggressive accounting practices that may result in disputable and/or inaccurate financial reports.

I. Create an organizational environment in which both clinical and leadership mistakes are minimized and, when they do occur, are disclosed and addressed effectively.

J. Work to ensure that the organization complies with all applicable laws and regulations.

K. Work with local, regional, statewide and federal organizations to ensure adequate response to identified public health emergencies, including appropriate pre-planning and exercises of such plans.

L. Implement an organizational code of ethics, including conflict of interest principles and whistleblower protections, and monitor compliance.

Source: Reprinted with permission of the American College of Healthcare Executives.

M. Ensure that competent and effective ethics resources and mechanisms are available for staff, patients and families to address organizational and clinical ethics issues.

IV. THE HEALTHCARE EXECUTIVE'S RESPONSIBILITIES TO EMPLOYEES

Healthcare executives have ethical and professional obligations to the employees they manage that encompass but are not limited to:

A. Creating a work environment that promotes ethical and equitable conduct.

B. Providing a work environment that encourages free expression of ethical concerns and provides effective mechanisms for discussing and addressing such concerns.

C. Promoting a healthy work environment, which includes freedom from harassment—sexual or otherwise—and coercion of any kind, especially to perform illegal or unethical acts.

D. Ensuring a culture of inclusivity that seeks to prevent discrimination on the basis of race, ethnicity, religion, gender, sexual orientation, age and disability.

E. Promoting a clinical environment that intends to avoid discriminating behavior toward healthcare professionals and trainees from patients and families.

F. Working to ensure there is a process in place to facilitate the resolution of conflicts that may arise between workforce members or the individual and the organization.

G. Providing a work environment that promotes the proper use of employees' knowledge and skills.

H. Providing a safe, healthy and equitable work environment.

I. Ensuring clinicians and other staff are not subject to violence or any form of preventable harm by patients, family members or visitors.

J. Promoting a culture in which employees are provided fair compensation and benefits based upon the work they perform.

Source: Reprinted with permission of the American College of Healthcare Executives.

V. THE HEALTHCARE EXECUTIVE'S RESPONSIBILITIES TO COMMUNITY AND SOCIETY

The healthcare executive shall:

A. Work in partnership with other local organizations to meet the needs of the community.

B. Work to identify and seek opportunities to foster health promotion in the community.

C. Encourage and participate in public dialogue on healthcare policy issues, and advocate for solutions that will promote quality healthcare and improve the health status of the community and access to care.

D. Demonstrate and promote an understanding of the social determinants of health and encourage initiatives to address factors influencing them, such as education, housing, employment and similar issues affecting health, functioning, and quality-of-life outcomes and risks, while applying short- and long-term assessments to leadership decisions affecting both community and society.

E. Provide prospective patients and others with adequate and accurate information, enabling them to make informed decisions regarding services and their costs.

F. Work to support access to healthcare services to all people, particularly the underserved and disenfranchised.

VI. THE HEALTHCARE EXECUTIVE'S RESPONSIBILITY TO REPORT VIOLATIONS OF THE *CODE*

A member of ACHE who has reasonable grounds to believe that another member has violated this Code has a duty to communicate such facts to the ACHE Ethics Committee.

ADDITIONAL RESOURCES

Available on **ache.org** or by calling ACHE at (312) 424-2800.

1. ACHE Ethical Policy Statements

   "Considerations for Healthcare Executive–Supplier Interactions"

   "Creating an Ethical Culture Within the Healthcare Organization"

Source: Reprinted with permission of the American College of Healthcare Executives.

"Decisions Near the End of Life"

"Ethical Decision Making for Healthcare Executives"

"Ethical Issues Related to a Reduction in Force"

"Ethical Issues Related to Staff Shortages"

"Health Information Confidentiality"

"Impaired Healthcare Executives"

"Promise Making, Keeping and Rescinding"

2. ACHE Grievance Procedure

3. ACHE Ethics Committee Scope and Function

Source: Reprinted with permission of the American College of Healthcare Executives.

Index

Note: Page numbers in *italics* indicate exhibits.

Ambulatory patient classification (APC), 107

American Association for Physician Leadership (AAPL), 129–30

American Association of Colleges of Nursing, 107

American Civil Liberties Union (ACLU), 347

American College of Healthcare Executives (ACHE), 249; *Code of Ethics,* 34, 73–74, 127–28, 147–50, 164, 216–18, 250, 387, 461–62, 475–81; conflict of interest and, 49, 51; "Considerations for Healthcare Executive–Supplier Interactions," 49; "Ethical Decision Making for Healthcare Executives," 49; Ethics Self-Assessment, 6, 57, 461–73; Ethics Toolkit, 462; goal of eliminating health disparities, 328; "Healthcare Executives' Role in Mitigating Workplace Violence," 298; "Impaired Healthcare Executives," 96; *Leading a Culture of Safety: A Blueprint for Success,* 34–35, *35*; postgraduate fellowships and, 71, 83

American Hospital Association (AHA), 251; ethics audit, 254; goal of eliminating health disparities, 328; *Handbook for Hospital Ethics Committees,* 394–97; on mergers and acquisitions, 161–62, 165, 166; *The Patient Care Partnership,* 27; "A Patient's Bill of Rights," 172–73; Quest for Quality Prize, 244; Special Committee on Biomedical Ethics, 250; "Top Ten Principles and Practices of Great Boards," 161–62

American Marketing Association, 163

American Medical Association (AMA): *Code of Medical Ethics,* 33, 171, 405, 417, 424; conflict of interest *vs.* obligations and, 51; Council on Ethical and Judicial Affairs, 417–18; on ethical duty to report impairment in colleagues, 409; guidelines for preventing sexual harassment, 85–86; on gun violence, 206; on impaired colleagues, 96, 99; on reporting physicians deficient in character or competence, 130

American Medical Informatics Association (AMIA), 146

American Medical News, 31, 323

American Nurses Association (ANA): *Code of Ethics for Nurses,* 97; on duty of healthcare workers during an emergency or disaster, 436, 437; on laws to protect healthcare workers from violence, 206; Magnet Recognition Program, 128–29; on state-mandated nurse staffing levels, 125

American Nurses Credentialing Center (ANCC), 128

American Public Health Association (APHA), 359

American Rescue Plan, 358

ANA. *See* American Nurses Association

Analytic surveys, 399

ANCC. *See* American Nurses Credentialing Center

"An Even Deadlier Pandemic Could Soon Be Here" (Tuifeki), 345

Anger management consultant, 131

Animal Farm (Orwell), 101

Antitrust Division of the Department of Justice, 62

APC. *See* Ambulatory patient classification

APIs. *See* Application programming interfaces

Appeal procedures, 386–87

Apple Newton, 368

Application programming interfaces (APIs), 94

Applied ethics, 378–79

Arbinger Institute, 428

Aristotle, 12

Armada, A. A., 314, 316–17, 319

Arras, J., 444, 445

Ascension Health, 365

Ask Jeeves, 369

Association of American Medical Colleges (AAMC), 324, 328, 416

Association of Governing Boards (AGB), 51–52

Autonomy: bioethics and, 424; definition of, 377; emergency preparedness and, 444; faculty oversight and, 427; failures after completing training program and,

49; ethical dilemmas in healthcare and, 47, 224–25; governing board members and, 50–51, 237; information technology problems and, 139, 144–45; money and, 50; nondisclosure of, 247; policies and procedures for bid process, 53, 56, 224–25; standards of conduct that address, 50

Conflict of motive, 144–45

Conflicts of interest, research and, 428–29

Consent form, 182–83

"Considerations for Healthcare Executive–Supplier Interactions" (ACHE), 49

Consolidated Omnibus Budget Reconciliation Act, 358

Consolidation-Disruption Index, 429

"Conspiracy of silence," 25, 29

Consultants: information technology and, 139, 145–46; information technology problems and, 139, 145–46

Context, in values-based decision-making, 264, 266

Continental Healthcare, 157, 160, 456–57

Contingency surge capacity, 440

Contract research organizations (CROs), 430

Conventional surge capacity, 440

Conway, Jim, 243

Cooperation, in Tavistock principles, 391

Coordination: agreements, in healthcare emergency management, 439; interjurisdictional legal, 438–39

Cordova, R. D., 318, 319, 326, 327

Corporate inertia, 369

Cosby, Bill, 72

Cosgrove, Toby, 27

Cost-containment, 384, 388–89

Council on Ethical and Judicial Affairs (CEJA), 417–18

Couric, Katie, 457

Court of Common Pleas, Franklin County Ohio, Case #19 CR02735, State of Ohio vs William S. Husel, 233–34

COVID-19 pandemic: analysis, 344–46; attacks on healthcare workers and, 433; clinician burnout and, 95, 284–85;

deaths attributed to, 341, 346, 353; ethical considerations and challenges in, 341–49; evolution of, 346–48; healthcare ethics committees and, 396; hope, community engagement, and resilience during, 356–57; ill effects of, on health of survivors, 205–6; improve health outcomes for most vulnerable populations, 359–61; information technology and, 274, 331–39; initial response to, 341; intellectual integrity and, 429; issues related to, 342–44; lockdown, 336, 338, 339; long COVID and, 341; merger activity and, 166; misinformation and, 345, 348, 349, 356, 360–61; nation's (US) public health response to, 345–46; "new normal" and, 207–8, 338–39, 342; racism and health inequities during, 343, 353–55; *Rapid Expert Consultation on Crisis Standards of Care for the COVID-19 Pandemic*, 440; relief efforts, 358–59; staffing crisis and, 283–88; steps for the future, 348–49; vaccines for, 342, 344, 345, 348, 349, 356, 358, 360, 363; violence in the workplace and, 296; visitors for patients who were infected with, restrictions on, 285, 342–43

CPR. *See* Cardiopulmonary resuscitation

"The crappy paper" problem, 428–29

Creativity, encouraging, 366–67

A Crisis in Health Care: A Call to Action on Physician Burnout (Massachusetts Medical Society), 94–95

Crisis standards of care (CSCs), 439–41; examples of events that cause, 439–40; planning, key elements forming basis for, 440; policies supporting move to, 441; purpose of, 439; surge capacity and, categories of, 440

Crisis surge capacity, 440

CROs. *See* Contract research organizations

Cross-cultural medicine, 324

Crown, Patricia, 321

C-suite: aging workforce and, 316; chief innovation officer in, 365. *See also* St. Cecilia Medical Center case study

C-suite, gender discrimination and. *See* St. Cecilia Medical Center (SCMC) case study

Cuban, Mark, 85

"Cultural blindness," 319

Cultural competency: training, 303, 319, 328; workforce diversity and, 170, 175–76

Cultural individualism, 444

Culture, of innovation, 366–72; encouraging creativity, 366–67; establishing value, 367–69; ethics issues, 371–72; facilitating change, 370–71

Culture and ethnicity, 319–20; data collection and, 319; patients and, 319–20; workforce and, 320

Culture issues, mergers and, 161, 162–63

Curiosity, in creative individuals, 367

CVS, 364

CWOs. *See* Chief wellness officers

Cybersecurity & Infrastructure Security Agency (CISA), 334

Dallas Mavericks, 85

Dana-Farber Cancer Institute, 40–41

Daniels, Stormy, 72

Darwin, Charles, 8

Data: culture, ethnicity and, 319; for HEC evaluation, 399–400, 403; intellectual integrity and, 429

Days in receivables, revenue enhancement and, 114

DeChant, Paul, 284

Decision-making, ethical: accelerating process of, 370; based on value, 259–60, 264, 266, 267; context, 264, 266; during crisis, 434–41; deciding, 268; decision-making ellipse, 264, *265*; framing, 266–67; medical errors and, 24; naming and clarifying, 267–68; reporting, 268–69; weighing, 268

Decision-making ellipse, 264, *265*

Decision Sciences Institute (DSI), 8

Declaration of Helsinki, WMA, 428, 430

Demographics, diversity and, 314

Department of Anthropology at the University of New Mexico, 321

Department of Medicine Health Equity Committee, 343

Department of Veterans Affairs, 31

Descriptive surveys, 399

Deselection, 384

Diagnostic and Statistical Manual (DSM-5), 405–6

Disaster, definition of, 434

Disaster ethics, 445

Disaster triage, 437–39

Disclosure of information, 385

Discrimination: based on socioeconomic class, 197, 204–5; against a class of patients, medical errors and, 24, 37–38; disruptive physician behaviors and, 131; patient rights and, 172–73

Disincentives, 384, 385, 386, 390

Disproportionate Share Hospital (DSH) payments, 106, 114

Disruptive behaviors, definition of, 131

Disruptive innovations, 363–64

Disruptive physician behaviors, 124, 129–32

Distributive justice: definition of, 377; in emergency preparedness, 444

Diversity, 313–29; aging workforce and, 316; business case for, 327–29; change and, drivers of, 315–16; culture and ethnicity and, 319–20; definition of, 316–17; demographics and, 314; gender and, 321; generation divide, 321–23; global economy and, 315–16; healthcare's public image and, 316; immigration patterns and, 314; international medical graduates and, 316; key actions to hardwire, 329; laws and regulations and, 314–15; limited English proficiency and, 315; management and, 313–29; multicultural professionals and, 323–24; opportunities for healthcare leaders and, 325–27; overview of, 313–14;

Environmental Protection Agency, 62

EOPs. *See* Emergency Operations Plans

Equal Employment Opportunity Commission (EEOC), 457–58

Equal liberty, in emergency preparedness, 444

Equipment storage and maintenance, management's responsibility for, 196, 200

Equitable treatment, 53, 147, 278

Equity, crisis management and, 435

ERISA. *See* Employee Retirement Income Security Act

"Errors in Converting Principles to Protocols: Where the Bioethics of U.S. Covid Vaccine Allocation Went Wrong" (Parker), 345

Ethical behavior, elements of, 251–54

Ethical culture, in "from-to's" of ethical governance, *252–53*; legacy, *253*; mindfulness, *252*; respect, *253*; tenacity, *253*; voice, *253*

Ethical decision making: barriers to, 4–6; framework for, 7–13; tools for, 13

"Ethical Decision Making for Healthcare Executives" (ACHE), 49

Ethical dilemmas in healthcare, 45–64; adherence to professional codes of ethical conduct and, 48, 57–58; adherence to the organization's mission statement, ethical standards, and values statement and, 48, 56–57; case study (*See* Qual Plus HMO case study); conflicting moral demands and, 48, 59–64; discussion, 49–64; ethics issues and, 47–48; justice and fairness and, 48; legal implications, 48; management's role and responsibility and, 28, 53–54; organizational implications and evaluating the effectiveness of ethics committees and, 48, 58–59; use of organizational resources and, 48, 54–56. *See also* Conflict of interest

Ethical responsibilities, understanding, 3–13. *See also* Ethical decision making

Ethical standards, adherence to: cause and, termination for, 215, 216; ethical

dilemmas in healthcare and, 48, 56–57; gender discrimination and, 69, 72–73; information technology and, 139, 143–44; medical errors and, 23, 28–32; nurse shortage and, 124, 125–26; physician impairment and, 91; workforce reduction and, 109

Ethical succession, in "from-to's" of ethical governance, *253*

Ethics: definition of, 3; intersection of governance, management and, 237–54; morals *vs.,* 3–4; relationship between management and, 4, *4*

Ethics and Compliance Initiative (ECI), 59–60, 62, 275–76

Ethics and management lessons learned from Hurricane Katrina, 193–210; case study (*See* Memorial Medical Center case study); discussion, 197–209; emergency preparedness planning, 196, 197–98; environmental racism and discrimination based on socioeconomic class, 197, 204–5; ethics issues, 196–97; failure of federal, state, and local government agencies to mount an organized, coordinated response to Katrina, 197, 202–4; lessons learned, 209; management's ethical responsibility to care for the caregivers, 197, 205–6; management's responsibility for safe equipment storage and maintenance, 196, 200; management's responsibility for staff education and training in ethics and ethical conduct, 196, 200–202; management's responsibility in construction and maintenance of buildings, 196, 198–200; new normal, integration of public health and healthcare delivery, 207–8; preparing for human-created disasters and gun violence, 206–7

Ethics audits, 254

Ethics consultation, 49, 251, 396, 402

Ethics guidelines, 395

Ethics issues: in culture of innovation, 371–72; ethical dilemmas in healthcare and, 47–48;

Great Ormond Street Hospital, 179–80, 185, 189

"Great resignation," 283–88. *See also* Burnout

Greenspan, B., 126, 282

Green Team, 208

Greer, T., 150

Grills, C., 355, 356

Gross domestic product (GDP), 416

"Guilt by association," 16

Gun violence, 206–7

H5N1 strain, 345

Haden, J., 279

Hamm, G., 31

Handbook for Hospital Ethics Committees (AHA), 394–97

Hand v. Tavera, 389

Harassment, disruptive physician behaviors and, 131

Harm reduction, in emergency preparedness, 444

Harvard Business School, 41, 86, 300, 345, 364

Harvard Global Health Institute, 94

Harvard T. H. Chan School of Public Health, 94, 348

Hastert, Dennis, 203

Hazard vulnerability analysis (HVA), 442

HCA Healthcare, 249

HCPro, 428

Health Affairs study, 208

Health Care and Education Reconciliation Act, 393

Healthcare coalitions, in interjurisdictional legal coordination, 439

Healthcare delivery: fee-for-service model of, 380; new normal and, 207–8; role and integration of public health within, 353–61

Healthcare emergency management, 433–49; all-hazards approach to, 441; disaster triage and the allocation of scarce medical resources and, 437–39; duty of healthcare workers to respond and, 436–37; ethical

decision-making during crisis and, 434–41; formal (written) coordination agreements in, 439; mitigation phase of, 442–43; preparedness phase of, 443–46; recovery phase of, 447–48; response phase of, 446–47. *See also* Crisis standards of care

Healthcare ethics committees (HECs), 393–403; COVID-19 pandemic and, 396; effectiveness of, evaluating, 48, 58–59; evaluation strategies, 397–402; functions of, 394–97; overview of, 393–94; practical application and, 402–3; termination for cause and, 216, 220–21

Healthcare Executive, 343, 462

"Healthcare Executives' Role in Mitigating Workplace Violence" (ACHE), 298

Healthcare Innovators Professional Society (HIPS), 365

Healthcare Leadership Excellence: Creating a Career of Impact (Rice and Perry), 4

"Healthcare Management Ethics" column, 462

Health expenditures, 357

Health impact pyramid, 357, *357*

Health inequities, racism and, 354–55

Health Insurance Portability and Accountability Act (HIPAA), 57, 143, 334, 387

Health Professional Recovery Program (HRRP), 97

Health Research & Educational Trust (HRET), 328, 329

Health Resources and Services Administration, 359

Heartland Healthcare System case study, 135–52; ethics of managing people and, 273; follow-up on, 456; legal perspectives, 229. *See also* Information technology

Hébert, P. C., 36

HECs. *See* Healthcare ethics committees

Hedonism, 278

Hegel, G. W. F., 191

The Help (movie), 355

Henry Ford Allegiance Health (HFAH), 57–58

Henry Ford Health System, 40, 302

Improvement, in Tavistock principles, 391
"Improving Access to Services for Persons with Limited Language Proficiency," 328
Incident Command Structure (ICS), 358–59
Inclusive (process value), 435
Independent engagement, in "from-to's" of ethical governance, *252*
India, CROs in, 430
Individual liberty, crisis management and, 435
Information technology, 331–39; adherence to the organization's mission statement, ethical standards, values statement and, 139, 143–44; case study (*See* Heartland Healthcare System case study); communication and, 151–52; conflict of interest and, 139, 144–45; consultants and, use of, 139, 145–46; discussion, 139–52; ethics issues, 138–39; justice and fairness and, 139, 146–47; lessons learned and, 147–50; management's role and responsibility and, 138, 140–41; organizational implications and, 138, 141–43; strategy, flexibility and, 150–51
Informed consent, 22, 183, 184, 371, 444
Innovation, 363–72; change and, facilitating, 370–71; creativity and, encouraging, 366–67; culture of, 366–72; current initiatives, 364–66; definition of, 363; ethics issues and, 371–72; types of, 363–64; value and, establishing, 367–69
Innovation centers, 364–65
Insanity, definition of, 363
In-service exams, 422
Instagram, 345
Institute for Diversity in Health Management (IFD), 328, 329
Institute for Healthcare Improvement, 34, 205, 343
Institute for High Character Leadership, 3
Institute of Medicine (IOM): on diversity in the US, 313, 319; on duty of healthcare workers during an emergency or disaster, 436; *To Err Is Human* report, 28, 29–30, 41, 116

Institutional review boards (IRBs), 428
Insurance agreements, revenue enhancement and analysis of, 115
Intellectual integrity, research and, 429
Intent to kill, 233–34
Interactive Patient Care System, 365
Interdisciplinary committee, 360
Interjurisdictional legal coordination, 438–39; healthcare coalitions in, 439; local governments in, 439; nations in, 438; states in, 438
Internal evaluation, 399–400
International Emergency Management Group (IEMG), 438
International Federation of the Red Cross and Red Crescent Societies (IFRC), 345
International Labor Rights Fund, 315
International medical graduates (IMGs), 316, 323
International Society for Vaccines Board, 344
Interviewing potential employees, 280–82
Investor-first model, 378
IOM. *See* Institute of Medicine
IPad, 368
IRBs. *See* Institutional review boards
Issues wheel, 9, *10*
Italie, L., 79
Ivan, Hurricane, 194
Iwanabe, K. E., 318, 319, 326, 327

Jacobs, L. M., 436
JAMA Pediatrics, 341
James Bond films, 317
Jennings, B., 444, 445
Job descriptions, 283
Jobs, Steve, 363
Johns Hopkins study, 30
Johnson, Timothy, 41
Johnson & Johnson, 358
The Joint Commission, 29, 41; accreditation standards, 298, 328; award for improving patient safety and healthcare quality given by, 241; Betsy Lehman case and, 41; codes of conduct for physician behavior,

Picasso, Pablo, 366

Picoult, Jodi, 458

Pipher, Mary, 188

Policies: for bid process, 53, 56, 224–25; ethics, 394, 395–96, 402; HECs' development of, 395–96; patient demands and (*See* Hurley Medical Center case study); personnel, 129, 278–79; physician impairment and, 91, 99; supporting move to crisis standards of care, 441; workforce diversity and, 170, 174–75; zero tolerance, 40, 131, 477

Postgraduate fellowships, 71, 83

Post-medical school training. *See* Graduate medical education

Pou, Anna, 199, 459

Poverty, diversity and, 316

"Power of authority," 78

The Practice of Control (workbook), 131

Preparedness phase, of emergency management, 443–46; activities of, defining and prioritizing, 443–44; application of ethics principles in, 445–46; ethical goals of, 444–45

Presbyterian Healthcare Services, 208

Privacy, crisis management and, 435

Probationary periods for newly hired employees, 282, 290

Problem resolution, workforce reduction and, 110–13

Process standards, self-assessment and, 401

Process values, 435

Professional codes of ethical conduct, adherence to: ethical dilemmas in healthcare and, 48, 57–58; gender discrimination and, 69, 73–74; medical errors and, 23, 32–37; physician impairment and, 91, 96–97

Professional competence, commitment to, 379

Professionalism: in coursework of university programs, 77; emergency preparedness and, 444; modeling, for residents in training, 427; negative employees and, 294; public health, emergency

preparedness and, 444; redeeming value of, 279; role of physicians and, 37; workforce diversity and, 326

Program evaluation, 398–99

Program Evaluation Committee, 426

Proportionality, crisis management and, 435

Prudential algebra, 8

Pruitt, J., 282

Public accountability, in emergency preparedness, 444

Public health: within healthcare delivery, 353–61; hope, community engagement, and resilience and, 356–57; improving outcomes and, 359–61; new normal and, 207–8; overview of, 353–54; pandemic relief efforts and, 358–59; racism and health inequities and, 354–55

Public image of healthcare, diversity and, 316

Quality: clinical, workforce reduction and, 110, 116; ensuring, 386

Quality Interagency Coordination Task Force, 28–29

Qual Plus HMO case study, 45–64; ethics of managing people and, 273; follow-up on, 452–53; legal perspectives, 224–25. *See also* Ethical dilemmas in healthcare

Quest for Quality Prize, 244

Questions: generated based on the ethical principles, 419, 420, 421–22; in interviews, 280–81

Rabkin, M. T., 248

Race: diversity and, 317–18; patients and, 318; workforce and, 317–18

Racial and ethnic disparities in healthcare, 343

Racial violence, 355

Racism: based on socioeconomic class, 197, 204–5; COVID-19 pandemic and health inequities, 343, 353–55; health inequities and, 354–55; links between poor health and, 204

Racism and Health (website), 343

Self-awareness, emotional intelligence and, 277–78

Self-discipline, 278

Self-management, emotional intelligence and, 277, 278

Senge, Peter, 370

Sentinel Event Alert (The Joint Commission), 130–31, 245

Service, commitment to a spirit of, 379

Settler colonialism, 354–55

"Set Up to Succeed" (Clarke and Barch), 249

Severe acute respiratory syndrome (SARS), 434–36

Sexual harassment, EEOC's definition of, 78

Sexual orientation, diversity and, 315, 324–25

Sham bank accounts, 291–92

Shanafelt, T. D., 245

Shelkin, Pete, 139

Shootings: active shooter and, 434; mass, 207; workplace, 433

Shrader, A., 326

SHRM. *See* Society for Human Resource Management

Sibson Consulting study, 289

Sins of Omission: How Government Failures to Track Covid-19 Data Have Led to More Than 1,700 Health Care Worker Deaths and Jeopardized Public Health (National Nurses United), 342

Slate, 203

Slavery, 355

Sloan-Kettering Institute, 417

Small Great Things (Picoult), 458

Social awareness, emotional intelligence and, 277, 278

Social determinants of health, 243, 250, 354, 387, 480

Social good, fostering, 387

Social skill, emotional intelligence and, 277, 278

Social values, 400

Society for Human Resource Management (SHRM), 79, 215, 289

Soklaridis, Sophie, 85

Solidarity, crisis management and, 435

Special Committee on Biomedical Ethics (AHA), 250

Stakeholder model of business ethics, 378

Stakeholders: disaster triage and, 438–39; new diversity of, 325–27

Standard of care, 201, 228, 233, 424, 439

Stanford University, 343, 345

Starbucks, 367

Statement on Conflict of Interest (AGB), 51–52

States, in interjurisdictional legal coordination, 438

Stewardship, 379; of community resources, mergers and, 161, 164; crisis management and, 435

Stockett, Kathryn, 355

Strategy, information technology and, 150–51

Strengthening Ethical Wisdom: Tools for Transforming Your Health Care Organization (Gilbert), 251, *252–53*

"Stretch goals," 290–91

Structural racism, 354–55

Structure standards, self-assessment and, 401–2

Study participants, safety and consent of, 428

Substance use disorder: age at first presentation for treatment of, 406; alcohol use disorder, 407; benzodiazepine misuse, 407; cocaine use, 407; criteria and definition, 405–6; drugs abused by physicians, 407–8; gender difference in, 406; injectables, 407; marijuana abuse, 407; opioid abuse, 407; personality disorders and, 408; physician burnout and, 408; prevalence of, among physicians, 406; risk factors for, 408; specialties of physicians receiving care for, 407; tobacco use, 407. *See also* Impaired healthcare professional

Substantive values, 435

Suddath, C., 289

Suicide by firearms, 206, 347–48

Summative program evaluation, 398

Survey research, in program evaluation, 399

Sutton Memorial Hospital, 155, 230, 238, 456–57

About the Author

Frankie Perry, RN, MA, LFACHE, has held senior positions in both nursing and hospital administration. She served as assistant medical center director of Hurley Medical Center in Flint, Michigan, for several years; as executive vice president of the American College of Healthcare Executives (ACHE); and as a national and international healthcare consultant with engagements in Cairo, Egypt; Doha, Qatar; and Mumbai, India, among other locations. She currently serves as faculty for the University of New Mexico. Perry has authored many articles on ethics and healthcare manage-ment and in 1984 received ACHE's Edgar C. Hayhow Award for Article of the Year. Her book *Management Mistakes in Healthcare: Identification, Correction and Prevention*, coedited with Paul B. Hofmann, DrPH, LFACHE, was published by Cambridge University Press in 2005. Her self-study course *Healthcare Leadership That Makes a Difference: Creating Your Legacy* was published by Health Administration Press in 2012, and *Healthcare Leadership Excellence: Creating a Career of Impact*, coauthored with James A. Rice, PhD, FACHE, was published by Health Administration Press in 2013. In addition, she teaches an online seminar, "Practical Strategies for Decision-Making in a Dynamic Environment," for ACHE. In 2008, she received an ACHE Regent's Award in recognition of significant contributions to the achievement of the goals of ACHE and the advancement of healthcare management. In 2011, she became the first female recipient of ACHE's Lifetime Service Award. She is a past member of the board of directors of the Commission on Accreditation of Healthcare Management Education.

About the Contributors

Robert S. Bonney, JD, MSPH, MBA, LFACHE, is a retired healthcare executive and Life Fellow of the American College of Healthcare Executives (ACHE). In addition to his extensive hospital experience, he has been an active participant on and contributor to numerous boards and committees, including current roles on the boards of Rockhurst University and Presbyterian Manors of MidAmerica. He has been active with the Commission on Accreditation of Healthcare Management Education, where he currently is a Master Fellow and serves on the Governance Committee. Mr. Bonney has taught more than 100 courses at the University of Kansas, Texas Tech, the University of Missouri–Columbia, and the Harvard School of Public Health. He has numerous publications. Mr. Bonney was named Professor of the Year five times at the University of Kansas Medical Center Health Administration Program. He graduated *summa cum laude* from the Detroit College of Law (now Michigan State School of Law) and earned master of science in public health and master of business administration degrees from the University of Missouri–Columbia. He served in the US Air Force as a Minuteman missile launch control officer.

Melissa Cole, DNP, MSW, RN, RN-BC, FACHE, NEA-BC, was on the faculty of the University of New Mexico (UNM) College of Nursing. She was a nurse for 35 years and a social worker for 30 years, working primarily in leadership positions. Her research at UNM included ethics in nurse leadership. Dr. Cole served as president of the New Mexico Chapter of the American College of Healthcare Executives and as a board member for five years. She was an active member of several healthcare and service organizations. She was a board-certified informatics nurse and advanced nurse executive. She received her master's in social work degree from the University of Michigan and her doctor of nursing practice degree from UNM. Regrettably, Melissa Cole died in 2023.

Tracie C. Collins, MD, MPH, MHCDS, is a professor and dean of the College of Population Health at the University of New Mexico (UNM). From February to

August 2021, she served as New Mexico Secretary of Health before returning to UNM to serve as dean of the College of Population Health, bolstering the state's public health and pandemic-response leadership. Dr. Collins has served in significant academic leadership roles, in addition to providing clinical care and conducting and overseeing clinical research. She has also lectured in Nepal and Kenya. Prior to her tenure at UNM, she held faculty leadership positions at the University of Kansas, the University of Minnesota, and the Baylor College of Medicine in Texas, where she also served as director of the General Internal Medicine Consult Service of the Michael E. DeBakey VA Medical Center in Houston. From 2010 to 2012, she was chair for the Disparities Task Force, Society of General Internal Medicine. From 2013 to 2016, she served as president-elect, president, and immediate past president for the Association of Chiefs and Leaders of General Internal Medicine. Dr. Collins has produced more than 100 peer-reviewed publications over the course of her career. She earned a doctor of medicine degree from the University of Oklahoma, a master of public health degree from the Harvard School of Public Health, and a master of health care delivery science degree from Dartmouth College.

Rebecca A. Dobbs, RN, PhD, has extensive experience in critical care nursing; aeromedical evacuation; nursing administration; health services administration in both the government and private sectors; and emergency management program development, oversight, and evaluation. She serves as a subject matter expert in the areas of healthcare contingency planning, hospital emergency management program development and evaluation, and exercise program development. She has been a Certified Emergency Manager, a Certified Healthcare Emergency Professional, and a Fellow of the American College of Healthcare Executives (ACHE). She is a past ACHE Regent for New Mexico.

Glenn A. Fosdick, MHSA, LFACHE, has had a distinguished career in hospital and health system administration spanning more than 40 years. From 2001 to 2014, he served as president and chief executive officer of the Nebraska Medical Center in Omaha. Previously, he served as executive vice president and chief operating officer and then, from 1995 to 2001, as president and chief executive officer of Hurley Medical Center in Flint, Michigan. He also held administrative positions at Buffalo General Hospital in Buffalo, New York, and Genesee Memorial Hospital in Batavia, New York. He earned a bachelor's degree in business administration at the State University of Buffalo, New York, and a master's in health services administration at the University of Michigan–Ann Arbor. He is a Life Fellow of the American College of Healthcare Executives (ACHE) and served as the ACHE Regent for Nebraska. He has received numerous awards, including an ACHE Management Excellence Award in 1998 and an ACHE Regent's Award in 2013. He remains active on health system and health-related boards.

Howard J. Gershon, LFACHE, is a founding principal of New Heights Group in Santa Fe, New Mexico. He has spent more than 35 years as a healthcare consultant, specializing in strategic planning, market research, program development, and facility development for clients throughout the United States. He is a Life Fellow of the American College of Healthcare Executives (ACHE) and a past ACHE Regent for New Mexico. He is also a Fellow and past chair of the board of directors of the American Association of Healthcare Consultants. He has served on the board of the Health Services Management and Leadership Alumni Association at The George Washington University, is listed in *Who's Who in Health Care*, is a member of the *Strategic Health Care Marketing* editorial advisory board, and has participated as a panel member or speaker in workshops and seminars on various hospital- and health-related issues. Mr. Gershon is a frequent contributor to the healthcare literature, with articles and quotes appearing in *Hospitals & Health Networks, Healthcare Executive, Modern Healthcare, Health Care Strategic Management*, and the *Journal of Healthcare Management*.

Joan McIver Gibson, PhD, is a philosopher and consultant in applied ethics, bioethics, and values-based decision making. She has more than 35 years of teaching, training, consulting, and administrative experience in a variety of settings, including universities, business, state and federal government, healthcare, community, and research organizations. She has written several books and articles, including the book *Pause: How to Turn Tough Choices into Strong Decisions*.

Walter P. Griffin, JD, maintains a general practice, including personal injury law, mediation, business law, and general litigation. He attended Tulane University of Louisiana and is a graduate of the Wayne State University School of Law. He was first lieutenant in the Judge Advocate General's Corps of the US Air Force. He maintains memberships in the Genesee County (Michigan) Bar Association (of which he is a past president), the State Bar of Michigan (of which he is a past chairperson of the Negligence Law Section), the American Bar Association, and the Michigan Defense Trial Counsel (of which he is a past president), and he is a Fellow of the American College of Trial Lawyers. He was the recipient of the 2001 Michigan Trial Lawyers Association Respected Advocate Award for Defense Counsel and was named the 2007 Distinguished Case Evaluator of the Year by the Genesee County Bar Association.

Paul B. Hofmann, DrPH, LFACHE, is president of the Hofmann Healthcare Group Moraga, California. He has served as executive vice president and chief operating officer of the Alta Bates Corporation, a diversified nonprofit system in northern California; executive director of Emory University Hospital in Atlanta, Georgia; and director of Stanford University Hospital and Clinics in Palo Alto, California. He has also served as a Distinguished Visiting Scholar at Stanford University's Center for Biomedical Ethics. He has been nationally recognized for his significant contributions to the field of healthcare ethics and received the Lifetime Service and Achievement Award from the American College of Healthcare Executives in 2023. He is a well-published author and coeditor (with Frankie Perry) of the book *Management Mistakes in Healthcare: Identification, Correction and Prevention* (Cambridge University Press, 2005).

C. Rod Pattan, MD, is a graduate of Wayne State University School of Medicine. He has been board certified in Family Practice and in Obstetrics and Gynecology, completing his residency in the former in 1990 and in the latter in 1993. He has experience both in private practice and as faculty for residency programs and served as residency program director for an ob-gyn residency in Michigan from 2000 to 2007. He has also been a colonel in the US Army, with duties that have included the training of residents in ob-gyn and other primary care specialties.

James A. Rice, PhD, FACHE, is an internationally recognized authority on healthcare policy, governance, and strategy development. He is director of a large international leadership development program with Management Sciences for Health, supported by the US Agency for International Development (USAID) in Washington, DC. Dr. Rice also serves as vice chairman of The Governance Institute. He holds faculty positions at Cambridge University and the program in health administration at the University of Minnesota's School of Public Health.

Richard H. Rubin, MD, FACP, is professor emeritus of medicine at the University of New Mexico (UNM) School of Medicine. He was a coeditor of *Medicine: A Primary Care Approach* (W. B. Saunders, 1996), a textbook of primary care medicine directed at a medical student readership. He received the Arnold P. Gold Foundation Humanism in Medicine Award (selected by the students of the UNM School of Medicine) in 2006 and the Laureate Award from the New Mexico Chapter of the American College of Physicians in 2007. He is currently a member of the volunteer teaching faculty at the Oregon Health and Science Center in Portland.

Pete Shelkin, MSHA, CISSP, PMP, FHIMSS, is president of The Osuna Group LLC, where he provides interim management, strategic planning, and other health information technology (IT)–related consulting services to healthcare organizations nationwide. He has extensive experience providing IT leadership for health plans, hospital systems, academic medical and research centers, and clinic groups in chief information officer, chief technology officer, and consulting roles. He has also lectured as an adjunct instructor for The Ohio State University's School of Allied Medical Professions and has served on the board of directors for industry groups such as the Healthcare Information and Management Systems Society and the Personal Connected Health Alliance.

J. Mitchell Simson, MD, is an associate professor of internal medicine at the University of New Mexico School of Medicine. Previously, he was in private practice and worked for the New Mexico Department of Health as a staff physician at Turquoise Lodge, an alcohol and drug inpatient rehabilitation program. He is board certified in Internal Medicine and Addiction Medicine.